Library of
Davidson College

UNIVERSITY OF CAMBRIDGE
ORIENTAL PUBLICATIONS

NO. 16

STUDIA SEMITICA
VOLUME I

UNIVERSITY OF CAMBRIDGE ORIENTAL PUBLICATIONS PUBLISHED FOR THE FACULTY OF ORIENTAL STUDIES

1 *Averroes' Commentary on Plato's Republic*, edited and translated by E. I. J. ROSENTHAL
2 *FitzGerald's 'Salaman and Absal'*, edited by A. J. ARBERRY
3 *Ihara Saikaku: The Japanese Family Storehouse*, translated and edited by G. W. SARGENT
4 *The Avestan Hymn to Mithra*, edited and translated by ILYA GERSHEVITCH
5 *The Fuṣūl al-Madanī of al-Fārābī*, edited and translated by D. M. DUNLOP
6 *Dun Karm, Poet of Malta*, texts chosen and translated by A. J. ARBERRY; introduction, notes and glossary by P. GRECH
7 *The Political Writings of Ogyū Sorai*, by J. R. MCEWAN
8 *Financial Administration under the T'ang Dynasty*, by D. C. TWITCHETT
9 *Neolithic Cattle-Keepers of South India: a Study of the Deccan Ashmounds*, by F. R. ALLCHIN
10 *The Japanese Enlightenment: a Study of the Writings of Fukuzawa Yukichi*, by CARMEN BLACKER
11 *Records of Han Administration*, vol. I, *Historical Assessment*, by MICHAEL LOEWE
12 *Records of Han Administration*, vol. II, *Documents*, by MICHAEL LOEWE
13 *The Language of Indrajit of Orchā*, by R. S. MCGREGOR
14 *Japan's First General Election, 1890*, by R. H. P. MASON
15 *A Collection of Tales from Uji*, by D. E. MILLS

ALSO PUBLISHED FOR THE FACULTY

Archaeological Studies in Szechwan, by T.-K. CHENG

CAMBRIDGE ORIENTAL SERIES

1 *Modern Arabic Poetry: an Anthology*, by A. J. ARBERRY
2 *Essays and Studies presented to Stanley Arthur Cook*, edited by D. WINTON THOMAS
3 *Khotanese Buddhist Texts*, by H. W. BAILEY
4 *The Battles of Coxinga*, by DONALD KEENE
6 *Studies in Caucasian History*, by V. MINORSKY

(This series was first published by Taylor's Foreign Press and then by Vallentine, Mitchell & Co. There was no number 5.)

ERWIN I. J. ROSENTHAL
STUDIA SEMITICA

VOLUME I
JEWISH THEMES

CAMBRIDGE
AT THE UNIVERSITY PRESS
1971

Published by the Syndics of the Cambridge University Press
Bentley House, 200 Euston Road, London N.W.1
American Branch: 32 East 57th Street, New York, N.Y. 10022

© Faculty of Oriental Studies, University of Cambridge 1971

Library of Congress Catalogue Card Number: 70-116836
Standard Book Number: 521 07958 6

Printed by offset in Great Britain
by Alden & Mowbray Ltd at the Alden Press, Oxford

CONTENTS

INTRODUCTION *page* vii

PART I · THE HEBREW BIBLE AND ITS EXEGESIS

1 Some aspects of the Hebrew monarchy 3
(*Journal of Jewish Studies*, vol.IX, nos.1 and 2, 1958, pp.1–18)

2 Don Isaac Abravanel: financier, statesman and scholar, 1437–1937 21
(*Bulletin of the John Rylands Library*, vol.21, no.2, October 1937, pp.445–78)

3 Rashi and the English Bible 56
(*Bulletin of the John Rylands Library*, vol.24, no.1, April 1940, pp.138–67)

4 Saadya Gaon: an appreciation of his Biblical exegesis 86
(*Bulletin of the John Rylands Library*, vol.27, no.1, December 1942, pp.168–78)

5 Saadya's exegesis of the Book of Job 97
(*Saadya Studies*, ed. E.I.J. Rosenthal. Manchester University Press, 1943, pp.177–205)

6 Sebastian Muenster's knowledge and use of Jewish exegesis 127
(*Essays in Honour of Dr J.H. Hertz* [Chief Rabbi]. Edward Goldston, London, 1943, pp.351–69)

7 Edward Lively: Cambridge Hebraist 147
(*Essays and Studies Presented to S.A. Cook*, ed. D.W. Thomas. Taylor's Foreign Press, London, 1950, pp.95–112)

8 Anti-Christian polemic in medieval Bible commentaries 165
(*Journal of Jewish Studies*, vol.XI, nos.3 and 4, 1960, pp.115–35)

9 *Jüdische Antwort* 187
(*Kirche und Synagoge*, ed. K.H. Rengstorf and S. von Kortzfleisch. Ernst Klett Verlag, Stuttgart, 1968, pp.307–62)

10 The study of the Bible in medieval Judaism 244
(*The Cambridge History of the Bible*, vol.2, ed. G.W.H. Lampe. Cambridge University Press, 1969 (completed 1957), pp.252–79)

Contents

PART II · MEDIEVAL JEWISH RELIGIOUS PHILOSOPHY

11 Maimonides' conception of State and Society 275
    (*Moses Maimonides*, ed. I. Epstein. The Soncino Press, London, 1935, pp.191–204)

12 Avicenna's influence on Jewish thought 290
    (*Avicenna: Scientist & Philosopher*, ed. G.M. Wickens. Luzac & Co., London, 1952, pp.66–83)

13 Torah and *nómos* in medieval Jewish philosophy 309
    (*Studies in Rationalism, Judaism & Universalism*, ed. R. Loewe. Routledge and Kegan Paul, London, 1966, pp.215–30)

PART III · *WISSENSCHAFT DES JUDENTUMS*

14 Ismar Elbogen and the New Jewish Learning 327
    (*Year Book VIII*, The Leo Baeck Institute, Horovitz Publishing Co. Ltd., London, 1963, pp.3–28)

APPENDIX OF ADDITIONAL NOTES 353

INDEX 355

Acknowledgements are due to the editors and publishers of the works listed above for permission to reproduce the papers in this volume.

INTRODUCTION

The collection here offered contains the majority of my contributions to periodicals, *Festschriften*, memorial volumes, and papers read at international congresses. They cover a period of more than thirty-five years and are the result of research in two adjacent, inter-related fields of study: Judaism and Islam. The studies are here distributed over two volumes for the convenience of those readers who are more interested in only one of the branches of Semitic studies. But owing to the languages employed in the various texts upon which the studies are based, as well as to the subject matter, some of the studies included as chapters in volume I could just as well be put as chapters in volume II or vice versa. For the subjects treated are, in fact, closely interconnected both in language and subject matter.

Thus, Arabic language and grammar and lexicography are of great importance for the exegesis of the Hebrew Bible. For the science of Biblical exegesis among the Jews in the Middle Ages and later was decisively influenced under Islam by Arab grammar and lexicography (cf. my *Judaism and Islam*, London and New York, 1961, part two, for a general account), although Hebrew grammatical and interpretative canons go back to the Tannaim and Massoretes. Yet, the decisive development of the literal interpretation of the Hebrew Scriptures to a fine art and a sharp weapon in their defence and for the preservation of a living Judaism began with Saadya Gaon (882–942) whose Arabic Bible translation became authoritative and whose linguistic attainment and commentaries made possible the flowering of Bible study in East and West during the later Middle Ages. For this reason chapters 4 and 5 of volume I are included in that volume: Saadya's literary activity on behalf of Judaism was necessitated as much by the defence of Rabbinic Judaism against Jewish heretics and rationalists as against Muslim and Christian attack. Philosophical Bible exegesis also begins with him under the impact of *Kalām* and reached its peak in the context of medieval Jewish religious philosophy greatly influenced by Islamic philosophy which transmitted and at the same time transformed Greek and Hellenistic philosophy. Chapters 11 and 12 of volume I belong as much, therefore, to volume II ('Islamic Themes'); but since they are concerned with Judaism in the first place they are included in 'Jewish Themes'.

Introduction

On the other hand, important works of Islamic philosophy are extant—sometimes solely—in Hebrew translations. In the case of Averroes, the Arabic originals of his commentaries on Plato's *Republic* and on Aristotle's *Nicomachean Ethics* have so far not been discovered. Without their Hebrew versions the work of Averroes, the Muslim religious philosopher and the commentator of Aristotle in particular, could not be understood and appreciated. Since his *Commentary on Plato's 'Republic'* forms an integral part of his thought—together with those on Aristotle's *Corpus* and with his extant philosophical-theological writings—volume II, chapter 4, partly based on it, belongs to 'Islamic Themes'.

In passing it may be noted that volume II, chapter 3 is an extension of my earlier study 'Politische Gedanken bei Ibn Bâǧǧa' (in *Monatsschrift für Geschichte und Wissenschaft des Judentums*, 1937) which, in the absence or through inaccessibility of the Arabic originals, was based on their Hebrew translations and is not included in the present collection. The Hebrew translations of some of Alfārābī's political writings are also not without value for a better understanding of his thought.

So far, we have mainly touched on the linguistic connection between the two volumes. Of greater significance is undoubtedly their thematic interrelatedness. Jewish philosophy within the limits of normative Judaism begins much earlier, with Philo of Alexandria who already clearly recognized the fundamental problem posed—by untrammelled rational inquiry—to a religion centred in a law for which divine revelation is claimed and which is thereby perfect, immutable and permanently valid and obligatory. In that it is far superior to and divided from the *nómos*, the man-made law of Greek philosophy. In the Middle Ages no less the confrontation between revelation and reason principally took the form of the contrast between divine and human law in both Islam and Judaism. The occasion for its emergence in Judaism was—apart from Saadya and a few other Jewish thinkers in the Muslim East—the living contact of Jewish thinkers with Islamic philosophy in Muslim Spain. The common ground between Jewish and Islamic philosophy and between both and Greek-Hellenistic philosophy was the concept of law and its basis in justice, the foremost virtue in state and society. It was this concept which secured to Greek-Hellenistic philosophy an entry into Islam and Judaism.

The study of the political philosophy of Plato and Aristotle enabled the *falāsifa*—on the basis of the religious and political unity of Islam as faith and a way of life—to see more clearly the political character and significance of the *Sharīʿa* of Islam and, in turn, enabled the Jewish religious philosophers—

Introduction

despite the absence of an independent Jewish polity—to see, with the help of these *falāsifa*, the political significance of the Torah. The *falāsifa* had the difficult task to reconcile not only the demands of the *Sharī'a* with a very different political reality, but also with the metaphysics of Aristotle and with the political philosophy as expressed in his *Nicomachean Ethics* and even more in Plato's *Republic* and *Laws*. To some extent, Messianism with its promise of a restored, ideally just and perfect Jewish polity took for the Jewish philosophers the place of the actual and ideal Islamic state of the *falāsifa*. (We are not concerned with the theory of the *khilāfa* as part of the *Sharī'a* in this context, but rather with the *Sharī'a* and Torah in relation and contrast to the *nómos* of Plato and Aristotle.) As is clear from volume II, chapters 3–5, there is neither uniformity of attitude among these three Muslim philosophers nor absence of ambiguity or inconsistency in their utterances. But despite the brilliantly argued plea for the primacy of philosophic truth and the subordination of religion to philosophy in the case of Alfārābī and Averroes I still hold to my basic position—at any rate with regard to Averroes—while in the case of Alfārābī a fresh attempt must be made since we now have a critical edition of his *K. al-milla al-fāḍila*. Briefly this position is that I am convinced, from my reading of the relevant texts and from the standpoint of Islam, that rationalism with its sovereignty of human reason is not reconcilable with Muslim (or Jewish) faith in the Middle Ages. I would term the position of, say, Averroes and Maimonides, intellectualism. The difference between rationalism and intellectualism in the Middle Ages is that the latter starts from the sovereignty of God and the primacy of revelation and his law. Rationalism does not restrict free, independent rational speculation and does not exempt the prophetic nature and activity of Moses and Muḥammad respectively from the psychological theory of prophecy and from the other prophets. Certain religious doctrines must be accepted by all believers, elite and masses alike. Hence, the ideal religious state and its law—*Sharī'a* or Torah—are superior to and not identical with the ideal *pólis* and its *nómos*. A closer study of Alfārābī's *k. al-milla* and a comparison of it with his other political writings *may* result in a modification of my views. In my *Political thought in medieval Islam* (p. 163) I left open a decision whether Alfārābī understood the concept of the future life in the traditional Muslim or in the esoteric, philosophical sense. At present I still doubt the correctness of applying esotericism to the interpretation of religious philosophers who were, to my mind, Muslims or Jews first and disciples of Plato and Aristotle and their successors in Hellenistic philosophy second, certainly in political philosophy. It all depends on

Introduction

whether the *Sharīʿa* was accepted as superior to the *nómos* or identified with it as only equal. As long as those living under the *Sharīʿa* or the Torah hold that only divine law guarantees man the Highest Good as the aim of politics in the shape of well-being in this world and happiness in the next it seems difficult to maintain the primacy of philosophic truth which is accessible to the metaphysician exclusively. For religion and philosophy teach the same truth, only by different means. It is true that the love of God as the realization of man's Highest Good is the highest stage in the quest for happiness, above and beyond the knowledge of God (cf. volume I, chapter 13), but this is still within intellectualism, to my mind, and, although the *amor Dei intellectualis* is clearly reserved for the intellectual elite and out of reach of the masses, all believers can reach their respective stages of happiness through obedience to the divine law: the Jew by fulfilling the commandments (*miṣwōth*), and the Muslim by observing the *Sharīʿa*. Averroes did not for nothing reproach Plato that he neglected the third estate.

Thus, in a very real sense, the philosophical interpretation of Scripture is only a part of the paramount demand on all believers to acquire *ʿilm*, knowledge (which includes philosophy for the intellectual elite), and at the same time to live the commandments of religion (*ʿamal*), that is, intellectual understanding and ethical behaviour.

Thus political philosophy in medieval Islam and Judaism is only a special application and extension of Scriptural exegesis which also lies at the root of volume II, chapters 9–11, posing the question of the nature of Islam and its place in a modern national state.

In volume I, chapters 3 and 6–9 are extensions of Jewish Biblical exegesis into the question of Jewish–Christian relations centred in Biblical exegesis, or at least starting from it. Chapters 3, 6 and 7 deal with a special aspect of this Jewish exegesis in that they trace its presence in the English Bible culminating in the Authorized Version (the King James Version) and its impact on sixteenth-century Christian Hebraists. *Hebraica Veritas* was their battle-cry, and in their attempt to establish it and to secure through it the Word of God and the Reformation they made good use of Jewish exegesis. Since the concept of *Hebraica Veritas* is closely linked with the principal question at issue between Christians and Jews, namely, who was the *Verus Israel*, the adherents of the Old or the New Covenant, these chapters are part of the wider complex of the 'dialogue' between the Church (both Catholic and Protestant) and the Synagogue. As such, it begins with the Church fathers, as is well known. But it reached new heights in the later Middle Ages, thanks to the refinement of Biblical exegesis, chiefly charac-

Introduction

terized by the plain meaning of Scripture on which the Jews took their stand against a militant Church trying to convert them to the Christian faith. This 'dialogue' is not confined to the commentary literature (with which chapters 3 and 6–8 are chiefly concerned), but extends to religious disputations forced by the Church on the Jews and is never free from polemic and apologetic. Hence, we cannot expect a real dialogue which can only take place on the basis of the equality of both partners. These disputations, together with polemical writings by Jews, including an attack upon the New Testament, are adduced—in addition to medieval Jewish Bible commentaries and views of religious philosophers—in chapter 9, a contribution to a composite work *Kirche und Synagoge*. The subtitle of this work—'A Handbook on the history of Christians and Jews'—reflects its concern with Christian–Jewish relations from New Testament times to 1930. The story of these relations is amply documented with source material in translation.

My chapter is called '*Jüdische Antwort*' because the Jews were throughout on the defensive and wrote in the first place an 'answer to the Christians' (chapter 8) in defence of Judaism and in order to fortify and encourage the Jews to remain loyal to their ancestral faith, the continuing valid truth of which they staunchly maintained. The Christians naturally insisted on having the only true faith and, largely with the help of Jewish converts to Christianity, hoped to convince the Jews by challenging them to answer specific questions. The questioners at these disputations supported their contention that Jesus was the Messiah promised in the Old Testament with arguments taken from the haggadic (i.e. non-preceptive) part of Talmud and Midrash. The Jews not only denied these claims, taking their stand on the non-obligatory character of stories as opposed to the obligatory part in form of laws and regulations, but tried—though in vain—to bring the discussion round to the nature of God. For they denied the doctrine of the Trinity and with it the divine nature of Jesus Christ. For the Jews, the messianic prophecies in the Old Testament were not fulfilled during the Second Commonwealth—in the lifetime of Jesus—but the Messiah was still to come. Nor would they agree that the New Covenant had superseded and annulled the Old: the Torah was God's perfect revelation through Moses and retained its validity and obligatory character to the end of time.

These basic differences in attitudes and the consequent understanding of the Bible—for the Jews Holy Writ, the perfect, complete and eternally valid revelation of God, for the Christians the Old Testament as an integral part of Holy Writ, incomplete, but completed and fulfilled in the New Testament through the life and death of Jesus Christ—are treated at length. It is

Introduction

to be noted that the Jewish answer is neither an academic exercise nor a purely literary activity of the learned. It has its place in the daily struggle for Jewish survival, its *Sitz im Leben*, of which it is the literary expression. This is made clear in volume I, chapter 8, illustrated from certain literary expressions. '*Jüdische Antwort*' places this literary war in the context of the social and economic life of medieval Jewry no less than in that of the relentless missionary activity of the Church which reached its climax in the so-called religious disputations forced on an unwilling Jewry at bay. In fact, these disputations were little less than trials of people accused of blindness and obstinacy. The Jewish spiritual leaders were summoned before a tribunal consisting of the highest dignitaries of Church and State who employed Jewish converts to Christianity in their intimidating attempt—in the form of question and answer—at convincing the leaders of the truth of the Christian interpretation of the messianic prophecies of the Old Testament so that they would have to abandon their (Jewish) interpretation, acknowledge the Christian truth and draw the logical and moral consequences: conversion of their own person together with the Jewish masses whom they led and represented. It is not without significance that the Church chose this unequal contest at least partly as a means—hoped to be effective and successful—to combat and eradicate judaizing tendencies among its heretical adherents.

Apart from the theological 'dialogue' political and economic pressure became stronger and more dangerous. The necessary, but odious Jewish occupations of moneylending and taxfarming, combined with uncertainty of the right of domicile, the threat of expulsion and repeated exactions of heavy taxes and special payments for the privilege to exist and earn a living, made the Jewish position ever more precarious. Church and State combined in harassing the Jews who aroused the hostility of the Christian masses with the result that conversions to Christianity increased with increasing pressure and had a demoralizing effect which cramped the mental and physical powers of those called upon to answer Christian attack and argument.

Naturally, this state of affairs is more hinted at than openly reflected in the vast commentary literature which was obviously determined by the Biblical texts which the Jews had to interpret in defence against Christian claims that the promised Messiah had already come in the person of Jesus, son of God, whose advent had superseded and annulled the Law of Moses. The medieval Jewish commentators had recourse to the plain meaning of Scripture with the help of grammatical accuracy and historical argument. The religious philosophers, particularly Saadya, Maimonides and Albo, one of the Jewish leaders at Tortosa, whose views are adduced in extensive quotations, mainly

Introduction

relied on logic in their exposition of the simple, absolute unity of God making full use of philosophical arguments borrowed from Aristotle. The argument from history is also employed, alongside with that from personal experience. The anti-anthropomorphism is naturally very much to the fore in the refutation of the divine–human nature of Jesus Christ, and Maimonides in particular is at pains to demonstrate the untenability of the doctrine of the Trinity or Tri-unity with the help of his distinction between God's essence and his attributes which are attributes of action, not of essence. (In this connection the rigorous exercise of censorship by the Christian authorities deserves mention since we can often only discover the true, full meaning of his views, and those of the Bible commentators, thanks to the chance survival of uncensored manuscripts.)

As far as the religious disputations at Paris, Barcelona and Tortosa are concerned, reliable evaluation of their arguments is somewhat hampered by the paucity of full Hebrew reports. This applies in particular to Tortosa of which disputation we have a Hebrew report only of the first five of sixty-nine sessions, but a full Latin protocol. The theological argument apart, we learn a good deal about large-scale conversions of Jews after the several sessions, about the state of mind—anxiety and uncertainty—and the difficult physical condition of the Jewish learned 'participants'.

Of the polemical writings a treatise by Efodi demands special attention since it is directed against the New Testament and shows an understanding of Christian doctrines, especially of the Trinity and of the Transubstantiation, much more profound than anything Jews have written before and for a long time after him. This work deserves detailed examination. Lastly, Isaac Troki's treatise is briefly discussed which does not advance beyond Efodi's, but is important since it reflects the attitude of protestantism at the end of the sixteenth century (which is, however, no different from that of the Catholic Church). It was widely read and overshadowed Efodi's tract written almost 200 years earlier before the invention of printing. Moreover, Efodi is still in the direct line of polemicists who had to face up to the fact that even their personal friends forswore the faith of their fathers. The point was made before that the Christian 'questions' were put by Jewish converts to the dominant religion in the majority of cases which embittered the Jewish defenders and sharpened the polemic between Jews and Christians in the late Middle Ages.

It was thought advisable to give this rather fuller summary of volume I, chapter 9, because it is written and republished in German as part of a German publication which is directly concerned with a real dialogue on

Introduction

equal terms in the wider context of the self-critical examination of Christian-Jewish relations in the new Germany after the disastrous Hitler regime.

Today, when a real dialogue is being attempted, the arguments put forward by medieval Jews having to face the combined might of the Church and State in adverse circumstances are still worth consideration. For they demonstrate the theological irreconcilability of the Jewish truth and the Christian truth. Yet, at a time when organized religion—be it Judaism, Christianity or Islam—is fighting for its very life it *may* be possible to come together on the ethical plane, eschewing doctrinal differences. For today, as in the Middle Ages, in the Reformation and since, logic is not always the best guide and persuader where faith and 'ideology' are concerned.

This lesson is also clear from volume I, chapter 14, since the New Jewish Learning (*Wissenschaft des Judentums*)—exemplified in Ismar Elbogen—arose in a 'liberal' age against the background of the Enlightenment and the French Revolution at first in support of the emancipation of the Jews and their civic equality. It applied to the sources of Judaism the literary and historical criticism of modern Europe and presented Judaism as a rational faith in our time. In this necessary task the *Wissenschaft des Judentums* could not always free itself from polemic and apologetic because it has its *Sitz im Leben*: the equality of Jewish citizens of a national secular State whose majority are Christians, be they believers or not. Whether it has succeeded to supply the essential intellectual affirmation of faith (other than orthodox, traditional Judaism) is still an open question.

Islam is today faced with the same problem: the acute crisis of Faith. The secularization of Islam is as serious a danger to its meaningful survival as a force in the modern national States of Muslims which have arisen from the end of the First World War onwards, as is that of Judaism and of Christianity. This serious problem is at the root of the three last chapters of volume II, the last of which was originally intended by the editor of *The Muslim World* as an introduction to a special issue of the journal (hence, its brevity).

All the studies are here reprinted in a facsimile of their original form, and their original pagination is included at the foot of pages, in brackets, to enable the reader to follow up cross references within individual chapters (continuous pagination for each of the volumes precedes this original pagination). Owing to the technical process of production only misprints could be corrected and it was not possible to make the transliteration of Hebrew and Arabic uniform throughout both volumes. But there should be at least uniformity in the individual chapters. A few additions, mostly of a bibliographical

Introduction

nature, have been printed in an appendix at the end of each volume: reference to an additional note in the appendix is indicated in text or footnotes by the use of a dagger symbol.

It is my pleasant duty to thank the Publications Committee of the Faculty of Oriental Studies, Cambridge University, and in particular, its chairman, Mr E. B. Ceadel, for agreeing to republish the twenty-five studies in book form. I should also like to thank those concerned with the production of these two volumes for their care and understanding help.

E.I.J.R.

Pembroke College, Cambridge
August 1969

PART I

THE HEBREW BIBLE AND ITS EXEGESIS

I
SOME ASPECTS OF THE HEBREW MONARCHY

THE occasion for this paper is Professor Geo Widengren's important contribution to the controversial question of kingship in ancient Israel, published in the *JSS* (2, 1, Jan. 1957) under the title *King and Covenant*. His article follows earlier comprehensive investigations into the character and significance of kingship in Israel—seen in the context of divine kingship in the Ancient Near East—entitled *Sakrales Königtum im Alten Testament und im Judentum*, which in turn is but one line of the author's valuable researches into this problem from the point of view of comparative religion. It might, therefore, appear presumptuous to examine *King and Covenant* exclusively from the point of view of the Hebrew Bible alone in an attempt to see what the O.T. itself has to say on the problems of origin, character and functions of the king in relation to God and people.

Yet, such a procedure is necessary and essential if we want to understand this institution in Israel and arrive at a balanced interpretation. Leaving aside text-critical questions of different sources and revision born of definite attitudes, we obviously find reflected in the Hebrew Bible the struggle waged by its writers for Hebraic monotheism against paganism in its Egyptian, Assyrian-Babylonian and particularly Canaanite forms. Naturally, the institution of kingship reflects this contrast and struggle decisively. Needless to say that in face of the enormous literature on the subject[1] the present paper can only touch on some aspects of the problem: hence Widengren's article serves as a point of departure as well as a point of reference. For king, covenant and *Torah* are the central problem of the Hebrew monarchy and their interrelationship determines the course of Hebrew history and its continuation in Judaism. Because this is so it appears to me imperative for reasons of method and

---

[1] In particular A. R. JOHNSON, *Sacral Kingship in Ancient Israel*; MARTIN BUBER, *Königtum Gottes;* N. W. PORTEOUS, *The Kingship of God in Pre-exilic Hebrew Religion;* Y. KAUFMANN, תולדות האמונה הישראלית I,3, pp. 686 ff. (ch. מלכות האלהים); E. GOODENOUGH, *Kingship in Early Israel* (*JBL* 48 (1929)); C. R. NORTH, *The religious aspects of Hebrew Kingship* (*ZAW*, 1932); H. FRANKFORT, *Kingship and the Gods* (especially Epilogue: The Hebrews); JOH. PEDERSEN, *Israel*. These studies are singled out because they have a special bearing upon the problem under discussion in this paper.†

clarity to restrict our inquiry to the Hebrew Bible and not to draw upon its later Greek and Aramaic versions nor on Rabbinic sources, in particular the Mishnah. Scriptural proof is needed for Rabbinic institutions and practices, but Mishnaic accounts of the celebration of *Sukkoth* and the part of the king in it (*Soṭah* vii: 8) do not allow us, to my mind, to draw conclusions as to O.T. practice.[2] While they may well reflect earlier usage there is no certainty that functions and ceremonies were continued without change and modification.

Two lines of approach are possible in relation to the Hebrew monarchy. We can look upon kingship as the natural development out of the tribal organisation and see in the king the continuation of the charismatic leader, but not his replacement by an institution taken over, though perhaps in a modified form, from surrounding patterns. Or, we may assume that late kingship is deliberately traced back to royal traits in Moses and Joshua, unless we assume the opposite and see in the story of Moses, Joshua and the Judges a deliberate attempt at reading into the past, by the literary method of flash-back, a contemporary situation. This latter method may yield results in the field of textual and literary criticism of the O.T., but it is unhistorical and runs counter to known political and historical reality.

The first point I want to make is that if we look at the O.T. as a whole and on its own ground the intention seems to stress the historical continuity throughout biblical history from Moses and Joshua through the Judges to David, Solomon and the house of David. Two traditions are woven together, the desert and the settled, largely urban civilisations, with their contrasts unresolved. The link is provided by the concept of the covenant between God and the people.

How, then, did kingship arise in Israel? There is a possibility that Ugarit served as a model. I. Mendelsohn[3] has recently adduced

---

[2] In view of WIDENGREN's use of this *mishnāh*, p. 20. For the same reason, it seems to me inconclusive to adduce the Samaritan *Sukkoth*-liturgy for the part played by the king in the ritual of the Northern kingdom (*Sakrales Königtum*, pp. 41 ff.).

[3] Cf. I. MENDELSOHN, *Samuel's Denunciation of kingship in the light of the Akkadian documents from Ugarit* (*BASOR* 143, Oct. 1956, pp. 17 ff.). He holds that Samuel's account represents an authentic description of the semi-feudal Canaanite society as it existed prior to and during the time of Samuel. He concludes: " In view of the evidence from the Akkadian texts from Ugarit it seems obvious that the Samuel summary of ' the manner of the king ' does not constitute ' a rewriting of history ' by a late opponent of kingship but represents an eloquent appeal to the people by a contemporary of Saul not to impose upon themselves a Canaanite institution alien to their own way of life."

evidence that Canaanite kingship exactly corresponded to the description we have in *I Sam.* viii. Samuel's warning reflects the state of affairs in Canaan. Whether we assume that kingship in Israel is influenced by the Canaanite pattern or not, the Ugaritic parallel strongly militates against the view held by some scholars that the anti-monarchical passage in *I Sam.* represents a projection from the time of the late monarchy back into its beginnings. A. Alt[4] contends that neither the Philistines nor the Canaanite small states led by an aristocracy could have influenced the Israelite tribes. More likely a parallel would be found among the peoples inhabiting the borderlands towards the Syrian-Arabian desert, Edom, Moab, Ammon and Aram, and Alt points to *Nu.* xx. We might also think of *Gen.* xxxvi, where the kings of Edom mentioned in vv. 31 ff. are not Esau's descendants, consequently not those promised to Abraham and Sarah (*Gen.* xvii: 6, 16). But Alt favours another alternative, advocated earlier by Kaufmann etc.,[5] namely, that the establishment of an Israelite monarchy arose quite naturally and necessarily out of the political situation created by the subjugation of the territory of the tribes by the Philistines. This view is, no doubt, correct—it is shared by Noth in recent studies.[6] For we must bear in mind that judges as charismatic leaders rose to defend against attack one or more, but never all the tribes (even though they were linked in a confederacy). Having successfully overcome such an emergency these military leaders were appointed judge-rulers in peace. Philistine encroachment necessitated a more permanent and comprehensive national leadership which could guarantee a settled life in peace and independence. We must also remember that Joshua died before his task was completed and did not even nominate a successor. Only Saul and David later succeeded in establishing the settlement begun by Joshua, and they did so with the support of the whole confederacy of tribes.

Why was kingship opposed in these circumstances which imperatively demanded strong, efficient leadership? How can we account for the anti-monarchical tendency expressed so forcefully

---

[4] Cf. A. ALT, *Gedanken über das Königtum Jahwes* (1945) in *Kleine Schriften zur Geschichte des Volkes Israel* (1953), especially pp. 15, 21-29.
[5] See above, n.l. and S. TALMON, משפט המלך (*I Sam.* viii) in ספר בירם (1956).
[6] E.g. in his *Geschichte Israels* (1950) and particularly *Gott, König, Volk im Alten Testament* in M. NOTH, *Gesammelte Studien zum Alten Testament* (1957) which came to my notice only after I had written this paper; but I have now used it for preparing the paper for publication.

in *I Sam.* viii and xii? If we take such passages as *Hos.* vii: 7 and viii: 4 into additional consideration we are led to the conclusion that there the desert tradition asserted itself, represented in its purest form by the Rechabites. It is an attitude and tradition fostered by Moses and Joshua, the instruments of the divine will and guidance, which found expression in the concept of the kingship of God over Israel. For this reason the Exodus from Egypt under God's providential leadership is of such paramount importance in its frequent recurrence, introduced by a form of the verb זכר, remember.[7]

The *Samuel* passage may also reflect concern about the historical continuity which was threatened by the transition from nomadic existence in the years of the wandering through the desert, to settled urban life under a human king ruling as an absolute master, in contrast to the divine king who referred to Israel as his son and firstborn.[8] But allowing for the preservation in the O.T. of the desert tradition there is nothing incongruous in linking the kingship of God with the redemption from Egyptian bondage and both with the pre-monarchical period of Israel's history. Buber's claim[9] that מלך denoted " originally not necessarily ' king ' but ' leader ' ", cannot easily be substantiated since, apart from the meaning in Aramaic " to counsel," מלך—like Arabic *malaka*—clearly means " to possess, to own", an appropriate term to express God's relationship with Israel. This is supported by such passages as *Ex.* xv: 17 (קנית) and *Deut.* iv: 20 (עם נחלה).

The close interrelation between the divine and the human king has often been stressed, particularly through the expressions *father* for God and *son* for the human king. Passages like *II Sam.* vii: 14 with its parallel *I Chr.* xvii: 13 do not make a divine being of the human king, but rather indicate that the king represents Israel which is called God's son in the passages quoted previously. To my

---

[7] Cf. JOH. PEDERSEN, *Israel*, p. 664. This is not the place to enter into a discussion of his views on the monarchy in Israel (I-II, pp. 22 f., 37 f.) nor of his evaluation of Moses and the patriarchs as projections from the late and post-regal period (III-IV, pp. 662-66), but cf. CASSUTO and KAUFMANN. Cf. also BUBER, *op. cit.*, p. 120 against MOWINCKEL.

[8] See also *Deut.* xiv: 1. *Hos.* xi: 1 and *Jer.* xxxi: 9 may well go back to *Ex.* iv: 22. This *Exodus* passage, seen in its context, may possibly mean a claim to equality for Israel with Pharaoh: both are adopted sons of God. The same may apply to *Ex.* xv: 18 proclaiming the kingship of God; in both cases it is not possible to prove conclusively an early or late date.

[9] *Op. cit.*, p. 49. But his treatment of God as king is most instructive and convincing; see particularly pp. 52 ff., 58 ff., 65 and the whole fifth chapter.

mind it can no more be connected with the Egyptian or Assyrian god-king, than the husband-wife relationship of God and Israel with a female consort of God. It is a metaphor to express the close personal relationship between God, the divine, and Solomon, the human king. The O.T. knows of no deification of the earthly ruler. This applies no less to the expression used of Solomon sitting on the throne of God (*II Chr.* xxix: 23, also *ibid.* ix: 8); it does not make him into a divine being, the more so since in other passages (*I Chr.* xxviii: 5) the expression " kingdom of God " is used of the throne on which Solomon and the sons of David are to sit (*II Chr.* xiii: 8). While the possibility cannot be ruled out that different sources are here represented by different expressions which the Chronicler did not succeed in harmonising[10], it can be claimed with equal justification that the throne occupied by the descendants of David belongs to God as the supreme king whether it is called " the throne of God " or " the throne of the kingdom of God."

To my mind, the terminology is intentional and is used to express the continuity from the prophetic lawgiver and leader under God through the charismatic judges to the kings of the house of David with the divine promise of eternal rule over God's people Israel. Kingship is the natural development after the transition from nomadic and rural to urban settlement and civilisation and expresses the unity of the tribes under God who owns them. This is what the O.T. teaches, irrespective of what it implies or conceals under a diversity of sources and traditions. Noth[11] has plausibly argued for a definite element of opposition against the kingship-ideology of the Ancient East persistently noticeable in the Hebrew concept of kingship, and I am in entire agreement with him. I hold that the charismatic leader of pre-monarchical Israel is continued in the king: both are chosen by God—*Deuteronomy* xvii will occupy us presently. The institution of human kingship does not necessarily constitute a rebellion against God and the rejection of his supreme kingship. But, no doubt, it constitutes a threat to pure Yahwism by its political entanglement with the great empires and with their gods as an unavoidable consequence. Apart from the adduced *Samuel* passage (and perhaps the *Hosea* one) there is no hostility to

---

[10] Perhaps they did not strike him as contradicting each other?
[11] See his *Geschichte*, pp. 122 ff., 142 ff., and especially his *Gott, König, Volk*, pp. 206 ff., 211 ff., 216 ff., 221 ff. cf. also H. FRANKFORT, *op. cit.*, especially pp. 338 ff., 342 f.

kingship as such. On the contrary, it is glorified in the promise to Abraham, Sarah and Jacob and, particularly, to David and Solomon "for ever." It finds its culmination in the Messianic promise and hope.

What constitutes the right kind of kingship is stated in *II Kings* xviii: 5f. and xxiii: 25 in the author's verdict on Hezekiah and Josiah respectively. Significantly, the good king's characteristic achievement is seen in his scrupulous observance of the Torah of Moses, thus not only linking kingship with the Torah, but also the king with Moses. Add to these two passages David's charge to Solomon (*I Chr.* xxii: 12f.) and Isaiah's description of the ideal king-Messiah (xi: 2f.) with its echo in Solomon's request for wisdom and insight (*II Chr.* i: 8 ff.)[12].

The continuity between the charismatic leader and the king is exemplified by the רוח (spirit) of God resting on both and conferring power and authority upon them. This רוח enables them to function as military leaders and judges on behalf of God the King. The first human king, Saul, receives this spirit by being anointed by Samuel. When the same prophet anoints David, the divine spirit departs from Saul and enters David. The king functions as judge and military leader as the anointed of God (משיח יהוה): he is consecrated to the service of God in obedience to His Torah, that is, if we assume at least the existence of the Pentateuch, especially Deuteronomy in the time of Solomon.[13] I can see no compelling reason against such an assumption.

It appears that the act of anointing secured the succession in the family of the anointed king. According to the Bible, after David only Solomon is anointed by Zadok the priest in the presence of Nathan the prophet,[14] and later Joash, Jehoahaz, and Jehu of Israel. In these cases, special reasons existed for this practice: Adonijah's usurpation could only be countered by the anointing of Solomon; Joash became king in place of Athaliah who had usurped the throne after her son's death, through the priest Jehoiada's revolution (*II Kings* xi: 12) (Jehoiada's wife had saved Joash her nephew); Jehoahaz was made king by the עם הארץ[15] after Josiah's

[12] I am not concerned with the relative date of these passages but with a common attitude to king and kingship.
[13] So e.g. E. ROBERTSON, YEIVIN; ZEMIRIN thinks of a possibly earlier date during the period of the Judges or at the beginning of the monarchy.
[14] Unless NATHAN is interpolated.
[15] See on the עם הארץ now WÜRTHWEIN, *Der 'Amm ha'arez im Alten Testament* (1936).

death (*ibid.* xxiii: 30); and Jehu was anointed by a disciple of Elisha to destroy the house of Ahab (*ibid.* ix: 6). Normally, succession was secured either by designation—Solomon by David—or by election—Saul and David. The term used is in most cases the *hif'il* of מלך, in Jotham's parable משח.

Anointing is equivalent to the divine choice or approbation. This is clear from *Deut.* xvii: 15: the choice of the king by God is an essential condition for the legitimate exercise of his office after his election by the people. This divine choice is mediated to the people by a prophet who anoints the chosen candidate (Samuel, Elijah, Elisha) unless the (high) priest does it. We have seen one king succeed to the throne through election by the עם הארץ. They, together with the elders, play an important part during the monarchy, not only in this matter but in covenant ceremonies—already in the days of Joshua at Shechem, as before at Sinai—and in matters of legislation. The institution of elders is frequently met with in tribal organisation and it is not impossible that we find the prototype of the organisation of the monarchy in Israel in pre-historic Mesopotamian society, which Thorkild Jacobsen calls " primitive democracy ". It had a council of elders and a general assembly of the free male citizens who could choose a king.[16]

Next to the principle of continuity of authority in ancient Israel—which suggests an internal development rather than outside influence and the conscious adoption of ancient Near-Eastern kingship-ideology—the designation of the human king by the term נגיד points, to my mind, in the same direction. It maintains the clear distinction between the divine king and his anointed of the house of David. This נגיד—usually translated by " captain ", " prince " or " ruler "—is literally " set in front ", hence he is in front, at the helm, or in charge of people and institutions.[17] I am only concerned with its use for the king. The first passage where it so occurs is *I Sam.* ix: 16 which belongs to the version of Saul's election favourable to the institution of kingship. God says to Samuel: " . . . thou shalt anoint him to be a נגיד over my people Israel, that he may save my people out of the hands of the Philistines . . . "

[16] *Primitive Democracy in Ancient Mesopotamia* in: *JNES*, II: 3 (1943). Historic Mesopotamia was, by contrast, organised along autocratic lines.

[17] נגיד is passive in form, but comes to have an active meaning like פקיד, נביא, נשיא. All passages where נגיד occurs were examined in the Hebrew Bible, LXX and Targum. Although the versions would confirm my view, I cannot adduce them since I do not consider it sound to go outside the O.T. for the purposes of this paper.

Military leadership is thus clearly indicated. Samuel obeys God's command and tells Saul: " for the Lord hath anointed thee to be a נגיד over his possession " (x: 1).

No doubt, נגיד is equivalent to " king ". But it is significant that the term נגיד is used whenever God commands a prophet to anoint a king or whenever He himself speaks to a king (Saul, David, Jeroboam, Baasha), either directly or through a prophet. I would draw the inference from this that, seen from the viewpoint of the divine king, the earthly ruler—who is demanded by the people as a king just as all the nations have one (*I Sam.* viii, *Deut.* xvii: 14)—is in Israel not a king ruling with absolute authority nor a godlike being as among the peoples in whose midst the children of Israel dwell. Absolute power and authority belong to God alone, the supreme king over Israel and the world. The human king is only a נגיד over the people of God. Is this not indicative of the pure theocracy of the kind we find in *Daniel* ix: 25 in the term used of the Messiah, משיח נגיד, and in passages like *I Chr.* xxviii: 4 (where נגיד is used in parallel with מלך), or *II Chr.* vi: 5? (In the parallel story *I Kings* viii נגיד does not occur.) There may be equal significance in the fact that Isaiah does not call the Messiah " king " either, when he announces the scion of David (ix and xi). When, on the other hand, Solomon says to God והמלכתני (*II Chr.* i: 8 f.) and God uses the term המלכתיך (*ibid.* v. 11), I do not think that this seriously militates against such an interpretation, the more so since *I Chr.* xxix combines המליך with משח לנגיד (v. 22). The next verse contains the phrase: " and Solomon sat on the throne of God ". We met a little earlier other passages with alternating expressions as regards the throne, to which may be added *II Chr.* vi: 10, where Solomon says of himself: " and I sat on the throne of Israel as the Lord promised ".

Even allowing for the Chronicler's inability or unwillingness to harmonise his sources, mentioned earlier, one thing seems to me to be quite clear: the kingship of David and Solomon is seen as coming under the supreme kingship of God. This is expressed, if I am not mistaken, by the term נגיד. It suggests to me a meaning not far from that of *khalīfa* (vicegerent), used in the Qur'an of David (*Sura* xxxviii: 25)[18]. Yet this requires investigation, quite apart from the fact that we must base upon the Hebrew Bible our

---

[18] One might also think of *amir al-mu'minin*, but the same reservation applies here, too.

attempt at explaining the character and meaning of kingship in ancient Israel. But it is safe to conclude from the relationship between God and the "נגיד over his people Israel" that as long as the king serves his divine overlord alone, being conscious of his duties and responsibilities to God and his people, he is granted the divine king's protection. This is expressed in the promise to David.

However, there is one passage which apparently contradicts my claim that the term נגיד is only used by God. We read in *I Kings* i: 35 of David: "him (Solomon) have I charged (appointed, צויתי) to be a נגיד over Israel and over Judah". Though "over Judah" may be suspicious, the awkward fact remains—also noted by Alt[19]—that David here seems to usurp the authority of God. It is probable that the act of anointing commanded by David evoked in the writer the association with the appointment as נגיד. David acted in an emergency; he had to prevent Adonijah from becoming effective ruler. Naturally Solomon could be anointed to the kingship only in the same terms as his father David before him whom he was to succeed. Yet, this explanation does not account for the addition " and over Judah ", unless we understand it as foreshadowing the events after Solomon's death and/or as linking Solomon's succession with the establishment of David's kingship over Judah and Israel.

II

A brief consideration of Samuel's opposition to a human king in *I Sam.* viii and xii and in relation to the "law of the king" in *Deut.* xvii will lead us to take issue with some of Widengren's interpretations and opinions. It has long been recognised that there is a close connection between *I Sam.* viii and *Deut.* xvii; it is

---

[19] *Op. cit.*, p. 44, n.l. and p. 62, n.l. ALT speaks of a " certainly intentional misapplication of the term נגיד " in this passage " since only YHWH could make such a disposition and only over Israel, not over Judah". But I cannot see how YHWH could be limited to Israel nor can I agree with ALT's interpretation of the term נגיד as " der von Jahwe Kundgegebene," understanding the term not only passive in form but also in meaning and distinguishing the מלך from נגיד. The contrast between " religiösem Nimbus ", i.e. a religious charismatic leader appointed by YHWH, and a profane מלך acclaimed by the people, " so dass die göttliche Weihe und die menschliche Würde klar von einander geschieden bleiben " (p. 23) cannot be maintained in this form in any of the passages concerned. Cf. also J. VAN DER PLOEG, *Les Chefs du Peuple d'Israël et leurs Titres* in *R.B.* lvii, 1950, pp. 45 ff.

obvious from the use of identical terms in both passages.[20] The operative clause is והיינו ככל הגוים; we also note the double function of the king as judge and military leader.

It has often been said that *Deut.* xvii: 14, 15 is not a command, but constitutes permission, just like *Deut.* xxi: 10 ff. in the case of the female prisoner in war. This is deduced from the conditional statement: " and if you say ". A definite commandment concerns only the manner of electing a king and also his duties. Here the crucial point is that the people must set over themselves God's chosen. In fact, this describes precisely the situation which had arisen at the time of Samuel in respect of Saul and David. Both were anointed by Samuel by order of God. Further, the following verses (xvii: 15b, 16 and 17) fit Solomon's reign so perfectly that I am inclined to assume, with some scholars, that the *Samuel* passage goes back, though perhaps not in its present literary form, to Samuel and the passage in *Deut.* is modelled upon it.

Next, we must consider the conditions imposed on the would-be king in vv. 18-20. He must write a copy (משנה) of the Torah according to the book in the possession of the levitical priests, he must have it always with him and " read in it all the days of his life that he may learn to fear the Lord his God, to keep all the words of this Torah and these statutes to do them ". This is self-explanatory.

[20] Not so S. R. DRIVER in his *Commentary*, pp. 209 ff. who only allows a literary connection. The " law of the king " deserves a separate study, particularly in view of WIDENGREN's positive attitude to K. GALLING's " very attractive hypothesis " that *Deut.* xvii: 14-20 forms part of the " *Urdeuteronomium* " from the Northern kingdom (*King and Covenant*, p. 15, n. 2). GALLING developed this idea in his *Das Königsgesetz im Deuteronomium* (*Theol. Literaturzeitung*, 1951, nr. 3, pp. 134 ff.). In his opinion " there stands the charismatic king-ideology of the North behind *Deut.* xvii: 14-15a ". 15b points to the North, a view shared by GRESSMANN who otherwise assumes a southern origin for the " law of the king ". I am inclined to see in v. 15b a reference to Solomon: this injunction was to prevent a son of one of the foreign wives of Solomon from the succession to the throne. GALLING sees, with STEUERNAGEL, a reference to slave trade in v. 16 (return of the people to Egypt). GALLING refers v. 17a not, as is usual, to Solomon, but to Ahab and Jezebel (*I Kings* xvi: 31 ff.). But there is good reason to retain the application to Solomon, especially in view of v. 15b. GALLING considers vv. 18 f. as secondary, holding at the same time that they would suit Jeroboam II. The whole passage is held by him to have come from the North to Judaea towards the end of the eighth century, and he wishes it to be understood as " a prophetic warning constituting a complement, positive within limits, to the complete rejection of kingship by Hosea ". With PEDERSEN, etc. I am inclined to see in Hosea's hostility an echo of the Rechabite attitude. Hosea's hostility is, to my mind, not absolute and fits well the surviving desert tradition of Israel. But I entirely agree with GALLING's view that for *Deuteronomy* the state is a *civitas Dei* which can be realised and is not an utopia. (cf. his *Die israelitische Staatsverfassung in ihrer vorderorientalischen Umwelt* (1929), p. 63).

It seems to me also to underlie the praise given by the author of *Kings* to Hezekiah and Josiah. I would only stress that the king is bidden to *read* in the Torah which is a copy of the original in the possession of the priests. For Widengren claims that the king was the possessor and teacher of the Torah.

Since he makes the same claim for Joshua, it is necessary, before looking at the texts of the Bible, to explain why Widengren puts such an interpretation on them. It seems to me that he must establish a connection between the Israelite " king " and the Babylonian king in order to fit the Israelite ruler into the kingship pattern of the ancient Near East with an important ritual function in the foreground. Widengren makes the Babylonian king ascend to heaven at his enthronement when he is presented with the two tablets of destiny.[21] It is quite possible that this myth has percolated into Canaan; it is already much less likely, even improbable, that it should have served as a pattern for Moses' ascension to the mountain of the Lord in order to receive the two tablets of stone of the covenant between God and the people of Israel. On the contrary, it may well be that the formulation in *Exodus* xix is in deliberate opposition to such a Babylonian myth. But in any case there cannot be a correspondence between a myth and the fact of revelation accompanied by the conclusion of a covenant. Nor are the tablets of the same nature or kind. In calling revelation an historical fact I simply mean that as such it meets us in the pages of the O.T. and reflects the consciousness of its writers. This is independent of the results of *Quellenscheidung* and of tendentious editorial revision.

In *Deut*. xxxi: 9, 10 Moses commands the levitical priests and the elders to read this Torah in the hearing of all Israel on the feast of Tabernacles in the year of release. Widengren rightly stresses the importance of the Torah—this is one of the most valuable features of his study—and its reading; he rightly brings this passage into connection with *Josh*. viii: 34 f. But how can this make Joshua the possessor of the " book of the law " which he inherited from his predecessor Moses?

That there is parallelism between *Josh*. i: 7 ff. and *Deut*. xvii: 18 f.[22] is correct, yet, to my mind, neither the commandment nor the situation are identical. In the first place, the king is commanded to write a *copy*, as I have already emphasised. We know from *Deut*.

[21] Cf. *op. cit.*, p. 17 with nn. 3-6.
[22] Cf. *ibid.*, p. 15 with n.l.

xxxi: 26 that Moses ordered the Levites in charge of the ark of the covenant of God to deposit the " book of this Torah " there as a witness. If the Levites were the keepers of the Torah, how can Joshua have " inherited this law from his predecessor Moses "[23] any more than the people as a whole?

Moreover, Joshua is obliged to consult the priest in an emergency or a difficulty; he has no direct access to God as Moses had. The priest was the mediator between Joshua and God, by means of the *Urīm we-Thummīm*. Joshua is only the charismatic leader, but he has not inherited the Torah; it is an inheritance bequeathed to the whole people as we know from *Deut.* xxxiii: 4. The parallelism between king and charismatic leader can be explained by the post-Mosaic situation which made knowledge of and obedience to the Torah binding upon the leader as head of the people. Whoever is responsible for the Octateuch in its present form has—so it seems to me—been at pains to show the continuity from Moses through Joshua and the judges to Saul, David and beyond, not only in leadership as such, but in a leadership born of knowledge of and obedience to the Torah.[24] It is neither a case of identity nor can we speak in terms of a typology. Moses is not " the *typos* of the Davidic King . . .",[25] nor Joshua " the prototype of the Israelite ruler ",[26] as Widengren holds. Much of the correspondence—the parallelism —is due to the hand of the Deuteronomist. Charismatic leaders have the same duties as the kings, but that does not make the one the *typos* of the other. The king is, after all, "the anointed of the Lord ". But we can safely say that the Octateuch emphasises continuity by deliberately building the history of Israel round the covenant and the Torah as the permanent centre of gravity, the guiding idea, the *Leitmotif* as it were, whereas leaders and rulers come and go.

Of equal significance is the connection between the reading from the Torah on important occasions and the conclusion of the covenant between God and the people as a renewal of the Sinai-covenant.

---

[23] Even so Joshua as the charismatic leader made a covenant on behalf of the people at Shechem, gave them laws and wrote into " the book of the *Torah of God* " (*Josh.* xxiv: 25 f.).

[24] See e.g. *I Kings* ii: 3: David's charge to Solomon.

[25] Cf. WIDENGREN, *op. cit.*, p. 18. That Abraham b. Ezra, e.g., interprets the passage *Deut.* xxxi: 15 מלך ויהי בישרון by identifying מלך with Moses cannot be adduced as evidence for O.T. times. WIDENGREN does not refer to this interpretation.

[26] Cf. *ibid.*, p. 15.

Here, too, there is continuity: Moses makes a covenant with God, i.e., on behalf of the people (כרת ברית ל'),[27] Joshua at Shechem, Jehoiada at the proclamation of Joash as king (*II Kings* xi), King Josiah after the discovery of the book of the covenant (*II Kings* xxiii: 2 f.). It is possible, even probable, that Joshua made the covenant at Shechem on *Sukkoth* and read the Torah in accordance with *Deut.* xxxi: 10, as Widengren stresses. Presumably Joshua acted as one of the elders who, together with the levitical priests, are there charged with the reading. But it seems to me a little speculative when Widengren makes Josiah's covenant-ceremony coincide with the celebration of Passover. He cites Professor Hooke[28] in support of his identification of Passover with the New Year festival, i.e. *Sukkoth*, because he wants to bring Josiah's reading of the Torah in line with the prescribed reading on *Sukkoth*. Here several difficulties arise. In the first place, Professor Hooke offers no conclusive evidence for his identification of Passover with New Year. Next, the reading of the Torah on *Sukkoth* is commanded for the year of release, though this need not necessarily exclude a public reading in the case of Joshua or Josiah.

However, *II Kings* xxiii in its present form poses a number of awkward questions which must first be faced before we can accept Widengren's contention that Josiah concluded the covenant on Passover. It has long been seen that vv. 4-20 intervene between vv. 1-3 and v. 21. The emphasis that no Passover was celebrated like this from the days of the judges, makes plausible the assumption that it was the result of the discovery of the " Book of the Covenant ". vv. 4-20 are taken to constitute the reform of Josiah which, as is widely agreed today, preceded the discovery of the book in the eighteenth year of King Josiah.[29] While thus the sequence of events as recorded in this chapter is open to question, the account

---

[27] Cf. J. BEGRICH, *Berit* in: *ZAW*, 1944, pp. 1 ff. who holds that " the *berit* is altogether one-sided. Only the Powerful binds himself to the less powerful " and that a mutual covenant is a later development. He was anticipated in this view by BUBER (*op cit.*, p. 127). See also JOH. PEDERSEN, *Der Eid bei den Semiten*, pp. 51, 60. It seems doubtful whether this distinction on the assumption of a development can be upheld since the very concept of " covenant " pre-supposes a mutual undertaking of two partners even if they are so unequal as God and the people of Israel. But I am more concerned with the exact meaning of ל in contrast to את since it is important to note that the partners are God and Israel and that Moses, Joshua, David and Josiah only mediate the covenant, ברת... ל. Cf. WIDENGREN, *op. cit.*, pp. 23 ff. with notes in which he discusses BEGRICH.
[28] S. H. HOOKE, *The Origins of Early Semitic Ritual* (1938), p. 47.
[29] The latest discussion of this problem is to be found in a careful, well-documented study by S. ZEMIRIN in his book יאשיהו ותקופתו (1952).

of individual events may well be correct. It stands to reason that the king first read the Torah, then concluded the covenant before God and after that commanded the people—as a token of his and their willingness to observe all the commandments—to celebrate a Passover in the prescribed fashion. If this sequel is correct, then the covenant ceremony cannot have taken place on Passover. It is more likely that the discovery of the book occasioned the king's action in calling for a special assembly after he had consulted the prophetess Huldah. There is, as far as I am aware, no evidence for Widengren's view that the celebration of Passover in the month of *Abib/Nisan* coincided with the celebration of the New Year festival, the *Akītu* festival in Mesopotamia, nor for Prof. Hooke's contention that it (Passover) lasted eleven days like this *Akītu* festival.[30]

Reading of the Torah and covenant ceremony can, therefore, not have taken place on New Year unless the assumptions of these two scholars can be raised to a certainty. Nor does the description of Passover in the Pentateuch lend itself to such an identification with the New Year festival.[31]

Returning once more to the question of the various covenant ceremonies, the salient point in all is that the people pledge themselves to fulfil the commandments of the Torah. The king (as once Moses and Joshua) is only the mediator of the covenant between God and the people, and his part must not be overrated. It is obvious that the head of the people should be instrumental in so vital a matter which was equally binding on him and the people.

During the monarchy, we have on record only one instance of another person acting as mediator of a covenant: according to *II Kings* xi: 17 the priest Jehoiada, after the crowning and anointing of Joash (v. 12) and the elimination of Athaliah, makes " a covenant between the Lord and the king and the people that they should be the Lord's people . . . ". This can be explained by the circumstances of the revolution which necessitated the anointing of the new king to re-establish the Davidic line, and the renewal of the covenant interrupted by Athaliah's usurpation of the royal power and authority. Another contributory factor to Jehoiada's exercise of the royal prerogative may have been the fact that Joash was a minor. This may also explain the presence of the phrase ובין המלך which

---

[30] *Op. cit.*, p. 48.
[31] And this in spite of the discrepancies and contradictions in the various accounts of the festival in the Pentateuch.

separates "the Lord" from "the people". The addition "that they should be the Lord's people," not only shows that the two parties to the covenant are God and the people, as on all other recorded occasions of covenant ceremonies, but also the determination to return to the worship of God, as the continuation of the chapter indicates.

It is noteworthy that according to *II Chr.* xxiii: 18, Jehoiada exercises the functions of David by appointing levitical priests to officiate in the Temple, " as it is written in the law of Moses ". Moreover, he was buried " in the city of David among the kings " (*ibid.* xxix: 16). Was this in recognition of his services, as the Chronicler says, or perhaps rather because he was, in fact, the effective ruler during the king's minority, a self-appointed regent?

We have seen earlier on that Widengren lays stress on the king being the possessor of the book and why he wants to have it so. Of greater importance is his further claim that the king was also the teacher of the Torah. Now, whenever the reading of the Torah is mentioned, either as a command (*Deut.* xvii) or as part of a ceremony (*II Kings* xxiii), the king, as before Moses and Joshua, *reads*; he never teaches or expounds.[32] This is so because the accredited teachers of the Torah were none other but the levitical priests. Ezra is the first O.T. personality of whom it is stated that he not only read, but also explained the Torah. But then he was himself a priest and he was assisted, according to *Neh.* viii, by his priestly colleagues.

Widengren bases his view on a passage he rightly considers important and wrongly neglected, *II Chr.* xvii: 7-9. But, to my

[32] WIDENGREN, *op. cit.*, pp. 18 f. stresses the connection of Moses' reading from the book of the covenant before enacting the covenant with the covenant ceremony of Josiah (*II Kings* xxiii). Following MOWINCKEL, he sees in this correspondence a projection from the days of the monarchy back into the period of myth and mythology before the settlement. Moses is alleged to have performed the same ritual as that obtaining in the royal temple in Jerusalem. To my mind, the connection with the deliverance from Egypt and the proclamation of a basic law of corporate and individual conduct as the content of the covenant makes Moses and his work an historical fact. *Ex.* xxiv: 5-8 can well be a plausible contemporary historical record—even if its literary form is later. There is no compelling reason to see in this passage a *replica* of a ritual enacted at the royal temple by the king. Cf. also BUBER, *op. cit.*, pp. 119 ff. with the relevant notes, against MOWINCKEL; A. WEISER, *Glaube und Geschichte im Alten Testament* (1931), against myth and mythology, especially pp. 23 ff., 28, 30 ff., 39, 44, 49, 51. In the last named passage WEISER rightly stresses history as an experience in the time of Moses and repudiates the view of those who deny the existence of a genuine historical consciousness at that time and assume instead a later transformation of an original myth and mythological thinking into history and historical thinking.

mind, this passage does not " show one of the rulers of the Judaean kingdom [Jehoshaphat] consciously acting in the capacity of an instructor of the law ". It says that the king sent[33] for his commanders[34] to teach, *and with them* Levites and priests. " And they taught in Judah, and with them was the book of the Torah of YHWH . . . " The teachers of the Torah are here, as always in the Bible, the levitical priests. The שרים were, what we would call today, law-enforcement officers whose task it was to see that the teachers were obeyed. But Widengren is right when he says that " the king . . . is also responsible for the teaching of the *Torah* ". This is, however, not the same as being himself מורה, the teacher, the instructor. The king only acts as reader.[35] He is bound to the law and under its authority, he must know it so that he can observe it and rule in justice and righteousness. As head of a religious state, he is ultimately responsible for its teaching and observance.

This includes the regulation of the cult. Since the Bible knows no distinction between temporal and spiritual, but only between profane and holy in Israel, it stands to reason that the consecrated king, the משיח יהוה, is responsible for all functions and institutions of the religious state. Hence his prerogative to appoint priests and regulate the service in the Temple in every detail.

David brought the ark of the covenant to Jerusalem, and Solomon placed it in the Temple he had built. Significantly, tradition and continuity prevailed, and the ark—symbol of God leading his people from bondage to freedom and independence, and of the wandering tribes—found a home in the Temple, symbol of a united Israel under God. A link was established between the desert past and the urban monarchical civilisation: it illustrated the continuity of divine guidance and presence.

Cult and ritual are important, nobody would deny it.[36] But they are only one facet of Israelite life, and if we look at the king's part

---

[33] Maybe . . . שלח ל means " commissioned ".

[34] שרים here does not mean " princes " but is equivalent to שוטרים as in *Deut.* i: 15; cf. also *Deut.* xvi: 18. It means elsewhere "captains ". Cf. also J. VAN DER PLOEG, *Les Šoṭerim d'Israël* in: Oudtestamentische Studien X, 1950, pp. 185 ff. and idem, *Les Chefs du Peuple d'Israël et leurs Titres* in: *R.B.* lvii, 1950, pp. 40 ff.

[35] Cf. WIDENGREN, *op. cit.*, p. 21. Cf. also p. 23, where he stresses the cultic character of the study of the law by the king and his part in the New Year ritual as reader of the *Torah*. To my mind the ritual, cultic element is overstressed and *Ps.* cxxxii has no connection with the injunction contained in *Deut.* xvii:18-20.

[36] It is the unquestioned merit of A. R. JOHNSON, *op. cit.*, and his other studies to have made this clear.

in it we realise how important the Torah is within this ritual. Next to sacrifice, the reading from the Torah occupies a central position. Whether the king was the reader on all occasions or only on special feasts, we do not know, nor is there any evidence that he recited the so-called royal psalms himself, let alone that he enacted the ritual drama of the dying and rising god. It seems extremely doubtful whether such a deliberate imitation of foreign cults reminiscent of foreign domination, such an insult to God, would ever have been tolerated if we remember that the whole tenor of the Bible is an unceasing and unremitting fight against Ba'al in any shape or form. Nobody will deny the presence of Canaanite elements in the psalms. But, basing our ideas of Israelite kingship on the historical and prophetic books—a method practised by M. Noth so convincingly[37] —we may well doubt whether these elements were anything but a literary borrowing, devoid or deliberately stripped of their original connotation. Their cosmic-mythological imagery is no proof that their essentially mythological character and meaning have been preserved and consciously accepted.

The cultic function of the king is attested for his reading of the Torah. It served to remind him and the assembled people of their respective obligations to God under the covenant expressed in the Torah. All royal functions ultimately derive from this covenant relationship between God and His people Israel. The Torah is the divine charter and constitution, and not the work or property of the king who is, after all, only a link, admittedly an important link, between the two partners in the state. In theory at least, next to the Torah, it is the people represented by the elders and the עַם הָאָרֶץ who have to qualify under royal leadership for the fulfilment of the divine promise.

That the political reality was entirely at variance with this ideal demand does not invalidate this pattern. The O.T. itself testifies in the prophets to the gulf that existed between ideal and reality. It is not accidental that David became the pattern and symbol of the Messianic kingdom of the future, David whom the divine king set on the throne as a נָגִיד over his people Israel.

[37] Cf. his *Gott, König, Volk*, pp. 208 (in particular), 214 ff. (stressing the element of "remembrance" forcefully, and rightly so), 223-226. Since this paper is intended to rectify certain claims made in WIDENGREN'S *King and Covenant* a consideration of the so-called royal psalms was not called for. Moreover, I fully concur in NOTH's view, just referred to (p. 208) that it would not be safe to accord to [poetical] allusions in the Psalms the same historical value as to the historical books.

In this whole complicated question it is, as in all matters of human life with its contradictions and inconsistencies, largely a question of emphasis and of preserving a balance. Between historical memory and messianic expectation and redemption, the Davidic king holds sway as the משיח יהוה, not as the annual enactor of the ritual drama of the dying and rising god of nature. He, together with his people, is charged under the covenant to obey the God of love, justice and righteousness by observing in knowledge and action the commandments, statutes and ordinances of the Torah.

In conclusion it may be helpful to summarise the main points of my argument. Widengren's justified emphasis on the close connection between king, covenant and Torah is in itself a warning against stressing the cultic function of the king as much as he does, the more so since the O.T. itself offers no support for the view that in this the king of ancient Israel conforms to the Near Eastern pattern. Next, the kingship of God severely limits the sacral character of the human king and makes him primarily the instrument, the vicegerent of God, expressed in the term נגיד. Then, again within the confines of the O.T., neither Moses nor Joshua are the *typos* of the Davidic and Northern Israelite ruler respectively, but are charismatic leaders some of whose functions were taken over by the king after his nation-wide rule was established, for reasons to be found in the contemporary historical situation. Among them the military and judicial functions of the man chosen by God are paramount. Further, against this background, the claim advanced by Widengren that the king was the possessor and teacher of the book of the Torah of God must be considered unproven and actually contradicted by the O.T. itself. Lastly, in the matter of the all-important covenant relationship between God and the people of Israel, the king is merely the mediator in his capacity as head of a religious state.

2

DON ISAAC ABRAVANEL: FINANCIER, STATESMAN AND SCHOLAR, 1437-1937[1]

I.

THE Christian reconquest of Spain during the first half of the thirteenth century inaugurated a vigorous Crusade of the Church for a united Christian nation. Islam retreated to Granada, the southernmost part of Andalusia.

[1] A lecture delivered in the University of Manchester on 24th May, to commemorate the quincentenary of his birth.

As only those works of Abravanel which are quoted were available for the preparation of this lecture a final judgment on his real significance must be deferred to a comprehensive monograph, based on the whole literary remains extant and the literature on Abravanel, which the present writer intends to write in due course. The following studies could, with regret, not be used, as they were, or still are, not accessible. For the life- and political-history of Abravanel: F. Baer's *Die Juden im christlichen Spanien II*; for Abravanel as religious philosopher: Jakob Guttmann's *Die religionsphilosophischen Lehren des Isaak Abravanel*, Breslau, 1916; for the Biblical exegesis of Abravanel: S. Grünberg's *Eine Leuchte der Bibelexegese um die Wende des Mittelalters*, Berlin, 1928, which the author kindly sent me on request, but too late for inclusion in this paper. The *M.G.W.J.*, 1937, Heft 3, also contains two articles on Abravanel by S. E. Urbach on *Die Staatsauffassung des Don Isaak Abrabanel*, and by J. Bergmann on *Abrabanels Stellung zur Agada*. The former is a notable contribution (see p. 464, note 2). This came to my notice only after my paper had been sent to the printer. Be it noted here generally for the whole paper that many questions and aspects of Abravanel's teaching could not be dealt with, and others which deserve a fuller treatment could only be touched upon. This will be given them in the intended monograph, in which some views propounded here may need revision after a more careful study of Abravanel and his predecessors has been made. A comprehensive history of the Jewish exegesis in the Middle Ages (Bacher ends with Maimonides) is a serious *lacuna*. To assess Abravanel's own contribution to Biblical exegesis it is indispensable to compare his commentaries in a very detailed analysis with the previous exegesis. The present paper is therefore only a modest attempt to make a small contribution to that problem.†

Jewish themes

The whole country of Spain, though divided politically into Castile, Aragon and Navarre, was now opened up for an extensive Christian propaganda, led by the zealous Dominicans, who called upon the Christian monarchs to dissociate themselves from the Jews and to assist the Church in purging the peninsula from both Muslim and Jewish infidels. It is true, the Laws passed by the Lateran Council of 1215 and repeated by subsequent papal Decrees were directed against these two sections of the Spanish population alike, but in practice it amounted in the first place to a life and death struggle against the Jews. In accordance with the discriminating laws of the Church, the kings issued decrees and made laws against their loyal Jewish subjects. They found it, however, very difficult to put these laws, suggested to them by their Christian conscience and the active Spanish clergy, into practice. For the Jews fulfilled an important and indispensable function in the political and economic life of Spain. Represented in all classes of the population, they formed, in particular, a large part of the middle class engaged in crafts, trade, and commerce and were prominent among the king's financial advisers, and tax farmers. The wars against the Moors were costly and so were later Dynastic troubles. In any case it was the Jewish treasurer or financial advisers and agents who had to supply the necessary money. He who is in charge of the financial administration usually wields considerable political influence as well. It is easy to understand that the Spanish nobility intensely disliked Jews to occupy such key positions by virtue of their ability and loyalty which they themselves claimed by virtue of their birth and position. That the royal house made use of Jewish doctors created additional ill-feeling and the fact that Jews were prominent among the tax farmers made them unpopular among the masses. To complete this dismal picture one need only think of the luxurious life of the few Jews who had risen to high positions and lived just like the other Spanish Grandees. The crown, however, felt that the Jews were necessary for a smooth functioning of the administration, and were not prepared to dispose of their services. I cannot trace here the development of the " Jewish question " leading up to the disastrous events

Don Isaac Abravanel

of the year 1391, in which the excited mob, led by a fanaticised clergy, indulged in a cruel massacre of the Jews throughout Castile. Thousands preferred death to baptism, but a considerable number took baptism, many of them in the hope of returning to their inherited faith after order had been restored. Among the latter we find the grandfather of Isaac Abravanel who escaped death in Seville, where the family had lived for generations, by embracing Christianity. But he fled to Lisbon and returned to Judaism. The Church was not dissatisfied with the result and the success seemed to justify their methods. They thought that the day could not be far off when all the Jews would, either by persuasion or force, adopt the dominant religion. The political authorities deplored such outbreaks of violence and in most cases intervened successfully to avoid a complete annihilation of the valuable Jewish element. They were, naturally, not opposed to a peaceful propaganda among the Jews. At first tolerance of other religions prevailed in Spain, the Jews enjoyed religious autonomy and an organisation in communities of their own. Although the Government made this concession for reasons of better control and a guaranteed regular income, from taxes and tributes, the Jews benefited from this system and could maintain their cultural autonomy. Gradually the Government gave way to clerical pressure and lent their authority to religious disputations. The Jews had even to attend in their own synagogues missionary sermons by Dominicans (and later also Franciscans). Invitations to public disputations could not be refused, but the Jews had to be very careful in their replies to questions which they had to answer and could not attack openly the Christian dogma. The first disputation took place in Barcelona in 1263, in the presence of the king of Aragon. Raimund Pennaforte, head of the Dominican order in Spain and confessor of the king, was in the chair. Pablo Christiani, a zealous convert, could not convince his Jewish opponent, Nachmanides, that the Messiah had already risen in the Divine Christ, by his martyrdom and death the Saviour of mankind, and that the Torah of the Jews had been abrogated thereby. Despite his victory, Nachmanides was sent into exile because he had repeated in a treatise what he had answered to his opponent. The Church could not suffer defeat, thus the fate of the rabbi should prove to the Christian world at least the superiority of Christianity as interpreted by the Dominican. The Jews were intimidated incessantly by predicant monks and were exposed to all sorts of humiliation, from the exclusion from holding public offices down to the badge on their outer garments and other distinctions from the Spaniards. They were also forbidden to employ Christian servants. Although these restrictive laws were temporarily rescinded, it was this stigma of outcasts from Spanish society which weighed heavily on the Jewish mind. Discriminating laws, Dominican propaganda, a mob, ready at any moment to fall upon the Jews in the name of Christ, but in reality in the hope of rich spoil, they altogether undermined the Jewish resistance, especially in the higher circles of society where assimilation to the Spanish way of life prevailed. No wonder, that many accepted Christianity hoping to escape spiritual torture and social degradation. The Church did not fail to influence their souls so that their conversion should be followed by sincerity and active participation in their new faith. For it did not escape the ever vigilant eyes of the clergy that secretly these New Christians (Marranos) practised their old faith, that they kept friendship with their relatives and Jewish friends. This behaviour threatened to deprive the Church of the fruits of Dominican efforts. The old problem remained, and another disputation was held in Tortosa in 1413 with the object of effacing all traces of Judaism by complete surrender. A new phase in the struggle began with the united efforts of the archbishop Paul of Burgos, formerly Rabbi Solomon Hallewi, the unscrupulous Vicente Ferrer and Benedict XIII. Among the defenders of Judaism was Joseph Albo (1380-1440). Geronimo de Santa Fe, formerly R. Joshua of Lorca, fought for the Church. The question of the Messiah was again the centre of discussion, which ended without the expected result. Terrorism and intimidation continued, although the Jews enjoyed a temporary respite during the four decades following upon Tortosa. Only the union of Aragon and Castile through the marriage between Ferdinand and Isabella in 1474 opened the last phase, ending, as is well known, with the expulsion of the Jews from Spain in 1492. This time the Marranos were the target of the combined attack of State and Church. The decisive march towards a united Christian Spain began with the introduction of the Inquisition in Spain under Torquemada, the Dominican confessor of the queen. Countless victims demonstrated again and again to their judges that the Church could only secure the unconditional surrender of all the Marranos with their families by a complete removal of the Jews. For these were the real obstacle to the effective cure of the New Christians from the Jewish "disease." The conquest of Moorish Granada inspired the leaders with such enthusiasm that the king felt impelled to issue the fatal decree in 1492, that all Jews throughout his kingdom had either to embrace the so visibly victorious faith or leave the realm within three months. The damage which would ensue for the financial and economic life in general was, at least for the time being, negligible compared with the great moral success of eliminating the stubborn Jewish heresy from the distinctly Christian Spanish nation.

II.

Into such a world was born Don Isaac Abravanel in 1437, in Lisbon, where his father acted as financial agent to the Court.[1] Isaac received an extensive education in Jewish and secular learning, which enabled him to gain distinction as a writer so great that he can be regarded as the last prominent scholar of the Spanish period in Jewish history. He served king Alfonso as financial adviser till the monarch's death in 1481. He tells us that he enjoyed royal favour and the friendship of the ministers and courtiers, which speaks for his personality. Being a man of refined culture with a genuine interest in philosophy and theology, his house became the meeting-place of nobles and scholars. This was valuable for the shaping of his thought, despite his self-accusations that he had—in the company of kings, princes and nobles—neglected study and learning.[2]

[1] This short biographical note is based on the editor's Hebrew preface to Abravanel's *Commentary on Daniel*.

[2] Abravanel's preface to his commentary on *Kings* contains an even stronger self-accusation for having forsaken the kingdom of Judah and Israel, his heritage

Jewish themes

Alfonso's successor, suspicious of the friends and advisers of his father, persecuted and put them to death. Abravanel speaks of intrigues and calumnies at Court to which he would have fallen victim had not one of his noble friends warned him to evade going to Court on the royal request. He fled into Castile; this confirmed the king in his suspicion that Abravanel had conspired with his close friend, the Duke of Braganza, against the king. The accusation was entirely unfounded, but the king confiscated Abravanel's whole property. Finding that *Torath haShem* was better than thousands of pieces of gold and silver, Abravanel devoted his leisure to study and teaching and began his *Commentary on the Early Prophets*. He had just begun his Commentary on the book of *Kings* when he received a summons to Ferdinand of Castile, in 1484, which resulted in his appointment as financial adviser and treasurer to the Crown,[1] an office he held until the expulsion. Their Catholic majesties would certainly not have employed a Jew if he did not serve them loyally and in the interests of the country. Both the king and the queen showed him their favour and it is largely due to his skill and resourcefulness that Ferdinand could finance and conduct the "Holy War" against Granada. It adds a touch of irony to the tragic story of the expulsion that Abravanel should have so conspicuously contributed to the successful campaign against the Moors, since Ferdinand's victory was the immediate cause of his anti-Jewish measures, and, moreover, that Abravanel served a queen whose confessor was Torquemada. Abravanel tells the story of that expulsion in passionate terms, speaking of the king who wished to bring under the wings of his God who had given him victory over Granada, the people who walk in darkness, the scattered Israel, and to win back to his religion the backsliding daughter or to send them forth to another country. In vain did he offer his own, and all the money and possessions of the Jews. Equally fruitless was the intervention of his friends, the Spanish grandees, for the queen stiffened the king, and the

—the Abravanels claimed Davidic descent—and the interpretation of their history for worldly honours and service of other kings.

[1] *Loc. cit.*, and esp. Abravanel's preface to *Joshua* in his *Commentary on the Early Prophets*, Hamburg, 1687.

decree was made public. On the appointed day 300,000 Jews led by their God, left Spain without clear object.[1] He describes vividly the many misfortunes the exiles had to endure on the high seas and on land, how they were robbed and slain, died of hunger and pestilence, until within a few years their number had dwindled to ten thousand.[1] He himself came to Naples with his family where he wrote his Commentary on *Kings*. Living honoured and in peace among the great he served King Fernando. When Charles of Anjou sacked Naples, Abravanel accompanied Alfonso, Fernando's successor, into exile. His house with his valuable library fell a prey to pillaging French troops. After the king's death he found a refuge in Corfu, from there he wandered to Monopoli, where he wrote most of his books.[2] At last he found a home with his son Josef in Venice, where he rendered once more public service in negotiating a commercial treaty between the Republic and Portugal about the trade in spices. His advice was eagerly sought until his death occurred in 1508. Among the chief mourners who brought his dead body to the Jewish cemetery in Padua were the leaders of the city. The man who experienced so many vicissitudes in his life could find no rest even in death, for in 1509 the cemetery was destroyed. Abravanel had served the kings and princes wherever he lived. The experience he gained in his political career found expression in his commentaries and other writings. To these we now turn.

III.

To do justice to the literary work of Abravanel we must place it within the history of his time. He lived at the close

---

[1] Comm. on *Daniel*, 5b. 1; 6b. r.; 7a. 1. Preface to *Kings* and Introduction to Comm. on *Deuteronomy* (in *Comm. on the Pentateuch*, Venice, 1579). Esp. the Comm. on *Daniel* contains frequent references to contemporary Jewish history, including the Marranos.

[2] A full list of his extant works is given in J. Fuerst's *Bibliotheca Judaica*, pp. 11/15, or in *Jew. Enc.* s.v. *Abravanel*. Abravanel refers frequently in his Comms. to his historical work *Yamoth 'Olam* from Adam to his own day, the loss of which is the more to be regretted as it could throw light on Abravanel as historian. We could also learn how he used his knowledge of ancient history and his own political experience in addition to his many remarks in his Comms. He also refers when discussing prophecy to his treatise *maḥaze Shaddai* which is also lost.

of an epoch rich in individual scholars whose achievements in philosophy, science and medicine bore fruit outside Judaism as well, and form an integral part of mediæval culture and civilisation. Abravanel exerted an influence on Biblical exegetes, especially in the seventeenth and eighteenth centuries, next in importance to Maimonides (1135-1204). But the age of Abravanel was no longer that of Maimonides. The unfavourable atmosphere of persecution and humiliation to which Judaism was subjected left an indelible mark upon the attitude of the Jewish thinkers to the tendencies which had arisen following upon Maimonides. Attack from without, disintegration within, made it imperative for the responsible teachers of Judaism to insist on the strictest adherence to traditional teaching and interpretation, and on rigid observance of the traditional Jewish form of living. Moreover, the days when Muslims, Jews and Christians laid more stress on the binding than the separating features of their systems irrevocably belonged to the past. The tendency to harmonise Revelation and Reason gave way to the subordination if not surrender of speculation. This general process did not pass unnoticed in the Jewish camp. Even without it the Jews could not tolerate free thought undermining the fortress of tradition, and they had to struggle for the maintenance of their religion which was discredited as inferior. They honestly believed that they could achieve this only by reasserting the sole and sufficient authority of Written and Oral Torah. Speculation could not be banned but it had to be limited. There was and is only one truth, that of revelation. Speculation can and must help to bear out this truth, but no longer must Scripture be interpreted to satisfy human reason, if need be by ascribing an esoteric, hidden meaning to Scripture. Reason should help to establish the literal meaning in order to interpret tradition for a persecuted people to sustain them in their inherited faith, to give them strength and confidence in a better future, but first of all to make their plight tolerable by expounding to them the truth and beauty of their own religion. It was necessary to make the people immune against the temptations of the Church and the promises of a better life, both spiritually and materially. The Rabbis of the day fought those who dissolved Judaism into a philosophic system, into pure Ethics and Metaphysics. No wonder that the character of contemporary Jewish literature is apologetic and polemic in the first place. Defence is necessarily conservative. No doubt, those who did not believe in the values of philosophy and science, and consequently wished all secular study to be banned, were reactionary. But the conservative majority saved Judaism from destruction, and handed it down intact to following generations. They did not despise philosophy but at the same time they did not allow Aristotle an authority equal (or even superior) to that of the Torah.

IV.

In such an atmosphere Abravanel grew up. Quite naturally he stands on the shoulders of his predecessors and makes ample use of their interpretations of the Bible. He consulted the sages of the Talmudic period whose authority he acknowledged and, where possible, followed. There are, however, instances where he disagrees or offers an alternative interpretation by expounding the literal meaning of the passage in question. He frankly admits this his indebtedness, but he neither follows nor rejects earlier findings blindly. He uses his own judgment, supported by grammatical knowledge and wide experience in the world of affairs. He is undoubtedly greatly influenced in his exposition of the Pentateuch, the Earlier and Later Prophets, and of Daniel by Maimonides, Nachmanides (1194-1270) and Gersonides (1288-1344), and to a lesser degree by Rashi (born 1040) and Ibn Ezra (1091-1167). But he uses them critically and upholds his own against them. His commentaries are far more than a mere compilation, or a convenient summary of earlier views. This is as true of his method as of his comments in detail.[1] He reminds one rather of the modern style of Biblical commentaries with their critical discussion of prior exegesis. Thus, whole chapters in his Commentary on *Daniel*, e.g. deal

---

[1] Cp. the devastating verdict of the eminent Steinschneider in his *Polemische und apologetische Literatur der Juden etc.*, Leipzig, 1877, p. 375, with n. 55 to the contrary.

with such critical discussions, followed by a sound criticism of their attitude to and interpretation of individual passages. After giving his reasons for and against in a clear exposition he states his own view. Such scholarly procedure is something novel in the history of Biblical exegesis, Jewish as well as Christian. Expressing his disapproval of preceding Jewish exegesis in unmistakable terms he is nevertheless not so conceited as to fancy himself in sole possession of the truth, but admits other interpretations as also possible and good. This measure of objectivity prompted him to introduce into Jewish exegesis an element hitherto unknown. He made a careful, extensive study of the exegesis of the Church fathers and mediæval Christian scholars. This cannot be dismissed by a reference to the apologetic and polemic character of contemporary Jewish literature. True, the Messianic prophecies had to be defended against the Christian claim that Isaiah's predictions pointed to Jesus, and that Daniel's Fifth Empire referred to the reign of the Antichrist, to quote only two obvious examples. But the numerous quotations of, and references to Jerome and Nicholas of Lyra in the first place, and occasionally to Isidore of Seville,[1] Porphyry, Bede, Leo Africanus and Albertus Magnus and even to the above-mentioned Paul of Burgos and other renegades throughout Abravanel's commentaries, cannot be attributed to such a tendency. Thus we believe there is good reason to ascribe this scholarly attitude to the coming of the new age, and to see in this readiness to look for truth where it can be found, be it even in quarters antagonistic or openly hostile to Judaism, the beginning of scholarship for its own sake which characterizes the Renaissance. This is confirmed by Abravanel's use of Latin Chronicles dealing with the history of the Assyrians, Babylonians, Medes and Persians,[2] as well as with that of Roman antiquity. His material far exceeds what he found in Josef

---

[1] Comm on *Daniel*, 53a. r, the sage *Isidro*. For want of space I cannot give references for all names and statements. Porphyry is in this commentary twice referred to as a Christian, once rightly styled a Greek philosopher. Probably Jerome is the source for Abravanel's acquaintance with Porphyry's *Commentary on Daniel* which is no longer extant.

[2] Frequently referred to as the *Chronicles of the Kings of Persia*, e.g. in *loc. cit.* 41a. r., giving preference to them against the sages.

ben Gorion's *Josippon* (Pseudo-Josephus).[1] Moreover, it generally is not merely embellishment but forms part of the argument, be it to prove the accuracy of the Biblical narrative, to explain it, or to provide a historical background. Though this knowledge and its application do not make Abravanel a humanist in the strict sense, they are characteristic of his personality which is otherwise so typical of the conservative tendency of that period in Judaism whose last representative Abravanel is. Through this side of his personality he clearly reaches over into the next age of human thought. A few examples may illustrate this. He speaks of the various forms of the constitution of Ancient Rome, quotes Vergil, Ovid and other Latin authors in commenting upon Nebuchadnezzar's dream in *Daniel*, and states, in this connection, that Circe knew how to change man into an animal.[2] Or the expression *as the appearance of horses*, used for the army in *Joel* ii, 4 reminds him of the centaurs whom Hercules had captured.[3] It may be argued that all these are minor details without significance, testifying merely to a certain degree of *Bildung* of the author Abravanel. Taken individually by themselves, this cannot be denied, but grouped together, they make a whole which cannot be overlooked if seen in connection with what can only be called the beginnings of research and of a strictly scientific approach. Not only does Abravanel trace the story of the queen of the Amazons and Alexander the Great, told by Gersonides, back to *Josippon* as the primary source, but he shows a truly scholarly mind in a significant text-critical remark on a passage in the 39th chapter of the *Pirke d'R. Eliezer*. This forms the first part of Abravanel's *Yᵉshuʿoth Mᵉshiḥo*, in which he collected all the Midrashic-Talmudic evidence for the Messiah. In certain editions, he informs us, he found a variant reading and expounded the

---

[1] I could only use the Latin translation, ed. Oxford, 1706. Abravanel's sources in addition to the Josippon (s. Book. VI, ch. xliii, for various constitutions of Rome, elaborated by Abravanel) must yet be found, especially what is meant by the " Chronicles of the Latins," etc.

[2] Comm. on *Dan*. 33b. l./34a. r.

[3] Also mentioned in A. Merx: *Die Profetie des Joel*, Halle, 1879, a model comm. which should find successors for all the Biblical books! It is noteworthy for a balanced judgment on Abravanel as a commentator.

passage also according to this variant, adding *if it is correct*.[1] Quite clear and convincing a case for the scientific approach is presented in his attitude to such questions as date and authorship of the *Earlier Prophets* or some of the Hagiographa. In order to realize the characteristic novelty of his method a few remarks are necessary on Abravanel's attitude to his Jewish predecessors as he describes it himself, in contradistinction to his own method of Biblical exegesis. This he defines as an attempt to bring out the clear, literal meaning of the text (*Pᵉshaṭ*) by laying stress on the general meaning and import of the Biblical books. He deplores the method of Abraham ibn Ezra and of Nachmanides who like to speak in riddles, as well as that of Gersonides who aims at expounding the moral value of the narratives. He especially carps at the latter method, which he considers vain in so far as the words of the prophets themselves are valuable ethically and intellectually. He likewise condemns Ibn Ezra for his grammatical exegesis and the superficiality of his literal interpretation which by its brevity is insufficient for the true explanation of the real meaning of Scripture. But in reality he follows him often in detail, expressly stating so! (He would have done well to adopt his brevity also!) Rashi is, for him, over-dependent on the Midrashic explanations of the sages, a point which is nearer to the truth though rather one-sided.[2] He naturally acknowledges Rashi's explanation where he finds it good. His own use of the haggadic material of the sages distinguishes him from Rashi in that he subjects this material to criticism and tries to find the reason for such an interpretation which he very often adopts. But it is different with Nachmanides who states in the Preface to his Commentary on the Torah, in strikingly similar terms, his intention to expound the true sense of the Law. But we venture to think that Abravanel is more consistent in putting

[1] 2a. r. Note also the importance of the Exodus from Egypt as the prototype of the future ultimate Redemption, which will also take place in the night of *Passover*.

[2] *Comm. on Early Prophets*, Introd. 4a. r./l., where he also blames R. D. Qimḥi for not giving references to earlier commentaries, Midrashim and sayings of the sages, quoted by him.

his method—which is, in principle at least, also that of Nachmanides—into practice as is amply testified by a large number of dissenting interpretations.[1] He differs more widely from Gersonides, though he follows his form of interpretation by first explaining the words and then giving the meaning of the passage or a larger section. A comparison of the two comments on the first verses in *Genesis* e.g., however, shows that, although most of the twelve words which Abravanel thus explains are also explained by Gersonides, Abravanel keeps much more within the limits of a linguistic and literal interpretation, whereas Gersonides rationalizes as a metaphysicist. The fact that Abravanel makes ample use of philosophical terminology must not lead us to assume that his interpretation is philosophical and aims at the esoteric meaning of Scripture. He does not see any need to write a rational guide to the perception of God on the basis of Scripture like Gersonides. Nevertheless, it would be wrong to look in Abravanel's commentaries for an exclusive application of the method of *Pᵉshaṭ*. He gives sometimes symbolical and figurative explanations [2] but makes it clear

---

[1] E.g. in the question what God created first (s. *Comm. on Pentateuch*, Introd. to *Genesis*), where he also criticizes Ibn Ezra, Gersonides and Rashi. Or, in the question of the creation of the angels, where he censures also Maimonides and Baḥya. In commenting on the meaning of *the light* (*ha'or*) the views of Nicholas of Lyra and of the commentators of the nations are in addition refuted. Abravanel finds the sages of the *Gemara* more helpful, who *know the way of God*, a very characteristic attitude. Other similar phrases run: *the views of these Rabbis* (Maimonides, Nachmanides etc.) *do not agree with the testimony of Torah nor with the words of the sages ;* or, *such an interpretation is strange to the literal meaning of Scripture.* Disagreement with Nachmanides, Gersonides, etc., is especially important in the question of the revelation of the Torah to the whole nation. In his comment on *Deut.* xxviii, 15 ff., Abravanel fiercely attacks Nachmanides because for him these verses point to the first Temple, its destruction and the Babylonian exile, as well as to the second Temple. This is intolerable for Abravanel, who nowhere admits any reference to the second Temple and a second exile, for the return from Babel was not the promised Redemption. The Deuteronomic passage, as all other predictions, refer to the final Redemption. The Jews still live in the first Exile, the second Commonwealth was only an episode. Cp. also Comm. on *Daniel*, 61b. l.

[2] Cp. his identification of the angels with the Separate Intelligences (Comm. on *Genesis*, Introd.) or the expression in *Ezekiel* xi, 19, *heart of stone* (*Yᵉshu'oth Mᵉshiḥo*, 39b. l.). Especially the last example is instructive for Abravanel's concession to the figurative method if a literal meaning is incompatible with

that such a meaning is additional to the verbal significance of the particular passage. He admits a deviation from the *P'shaṭ* only in such very rare cases where the literal meaning is evidently contrary or inaccessible to human reason, thus distinguishing himself sharply from Maimonides and also Gersonides. This difference is the result of Abravanel's conviction that the divinely revealed Torah is essentially clear in its own terms, and that man can understand the obvious meaning of Scripture with the help of traditional exegesis and his own discerning faculty. By no means must he read into the Bible philosophical theories, which are foreign to Scripture, nor rationalize the Biblical narratives. Despite his indebtedness to previous Jewish exegesis, there is in his clear reasoned argument, combined with a deep knowledge of affairs and a systematic treatment of particular problems arising out of the text, sufficient originality in his commentaries to claim for him high rank as a creative exegete. A number of questions and doubts dealing with the general contents of the books and real difficulties of the text introduce his comments. By that he achieves a unity of treatment of that text and indicates that a solution of these questions brings out the meaning, importance and teaching of the book. Further, he can thus best deal with the various opinions expressed by his Jewish and Christian predecessors and also present his own views. If many of the questions are thus given by his careful study of previous exegesis with the view of answering them satisfactorily, it may be argued that Abravanel kept strictly within the limits set for him by his mediæval milieu. The only advantage of his method would then be a systematic presentation. This should not be belittled, for his method of

reason. Or the four beasts in *Daniel* are explained as *heavenly princes* (Comm. on *Dan.*, 14a.). For a symbolical interpretation *see* Comm. on *Leviticus*, Introd., where he adduces in addition to Gersonides, whom he here praises, two more reasons for the choice of the three kinds of cattle : (1) *baqar* points to Abraham (cp. *Genesis* xviii, 7), *ḳebhes* to Isaac, and '*ez* to Jacob (cp. *Gen.* xxvii, 9), whereas by *gozel* and *tur* Moses and Aaron are meant. (2) These kinds of cattle and birds were chosen as symbolic for the Israelite nation in connection with such passages as *Amos* iv, 1, or *Hosea* iv, 16. Because of Isaiah's comparison (in ch. liii) with *ṣon* and *raḥel* the Israelites are commanded to offer these kinds as a substitute for their own flesh and blood.

adducing every available piece of evidence, positive as well as negative, is in itself a first step in scientific research. But this procedure which is a novelty in Biblical exegesis is outweighed by the courageous manner in which Abravanel lays his finger on real difficulties in the text as not even Ibn Ezra has done before him. He thus laid the foundations of the historico-critical " Einleitungswissenschaft". Whether these questions and doubts are due to scholastic influence cannot easily be determined. An obvious comparison with the frequently quoted Nicholas of Lyra's *Postillæ* [1] to the Pentateuch has so far not convinced us. The fact that he lived at the end of an epoch, the characteristic feature of which was the endeavour to maintain and safeguard a rich heritage, and to repair the breaches and cracks in the wall of tradition, quite naturally suggested to a man of affairs the need to sum up what had been achieved hitherto, and to add to it wherever he had something relevant to say. For, although there was a genuine desire for study and learning in him, he was, as a realist, conscious of the necessity to sustain the shattered hopes of his generation, to strengthen their courage, and to support them in their effort to hold out and survive the tragedy of the expulsion. He intended by expounding to them the good tidings of the *prophet* Daniel " to rouse his people Israel from the sleep of Exile " so that they might take to heart the promises of Redemption to fill the downhearted with new confidence.[2] But that Abravanel, in addition, could appeal to Christian Bible scholars (Buxtorf the younger, Buddeus, Carpzow and others) and command a place in the science of exegesis outside Judaism as well, is due, not so much to the fact that his criticism of the Christian claim on the Old Testament as pointing to the Messiahship of Jesus represented an important challenge which they felt impelled to refute,[3] but rather to his novel approach to the composition, date and authorship of the Biblical books. For this is much more important. His investigation into the general character and meaning

[1] Edition Bale, 1506. For Rashi's influence on Nicholas see A. J. Michalski in a careful study on *Lev.*, *Num.* and *Deut.* in *ZAW*, 1915/16 in addition to the literature quoted in *Encycl. Jud.*, Band x.
[2] Comm. on *Dan.*, 7a. l./8a. r. [3] See Fürst, *loc. cit.* (n. 6).

of Scripture is executed under the four categories of Greek philosophy: Purpose, Matter, Agent or Author, and Form.[1] Applying the first, second and fourth categories to the question of the division of the Canon he contrasts the traditional Jewish division into Law, Prophets and Hagiographa with the Christian division into four parts (legal, historical, prophetic and Wisdom literature). He objects to their classification of David among the prophets with his book of Psalms and to *sapientes* as designation of the Hagiographa, thus putting them on the same level as the writings of Aristotle and other philosophers, whereas in reality they are composed with the aid of God (*b^eruaḥ haq-qodesh*). He himself divides the Canon according to the time of the composition of the several books. Chronologically the Law comes first as being written before the entry of Israel into Canaan. All books written during the period of the Hebrew monarchy in *Ereṣ Yisrael* before the Exile are assigned to the second group.[2] The third group belongs to the period following upon the destruction of the Temple, the Exile and subsequent return.[3] Here is at any rate an attempt to apply one guiding principle to the whole corpus of Scripture while evading the question of growth and close of the Canon, and avoiding giving reasons for placing the several books according to subject matter and form.[4]

The discussion of authorship reveals considerable critical acumen. Thus, he states that because of seven passages containing the phrase *unto this day*[5] Joshua could not have written his book, for this phrase denotes clearly that the book was written after the events had happened. He is confirmed in that opinion by the narrative of the lot of Dan which must also belong

---

[1] E.g. in his comment on *Exodus* xix, and in his Introd. to Comm. on *Levit*.

[2] I.e. Joshua, Judges, Ruth, Samuel, Kings, Isaiah, Jeremiah, Lamentations, Hosea, Joel, Amos, Obadiah, Jonah, Micah, Nahum, Habbakuk and Zephaniah. This is, he avers, in accordance with the character of the Scriptures and of the statement of the sages in the *Seder 'Olam* (*Rabba*), frequently quoted by him. Its influence on his historical comments will have to be defined. The Psalter, Proverbs and Qoheleth belong to this same period.

[3] I.e. Ezekiel, Esther, Ezra, and Chronicles (written by Ezra). After the return from exile were written Ḥaggai, Zechariah and Mal'achi.

[4] Preface to *Joshua*, 1b. r./2a. l.

[5] *Loc. cit.* 2a. l./b. r. bottom. Quoted in their order of occurrence they are: iv, 9; v, 9; vii, 26; ix, 27; xiv, 14; xv, 63; xvi, 10.

to a much later date, for the war of Dan falls in the period of the Judges towards the end.[1] Samuel wrote it as well as *Judges*, whereas he wrote of his own book only those chapters which deal with events in his own day. The other portions of *Samuel* were written by the prophets Nathan and Gad. It was Jeremiah who collected the whole material and made the present book of *Samuel* out of it. In doing so Jeremiah—according to Jewish tradition, shared by Abravanel, the author of the book of *Kings* —undoubtedly added words to explain statements and facts as he understood them on the basis of his own experience, and therefore he said *unto this day*.[2] But not only experience but also God guided the prophets who worked upon older chronicles when they collected and selected their material. Otherwise they would not have been able to distinguish truth from untruth, and what is necessary from what is not. For it is the way of scribes and recorders to praise or criticize more than is fitting out of love and hatred. Therefore, the prophets could write everything in truth and perfection only by being taught by God. In that way Abravanel vindicates the prophetic character of these four books.[3] The discussion why the book of *Ruth*—written according to Jewish tradition by Samuel— is placed in the Canon under the Hagiographa and not under the prophets, serves as another example of Abravanel's positive and creative criticism. From a chronological point of view these stories should be written in *Judges*. But *Judges* deals primarily with the happenings to Israel and the judges in general. Thus, particular things which happened to Jews in

---

[1] Cp. *Judges*, xviii, esp. *v.* 31 and xix, 47, with the whole section from 40 ff. Similar reasons are advanced for the view that Samuel did not write his book (cp. v, 5 and vi, 18); before all the phrase in ix, 9 : *for he that is now called a prophet was beforetime called a seer* clearly points, for Abravanel, to a much later date after Samuel's death when the customs had changed. This example, together with another *to this day* (II. *Sam.* vi, 8) betray considerable understanding of the chronological and historical problems in these books. Against Jerome's name *Regum* for the book of *Samuel* Abravanel defends the name *Samuel* for the perfect judge and David as the perfect king, the more so since Samuel had written the part dealing with Saul and David.

[2] *Loc. cit.* 2b. r.

[3] 2b. l. The profound problem of prophecy and its difference from *ruaḥ haq-qodesh* was discussed only by Maimonides in his *More* II, ch. 45, wherefore Abravanel discussed it at length in his lost treatise *maḥaze Shaddai*.

this period but did not affect the whole of Israel are left out. Now, Samuel was personally interested in the family history of David, therefore he traced this history back and wrote *Ruth* as a separate Scroll after he had completed *Judges*. As he did so of his own free will and was not commanded by God, such a book composed in honour of David could not be put on the same level with the prophetic writings.[1] This argument shows at least that Abravanel felt a real difficulty and he betrays a critical mind in his attempt to solve it. For him, the several Biblical books formed an organic unity, consequently he wished to bring out the meaning of the book as a whole rather than of the single words. His problem, therefore, was to explain why sections or passages—seemingly out of place for various reasons (historical, chronological or those of character or contents of the book)—occupy their present position, and justify it. Thus he explains the position of Psalm xviii in II. *Samuel* xxii, arguing that it was fitting that David should express in a general song his thanks to God for His visible support in all his battles, and for the successful completion of the wars.[2] Struck by the numerous variants in Psalm xviii in the Psalter as compared with the same in *Samuel*, Abravanel explains the divergence by making a distinction between two recensions resulting from the different time, circumstances and purpose. In *Samuel* we have a spontaneous dialogue between David and his Creator, composed in David's youth. But when David composed his

---

[1] *Loc. cit.* 3a. r. Here Abravanel puts and answers the question why *Chronicles*, containing many prophetic stories, is placed with the Hagiographa: (1) Its authors were Ezra and Nehemiah, who were no prophets. (2) They had not received the Divine command to write it. (3) Not by means of prophetic inspiration did they write it but culled the stories from the prophets and Hagiographa which were in their midst, changing facts and proper names in order to improve the understanding of these stories. Moreover, Ezra intended by writing *Chronicles* to set a monument to David and his house as there were left only the two tribes of Benjamin and Juda and as Zerubbabel was of the house of David. He continued the story in *Ezra* (return from Exile, building of the second Temple). As he considered both books as one, the last words of *Chronicles* are actually the beginning of *Ezra*. Having the glorification of David in mind, Ezra left out everything which could be detrimental to his memory. In this way Abravanel solves the difficulties of repetitions or omissions in *Chronicles* compared with *Samuel*. (Preface to *Samuel*, 47a. r./l.)

[2] *Ibid.*

book of *Psalms* in lonely old age he made several changes in the wording in order to make it more intelligible to the lonely soul in prayer. Moreover, apart from his desire to make an originally intimate dialogue accessible to the understanding of the community, literary and stylistic considerations prompted him to improve the expression in accord with poetic custom.[1] Abravanel ranks Jeremiah next to Moses, the unsurpassed prophet, as regards perfection of Imagination, but he is aware of his stylistic shortcomings. These he tries to explain by pointing out that Jeremiah had to enter upon his prophetic career when still young. He had not yet mastered the language, the right arrangement of words, the beauty of metaphor (this is hardly justified!), therefore he rightly said: *Ah Lord God, behold, I cannot speak: for I (am) a child.* Isaiah was of royal blood, enjoyed an excellent education at Court, and therefore knew how to write beautifully. The other prophets prophesied in mature age, experienced in the affairs of the world, whereas Jeremiah, descended from the priests of Anathoth, a small provincial place, could only use a language corresponding to the stage he had reached when he was commanded to prophesy.[2] In this connection we must mention Abravanel's attempt to explain the divergence between the same stories told in *Kings, Chronicles, Isaiah* and *Jeremiah.* He distinguishes between the

[1] Comment on II. *Samuel* xxii, p. 100a. r./l. He thus explains the change of the second *kaf* (*Sam.* v. 1) into *yad* in the psalm, repeating this process systematically for all the variants. Another example of his tendency to deal with a question in its proper place completely and systematically is served in his *Mashmiʿa yᵉshuʿah* when he comments on *Obadiah.* As this book deals exclusively with *Edom,* Abravanel discusses here all prophecies directed against Edom collected from the other prophets under the following aspects: to whom, to what event, and to what date do they refer, did they come true or have they still to come true. This is of greatest importance for their bearing on the coming of the Messiah (58b. l.).

[2] Comm. on *Jeremiah* in: *Comm. on Later Prophets*, Amsterdam, 1641, p. 96a. r./l. The phrase: *thus far (are) the words of Jeremiah* at the end of ch. li. suggests to Abravanel that Jeremiah could neither have written the last chapter in his book nor in *Kings.* Ezra or the "Men of the great Assembly" transferred the last chapter of *Kings* to the end of *Jeremiah* when they collected the books and arranged the Canon for two reasons. (1) The reader thus knew that Jeremiah's prophecy of the destruction of Jerusalem had come true and (2) to link it up with the book of *Ezekiel* (Introd. to *Comm. on Early Prophets*, 3a. l./b. r.).

historical and the prophetic treatment of these stories, corresponding to their respective purpose and context. Thus, Jeremiah narrates in *Kings* the story of Hezekiah as part of the history of his reign, whilst Isaiah told it under the aspect of prophecy. Or a story is used as a sort of historical background and as a verification of a particular prophecy. The prophets used the *Chronicles of the kings of Judah* which were written down simultaneously with the events, but for their own purposes.[1]

Illustrations by means of comparison between Jewish, Roman or contemporary institutions and offices, and a keen political sense enrich Abravanel's exposition of details, such as his remark on I. *Kings* iii, 1 ff. that Solomon married the daughter of the Egyptian Pharaoh, not because he loved her and was enamoured by her beauty, but for political reasons. It was advisable to gain peace with and the friendship of a great power by such a dynastic marriage.[2] How contemporary events occupied his mind and directed his thought is evident from remarks and comments in his Commentary on *Daniel* (*Ma'y^ene hay-y^eshu'ah*) and in his two other Messianic treatises (*Y^eshu'oth M^eshiḥo* and *Mashmi'a y^eshu'ah*). The meaning and first aim of the visions of Daniel is to encourage, by the parable of the four empires which will be destroyed, the people of Israel to return in repentance to God and to obey Him. That this is addressed to his own generation is evident from the comment on Daniel's character: *and we learnt also (a lesson) for the affairs of the nation in Exile that it is fitting to act like Daniel in holiness and segregation, in seeking (the company) of the wise, in meditation on the Torah and in true and loyal service of*

---

[1] As note 2, p. 463.
[2] Comm. on *Kings*, 10b. 1. The Commentaries on *Deuteronomy, Samuel, Kings* and *Daniel* contain much material for Abravanel's political thought together with theoretical statements on political philosophy in his Comm. on Maimonides' *More*, e.g. I hope to deal with this problem in full in the monograph, with special regard to the question in how far Abravanel's own political experience led him to accept or reject the current theory, influenced by Plato. He draws a parallel between the recorder in I. *Kings* iv, 11 ff., and the Roman *procurator fiscalis* or between the *king's friend* and the *major domus* (loc. cit., 17b. r.). The life at Solomon's Court is illustrated by references to Court officials and practices in contemporary Spain and France.

kings.¹ Interesting is his interpretation of the sufferings of the Marranos and of contemporary history: *that in the midst of all the anguish and persecutions many of our nation leave the religious community and this is heresy, for through the wickedness of the (Christian) nations hundreds of thousands of Jews have forcibly left the Lord* . . . " *until all kingdoms are changed to heresy* " shows that this refers to all nations in general or to the wicked in particular, be it to Rome where our own eyes see in the kingdom of Spain that heretics increase and where they burn them because of their heresy ' in thousands and myriads '. . . . Also all the priests and bishops of Rome in this time run after profit, accept bribes and do not care for their religion, for heresy shines out on their forehead. . . .² He saw in those happenings clear signs of the times, indicating the birthpangs of the Messiah, for he lived in the expectancy of the Messiah, of the end of the Exile and of the promised Redemption (*Gᵉulah*). The prophecy of Daniel was about to come true. Rome, the fourth empire, was in a state of sinful corruption the end of which was death and destruction, and the fifth empire, that of the king Messiah would then dawn upon mankind and bring Redemption to the righteous of the Jews and all nations. Therefore Daniel is set as an example to the Jews. As he was saved by God so Israel will witness Redemption if they but follow Daniel.³

Abravanel's Messianic treatises owe their origin to two reasons. The first practical reason was already stated: he wanted to encourage his fellow Jews by an appeal to be prepared, morally in the first place, for the imminent coming of the Messiah sent by God, who would deliver them from all their sufferings. The second reason is one of defending the current Jewish view on the Messiah against Dominican attacks, more satisfactorily than Nachmanides. Thus, the problems discussed in the *Yᵉshu'oth* and *Mashmi'a* correspond exactly to the questions in the Disputation of Barcelona. Moreover, Geronimo de Santa Fe had again tried in vain to prove from

---

¹ Comm. on *Dan.*, 25a. r. Another similar exhortation is on 38b. r.

² *Yᵉshu'oth Mᵉshiḥo*, 21b. l./22a. r. and Comm. on *Dan.*, 87a. r./l. The standard work on the Marranos is: *History of the Marranos* by Dr. Cecil Roth, 1932. ³ As note 1 above.

Talmud and Midrash Christ's divinity and Messiahship and had afterwards repeated his claims and accusations in two treatises. This fact alone necessitated a competent Jewish reply. Abravanel polemises against Nachmanides who held that no Jew was obliged to believe in the *Haggadah* when Pablo Christiani quoted certain *haggadoth* which seemed to support the Christian claim. Abravanel investigates in systematic manner the whole haggadic material and seeks an answer to the controversial points raised in the Disputations.[1] He had to show that, apart from the Messianological passages in the Bible, there are in Talmud and Midrash unmistakable Messianic predictions which can claim an authority equal to the Biblical ones if they are correctly interpreted. In this attempt he marks a definite advance on his Jewish predecessors and with great exegetical skill he succeeds in vindicating the Jewish point of view. In addition, he rightly points out in his preface to the *Yᵉshuʿoth that the commentators of the Talmud (as is known) do not comment on the haggadoth but are only engaged in the exposition of the miṣwoth (Commandments) in making clear what is forbidden and what is allowed.* This statement testifies to the tendency of these centuries when, under the influence of the French and German schools of Rabbis, study centred almost exclusively upon the Talmud and the exposition of *Halakhah*. Abravanel could claim to fill a real gap in contemporary Jewish literature.[2] All the haggadic evidence was collected and systematically sifted in respect of four questions. The first question, whether the Messiah had already come, or whether the appointed time for his coming was drawing near, shows how real such an investigation was at that time. The third question dealing with his nature (whether divine or as mere man, like one of us, or another separate intellect), and the fourth whether the Torah will be abrogated in its entirety or in parts when he comes,

---

[1] Abravanel admits that the Rabbis had no power to refute the Dominican claim freely. Therefore he interprets these *haggadoth*. The Rabbis would have exposed themselves and their communities to real danger had they done so.

[2] He mentions R. Solomon ben Abraham Adret (1235-1310) and R. Yedayah ha-Bedarsi (*ca.* 1270-*ca.* 1340) who began to deal with the *Haggadah*, but they had not treated the *haggadoth* he himself is going to interpret.

are both no less vital though of a more polemic nature.[1] Here Abravanel is forced to relinquish the literal meaning of the passages and to aver that the first rabbis spoke in riddles and similes in order to instruct us in the aim of the stories rather than in their verbal meaning.[2] In his *Mashmi'a* he naturally quotes the same passages as do his Jewish predecessors in their Messianic treatises.[3] But his treatment singles him out by the completeness and systematic arrangement of the material which is discussed in the light of the four questions. His argument is broader, including frequent references to past and present history, especially that of ancient Rome, both heathen and Christian. He emphasizes again and again the epoch-making conversion of Constantine the Great, and—quite in keeping with the teaching of the mediæval Church—that Constantine had surrendered the rule over Rome to Pope Silvester. This agrees well with the interpretations of the prophecies against Edom and in particular of Daniel's fourth Empire (Rome = Edom). His knowledge of Roman history enabled him to give the prophetic and haggadic predictions a more concrete and therefore a more convincing interpretation.[4]

It still remains to show what sources he used. He himself cites only *The Chronicles of the Latins*, Josef ben Gorion and the Latin text of Flavius Josephus as furnishing some information. Though Abravanel distinguishes between the two he is inconsistent in his judgment, or rather condemnation, of Josephus.

[1] He refutes frequently the views of Nachmanides, and as far as he argues on philosophical grounds also Maimonides.

[2] Here he follows Maimonides (*More*, ii, ch. 47).

[3] For a full treatment of Abravanel's Messianism *see* J. Sarachek: *The Doctrine of the Messiah in Mediæval Jewish Literature*, New York, 1932. This book makes it unnecessary for me to reproduce here a summary based on a careful study of the three Messianic treatises carried out before I had access to Sarachek's book. Unfortunately the development of thought and argument in the various authors is not worked out in the study nor is the influence of the earlier on the later writers clearly indicated by references so that a critical study of Abravanel's own contribution and his indebtedness to previous authors must be reserved for the monograph. As a basis Sarachek's book is very useful as regards the material. I regret that I could not use A. H. Silver's *A History of Messianic Speculation in Israel*, New York, 1927.

[4] His acquaintance with Christian Dogma and doctrines can be seen from passages like 66a. l. and 75a. l. in his Comm. on *Daniel*.

Moreover, his historical sense, otherwise good, failed him in that he takes Josippon in most cases where he uses him as a historical source in the strict sense. He does so, however, with the critical reserve peculiar to him when statements found there do not tally with tradition or Latin histories.[1] His knowledge of Roman history, which filled him with admiration for that ancient Rome whose rule *is far above all other rule like Heaven is above Earth, in wisdom and bravery*,[2] he found particularly useful in interpreting Daniel's visions in keeping with the course of history. Contrary to Gersonides [3] he identifies the *small horn* with the Pope. Papal rule began in Rome—after the destruction of Jerusalem—by a disciple of Jesus and it is called *small* because it was small at the beginning. In those days the emperor ruled over Rome and the Pope taught only the Christians there. Therefore Daniel says *among them* and not *after them*. This small horn survives the three earlier beasts and their empires! The fifth empire is that of the king Messiah—not of the Antichrist as the Christian interpreters, who identify him with the small horn, would have it. This period inaugurates the ultimate Redemption. This will not be followed by an Exile, for from now on Israel, which will not perish like the four empires, will serve God faithfully for ever.[4] Abravanel made ample use, too, of his knowledge of

---

[1] Before basing an exposition of Abravanel's attitude to either of the two on passages like 65a. r./l., 75b. r. or 39b. in his Comm. on *Daniel*, and 40a. r. in his Comm. on *Kings*, I want to collect further evidence. For there is not only constant confusion between Josephus and Josef ben Gorion but a comparison between both, Abravanel and the relevant passages in *Chronicles*, e.g., involves text-critical problems as well.

[2] Comm. on *Dan.*, 42b. r. A similar statement (16a. r.) is made to prove the identity of Rome and Edom, i.e. that Rome not only rules all nations politically but, through the Pope, also their beliefs.

[3] Who identified the small horn with Constantine. Abravanel states the impossibility by asserting that this was one of the greatest Roman emperors. Abravanel was familiar with the history of Rome under the consuls and Caesars before Christ and after and with the persecutions of the Christians (*see loc. cit.*, 43a. r./44a. r.).

[4] Again Gersonides is censured with amazement that he identified the *son of man* with the king Messiah and the *Ancient of days* with either the Roman Senate or the Pope: *This is mere fancy and the truth is that God alone is the agent of Israel's Redemption.*

Persian history, both before and after Alexander the Great, and of that of the Diadochoi. Thus he attacks Gersonides, who finds his explanation of the *he goat* in Alexander's illegitimate birth. Abravanel, thanks to his better knowledge of history, sees in that term a reference to the relative unimportance and insignificance of Macedonia in its early stages.[1] A large part of this Commentary consists of a critical analysis of the views of his predecessors, both Jewish and Christian. Of special importance in this respect is Abraham bar Chiyya (1065-1136) whom he quotes frequently and to whom he is indebted, like his predecessors, for his astronomical or rather astrological knowledge. He does not hesitate to disagree with his source if his own judgment leads him to other conclusions. Yet he borrows completely bar Chiyya's conception and construction of Jewish history in accordance with the course of the planets and follows the parallelism between the periods of World history and the six days of Creation.[2] The agreement between Scripture and astronomy, respecting the termination of the Exile, is clear evidence to Abravanel of the truth of Scripture, and of the right to use astronomy to this end. Turning to his criticism of the Christian exegesis given in special chapters Abravanel polemises in particular against Porphyry, who interpreted the *small horn*[3] and other prophecies as pointing to Antiochos Epiphanes and the Maccabees. Nicholas of Lyra, counted first among the Christian commentators, is followed where he agrees with Jewish tradition and not with Latin, but Abravanel criticizes his chronology.[4] He censures the Church's method of referring all good predictions to the Christians and all bad ones to the Jews.[5] Paul of Burgos with his master Raimund di Martini are refuted and charged with an interpretation of the stories not according to their proper meaning but according to what they wanted them to mean![6]

Abravanel's own exposition must be reserved for a more

[1] *Loc. cit.*, 41a. r. and 53a. r./54b. l.
[2] See *Sefer megillath ham-megalleh*, ed. Guttmann-Poznanski, Berlin, 1924.
[3] See n. 1 above. Albo and others are likewise blamed for referring Daniel's visions to the second Temple. [4] Comm. on *Dan.*, 66a. r.; b. l.
[5] *Loc. cit.*, 75a. r. [6] *Loc. cit.*, 67a. l.

comprehensive treatment of the subject, but it is characteristic and important for his thought that he counted Daniel among the *prophets*. In opposition to Maimonides and other Jewish authorities he proves that the visions bear all the criteria of true prophecy.[1] Thus Daniel—together with the other prophets—supplied him with valuable additional proof for the future Redemption. Taking the visions as predicting future events, he could make the prophecy of the four empires the backbone of his interpretation. The fall of the fourth, accompanied by strange and terrible happenings, would illustrate one of the pillars of the advent of the Messianic age, God's vengeance upon Israel's enemies. Necessarily connected with that age is also Resurrection.[2]

He expresses a confident hope and firm belief in the approaching salvation of his people and all the righteous on earth in these words: *the rod has blossomed, a staff has risen in Israel, the time of the nightingale has come. A vine is before my eyes as if in bloom. Therefore I say, our salvation has drawn near . . . and even if many troubles meet us, they are the birthpangs of the Messiah; this is a time of anguish for Jacob but there will be a saviour and the kingdom will be unto God; His kingdom is an everlasting kingdom and His rule from generation to generation.*[3] Because he saw many despair of the coming of the Messiah he wanted to prove it from the plain straightforward meaning of Scripture. He addresses the *Apikorsim* in the first place,[4] i.e.

---

[1] Abravanel finds support for his view in the *Seder 'Olam* (as well as in the Christian Church). His proof occupies many pages (16b. l./20a. r. and *pass.*). Most of the argument forms a refutation of Maimonides' theory of prophecy. Abravanel distinguishes between prophetic and natural dream and thus refutes Maimonides' view of a common source for prophecy and dream and shows that Maimonides wrongly quotes Aristotle in favour of his view. Anticipating the few remarks made on that question later on in this paper it must be noted that Abravanel takes up this point again and again throughout his commentaries (e.g. in defending Solomon against Maimonides who would deny him prophetic visions, see Comm. on *Kings*, 11 l.). Abravanel takes the traditional, conservative view of the miraculous supranatural character of prophecy against the psychological view of Maimonides who explains prophecy as a natural phenomenon (see Abravanel's Comm. on *More*, II, chs. 32-7 in particular).

[2] Following Maimonides who held that these passages were the clearest of all in Scripture on Resurrection.

[3] *Mashmi'a yᵉshu'ah*, 2a. r./3a. l.   [4] *Loc. cit.*, 83a. l.

here those who disregarded with scorn and contempt the predictions of Scripture. He therefore collected only unmistakable evidence and left out the Hagiographa, the plain literal meaning of which did not necessarily yield Messianic material. Daniel is the most important of the 17 *announcers of good tidings;* Zechariah is the most convincing of the Minor Prophets, and from Isaiah he derives 14 principles by which he inquires into the prophecies of Redemption in all the prophets. The Pentateuch is naturally also included. Next to his primary aim, just discussed, Abravanel wishes to prove convincingly that none of these prophecies refer to the return from the first Exile, the building of the second Temple and the second Commonwealth, but clearly and exclusively to the final Redemption *at the end of days.* They can also not be interpreted in the way of the Christian commentators. He sets the concrete, literal meaning against the Christian claim that the real meaning is the spiritual Redemption, the salvation of the soul effected by Christ's martyrdom and death. Abravanel insists on the actual Redemption in flesh as well as in spirit. (Therefore he stresses Divine vengeance, resurrection and ingathering of the exiles almost coinciding with it.) If the Christians referred the term *Edom* to the Children of Israel because of their sins, they overlooked the fact that immediately following the prediction of vengeance upon Edom is given consolation and comfort for Israel.[1] Here we meet again Abravanel's insistence on the unity of Scripture as a whole, including its single passages. Jesus, for him, is not the promised king Messiah of Davidic origin,[2] nor has he fulfilled the prophecy that after the Redemption most of the nations will turn to the one true God, acknowledge and worship Him and study His Law. For history shows that only a part of the world—chiefly coerced by Constantine—embraced Christianity, whilst more than half of the inhabited Earth is in the hands of the Muslims. The disunion among the Jews in the Second Commonwealth excludes the reference of this prophecy to the Second Temple.[3]

[1] *Loc. cit.,* 30b. l.
[2] *Loc. cit.,* 31b. r./l. He points out—in reference to Matthew i—that in the time of the second Temple husband and wife need no longer be of the same tribe as there was no longer a division of the land.   [3] *Loc. cit.,* 32a. r.

V.

Apart from the pedagogic and apologetic-polemic significance of these Messianic treatises, they throw light on the personality of their author and his attitude to Judaism. How is it possible, we may ask, that such an eminent statesman, such a successful political negotiator had no constructive policy in mind to better the lot of the Jews in his day? Why did he not try to organize a well-ordered exodus from Spain and keep the exiles together and settle them, or at least part of them, in Palestine or the neighbouring countries? Such an idea never entered his mind. A clue to the reason may be seen, perhaps, in Abravanel's denial of the opinion of the sages that Daniel went up to Jerusalem.[1] His explanation is that Daniel did not wish to go to Jerusalem because the Exile was so long and Redemption so very far off. Zerubbabel also returned to Babel from Jerusalem, for which he constantly prayed as well as for Redemption. Exactly the same attitude we find with Abravanel. He was, as we have seen, so convinced of the approaching end of the Exile, and was so certain about God's own deliverance by sending the promised Messiah, that the only thing for the Jews to do was to suffer patiently under foreign rule and oppression and to return to God before He would restore them to their own country. Suffering is God's punishment for their sins. If they repent and reform their ways God in His infinite mercy will deliver them. For, and here we reach the ideological structure the practical outcome of which is this in the political sense passive attitude, Israel is guided by God's particular Providence. God will never abandon His chosen people. He is the God of all the Earth and His Providence watches over all mankind, but only in a general way. Israel, He has chosen among all nations, not to grant her privileges but to serve His Supreme will, embodied in the Torah. If history is the manifestation of God's will and rule, Israel's history is the reaction to this Divine will. It is well with Israel when she obeys God; if she rebels by serving strange gods, He who by covenant has chosen her will also

[1] Based on Josippon, Book I, ch. iii, who lets Daniel die in Susan (*see* Comm. on *Dan.*, 68a. r.).

punish her. But as Jacob is His first born son, He will again and again show mercy upon the repentant Israel. This idea is common to Judaism throughout the Middle Ages, based upon the prophets and the later sages. Abravanel seems to be indebted to Yehudah Hallewi's (1080-1141) *Kusari* for the shaping of his thought of God's particular Providence.[1] His wide though perhaps superficial knowledge of ancient history confirmed his belief in this Divine Providence, for he saw that the might of Rome, the beauty of Greece, the powers of Assyria, Babylonia and Persia had all flourished and perished. Israel alone among these ancient nations had survived, without political organization, without a land, scattered among the nations to testify—not least in her sufferings at their hands —to the will of God, to His might and glory, which will restore her in the days of the Messiah to her land.[2] In this way Abravanel interpreted his own times, like all Jewish thinkers who saw in the continuity of Jewish history the manifestation of a Divine plan and who attributed the Jews' suffering, in the first place, to their own shortcomings, and to the neglect of God's positive commandments. Hence his exposition of the Bible, hence his Messianism, which seems so theoretical because it is propounded with so much learning. Nations perished because they were guided by their own laws and customs (through which alone, to his mind, they are distinguished from each other). Israel survived because she still upheld *Torath haShem*, the Law of (the one) God. Every nation has its heavenly prince and star to guide its destinies, and heavenly bodies determine their movements and actions. But Israel is singled out, since her guide is God alone. The body of Israel is like that of all other nations, but in her soul she is distinct from them, for Israel stands under God, the other nations under the heavenly bodies although naturally with the consent and

[1] *Loc. cit.*, 24b. r. Yehudah Hallewi and Abraham bar Chiyya must be considered as likely sources for Abravanel's conception of Jewish history in general.

[2] Abravanel is completely in accord with Maimonides, who at the end of the *Hilkhoth mᵉlakhim* in his *Mishne Torah*—quoted by him—describes the Messianic kingdom as a real earthly kingdom, invested with all the political power necessary to guarantee a reign of peace and justice for all mankind.

knowledge of God. They depend on the natural order, but Israel depends exclusively on God, who may, by His special Providence, do good or evil to Israel according as she deserves. In other words, God can hinder the action of this heavenly agent or can add to it at times. Israel is thus governed by a miraculous order superior to, and independent of, nature. Whether God annuls planetary constellations in the case of Israel depends on how she fulfils the Torah and its commandments.[1] Abravanel cherished the same faith and belief as every Jew of his age. But whereas the masses did so in a naïve, none the less, strong and sincere, belief, strengthened by the hope of seeing with their own eyes the promised Redemption and thus being visibly recompensed for their sufferings, Abravanel had arrived by his study at an almost scientific corroboration and justification of that faith innate in every Jew. It was the same during the Crusades with the French and German Jewries.

VI.

No account of Abravanel would be complete without at least touching upon his attitude to Maimonides. In all questions of principle, of fundamental teachings in Judaism, Abravanel is indebted to Maimonides, even where he differs from him. Whenever Maimonides' views can be harmonized with the plain meaning of Scripture and with the sayings of the Talmudic sages, Abravanel follows *the master, the great teacher*. Only if this is impossible does he deviate from him. In his treatise *Rosh Amanah* Abravanel defends Maimonides' thirteen articles against Albo and Crescas (1340-1410), although he holds the reasonable view with regard to dogma that in the face of the equal importance of every precept of the Torah and of the equal authority of its teachings no precedence or preference should be given to particular principles. This attitude is well in accord with Abravanel's view of the unity of Scripture, repeatedly stated.

There are, however, three questions of particular importance in which he strongly opposes Maimonides: prophecy, the

[1] Comm. on *Dan.*, 83a. r. and esp. 88a. r./90b. r. *See* also n. 1, p. 473.

interpretation of the Creation story and that of Ezekiel's vision of the Heavenly Chariot. Abravanel holds that the vision of the Chariot has nothing to do with the natural or metaphysical sciences, as Maimonides and his followers claim, but it is, by its position of preceding the prophet's warning of punishment by Exile, part of that matter. The vision points to the same four world empires as Daniel's four beasts.[1] Abravanel is convinced that Maimonides himself felt the difficulty of his explanation, but that he relied on his own mind and rational investigation. Instructive for Abravanel's attitude is his remark that he who is not convinced of the *Creatio ex nihilo* by (philosophical) proof should accept it by way of tradition from the prophets. *There is no harm in this.*[2] In sharpest contrast to Maimonides is Abravanel's traditional view of prophecy and its origin. A few words at least must be said on this point. Maimonides sees in prophecy a natural phenomenon, open to every person endowed with perfect imagination and perfect intellect. God lets emanate the active intellect on to the rational and imaginative faculties alike and thus makes man a prophet.[3] He differs from Alfarabi only in that God can withhold the gift of prophecy, especially if preparation for it is lacking in the person naturally destined for it. Abravanel dismisses the psychological explanation of prophecy and makes God the sole active force in endowing man with the gift of prophecy, contrary to Maimonides' negative power of withholding. By pointing to Amos, Abravanel denies that intellectual preparation is necessary. If prophecy were a natural phenomenon why is it only to be found in Israel and why were not the great philosophers, so perfect in virtues and thoughts, worthy of being prophets?[4] He also makes due allowance for the miraculous element, as e.g. when he insists,

---

[1] *Loc. cit.*, 15a. r. Abravanel marshals 28 objections against Maimonides' interpretation at the end of his Comm. on the *More*, 71b. ff. (ed. Warsaw).

[2] *Loc. cit.*, 73b. to the end. Abravanel explains that Maimonides could not deal in his *More* with the principles of the *Coming of the Messiah* and the *Resurrection* as they belong to the category of *Reward* and *Punishment* and are thus included in the principle of *Providence*. As they are, moreover, derived from tradition (*Qabbalah*) they cannot be expounded by metaphysical investigation (*'Iyyun*). For this reason Maimonides expounded them in his letters.

[3] *More*, II, ch. 37. [4] Abravanel's Comm. to *loc. cit.*, 79 ff.

against Maimonides and Nachmanides, on the whole nation having seen God at Sinai, listened to His voice and heard as well as understood all the Ten Commandments. He quotes Ibn Ezra in his support.[1]

These few examples show that there is a divergence in principle which is partly at least due to the developments which took place in Judaism following upon Maimonides. In the deplorable fight between Maimunists and Antimaimunists Abravanel occupies a middle position. He admires the work of Maimonides and acknowledges his indebtedness to him on almost every page and refrains from decrying the pursuit of philosophy and secular sciences as the Antimaimunists did. But he does not consider philosophy, as rational speculation, an equal partner to the Torah and Rabbinic tradition. He makes use of a philosophical argument if it helps to support tradition, to bring out the real, plain meaning of Scripture. He does not belittle human reason, yet he does not allow it free play to get the upper hand. Maimonides assigned an important place to moral virtues and insisted on the performance of the Commandments as a means to moral perfection, but maintained that the highest good and ultimate happiness and perfection consisted in the true perception of God leading to an imitation of His ways, thus again resulting in action. He allowed Reason to interpret Scripture according to rational standards (sometimes clearly ruling out the original, literal meaning). Abravanel makes such a concession only in so far as Reason can support tradition, with Scripture as the unique basis. This is not the place to argue whether the observance of the Commandments is of equal importance with or even superior to a rational perception of God. But the statement that although the intellect and imagination of the prophet must be sound, it is his moral perfection and his freedom from the defects of his animal desires which make him fit for prophecy,[2] rather points in that direction. Abravanel likes to style himself

[1] See n. 1, p. 470, and n. 1 second half, p. 457.

[2] See n. 4, p. 475, 6th premise. This is directed against Muhammad, with his excessive lust. Is Abravanel here making a concession to Maimonides by admitting preparation, even if it be moral and not intellectual?

and those who sympathise with him in their interpretation of Scripture as *the true representatives of Torah* or as *the community of the believers*[1] against the philosophers. He goes even so far as to despise those, like Maimonides, Ibn Ezra, Gersonides, etc., who tried to harmonize the words of the sages with the views of Aristotle and his disciples and their sophistry, *for I know that the way of the sages of Israel in their wisdom received by tradition is as far removed from the ways of the philosophers in their speculations and thoughts as East is from West.*[2] Nevertheless he did not hesitate to accept individual interpretations of these very men he had so violently denounced—if they were in accord with tradition! He can say of Maimonides that his interpretation of prophecy is as far above his own—which agrees with tradition —as Heaven is above Earth,[3] and accept with praises his interpretation of the meaning and character of the sacrifices.[4] This is not lack of sincerity or truthfulness on his part, but rather the outcome of his empiric nature and of his search for truth where it may be found. It would be wrong to set off one statement against another contradictory one, for, seen in the whole of his work and of his personality, they form nevertheless a unity. For an unswerving faith and a sincere loyalty bind these seemingly divergent statements and moods together. The man who stands in the middle between those who merely accepted and handed on established tradition and those who claimed the right to examine tradition with autonomous human reason is by no means a mediocrity. A man of wide learning, he has incorporated in his mind the conflicting tendencies of his day. He is at home in tradition as well as in philosophy and history, and makes use of all his tools in a manner appropriate to the task of the moment. He is the last representative of the mediæval epoch and at the same time the first Jew to apply a scientific method to the interpretation of the teachings of Judaism. He is a moderate conservative eager to maintain the *status quo* in Judaism. To this end he not only sums up in a final form what previous generations taught but, in method and exposition, adds something of his own. Granted that

[1] As note 2, p. 476.
[2] *Yᵉshuʻoth Mᵉshiḥo*, preface, 9b. l.
[3] As note 2, p. 476.
[4] Introd. to Comm. on *Leviticus*.

Abravanel as a commentator is indebted to the exegesis prior to his day in many points of detail, even in method perhaps, there remains nevertheless an outstanding contribution to Biblical exegesis as a science. He was, indeed, the first to understand and practice exegesis as such. He tried to understand men and their intentions by making due allowance for their character, position and milieu. Systematic treatment, sound criticism of his predecessors, independent mastery of the accumulated knowledge, a scholarly enthusiasm to clear away doubts and to see and solve real difficulties, the desire to understand the Bible as a whole and to bring out the real meaning of its several books in their true historic setting, are qualities all peculiar to himself. This is mainly the result of his practical experience as a statesman and diplomat who witnessed important developments in Spanish and Jewish history. Knowledge thus gained he threw back to the past history of his people, which he saw, partly at least, in the light of the history of the world powers. The occasional references in the Bible saw in the world powers instruments of God's will in His plans with Israel. In addition to that Abravanel learnt to understand and judge the nations by their own standards as he saw them through the chronicles of the Latins. With a great love for his people, whom he tried to serve all his life, especially by expounding to them their spiritual heritage, he combined the humanist's admiration for the Classics and foreshadowed in important beginnings the scholarship of the Renaissance. All students of the Bible are thus indebted to him for his courageous attempt to apply a strictly scientific method to the interpretation of the Old Testament, to bring out its plain, clear meaning, and to realize and to solve its difficulties. Our difficulties in respect of the Bible are other and so are our methods of removing them, yet our approach should still be that of Abravanel: the will to understand and to live its message of beauty and truth, and to see in it a great record of what the right relations should be between man and God and man and his fellow.

3

RASHI AND THE ENGLISH BIBLE[1]

RABBI SHELOMOH BEN YIÇHAQ, commonly called by the Jews by juxtaposition of his initials RASHI, and by Christian exegetes of the Old Testament Rabbi Salomon, was born in 1040. In normal circumstances this present year would have seen elaborate commemorations of the nine hundreth anniversary of his birth by the Jews all over the globe, among whom he holds not only a place of honour second to none of their old teachers but is in fact a household word. For traditional education as well as traditional exegesis of the Old Testament has been bound up with the writings of Rashi since they were first copied and then printed unto our own day. And although his chief importance within Judaism consists in Rashi the commentator of the Talmud, his popularity among the masses of devout Jews derives from Rashi the interpreter of the Old Testament. Hundreds of manuscripts of his Commentary on the Old Testament are extant, and the first dated printed Hebrew book is this Commentary, published in 1475. As a Bible commentator Rashi found his way into Mediæval Christian exegesis, into the works of the Hebraists among the Humanists, and into the principal translations of the Old Testament into the Latin and the vernacular tongues in the sixteenth and seventeenth centuries.

In a study on Don Isaac Abravanel, published in October, 1937, in this BULLETIN, I drew attention in a footnote to Rashi's

[1] I should like to thank the Librarian very much for his encouragement and advice and the facilities offered me to consult the unique collection of English Bibles in the Rylands Library. In no other place would I have been able to complete such a study in so short a time. No less am I indebted to both Mr. Vine and Mr. Taylor for invaluable help in bibliographical matters.

influence on Nicholas of Lyra.[1] It so happens that this year is also the six hundredth anniversary of this Commentator who not only derives his method of literal interpretation, by his own testimony, from Rabbi Salomon, but quotes him so frequently in his own interpretation that the great Johannes Reuchlin hyperbolically wrote that not many pages would remain over if one were to cut out Rashi from Nicholas' *Postillae*. A perusal of three German studies on Rashi's influence on Nicholas of Lyra [2] gave me the idea to examine the *Authorized Version* of the English Bible from the viewpoint of Rashi's exegesis in it. From 1937 onward I paid special attention to passages which reminded me of Rashi. Not until some weeks ago had I concentrated on this problem, and it may not be quite out of place to recount briefly the way followed. For this may lend additional weight to the conclusions drawn from the inquiry. Direct influence of Rashi on any of the translators of the English Bible, from Tindale down to the *Authorized Version*, seemed unlikely at first. Nicholas of Lyra appeared to be the natural intermediary. Beginning with the German studies referred to already,—which are, however, concerned with comment, not with translation—I soon extended my search for parallels over a large part of the Pentateuch and the Earlier and Later Prophets, particularly the more difficult and obscure passages where a translator would obviously have recourse to Jewish exegesis prior to the existence of a reliable dictionary as the result of systematic study of the Hebrew language. In this way parts of *Samuel, Isaiah, Jeremiah,* the whole of *Amos* and *Micah* and a number of *Psalms* were examined. Despite the fact—too often overlooked—that every translation is at the same time interpretation, I did not expect to find too many instances of borrowing from Jewish, in particular Rashi's exegesis. Moreover, a good many borrowings

---

[1] P. 459, n. 1.

[2] A. *Siegfried*, Raschi's Einfluss auf Nicolaus v. Lira und Luther in der Auslegung der Genesis in *Archiv für wissenschaftliche Erforschung des Alten Testaments*, Halle, 1870-71.

Maschkowsky, Raschi's Einfluss auf Nicolaus von Lira in der Auslegung des Exodus in *Z.A.W.*, 1891-2.

A. J. *Michalski*, dto. der Bücher Leviticus, Numeri und Deuteronomium, in *Z.A.W.*, 1915-16.

go back to St. Jerome's *Vulgate*. St. Jerome often adopts the Aramaic rendering of the *Targum* transmitted to him with Rabbinic interpretations by contemporary Jews. All these passages naturally had to remain outside the scope of our inquiry.

Working from the *Authorized Version* backwards I examined its passages with a Rashi-background in Tindale, Matthew and Coverdale. It became soon evident that neither Nicholas nor Luther, who is commonly held to have influenced Tindale in his translation, could be the source for the English rendering based on Rashi. (Whether Tindale really followed Luther or whether both drew directly from Nicholas in such passages where they agree is a debatable point which deserves careful consideration.) Where could the contact with Jewish exegesis have been effected?

If we remember that Tindale spent many years on the Continent, chiefly in Worms, Marburg and Antwerp, it would only be natural that Jews acquainted him with their own interpretation if he made contact with Jews. The great popularity which Rashi enjoyed as interpreter of Scripture plausibly accounts for the transmission of his exegesis as the accepted Jewish one. Rashi and the Targum were the principal sources for the majority of Jews (and still are to a large extent). Only the more learned among the Jews would consult R. David Qimḥi, Ibn Ezra, Nachmanides or Gersonides. In fact, there are among the passages examined by us many which must have accepted the Targumic rendering. All these remain outside our present study. But it must be emphasized that Targum and Rashi are the principal sources of information for the translators from the original Hebrew Old Testament. In this connexion it must not be forgotten that Rashi himself depends to a considerable degree on the Aramaic version. Frequently he puts the Aramaic into his Hebrew, as it were, without acknowledging his source, or at least receives his cue from the Targum.

Yet, even if we could trace individual Jews who supplied Tindale with information, this would in no way explain so many more faithful reproductions of the Hebrew original in the *Authorized Version* not to be found in the earlier English versions. The real turning-point is reached with the *Genevan* and the

Bishops' Bibles, but to a large extent already with Coverdale's *Great Bible* of 1539.

We shall return to the *Great Bible* later. Still looking for direct Jewish influence we thought of finding it with no great difficulty in the assumption that the translators of the *Genevan Bible* in the course of their exile had met with Jews whom they consulted for their translation. The problem is, however, complicated through the great influence exerted by Calvin and the Swiss reformers on them. A number of the Bishops and divines who undertook the *Bishops' Bible* had been exiles, mostly in Switzerland, during the reign of Queen Mary. At least two of the principal translators of the *Genevan Bible* must have been good Hebraists. William Whittingham did not return to England with the other reformers at the accession of Queen Elizabeth but supervised the whole work in Geneva.[1] Although there is no definite statement that he knew Hebrew it may be assumed that he would not have undertaken such a task without a knowledge of Hebrew. Of the other, Anthony Gilby,[2] we know that he not only translated Commentaries of Calvin and Theodore Beza but wrote Commentaries of his own on *Micah* and *Malachi*. Unfortunately we were not able to secure copies of these. They would clearly throw light on their author's work as a translator, and at the same time give us an answer to our question: Did Gilby have a direct knowledge of Jewish exegesis?

We fared not much better with the translators of the *Bishops' Bible*. However, the *Zürich Letters*[3] reveal one point of interest for our problem, i.e. the contact of the English reformers with scholars like Bullinger, Bibliander and Wolfius. Bishop Parkhurst praises in letters to John Wolfius the latter's learned commentaries,[4] and Bishop Sandys as well as Parkhurst speak highly of Bullinger's Commentaries.[5] The *Parker Correspondence* which

[1] *D.N.B.*, s.v. [2] *Ibid.* [3] Edited by the *Parker Society.*

[4] Second Series, Camb. 1845, p. 127, on *Kings*, encourages W. to publish his discourses on *Deut., Judges, Ruth,* etc. P. 177 praises Comm. on *Nehemiah*; p. 199 urges publication of Comm. on *Esther* and lectures on *Ezra*.

[5] *Zürich Letters*, 1558-76, Camb. 1842. On p. 145 Sandys' letter to Bullinger about the latter's ' very learned Comm. on prophet Daniel ', speaks also about copious MS. Comm. on *Genesis* and *Exodus* by Bibliander. R. Hilles writes Bullinger about his homilies on *Isaiah*. Grindal and Parkhurst do likewise, with praise.

we consulted next yielded a most interesting and important result. Among the instructions issued by Archbishop Parker for the translation are two of special relevance to our problem. The first enjoins upon the revisers, whose list with the books allotted to them we find on pp. 334 ff., " to follow the common English translation used in the churches and not to recede from it but where it varieth manifestly from the Hebrew or Greek original."[1] And the second rule points to the sources to be consulted for that purpose, in the words : " Item, to use sections and divisions in the text as Pagnine in his translation useth, and for the verity of the Hebrew to follow the said Pagnine and Münster specially, and generally others learned in the tongues." Parker himself 'revised' the books of *Genesis* and *Exodus*.

It is the more astonishing to find Bishop Sandys, one of the translators, taking exception to Münster in his letter to Parker : " The setters forth of this our common translation followed Münster too much, who doubtless was a very negligent man in his doings, and often swerved very much from the Hebrew." Does Sandys mean by "this our common translation" the work upon which the team under Parker, including himself, was engaged or rather the *Genevan Bible* which, however, never received the official sanction of the Church, or perhaps most likely of all, does he refer to Coverdale's revision of Matthew's Bible, known as the *Great Bible*? For was not the *Bishops' Bible* a revision of the *Great Bible*, though, in the words of Dr. Guppy " it shows that good use was made of the ' Genevan Version ', for some of the best and raciest of the notes in the ' Bishops' Version ' are taken from it verbatim, without acknowledgment " ?[2] I must leave the decision of this matter to those who can speak with authority on the history of the English Bible. For our problem here it is of little concern since Sebastian Münster appears to have been godfather to the *Great Bible* no less than to its successors.[3] Not only had Coverdale in all

[1] A similar statement is contained in Parker's letter to Queen Elizabeth accompanying the volume of the Bible presented to the Queen (p. 337).

[2] Dr. Henry Guppy : *A Brief Sketch of the History of the Transmission of the Bible down to the Revised English Version* 1881-95, p. 53.

[3] See *Catalogue of the British and Foreign Bible Society*, I, p. 21. It says, " A revision by Coverdale of Matthew's Bible, which he corrected chiefly by the aid of Sebastian Munster's Latin translation of the Hebrew Old Testament."

probability a hand in the *Genevan Version*, but this version betrays without any doubt the influence of Sebastian Münster as well as that of Leo Judae.[1] Anybody who has ever looked closely into the translation of Sebastian Münster must recognise the soundness and wisdom of Archbishop Parker's injunction. Parker, together with Bishop Grindal, can also not have shared the apprehension of the Church against the popular *Genevan Version*, for we find among his Correspondence a letter addressed jointly with Grindal to Sir William Cecil upon the subject of renewal of the licence of John Bodley to reprint the *Genevan Version*. In it they say: " So it is, that we think so well of the first impression, and review of those which have sithence travailed therein, that we wish it would please you to be a mean that [the licence may be renewed]. . . . For, though one other special Bible for the Churches be meant by us to be set forth, as convenient time and leisure hereafter will permit: yet shall it nothing hinder, but rather do much good, to have diversity of translations and readings." Surely, a remarkable admission which betrays no mean quality of the chief-editor of the *Bishops' Bible*!

Before discussing the character of the Latin translations of Sebastian Münster, Leo Judae and Santes Pagnino with special consideration for possible and actual influence of Jewish exegesis, we must proceed to glance briefly at the makers of the *Authorized Version*. The information concerning them in Anderson's *The Annals of the English Bible*[2] and the *Dictionary of National Biography* goes back in its bulk to Anthony à Wood's *Athenae Oxonienses*. Histories of Oxford and Cambridge University are no more explicit on the attainments of those among the translators who were Regius Professors of Hebrew. The greater number of them, led by the Puritan leader Dr. John Rainolds, to whose initiative at the Hampton Court Conference in 1604 we owe the *Authorized Version*, appear to have been noted Hebrew scholars. Some of them are granted with extensive knowledge of cognate Semitic tongues, Chaldaic [which is Aramaic], Syriac and Arabic. It goes without saying that all of them were excellent Classical scholars.

[1] *Loc. cit.*, p. 61.   [2] Vol. II, p. 374.

If we single out a few of them it is because we believe that they could best answer our question of who was acquainted with Rabbinic exegesis. Wood informs us that Richard Kilbye, who was Regius Professor of Hebrew at Oxford, wrote a Commentary on the Book of *Exodus,* "the chief part of which is excerpted from the monuments of the Rabbins and *Hebrew Interpreters.*" According to the *D.N.B.* Edward Lively, Regius Professor of Hebrew at Cambridge, left *Annotations to the first five of the Minor Prophets* as well as a Commentary on Peter Martinius' *Hebrew Grammar.*† It may well be that among the unpublished manuscripts left by Dr. John Overall, a correspondent of Hugo Grotius, material bearing on our question is to be found. He was for a time Librarian of St. John's and Christ's Colleges, Cambridge. Dr. John Rainolds left *The prophecie of Obadiah opened and applied, etc.,* as well as *Sermons on the Prophecies of Haggai,* "never before printed, being very usefull for these times." Of both we shall speak later, whereas we could not see Kilbye's nor Lively's Commentaries. Of Dr. Miles Smith,—together with Bishop Bilson the final examiner of the whole work,— Wood says : "He ran thro' the *Greek* and *Latin* Fathers, and judiciously noted them in the margin as he went. The Rabbins also, as many as he had, with their glosses and Commentaries, he read and used in their own idiom of Speech. And so conversant he was, and expert in the *Chaldaic, Syriac,* and *Arabic,* that he made them as familiar to him, almost, as his own native tongue. *Hebrew* also he had at his fingers-ends." [1]

It would constitute a valuable contribution to the history of Hebrew scholarship in the sixteenth and seventeenth centuries if light could be thrown on the competence of the translators, chiefly those whose literary remains contain Biblical commentaries and Hebrew Grammars, as for instance Bishop Alley, one of the translators of the *Bishops' Bible,* Gilby (*Genevan*), Kilbye, Lively and Rainolds (*Authorized*). The latter's acquaintance with Rashi is evident from two quotations with which we shall deal later. But another question requires an answer as well, i.e. who were the instructors of these Hebraists and by which books were they guided? An answer to the last question may

[1] *Athenae,* p. 490.

be found by an investigation into the bequests of manuscripts and printed books made by our translators to the Oxford and Cambridge Colleges. Archbishop Parker, e.g., left among others "50 books chiefly consisting of commentaries upon the Old Testament and the New Testament."[1] That Parker took a personal interest in the advancement of Hebrew Studies is shown by a letter, addressed jointly with Bishop Grindal to the Vice-Chancellor and Heads of Houses at Cambridge in 1569 recommending to them Rodolphus Cavallerius, "otherwise called Mr. Anthony" [Chevalier].[2] We find among Parker's correspondents another Hebrew Professor, Immanuel Tremellius, a convert from Judaism.[1] And in 1574 Parker promises to do "the best I can to other of my Cambridge brothers, to contribute some increase of living to that Hebrew reader."[3]

Until this question of books is decided one can only surmise, though not without foundation, that Reuchlin's *De Rudimentis Hebraicis* must have been the main source of information for the English Hebraists no less than for those on the Continent. This fundamental work was published for the first time in 1506. It drew largely on Rashi's *Commentary*, published, as stated before, in 1475, and for the dictionary embodied in his work Reuchlin made ample use of R. David Qimḥi's *Book of Roots* (*Sefer haShorashim*), published in 1480.[4] After years of private studies, Reuchlin obtained his first teacher of Hebrew in 1492

---

[1] See Strype, *Life of Parker*, II, 475.

[2] *Parker Correspondence*, p. 348 f. The same is referred to in a letter of Rodolph Zwingli addressed to Bishop Sandys thanking him for the Hebrew knowledge he (Zw.) acquired at Cambridge from Anthony Chevalier and Immanuel Tremellius (*Zürich Letters*, 2nd Series). Chevalier, a French Protestant Refugee, occupied the Chair of Hebrew at Cambridge under Edward VI. He contributed Latin translations of Pseudo-Jonathan's Targum on the *Pentateuch*, corrections of Targum on the *Earlier and Later Prophets* to Walton's Polyglot. Left also Rudimenta Hebraicae Linguae. See *Athenae Cantab.* I, 306-8. Tremellius was Regius Professor of Hebrew at Cambridge, 1549-52 (*J. P. Mullinger*, The University of Cambridge, pp. 416 ff.). See also *Athenae Cantabrigienses*, I, 425, and D.N.B., s.v.

[3] *Parker Correspondence*, p. 468. The reference is to Peter Bignon, but Edward Lively was appointed. See Strype, *op. cit.* II, 379.

[4] See the full study by Dr. *Ludwig Geiger*, Johann Reuchlin, etc., Leipzig, 1871, especially pp. 105 ff., and based thereon *S. A. Hirsch's* essay on Reuchlin in *A Book of Essays*, London, 1905.

in the person of Jacob ben Yeḥiel Loans, body-physician to Emperor Frederick III, and later in Rome he studied under Obadiah Sforno of Cesena. According to Geiger, Reuchlin follows closely the arrangement of Qimḥi, whose grammar (*Sefer haMikhlol*) he mentions once in his *Rudiments* and whose Commentaries he uses freely. He also quotes Maimonides. But he holds Rashi as the *Ordinary Interpreter of Scripture* (*ordinarius scripturae interpres*) in special regard and often accepts his interpretations. Reuchlin was well known among the English reformers. One of his disciples was Conrad Pellicanus, the teacher of Sebastian Münster, who speaks very highly of his master in the Preface to his Latin translation of the Old Testament.[1] Sebastian Münster undertook a second impression of Reuchlin's *Rudiments* in 1537, with considerable changes. As regards Sebastian Münster's translation we may do well in quoting his own words to show to what an extent he allowed himself to be guided by Jewish exegesis. In his Preface he admits: " Consuluimus . . . in Pentateucho ex Heb. scriptoribus Chal. [daeum] interpretem, Rabi Salomonem [Rashi], David Kimhi, Ibn Ezra, R. Menahem [ben Saruq, the Grammarian and author of a Hebrew dictionary],† . . . Mosen Gerundensem [Nachmanides] . . . et quosdam alios : et cuius expositio in obscurioribus locis nobis commodior visa fuit, hunc sequuti sumus." In other words, he consulted the Targum and the Rabbinic mediæval Hebrew commentaries in order to arrive at a better understanding of the obscure passages in the Pentateuch (and we may add, the same applies to the other parts of the Bible), and he follows the best explanation. Of value and interest is his observation on the importance of the Targum for Jewish exegesis : " Facimus autem saepiuscule Chal. aeditionis mentionem quod illa sit veluti asylum Hebraeis, ad quum confugiant, quando aliquid obscurum et senticosum occurrit. Nam illa luculenter explicat, quod in divinis libris minus clarum positum invenitur, ut saepe in nostris monstrabimus annotationibus." We venture to suggest that almost wherever we find a Targumic interpretation as the English translation from the *Great Bible* onward such a translation originates in Münster's Latin version

[1] Basel, 1534-35.

if he either translates like the Targum or, even if he should follow the *Vulgate* in a different translation, at least quotes the Targum in his annotations following upon each chapter. This is not the place to assess the critical value of Münster's version. But it ought to be stated, in view of Parker's instruction and of Sandys' adverse verdict that Münster was not only a sound Hebraist but well versed in Jewish exegesis as well. He does not follow the Rabbis blindly, he carefully weighs their interpretations in his mind and never forgets to mention dissenting views if he quotes Hebrew exegesis.[1] Who imparted this knowledge of Jewish exegesis which is exceptionally extensive and sound to Münster? We have heard before that Pellicanus and Reuchlin's *Rudiments* were his teachers. But not they alone. He like Reuchlin had his Jewish teacher, as he says himself in his Preface: " Mihi ab Hebraeo, qui me in Scripturis erudivit, ita expositum est." This *Hebraeus* was no other than Elias Levita. He may account for the authorities quoted other than those found in Reuchlin, notably Rashi and Qimḥi. For the ordinary Jewish teacher would rarely adduce Ibn Ezra, Nachmanides, Gersonides, etc., but would rather confine himself to the Targum and Rashi. Münster repaid his teacher by translating most of his grammatical works into Latin, and another of Levita's disciples and friends, Paul Fagius, published his Targumic Dictionary, the first of its kind, and also his *Tishbi* which he translated into Latin. Fagius who, together with Münster, did most to spread Levita's fame and to establish his influence on Hebraists, held the Chair of Hebrew at Cambridge in 1549,[2] preceding Immanuel Tremellius. It stands to reason that Fagius made use of Levita's treatises at Cambridge. But this has yet to be verified.

As far as possible at the moment we have answered the question of books used. Fagius as well as Tremellius partly answer for the other question: who were the instructors of the English Hebraists. Towards the close of the sixteenth century

---

[1] E.g. in *Gen.* xlix, 5, he adopts the Jewish interpretation, based on the Targum, in his translation of שׁוֹר by ' murus ' in these terms : " *Suffoderunt murum :* Hebraei exponunt hic שׁוֹר pro חוֹמָה muro, et non pro tauro, praeter unum Rab. Sal. qui per taurum docet intelligendum Joseph."†

[2] *See* Mullinger, *op. cit.*, and *Athenae Cantabrigienses*, I, 95, 538.

we find at Cambridge another baptized Jew, Philip Ferdinand,[1] giving Hebrew private lessons. That Tremellius had acquired a considerable knowledge of Jewish exegesis prior to his conversion can easily be gauged from his Latin translation of the Old Testament. From my perusal of his version I am inclined to think, however, that his use of Hebrew exegesis must at least partly be attributed to Münster's transmission whose arrangement he seems to follow by adding linguistic and exegetical notes at the end of chapters. His translation is said to have enjoyed wide Protestant approval. A study of his literary remains would establish his scholarship. He wrote among other works a Commentary on *Hosea*, a Chaldaean and Syriac Grammar, and translated the *XII Minor Prophets* in Aramaic into Latin. Rainolds on *Obadiah* attacks his translation,[2] but we shall find traces of it in the *Authorized Version*.[3] Finally, " in 1608 " we find that " two Jews, who were not members of the University, were allowed to read in the Bodleian Library, viz. James Wolfgang, who is described in the certificate of admission as " a man well deserving in the Hebrew tongue and a convert from Judaism," and James Levita, ' Judaeus Orientalis '.[4] In the following year Isaac Casaubon meets Jacob Barnett whom he recommends to Oxford, where Kilbye licensed him to lecture in Hebrew.[5] Only Kilbye's Commentary [6] can show us whether Barnett influenced him. Wood's remark rather suggests it.

One thing before all will be clear from this fragmentary sketch of the state of Hebrew studies in this country in the sixteenth and seventeenth centuries : without a close investigation of hitherto unpublished or at least unused evidence it will not be possible to decide the part which personal contact with Jews of more or less Jewish learning and the first systematic treatises on Hebrew Grammar and Lexicography played in

---

[1] *See* preceding note, and *Lucien Wolf*, The Middle Age of Anglo-Jewish History, 1290-1656, in *Papers, Anglo-Jewish Exhibition*, London, 1888, pp. 53 ff., particularly pp. 65 ff.†

[2] *See* later, p. 162. [3] *See* later, pp. 154, 159.

[4] A. Neubauer in *Collectanea*, Second Series, edid. M. Burrows. Oxford, 1890.

[5] On Barnett and his strange fate, *see* L. Wolf, *op. cit.*, and Neubauer, *op. cit.*

[6] *See* below, p. 162.

equipping the translators with their Hebrew knowledge, in addition to the help they derived from previous translations in accordance with their terms of reference. A complete answer will perhaps never be given. Yet the road leading to it runs through notes about ownership of Hebrew Manuscripts in the British Museum, the Bodleian Library and the Libraries of the various Oxford and Cambridge Colleges which have received bequests by Archbishop Parker and others. Records of these Colleges may yield some information as well as correspondence, published and especially unpublished of English divines and scholars with their opposite numbers on the Continent [1] and among themselves. The *State Papers* in the Record Office must also be consulted.

As far as the English translations are concerned, contemporary Latin translations made from the Hebrew original as well as Luther's German version, probably in the case of Tindale, certainly in the case of Coverdale in his Bible of 1537, will account for most of this influence of Jewish exegesis. Luther owes his acquaintance with Rashi mainly to Nicholas of Lyra. Tindale may have received help from Jews during his Continental stay. What is most remarkable is the fact that Coverdale approaches much nearer to Jewish exegesis in his revision of *Matthew's Bible*, thanks to Münster's Latin version, whereas in his own attempt, 1537, he is strongly influenced by Luther. The *Genevan Version* clearly shows the imprint of Münster. But not only will it have to be proved in every case whether this imprint is a direct one or comes through the *Great Bible*, but there is also Leo Judae's Latin Version of 1544 to be considered. That Leo is of Jewish descent is probable. His son says of this matter: "Nun möcht es wohl sein, dass vielleicht seine Vorfahren wären Juden gewesen, vom Judenthum abgestanden und Christen geworden, besonders weil dort im Elsass viele Juden wohnen." Though this is likely so the anyhow remote Jewish parentage does not appear to have left traces in the form of Hebrew and Rabbinic knowledge, for we are told by Leo's

---

[1] We are told, e.g., that Tremellius was in correspondence with " many of the most distinguished men of an illustrious age " (*see* L. Wolf, *op. cit.*).

Jewish themes

biographer [1] that he translated the whole Bible from 1538, assisted by Michael Adam, a convert from Judaism. Most likely, this convert supplied the Jewish exegesis found in Leo's translation.

Turning to the *Bishops' Bible* we recall Archbishop Parker's injunction to follow 'for the verity of the Hebrew the said Pagnine, etc.' Pagnino betrays considerable familiarity with Jewish exegesis in his Latin version (1528), must obviously have seen Münster's translation, but—as is only natural for a Dominican—follows the *Vulgate* much more than any of the other versions. That he took his Hebrew studies seriously and attained a certain efficiency is proved by the existence of a *Hebrew glossary*, first published at Lyons, 1529, and printed by Plantin at Antwerp in 1570 in an abridged form under the title *Epitome Thesauri linguae sanctae*.[2] In it he often quotes Rashi, R. Jonah [Ibn Djannāh], Qimḥi, R. Abraham (ibn Ezra?). Whether this work rests on Pagnino's own research, based on Qimḥi's *Book of Roots*, or is modelled upon Reuchlin's *Rudiments*[3] is a matter for close investigation. His knowledge of Hebrew was certainly considerable.

As stated above, Tremellius' Latin translation is to be taken into account for the *Authorized Version*. Where this *Authorized Version* stands on its own, the source must be sought in the scholarship of the translators. Here is a profitable field for

---

[1] In: Leben und ausgewählte Schriften der Väter und Begründer der reformierten Kirche IX. Edid. K. R. Hagenbach, etc. Elberfeld, 1861.

[2] The Hebrew title is: קֹצֶר אוֹצָר לְשׁוֹן הַקֹּדֶשׁ, Anthony Chevalier, see n. 2, p. 145, published emendations of it. We have consulted the Rylands copy of it.

[3] Since this paper was sent to press we have been able to consult the original *Rudimenta Hebraica*, 1506. Dr. Geiger's views are fully borne out. As regards Pagnino, it is not always possible to decide whether he used Qimḥi or only Reuchlin in the cases where both Qimḥi and Reuchlin coincide. But so much is certain that Pagnino follows Qimḥi much more closely by citing all the words derived from one and the same root. As a rule he only shortens the argument or substitutes for an authority named by Qimḥi *alij*. He also introduces every letter by *Litera* א, e.g., just as Qimḥi writes אות האלף, etc. Contrary to Reuchlin he brings at the end of each letter of the Hebrew alphabet, just like Qimḥi, all the *quadriliterals* mentioned by the latter in exactly the same way. These two last mentioned points suggest rather a direct perusal of Qimḥi by Pagnino. But his *Thesaurus*—we had only the *Epitome* at our disposal—must be carefully examined for this question.

research. The possible lines of approach have been tentatively suggested above.

A number of characteristic examples may supplement the foregoing pages.

II. RASHI'S INTERPRETATION FOLLOWED IN THE ENGLISH VERSIONS.

A. *In the Translations.*

1. *Genesis* xlix. 5 כלי חמס מכרותיהם

Rashi offers two explanations which both find their echo in the translations. He says : ' an expression for weapons. The sword in Greek (*means*) μάχαιρα (*Tanḥumā*). Another explanation is (*Ber. R.*) in the land of their sojourn they are wont to weapons of violence, like *Ezekiel* xvi. 3. And this is the translation of Onqelos.'

מכרותיהם. לשון כלי זיין. הסייף בלשון יוני מכי״ר (תנחומא).
דבר אחר: (ב״ר) בארץ מגורתם נהגו עצמם בכלי חמס כמו יחזקאל
טז״... וזהו תרגום של אונקלוס.

T(indale) : weked instruments are their wepons.
C(overdale) : their deadly weapons are perlous instrumentes.
M(ünster) : vasa violenta in habitaculis eorum.
In a note he quotes, just like Rashi, two opinions, the one following the Targum, the other seeing a Greek word in it.
GR(eat Bible) : cruell instrumentes in their habitacions.
(Leo) *J*(udae) : arma violenta macherae eorum. *Marg.* Quidam legunt, habitatio eorum.
G(enevan Bible) : the instruments of crueltie are in their habitacions. *Or*, their swordes are instruments of violence.
P(agnino) : . . . in habitationibus suis. The other meaning is quoted in his *Epitome*.
B(ishops' Bible) : are cruell instrumentes in their habitations.
A(uthorized Version) : instruments of cruelty are in their habitations. *Or*, their swords are instruments of violence.
R(evised Version) : weapons of violence are their swords.
TR(emellius) : instrumenta violentiae conventiones eorum. He explains this in a note : hoc est pactionibus illis quibus cum Schecemitis convenerunt. This agrees with Ibn Ezra's own

explanation who says, after reviewing and rejecting existing interpretations: after they had concluded an alliance with the Shekhemites they murdered them cunningly.

שאחר שהכניסו אנשי שכם בברית הרגום במרמה.

Tindale, "Matthew" (who is not specially mentioned) and Coverdale follow the *Vulgate* with Jerome's explanation *arma eorum*, which is also the one view propounded by Rashi who himself quotes the *Midrash*. St. Jerome may well have heard it from his Jewish helpers. *GR*, following upon *M*, introduces the other Jewish view. *J* adopts the first in his translation and brings the second in his note. *G* and *A* bring both, *B* follows *M*'s and *P*'s translation, and *R* goes back to the older translations, substituting 'weapons' for 'instruments'. *TR* goes his own way by adopting Ibn Ezra's view which is comparatively rarely represented in the translations.

2. *Genesis* xlix. 10. ולו יקהת עמים

Rashi explains this phrase by *an assembly of peoples*.

אסיפת העמים.

Lyra accepts the rendering of the *Vulgate* but says: In Hebraeo autem habitur sic: Et erit ei aggregatio gentium.

T: to whom the people shall herken.
C: and unto him *shal* the people fall.
M: et ad illum aggregatio (erit) populorum.
GR: unto hym shal the gatheringe of the people be.
J: et ad illum gentes confluent.
G: and the people *shal* be gathered unto him.
P: Et ei erit aggregatio populorum.
B A: unto him shall the gathering of the people be.
TR: et sit ei obedientia populorum.
R: unto him shall the obedience of the people be.

Here again Rashi is introduced by *M* whose translation is adopted by *GR* which in its turn is followed by *B* and *A*. *G* only exchanges the noun for a verbal clause, perhaps under the influence of *J*. *P* either follows Rashi directly or via Lyra's explanation. He quotes Rashi in his *Epitome*.

T TR and *R* seem to follow the Aramaic rendering, for we read in the Targum *and to him shall obey the peoples*.

ולה ישתמעון עממיא.

Rashi and the English Bible

3. *v.* 26. עד־תאות גבעות עולם

Rashi explains תאות by קצות 'ends' and the whole phrase by *unto the end of the boundaries of the everlasting hills.*

עד סוף גבולי גבעות עולם.

T C : after the desier of the hilles of the worlde.
M : usque ad extremitatem collium mundi.
GR B : unto the utmost of the hilles of the worlde.
J : usque ad desiderabiles colles qui iam olim fuerint. But he explains: quidem legunt usque ad terminos collium vel circuitum.
G : unto the end of the hilles of the worlde.
P : usque ad terminum collium perpetuorum. But cp. his *Epitome s.v.* אוה giving 'desiderium', but not quoting this passage. He may follow Lyra in his translation.
TR : usque ad finem collium saeculi.
A R : unto the utmost bound of the everlasting hills.

T C J translate the word in its usual meaning, following the *Vulgate*. But *J* reproduces Rashi in his note and *M* introduces it into all subsequent translations. *P*'s translation is more correct as 'mundi', 'of the worlde' would require העולם in the Hebrew text. But whereas these versions reproduce the text only, *A R* include Rashi's explanation in their rendering as well.

Of other examples in *Genesis* the following may be noted: iv. 1 ; ‡xxxvii. 35 ; L. 5.

4. *Exodus* xiv. 20 ויהי הענן והחשך ויאר את־הלילה

Rashi says to ' and it was a cloud and darkness ' *for Egypt* (למצרים); to 'and it lit up' *a column of fire the night for Israel* (לישראל).

Based upon Rashi directly or through the transmission of Lyra *J* adds in brackets [Aegyptiis] and [Israelitis].

M in annotating this verse explains thus and says : " Et haec est expositio Chal. interprete et R. Abr. Sepharadi."

TR : illis erat nubes et tenebrae, *his* autem illustrabat noctem ipsam.

A : and it was a cloud and darkness *to them* but it gave light by night *to these.*

TR undoubtedly is the source for *A*, the only English version which inserts these words for the sake of clarity. Rashi as often follows the Targum.

5. xix. 13   במשך היובל

Rashi *if the horn draws out a long sound*

כשימשוך היובל קול ארוך.

T C: when the horne bloweth.

P: quum perplixum sonitum dederit buccina. *Epitome*: 'Cum protraxerit (.i. longiorem sonitum dederit) cornu.'

M: cum prolixius buccina sonuerit. He explains במשך exactly like the Hebrew Commentators.

GR: when the trompe bloweth longe.

J: Quum protractus fuerit Jobel.

G (B): when the horne (trumpet) bloweth long.

TR: cum tractim sonabit cornu. His note runs: id est, audietur continens unius toni sonus.

A R: when the trumpet soundeth long.

Here again it is *M* who introduces a translation which in Archbishop Parker's phrase follows closely *the verity of the Hebrew*.

For other examples in *Exodus* see i. 11; ii. 16, 25; xii. 8, 9, 21; xxi. 10; xxii. 18, 28; xxiii. 1; xxv. 2, 39. xxi. 10 and xxii. 28 are particularly instructive.

6. *Deuteronomy* xxxii. 15   כשית

Rashi: כשית is like כסית. It is the expression of Job xv. 27, for he has covered his face *with his fatness*.

לשון (איוב טו) כי כסה פניו בחלבו.

All English versions translate *with fatness* undoubtedly under the influence of Rashi's explanation.

7. *v*. 42.   מראש פרעות אויב

Rashi: because of the transgression from the beginning when the enemy broke in, for when the Holy One, blessed be He, punishes the nations he avenges upon them their iniquity and the iniquity of their fathers from the very beginning of their onslaught upon Israel.

מפשע תחלת פרצות האויב כי כשהקב"ה נפרע מן האומות פוקד
עליהם עונם ועונות אבותיהם מראשית פרצה שפרצו בישראל.

T: ' and of the bare heed of the enemye.'

C: and in that enemies heade shall be discovered.

M: idque propter sanguinem occisorum et captivitatem (eorum) a capite ultionum inimici. His explanation is: et eum captivum abduxerunt, incipiamque ulcisci a capite et initio primae iniuriae quam hostis intulit.

GR: and for their captivite, sens the beginning of the wrath of the enemye.

J: ab hosti summatim ultiones rependam. He adds in the margin: Alii legunt a capite nudatorum, alii, a capite ultionem hostis.

G: when I beginne to take vengeance of the enemie.

P: reddam ultionem hostibus meis.

B: since the beginning of the wrath of the enemie.

TR: confossorum et captivorum, inde a principio erunt ultiones inimici. He explains this: *Inde a principio*. id est cum ultionem sumam de inimicis, nihil impunitum relinquam eorum quae inde a principio contra me commiserunt.

A: from the beginning of revenges upon the enemy.

R: from the head of the leaders of the enemy (*or*, the hairy head of the enemy).

Rashi arrives at his explanation by taking the Hebrew root פרע in the meaning it has in Aramaic as *avenging punishment*. Moreover, he takes ראש to mean 'beginning' and not 'head.'

T C J in his first alternative base their translations upon the *Vulgate*: et de captivitate nudati inimicorum capitis.

M strikes the middle between *Vulgate* and Rashi. He takes ראש, both as 'head' and as 'beginning', thus working his two sources together. His explanation follows the *Vulgate* in the first part, but from *incipiamque* it is abbreviated Rashi. *GR* derives from *M*.

J likewise combines *Vulgate* and Rashi. *P* agrees with *J* and *B* with *GR*. *G* seems to reproduce the second half of *M*'s explanation in an abbreviated form. *TR* retains some of the *Vulgate* but the second part of his translation and his explanation are clearly modelled upon Rashi. *A* is Rashi contracted. And *R* is in favour of yet two other possible meanings of the root פרע

8. xxxiii. 29. ויכחשו

Rashi. *like the Gibeonites,* כגון הגבעונים. He takes ויכחשו like the Targum, ויכדבון. He is followed by Lyra.

T : shal hyde themselves from the.
C : shall pyne awaye.
M : debilitati sunt inimici tui erga te.
B (GR) : have lost their strength to the (warde).
J : Et mentientur tibi inimici tui.
G : shalbe in subjection to thee.
P : negabunt (like *Vulgate*).
TR : Sic reddantur abjecti inimici tui tibi. In marg. : *Heb.* mendaces.
A : shall be found liars (*or,* shall be subdued).
R : shall submit themselves unto thee (marg. yield feigned obedience).

J is the first to follow Rashi, either directly or through Lyra. *M* is followed by *GR* and *B*. *A* follows ultimately Rashi in the text, in the margin, however, *G* and *TR*.

Among other examples in *Deuteronomy* the following may be mentioned : xxxii. 17, 18 ; xxxiii. 12, 27.

9. *Micah* i. 9. כי אנושה מכותיה

Rashi : *for she is sick of her wounds.* כי חולה היא במכותיה
T/M (for Tindale-Matthew) *C GR B* : is paste remedy.
M (J) : quia (quoniam) desperata est plaga eius.
P : quia desperatae sunt plagae tuae.
G : for her plagues are grieveous.
TR : aegra fuit *Shomron* plagis suis.
A : for her wound is incurable (*or,* she is grieveously sick of her wounds).
R : for her wounds are incurable.

A adopts Rashi's explanation in the margin. *TR* brings here R. David Qimḥi's interpretation, without naming his source as he did with Ibn Ezra above. Qimḥi says *ad loc.* among other things : the plague that fell upon Samaria and came as far as Judah.

המכה החלה בשמרון ובאה עד יהודה.

10. iii. 5. וקדשו עליו מלחמה

Rashi, rendering the Targum into Hebrew without acknowledgment, says: *and they prepare war against him.*
    והזמינו עליו למלחמה.

T/M C GR: they preach of warre.

M: adornant. But he quotes the Targum in the note thus: contra hunc excitant bellum.

J: bellum denunciant.

P: praeparant bellum.

G B A: they even prepare war against him.

T R: indicunt bellum.

R: like *A*, but has in the margin: *Heb.* ' sanctify.'

P G B A are clearly influenced by Rashi, possibly through the medium of *P* or of *M* in which latter case it would be correct to attribute the influence to the Targum. If *P* is responsible this would constitute the only case we have come across of *P*'s influence; cp. also his *Epitome*.

11. v. 3. לכן יתנם

Rashi, possibly taking his cue from the Targum's יתמסרון *they will be handed over* explains: *he will give them into the hands of their enemies.* יתנם ביד אויביהם

T/M C GR: whyle he plageth them.

M: in a note *ad loc.* says before the Messiah is born into the world *tradet deus Jehudaeos in magnas afflictiones*.

G B A: Therefore will he give them up. Targum or Rashi are behind this translation.

TR: exponet *quidem* eos.

12. *Amos* v. 12. ואביונים בשער הטו

Rashi: ' in the gates of your courts they pervert the right of the poor.' בשערי בתי דיניכם הטו משפט אביונים

T/M C GR: ye oppresse the poore in judgment.

M: et pauperum (causam) in porta pervertunt.

J: ut deijiciatis pauperem in foro (foro, Ebr. nam fora in portis erant).

G B: and they oppresse the poore in the gate.

TR: et egentes in porta pervertentium.

P: et pauperum iudicium in porta perverterunt.

A (R): and they turn aside the poor (needy) in the gate *from their right*.

Here again Rashi is behind *A R*, whilst *P*'s *iudicium* also comes from Rashi.

Other examples of Rashi's influence are: *Micah* ii. 3; iv. 13; vi. 3, 13. *Amos* vi. 4; ix. 1, 9.

To assess the imprint of Jewish exegesis properly we must not limit our inquiry to Rashi. A systematic investigation must comprise the Targum as well as all the Mediaeval Hebrew Commentators. A few examples may illustrate this.

13. *Deuteronomy* xxxiii. 7.   ידיו רב לו

   Ibn Ezra: *let his hands be sufficient for him*.   יספיקו לו ידיו
   T: let his handes fyght for him.
   C: let his handes multiplye.
   M: manus eius sufficiens est sibi.
   GR B: his handes shalbe good ynough for hym.
   J: manus eius multae erunt.
   P: contendent sibi.
   G A: let his hands be sufficient for hym.
   TR: manibus eius satis *sit* ei.

T and *P*, following the *Vulgate*; *C* and *J*; *M G A* and *GR B TR* agree with each other. *M* accepts the interpretation of Ibn Ezra tacitly and hands this down to all subsequent English versions.

14. *I Samuel* xx. 4.   מה־תאמר נפשך

   Targum: *What is the desire of your soul*.   מא רעוא נפשך
   T/M (C) GR: whatsoever thy soul (heart) desyreth.
   M: quidquid dixerit anima tua.
   J: quidquid pro voto desideras. Note: Ebr. quid dixerit anima tua.
   G: requireth (Heb. sayeth).   *B*: desireth (Heb. sayth).
   TR: quod sit desyderium tuum. Marg.: Hebr. quis sit animus tuus. sic animus pro desyderio *Ps.* 27. 12 et alibi frequenter.
   Λ: whatsoever thy soul desireth (*Heb.* speaketh, or thinketh).
   R: like *A* (*Heb.* saith).

In this case *T/M* already follows the Targum. Perhaps Tindale owes this acquaintance with the Targum to personal instruction from Jews? *TR* makes a plunder, for it is not נפשך that means 'wish' but the verb אמר is rendered by the noun רעוא 'will, pleasure'!

15. *Micah* vi. 9. ותושיה יראה שמך

R. David Qimḥi: the man of wisdom . . . said the prophet: " if I announce your words in the midst of the city he who is the man of wisdom among them alone shall see in his innermost heart your honoured name . . ."

ואיש תושיה . . . אמר הנביא כשאני קורא דבריך . . . בתוך העיר מי שהוא איש חכמה ביניהם הוא לבדו יראה בתוך לבבו את שמך הנכבד . . .

Rashi explains similarly " who sets his heart *upon the task* to understand and see your ways."

אשר נותן לב להתבונן ולראות דרכיך

T/M C GR: that thy name may be righteousnesse.

M: et (vir) salutis videbit nomen tuum. He explains: Est autem תושיה non salus sed existentia, et id quod firmum manet, quales sunt electi et praeordinati ad salutem. Hebraei tamen exponunt חכמה sapientiam, quae sola in mundo inferiori permanet. . . .

J: quique ratione praeditus est, videbit nomen tuum. *marg.* alij legunt, timebit. Does he mean Pagnino by ' alij '?

G A: and *the man of* wisdom shall see thy name.

TR: nam quod res est videt nomen tuum.

A marg. *Or*, thy name shall see that which is.

B: the man that shalbe saved consydereth thy name.

P: et vir sapiens timebit nomen tuum. In his *Epitome* he gives also other meanings quoting Qimḥi.

GR does not follow *M* in this case. But *M* borrows (vir) from Qimḥi as well as his explanation. And it is this Jewish exegesis which found its way into *G* and *A* whilst *A* follows *TR* in the alternative translation of the margin.

J may equally well be influenced by Rashi or Qimḥi.

Apart from Rashi the Targum, Qimḥi and Ibn Ezra will be the principal exponents of Jewish exegesis in the English versions. It is for this reason that we gave the last three examples.

Jewish themes

B. *In the Notes of the Genevan and the Bishops' Bibles.*

16. To *Genesis* xlvii. 21, 'he removed them from one end ... of Egypt to the other end.'

Rashi: *as a reminder that they had no longer any share (or portion) in the land.* לזכרון שאין להם עוד חלק בארץ

M: Seu ut Hebraica habent: in signum quod nihil proprij amplius haberent in terra.

G: 'By this changing they signified that they had nothing of their owne but received all of the kings liberalitie.'

B: This was a token that they had no proprietie more in the lande.

B is a literal translation of *M* who, in his turn, translates Rashi.

17. To *Genesis* xlix. 10, 'until Shilo come.'

Rashi: *the king Messiah whose will be the kingdom.* And thus Onqelos translates. מלך המשיח שהמלוכה שלו

P translates: donec veniat Messias. In his *Epitome* s.v. שיל׳ refers to this passage and translates Filius eius, quoting 'Tharg. Christus.'

J: in the margin we find: Shilo, felicitator.

M: quotes משיח שילו, based on Targum.

B: Shilo, Messias is here promised.

TR: usquedum venerit filius eius. *Heb.* secundae eius, hoc est, Christus, ut Chaldaea paraphrasis utraque (i.e. Pseudo-Jonathan as well as Onqelos), et Hebr. interpretes fere omnes consentiunt.

B may derive from *P*, *M* or Rashi. *TR* follows Pseudo-Jonathan זעיר בנוי *the youngest of his sons.*

18. To *Exodus* xxi. 6, 'and he shall serve him for ever.'

Rashi: until the Jubilee, or not so but for ever? Therefore Scripture teaches (*Leviticus* xxv. 10): *and ye shall return every man to his family.* This shows that 50 years are called עולם; but not that he serve him all the 50 years, nay, he shall serve him until the Jubilee be it near at hand or far off.

עד היובל או אינו אלא לעולם כמשמעו· ת״ל ואיש אל משפחתו תשובו מגיד שנ׳ שנה קרויים עולם ולא שיהא עובדו כל נ׳ שנה אלא עובדו עד היובל בין סמוך בין מופלג·

M: Id est, usque ad iubileum: sive is annus prope fuerit, sive longe abfuerit. Sic enim Hebraei communiter exponunt hunc locum.

B: The worde in Hebrue dooth not always sounde perpetuitie, sometyme it is taken for a long continuance for in this case they were never set free tyl the yeare of Jubilee, whiche was a tyme of generall pardon.

TR also explains until the Jubilee.

The origin of the note in *B* is quite clear.

19. To *Exodus* xxix. 24, ' and shalt wave them for a wave offering.'

Rashi: He waves forward and backward unto Him who possesses the four sides of the world. . . He waves upward and downward unto Him who possesses Heaven and Earth.

מוליך ומביא למי שד׳ רוחות העולם שלו מעלה ומוריך למי שהשמים והארץ שלו.

M: Siginifcat הֵנִיף aliquid in sublime porrectum, hinc inde ad quattuor mundi plagas movere, et quasi ventilare.

B: ' This sort of offering after the priest had lyfted it up, was moved into every side of al coastes, to signifie that God was Lorde of al the earth. It was muche lyke to the manner of blessings used in papistes churches over the chalice.'

Here *M* alone does not account for *B*. It must therefore be assumed that the writer of the note had a first-hand knowledge of the original Rashi.

Attention may be drawn to another notable instance of Rashi serving as interpreter, i.e. *Exodus* xxi. 10. Other examples are xxii. 18, 25, 28.

20. *Isaiah* xli. 1. איים ' Islands.'

Rashi: Islands. Idolators to reprove them.

איים. עכו״ם להוכיחם על פניהם.

B: By the Ylandes, God meaneth the Gentles whom he reproveth for their idolatrie.

21. *v*. 5. ' The isles saw *it* and feared.'

Rashi: The idolators. the wonders I am performing. . (*or*, powerful works). עובדי עכו״ם הגבורות שאעשה וייראו

G: considering mine excellent workes among my people. 'and came.'

Rashi: they assembled themselves to fight.

זה אצל זה נאספים להלחם.

G: they assembled themselves and conspired against me to maintain their idolatrie.

Both notes go back to Rashi.

22. *v.* 25.

Rashi: and Cyrus shall, etc. וכורש העירותי...

G translates: from the East sunne shal he call upon my name. 'he' in *marg*. That is, Cyrus. So also *B*.

These examples may suffice to show that Rashi did not only supply the translation of many a passage but also furnished a number of notes for the better understanding of both the *Genevan* and the *Bishops' Bibles*.

That Rashi's influence could not be limited to the actual translations but ought to have extended to the writings of the translators dealing with the Old Testament appears to be a safe assumption.

We may therefore be allowed to conclude this study with a short paragraph on

C. *Rashi's Interpretation in English Biblical Commentaries.*

As stated above we were unable to procure copies of the Commentaries written by Gilby of the *Genevan* nor Kilbye and Lively of the *Authorized Version*. But we were able to consult John Rainolds' treatises on *Obadiah* and *Haggai*.[1]

23. In his commentary on *Obadiah* Rainolds translates i. 9, איש מהר עשו by 'the valiant of the mount . . .' Commenting on this verse he polemises against Tremellius' translation 'every one of the mount . . .' He continues: 'But sith the Hebrew word איש signifieth a valiant man, differing from אדם as *vir* doth from *homo*, and ἀνήρ from ἄνθρωπος. . . .'[2] Now we find in Rashi *ad loc.* 'Every valiant man, כל איש גבור

[1] First published Oxford, 1613, resp. London, 1648. The edition used for this paper is dated 1864 and appeared in Nichol's Comms.

[2] *Obadiah*, p. 20. On p. 39 he rails against 'the frantic dreams of Jewish rabbins' who refer the captivity of *v.* 20 to Titus, etc.

24. Commenting on *Haggai* i. 8 he refutes the Jewish interpretation that the missing ה in ואכבד signify that 'the latter temple was greater than the former.' He goes on : ' Some of them will say in regard of the building, others in respect of the continuance, for that as they account this stood ten years longer than the former which is laid down by the author of their ordinary gloss. . . .'
" Nay, they are convinced of madness by the same rabbin, for on the same word, because the Hebrew word wanteth the letter ה, which in number standeth with them for fifth, he saith it is a note of mystery ; for that this latter temple wanted five things which the former had : (1) Urim and Thummim ; (2) the ark of the covenant ; (3) fire from heaven ; (4) the sign of God's glory ; (5) presence of the Holy Ghost ; and this is proved, alleging a place of Talmud, which is among the Jews as the decretal among the papists, the author thereof would no more err, than can the pope ; a Talmudical fancy ; for although ה were wanting (as it is not in those copies which are received without points) ;[1] but if it were by their fault that copied out of the book, what reason that there would want five things because ה signifieth five in numbering, which is nothing but a sottish and cabalistine toy ; for even this temple wanted more than these five things, as they also confess, even in the same book, for there was not the cup of manna, and therefore not only five, but eight or nine more were wanting . . . etc."

We quoted this lengthy tirade in full because it allows us a glimpse into the mind of one of the principal figures of Puritan Biblical scholarship. His knowledge of the Talmud must not have been substantial if he could seriously hold such views! But he must obviously have combined with a militant outspokenness a sound knowledge of the Hebrew Bible and of Jewish exegesis, notably of Rashi whom he calls *the author of their ordinary gloss*, just like Reuchlin. For he actually quotes Rashi's comment on *Haggai* ii. 9 : רב ושמואל חד

[1] The Massoretic text distinguishes between ואכבד K^e*thib* and *Qere* ואכבדה. The quotation occurs in his *Haggai*, p. 30. His reference to Josephus goes back to Rashi in this instance. But there are other references to Josephus throughout his *Commentary* which suggest that he read Josephus just as he read and quoted other classical authors.

אמר בבנין וחד אמר בשנים ששני בית ראשון ת״י ובית שני ת״ך
Rab and Sh{e}muel (are of different opinion), the one says with regard to the building, the other says with regard to the continuance, for the first temple stood 410 years and the second 420. And what Rainolds says about the five things, this is literally taken over from Rashi *ad loc.* : " the missing ה accounts for five things which were in the first temple but not in the second : חסר ה״א כנגד ה״ דברים שהיו במקדש ראשון ולא במקדש שני ארון אורים ותומים ואש ושכינה ורה״ק ; the ark, Urim and Thummim, Fire, Divine Presence and Holy Spirit." Now, the *Athenae Cantabrigienses* inform us that Drs. Airay and Rainolds secured a position for the aforementioned Philip Ferdinand as teacher of Hebrew in several Colleges and Halls. Both scholars acted as a sort of tutor to Ferdinand who removed to Oxford in 1596.[1] His knowledge of Hebrew must have been extensive and is attested to by J. Scaliger who was his pupil in the Talmud.[2] We venture to suggest that this former Polish Jew, steeped in Hebrew and Aramaic literature, showed gratitude to his benefactor Rainolds by acquainting him with Jewish exegesis. But without a record for it as yet nothing more definite can be asserted. It may be that a perusal of Ferdinand's literary remains may throw some light on this point. Any future research into the state of Hebrew scholarship in Elizabethan England will have to concentrate on correspondence such as the letters of Scaliger, Casaubon and other famous contemporaries. Though John Selden reaches over into the second half of the seventeenth century it is just likely that among his vast collection of letters material bearing on this question may be found. Generally speaking there should be no lack of material in a century noted for the high quality of its scholarship. And although Hebrew studies could not compete with Classical scholarship their significance cannot be doubted, both as regards mere scholarship and particularly by their bearing upon the genesis of the monumental *Authorized Version*. A monograph on Hebrew scholarship in Elizabethan England is not only a contribution to the history of learning but also to the history of the English Bible. And although much of the advance of the

[1] P. 239.   [2] *Ibid.*, p. 549. Where his writings are enumerated.

standard Version of King James is due to Sebastian Münster, it is obvious that even the perusal of his learned notes was only possible for men with an adequate knowledge and understanding of Hebrew. And although Ferdinand and Tremellius, Kilbye, Lively and Rainolds could not vie with Reuchlin, Münster and Fagius in fame perhaps, these scholars after all provided the background for Pococke. A study of their literary remains may well show that their attainments were considerable, and such a study should be made.

That the labours of the Mediaeval Jewish exegetes bore fruit in the works of these Hebraists of the sixteenth and seventeenth centuries, and not least in their Latin and English Versions of the Hebrew Bible, even the limited number of passages quoted in the foregoing pages should convincingly demonstrate. The English Bible as a literary monument is without rival. Its influence on English style has been recognized by competent judges. Still more obvious and significant is the great moral force which has gone forth from its pages and has so conspicuously helped to mould and shape the English character. It is therefore well to remember that the foundations for this monument were laid by men who saw in the promulgation of God's Word in the vernacular a powerful weapon for the attainment of Christian liberty and freedom. And it is to their lasting credit that in their fierce struggle for reform, helped by the spirit of Humanism and the zeal of the reformers with whom they established contact when in exile on the Continent, they did not spare energy nor industry to turn to the Hebrew fountain and bring it to life in their own tongue. In this task they were assisted by Jewish exegesis, directly or indirectly, through the instrumentality of Latin translations, among which that of Sebastian Münster occupies first place.

To follow up their labours and to assess their failure or success is an academic matter. Yet even the historian who patiently follows the translators of the sixteenth and early seventeenth centuries on their wanderings through the Bible and watches them at work liveth in the present. Witnessing the tragic persecution of the descendants of these Mediaeval exegetes and teachers he cannot but marvel at the coincidence that the descendants of Parker and Rainolds, of Grindal and Kilbye should have again to defend those Rights of Man to which the Bible bears testimony, that Bible which these his forbears introduced to all Christians of their own and all subsequent generations !

It had seemed to me to be a worthy tribute to the memory of one of these teachers on the occasion of the ninth centenary of his birth to recall the services which his interpretation has rendered to the perfection of the English Bible. The same qualities which have endeared Rashi to his people, which have enabled him to teach generation after generation the beauty and truth of their Bible, have also commended him to the Christian student of the Hebrew Bible and to the Christian teachers of their nations. Nobody has set Rashi a finer memorial than that great Humanist Reuchlin in calling him the *Ordinary Interpreter of Scripture*, the echo of which apt characterisation we heard in Rainolds' *author of their ordinary gloss*.[1] It is the simplicity of diction, the directness of approach, the distinction between the literal sense and the homiletic lesson, the attention to grammar—faulty as it sometimes may seem to us moderns—and at the same time the ease with which the often drawn-out Rabbinic interpretation is set forth and brought home to the ordinary reader, it is all these peculiarities of his Commentary singly and all combined which have appealed to the Christian exegetes from the fourteenth century onward. And it is surely no coincidence

---

[1] Cp. also S. A. Hirsch *Early English Hebraists: Roger Bacon and His Predecessors* in : A Book of Essays, London, 1905, and his *Presidential Address*. (Jewish Historical Society of England *Transactions VII*, London, 1915, pp. 1-18). These are the first studies on Hebrew Scholarship in thirteenth- and fourteenth-century England. This subject has now been taken up by Miss Smalley. See her *Hebrew Scholarship among Christians in Thirteenth-Century England, as illustrated by some Hebrew-Latin Psalters*, Lectiones Series, No. 6, London, 1939.†

Hirsch, in his *Presidential Address*, mentions quotations of Rashi by the Franciscan Henry of Costessy in his *Expositio super Psalmos*, written *ca.* 1336, alongside with quotations from other Jewish authorities. William de la Mare, a contemporary of Roger Bacon, in his *Correctorium Vaticanum* [of the text of the *Vulgate*], cites the *Perush* [Commentary] by which is almost certainly meant *the* Commentary of Rashi (*s.* Hirsch, *ibid.*, p. 12).

It remains to be seen whether the English Hebraists of the sixteenth and seventeenth centuries knew of and used these earlier, mainly Franciscan Commentaries and other Hebrew and Biblical studies.

that his Commentary was the first dated printed Hebrew book, a fact which must have largely contributed to the popularity of Rashi's interpretation at a time when 'Back to the original sources' was the battle-cry of the educated. Though Rashi's achievement in the field of Talmudical exegesis by far outdistances his fame as a commentator of the Bible, it is the same quality in both which accounts for his success. Yet, seen in a wider perspective, it is Rashi the Bible-commentator who will live in the minds and memories of men not confined to Jews and Judaism.

All those who value culture and civilization, in particular those who see in Christianity and its teachings the highest ideal for our endangered civilization and who believe that the realization of the Biblical ideal—and after all the Old Testament forms part of it still—is the only road to salvation, would do well to remember that Rashi furnished many a brick to the building of the moral wall which we feel called upon to defend and make into a secure reality.

The last decade of his life was overshadowed by the savage persecutions of the first Crusade and its aftermath. There is great relief in the thought that a more humane generation of Christians have at a time of grave trial vindicated the genius of a persecuted people and have thus enriched a work which they set up as a standard for all times through the toilings of a devout man of God who lived what he taught : Rashi.

4
SAADYA GAON: AN APPRECIATION OF HIS BIBLICAL EXEGESIS[1]

I.

SAADYA'S exegesis of the Old Testament, both in his Arabic translation of it and in his commentaries on several books which have survived, represents the first systematic attempt at setting out in coherent treatises its legal, ethical and theological teachings. To achieve this, Saadya has made extensive studies of Hebrew grammar and lexicography: he wanted to establish the plain meaning of Scripture. He became thus the founder of Hebrew philology among the Jews. Besides, as is to be expected from the head of the principal academy of traditional learning, he brought the traditional interpretation of the Bible fully to bear on his own investigation of the text. Being, moreover, steeped in the culture of his Islamic surroundings, he made full use of the secular knowledge of his age, which spread as the result of the renaissance of Greek science and Hellenistic philosophy, and applied the findings of reason to the text: especially if the literal meaning would be incompatible with reason, Saadya

---

[1] The reader may wish to consult the following works: H. Malter, *Saadia Gaon, his Life and Works*, Philadelphia, 1921, where a full Bibliography is given. For Saadya's Biblical exegesis in particular, W. Bacher, *Die Bibelexegese der jüdischen Religionsphilosophen des Mittelalters vor Maimuni*, Budapest, 1892, is very important. Cf. also H. Hirschfeld, " The Arabic portion of the Cairo Genizah at Cambridge," in *J.Q.R.*, XVII, 712 ff., and XIX, 137 ff., and B. Heller's study of Saadya's Version of " Proverbs," in *R.E.J.*, XXXVII, 72-85, 226-251. A volume of *Saadya Studies*, edited by the present writer, to be published by the Manchester University Press, is in the press. It will contain hitherto unpublished fragments of Saadya's *Commentary on Leviticus*, edited and described by J. Leveen, and an article by the present writer on *Saadya's Exegesis of the Book of Job*.† The last-named article gives a detailed account of the exegetical method of Saadya. It cannot be repeated here. Saadya's " philosophical" work, *Book of Beliefs and Convictions*, which contains much material on the subject discussed in the present article, has not been drawn upon, nor his *Commentary on the Sefer Yeṣirah*.

would bring out the inner meaning of a word or passage. As a teacher he was determined to make his generation understand the lesson of the Bible in a language they spoke and understood: Arabic. Fierce opposition on the part of the Karaites, who rejected Jewish tradition and fought it by going back to the Bible which they closely examined, made a fresh authoritative interpretation of the Bible necessary. This interpretation was not only to vindicate the orthodox tradition but aimed at a revival of Rabbanite Judaism.[1] The message of the Bible as the eternal fundament of Judaism had to be interpreted afresh so as to answer the doubts and confusion caused not only by the Karaites, but also by adherents of philosophical schools as they were found among the Muslims. The battle between orthodoxy and enlightened philosophical free-thinkers was in full swing in Saadya's time: scepticism and confusion found their way also into the Jewish camp. The clear, unmistakable teachings of the Bible were to be once more the true guide to a full, moral life. The precepts of the Bible setting out a way of life with clear injunctions for the relations between man and man and man and his Creator were to be made accessible to every Jew: hence Saadya's life-long work on the Bible, including his great so-called philosophical *magnum opus*. Even in this work, the first systematic exposition of the basic ideas of Judaism, the theologian and teacher takes first place, only that Saadya employed the philosophical method and philosophical argument. This *Book of Beliefs and Convictions* is actually a primer of Theology *more philosophico*.

[1] Saadya contrasts at the end of *Prov.* viii the *believers in the* (absolute) *unity (of God)* and the *Rabbanites* with the *heretics and dissenters*, having especially the Karaites in mind. In his comment on *Prov.* ix he gives this definition of the Rabbanites: *they have revised the Bible, (have stated) how many chapters, verses and words it has, have divided it into parts and portions and counted the words . . . they then guarded the tradition, vested with them by the prophets of God concerning the (Divine) Law (Torah), the laws of inheritance, judgments, (things) permitted and forbidden and the other laws.* . . . A similar statement is contained in one of the Fragments published by Hirschfeld (*l.c.*) and translated by him in these words: *Now we Rabbanites are the first class of Israelites who derive their appellation from the prophets of God who follow their footsteps and preserve their tradition for future ages; these sectarians, however, differ from each other.* . . . This is naturally in complete agreement with the Rabbis.

II.

The most important and interesting feature in Saadya's exegesis is that he prefaces every book he comments on by a lengthy Introduction in which he expounds the lesson of the book, its principal idea, its structure and his own aim in explaining it. To this he adds some general remarks about the principles to be observed by the translator and commentator.[1] The actual comment is not just a gloss to every verse but—apart from linguistic notes on the meaning of words, their derivation and connotation in the context—an exposition of the meaning of a verse, a group of verses or a whole chapter. He traces the connexion of one chapter with another preceding or following one, and defines the contribution certain phrases or more extensive literary or logical units make to the basic idea of the book: e.g. the principle of the Justice of God in his dealings with man in *Job*, or the problem of acquiring knowledge in *Proverbs*. His comments are to the point, concise and lucid,[2] and no verse or phrase is too obscure to receive a plausible explanation be it readily reconcilable with the wording or not. In making the distinction between the plain, literal exoteric meaning of a word (*ẓāhir*) and the inner, hidden, esoteric meaning (*bāṭin*)[3] Saadya

---

[1] *See* my paper on *Job*, l.c.

[2] Hirschfeld quotes in the just mentioned Fragment a statement which is symptomatic for Saadya's method: *I must first reproduce the explanation given us by the prophets ... and recount the sum total of forbidden marriages mentioned in Bible and Tradition. This will be followed by those added or deducted by the innovators and to show their error.* It brings out clearly the dual purpose of Saadya's exegesis: to define the accepted Rabbanite *Halakah* and to maintain tradition against the Karaites, at the same time refuting their interpretation as erroneous innovation.

[3] *See* my paper on *Job*, l.c. A good example is furnished in his comment on *Prov.* xxiv. 27. He first gives the literal interpretation and then explains the verse figuratively, bringing out the hidden, inner meaning: first man must satisfy the demands of nature (food, clothing, dwelling, etc.) in this world before he can reach the things of the world to come for this is so determined by Providence. The same applies to science where there is necessarily a preliminary science for the more advanced one as *the Greeks*, says Saadya, *call this introduction Isagoge to Logic, astronomy, geometry and medicine.* And then Saadya applies this same principle to the relation between the rational and the revealed laws: *the attachment of the servant (of God) to Sabbath, festivals, etc., is of no benefit to him unless preceded by (the practice of) the rational laws like right, justice, equity.* . . .

expressly limits the latter, figurative explanation to passages the literal interpretation of which would run counter to Reason and established Tradition. Thus he concludes his Introduction to his version of the Pentateuch with the statement that it is *a simple, explanatory translation (tafsīr) of the text of the Torah, written with the knowledge of reason ('aql) and tradition (naql)*. Another feature of his commentaries is that Saadya often digresses into the discussion of philosophical or theological questions in little excursuses wherein he employs the means of contrast in order to drive home his point, to bring out the importance of an idea, e.g. Nature versus Reason (Introduction to his version of *Proverbs*),[1] or the telling contrast between transient riches and durable wisdom and knowledge (comment on *Prov.* iii. 18),[2] or the contrast between God's wisdom and that of man on the Four Elements (comment on *Prov.* xxx. 3). Another characteristic feature of Saadya's explanation is that he aims in his definitions of the nature and meaning of basic ideas like *wisdom, instruction, knowledge* at completeness and clarity to the exclusion of all ambiguity and vagueness. He achieves this by analysing the various *aspects* of *Wisdom* in his comment on *Prov.* viii. 21 : here he enumerates eight constituent parts or modes of *ḥokmah*. In the beginning of his *Commentary* he distinguishes four *kinds* of *Wisdom*.[3]

---

[1] *See* Saadya's version of *Proverbs*, edit. H. Derenbourg, Paris, *Introd.*, p. 6.

[2] Saadya makes many comparisons, e.g. whereas *riches need a master to guard them, wisdom guards him who possesses it*. Or, *riches just gained perish, but the gain of wisdom is durable*. . . .

[3] Among the *eight* aspects are : counsel ; excellent discernment without which the power of the mighty is useless ; kings, their ministers and advisers need it for their administration ; judges and jurists for their decisions. It is equally essential for those who aspire to worldly gain and riches : for without it they know not justice nor equity in their commercial activities and trade becomes robbery. Of the four *kinds* of wisdom are *discernment* (*tamyīz*, for: *lĕhābīn imrē bīnah*) ; the reception of learning taught (for : *laqaḥat musar sekhel*). In another passage Saadya distinguishes twelve meanings of wisdom to be found in *Proverbs*, giving wisdom now a philosophical object (*observation, reflexion, deducing the particular from the general, etc.*), now a theological connotation (being contained in *stories of the end of the good and the wicked*, or, *in command and prohibition*). There are, moreover, distinctions between various kinds of knowledge : comprehension is defined as *the acquisition of knowledge by man's learning the principles and roots of the sciences from him who preceded him*. (Note the importance of tradition !)

Here is not the place to treat of Saadya's *Theory of Knowledge* in full.[1] Suffice it to refer to his view that knowledge has three roots : sense-perception, reason or rational perception, and necessary logical deduction. This type of knowledge is, so-to-speak, *secular* knowledge of the philosopher. It is contrasted with the knowledge of the *religious* thinkers who, as members of the *community of the believers in the* (absolute) *unity* (of God), supplement the three roots or constituent elements by a fourth : *true* (and trustworthy) *tradition* contained in the *Torah* and the *Books of Prophecy*. Saadya insists on the complementary unity of Reason, *Torah* as the book of Divine Instruction, and Tradition. This tradition (*khabr, naql* or *āthār*) contains not only the three elements just mentioned which could not guarantee the character of absolute proof as man's experience and reason is imperfect. It possesses the additional quality of truth because it derives from the prophets who were worthy to receive divine instruction by revelation. This axiom of the revealed truth stands at the beginning of mediæval philosophical speculation and forms its heart and centre. In this sense must we understand Saadya's statement in his *Introduction* to his version of the *Pentateuch* that God has given man two other proofs—in addition to the *Torah* and the Prophets—Reason which precedes it and Tradition which follows it. *With the help of the argument from reason man realises that God who created everything out of nothing is One, Eternal and Unique, free from Matter, possessed of Free Will and* (absolutely) *Just*. Tradition confirms this by furnishing the knowledge

For a full account cf. *Introd.*, pp. 6 ff. This mixture of philosophical and theological speculation is characteristic of Saadya, who is primarily a theologian. The interpretation of such passages is made difficult by the fact that terms like *ḥikmatun, ma'rifatun, 'ilmun* mean not necessarily the same thing in different contexts. Theological concepts, on the other hand, are unequivocal. In *Proverbs*, as in *Job*, the same problems are discussed as in Saadya's philosophical work. Yet, whereas the argument is philosophical in the *Book of Beliefs*, it is predominantly theological in *Job* and mixed in *Proverbs*, with a predominance of philosophical excursuses.

[1] *See*, on this point especially, Bacher, *l.c.* ; Guttmann, *Die Religionsphilosophie des Saadja*, Göttingen, 1882 ; Ventura, *La philosophie de Saadia Gaon*, Paris, 1934 ; S. Rawidowicz, " The Idea of the Purification of God," in *Saadya Studies, l.c.* I follow Bacher, who cites the *Book of Beliefs*, supplemented by passages in the Biblical commentaries of Saadya. Bacher deals with the great influence Saadya has exerted on Baḥya on pp. 59 f.

derived from the tradition of the prophets who came after the *Torah*[1] and were, in their wisdom and experience of human life, responsible for the traditional laws which are not in conflict with Reason. The antagonist of Reason is *not* Revelation but Nature. Saadya, in his *Introduction* to his version of *Proverbs*, says that *God has written, through Solomon, a book* (i.e. *Proverbs*) *to instruct man who needs guidance* (*tadbir*) *in these matters of Reason versus* Nature. *If man's Reason rules over his nature he is truly human, if it is the other way round, his actions are like that of beasts. Though Nature comes first in the building up and in disposition, it is Reason which decrees what to do and then man does it ; if it decides something should be left, then man does not do it.*

We owe to Saadya the distinction of the Commandments of the Bible : those demanded by Reason and those commanded by God through Revelation. This classification has been accepted by subsequent Jewish thinkers until Maimonides attacked it as emanating from the *Mutakallimun*, the Muslim dialectic theologians. *Nature*, says Saadya in the same passage from which we have just quoted, *is not prone to provide knowledge in religious matters*, i.e. in these two groups of commandments. By the *rational laws* Saadya means *the command to do everything which is approved by Reason, like Righteousness, Truth, Justice, Equity, Good Deeds and the like, and to prohibit everything of which Reason disapproves, like lie and falsehood, theft, immorality and the like.* By the *Commandments of Revelation* he means *the laws which the prophets have announced ; purity, sacrifices, Sabbath, Festivals,* etc.[2] *Nature tries to keep man off these things as it is tiring and*

---

[1] Saadya naturally adheres to the traditional view that the Rabbis were the successors of the prophets.

[2] In his comment on *Prov.* xxix. 18 f. Saadya admonishes his readers to *listen to what God announced through his prophets on matters of Sabbath, Festivals, Fasts, purity and inheritance*—the laws of inheritance, on which Saadya has written a whole treatise, still extant and published in the *Œuvres complètes*, are very frequently mentioned as of great importance, and always in connexion with the other laws of revelation. Saadya, in this comment, stresses the unity and connexion between the two groups of laws : *it is necessary that the announced* (*khabariyya* for the usual *samā'iyya*) *laws precede the logical laws* (*mantiqiyya* for the usual *'aqliyya*) *: justice, right, equity, and love thy neighbour as thyself.* The last commandment is not included in the other references elsewhere to the rational laws. Moreover, the order of the two groups of laws is reversed here,

troublesome to learn by study and investigation, etc. It belongs to the functions of Reason to direct man's attention to pushing back and silencing Nature so that he (can) seek wisdom. If Nature tempts man to do evil, Reason warns him of the result of such action : grief, evil and misfortune in this world and punishment and evil in the world to come.[1] Ḥokmah is here understood in the traditional sense of study (of the all-embracing Torah in the wider sense) in order to do good and shun evil.

III.

It is clear that Saadya as a religious teacher was concerned with the right behaviour of man as a religious person, first and foremost. Yet, as a son of his age, he was not satisfied with a blind faith and a mechanical observance of the commandments. The supremacy of Reason over Nature was to be secured only by constant striving : it alone guaranteed man *happiness*. This happiness man cannot reach by his own exertions, by employing his rational faculty unaided : it is possible only through a study of the *Torah, the aim of which is to make the servants (of God) entirely happy ; for the Torah forms a collection of the three kinds (of instruction) and is therefore of utmost perfection and ultimate authority. God tells his servants to do justly and to refrain from evil.*[2] Intelligent faith and conscious, willing observance were to be achieved only by study, and study requires instruction (*ta'dib*). Saadya distinguishes three kinds of instruction : The first is

cf. p. 170, n. 3. Precedence of the rational over the revealed laws in time seems to be implied in Saadya's interpretation of " *the fear of the Lord is the beginning of knowledge* " : *it is not meant that the fear precedes knowledge for it would be absurd that there should be fear without knowledge*. Precedence is temporal, not qualitative.

In the Fragment quoted on p. 169, n. 1 and p. 170, n. 2, Saadya states (Hirschfeld, *l.c.*, p. 721) that the prophets are necessary not only to explain the practice of traditional regulations, but also that of the rational laws. The supremacy of Revelation could not be expressed more clearly and convincingly. We agree with M. Lambert's statement in his Introduction to his edition of Saadya's *Commentary on the Sefer Yesirah* that Saadya " reste *tout à fait indépendant de cette philosophie grecque qu'il connaît si* bien. Bien supérieur en cela à Maimonide. . . . Saadya reste toujours fidèle à l'esprit du judaisme." Yet, we would qualify the reference to Maimonides who is, we believe, no less true to the spirit of Judaism than Saadya.

[1] See *Introd.*, pp. 3 f. [2] *Ibid.*, p. 2.

simple command and prohibition: *do this and refrain from that*. The pupil is not informed of the consequences connected with command and prohibition. The second method consists in telling the pupil that he has the choice between reward for obeying and punishment for disobeying command and prohibition. *This is stronger than the first for he can imagine the happiness or misfortune he will meet with in every deed he chooses.* The third kind consists in adding to the preceding way *the story of those people who obey the commandments, for their reward and their happiness are the best, and the story of those people who injure themselves with their disobedience and are punished and unhappy. This way is stronger than the two first ones, for experience and test come to him who obeys . . . and it takes for him the place of a testimony*.[1] One must always learn. Unlike the craftsman who does the same amount of work every day, the student learns little in the first year, twice as much in the second, etc. . . . *therefore the seeker after wisdom must needs be patient . . . likewise prayer and good deeds demand zeal and patience* (comment on *Prov.* viii. 36).[2] This seeker is warned by Saadya not to inquire into two things: Creation (*'ilmu-l-ibdā'i*) and Revelation (*wal-ikhtirā'i*). Both these terms stand undoubtedly for the Hebrew *ma'aseh bĕrēshit u(ma'aseh) merkabah* of the Rabbis. They are for God, not for man. But the wise say to the seeker: *inquire into God's commandments and prohibitions and into what your fathers have handed down*. In other words, wisdom is interpreted as the contents of both, the written and the oral *Torah*. Saadya called *Proverbs* the *Book of the Seeker after Wisdom*, for it gives him *advice how to obtain it*.[3]

IV.

In each *Introduction* we find, too, a short description of the contents of the book, its difficulties, and consequently Saadya's special attention is focussed on clearing up those difficulties. Thus, he singles out for special treatment the story of Satan,

[1] See *Introd.*, p. 2.   [2] Cf. also comment on xix. 18.
[3] *Introd.*, p. 11. Cf. also my paper on *Job*, how Saadya justifies the title of *Theodicy* there.

who he is, what he says and how he behaves, for he finds that all these points cause considerable difficulty to the reader of *Job*. Next, he points to the sufferings of Job although he was *perfect and upright*, as causing doubt and confusion. Likewise difficult is the understanding of the sequence of speech and answer as between Job, his friends and Elihu : how the discussion progresses between them, whether and how they understood each other and in what their opposition to each other consisted. Saadya answers all these doubts and difficulties with the help of metaphor, rational interpretation, another passage in *Job* or from another book of Scripture, or with the help of true prophetic tradition. The similes of *Proverbs* serve the same object of instruction : *this is the way how Reason brings near to Nature what is* (originally) *alien to it*. This is done by four devices : (1) simile (Hebrew : *mashal*) ; (2) interpretation of similes (Hebrew : *mĕliṣah*) ; (3) similes which God has coined through his prophets (Hebrew : *dibrē ḥakhamim*) ; (4) parables which God has coined as another (metaphorical) rendering of a simile and its interpretation (Hebrew : *ḥidot*). As such parables or similes, Saadya conceives the proverbs : hence he often explains them by way of comparison. Like a father chastises his son for his benefit, so God punishes his servant in justice.[1] To vi. 23 *the commandment is a lamp and the law is light*. Saadya stresses the contrast rather than the comparison : *the lamp goes out quickly but the light of the sun does not vanish except together with the world ; likewise the father perishes, but not the Torah. And if the lamp is for one's house in particular, so is the father for his son alone, whereas the light is for the whole of creation, just as the Torah is for them all* (i.e. created beings). Commenting on xxv. 5 Saadya calls the king one of the *rochers de bronze* (lit. *columns*) of the world. He cannot establish *his rule except through justice and equity in his political and legal administration, therefore he must remove all unjust persons from his presence.* . . . On xxix. 12 Saadya's comment is that *the ruler must be just and straight more than any other man, for his bad example corrupts his princes, the princes those who are subordinate to them, until the whole nation is*

---

[1] *See* comment on *Prov*. iii. 11 f. God is just, not unjust, the theme of *Job*. Cf. also the example quoted on p. 171, n. 2.

bad.¹ With reference to xxviii. 2 Saadya declares himself in favour of the monarchy: *it stands to reason that the perfect government is only one that is in the hands of one man, but the government in a democracy cannot be perfect because of their differences and mutual opposition.* It is interesting to find here an echo of Plato's *Politeia* and the influence of the absolutistic rule of the contemporary Abbasid caliphs.

Mention must at least be made of frequent references to the Aramaic of the Targum in his linguistic notes.²

V.

A few remarks on how Saadya divided the *Book of Proverbs*, how he occasionally re-arranged the verses in a chapter, and on the order and disposition of the *Pentateuch* may conclude this short survey.

Saadya divides *Proverbs* into three parts: (i) chapters i-ix; (ii) chapters x-xxiv, bearing the heading: *similes and instructive sayings*; (iii) chapters xxv-xxxi.³ As an example of re-arrangement of verses may be quoted chapter ix. Saadya translates *vv.* 1-9, then follow *vv.* 13-18, then he brings a comment and ends up with the translation of *vv.* 10-12.

As to the order and disposition of the *Pentateuch*, Saadya thinks that *fittingly the commandments should occupy first place, followed by the consequences* (reward and punishment for obedience and disobedience respectively) *and then the stories* (i.e. history). *But,* he goes on, *as the Torah was not sent down by God in his wisdom until men were complete in numbers, God had to make known to them the substance of past history so that men imitated what was praiseworthy in the actions of their predecessors . . . and kept away from what was blameworthy. . . .* We have here an early mediæval example of the pragmatic conception of history.

---

¹ Cf. also *v.* 16.
² Cf. comment on xxiii. 2 and instances quoted in my paper on *Job*. Other linguistic comments are found in his notes on i. 18, 23; vi. 33 and *passim*, also frequently in *Job* and *Isaiah*.
³ Cf. subdivisions in modern critical commentaries, e.g. W. O. E. Oesterley, *The Book of Proverbs*, in the *Westminster Commentaries*, who finds *ten* different collections incorporated in the book (*Introd.*, xii. ff.).

Saadya's translation of the Bible became the authoritative Bible of the Arabic-speaking Jews. His comments made a deep impression on subsequent commentators of the Bible and exerted a lasting influence which was equally fruitful whether they were accepted or rejected. His method of prefacing general introductions with descriptions of the contents, the form and the meaning and message of the books of the Bible as well as with a statement on and an enumeration of their difficulties was not fully taken up—despite Nachmanides and Gersonides—until Mediæval Jewish exegesis found its last great exponent in Don Isaac Abravanel.[1]

These few pages, we hope, have shown that at the beginning of Jewish Biblical exegesis there stands a pioneer of outstanding ability who can hold his own against all successors in this and in other fields of Jewish traditional learning.

[1] *See* my article on Abravanel in this BULLETIN, Oct. 1937, pp. 445-478.

5
SAADYA'S EXEGESIS OF THE BOOK OF JOB[1]

THE name *kitābu-l-taʿdīl*, *Book of Justification* (of God), which Saadya has given to the *Book of Job*, indicates the purpose and contents of *Job*. Saadya sees in it an exposition of the problem of *Theodicy*; it gives an answer to the pressing problem of the suffering of the righteous whilst the wicked prosper, based on the belief in the absolute justice of the omnipotent, omniscient, one and only, free-willing Creator-God. It is therefore not surprising to find so many passages from *Job* used as proof-texts for the views Saadya propounds on the nature and attributes of God as well as on His relations with Man in his *kitāb al-amānāt* and in his *Commentary on the sefer yeṣirah*.[2] The exegesis of the *Book of Job* is primarily concerned with the suffering of the righteous and pious man sent to him by a gracious God not as a punishment but as a test of man's unswerving faith and trust in God, his fatherly benefactor and guide.[3] Saadya is thus not only bent on

[1] This paper is based on Derenbourg's edition of the Arabic text forming the fifth volume of the *Œuvres Complètes*, with Hebrew notes by W. Bacher, Paris, 1899. Many of the translations of Saadya have been rendered into Hebrew by Bacher in his notes, but he has not discussed them. I have therefore not explicitly stated when Bacher noted an addition or a change compared with the Hebrew text of *Job*. In a great number of cases Bacher has not noted Saadya's peculiarities. A few Genizah fragments in the Bodleiana-Oxford which were not accessible to the editors of the text have been consulted. I hope to deal with them in a separate paper: they throw no fresh light on the questions dealt with here. An appreciation of Saadya and his work as an exegete, his aims and method appears in the *Bulletin of the John Rylands Library* (Manchester, Vol. 27, No. I, pp. 168-178). As owing to war-time conditions the necessary literature was not available, I had to limit myself to an exposition of Saadya's *kitābu-l-taʿdīl*. Saadya's influence on later commentators of *Job* must remain outside the purview of this paper. Much material on this question has been collected by Bacher in his notes already. Severe restrictions on space necessitated by war-time conditions have forced the present writer to leave out Saadya's philosophical comment which is, however, only a small part of his otherwise mainly theological comment.

[2] Lack of space does not permit me to include these two works in our inquiry. The comment on *Job*-passages in them does not materially differ from the text under discussion.

[3] *See* Saadya's *Introduction*, p. 4.

explaining the nature and attributes of God, as far as this is possible for man who is in every respect inferior to his Creator, *i.e.* on writing a learned treatise on Theology. His aim is just as much to guide and to instruct, in a practical manner, his generation by setting out the *lesson* of the book. It is for this lesson that God has made known to us this history of Job, *the prophet*.[1] The three friends hold opinions against which we must guard ourselves, whereas Elihu's view is praiseworthy, based as it is, on sound reason and just argument.[2] Because many people have failed to understand the lesson of the book and have consequently been led into doubt and error, Saadya set himself the task of explaining the difficult book, both through a clear translation and accompanying comment.

I. The Version

In perusing Saadya's Arabic version and comment we must therefore bear in mind the eminently practical purpose this teacher of his nation followed. The translation is a classical example of the truism that every translation is at the same time, interpretation, a point which is not sufficiently appreciated in the case of the principal ancient versions in relation to the Massoretic text.[3] We must therefore expect a number of changes necessitated by Saadya's intention to make the meaning of the Hebrew clear and intelligible. Disregard for poetical form and diction, change of word-order, of tense and person of the verb employed, of active into passive form and *vice versa*, addition of words or whole phrases in innumerable cases, change of interrogative clauses into conditional or causative ones and *vice versa*, of main into dependent clauses, linking up of verses and chapters as well as joining one half of the same verse more closely to the other. Yet, nowhere are these devices employed in an arbitrary fashion; they are all conceived as necessary means to the unity and unification of the book as a whole, from the literary as well as from the logical point of view. The unity of the book is an axiom with Saadya, in its form no less than in its content as every attentive reader will find. Moreover, in its treatment Saadya makes no distinction between one book of Scripture and another, at least as far as the translation

---

[1] *See* Saadya's *Introduction*, p. 4.
[2] *L.c.* p. 6.   [3] *See* below, p. 195.

is concerned. He follows *three principles by which the interpreters explain all the books of God: rational argument, the use of the language of the people among whom the book (originated) and the reasons embodied in the traditions handed down from the prophets of God through the earlier (sages). The foremost in every translation is the known* (and commonly accepted meaning) *of the words . . . except that it is incompatible with Reason or that Tradition rules it out. The next is the figurative expression in use among the nation.* This method is to be employed if neither Reason nor Tradition admit of literality, yet the metaphor must be within reach of the common man and applied *with equity (bi-'inṣāf)*, *i.e.* in right measure and manner. In other words, the method of *ta'wīl*, here called *madjāz*,[1] is applicable. But whereas *ta'wīl* refers to the commentary, to explaining a word or phrase not according to its plain, simple meaning (*ẓāhir*), but bringing out its implied, hidden (*bāṭin*) sense, *madjāz* refers to the *translation*. This method is frequently employed by Saadya and shows how sensitive his logical mind was to what is rationally inadmissible.[2] Needless to say Saadya carefully avoids anthropomorphism, herein displaying much more consistency than the *Targum*.[3] There are, finally, to be considered a number of deliberate changes in the translation, due either to the obscurity of the original text or to Saadya's theological concepts.

Literary Means.

Saadya aimed at providing his generation of Arabic-speaking Jews with a clear, readily understandable Arabic version of *Job*. He sees one of the principal difficulties, which prevent such a ready understanding for many readers, in the prolixity of the discourse.[4] Consequently, he tries to bring out in his translation already the real meaning of the verse. This can be achieved in various ways: by stressing the essential part of the verse or a combination of verses, by using appropriate particles, *e.g. walima* (ii. 11), *amma* (ix. 23), *falamma* (ii. 12), *li'annahu* (ix. 4), *faqad* (xvii. 1), *lakinna* (xxviii. 23), *bal* (xxiv. 14) for contrast, *aw* (iv. 10), *iḏ* (xxii. 23), *fa'iḏa* (v. 5), not to forget the frequent substitution of *ḥatta* for simple *wĕ* or *waw conversive*. In a great many cases a comparison is

---

[1] *Introduction*, p. 7.
[2] *See below*, on Saadya's rationalism, p. 183 f.
[3] *See below*, p. 186 f.   [4] *Introduction*, p. 7.

introduced by *kayfa*, *ka'anna*, *waka'anni* (iii. 25), *kaḏaka* (vi. 7, vii. 9), *wakama* . . . *kaḏaka* (xxxvii. 22), *wakayfa* . . . *ka-* (xvi. 21). In many cases Saadya gives the verse a metaphorical meaning. He turns a statement of fact, which is obviously impossible on logical grounds, or highly improbable, into a simile by introducing an element of comparison, e.g. *ka* (xli. 26), *miṯlu* (*ib.* 25), *wanaẓiruha* (vi. 2). This is done quite systematically, arising as it does out of Saadya's rationalism of which we shall speak later.

It is noteworthy that Saadya joins almost every verse to the preceding one, be it by simple *wa* or by *aw* or *fa*, or by one of the particles mentioned before, to which may be added *lau*, *layta*, *hal*, *la'amri*, *illa an*, *mimma*, in order to bring out the inner relationship in which, to his mind, the verse stands to the preceding or following one : relative, restrictive, conditional, consecutive, causative, concessive, temporal, interrogative, expressing wish or oath. The underlying idea is to bring about coherence of form and contents and to show the unity of the book. A few of the more elaborate devices may be quoted : *wa'aqūlu* (ix. 22), *wata'lamu annahum* . . . (xxii. 29), *wa'ata'allā* (xxx. 25), *as'alu-llaha an* (xxxi. 6), *wamimmā sabīluhu an* . . . *liḏalika* (xxxvi. 15), *wahal shāhadta* (xxxviii. 12) and *v.* 13 begins, to mark its close connexion with *v.* 12, with *aw tafhamu-l-qudrata*. *Wahal ta'rifu kayfa* (xxxix. 13), *wamin al-ṭā'-iri mun* (*v.* 14), *faman ḏā* (xl. 24).

These examples, by no means exhaustive, show clearly how consistently Saadya underlines the intended meaning by introducing verses in this way. The same applies to the second half : for *ka'asher* of the Hebrew text of xxix. 25 Saadya has *wahum bayna yadayya kaman*, thus changing the subject and with it the sense. Or, again with a change in meaning, yet making for clarity, in xxxiv. 9 for *birěṣoṯo 'im elohim* Saadya translates *an yu'awwiḏahu-llahu: that God recompense him*. In xxxvi. 2 Saadya supplies the implied verb by adding *baqiya* and the addition of *alayka* heightens the effect of obvious clarity.

This is one of many instances where additions destroy the terse, poetical diction and turn an abrupt phrase into a rather prosaic statement of fact. Moreover, the rhythm is tampered with and the balance of the *stichoi* upset. Yet, to repeat, we must remember that Saadya made his version of Job for ordinary readers. His aim was to convey the meaning of this highly didactic book rather than to do justice to its literary form. On the other hand, Saadya sometimes adds a subject or a verb, often a qualifying adjective or whole phrase, to restore a balance needed in prose or for the sake of complete clarity where such a correct parallelism is out of place in a poetic context. There are the familiar means of linking verses, e.g. xxi. 6, *wama' a hada*, to effect a link with the previous verse, or *fahum yaquluna* (v. 17). A subject and at the same time a contrast is supplied by the addition of *al-ṣaliḥin* in the first half of v. 16 to go with *al-ẓalimin* of the second *stichos*. For the Hebrew *lā yaʿănennu* (ix. 3) Saadya has *lā yuṭīqu an ...* to emphasize the impotence of man. He provides, as subject of xxiv. 16, *wal-sāriqu minhum* to bring the verse in line with the two preceding ones: *murderer, adulterer*, and v. 16 *thief*. As the second *stichos* of xxii. 17 is incomplete Saadya adds as governing verb *wayastaqillu:ia: and they show proud contempt for*. Or (xxvii. 15) he adds the reason why his widows will not weep, *'alayhim min shuġlihinna bimaṣā'iba ukara: over them as they are preoccupied with other misfortunes*. In xvii. 12 Saadya adds to the first *stichos*: *bil-sahari* and to the second: *bil-sadari*, not satisfied with copying the *Targum*.[1] He thus not only escapes literalness and excludes the erroneous belief that *man* can change night into day, but explains at the same time that *sleeplessness* is the cause of the first statement and *giddiness* that of the second, giving medical reasons in his comment. Likewise, in xiii. 14, a qualifying *min al-alami* added to the first half and *min al-ru'bi* to the second explain Job's action. The addition of *biġairi maraḍin* in xxi. 13 accentuates the suddenness of their death, implied in the Hebrew *ubĕregaʿ*. To exclude any ambiguity Saadya adds to *wĕlissu el-eluuh panĕka* of xxii. 26 *shāfiʿan*. And although the first half of xxxi. 9 makes the object of the action of the second half very obvious Saadya adds *bisababiha*. Although he often disregards the basic *parallelism of members* his additions are not seldom governed by the same principle, as e.g. xxxviii. 19, where *ṭābitan* of the first half corresponds with *dā'iman* of the second. The parallel *or* ‖ *yareaḥ* of xxxi. 26 is more appropriately rendered by Saadya *shamsan* ‖ *qamaran*.

The question of xiii. 24 is turned into an imprecation, and the rhetorical question of xxvi. 2, implying a negative answer,

[1] *See below*, under *Targum, ad loc*. p. 189.

is in Saadya's version a negative statement of fact, emphatically introduced by the expression of oath: *la'amri*. Cp. also x. 3. A statement of fact in xxxiii. 18 is, by the introductory *fa'in huwa fa'ala dalika*, transformed into a conditional clause and thus linked up with the preceding verses. Incidentally, this introductory phrase destroys the balance of the verse.

Saadya translates the Massoretic *tohŏlah* in iv. 18, meaning *sin, error*, by *lam'an: splendour*, deriving it from *halal: to shine*, and understanding it as *tĕhillah*.[1] This is evident from his reference to *Is.* xlii. 8 as a parallel and to *Is.* xiii. 10 for the verb from which it is derived in the comment on our verse. Cp. also xvii. 11. *mōrāshē* is understood by Saadya in the sense of *marĕshē* and xxxiii. 18 *shālah* in the sense of *shilluah* (*ṭard*), *exile*.

Further, there are instances of a slight change in the order of words, *e.g.* iii. 14, Saadya translates as if the text were '*im malkē ha'areṣ wĕyo'aṣeha*. Also xxviii. 2, where Saadya not only makes *nĕhushah* change places with *wĕ'eben*, but parallel with *mē'afar* understands *mē'eben*. xxxiii. 23, Saadya draws *one in a thousand* to the *good deed*[2] he has added and translates: *If he has one good deed out of a thousand then it*, *i.e.* the good deed, *is like an angel*, which makes excellent sense but is not a literal rendering.

Deliberate Deviations.

xvi. 4. The Hebrew obviously suggests that Job would behave in like manner and speak against his friends if they were in his shoes. This seems to run counter to Saadya's idea of Job for he adds *ṣahīhan* after *bĕmillim*, *i.e.* he would speak *true*, just words and he would shake his head not in disapproval but *tahzīnan* (another addition!), *in sadness*. The self-righteousness of Job, expressed in xxi. 16, is eliminated by Saadya by rendering *menni* by *'anhum*, *i.e. the good*. Saadya repeats this translation in the same passage in xxii. 18. In xxii. 30 *wĕnimlaṭ* is changed into the second person by Saadya, thus referring to Job whose deliverance is likened to that of the island by *kadāka*. The difficult *bĕshelah* of xxxvi.

---

[1] Further instances are: iii. 6, xii. 18, xvi. 5, xvii. 12, xxi. 2, 13, xxviii. 15, 17, xxxiv. 3. These are dealt with under the heading *Targum* as Saadya obviously follows the *Targum*. See also Table II. It is a question of interpretation, not of reading a different text.

[2] *See below*, under Targum, *ad loc.* p. 190.

12 is rendered *fī ba'ti*, and is taken up again at the end of the verse by *bihi*. We venture to render Saadya's translation: *But if they do not hear (obey) they will be passed over at the resurrection and they will die without knowledge thereof.*[1] In *v.* 20 Saadya treats *taḥtam* as if it were *taḥteka*, adding *fī alamika*. Saadya uses in xxxvii. 1 the suffix of the third person plural for the Hebrew first person sing. In xl. 15 *bĕhemot* is for Saadya not the primeval monster but *some animals, ba'ḍu-l-bahā'ima*, and the first half of *v.* 19, *hu reshit darkē-el*, Saadya renders by *huwa awwalu ma kalaqa-llahu min al-bahā'imi*. *Darkē-el* usually mean for Saadya the attributes of God, hence his departure from the Hebrew text. For xli. 14, *tādūṣ dĕ'abah*, Saadya has *tuhtafu-l-shadjā'atu*. This interpretation brings out the parallelism with the first half of the verse, yet we are unable to see how Saadya could have arrived at it.

It appears that Saadya understood the phrase *bĕmordē or* in xxiv. 13 in the form of *bĕredet ha'or*, judging by his rendering *iḍa warada-l-nuru*.[2]

Minor changes which ease harshness of the Hebrew original will be discussed in separate surveys dealing with Saadya's relation to the *Targum* to *Job* and with agreements between Saadya and one or more of the principal ancient versions.

The large number of similes and expressions of comparison practically all fall under the category of Saadya's Rationalism and/or his conception of God. It must be borne in mind that Saadya is primarily a theologian and that his rationalism has its basis in Theology and not in Philosophy in the strict meaning of the term. It is therefore for purely practical reasons that we treat of his rationalist theology under two different headings in demonstrating how it influenced his Arabic version of *Job*.

Deviations due to Rationalism.

Saadya's translation of the second half of ix. 25, *waka'annī lam ara fīhā kairan*, is due to two principles consistently adopted by Saadya, the one being to exclude what is logically impossible: here *days* cannot see, therefore the change to *I have not seen;* the other to avoid exaggeration and overstatement: here therefore the qualifying, restrictive *and it is as if*. Saadya calls this *hyperbole* in his comment on xii. 7,

[1] Against Derenbourg's *ils passeront par l'insomnie* . . . .
[2] Further examples of deviations are to be found in the section *Targum*.

where he translates *shĕ'al-na* by *walau amkana an tas'ala: and if it were possible.* . . . Or, by inserting *katiruha* as subject of *wayyiklu* (scil. *yomay*) in vii. 6 he blunts the edge of the obvious exaggeration of the Hebrew text. Of the same type is his rendering of *yamut* (xiv. 8) by *wakāda an yamuta: almost.* Another example is xvi. 5. As the Earth is not a living creature Saadya translates xii. 8, *la'areṣ* by *liwaḥshi-l-ardi*, thus, moreover, effecting an exact parallel with *dĕgē hay-yam* of the second *'stichos*. Again the inanimate Earth in xx. 27 is turned into *ahlu-l-ardi* and likewise Heaven into *ahlu-l-samā'i*. Cp. also xv. 35.[1] It is very likely that Saadya was guided by theological considerations to avoid personification of Earth and Heaven and their rivalry with God. The same two reasons prompted Saadya to deny speech to *Tehom* and *Yam* in xxviii. 14, which he renders *walau amkana 'an yas'ala-l-ġamra laqāla . . . wakadalika-l-baḥru lau djāza an yaqūla laqāla.* . . . The addition of *ka* in xx. 27 and xxii. 16 eliminates the awkwardness of literality. xxii. 6, *bigdē 'arumim*, literally is impossible, therefore Saadya renders the phrase: *tiyāba qaumin fayaṣiruna 'urātan: . . . the garments of people so that they become naked.*

The insertion of *mitlan* and *shibhan*, respectively, in xxix. 6, and of *mitlan* in *v.* 14, fulfils the same function. Or, in *v.* 15 Saadya avoids literalism by rendering *'ēnayim* through *maqama-l-'aynayni*, likewise for *feet* and for *father* of the following verse. This may seem to go rather too far, but it shows the single-mindedness of purpose and thoroughness of method of a conscientious teacher. To leave no doubt that xxx. 7, 9 and 29 must be understood metaphorically, Saadya employs such phrases as *fayushbihuna-lladina*, or simple *ka* respectively *waka'anni*. Cp. also xxxi. 18. As *loins* cannot bless, Saadya renders *v. 20, if he does not bless me for the heat of his loins.* As the *hand* cannot kiss *the mouth*—which is the literal rendering of *v.* 27—Saadya changes the order of words [2] and translates the verse as a consequence of *vv.* 24-6 which he introduces by *wa'in* as conditional clauses. As *yāmim* cannot speak Saadya renders it *dawī-l-a'mār*. Similarly, in xxxviii. 41 he inserts *ka'annahum*, as young ravens do not cry for assistance to God when they are hungry!

[1] *See also* section *Targum*. In a number of cases this rationalization begins with the *Targum* already.
[2] Other examples were cited above, p. 182.

Deviations Resulting from his Conception of Divine Nature.

Saadya has taken great pains to represent God throughout the *Book of Job*, as indeed, in all his writings, as the unique Creator-God whose nature is beyond human understanding, whose attributes of absolute Power and Free Will, of supreme Justice and Wisdom are made evident in the *kitābu-l-ta'dīl*. His translation carefully avoids anything which, through ambiguity or adherence to literalism against the dictates of Reason or Tradition, might impair the absolute Oneness of God, who is the sole Agent in the world, and neither shares with nor delegates to anybody His power of decision and action. As *El* he is *Al-Tā'iq*, the (*All*) *powerful;* as *Eloah* or *Elohim* he is *Al-ilāhu;* as YHWH he is *Allāhu*, and as *Shadday* he is—in agreement with Tradition—*Al-kāfī: He who is sufficient* (*in himself*). Yet, there are cases where *Elohim* is rendered by *Rabbun: Lord*, so, e.g., xxxii. 2, *mē'elohim*, is translated by *min rabbihi*. It may be that Saadya wishes to express the close relationship between man and God as that between the slave and his master. Cp. also xvi. 21. In xxxii. 8 *Shadday* is rendered by *al-ilāhu*, whereas in the same phrase *nishmat Shadday*—where *nishmat* is replaced by *amr* in both cases, to avoid anthropomorphism—in xxxiii. 4 we find the familiar *Al-kāfī*. And yet in the same verse we find *El* rendered by *Allahu* and not by the usual *Al-tā'iq*. Just as *nishmat* gives way to *amr* so *ruaḥ* is rendered by *rūḥ ḥikmati-* . . . xxxi. 14, *El* is rendered by *Al-kāfī*.[1] The exalted majesty of God, His power of working signs and miracles, His greatness, which we cannot fathom, are expressed by Saadya in his rendering of xxiii. 3, *těkunato* by *ġāyatihi*—to avoid giving God a *seat*. xxxvi. 27 is introduced by *wamin āyatihi annahu* . . . whereas v. 26 accentuates the Hebrew *sagī wělō neda'* by expressing the simple *wě* through *fauqa min*. The whole phrase runs: *Ya'lamūna anna-l-Tā'iqa katīra-l-waṣfi fauqa mā na'lamu.*[2]

A few more cases of avoiding corporeality and limited

---

[1] In xxxiii. 6 *lā'el* is not rendered by *fil-Tā'iqi* but by *fil-ṭāqati*. This is either intentional to avoid all reference to God by rendering it impersonally, or may it be a scribal error? No doubt Saadya's rendering makes good sense, *I am as regards power* (*ability*) *on your level*, i.e. on a par with you.

[2] Under *Targum*, below, more examples of avoiding anthropomorphism will be found.

finality may conclude this survey: ix. 11, *yaʻăbor*, Saadya adds *tadbīruhu: his regimen*, making it the subject of the verb. Or, *mipiw* of xxii. 22 is rendered by *min umūrihi*. xxiii. 11, *baʼăshuro*, refers to God; Saadya translates *tamassakat. biqadami nabiyyihi: my foot has fastened on the footstep of his prophet*. Or (xxiv. 1), *yomaw*, referring to God, has become with Saadya *ayyāma waʻdihi: the days he has promised*. xxvii. 2, *ḥay-el:* Saadya *waḥaqqu-l-Ṭāʼiqi*, v. 11 *yad-el : qudrat*. ... xxxvi. 7, *ʻēnaw :* Saadya *ʻināyatahu, providence*. xxxvii. 2, *wĕhegeh mip-piw:* Saadya *wadarsun min qaulihi*. xl. 9, *zeroʻa : sulṭanun*. xlii. 5, *shemaʻtīka*, cannot be translated literally, therefore Saadya renders it by *waqad kuntu asmaʻu biqudratika ḵabaran*, and the personal suffix *ka* of *raʼatka* is rendered by *hā*, referring to *qudra, I have seen it, raʼaytuhā*.

As God and man cannot be compared with each other, God being not only infinitely greater than man but greater on quite a different plane, Saadya renders xxxiii. 12, *yirbeh eloah mēʼenosh* by inserting *qudra : .qudratu-llahi aktaru min al-insāni*. *Qudra* is for Saadya one of the principal attributes of God; His Power is indivisible, absolute and, to repeat, exclusive to Himself. He does not share it with nor delegate it to any other being. Therefore Saadya would not admit that in ii. 7 Satan is the subject of *wayyak*. No, God is the only active force, consequently Saadya inserts *allahu* and makes the second half of the verse the dominant part, the main clause, by starting the verse with *falamma* for Hebrew *wa*: *When the adversary had left the presence of the Lord the Lord smote Job*. ... And he adds this comment to the verse: *The action is related to God, be He exalted, as there is no agent except He!*

Saadya's Indebtedness to the Targum.

In turning to the question of Saadya's sources the subsequent list of passages, covering the whole *Book of Job*, arranged in parallel columns, proves beyond any doubt the great indebtedness of Saadya to the *Targum to Job*. What was established in respect of the *Targum Onqelos* with regard to Saadya's version of the *Pentateuch* [1] applies in a much higher degree to Saadya's indebtedness to the *Targum to Job*. Saadya steers clear of *Midrashic* interpretation, and translates whenever possible according to the plain meaning of the text. Only

[1] See A. Schmiedl in *MGWJ*, 1901, pp. 124 ff., and 1902, pp. 84-8, 358-61.

in very few cases we find traces of the *Targum*'s freer, Midrashic, explanatory rendering in Saadya's comment. He shares the *Targum*'s aversion against anthropomorphism but by far surpasses the *Targum* in consistency and systematic thoroughness. He shares with the *Targum* the rationalist approach expressed in the use of particles of comparison to give the verse a metaphorical turn. But he has, if he learnt from the *Targum* in this respect, developed this practice into a fine art. He has left the *Targum* far behind in this respect as well as in his struggle against anthropomorphism. The same applies to his much greater care in emphasizing the uniqueness of God and in avoiding the personification of Earth and Heaven, Death and Destruction. Similar tendencies in contemporary Islam may have sharpened Saadya's eyes for these matters, but one will do well to remember and to stress the Jewish background. Saadya's choice of Arabic words for their similarity in sound has often been mentioned. But there is ample evidence in our list that Saadya frequently chooses a word for its identity or resemblance with the Aramaic. This is only natural for a man who was at home in all three languages and maintained that there was close affinity between Hebrew, Aramaic and Arabic as well as unbroken continuity between Biblical and post-Biblical Hebrew. The unity of the Hebrew language is for him as much an established fact as the unity of the *Book of Job* or the Bible as a whole. The same root is used in the *Targum* and by Saadya in the following passages of our list : vii. 1, 5, xiv. 6, xv. 6, 33, xix. 23, xxi. 13, 20, xxx. 29, xxxii. 2, xxxiv. 34, xxxviii. 40, xl. 21, 22, 30, 31.

Agreement with Other Versions.

Apart from the agreement between Saadya and the *Targum*, the comparative list shows considerable *consensus* with the various *Greek* versions, especially the *Septuagint*, and with the *Vulgate* and the *Peshitta*. Where *Vulgate* and *Targum* go together, or *Peshitta* and *Septuagint* and/or *Vulgate*, one might suppose an influence of the one on the other or others. If we assume that Saadya knew neither Greek nor Latin how, then, can we explain agreement between him and either the Greek or Latin version ? It is hardly possible to imagine that all the versions had the same text or texts in front of them and that some chose one reading and others another. This is the more

Jewish themes

TABLE I

SAADYA'S DEPENDENCE ON THE TARGUM TO JOB

1. Agreement

Chapter.	Verse.	Mass. Text.	Targum.	Saadya.
i.	5	הקיפו	שלימו	אנתהת
		ויקדשם	וזמננון	פיטّהרהם או פّיעדّהם o
				Textus receptus
				פיטّהרהם
		ברכו	ארגיזו	טענו
	12	מעם פני	מן קדם	מן בין ידי
	14	על ידיהם	על סטריהון	אלי גֹאנבהא
	19	מעבר	מסטרי	מן גֹאנב
	21	שמה	לבית קבורתא	אלי אלקבר
ii.	4	עור	אברא	עצֹו
	8	אפר *dust*	קטמא *ashes*	רמאד
iii.	3	הרה	איתברא	ולד
	6	יחד	יתיחד	ינתמע
v.	7	לעמל	למלעי באוריתא	¹ללעّמל באלטّאעّה
vi.	3	לעו	*Lagarde* אשתלהין	מנגّךّ
			Miqr.Ged. משתלהין	
	6	חלמות	חלמונא	²אלבדّךّ
	12	אבנים	היך אבניא	כקוّהّ אלחّגֹארהّ
		נחוש	כנחשא	כאלנחאם
	20	בטח	אתרחיצו	ותّקו
	21	לו	כלא הויתון	כמא לא תכונו
?	25	נמרצו	נמליצו – בסימין	³אّעّדّّבّ
vii.	1	שכיר	אגירא	אלאגّיר, *instead of*
				the usual ⁴שّאכّריّ
	5	ודמאס	ואיתמסי	⁵וّתّمّاسّي
ix.	2	אמנם	ברם בקושתא	חّقّا
	27	אמרי	אימר	قّلّتّ
		פני	רוגזי	נצّבّي
x.	16	תתפלא	תדיין	תנתצّףّ

¹ Bacher quotes *Targ.* in his note. Though the rendering is not wholly corresponding, one is justified in claiming *Targumic* influence.
² *See* Comment *ad loc., below,* p. 200.
³ But ר and ל interchange. ⁴ Also xiv. 6.
⁵ The root is מסי, not מסס as Kittel says.

108 [188]

Saadya's exegesis of the Book of Job

TABLE I—Continued

Chapter.	Verse.	Mass. Text.	Targum.	Saadya.
xi.	14	באהלך	במשכנך	פי כבאך
	17	חלד	נושמך	עמרך
	18	וחפרת	ותתקין בי קבורתא	¹ואדא אבתנית ביתא
xii.	18	מוסר	שושילתא	רבאטאת
	23	גוים 2nd	לאומיא	אלאמם
xv.	2	קדים	היך רוח קדומא	כריח אלקבול
	6	יענו	יסהדון	ישהד
	18	מאבותם	מן מסורתא דאבהתהון	מא נקלוה מן אבאיהם
	26	בצואר	בתוקפא	בענק קﬢ
	33	יחמס	יתר	וינתר
xvi.	5	יחשך	יתמנע	ינצﬢ
	21	ובן־אדם	ודיך אנש	כאסתקבאלה
xvii.	6	למשל	למתלין בי	תמתילא לי
	12	ליום	היך יממא	כאלנהאר
xix.	23	ויחקו	ויתרשמון	תרסם
	27	ראו	יחמון	תנטר
	29	שדין	דדיין קשוט Lag.	אן אלחכם חק
xx.	22	במלאות שפקו	תתמלא סאתיה	¹ואדא אמתלא קפיזה
	23	חרון אפו	תקוף רוגזיה	מן שדה נצבה
	26	אש	נור דנהנם	נאר, but in his comment, הי נאר נהﬢם
	27	ארץ	דירי ארעא	אהל אלארץ
xxi.	13	יחתו	נחתין	ירדון
	20	כידו	תבירייה	תבארה
xxii.	8	איש זרוע	גבר נצחון	דו אלדראע אלגאלבה
	9	ידכא	תשפך	תוזדה צעפא
	11	חשך	בחשוכא תשרי	תכון פי אלטלאם
	16	ולא־עת	בלא עדנהון	בניר וקתהם
	20	קימנו	מיקום	אנאמהם
	24	בצור	היך טינרא	כצואן
		אופיר	דהבא דא'	דהב א'
xxiii.	2	מרי	מריר	מכאלף

¹ Saadya follows the *Targum* and Bacher is not right *ad loc.*
² Bacher refers to *Targum* in his note *ad loc.*

TABLE I—Continued

Chapter.	Verse.	Mass. Text.	Targum.	Saadya.
xxiv.	5	הן פראים בפעלם	היך דין כמדוריא *Lag.* כמרדיא לעובדיהון	כאנהם וחוש אלי צנעתהם
	17	צלמות	היך טולא דמותא	כאלנבם
	18	על־פני	למשט על	כאנה תגרי עלי
xxvi.	5	רפאים	גבריא	אלמשנוא
	7	על בלימה	מדלית מידעם	לא עלי שי
	10	חק חג	גזר למשרי רקיע	רסם חגאבה
xxviii.	4	מעם־גר	מן אתרא די מזדלח	מן חית תגרי
	8	שחץ	אריון	אלסבאע
	15	סגור	דהב סגין	אלאבריז
	17	כלי	מאני	סאיר אניה
	22	אבדון ומות	בי אבדנא ומלאך מותא	אהל אלהלאך ואלמות
xxix.	6	בחמה	בלואי	פי אלסמן
	23	ופיהם פערו	והיך ארדסיא דפומהון	וכאנהם פערו
	25	כאשר	היך כמן ד'	כמן
xxx.	27	קדמני	דמא אקדימו	ממא תלקאני
	29	יענה	נעמיתא	נעאם
xxxi.	32	ארח	אכסנאי	ציף
xxxii.	2	צדקו	זכאותי	זכי
xxxiii.	14	ובשתים לא ישורנה	ובתניתא לא איצטריך למסכי	ולא יחתאג אן יתהר אלתאניה
	17	מעשה	מן עובדא בישא	מן פעלה אלסו
	23	עליו ן	עלוי זכותא	עמל צאלח
xxxiv.	16	בינה	תתבין	תפהם
	34	שומע לי	יקבל מני	יקבל מני
xxxvi.	30	אורו	מיטרא	סגלה, comment ואלסבל פהו אלמטר
	32	כסה־אור	מנע מטרא	¹ מנע סגלהם
xxxvii.	10	מנשמת־אל	ממימר אלהא	מן אמרה
xxxviii.	7	בני אלהים	כתי מלאכיא	אלמלאיכה
	21	ידעת	הידעתא	והל עלמת
	26	לא איש	דלית בה גבר	לא אנסאן פיהא
	40	למו־ארב	מטול לכמנא	מכמנעא

¹ Cp. also xxxvii. 11.

Saadya's exegesis of the Book of Job

TABLE I—Continued

Chapter.	Verse.	Mass. Text.	Targum.	Saadya.
xxxix.	8	יתור	יאלל	ירום
	10	עבתו	בַּאשׁליה	בּמקאט
	27	על־פיך	על מימרך	באמרך
xl.	12	הכניעהו	וַתברניה	ואהזמה
	18	נחשה	היך פצידי נחשא	כצלאבהֿ אלנחאם
	21-2	צאלים	טלליא	אלמטֿלהֿ
	24	אף	נחירידֵהּ	אנפה
	30	כנענים	תגריא	אלתנّאר
	31	בשכות	במטללתא	פי אלטֿלאל
xli.	22	חרש	היךְ חספא	כאלכֿסף
		חרוץ	דהבא סנינא	אלדהב
xlii.	9	צפר	וצפר	וצפר
	10	רעהו	חברוי	אצחאבה

II. Influence

xi.	12	ועיר פרא אדם	ועילא. היךְ בר נש	אלאנסאן כַּנחש וחש¹
xv.	15	ושמים	ואנגלי מרומא	יאהל אלסמא²
xvii.	1	קברים לי	קבורן מתקנן לי	יתמנّי לי אלקבור³
xx.	17	נחלי דבש	נחליא דמן דובשא	ואהידיّהֿ נעים כעסל⁴
xxiv.	29	פנים	שכנתא	רחמתה⁵
xxxvi.	5	ימאס	ירחק צדיקיא	יוחד פי בלקה⁶
	22	מורה	מלף תריצותא	ידאל עלי אלביר⁷
	32	כפים	חטוף ידא	אעמאלהם⁸

¹ The comparison is there but applied differently.
² Saadya may be influenced by the *Targum*, but does not follow the midrashic interpretation. Also xx. 27. In his comment Saadya lets Ṣophar speak of the intervention of angels.
³ Though not identical, both supply the missing verb.
⁴ If דמן would be read as דָּמָן the כ *comparationis* of Saadya comes from the *Targum* (*Miqr. Gĕd.* point דְּמָן).
⁵ Not the same, but both avoid anthropomorphism.
⁶ Both add an object, but Saadya is not so exclusive.
⁷ Both add an object.
⁸ The same idea is in both their rationalist minds.

Jewish themes

TABLE II

SAADYA IN AGREEMENT WITH ONE OR MORE OF THE ANCIENT VERSIONS BASED ON KITTEL'S *BIBLIA HEBRAICA* [1]

Chapter.	Verse.	Mass. Text.	Saadya.	Ancient Versions.	K[ittel].
iii.	6	יֵחַד	יֵחַד	STΣ	quotes Saadya as well and compares with Gen. xlix. 6
	11	מרחם	ברחם	GV	so K.
v.	5	צמים	צמאים	ΣSV	so K.
vi.	25	נמרצו	?נמלצו	T	so K.
viii.	14	יקוט	חבל השמש		K. refers to Saadya and to Is. lix. 5 and suggests קורים or כחוט
	19	יצמחו	יצמח		so K.
ix.	27	אמרי	אמרתי	GTV	so K.
xi.	7	תמצא	תבלב		K. sugg. either תנע or תבא
	8	גבהי שמים	גבהה משמים parallel with עמקה משאול		so K.
	14	באהלך	באהלך		so K., with vrs. ca. 40 MSS.
	17	חלד	חלדך	GT	so K.
xii.	4	אהיה	יהיה	GS	K. : GS ; I?M.
	8	לארץ	לחית הארץ		so K. who strikes out שיח
	18	מוסר	מוֹסְרִי	TV	so K. *vel* מוֹסֵר
	23	2nd לגוים	לאמים	TS	so K.
xvii.	6	למשל	למשל	G'AΘΣTV	so K.
	10	כלם	ואולם אתם	SV	כלכם so K.
	11	[2]מרשי = ניאט	מורש		K. cps. Syr. *marsho*
xviii.	2	קנצי	קץ	G	so K. but he is wrong to credit T with sing.
	9	בעקב	בעקבו	SV	so K.

[1] The Sigla used are those of the *Biblia Hebraica*, 3rd edition, Stuttgart, 1937. Both apparatuses were perused. See also the separate treatment of the dependence of Saadya on the Targum.

[2] Saadya explains *niyāṭ* as the cords by which the heart is suspended.

Saadya's exegesis of the Book of Job

TABLE II—Continued

Chapter.	Verse.	Mass. Text.	Saadya.	Ancient Versions.	K[ittel].
xix.	27	ראו	יראו	T	so K. but overlooks T.
		ולא	לא		so K. with Old Babyl. MS.
xx.	25	שָׁלַף	in his comment שלף חץ		K. sugg. as an alternative.
	28	יבול	מבול in his comment		K. sugg. יבל or מבול
xxi.	2	תנחומתיכם	תנחומתכם	GSTV	so K.
	13	יֵחַתּוּ	יֵחָתוּ	(G)ΣSTV	so K.
	28	אהל	does not translate it		K. sugg. to delete it.
xxii.	9	וּזְרֹעַ	תדבא	GTSV	so K.
	20	קימנו	יקמם	ΘSTV	so K.
	24	ובצור	וכצור	ΘST (V?) + 65 MSS.	so K.
	30	ונמלט	וְתִמָּלֵט	Θ	so K.
xxiii.	3	ידעתי	אדעהו		K. quotes MS. ידעתיו
	12	ולא	לא	GV	so K.
(?) xxiv.	4	יחד חבאו	(?) ויתחבאו		so K.
	22	בחיין	בחייו	GΣV	so K.
xxvi.	12	רגע	נער	S	so K.
xxvii.	10	יקרא אלוה	יקרא אל־אלוה	S	so K.
	18	כעש	כעכביש	GʳS	so K.
	23	עלימו	¹עלין		so K.
xxviii.	11	מִבְּכִי	²נִבְכֵי		K. sugg. נבכי or מבכי
	15	סגור	(זהב) סגור		so K., see Gesenius, s.v.
	17	כְּלִי	(כָּל־)כְּלִי	ΘΣTV	
xxix.	4	בסוד	בסוך (?)	GΣS	so K.
	6	בחמה	בחמאה	GTV	

¹ Saadya also reads כפיו.

² Saadya uses the same Arabic word, מניך for xxxviii. 16 נבכים, as noted by Bacher.

Jewish themes

TABLE II—Continued

Chapter.	Verse.	Mass. Text.	Saadya.	Ancient Versions.	K[ittel].
xxx.	11	שָׁלְחוּ	שלח	GV	
	12	ימין	ימיני		so K.
	15	תְּרָדֵף	תְּרָדֵף or נִרְדָף		K. תְּרָדֵף vel תֻּנְדָף, cf. G.
xxxi.	5	שוא	מתי שוא	GS	
	12	כי	does not translate it		K. sugg. to delete it.
	18	כְּאָב	כְּאָב	GV	
	32	אֹרַח	אוֹרַח	G'ASTV	so K.
xxxii.	9	רבים	רב ימים	GS(V)	so K.
xxxiii.	8	מלין	מליך	G^xAS	
	17	מעשה	ממעשהו הרע	T (G similarly)	K. ממעשהו, cf. STV
	32	צִדְקֶךָ	צִדְקָךְ		K asks whether to read thus.
xxxiv.	3	לֶאֱכֹל	לֶאֱכֹל	GSV	so K.
	16	בינה	תבין	G'AΣSTV	so K.
xxxv.	3	לך	לי		so K.
	10	עֹשָׂי	עֹשֵׂינוּ		so K.
	13	ישורנה	ישורנו		so K.
xxxix.	8	יָתוּר	יָתוּר	ΘTV	so K.
	10	עבתו	בַּעֲבֹת	T	so K., yet does not mention T.
	16	ללא	כְּהֵם לא		K. כְּלֹא
	21	יחפרו	יחפור	GSV	so K.
	24	כי־קול	בקול		so K.
xl.	12	הכניעהו	והכניעהו	TV	
	24	אף	אפו	T	so K.
xli.	2	לפני	לפניו	T	so K.
	10	עטישותיו	עטישותו		so K.
xlii.	7	כעבדי	בעבדי		so K. with many MSS.
	8	כעבדי	בעבדי	G	
	9	צפר	וצפר	GTSV	so K., who omits T.
	10	רעהו	רעיו	T	so K., who overlooked T.

unlikely since we cannot discover either uniformity or a guiding principle in their method of selection. In the light of our tables, it may seem presumptuous to draw any definite conclusions. Yet, we venture to suggest that it is unsafe to deduce from these versions that they are based on a different or even a better text than the Massoretic text. They are all translations. As such they are interpretations, as is the Massoretic text.[1] Late as this text is in its final form its traditional form has been adhered to most carefully, certainly more carefully than that of any other version. We are therefore inclined to find the explanation of the far-reaching agreement between Saadya and the ancient versions—the agreement between Saadya and Kittel's *Biblia Hebraica* without the versions as intermediaries must be set on one side—in a common tradition of interpretation. They all go back, we suggest, to one or other of the ancient Jewish schools of interpretation. This may help to explain why we find Saadya now in agreement with GSTV, now with T, now with GV or GS or S, to mention only the principal versions. But we must reiterate that the versions are interpretations and therefore not reliable guides to the ideal archetype of the Hebrew text. This does not minimize their value for the *understanding* of the text, but it does likewise not justify emendation of the Massoretic text in the light of their rendering. The other conclusion is that Saadya's version could legitimately claim a place equal to the more ancient versions in the *interpretation* of the text, and that it is neither of greater or lesser help for the *constitution* of that text! It may well be that his version as well as the more ancient ones is the product of an eclectic process of selection from a body of traditional exegesis. Considering the freedom with which Saadya treated the Massoretic text, it may well be that he either returned to a Pre-Massoretic tradition of *interpretation* —which was the same as that underlying the ancient versions —or, that in those instances where the link is not supplied through the *Targum*, he arrived at his translation by his own effort. It may be interesting to compare his translation with *Kittel* in that respect. After all, these instances of agreement with all or some or one of the versions cover only a fraction of the *Book of Job*. Most marked is the influence of the *Targum* which is, however, quite natural. For the many

[1] *See* H. Nyberg, *Studien zum Hoseabuche*, Uppsala, 1935-6, *Introduction*.

deviations which are his own the reason must be sought in his desire to produce an intelligent and intelligible version of the original.[1] They do not suggest that he translated from a text other than the Massoretic text. Moreover, most of the deviations common to Saadya and the versions are slight inasmuch as they only make easier the text as handed down in the Massoretic text: they clearly bear the mark of the interpreting translator. That they actually are due to a different consonantal text is, we venture to suggest, most unlikely, except where there is evidence of variant readings from old manuscripts. Scribal errors in transmission must naturally also be taken into account.

II. THE COMMENTARY

General Character.

Saadya is to our knowledge the first Jewish exegete to have prefaced a coherent commentary with an Introduction setting out the aim and purpose of the book under discussion. He stresses in concise language—to turn to *Job*—God's Grace and its difference from human grace in quality and quantity. God's *Djūd*[2] is without limit or end, the *Creatio ex nihilo* His greatest *faḍl*.[3] The suffering of man, his being punished spring from God's grace, they are for his good in that he fears God and His vengeance should he depart from His way as laid down in *Commandment* and *Prohibition*.[4] God inflicts suffering (*ālām*) for three reasons: Moral and intellectual instruction (*ta'dīb watafhīm*), which is likened to the chastisement a father applies to his son; Punishment (*'uqūba*), out of regard for the sinner to turn him from his sin, also called Purification (*tamḥīḍ*); Test and Examination (*balwā wamiḥna*). Of this last kind is Job's suffering. Although all five, Job, his three friends and Elihu, do not attribute injustice to God, the three friends have erroneous views on the nature, purpose of and reasons

[1] See above, p. 178, and Saadya's *Introduction*, p. 7.
[2] Literally, *generosity, liberality.*
[3] Literally, *grace* or *favour. Introduction*, pp. 2 ff., contains a long, most noteworthy discourse on the *Grace* of God.
[4] The most important chapter in the *Amānāt* bears this title. Throughout that primer of theology, *more philosophico*, all the questions touched upon in this section (Divine nature and attributes, theological concepts like Repentance, Recompense in the World-to-come, etc.) are systematically treated.

for suffering. Elihu has a proper conception, *i.e.* God means well with His servant for three reasons: Repentance (*tawba*) after sin; merits of the servant (*ḥasanāt, good deeds*); *test and examination*.¹ It is clear from this that Elihu is the principal witness to the right conception, consequently his speeches are the most important part and are therefore much more fully commented on than those of the three friends, provided we possess the commentary in its entirety more or less. The comment on the friends' speeches shows that they are wrong and that Job is right in thinking of himself as a *Ṣaddīq*. The architectural structure of the book is thus, at the same time, vindicated. Not only is every part necessary where it stands, but it forms part of a unity, in the formal as well as in the logical sense. The book is conceived on a plan, as it were, setting out to prove that Job's suffering is but a test of his sincere belief in the ultimate justice of God who alone knows why the wicked prosper and the righteous suffer in this world, who holds out reward in the world-to-come for the righteous who trusts in Him.² This proof is furnished by refuting the arguments of the three friends first, thus clearing the way for Elihu, God's speech and the final *dénouement* with the restoration of Job.

Saadya underlines the unity of the book by treating a group of verses as a logical unity, commenting on several taken together.³ He also sums up whole chapters and links them up with the following ones just as he does in his translation.⁴

His method of explaining one word of Scripture by another is the traditional one. But here, as in the case of the *Targum*, he goes far beyond his precursors, thanks to a closer attention to lexicography and grammar. He extends the scope of this method of citing scriptural verses or words as proof-texts for his own interpretation by including Post-Biblical Jewish literature, the *Mishnah* and *both Talmudim* as well as the Aramaic of the *Targum*. Thus, a large part of his commentary is but a justification of his translation.⁵ There is in our book

¹ See *Introduction*, pp. 2 f.

² *See* Saadya's *Commentary on Proverbs*, ch. xxx, where he discusses the different aims of Agur and Job due to their different problems.

³ The examples are too numerous to be enumerated, *e.g.* viii. 5-7, xx. 6-13, and those quoted *below*.

⁴ *E.g.* ch. viii. after *v.* 3.

⁵ Saadya usually starts with *fassartu, see* vii. 21, xvii. 6, xxxiii. 16, to quote a few instances at random.

very little philosophical comment.[1] On the other hand, we find what we might call structural comment showing the connexion between single or whole groups of verses and linking up verses in different chapters.[2] This is supplementary to the means adopted in his translation under the principle of "cause and effect." The remainder is theological comment in the narrower sense: a verse or a group of verses or a whole chapter are taken as an illustration of a theological idea: Divine Justice and the pedagogic significance of the suffering of the just and righteous being in the centre of his thought. God's Omnipotence and absolute Free Will are stressed no less than the importance of Repentance and the certainty of Recompense in the world-to-come. Saadya devotes special little sections, complete in themselves, to these topics which were for him questions of urgent concern. That they were discussed again and again in all speeches of the book was sufficient evidence for Saadya that they were cardinal problems

[1] Employing the term "philosophical" in its widest sense, as scientific in general not as metaphysical exclusively, we point to i. 6, on the faculties of the soul: Psychology; xxxviii. 6, *Creatio ex nihilo, Nature, Sustenance:* Physics (Natural Science), Economics; *v.* 19, Geometry, Astronomy; *v.* 32, stars, after the sun in *v.* 19, turning into Theology; *vv.* 39-41, God's Actions. It is here, as not seldom throughout the book, that Saadya strongly condemns those who believe in the eternity of the World, *al-dahriyyun*. Here and in his *Commentary on Proverbs* Saadya takes exception to the *Dahriyya* so often that we must assume that there was a body of Jews holding this, in his eyes, pernicious doctrine, for Saadya would not have taken every opportunity of combating this opinion were it confined to an Islamic sect. Comment on xxxix. 4 would fall under natural history.

[2] *E.g.* ix. 29, which, according to Saadya, is bound up with what precedes; xii. 12 is the application of the simile of *v.* 11. Ch. xxv., Bildad's speech, is necessary because Eliphaz did not give a satisfactory answer to the question why the wicked prosper. xxvi. leads on to xxvii, *see* comment on *v.* 14. Saadya's comment on xxxiii. 10 illustrates how he works on the assumption of the unity of the book. He refers back to xxix. 2 to end of that chapter, then to xiii. 26, leading on to the verse under discussion, xxxiii. 10 (Elihu), and contrasts it with Job's statements in xiii. 24 and 27. Or, in support of xxxii. 20 Saadya quotes xxi. 7 and xxii. 14 and 17. To xxxv. 16 he states that three Elihu-speeches are the answer to three speeches by Job, ch. xxxvi. is thus an addition. This view results from Saadya's statement in his *Introduction*, p. 8, that each speech receives an answer and that answer provokes another speech which in its turn must receive its answer until the three friends are silenced and Elihu takes the field. *See* also *n.* 2, p. 199.

affecting all men, not only Job as an individual who implores God repeatedly to make known to him his guilt, the reason for his suffering.[1] He therefore assembles all the passages relevant to the various problems in his notes thus emphasizing the unity of the book: the inadequacy of the three friends, their failure to see the problem of Job with his suffering on a higher plane where righteous and wicked alike are subjected to the incomprehensible will of God, their inability to convince Job or to be convinced by him made the introduction of Elihu indispensable. Once the ground has been prepared, these chapters provide the real discussion of the problem of Job. Yet, even Elihu is unable to answer Job's ever-recurring question, consequently God Himself intervenes a second time: something utterly unthinkable for Elihu.[2]

Not until Isaac Abravanel was Saadya's method of commenting, except for Gersonides to some extent, again practised among Jewish exegetes.[3]

Linguistic Comment.

To turn to Saadya's comments in some detail we give a few examples of his linguistic notes on single words of the text. ii. 6, *shĕmor*, Saadya explains it as *hishshamēr* and cites as parallels *Ex.* xxxiv. 11 f. and *Josh.* vi. 13. iv. 10, *nittāʿu*, is likened to *maltĕʿot*, *Ps.* lviii. 7, obviously assuming a root *lataʿa*. xxxvii. 1, *wĕyittar* from *attaru* of *Dan.* iv. 11.[4] vi. 22,

[1] Commenting on xxxvii. 24 Saadya says God addressed Job to make him recognize the word of Elihu to turn back from his opinion. ... Job made (repeated) efforts to make God disclose to him why He afflicted him (x. 2, xxiii. 35). But God did not let him know. He (Saadya) then considered carefully many of the tales of the *awwalun*, and he found that every one whom God afflicted asked his Master this question. Yet, none received a complete answer: Jeremiah (v. 19, xvi. 10) for bad deeds, Moses was not told so as not to weaken his patience with men (*Num.* ii. 16). ... But God told him something else (*Ex.* vi. 1), *Like that was Job and this is one of the attributes of God's Wisdom*. Cf. also p. 201 with *n.* 2, *below*.

[2] *See* end of *n.* 2, p. 198. xxxiii. 13-15: Elihu answers Job in these three verses on his words contained in xxvi. 5 and ix. 3, and tells him *God is too noble and exalted in His power that He answered man word for word . . . but only once not a second time*.

[3] *See* the present writer's "Don Isaac Abravanel," etc., in *Bulletin of the John Rylands Library*, October, 1937, pp. 445-78.

[4] Another example is xxiv. 11, *yashīru*, which Saadya derives from *ṣohorayim* against the *Targum* and the usual interpretation *to press oil*. Saadya destroys the parallelism with *yĕqābim dārĕku*.

in justifying his translation of *hăkī*, he quotes *Gen.* xxvii. 36 and xxix. 15 in support of taking it as a question, and remarks on the fact that the *hē* transforms the meaning of *kī*. v. 19, *běshesh* . . . *uběshebaʿ* are not to be taken literally but rather as description of a multitude, quoting in his support 1 *Sam.* i. 8, *Eccl.* vi. 3 and *Is.* vii. 23. Of *sěfīḥeha* (xiv. 19) Saadya says that *all plants* are meant by it and—according to a Fragment quoted by Bacher—states *he mentioned a part and means the whole*. xxvii. 7, *kěrāshāʿ oybī*, Saadya calls *kěrāshāʿ* in this phrase an *iknā*, *cognomen* like 1 *Sam.* xxv. 22, *oybī Dawid*. Interesting is his suggestion that xxii. 18, *mennī*, is to be understood as *mēhem*—he translates *minhum*—and v. 20, *qīmānu* as *qīmām*, although he translates *yěqumām!*   Three instances where a word is explained by its meaning in the *Mishnah* are: iii. 8, *liwyāṭān*: *min qaulihim fi-l-Mishnah* "*lā těʿorer ishāh liwyātah běmoʿēd*" (*Y.M. Qaṭ.* I, 80*d*); vi. 6, "*ḥallāmut*" is the egg ("*bayd*") like the expression of the *Mishnah* "*ḥelmōn mibĕfānīm*" [*Ḥul.* 64*ᵃ*] and in Syria [Palestine] one calls the yolk of the egg "*ḥelmōn*"; and xxi. 10, *'ibbar*: *yusammuna fi-l-Mishnah al-ḥāmila měʿubberet*[1] *wayaquluna lilwālidi mīluṭ wafīluṭ* like *Is.* lxvi. 7. The *Targum* is referred to in xviii. 3, *niṭminu*, in these words: *the translation of sittěmum pelishtim is ṭammonun pelishta'e*. xv. 29, *minlam*, gets this comment: *qad yufakkimuna fi-l-suryānī bi-l-nun millam/ minlam, ḥiṭṭin/ḥinṭin*. Cp. xviii. 2: *qinṣē mitlu qiṣṣē wa-l-nun tafkīman*. Saadya obviously did not count the *nun* as a rootletter.

The plain meaning of a word is explained in xxxi. 1, where Saadya translates *bětulah* by *bahkina*, which he explains by *djāriya ḥasana*. Cp. also xvii. 11. An *interpretatio ad sensum* is represented by *baṭṭ* as a rendering for *sīḥah*, xv. 4, which is explained as meaning *ṣalāt* and *raġba*, *prayer and fervent desire*, according to a Fragment. A figurative meaning is given to xv. 30 *běruăḥ piw* which, translated literally, is interpreted as *'iṣyān, rebellion*. Or (xxxvi. 16), where *dāshen* stands for *tawāb, recompense*, and *Is.* lv. 2 is cited in support. Likewise (xxxvii. 19) *ḥoshek*, for Saadya, means in this context: *in kana 'indaka hudjdjatun laysa muzlimatan qulhā* . . ., *i.e.* darkness stands for absence of proof. On xxx. 1 Saadya remarks by

[1] *Yěbamot*, xvi. 1. *Mishnah* includes, for Saadya, both *Talmudim* as these examples prove.

way of amplification—another characteristic of his comment—
their fathers be my shepherds.[1]

Rabbinic Background.

As to Job's parentage, the age in which he lived and whether he was a Jew or a non-Jew,[2] Saadya agrees with Jewish tradition (*naql*) that he was not of Israel, that he lived at the time *when our fathers were in Egypt*, and that Moses, by Divine command, made the story into a book for the nation (of the Jews).[3] Saadya gives the reasons *pro et contra* as regards lineage of the friends, and shows that the traditional view of the Rabbis—elsewhere called *al-awwalun = harishonim*—is in full concord with the Torah. Saadya differs, however, in his definition of Satan from the view expressed by Resh Laqish (*B.B.* 16a), that Satan, Evil Inclination and Angel of Death are identical. For Saadya Satan is *in truth a man*,[4]

---

[1] Other examples are: xii. 20, xix. 28, xxiv. 6, xxxiii. 16 a.o. As far as the *hapaxlegomena* are concerned, these are dealt with in Saadya's *tafsir al-sab'ina lafẓatan*. See the article by Professor S. Krauss in this volume. It is desirable that Saadya's use of grammatical terms which he has probably himself introduced into Hebrew national Grammar should be made the subject of a special study, the more so since Abu-l-Walid uses, to give only one example, the term *iḍmār* for *ellipsis* (see W. Bacher: *Aus der Schrifterklärung des Abulwalīd Merwān Ibn Ganāḥ*, Budapest, 1889, p. 2, *n.* 2), obviously influenced by Saadya. Some grammatical terms occurring in Saadya's *Commentary on Job* are the just mentioned *iḍmār*, xxxvi. 32, '*al-kappayim*, short for *'al-ma'āseh kappayim*. xx. 25, *ḥeṣ* is used as *kalimatun muḍmaratun*. xviii. 2, *tafkīm* (resonance) is used in commenting on *qinṣē* : *mitlu qiṣṣē wa-l-nun tafkīman*. xxvii. 23, Saadya applies the term *madjaz* (metaphor(ical)) to '*alēmō kappēmo*. xix. 28, *ḍamīr* (pronoun). xxix. 3, *hoshek* is rendered by Saadya as if it were *běhoshek*. In his note we read : the meaning is *in darkness* and the *bet* is *muktaṣar* (lit., *abbreviated*). Cp. also v. 6. xxvii. 7, *iknā*, see above, p. 200. The term *tabāluġ* for the more usual *mubālaġa*, *hyperbole*, is applied to xii. 7. See above, p. 183 f.†

[2] Only a few instances can be quoted. I. Schwartz in his *Tiqwat Enosh*, Berlin, 1868, has collected references to *Job* from *Talmud* and *Midrash*, and from *n.* 2, p. 202 onwards I have based my comparisons on his book. A systematic investigation of the Rabbinic background of Saadya's exegesis should be undertaken, following up what the learned editors of his works have already done in this respect. Saadya nowhere gives his sources (only sometimes refers to the *awwalun* generally).

[3] See *B.B.* 15 and 16.

[4] Cp. Saadya's lengthy note on i. 6. The Bodleian fragment is more explicit on this verse, but nothing new emerges for Saadya's views on Satan and the *běnē elohim*.

and he bases his view on 1 *Kings* xi. 14, *Zechariah* iii. 1 and *Ezra* iv. 5 f. He emphatically denies that Satan was an angel.¹ In the same passage he defends his translation of *bĕnē elohim* by *awliya'u-llahi*—based on *Ex.* iv. 22 and *Lev.* xxi. 9—against the usual *angels*. He further interprets *lĕhityaṣeb*, not in the sense of the *Targum* (and Jewish tradition generally) as assembling for *standing in judgment* but of *assembling* for *obedience and worship* (*lilṭaʻati walʻibādati*). From Saadya's comment on *v.* 7—comparing it to the answers to Abimelek (*Gen.* xx. 3) and to Bilʻam (*Num.* xxii. 9)—it must be inferred that he put Job on a par with Abraham ² and Israel. iii. 1, Saadya compares Job to Jeremiah. The same combination is found in the *Pes. r.*³ Saadya comments on vii. 9 that man is too weak to resuscitate himself. This interpretation is supplemented in three other comments (on xiv. 7 (especially Fragment), 12 and 14) by the insistence that only God if He so wishes can quicken the dead. This is obviously directed against the statement of Rabah (*B.B.* 16a) that *Job denied the Resurrection*. Saadya adds this comment to xxvii. 2: ... *wamaʻnā hesir mishpaṭi anna Iyob kāna ḥākiman fīmā bayna qaumihi* ... *falamma ḥalla bihi hadihi-l-muṣībatu zāla ḥukmuhu*. There is a parallel statement in *Pes. r.*⁴ Saadya states to xxxvii. 13 that God sends rain for three reasons: (1) as punishment (cp. 1 *Sam.* xii. 17); (2) for merit (*istiḥqāq*) concerning the land (cp. *Deut.* xi. 14); (3) as a favour (*tafaḍḍul*), (cp. 1 *Kings* xviii. 45). Cp. with this *Y. Taʻanit* 3 *bizĕkut haʼareṣ wĕhaḥesed wĕhayyissurin.*⁵

Nature and Attributes of God.

To xii. 23 Saadya says wherever creatures go the grace of God (*faḍl*) is upon them, and He grants them sustenance (*rizq*).

---

¹ This is based on the just quoted Fragment (*Bodl. Heb.* e. 74), *fakāna haʼulaʼi-l-awliyaʼu* ... *yadjtamiʻuna fīhā lilʻibādati waʼumuri-l-ṭaʻati.*

² *B.B.* 15b. See Sch[wartz] ad loc.

³ See Sch. ad loc. *hū hayā ēḥad mishshĕnayim shĕyeʼāreru wĕqillelu yoman shĕnoldu bahem.*

⁴ Sch. brings it to xxix. 17. Cp. also xxxvii. 7, where Saadya says: *fī qaulihi bĕyad kol adam yaḥtom arāda annahu yuʻarrifuhum ʼaʻmālahum waṣalāḥahum.* ... Sch. brings a passage from *Taʻanit* 11a which may be compared to our passage: *bĕshaʻat peṭirato shel adam* ... *kol maʻăsaw niftarin lĕfanaw* ... *weʼomrim lō ḥatom wĕḥotēm.* Cp. also xxxvii. 23, a similar statement in *Num. r. s.* 21 to Saadya's comment: *that is to say man does not reach nor attain all His attributes.*

⁵ See Sch. ad loc.

God is *al-bārī*, the Creator (vii. 21).¹ In that he is unique and from this quality result all his other attributes. Cp. the comment on xxxix. 30, *There is here* (in Nature, the created world) *no other Creator out of nothing (mubtadi'un), Former (ṭābi'un), Provider (rāziqun), Powerful master (qāhirun).*² God's knowledge is brought into relief by contrasting with it the impotence and weakness of man in Saadya's remarks on xlii. 6, that man's knowledge is insufficient to grasp *the subtle rule (tadbīr* ³) *of the Wise (al-ḥakīm), be He exalted, and His affairs (umūr* by way of command).⁴ Commenting on xxiv. 31-3 Saadya stresses God's complete liberty of action towards His creation. In his Omnipotence He can reward His creatures after He has chastised them. The cause for God's giving reward or inflicting pain is to be sought in His Free Will exclusively, according to the comment on xxxv. 4.⁵ For, says Saadya in his comment on vi. 8-10 (the three verses clearly expressing the idea of this whole section), *God does what He wants.* How completely spiritualized Saadya's conception is—in accordance with Jewish tradition—can be gathered from his statement on xxxv. 12-15 that God has neither advantage from man's righteousness nor harm from his sin. Saadya sees in ch. xli.—the description of Leviathan, the mighty monster—a symbol for the power of God, its master, in contrast to weak man, in particular to Job who learns from this description to answer God clearly. As the result, all who hear Job will know that it is the confession *that God is just who does no wrong and that it is necessary to submit to Him (taslīm ilayhi) for He does only what is best with His servants.* . . .

¹ In his comment Saadya says he translated *one will seek me* for *wĕshiḥartani* as the word cannot be referred to the Creator who does not seek anything. Here is a case of a passive in the impersonal sense for the active, in the Hebrew addressed to God, the Creator.

² Cp. also xl. 7.

³ Or *regimen* as translated *above*, p. 186. Cp. also the comment on xxv. 6 where Saadya puts in the mouth of Bildad these words: *the answer to your question, Oh Job, has to do with the Knowledge of God of which WE have no information nor do WE know it.*

⁴ Cp. xxxii. 8, *amr illahi* for *nishmaṭ shadday* (see above, p. 185). Is it possible that Yehudah Hallewi borrowed his term *amr illahi* from Saadya?

⁵ Cp. also comment on xxvi. 5.

God and Man.

Following upon this is God's restitution to Job of his earthly goods. Yet, this is made conditional upon Job's intercession on behalf of his friends. They had sinned against Job, their fellow-man, not against God, therefore Job must pray for them that God forgive them. For God is a gracious God. Out of His kindness he grants forgiveness for sin if the sinner repents, cp. xxxvi. 9. There the order is: *v.* 7 speaks of *ṭawāb* (Reward), *v.* 8 of *'iqāb* (Punishment), *v.* 9 of *indār* (Exhortation), and the acceptance of Repentance (*qubūlu-l-tawbati*) precedes *ta'wīḍ* (Recompense). The content of Recompense is more closely defined in a lengthy discourse after xxxiii. 29. God's grace (*ni'ma*) in the world-to-come is of three kinds: 1. After repentance (*vv.* 16 f.); yet there is no merit accruing to man after his repentance, no, God out of His grace bestows favour on him (*v.* 18). 2. The righteous turns to God in supplication and He answers him (*v.* 26), man confessing his sin (*v.* 27). 3. God inflicts sickness and pain upon him (*v.* 19). This is a good example of Saadya's method of summing up a whole chapter, or the important part of it, re-arranging the verses. Bacher quotes a fragment of a comment on ch. xiv., almost identical with the comment on xii. 6, which defines what constitutes a wicked man. Saadya distinguishes three kinds of rebels: those who are unjust in respect of property (thieves, robbers), the criminals and those who deny God. For the removal of injustice from God there are seven proofs contained in xxxiv. 17-19, three roots and four branches. The three roots are: fear and fright, ardent desire (covetousness) and ignorance. Saadya has a strong predilection for ideas or qualities or defects to occur in threes. Cp. also xxxviii. 31, *ḳilq, kulq, rizq*.[1]

Finally, a few examples of Saadya's conception of the nature of Reward and Punishment. In ch. xxi. after *v.* 26, Saadya explains, in contrast to xii. 6, that it is impossible for Job to accept the view of his friends *that Reward and Punishment take place in this world, for how can it be well with the kāfir for one hour even. Why do the wicked live? Then, we see the righteous die with a sad soul and they both (i.e. the righteous and the wicked) die. For, if reward and punishment were— as you say—in this world, how then are they both rewarded or*

---

[1] For further examples, *see above*, pp. 179, 181, 196, 197.

punished after they have both been dead in view of vv. 31 f. ? [1]
In xxxiv. 2 Saadya lets Job state that wisdom is a gift from God who punishes the rational (human beings) by withholding it from them. Elihu reproaches Job, says Saadya, in his comment on vv. 5 f., not for saying *God has removed my right* but for saying this and adding that God *will not recompense him for that in the world-to-come but rather deprive him of it in this (world)*. Saadya reads this interpretation into v. 6. In xxxv. 15 Saadya sees a clear reference to 'iwad (compensation) in so far as Job only counts his suffering and pities himself. *But if he knew that his rest will be great he would patiently bear what befell him.* Likewise xxxvi. 18 is explained as God's punishment. *Suffering in this world: its compensation is reward in the world-to-come for there is no wrath nor misfortune for they are an expression of ḥilm (clemency).*[2]

It would appear from these utterances on Reward and Punishment that in the view of Saadya, Elihu is primarily concerned to convince Job that there is a Hereafter, with Recompense in the form of rest (*rāḥa*) as the guiding principle. Thus, recompense is clearly lifted out of the realm of material gain into that of a blissful Life after Death.

Faith.

That this commentary no less than the translation reflect something of the personal attitude of Saadya to God and Life is evident. He has lavished his wholehearted attention and care on this labour of love; he has brought to bear on this great book his mature scholarship and spared no effort to elucidate a difficult work of art which is more than literature; it is an object-lesson in faith and trust in God who tests Job by inflicting almost unbearable suffering upon him: *If I were to defame Him, how, then, could I bear this suffering which is so strong that it hinders me from eating my food but that there is faith in Him in my heart. And even if He killed me Himself would I be constant towards Him* (laṣabartu lahu), (xiii. 14). Or to v. 19, *If he chose to judge me I would either remain silent and let Him kill me or I would seek Him and pray to Him in supplication.*

---

[1] Cp. also xxxiii. 29, dealt with *above*, p. 204.
[2] Cp. also comment to v. 16.

6

SEBASTIAN MUENSTER'S KNOWLEDGE AND USE OF JEWISH EXEGESIS[1]

SEBASTIAN MUENSTER has exerted a lasting influence on the English Versions of the Bible from the *Great Bible* onwards. In an earlier study on *Rashi and the English Bible*[2] I was able to show that whereas Miles Coverdale is strongly influenced by Luther in his own translation of 1537 he comes much nearer to Jewish exegesis in his revision of *Matthew's Bible* through making extensive use of Muenster's Latin translation. The *Bishops' Bible* is indebted to both the *Great Bible* and the *Geneva Version*. Both owe much to Muenster for their greater accuracy. Moreover, Archbishop Parker issued to the translators of the *Bishops' Bible* instructions one of which enjoins ". . . for the verity of the Hebrew to follow . . . Muenster specially. . . ." As Muenster was the principal medium of the transmission of Jewish exegesis, which is so evident both in the text and in the notes of the English Versions, a more detailed account of his considerable knowledge of Jewish grammatical studies and Biblical exegesis is surely called for. It is therefore the purpose of this short paper to describe critically the sources which Muenster used in his *Latin Bible*, in the translation of the Old Testament as well as in his numerous notes at the end of each chapter.

[1] Owing to pressure of work and wartime duties I have not been able to deal with the whole Old Testament but have had to confine myself mainly to the first three books of the Pentateuch for a detailed study of Muenster's translation. The second edition, Basle 1546, has been used as it is more fully annotated.

[2] Published in *Bulletin of the John Rylands Library, Manchester*, April 1940. See especially pp. 142 f.; 146 f.; many examples of Muenster as the intermediary between Jewish exegesis and the English versions are given from p. 151 onwards.

The battle-cry of the Hebraists of the sixteenth century was *Hebraica Veritas*. This phrase has, however, a double meaning. For these Hebraists are not only animated by a scholarly quest for Truth, they not only want to go right back to the original source, the Hebrew text, which they study with the help of Elijah Levita's Massoretic studies. They not only want to promote a true understanding of a correct text, supplied with an accurate, intelligible translation. *Hebraica Veritas* for them means, at the same time, a sharp weapon, forged, it is true, by much study and untiring effort, but forged to a purpose: to prove by a new, accurate understanding of the Old Testament the truth of the New Testament, the Messiahship of Christ. They are thus more than Reformers, than Protestants, they dispute the claim of the Jews to the Old Testament. They claim to understand the Old Testament better than the Jews themselves, who in their blindness and obstinacy refuse to recognize in Christ the promised Messiah and Saviour. For them as Christians the Old Testament points to and proves Christ. None expresses this more clearly than Muenster. Yet, none was better equipped for his task than this disciple of the Rabbis. Johannes Eck's warning against the " Rabi Muenster " pays eloquent tribute to this scholar whose translation another theologian characterized as more in agreement with the commentaries of the Rabbis than with those of the interpreters of the true Church.[3]

This new Christian zeal was greatly helped by the new art of printing. Bomberg occupies first place. But other printing presses in Venice and Constantinople have their share in making accessible to the sixteenth century Hebraists the treasures of Rabbinic literature. Without Bomberg's *Miḳraoth Gedoloth* Muenster's edition of the Hebrew text with the Massoretic accents would be unthinkable. His Latin translation with copious notes was made possible only by that Bomberg edition and the contemporary editions of the *Seder 'Olam*

---

[3] See L. Geiger, *Das Studium d. hebr. Sprache in Deutschland vom Ende d. XV. bis z. Mitte d. XVI. Jahrhunderts*, p. 7 f. It is the first systematic study of Hebrew scholarship in these times. This subject ought to be taken up more fully.

(*Rabba* and *Zuṭa*), *Josippon, Sefer (Seder) Ha-Kabbalah*, of the *Minor Midrashim*, of the Mediaeval Commentaries and Halachic works.

Muenster was not the first to undertake a new translation. He refers himself to predecessors like Santes Pagnino,[4] Luther, Steuchus[5] and others. But he makes it quite plain in his Prefaces, both Hebrew and Latin, that he has frequent recourse to the Jewish exegetes in his endeavour to give simply *Hebraicam veritatem*. They are for him sure guides to the true understanding of the plain meaning of Scripture. He uses them " not as oracles, but with discrimination." [6] And, we should add, with a strong Christian bias. He quotes dissentient views, linguistic as well as exegetical, so as to enable the reader to choose his own interpretation. Against Steuchus, he strongly defends his own adherence to *Hebraism* which even compels him to coin new Latin words.[7] He finds the Targum often to be more explicit than the Hebrew original and follows it frequently.[8] How highly he

---

[4] In my Rashi article, *loc. cit.*, I made Pagnino use Muenster; the text, p. 150, should read: " Muenster must obviously have seen Pagnino's translation ".

[5] Throughout his translation Muenster is very hard on Steuchus and takes him particularly to task for having charged Rashi with borrowing from St. Jerome.

[6] He goes on: *et quantum fieri potuit interpretatio ipsa hebraismo e regione posito, iuxta Hebraeorum mentem responderet . . . consuluimus . . . in Pentateucho ex Heb. scriptoribus Chal. interpretem, Rabi Salomonem, David Kimhi, Ibn Ezra, R. Menahem* (di Recanati presumably, in my Rashi article, p. 146, I ventured to suggest M. b. Saruk) *Mosen Gerundensem . . . et quosdam alios: et cuius expositio in obscurioribus locis nobis commodior visa fuit, hunc sequuti sumus.*

[7] He says: *nos tamen, qui versionem nostram e regione Hebraismi posuimus, noluimus ab Hebraismo recedere . . . Coegit autem nos interdum Hebraismus ipse, ut quo fidelius scripturam redderemus, compositionem latinam faceremus latinis auribus inconsuetam, ut est herbificare, pro herbam producere: reptificare, pro reptile multiplicare.* This is a clear indication of the earnestness of Muenster's endeavour to bring out the peculiar properties of Hebrew idiom and diction. It is something quite novel in his (and every) age. It is something which ought to weigh with every true translator. We might think of Buber/Rosenzweig and their views on and practice of translation.

[8] In his own words: *Facimus autem saepiuscule Chal. aeditionis mentionem quod illa sit veluti asylum Hebraeis, ad quum confugiant, quando aliquid obscurum et senticosum occurrit. Nam illa luculenter explicat, quod in divinis libris minus clarum positum invenitur, ut saepe in nostris monstrabimus annotationibus.* It is very likely that Elijah Levita, his teacher, who did such important work for a better understanding of the Targum, inspired him in his quite sound views on this matter. Significantly, Muenster calls Onkelos " *Chal. interpres,*" and *not* translator.

valued Ibn Ezra, Nachmanides, Gersonides, David Kimhi—and no doubt also Rashi, although he does not mention him in this context,—is clear from his statement that St. Jerome would not have needed a teacher if he could have used these commentaries.[9] He praises Nachmanides, D. Kimhi and Ibn Ezra for their cautious exposition of Scripture, bearing in mind the apposite dictum מי שאינו יודע מה למעלה ומה למטה ובספרים הופך דברי אלהים חיים which he tries to emulate.[10] He shows himself familiar with the basic *Rules of Interpretation*, employed by the principal Hebrew commentators. He pays attention to the *Tropi*, stresses the importance of *Nikkud*, following R. Menahem di Recanati whom he quotes frequently. Once, he also quotes R. Eleazar of Worms.[11] He cites R. Moses of Coucy's Preface to his *Liber Mitzwoth Maior* for the fact of the gradual recession of Oral Tradition and the ascendancy of Writing through the decrease of scholars, following upon the Galuth.[12] Muenster then refers to the Annual cycle of the Reading of the Torah, discusses *Lectio plenis et defectiva* and then quotes extensively from D. Kimhi's *Introduction* to his commentary on the *Early Prophets* on *Kethib* and *Kerē*. This quotation is followed by that of the contrary view of R. Jacob ben Hayyim of Tunis, the apostate corrector of Bomberg.[13] A comparison of Kimhi's text in the Bom-

---

[9] Yet Muenster forgets that he needed a personal teacher himself!

[10] He also quotes דברה תורה כלשון בני אדם and אחד במלות שונות
R. Menahem di Recanati is quoted with two important sayings:

1 . דברי תורה יש להם פנימי וחיצון גלוי ונסתר:

2 . ידוע הוא כי האותיות כשאינן נקודות יש להם פנים הרבה. אמנם כשהם נקודות אין להם רק משמעות אחד כפי הנקודה.

See Recanati's *Commentary on the Pentateuch*, edit. Venice, 1523 *section* ואלה המשפטים before comment on כי יפתח איש בור.

[11] To Lev. XII.2 on the sex of children, Muenster does not admit that he excerpted Eleazar's statement from Recanati, *ad loc*. See Recanati, *loc cit.*, beginning of *section* תזריע.

[12] See M. of Coucy's *Sepher ha-Mitzwoth ha-gadol*, edit. Venice, 1547, especially folio 3a r.

[13] Muenster quotes Hebrew and then translates it thus: *In captivitate prima corrupta sunt exemplaria, elicueruntque ex uno exemplari sic, et ex alio aliter: et ubi clarum non potuerunt habere sensum, scripserunt unam dictionem intra contextum,*

berg Bible of 1524, as quoted by Jacob ben Hayyim in the *Mikraoth Gedoloth* (Warsaw 1883) and in Muenster (Basle 1546) shows considerable variants in the first part of the passage.[14] Of grammatical studies he cites " Rabi Calonymos' *liber de accentis* "[15] and the *Grammar* of Abraham de " Palmis " (Balmes). In the notes to his translation, he very often quotes " R. Abraham Sepharadi " (R. Abraham Saba'), author of *Zeror ha-Mor;* the author of the " *Liber Nizahon* "; Moses of Coucy; a " sapiens R. Abraham " who is often identical with Abraham ibn Ezra, but sometimes both are quoted side by side. Recanati is frequently quoted for mystical and symbolical explanations which are sometimes called *pulchre*. On the whole, Muenster quotes accurately and translates correctly, but sometimes he blunders[16] or mixes up his authorities.[17] Once his inaccurate

---

et aliam ad marginem. Perierunt quoque exemplaria et distracta sunt: et morientibus sapientibus, qui tenebant scripturae sensum, conati sunt hi, qui erant de synagoge magna, restituere legem ad vetustatem suam invenientesque dissensiones in exemplaribus, adhibuerunt fidem pluribus exemplaribus consentientibus. Ubi vero claram cognitionem habere non potuerunt, scripserunt unam dictionem absque punctis, aut scripserunt in margine et non intra contextum. Jacob ben Hayyim opposes this view in the following terms: *Sententia illorum longe est a me. Nec enim adduci possum ut credam, et labiis confitear, Ezram scribam librum legis divinae atque libros prophetarum dubios, corruptos et confusos invenisse: quin magis sententia mea est, quod Ezras et collegae eius invenerint biblia sacra integra et illaesa, quodque Ezras iudicio suo cognoverit, qui libri scripti essent per sapientiam illam excellentem, et quare quaedam literae scriberentur, quaedam vero non: quare etiam dictiones quaedam extraneae scriptae essent: dimisitque eas in ipso textu ut scriptae erant adijciens in margine veluti glossam, quae naturam explicaret vocabuli extranei.* Muenster translated these two passages on the whole quite accurately, at least as far as the meaning is concerned.

[14] Here is the beginning of the quotation from D. Kimhi in Muenster's Hebrew
בגלות ראשונה נשתבשו הנסחאות והיו מוציאין בנסחא אחת כך ובנסחא אחרת כך,
ולא עמדו על בירורם וכתבו האחת מבפנים והאחרת מבחוץ וגם אבדו הספרים וגו':
[Kimhi on I K. XVII.14 reads נשתבצן for נשתבשו]
Bomberg and Warsaw read:
ונראה כי מלות האלה (כתיב וקרי) נמצאו כן לפי
שבגלות ראשונה אבדו....

[15] According to Bacher in Winter u. Wünsche's *Geschichte d. jüdischen Literatur*, p. 213, it is Joseph ben Kalonymos, grandson of Nakdan Shimshon, who wrote two didactic poems on the accents.

[16] To Gen. XLIX.10 he writes: *Sceptrum:sive, ut Hebraica habent: virga, scilicet regia ... Autor Libri Nizahon interpretatur dominatorem et ducem terrae.* In

quotation even looks like a deliberate change which may be due to his Christian bias.¹⁸ In some instances, his citations could not be traced.¹⁹ Quite apart from the innumerable occasions on which

---

reality Yomtob Lipmann of Mühlhausen, the author of the *Liber Nizahon*, states the exact opposite: לכן גם אשיב להם. ואומר שהם טועים בפשט הפסוק כי שבט האמור כאן אינו לשון מטה ומלוכה אלא לשון רידוי ושעבוד מלשון כי יכה איש את עבדו או את אמתו בשבט וגו':
The suffering will, however, not last for ever but will cease when the Messiah comes. Muenster agrees with Jewish traditional exegesis against Lipmann. Muenster quotes this work frequently, sometimes he notes with open displeasure the anti-Christian utterances of the author, e.g., to Gen. I.25 (see Lipmann, edition Nürnberg, 1644, p. 7, last paragraph. Muenster sums up the comment of pp. 7 ff., without quoting the hopeful passage about the Messiah.
¹⁷ To Exod. XXIII.5 he disagrees with Kimhi, but in fact it is Rashi's view. Kimhi does not say so in his *Book of Roots*.
Another example is Lev. XXVII.2, *see* below, p. 365, or Gen. XLIV.5, *see* below, p. 367 f.
¹⁸ To Exod. XII.17 Muenster quotes R. Abraham Sepharadi's designation for מצה as סימן חירות. In the text, however, we find סימן גאולה ! Has he deliberately changed to *Freedom* from Egyptian bondage what for Abraham Sabaʿ was a symbol for ultimate Redemption of a nation suffering in Exile? Only so can we understand why Muenster does not continue the quotation from the *Zeror ha-Mor* where its author states that the Commandment to eat unleavened bread for seven days is המצוה היותר עקרית שבתורה. Another instance for bringing the gist of Saba's comment only, without conveying the devotional character and moralizing tenor of it is Gen. L.19 (*see Zeror*, ed. Venice, 1546, p. 63b). Likewise, in citing this work to Gen. XXXIX.6 he brings only that the author said Joseph had such fine features although he ate only bread, but omits to mention what precedes this statement, i.e. that both Daniel and Esther learnt from Joseph that God would perform a miracle for them just as He did for Joseph (*loc. cit.*, 49b. l.). To Gen. II.3, on the other hand, we find a full and accurate quotation from Sabaʿ (*see loc. cit.*, 5a. l.). Christian bias is also apparent in his comment on Lev. XXV.5 שבתון where he militates against Jewish Messianism.
¹⁹ To Exod. XX.18 ערפל Muenster quotes חשך עב according to Kimhi as its meaning. Yet Kimhi in his *Book of Roots* does not say anything like it whereas Rashi explains it by עב הענן. The expression חשך. is somewhat strange. In his comment on Exod. XXIII.1 he brings the opinion of Moses of Coucy that we should follow the few witnesses who would save the innocent and not the many who have condemned him. I could not trace this in the *Sepher ha-Mitzwoth*. It is not to be found in any other Commentary but it may well come from Moses of Coucy's *Commentary* on the Pentateuch. Extracts of this Commentary are to be found in Eliezer

Muenster discloses his sources, there are many instances of unacknowledged borrowing, mainly from Rashi—whom Reuchlin, Muenster's foremost Christian predecessor, aptly called *ordinarius interpres Scripturae*—but also from D. Kimhi, Ibn Ezra, Nachmanides and R. Jacob *Ba 'al ha-Turim*, whose *Arba Turim* (once called "*Arba Tura*"(!)) are once quoted[20] and another time mentioned without being cited because of the absurdity of the statement. R. Abraham ha-Lewi is represented once with his "*Liber Kabalah*," so is Maimonides and twice the *Seder 'Olam*. Of Midrashic sources Muenster cites the "*Medras* ויושע" on several occasions, once the מעשה שאירע לר' יהושע בן לוי,[21] once the מעשה תורה, but not in the place he states.[22] Well-known sayings from the *Rabboth*-collections are naturally also represented. There are a few instances where the Talmud is quoted, once at least without the source being disclosed.[23]

It is amusing to see how he is sometimes on the defensive when quoting from the Midrash or from Commentaries: he excuses such quotations, often lengthy, as useful exercises for those among his readers who are students of Hebrew and whom he gives an opportunity to get into the Rabbinic idiom and to catch a glimpse of Rabbinic literature. This is usually accompanied by a biting remark about the absurdity or silliness of these *figmenta Judaeorum*! He is specially pugnacious where the Jewish interpreters refer a verse to

---

b. Yehudah's *Minhat Yehudah*, but this passage is not recorded therein. See also below, p. 361 with *n*. 33. Cp. also *n*. 22.

20 To Exod. XIII.16, together with Moses of Coucy (*loc. cit.*, p. 104).

21 Jellinek in his *Beth ha-Midrash* II, pp. XVIII ff. and 48–51 brings this Midrash under the title מעשה דר' יהושע.

22 To Gen. XII.1. It is more likely that his source was the Midrash מעשה אברהם See Jellinek, *loc. cit.*, II.119. Yet Muenster borrows from the מעשה תורה to Exod. VI.3 without disclosing his source when he mentions that three persons were created without sin. See Jellinek, *loc. cit.*, p. 94, lines 24 f. Naturally he introduces this Midrash by *delirant Hebraei qui scribunt*. Another quotation, also anonymous, is in his comment on Exod. XX.12 on יאריכון, in the name of "a certain Rabbi." See, *loc. cit.*, p. 94, lines 21 f.

23 See below to Exod. XXI.24, p. 362 f.

the Messiah still to come. It is here that he blames the Jews with obstinacy, with having a veil drawn over their eyes,[24] and similar flatteries. Yet such an attitude is understandable: he is a Christian, a son of his age. Such outbursts of a zealous fighter are timebound. But the recognition of the excellence of Jewish exegesis—which leads its attentive student to *Hebraica Veritas*—is therefore no less sincere. And indeed, it has borne choice fruit in that Muenster's *Latin Bible* has exerted a lasting and wholesome influence right down to the *Authorized Version*.[25] One might almost say that the perusal of Muenster's Version stimulates the closer study of Jewish Biblical exegesis and of the Hebrew grammarians and their works. It is only fair to say that the scholar in Muenster was stronger than the Christian, zealous for his faith, when he was bent on the task of translating especially difficult passages. He produced an imposing number of treatises on Hebrew Grammar and Lexicography and translated a large amount of Hebrew literature of all branches (linguistic, halachic, theological, scientific[26]). Though he is more erudite than original, his vast knowledge was turned to good account in his translation of the Old Testament, a work the avowed purpose of which was to make Christians understand the Old Testament as the foundation on which the New rests, for there is nothing in the New Testament that has not been forshadowed in the Old. Therefore it is most valuable.[27] Although all the prophecies of the Old Testament, for him, pointed to Christ in whom they were fulfilled, he could end his translation of the Torah with the unstinted praise of

[24] In an interesting biographical note in the midst of his comment on Gen. XLV.12 he says: *Judaei ipsi super quorum oculos velamen positum est in lectione veteris legis.* Therefore he understands the O.T. better than the Jews! But that he sees with clear, undimmed eyes, i.e., with those of a Christian seems to be a foregone conclusion!

[25] See my *Rashi and the English Bible*, loc. cit., pp. 151–61.

[26] Among them are translations of the principal works of his teacher Levita. Muenster and Fagius have not only spread the fame of Levita by their editions and translations of his works. They have also made him the authoritative guide in the study of Hebrew and Aramaic for generations. A new monograph on Levita is a desideratum.†

[27] In his Preface to the Pentateuch we read: *Magni igitur aestimandi sunt libri veteris testamenti, quod sint ceu fundamentum quoddam, quo novum nititur testa-*

Mosheh Rabbenu, under the heading מעלות משה. Nobody could improve upon this summary of Rabbinic opinion on the father of prophecy, the greatest and unequalled of all prophets.

There is no doubt, he deeply loved the old Testament: hence the immense labour he bestowed upon his translation, hence the zeal with which he studied the Hebrew commentaries, hence the interest in the Midrashim of the Patriarchs and of Moses, superficially hidden under the cloak of absurd " fairytales which make good exercises for students of Hebrew."[28] In good Rabbinic tradition he sees in the prohibition *not to seethe the kid in his mother's milk* a warning to be humane to the brute beast and the human being alike. The seven Noachide Laws are for him the charter of morality and international Law.[29] Or, he took great pains to ascertain the correct names of the forbidden animals in *Leviticus* and remarked that the German Rabbis often differ from French and Spanish Rabbis owing to the absence of certain species in one region and its occurrence in the other. He dares to differ from Jerome and the other Church Fathers, ancient and more recent, and puts his trust in the exegesis of Hebrew grammarians and commentators. If we compare the two editions of

---

mentum, unde certa argumenta novi testamenti peti possint. Siquidem nihil traditum est in novo testamento, quod non antea Mosaicae legis typis fuerit adumbratum . . . The Old Testament as the archetypes of and the arsenal for sure arguments for the New Testament: this is still the prevailing view among many Christian scholars.

[28] To Exod. XIV.27 he says: *Et quoniam cupimus studiosos iuuare in lingua, et deinde ostendere in quam reprobum sensum Judaei dati sunt subijciemus pauce ex illorum Medrasim* (follows a quotation). *Vide lector theologiam Hebraeorum. Possem hic absurdiora adijcere, nisi offenderem pias aures. Sic ludunt athei homines in scriptura sacra, vertuntque omnia in fabulas Luciani.* This is perhaps the strongest of many attacks scattered over his translation. And yet he is eager to accept the literal interpretation of the Rabbis and does not withhold praise from the Old Testament itself. Naturally, he would like to turn it into a Christian book. Here is an example of his sympathetic understanding: *Colligimus ex his* (the 140 blemishes, Lev. XXI) *quam integros et immaculatos dominus in veteri testamento voluerit habere ministros.*

[29] His summing up is: *Et hic est fons, ex quo manat totum ius civile et ius gentium. Nam si deus concedit homini potestatem super id quod minus est, ut sunt fortunae, familia, uxor, liberi, servi, agri. Magistratus ergo hic a deo instituitur et gladius datur ei in manus, in vindictum malorum, et laudem bonorum.*

his translation we see how the extent of his Rabbinic knowledge has grown in the interval. For, whereas he confines himself mainly to the commentators in the first edition, he adduces in the later edition more comment and further corroborative evidence from Midrashic and Talmudic literature.[30] His quotations are, to repeat it, on the whole surprisingly correct. The variants are, as a rule, unimportant, with some significant exceptions.[31] But a close investigation might yield some results for the possibility of an unexpurgated text. How seriously Muenster took his duty to give his readers a correct, fully annotated version of the Old Testament can best be seen when we consider his work on Isaiah. In his *Latin Bible* we find a translation of the text of Isaiah with full notes, culled chiefly from the Rabbis. But he also prepared a separate edition of the Book of Isaiah with a Greek and two Latin translations (one being the *Vulgate*, the other his own). Extracts from D. Kimhi's *Commentary* on Isaiah are added as an appendix. In the entire Bibles, he brings the Jewish views on all Messianic passages in full and tries hard to refute the Jewish interpretation, just as it was the practice in the Disputations of the earlier centuries. In the separate edition, however, he suppresses all references to Gog and Magog and to the coming of the Messiah and explains every prophecy of a Messianic nature in a Christological sense.[32] In this he is in line with the old-established interpretation of the Church, e.g. of such chapters as XI, XL, XLII or LI which have been taken to predict the Coming, Passion, Death and Redemption of Jesus. And yet he follows Jewish exegesis in the accurate translation of these Messianic chapters just as much as everywhere else.

---

[30] Often he quotes in the later edition the Midrash ויושע (see Eisenstein's *Otzar Midrashim*, New York, 1915, pp. 146 ff.), e.g. to Gen. XV.14; XXII.10; XLIII.34; XLV.12; L.19. Exod. III.14; VIII.12; XIV.27; XXIII.19. Lev. X.1. This Midrash was first printed in 1517 in Constantinople. A comparison has shown that Muenster quotes accurately.

[31] E.g. above n. 14 and especially 18.

[32] Jewish views which run counter to this tendency are passed over in silence in the separate edition. There is no mention, e.g., that Kimhi refers ch. XI to the *future* king Messiah.

Sebastian Muenster and Jewish exegesis

Without D. Kimhi's linguistic treatises and without the extensive training he received from the hands of Elijah Levita, Muenster would never have been able to understand, to appreciate, let alone to utilize Rabbinic literature. Without the Rabbis his translation would never have been nearer to the original nor would his interpretation of the Old Testament as the source and basis of Christianity have furthered the cause of the Reformers. They hailed his translation as the *Hebraica Veritas*. The *Authorized Version* is the most unimpeachable witness to this estimation of Muenster's work. No wonder therefore that it is Muenster more than anybody else who introduced the Targum, Rashi and Kimhi, Ibn Ezra and Nachmanides and a number of other Mediaeval authors into the English Versions. This alone would be a great service which has benefited Jew and Gentile alike. A further study of quotations from D. Kimhi and Moses of Coucy may perhaps result in establishing that Muenster used D. Kimhi's lost *Commentary on the Pentateuch* from Exodus to Deuteronomy as well as Moses of Coucy's *Commentary*.[33]

A number of examples may illustrate how Muenster worked Jewish exegesis into both his translation and notes:

---

[33] Though the majority of genuine quotations from Kimhi could be traced to the latter's *Book of Roots* there are some instances where Muenster must have used Kimhi's Commentary on Genesis. We could establish this fact for Gen. XVI.13 and XLIV.5 at least. *See* also above, *n*. 19. To Gen. XLIX.26 he probably used the *Book of Roots*—without disclosing his source— נזיר *id est, corona fratrum suorum*. Kimhi, *s.v.* נזיר says ראש אחיו ומעוטר whereas in his *Commentary* the explanation is: נזיר שר וגדול. We are engaged at present in an investigation of all Muenster's quotations from Kimhi. Apart from these two Genesis-passages we have to consider a passage in Muenster's *Epistola* which he prefaced to his edition of Abraham b. Hiyyah's *Sepher tzurath haAretz*, in which mention is made of Kimhi's *Commentary* in these words: *Scripsit mihi. superiori anni* (1545) *Andreas Masius*, . . . , *de multis libris Hebraicis, quos Romae vidit apud Judaeos, partim impressos et partim imprimendos, sed qui fere omnes sunt vel* אגרים *vel* פירושים *puta perush Rabi David Kimhi in* תורה. This does not convey the impression that Muenster saw and used this Commentary. At the present stage of our enquiry we cannot give a definite answer. The same applies to Moses of Coucy. In *n*. 19 above we quoted an example and to Lev. XXVII.2—which passage will be discussed below, p. 365, with *n*. 44—Moses of Coucy is quoted with an interpretation not to be found in his *halachic work*. We must leave this question open for the time being.

Jewish themes

A. *Quotations from Talmud and Midrash:*

At the beginning of Genesis he quotes the well-known Midrash of the seven things created before the creation of the world. He discusses that Kimhi mentions seven things and other exegetes seven different ones, some even ten. When discussing the institution of Sabbath he brings the Midrash that the Demons flee on Sabbath Eve into the far-away mountains only to return after nightfall on Sabbath.

To Gen. XII.1 the Midrash מעשה תורה is cited for the story of how Abraham burned the idols of his father Terah, whereupon Nimrod threw him into the burning furnace but God saved him by coming down from Heaven Himself.[34]

To Gen. XV.14 דן אנכי he quotes the Midrash ויושע about Uza and Michael arguing before God about the length of time the Israelites were supposed to remain in Egypt. God tells Uza that the 400 years mean not Egypt but "a land not of their own."[35]

In the Preface to his translation and in his comment on Lev. XXV he brings the Aggada of the world lasting for 6000 years.[36] He also notes the various views of the Rabbis as to the coming of the Messiah.

After quoting Nachmanides on Exod. III.14 he says the Hebrews deduce from this passage that the Divine Name was not to be pronounced and quotes "Talmud, Tr. *Helek* ההוגה ה׳ באותיותיו אין לו חלק לעולם הבא." It is for our question more important that he quotes the Talmud than that he brushes the statement aside as a silly superstition. None of these quotations occur in the first edition of 1534.

To Exod. XXI.24 עין תחת עין he brings the unanimous opinion of Jewish exegesis that this is not to be understood literally but that תשלום ממון *compensatio per bona externa* has to take place. He goes on to

---

[34] See n. 22 above.
[35] Cp. Eisenstein, *op. cit.*, p. 148r. l.
[36] Muenster cites *Sanhedrin*. It occurs on folio 97a, also slightly varied *Ab. Zara* 9a. As is to be expected, Muenster claims the 2000 years of *the days of the Messiah* for Christ. In his *Preface* he quotes this Aggadah already. But whereas there the world reverts to Chaos after 6,000 years, here the seventh millenium will be a *Sabbath of the Lord*. (It is the analogy of the seventh day, the seventh year, the seventh millenium.)

speak of five-fold compensation without disclosing his source. This source, however, is *M.B.K.* VIII.1 and *T.B.K.* 83b 84. Only the order of the five compensations is slightly different in Muenster: *damnum* (נזק), *sessionem* (שבת), *dolorem* (צער), *medicinam* (רפוי) *et confusionem* (בושת). The order in *M.* and *T.* is בנזק בצער ברופוי בשבת ובושת. Muenster's comment is based on Rashi and Nachmanides.

B. *Quotations from Historical Writings.*

These can be dealt with briefly. To Gen. L.19 he reproduces " Mose Gerundi's super Torah *Perus* " with a quotation from the *Chronicles of Joseph ben Gorion and other old books* about the conflict between Zapho ben Eliphas ben Esau and Joseph, how Zapho left Egypt for Italy after the death of Joseph, etc. This is, of course, Josippon. Muenster goes on to say—only in the edition of 1546—*et nos superiori anno illum Hebraice et Latine evulgavimus post editionem Constantinopolitanam. Antiquitates tamen Hebraice non vidimus.* Next comes the *Seder 'Olam* the second chapter of which is quoted to Exodus. To Exod. XII.40 he says that according to the *Seder 'Olam* and also to " R. Abraham halevi in his book קבלה " the children of Israel were for a period of 210 years in Egypt. Muenster obviously treats Abraham Ibn Da'ud's History as a primary authority without suspecting that the *Seder 'Olam* was probably the source of the *Seder ha-Kabbalah*.[38]

C. *Comments based on Jewish exegetes of the Torah.*

Phrases like *Et hanc expositionem huc retuli ex Gerundensi* (Gen. IV.20) alternate with a critical attitude towards some of the Jewish comments, e.g. *Nec curo quod Kimhi hic* עזב *pro* עזר *exponit.*[39] Yet, he can also say that a verse or a phrase are somewhat

---

[37] It is clear from Nachmanides' quotation (uncensored edit., Lisbon, 1489, but not to be found in the Horeb-edition of the *Torah*), that Jossipon must have been known also under other titles than *Sepher Joseph ben Gorion* in the Middle Ages. See on this point *Encyclopedia Judaica* (IX, 421). Abraham Saba' contrary to Muenster's assertion does not refer to this struggle (*see loc. cit.*, p. 63b).

[38] See Neubauer, *Medieval Jewish Chronicles*, ii (1895), p. 27 ff. and *Sepher ha-Kabbalah*, p. 25a. l.

[39] *See n.* 17 above.

obscure wherefore he wanted to render it more clearly with the help of the Hebrew commentaries. He finds the Targum particularly helpful, as can be seen from expressions like *reddidit Chal. interpres clarius hunc locum quam in Hebraeo habeatur, nam ita vertit: et aperuit Joseph omnes thecas in quibus erat frumentum, id quod nos per parenthesin signavimus.* (Gen. XLI.56). His rendering *horrea* for the Targumic אוצריא is also to be found in the *A.V.* as *storehouses*. Another instance is Gen. XLVII.22 חיק where he follows Onkelos' חולקא *pars* : *A.V.* translates *portion*.[40] On the other hand he has a lengthy note on Lev. XI.21, adopting Onkelos' דליה for לא, overlooking that the Kerē is indeed לו! [41] As stated above, he never tires of accusing the Jews of madness and stupid absurdity, in expressions like *delyramentum* or *taedet me hic referre figmentum Hebraeorum* (Lev. XX.6) or *Hebraei qui miri sunt in excogitandis prodigiosis figmentis* (Exod. IX.31) or, after quoting R. Abraham Saba', *sed post has nugas ad textum revertamur* (Lev. XVII.7).

Instead of quoting example after example where he brings the views of this or that Rabbi we will confine ourselves to those cases where he weighs one interpretation against another : so he brings the opinion of the author of the " *liber Nizahon* " : did God speak to Himself when he created Man or to the angels or, as Nachmanides holds, to the Earth?

To Gen. XVI.13 אתה אל ראי he states that the Christians and the Hebrews explain this obscure passage in different ways and goes on to quote at length the views of Rashi, Kimhi and Ibn Ezra without, however, taking sides. On the whole, he shows himself to be well informed where Jewish tradition is divided, as e.g. on Gen. XXV.6

---

[40] Another of many examples is Gen. XLV.24 אל תרגזו. Muenster follows Onkelos' תתנצון and translates *non contendatis* against *Vulgate* (*ne irascimini*). Rashi agrees with Targum. The rendering in A. V. *that ye fall not out* goes back to Muenster. To Exod. XXIII.18 Muenster says *Onkelos clarius vertit, sanguinem sacrificii pascalis.*

[41] He says : *Et nota quod Hebraei post Chal. interpretem exponunt hic* לא *pro* לו *ut non sit adverbium negandi sed aleph ponitur loco uau* (sic). The same thing happens to him with Lev. XXV.30.

הפילגשים he cites the Jewish view about concubines without *Kethubhah* and *Kiddushin* and classes Hagar among them. Keturah according to some was a legitimate wife (Nachmanides), but according to many others she is identical with Hagar (so Rashi). He himself agrees with Ibn Ezra that there were more than one as the text has *the sons of the concubines* in the plural. To Gen. XXXIX.6 הלחם he quotes Rashi who understood it to mean Potiphar's wife, but adds *expositio aliena a litera, etiam secundum multos Hebraeos*. One of these is Ibn Ezra.[42] To Exod. XXX.12 he comments on the value of the Shekel and thinks that the difference between Rashi and Kimhi arises out of the difference between ככר החול and ככר הקדש, the latter having twice the value of the former.[43] To Lev. XXVII.2 *secundum aestimationem animarum* he states that for Rashi the *Caph non esse servile, sed ociose superadditum ut* ערכך *idem sit quod* ערך whereas Kimhi treats it as a servile letter, referring to the priest who has to value *rem devotam*. In fact, Rashi does not say what Muenster quotes in his name; this is, however, stated by Ibn Ezra in the name of *all the grammarians*. Kimhi's view is implied in Ibn Ezra's continuation *yet some say that the* kaph *refers to the priest*.[44] There are also instances where he prefers Jewish interpretation to that of Steuchus whom he also attacks for his translation.[45]

Now follow a few examples of explanations for which no authorities are cited but which are all traceable to one or the other Jewish source:

Gen. II.20 שרץ *quasi* שהוא רץ *id est quod currit et semper movetur*. This is taken over from Nachmanides almost literally.[46]

Gen. XLV.8 לאב *capitur hic* אב *pater pro* מורה *instructore et directore*. Here Ibn Ezra is the source.

Gen. XLVIII.20 יברך *benedicat, non benedicatur* as the *Vulgate*

[42] *See* also *n.* 18 above (Saba').
[43] Muenster has taken this explanation, without acknowledgment, from Kimhi's *Book of Roots*, s.v. ככר !
[44] Moses of Coucy's explanation is ליתן ערך נפשות .
[45] E.g. to Exod. XXXIV.35.
[46] Nachmanides *ad loc.* ויתכן שהוא לשון מורכב יקרא שרץ שהוא רץ ורמש שהוא רומש הארץ לא ישקוט ולא ינוח.

translates. It is active, not passive and he bases his explanation *qui sunt futuri, benedicent filijs suis in te, dicentes*. . . . on Rashi. *A.V.* renders *bless*.

Exod. III.19 *alij exponunt* ולא *pro nisi*. This is Rashi and *A.V.* gives in the margin *but by strong hand*.[47]

Exod. VI.3 אל שדי according to some this is אשר די *cui est sufficientia*. This view is cited by Ibn Ezra disapprovingly in the name of Saadyah! Others, Muenster goes on, identify it with תקיף *fortissimus*. This must also go back to Ibn Ezra who records this view in the name of R. Samuel ha-Nagid.

Exod. X.11 ויגרש *subaudiendum est* מגרש *eiector. talis loquendi modus* לשון קצר *loquutio truncata*. So Rashi!

Exod. XV.26 חקות *statuta sine* טעם. Again Rashi!

Exod. XVII.8 ברפידים. He quotes some Hebrews who say it means *dissolutus manibus*. We find this view expressed by the *Ba'al ha-Turim* ברף ידים!

Exod. XIX.17 לקראת *in occursum (dei)*. In a lengthy note about the order he mentions first the firstborn, then the priests before the Levites, then the princes, the elders, the prefects, then the other Israelites, afterwards the minors, then the women and at last the proselytes. This is literally taken over from Ibn Ezra! Exod. XXI.10 is entirely copied from Rashi. Exod. XXV.18 כרובים *nomen compositum* כמו רביא *quasi puer*, adding רביא was more Chaldean than Hebrew. This is copied from Ibn Ezra! So is also Exod. XXIX.33 וזר *alienus. homo qui non est de genere sacerdotali*. Exod. XL.20 העדת *testimonium, intelligendum est tabulas legis*. This is Rashi. To Lev. X.1 Muenster asks why fire consumed the sons of Aaron and answers his own question by stating that they drank wine and refused to marry, etc. Both these reasons are given by the *Ba'al ha-Turim*!

---

[47] Likewise his explanation of Exod. IV.16 פה *os pro* מליץ *interprete*, אל הים *et deus pro* שר *principe vel* רב *duce* is taken from Rashi. Cp. also Gen. XXXV.8 where Muenster puts the question why Deborah is mentioned here and answers it exactly like Rashi: Rebecca had sent Deborah to fetch Jacob home. Deborah died on the journey. Rashi gives as his source R. Moses haDarshan.

To Lev. XVI.6 בְּיַד אִישׁ עִתִּי *per manum viri opportuni* he says that עִתִּי has the same meaning as מְזֻמָּן—this is Ibn Ezra!—or as הַמּוּכָן which he cópied from Rashi.⁴⁸

A few examples of his *linguistic* exegesis may conclude this survey:

In this point he is quite sound and capable of developing the knowledge which he gained from Kimhi's *Book of Roots* and from his teacher Elijah Levita. He can thus reject Recanati's *descensus* for נִיחוֹחַ in Gen. VIII.21 as the root is not נָחַת.⁴⁹ To Gen. XXVII.28 וּמִשְׁמַנֵּי הָאָרֶץ he says, following Kimhi in his *Book of Roots*, the *mem* was not a preposition but a denominative letter as it was not followed by a *Dagesh*.

Gen. XLIV.5 יְנַחֵשׁ בּוֹ *Nostri verterunt in quo augurari solet, ego vero sequutus sum Hebraeorum expositionem, qui* בּוֹ *pro* בְּעֲבוּרוֹ *exponunt augurando, inquit auguratur: hoc est, ut Kimhi post Rab. Jonam exponit, interrogat augures ...* He then quotes Ibn Ezra and others. Ibn Ezra, following R. Jonah (ibn Gannah), offers this explanation not Kimhi. Gen. XLVII.13 וַתֵּלַהּ *affligebatur. Heb-*

---

⁴⁸ To quote at least two more examples of borrowing from Kimhi without disclosing his source here is Muenster's explanation of Gen. XLIX.26 (*see n. 33 above*): *omni tempore quo steterit terminus collium mundi, erunt hae benedictiones super caput Joseph ...* Kimhi in his *Book of Roots, s.v.* אוה states: כל זמן שיהיה קיים גבול גבעות עולם תהיינה הברכות לראש יוסף.
Another example is Exod. I.21. Muenster says יאל equals רצה. This is taken from Kimhi's *Book of Roots, s.v.* יאל | An example of unacknowledged borrowing from Moses of Coucy may conclude this survey: To Exod. XX.8, 9 Muenster calls *mirabilia* what the Jews wrote about the Sabbath *quod non intelligant, quis verus sit sabbatismus.* He sums up these views and mentions among other things that the Jews wear different clothes, talk in a different way and eat different food. This is obviously taken over from Moses of Coucy's *Sepher ha-Mitzwoth*. p. 106 r.) without acknowledgment.

⁴⁹ Recanati, *loc. cit., section* נח says וזה ניחוח שנחת רוחו. Other examples of Recanati's exegesis, quoted by Muenster, are: To Exod. XI.4 Muenster quotes Recanati's explanation of *Middle of night as the hour of Mars as egregium commentum*: see Recanati, *loc. cit. section* בא אל פרעה. ואותה שעה היתה שעת מאדים וגו'. Or, Exod. XXIX.14 for a mystical explanation of sin-offering to mortify human passions and Lev. III.4—this is where he calls his explanation *pulchre*. Here Muenster gives a Latin summary of Recanati, *section* ויקרא : ועל כן לא היו מקריבין המוח והלב והריאה כי הם מיוחדים למחשבת החכמה.

raicam vocem תלה *cuius radix est* להה *Kimhi exponit pro* תשתגע *id est rabida facta est. Sed Rabi Saadias dicit* להה *idem esse quod* לאה *id est, fatigabatur terra*.... Muenster has simply copied from Kimhi's *Book of Roots*, where *s.v.* להה! Saadyah is cited!

Gen. XLIX.19 עָקֵב follows Kimhi's explanation סוף *A.V.* renders *at last*! Exod. XXV.9 יסד Muenster thinks the root to be rather נסך or יסד but certainly not סכך with Rashi. Exod. XXIX.37 יקדש *sanctus sit* against *sanctificabitur* of the *Vulgate. A.V.* renders *shall be holy*, Exod. XXXI.10 בגדי השרד *vestimenta ministerij*. The Hebrews, says Muenster, explain שרד by עבודה, but only in this passage. This is taken from Rashi; *A. V.* renders *cloths of service*. Lev. VIII.28 על העולה *post holocaustum*, following Rashi who takes על in the sense of אחר. Likewise Lev. IX.17 מלבד עולתו where he again adopts Rashi's explanation of מלבד meaning אחר.

These examples—though limited in number—show clearly how this devoted student of the Old Testament has explored—and on the whole to very good purpose—Jewish exegesis. His indebtedness to Jewish authorities, both well-known and lesser read, stands out clearly. Despite occasional criticism, Muenster regarded, in company with every other sixteenth century Hebraist, these Rabbis, grammarians and exegetes alike, as authorities close to the *Hebraica Veritas*. The soundness of his judgment outweighs his Christian bias which made him refute the Jewish view of Messianism and made him continually carp at the legends of the Jews, some of their customs and some of their theological views. Sound as his judgment is, it has by far not yet become the common attitude of the student of the Old Testament in the original tongue. And yet, one need only compare the *Vulgate*, early English translations and even Luther's German Version—which contains a good deal of Jewish exegesis through Nicholas of Lyra's *Postillae*—with the *Great Bible* and its successors and one will realize the improvement. This improvement, this being so much nearer to the letter *and* the spirit of the Hebrew Bible, is the result of Muenster's skilful, intelligent use of Jewish Biblical exegesis. As far as this exegesis is concerned with the literal meaning of the text not only but also with the basic teachings on the relations between God and Man and between Man and his Fellow, Muenster follows it unhesitatingly. He has thus set an indelible memorial to the best that the Hebrew genius of the Middle Ages has produced. That this memorial is not confined to his own Latin Version but is also traceable in the English Bible—which is definitely the richer for it—our earlier study on *Rashi and the English Bible* and this short paper may, we hope, have shown.

In his notes to Gen. XLV.12 in the edition of 1546 there is contained a most interesting biographical statement which ends with these words: *Haec volui hic obiter signare, ut posteri nostri sciant, quale exordium sumpserit Hebraismi studium apud Germanos.* Thanks to his labours and to Archbishop Parker's wise injunction the Bible is still respected in the English-speaking world, in a version as near to *Hebraica Veritas* as possible. And we ought to admit that Muenster successfully discharged his task which he described in his Preface as one " to show to everybody the beauty and excellence of the Torah " and that he undertook it, to quote again his own words, "לשם שמים and for the benefit of the Christians."

7

EDWARD LIVELY: CAMBRIDGE HEBRAIST

Cambridge made a notable contribution to Biblical studies in the sixteenth and seventeenth centuries, and the writings of its Professors of Hebrew and Divinity not only provided valuable aids for the better understanding of the Bible, but they also rank high as useful, accurate weapons in the struggle of the Protestants against the Church of Rome. A large share in the successful outcome of the religious controversy, apart from its political aspect, falls to Edward Lively, Regius Professor of Hebrew from 1575 to 1605, whose works[1] and lectures were

---

[1] All the known works of Lively have been used for this study. They are as follows:
(1) *Edvardi Livelei Hebræorum literarum in Academia Cantabrigiensi professoris, annotationes in quinque priores ex minoribus Prophetis, cum Latina eorum interpretatione, eundem opera ac studio, ad normam Hebraicæ veritatis diligenter examinata.* London, 1587.
(2) *A True Chronologie of the Times of the Persian Monarchie, etc.*, 1597. Written by *Edovard Livelie, Reader of the holie tongue in Cambridge.* Both expressions—Professor and Reader—are used; see also n. 3, p. 97.
(3) In manuscript: *Liveleianæ Commentationes in Martinium.* This is the superscription of MS. Ee.VI.23, University Library, Cambridge. Small quarto, paper, pp. 170. It is written and signed by one Richard Cradock. There was one Richard Cradock at Trinity in 1608 as a pensioner. He did not graduate, and was later a Counsellor-at-Law, according to J. and J. A. Venn, *Alumni Cantabr.* Venn also mentions a Richard Cradock at Clare College, pensioner 1580, M.A. 1588, deacon and priest 1593. I have been unable to discover who copied the *Commentationes.* There is no direct evidence that Lively actually wrote them. But there is indirect evidence to this effect from the editions of Martinius' *Hebrew Grammar* of 1612 and 1634, see n. 4, p. 97. I have found no reference in Lively's writings to these annotations, but they are in line with grammatical remarks in his other works, specially nos. 1 and 2. It is possible that Richard Cradock of Clare attended Lively's lectures and copied Lively's notes.
(4) *On the Translation of the Old Testament.* In manuscript, University Library, Cambridge, Add. 3066. Small quarto, on vellum, pp. 452 + vii. It is undated, but since it is dedicated to Sir Francis Walsingham, Principal Secretary to the Queen, it can be assigned to the years 1586–1590. Lively is credited with another treatise—*On the Canonical Books of the Old Testament*—preserved in a manuscript at Trinity College, Dublin. I obtained a microfilm of this manuscript, and ascertained that it is "the author's foul copy", not of this treatise, but of the treatise *On the Translation of the O.T.*, but without the Dedicatory Epistle to Walsingham. In it Lively says—"After some consideracon . . . it seemed good unto me to ioyne hereunto another treatise (though more briefly) being not my cheife intente concerning the canonical books of the same ould testament". This may have given rise to the ascription to him of a separate treatise. Since he devotes, however, considerable space in his treatise on the translation to a discussion of the Canonical books, it may well be that his "ioyne" means the same as "incorporate". But the possibility of a separate work cannot be excluded, although I have been unable so far to trace it.
(5) *Chronologia seu Notitia Temporum.* MS. Nr. 126, Trinity College, Dublin. Quarto, pp. 256. It has notes by Archbishop Ussher at the end. I obtained a microfilm of it. The last chronological table shows these dates: A.D. 638/41—Olympiad 354—A.M. 4582.

designed to vindicate the Reformers' stand upon the *Hebraica Veritas*.[1] He not only provided, as a skilful controversialist, adequate defence against Catholic attacks upon the English translation from the Hebrew original, but by his expert knowledge did much to further Hebrew studies in the last quarter of the sixteenth century in England. At that time the Protestant cause badly needed the support of the learned. Lively gave unsparingly of his time, energy and knowledge. Whilst all his writings, with the exception of his *Commentationes in Martinium*, reflect this burning heat of contemporary controversy, none does more so than his treatise *On the Translation of the Ould Testament*, in which he does for *Hebraica Veritas* what William Fulke of Pembroke did, a few years earlier, for the Greek New Testament in his *A Defense of the sincere and true Translations of the holie Scriptures into the English tong against the manifolde cavils, friviolous quarels, and impudent slaunders of Gregorie Martin, one of the readers of Popish divinitie in the trayterous Seminarie of Rhemes*.[2]

Limitations of space do not allow us to give a full-length biography of Lively. A few biographical details must suffice as a background to assess his attainment as a Hebrew scholar, and his influence upon his own and following generations.[3] He was first Scholar and then Fellow of Trinity College—according to his own statement,[4] thanks to the Archbishop of Canterbury— and when a successor had to be appointed to Thomas Wakefield, Lord Burleigh, the Chancellor, favoured Peter Bignon, a Frenchman. He appealed to the then Archbishop of Canterbury, Matthew Parker, to contribute, together with the other Bishops, to the stipend which he found inadequate, and Parker promised to help.[5] But the Vice-Chancellor and other Heads of Colleges pronounced Bignon ineligible since he was not a Master of Arts. In their opinion Fellows of Trinity should be preferred *caeteris paribus*. "By diligent search they found one there, namely, one Lively very fit and meet for that place." He was unanimously chosen, "being not only very toward in that tongue but also in all other arts and qualifications requisite for that Reader". They excused themselves to their Chancellor "that this preferring of one of their own would tend to encourage others to travail in that tongue, wherein, they said, they had divers of very excellent towardness. And that it tended to the honour and commendation of their University which had, they thanked God, as many as fit to occupy the places of all the ordinary lectures,

---

[1] See E. I. J. Rosenthal: *Rashi and the English Bible* (*Bull. of the John Rylands Library*, XXIV, 1, 1940), and *Sebastian Muenster's Knowledge and Use of Jewish Exegesis*, in *Essays in honour of the Very Rev. Dr. J. H. Hertz*, 1943, for the general background to this question, and also concerning English Hebraists.

[2] Published in 1583. The title of Gregory Martin's treatise is—*A discovery of the manifold corruptions of the Holy Sciptures by the Heretikes of our daies, specially the English Sectaries*, 1582. Lively refers to Fulke's treatise, presumably, when he says in his Dedicatory Epistle that others, more skilful than he, had defended the New Testament.

[3] For fuller biographical details see *DNB* XI, p. 1257 f. Also Cooper's *Athenæ Cantabr.*, *s.v.* Lively, and Venn, *op. cit.*, where Lively is stated to have been appointed to the Regius Professorship of Hebrew in 1575—which tallies with Broughton's continuous carping at the "30 yeares professor of Ebrew", and Archbishop Parker's letter of 1574; see n. 5 below—whereas according to J. Venn, *Admissions to Trinity College*, he succeeded Wakefield in 1580.

[4] Dedicatory Epistle to Archbishop Whitgift of his *A True Chronologie*. . . .

[5] *Parker Correspondence*, p. 468. Also Rosenthal, *Rashi*, p. 145.

Edward Lively: Cambridge Hebraist

as there was of any other country."[1] Lively occupied the Chair until he died in 1605, busily engaged on the translation of the Old Testament which had been decided upon at the Hampton Court Conference in 1604.[2] He had been chosen to head the Cambridge team of translators, and to be one of the scholars to whom his fellow translators should submit their observations on obscurities in the Hebrew.[3] The period in between these two momentous years of his life and career is devoted to sustained work on the linguistic and historical-chronological elucidation of the Hebrew Bible. This is clear from references to his published, and particularly to his as yet unpublished, grammatical, exegetical and chronological studies. Among his admirers we find Archbishop Jacob Ussher; the editors of revised editions of Martinius' *Hebrew Grammar*; Eyre, of Emmanuel College, and the illustrious Oxford Orientalist of the following century, the elder Edward Pococke.[4] There is only one dissentient voice—and this a rather loud

---

[1] Strype, *Life of Parker*, II, p. 379 f.

[2] Playfere, *Funeral Oration*, quoted in *DNB*, XI, 1258.

[3] Strype, *Life of Whitgift*, II, p. 30, quotes the king's letter to the Bishop of London containing this passage—". . . for the clearing of any obscurities either in the Hebrew or in the Greek and touching any difficulties or mistakings in the former English translations which we have now commanded to be thoroughly viewed and amended . . . that they send such their observations, either to Mr. Lively, our Hebrew reader in Cambridge, or to Dr. Harding, our Hebrew reader in Oxford, or to Dr. Andrews, Dean of Westminster, to be imparted to the rest of their several Companions. That so our said intended translation may have the help and furtherance of all our principal learned men within this our kingdom."

[4] Archbishop Jacob Ussher, on the year 3927 A.M., quotes Lively's *Chronologia* once in the third chapter, p. 32, of his *De Macedonum et Asianorum Anno Solari*, London, 1648, thus: "die XV mensis Adar, hoc est, aerae Christianae CLXVIII die XXII mensis Februarii, festum Purim cum die Sabbati concurrebat, quem idcirco magnum Sabbatum fuisse dictum scripsit, in Chronologia nondum edita, vir doctissimus Edovardus Livelius." In a letter to Eyre, Ussher inquires about 'Livelaeanum de authentica Scripturarum editione commentationem' [obviously MS. Dublin/Cambridge and, incidentally, a much better title than *On the Translation of the O.T.*] which he was daily expecting. Eyre answered that it and Lively's *Chronologia Latina* were to be published, and as soon as obtainable would be despatched by him to Ussher. Nothing came of the publication, and both MSS.—Mr. Lively's "foul" copies—were sent to Ussher. Guilelmus Coddaeus refers in the "Praefatio" to his edition of Martinius' *Hebrew Grammar* to the fact that "doctissimus Eduardus Liveleius Regius Hebraeae linguae Cantabrigiae in Anglia Professor iam ante aliquot annos huic fini [to improve upon it] egregie operam navavit, sed eius Notae nondum adhuc lucem aspexerunt." Sixtinus Amama in the "Praefatio" to his corrected edition of 1634, based on Buxtorf, and others, says: "Non paucos [defects] in ea observasse dicitur Ed. Livelaeus clarissimus, olim Cantabrig. Professor, sed quae adhuc sint ἀνέκδοτα." See also n. 1, p. 95. On Pococke, see n. 2, p. 105.

He is also mentioned by Père Richard Simon (1638–1712) in his *Histoire Critique du Vieux Testament* (Rotterdam, 1685). This important work, usually considered to offer the first critical treatment of the Hebrew text of the O.T., is in many respects anticipated by Lively's *On the Translation of the O.T.*, as the present writer hopes to show in a separate study later on. On p. 445 P. Simon discusses—among other modern versions and commentaries—Lively's *Annotationes in quinque priores ex minoribus Prophetis* in these words—"Le Commentaire de Liveleius est aussi fort literal sur les cinq premiers petits Prophetes, et on lui doit plûtôt donner le nom de Remarques, que de Commentaire." [This remark is uncalled for since "Annotationes" means precisely "Remarques".] "Il a trop affecté de paroître sçavant sans aucune necessité; ce qui convient mieux à un Rheteur, qu'à un Critique, qui doit expliquer en peu de mots le Texte de l'Ecriture, sans s'arrêter sur son discours d'autorités qui ne font rien pour son sujet. Il devoit aussi, ce me semble, se contenter de rapporter la Version du Texte qu'il jugeoit la meilleure, et ne pas s'amuser à rapporter celle des autres Interpretes, sans autre dessein que de les rejetter. Il est néanmoins bon d'examiner les anciennes Versions, et de les conferer avec les nouvelles: mais

and ugly one—that of Hugh Broughton.[1] His attack on Lively will be dealt with later on when we discuss the chronological writings of the "30 yeares professour of Ebrew". John Lightfoot, the most distinguished Cambridge Rabbinic scholar of the seventeenth century, mentions the opposition which Broughton's *Concent of Scripture* encountered "from Doctour Raynolds in Oxford[2] and Master Lively in Cambridge who both lectured against it. . . . It was some honour, to have two Opponents of so great Name, and Worth and Learning: but the greater their repute, and that most deservedly, the greater was his disadvantage that had to deal with them."[3] It is characteristic of Lively that he refrains from personal attacks upon Broughton, and contents himself with a scholarly rebuttal of erroneous opinions and interpretations, in marked contrast to the treatment he received from Broughton. His tone is always dignified, his language moderate— he pursues a middle way between frequent outbursts against the "papist adversaries" and deep personal regret at having to oppose the views of Joseph Scaliger whom he loved, and for whose scholarship he had the highest respect.[4] Protestants and Catholics fought relentlessly for the truth of Scripture, as they understood it from their particular point of view, and invective and abuse were employed as legitimate weapons on both sides. Lively prefers, on the whole, to hit out with well thought out arguments based upon linguistic and historical evidence skilfully chosen. But in face of their stubborn insistence on the Latin Bible as authentic Scripture his animosity is aroused, particularly against Genebrard, himself a noted Hebrew scholar, of whom he could write in connection with an incorrect Latin translation of Ps. xxxviii. 18—"how can it be justified by any but by a Genebrard who to please the pope can make all things of any thinge". Again, after a careful examination of the Latin Psalter[5] with its many mistranslations, the controversialist in him bursts out—"whosoever in reason and equitie considereth these places in the psalmes which I have brought to declare the corrupcon and naughtines of the Latin text, I doubt not but he will thinke we have just cause to travell further for a better translation and judge those exsamples

NOTE 4 *continued*
il est assez inutile dans de simple Remarques sur l'Ecriture, de faire la Critique des Versions de Pagnin, de Castalio, de Tremellius et de quelques autres Traducteurs modernes."

His strictures on Lively for parading his classical knowledge reveal the different attitude and consequent shifting of emphasis among Biblical scholars of the last quarter of the seventeenth century. They were Hebraists, and in the case of Pococke, noted Arabists. They rarely illustrated a point or meaning with quotations from Classical authors, and certainly did not attribute any authority to them.

[1] In his *Advertisement* (see p. 101 below), and in his *Principal Positions for groundes of the holy Bible*. . . .

[2] See Rosenthal, *Rashi*, p. 143, and pp. 162-4.

[3] Preface to his edition of Broughton's Works, 1662.

[4] "Joseph Scaliger a man of rare giftes, a great light of this age . . . speaking of Xerxes his passage into Greece *De Emendatione Temporum, Liber V* is so uncertaine and wavering in this poynt, that it is hard to finde in what iudgment he rested" . . . "For the truths sake I may not here omit one error of J. S., notwithstanding the reuerence and loue which I beare him, in regarde of his fruitfull paynes employed to the benefite of learning, and advancement of knowledge, whereby he hath well deserued of God his Church". [*A True Chronologie* . . . , p. 83 and 138.] We need only compare Broughton's criticism of Lively with these, and we have the measure of both, Broughton and Lively!

[5] Fol. 92a.

to be sufficient witnesses to show and testify as well the pitifull follie of ignorant and unskilfull papists as the great impudence and consciencles bouldnes of the learneder sort of them who seeing the truth like Giants sett themselves against it".[1]

In many ways he is typical of his age, very much alive to the religious issues as they affect the intellectual life of the nation no less than of the individual, especially the student, and determined to play his part as a responsible scholar. Steeped in the tradition of Classical Learning, he tries to apply it to his own subject and to use it for the better understanding of the Bible. In addition, he absorbed the writings and teachings of the Church Fathers, especially Jerome and Augustine. With this twofold tradition he blended the new knowledge which the Hebraists among the Reformers had been assimilating since the turn of the century, centred in the *Hebraica Veritas*. This battle-cry of the Reformers led to a new approach to the Old Testament, as is well known, and through that to a remarkable revival of Hebrew studies. These studies, it is true, were pursued in the first place for Christian ends, but the opening up of Rabbinic sources on lines similar to, though not identical with, the re-emergence of Classical texts, resulted in a more scientific method of Biblical study, with the help of grammar and lexicography. Needless to say, the Hebrew Language was studied because it was the original tongue of Holy Writ. Mastery of it made possible not only a better, but the only exact and true, understanding of the Word of God. It must also not be forgotten that the Catholics participated prominently in this revival of Hebrew studies, and were equally instrumental in making available, in Hebrew editions and in Latin translations, important post-Biblical Hebrew texts. But the principal impetus came from Elias Levita's grammatical, lexicographical, and Massoretic studies, partly made accessible to Christian Hebraists, both on the continent and in this country, by the translations of Sebastian Muenster.[2] Lively grew up in a tradition of Hebrew learning carefully planted and nurtured by such noted Hebraists as Fagius, Tremellius and Cevallerius, all of whom taught in the University of Cambridge.[3] His immediate predecessor, Thomas Wakefield, of Trinity College, also deserves mention in this connection.

It is only natural that the coming together of such varied traditions, each originating in such a diverse spiritual environment, has at times a rather curious, though none the less fascinating, result, and is more a delight for the cultural historian than an eye-opener for the Hebrew scholar. This is particularly striking in Lively's grammatical work, the unpublished *Commentationes in Martinium*.[4] It is more appropriate in his chronological-historical writings, where it is intentional, for Lively, following the lead of Jerome and Augustine, justifies the study and use of secular writers, especially the Classical authors. Before giving examples, he states in general terms what will even to-day be considered most apposite—"I must needes thereof greatly commend the wisdome of our forefathers, in ordering our universities. Where young scholleirs are first trained up in the studies of humanity before they enter into God his

[1] Fol. 98a.
[2] See Rosenthal, *Muenster*, p. 358, with n. 26.
[3] See n. 1, p. 96.
[4] See n. 1, p. 95.

schoole: that by that meanes comming furnished, and ready stored with many helps from their former learning, they may find a more easie waye and speedy course in that most graue race of divine knowledge, which is yet behinde [sic!] for them to runne. And surely so it is; and every one shall finde the experience hereof in himselfe. It is not to be spoken, how much and how cleare light, the diligent study and reading of Latin and Greeke writers; yeeld to the knowledge of holy scripture."[1] Of his examples at least one should be mentioned. As an illustration for Baal-zebub, the god of Ekron, he quotes Pliny, Pausanias and Solinus, who tell how the Eleans brought a sacrifice to Myagrus or Jupiter apomyios in order to rid themselves of flies. His summing up is equally instructive—"These writers then for many partes of Scripture are diligently to be sought into, and not as some rash braines imagine, to bee cast away as unprofitable in the Lordes schoole house: but especially for *Daniell* above all. In other places they may seem profitable: but heere they are necessary even by Hieroms judgment."[2] He will, therefore, use them as helps in the interpretation of Dan. ix. 24—27. This interpretation turns on the meaning of "weeks". "To the finding out hereof two thinges are most requisite: the one is a iust account of the times; the other, a true interpretation of the wordes in the originall tongue. If we faile in either of these, there is no hope to knowe what Daniell meant by his weekes: For neither good interpretation alone is enough without exact chronologie, nor this without the other serveth much to purpose."[3] It will readily be granted that these are sound principles of exegesis. Their application was called for by Mathew Beroald's erroneous exposition. He writes the correct exposition in English for "the upholding of truth, to the good of my countrie, and the benefitte of Christ his Church amongst us".[4] Just as the Hebrew Bible as a whole is the pure, authentic truth of God, so, for Lively, is the date of Daniel and of his prophecy as stated in the beginning of the book of Daniel "fortelling the coming of Jesus Christ, the Lord of life aboue 500 yeres before".[5] Of his very full explanation of the meaning of Daniel's weeks—the bane of all commentators—only the briefest account can be given here. We have to distinguish between a philological explanation of the word *shābhūʿa*, meaning either a week of seven days, or, as in Gen. xxix. 27, seven years, which enables him to arrive at the figure of 490 years, and a theological, chiefly christological, interpretation, with the help of other prophecies from the O.T. and also of N.T. passages. A similar example is his meaning "governour" for *māshīaḥ*, rather than Jesus Christ. He quotes in support of the general meaning "anointed" governor, or king, or priest, the mediæval Jewish exegetes Saadyah, Rashi, and Ibn Ezra. Another pillar in his defence are the Hebrew accents. He pleads their value for the right understanding of Scripture, and shows how interpreters get into difficulties and arrive at wrong conclusions if they ignore them. A case in point is the *'athnāḥ* under *shibhʿāh* in Dan. ix. 25, "which maketh onlie seven weekes, that

---

[1] *A True Chronologie*, p. 15.
[2] *Ibid.*, p. 22.
[3] *Ibid.*, p. 27.
[4] Dedicatory Epistle to Archbishop Whitgift.
[5] A Maccabean date would have been quite unthinkable for him. He was an unquestioning believer in the divinely revealed truth of every word of Holy Writ.

is 49 yeres distance from the commandment to Messias in plaine speech; so that it cannot bee applied to our blessed Saviour without straying and wresting which they who so understand it of Christ Jesus are driven unto. They are faine to use chopping and changing, adding and taking away, contrarie to the expresse commandement of God (in Deut. iv. 2): For first, whereas the original text after these words seaven weekes hath a rest, yea that rest which is usuall in the middest of a sentence, to signifie a pause after halfe the verse now alreadie ended: this pause by them is taken away, and the wordes without anie rest at all continued with the next following." He then takes up his opponents' charge that he makes too much of these "distinctions and rests", and says in conclusion—"Though all this were graunted, and though there were no vowels nore pointes at all, yet euen the uerie manner of the speech itselfe were enough to reproue their interpretation: for who euer read in the Hebrew Bible this kinde of speech; seven and threescore, and two for threescore and nine? It is not the custome of the holie Ghost to speake after that manner. If all the Hebrew Scripture from the beginning of *Genesis* to the end of *Malachie* be sought throughout, no one cleare example of the like can be founde."[1] In another passage he sums up his position in this matter thus—"Marke the wordes, consider their order and weigh well the rests. As I finde in the Hebrew so I have Englished, that is, the truthe of interpretation, be it understood as it may."[2]

It is convenient to deal here with Broughton's attack upon Lively, since it concerns mainly the interpretation of Daniel. "Master Lively", he tells us, "thirty yeares an Ebrew professour in Cambridge, denying that Duke accents give a noble distinction to the construction, perverteth Gabriels speech, *Daniel* 9, against all Christianitie, and against all Christian Hebrews, unto Judaisme so farre that he denyed any time for our Lords birth, baptism, or death to be told there, and continued sacrifice lawfullnesse, untill Jerusalem was destroyed.[3] None that ever was a Christian, saving Julian the Apostate, did so afore. Yet he was highly commended in the BB [Bishops'] libell four times nipping the Scottish mist.... Master Livelies terrour of thirty yeares profession made some learned BB commend his Judaisme and deniall of the Gospell by publick authoritie, and to triumph, how their own translation... and their owne exposition and all Christianitie was confuted. The king Athnach, even one Ebrew accent, for want of right skill, drove the thirty years professour in Hebrew and his Commenders to this great wisdome even by their authoritie to publish the defamation of their own truth in a very high degree." Space forbids to add all the other utterances of Broughton against Lively's interpretation of Daniel. Many pages of his queer pamphlet entitled *An Advertisement of Corruption in our Handling of Religion. To the Kinges Majesty* (1605), are devoted to a reckoning with Lively, especially disapproving of his chronology of the Persian kings employing Olympiads and using "auncientes rejected most strongly by both Testamentes, true old Greekes,

---
[1] *À True Chronologie*, p. 203.
[2] *Ibid.*, p. 171.
[3] Lightfoot's edition, p. 665. This sweeping allegation does not bear scrutiny. See p. 100, where Lively, as well as on the very title page, makes Daniel foretell the coming of Jesus Christ. But he denies that his Passion is so foretold, and that sacrifices must cease with Jesus' death.

and all Churches now".[1] Three times in different tirades Broughton demands that Lively "must recant". Once he appeals to the king himself—"And your M[ajesty] must compel him and his commender[2] to recant".

But one point of dispute between them is important enough to be discussed at greater length, since it raises a wider problem which was hotly debated in the sixteenth century and is still unsolved to-day. It is well known as "The Battle of the Vowel points".[3] Broughton devotes a chapter of his pamphlet to it under the heading "Of perverting the holy text of the Old Testament in 848 places", dealing with the closely related question of *Qerē* and *Kethībh*. He attacks David Qimḥi, the mediæval Jewish grammarian, lexicographer, and commentator, for his assumption, made in the preface to his commentary on Joshua, that the 848 marginal readings represent corrections of a corruption of the Hebrew text which took place during the Babylonian captivity, citing in his support Elias Levita and Barbinel [Abravanel].[4] We cannot enter here into this controversy, important as it is, not only from the purely scholarly point of view, but also because it has carried confusion into the Protestant camp, and seriously undermined their otherwise unassailable position and stand on the *Hebraica Veritas*. Suffice it, therefore, to confine ourselves to the issue between Broughton and Lively. The former writes thus about the latter—"Yet a learned man of Cambridge, M. Edw. Lively, maketh the margent the right reading, for Dan. 9 penned after *Babell* fell. . . . That his dealing is extremely dangerous to the authoritie of Scripture, For if in fiftie two yeares in *Babell* after the Temples fall, Moses and the Prophets had so many corruptions, in longer tyme more would grow. The learned man dealt here not learnedly. A professor of Ebrew 30 yeares might have shewed that the text was still most exact . . . and he should not weaken the glory of GODS Providence, whose watchfulnes hath preserved every letter of all the holy Hebrew that his Prophetes wrot for the use of all ages. . . . " Since Lively died in 1605, he could not defend himself against this misrepresentation of his views. He had expressed himself quite unequivocally concerning the purity and excellence of the original Hebrew truth in his treatise *On the Translation of the Ould Testament*.[5] For the question of vowel points in general, and *Qerē* and *Kethībh* in particular, we quote from this treatise the following statements—"This in the beginning I must advertise the reader of, that when we

---

[1] Other accusations are to be found on pp. 15, 19, 20 ff, 27, 29–31, 33 ff, such as— "Mast. Lively hath drawne Olympiads into our Ecclesiasticall authorities to make us a skoff to all Jewes of the world. . . . And Mr. L. never heard of any Jew that more regarded Olympiades, then we regard Lucianes true stories." Is this perhaps an echo of Muenster's reference in his comment on Ex. xiv, 27 to "fabulas Luciani"? See Rosenthal, *Muenster*, p. 359, n. 28. In another place Broughton charges him with "miraculous ignorance in Hebrew".

[2] Presumably Archbishop Whitgift.

[3] For a good discussion see C. D. Ginsburg's Introduction to his edition of Levita's *Masōreth Hammasōreth*, 1867, especially pp. 45–61.

[4] Levita deals with this assumption on pp. 106 ff. But he ridicules Abravanel's arguments as mostly untenable and shallow, a verdict which seems hardly just. Broughton refers to Abravanel's Commentary on Ezekiel. It should be Jeremiah. See also Rosenthal, *Muenster*, p. 354 f with n. 13 f.

[5] See n. 1, p. 95. Since it remained in manuscript, Broughton may never have seen it. But there is, as far as I am aware, no place in Lively's published writings which would warrant Broughton's baseless charges.

affirme the Hebrew booke [in the margin: bible] to be the authenticall trueth of the ould testament we do not mean them as they are now printed and pointed as though we thought nothing amisse therein, neither in letter nor pointe, or we thought it unlawfull to departe from them as Gregory Mart: affirmeth writing that we thinke the Hebrew that now is and as it is now pointed with vowells to be the true authenticall scripture which the holy ghost did first putt into the penns of those sacred writers."[1] He does not pronounce on the origin and date of the vowel points but, as is evident from this quotation, claims the right to disregard the Massoretic vocalisation if such a departure helps towards a better understanding of the Word of God. Tremellius, whom he esteemed highly, and Calvin are quoted as having introduced changes based on old manuscripts. But he vigorously refuted the charge brought against the Jews of having altered and falsified the Hebrew Bible. He commends the Jews for the care bestowed upon the preservation of the original text, and tries to explain—apart from the 848 instances of *Qerē* and *Kethībh* taken over from Elias Levita[2]—that neither *Tiqqūn Sōpherīm* nor *'Iṭṭūr Sōpherīm* mean a real change or alteration in these words[3]—"Those 17 places are recited in the smaler masoreth in the beginning of the booke of nombers. Of the 18th there is no mencon made which hath bred controversie which it should be my judgment is that it is in 10th verse of the ffirst chapter of Micheas where this reading I have rowled my selfe in the dust is said by the scribes to have bin thus changed and altered as now it is read roule thy selfe in the dust." He quotes "Aben Ezra that those places be now as they were at the first without any alteracon [see on Job xxxii. 3 and xii. 12]. Nor does R. Jacob in his Preface to the Rabbinic Bible believe anie change to have bin made in thos places by the Jewes." "According to the *Tishbī* of Elias Levita the scribes decreed that this should be the right reading of these places", he goes on to say. Therefore Levita thought *Tiqqūn Sōpherīm*, the ordinance of the scribes, "is meant to prevent an errour and doubt which might arise, just as the four words called *'Iṭṭūr Sōpherīm* that is that the scribes taking away objected also against the Jewes to argue their falsehood as though they had rased something out of their holy authenticall Bible but the trueth is they were called so not because anie iote or title of the holy text was taken awaye but to signify that certaine superfluous letters which upon mere coniecture by some were added to the originell should be putt out as in the 36 psalme where it is said thy Justice is like the mountains of God, thy Judgments as it were a great deepe, some thinking the conjunction copulative to be wanting in the later part of the sentens expressed the same for thy Judgments reading and thy Judgments as it were a great deepe. Heere therfor to correct that errour and to teach us that this sentence may stand well enough without that conjunction annexed the masoreth set these words in the margent *Iṭṭūr Sōpherīm* that is a detraction of the scribes as Rabi Nathan in his booke called Aruc declareth."[4]

---

[1] Fol. 29b.
[2] *Loc. cit.*, p. 115. *Tiqqūn Sōpherīm* from his *Tishbī*, p. 269 (Basle ed., 1557).
[3] Fol. 182 f. Originally the number varied between 17 and 18. The 18 are reproduced conveniently in J. Levy, *Neuhebr. u. Chald. Wörterb. über die Talm. und Midr.*, iv. p. 663 f. Lively's own supposition does not seem convincing.
[4] Basle ed., 1598, p. 112a.

Jewish themes

We pass now to a brief consideration of Lively as a grammarian. Though his notes on Martinius' *Hebrew Grammar*[1] do not reveal an original linguist, they do betray a thorough grasp of the varied problems arising out of the peculiarities of the Hebrew consonants and vowels, of etymology and elementary syntax. Lively draws, much more than Martinius, who states in his preface his indebtedness to David Qimḥi, on this dominant grammarian, and on the grammars of Abraham de Balmes and Elias Levita. He uses Qimḥi's *Mikhlōl* no less than the principal commentaries, especially those of Abraham ibn Ezra, expresses high regard for Junius Drusius, his teacher, Mercier, Cevallerius, Tremellius, Muenster, Calvin and Erasmus. Along with these authorities he goes to Julius Scaliger and Classical writers for grammatical terms and general linguistic problems, to which he correlates those peculiar to the Hebrew idiom. Last but not least, he brings his practical mind, trained on the actual Hebrew O.T., to bear on the clarification and amplification of the rather cryptic exposition of Martinius, who rarely goes beyond a sort of paradigm.

His recourse to Classical authors is naturally due to his upbringing, and is characteristic, as we remarked above, of his age. Partly he took his cue from Martinius himself. When he finds that a particular question needs special attention, he refers to others who had dealt with it, for example, to Reuchlin for the musical use of pauses, "de quo usu docte scripsit Reuchlinus".

On the whole he is justly critical of Martinius, although his *Hebrew Grammar* enjoyed great popularity, having gone through several editions. In discussing Martinius' "at *beneth*, pro quo est *bath*, facit *bānōth*," Lively remarks—"Sed ego potius existimo cum doctissimo Aben Ezra in comment. in 2 Exod. in singulari forma esse *banah*, unde pluralis regulariter banoth. Nam a masc. Ben filio fit regulariter Bana, unde Banoth. Si quis quaerat cur Hebraei Bath pro Bana usurpantur Respondet Aben Ezra ad vitandam ambiguitatem vocabularum. Nam est etiam verbum quod significat intellexit foemina."[2] Again, he objects to Martinius' statement that *māgūr* can have a plural of the first or second declination, for "magur tantum habet megurim: nam meguroth venit a megurah".[3] While he has not emancipated himself from classical grammatical method and terminology, he does stress against Martinius the difference between the Greek and Hebrew Dual.

The same soundness and competence can be discerned in his Commentary on the first five of the twelve Minor Prophets. While he freely acknowledges his indebtedness to earlier commentators like Drusius and Mercier, and to the translation of Tremellius, he does not blindly follow their translations and interpretations. These Prophets had been commented on by Mercier and by Drusius, and others, and we can therefore assess Lively's own work by a comparison with that of his predecessors. At once the reader is struck by the careful approach of

---

[1] See n. 4, p. 97. Lively used the Paris edition of 1580, as is clear from his quotations with page references.

[2] Fol. 33a; Ibn Ezra on Ex. ii. 2.

[3] Fol. 33b; we should read *māgōr*. There are other instances of his critical attitude to Martinius, e.g., 15b "nusquam reperita syllaba unius literae". Again, 59b, 60b, 78b. On '*asīthīnī*, which Martinius takes to mean *feci me*, Lively, Ezek. xxix. 3, says—"nam affixum quod hic adhibetur Iae personae, non retinet suam propriam significationem, sed est pro *li* mihi, ut doctissimus Tremellius, et alij interpretantur . . ." (75b).

Edward Lively: Cambridge Hebraist

Lively, by his painstaking labours to get as near to *Hebraica Veritas* as possible, chiefly with the help of Jewish commentators. Yarchius [Rashi] and Ibn Ezra are most frequently drawn upon, together with Qimḥi. Levita and Abraham de Balmes are also quoted, the latter once against Tremellius (on Hos. xi. 10). Muenster's influence is not apparent, except perhaps in some christological interpretations (e.g. Hos. xi. 1). Lively sometimes operates with interchange of radicals—for example *resīsīm* (Am. vi. 11) is equated with *reṣīṣīm*, the interchange between *sāmekh* and *ṣādē* being justified from Qimḥi's comment on this verse, and from his *Book of Roots*. Similarly in Hos. v. 11 he regards *ṣāw* as the equivalent of *shāw'*, basing his opinion on a remark of Rashi's on Nah. iii. 19. In fact it is in v. 18 that Rashi explains *nāphōshū* by *nāphōṣu*, since *zayin*, *shīn*, *sāmekh*, and *ṣādē* can all be interchanged. Broughton takes our Commentator severely to task for this, devoting a special chapter (8) of his *Advertisement* to it— *Of Tzau, an Ebrew worde in Hosea, rashly blamed*. Again he misrepresents Lively thus—"M. Lively writeth that the text is corrupt. Shau by him it should be. No Ebrew told him so, only he told himselfe so. By equall authoritie he might make a new Bible of his owne head." There is no word in Lively that the text is corrupt, and Rashi is after all an "Ebrew"! On the other hand, Edward Pococke quotes Lively's note in full in his own commentary on Hosea and adds—"according to the opinion of a very learned man, Mr. Lively, [there] seems to be no necessary proof at all [that *ṣāw* should be read as *shāw'*], since it may have the same meaning as *shāw'*".[1]

We consider next the sources Lively used and skilfully worked into his *Chronologia seu Notitia Temporum*, a major work which has remained in manuscript like his important treatise on the translation of the O.T. In its plan and execution it follows in some respects Joseph Scaliger's[2] *De Emendatione Temporum*, though Lively reserves for himself the right to independent judgment,

---

[1] P. 273. There is hardly a page in this almost 800 folio pages long Commentary without a reference to Lively, usually referred to as "a very learned man". On VII. 12 (p. 357) he calls him "a learned country-man of our own; taking the word in that signification also" [*shēma'*="report"]. The same applies to Pococke's Commentary on Joel. E.g., on iii. 9–11, he states—"I think therefore the plainest way to be that which the learned Mr. Lively takes". One example at least of Lively's peculiar way of comment must be quoted. On *qīqāyōn* (Jonah iv. 6) he has an extensive note referring first to Junius Drusius. The latter already quotes Dioscorides' *kiki*, Talmudic *qīq*, and Jerome. Lively gives Jerome's comment in full, comparing *qīqāyōn* with the Arabic "elcheroa. Idem affirmavit magister Samuel Hophnides Hebraeus, teste hic Quimquio, herbam esse *hanniqrā' bileshōn 'arabhī al kerwa*[*khirwa'* in Arabic]. Then he quotes "Talmud *beshemen qīq*. Nam *qīq* eo in loco [it is, though he does not say so, *B.T. Shabbath* 21a] idem valere quod *qīqāyōn* author est eruditus quidam Lakis". [R. Resh Laqish]. After that he quotes Classical authors—Dioscorides, IV, 158, Plinius, XV, 7, Herodotus [II, 94], ends up with Qimḥi (who *ad loc.* quotes the Talmudic discussion without source), and goes on to say that their descriptions do in fact fit this passage in Jonah. This is typical of him. He follows previous commentators, but where they say Dioscorides only, he gives the passage as well, and enlarges by adding Pliny and Herodotus, as well as the lengthy comment of Qimḥi in full and, in the end, achieves his purpose, which is to show that Classical authors, Church Fathers, Jewish exegetes, and contemporary Hebraists all agree in giving the word the required meaning.

[2] He argues with him about the chronology of kings Josiah and Jehoiachin. In another place (44) he quotes a passage from *T. B. Rosh hashshanah* as an argument against assigning a custom to Seleucid times and for a Babylonian/Persian date.

Jewish themes

and sometimes he contradicts Scaliger as he did in his *True Chronologie of the Times of the Persian Monarchie*. He is also indebted to Alfarghānī, who is dependent on Ptolemy's *Almagest*. Alfarghānī (Alfraganus in Latin) has been interpreted by Jacob Anatoli, who made a Hebrew translation out of a Latin one, but corrected it from the Arabic original, adding substantially to it, particularly on matters of the Jewish Calendar. This Hebrew version has been commented on by Christmann, who is quoted by Lively. The work is a mixture of Calendar, Chronological Tables and Chronicle, and a large number of authors (Classical, early Christian, Hellenistic, Jewish and contemporary) are incorporated in a work which, under the skilful hands of a purposeful scholar, became quite his own. To mention only a few principal sources, there is Eusebius, First Book of Maccabees, Josephus, Philo, Diodorus Siculus, not to speak of Xenophon and Herodotus. Josephus is used as a reliable source for Roman history no less than for the history of the Second Temple and the time of Jesus. Lively starts from the creation of the world and reckons 1656 years till the Flood, like *Sēder ʿŌlām Rabbā* and *Zūṭā* and Abraham b. Dā'ūd's *Sēpher Haqqabbālāh*. The prophets Jeremiah and Ezekiel are also historical sources for Lively, like the books of Samuel and Kings. While he is critical of Scaliger and his English contemporaries, especially of Broughton, whose *Sēder ʿŌlām* comes in for frequent censure, he gives unqualified credence to the mediæval Hebrew compilations just mentioned. Elias Levita's *Masōreth Hammasōreth* most likely acquainted him with these Hebrew Chronicles, and to some extent he was dependent in the use of his sources on what was available in print. Abraham Zakkut's *Sēpher Yūḥāsīn* is also referred to once. If one compares his own "Chronicle" with the works of Scaliger, Christmann, and later, with Ussher, one is at once struck by the extensive and full documentation in Lively. He follows up statements and opinions, traces them to their source and then uses that, and other more relevant sources, for his own purpose judiciously, and, as far as Hebrew sources are concerned, most accurately.[1] It is surprising to find him quoting from various tractates of

---

[1] He distinguishes between Josephus and Josippon (quoted as Gorionides). Abraham ibn Dā'ūd's *Sēpher Sēder Haqqabbālāh* is mostly quoted correctly as "Abraham Davidis filius", or, "Abraham Davison" in his *A True Chronologie*, or, "R. Abraham in sua Cabbalah", without page references, however. Once in this book (ed. Neubauer, p. 66) a quotation is attributed to him in the words "in Hebraice scripta R. Abrahamis historia legimus". Such a reference is usually concerned with the same author's *Dibhrē malkhē yisrā'ēl bebhēth hashshēnī* which is printed in the first edition of Mantua 1513, following on immediately on the *Sēpher Sēder Haqqabbālāh*. It is not edited critically and is missing from Neubauer's edition. I have verified several quotations in the Mantua edition and in the Prague edition of 1795. On fol. 48c, e.g., Lively refers to it as "R. Abraham in sua de rebus Judaicis historia", or "R. Abraham in sua historia Hebraica de rebus Judaeorum conscripta". The *Sēpher Sēder Haqqabbālāh* is once quoted as covering the time from the Exodus to the destruction of the First Temple. Because Lively usually translates Hebrew titles accurately into Latin—Talmudical tractates are thus quoted—*De Idolatria, De Tabernaculis*, etc.—it did not occur to me at first to look for the continuation *Dibhrē malkhē yisrā'ēl*, and so identify the quotations. The application of Daniel's prophecy to the period of the Second Temple, and the discussion of Jesus, no doubt appealed to Lively, who treated this and the other Jewish authors on a par with, if not as superior to, Classical authors and Church Fathers. See Elbogen, *Encyc. Jud.*, I, pp. 438–444, on Abr. b. Dā'ūd's historical writings. Lively also refers once to Abr. b. Ḥiyya, and quotes *Megillath Ta'anīth. Sēder ʿŌlām Rabbā* is quoted by its Hebrew or Latin title, "in maiore suo Chronico", with the number of the chapter.

Edward Lively: Cambridge Hebraist

the Babylonian, and also the Jerusalem, Talmud by chapter numbers, a practice not known from other writers, as far as we are aware, in the sixteenth century. The Talmud is quoted in connexion with sacrifices, especially on the Eve of Passover, followed by a lengthy discussion of the meaning of ʿerebh occasioned by the death of Jesus. Incidentally, it is worth noting that he quotes from an unexpurgated text of T.B. Sanhedrin ch. 6 (fol. 43a): "Jesum fuisse suspensum beʿerebh pessaḥ inquiunt Talmudici in parasceve pashatis ʿerebh eam ibi positam esse pro eo quod in evangelio Johannis παρασκευή dicitur." The same passage is quoted once more in Hebrew and Latin, against Broughton. Rashi and Ibn Ezra are adduced with comments to prove the meaning "eve" and its actual duration in hours, and in confirmation Maimonides' Mishnēh Tōrāh is repeatedly cited. Chapter references are given, and the Hebrew text is followed by an exact Latin translation.[1] Lively goes on to discuss the occurrence of Pentecost in relation to Passover, mentions the counting of the ʿOmer, and shows a good knowledge of Jewish feast days, of their appropriate sacrifices at their appropriate times, and of the Jewish Liturgy. He never omits to quote Talmudic texts, Maimonides, Rashi, Ibn Ezra, or Qimḥi in support of his views, and in order to refute attacks upon the veracity of the Rabbis of the Talmud. Often Josephus is employed as a witness. Apart from his interest in Passover on account of Jesus' death, he deals, as far as Jewish matters are concerned, mainly with problems of the Jewish year, discusses such terms as mōledheth and ʿibbūr in their philological meaning and their significance for the Jewish Calendar,[2] and treats at great length of the Sabbatical year (shemiṭṭāh) and Jubilee (yōbhēl), mainly in order to be able to compute the exact date of the destruction of the Second Temple. His sources are Maimonides' "tr. de Jubilaeis, cap. 10"[3] and "massekheth ʿArākhīn": hoc est exitus septimi anni".[4] How careful he was is apparent from this statement—"Objici hic potest quod R. Abraham in sua de rebus Judaicis historia[5] hanc templi desolationem refert non ad 9ᵃᵐ sed ad 10ᵃᵐ mensij praedicti", followed by the Hebrew text, the English translation of which runs—"and the Romans set fire to the Temple and captured it in the fifth month on the tenth day". He shows, with the help of Josephus, Bell. Jud., vii, 9, that the outer temple was burnt on the 9th Ab and the inner temple on the 10th, for

---

[1] Qorban Pesaḥ ch. 1, paras. 1, 3, 4, and ch. 10, para. 12. In his quotation from ch. 1, para. 5, the word ḥāmēṣ is inadvertently omitted. (For the Talmudical passage, cp. R. Travers Herford, Christianity in Talmud and Midrash, 1906, pp. 78–90). His evidence for the correct interpretation of ʿerebh is impressive. In addition to Maimonides, quoted as "R. Moses filius Maimonis" or Rambam, he mentions Ibn Ezra, Rashi, on Ex. xii. 6, "David Kimchi in suo lexico Hebraeo", R. Moses Nachmanides, Rabbi Nathan "in vetusto quodam Commentario dicto Mechilta" about the time between the two vespers, and goes on "item R. Simeon filius Jochaj in lib. antiquo Zohar". As regards the Passover eve he quotes, apart from Maimonides, Rashi on Deut. xvi. 2, 4–9, Ibn Ezra on Lev. xii. 3 for a special meaning and application of sunset, B.T. Abodah Zarah, ch. 1. To quote further references is not possible for lack of space, except for ʿarūbhthā in the Syriac New Testament. The relevant passages in Lively are fols. 40, 42a, 43 f.
[2] Fols. 3 f, 44.
[3] Fol. 48c. He even cites Joseph Caro's interpretation of Maimonides' meaning, printed in the margin of the Mishnēh Tōrāh, as confirmation.
[4] Fol. 12b.
[5] Abr. b. Dā'ūd's Dibhrē malkhē yisrā'ēl, Mantua ed., five pages from the end; p. 91a in Prague ed.

which he finds further proof in the fact, recorded by the Jews themselves,[1] that the destruction took place when Sabbath ended. "Exitus enim Sabbati dicitur illud tempus quod finem habet feriae 7ae et initium primae ... vel 9° die Ab desinente, vel 10° ineunte templum inflammatum fuisse." These examples must suffice to establish Lively's competence in the skilful application of Rabbinic texts in a way not usually found in the sixteenth century. Lightfoot and Pococke, almost a hundred years later, made extensive use of these texts which they provided with an English translation.[2] Lively's knowledge was not as wide as theirs—he had no Arabic, as Pococke—but his technical mastery of the texts, his understanding of them, and the use he put them to, earn him the reputation of the finest English Hebraist at the close of the sixteenth century.

Lastly, we have to examine his spirited defence of the Hebrew O.T. which is extant in the Cambridge MS. Add. 3066. The dedicatory preface to Sir Francis Walsingham already sounds the key note—"It is incredible that a translation should be better than the first originall scripture". In a translation "the fancies, errors and follies of a mortall man are many times sette downe instead of the truth of the everliving God". The Hebrew text is "a fountaine wherin the most cleare and perfect trueth of the ould testament is conteyned". The treatise proper starts with the bold assertion that Holy Scripture is "sett above all other learning and wisdome whatsoever or whersoever either in Greece or Egypt or Persia or Chaldæa or India". As proof is cited Deut. iv. 6, 8. He counters the Papists' charge against the Protestants of changing the Holy Scriptures, or omitting from them, or adding to them, by the accusation that they themselves leave out the Second Commandment of the Decalogue because it runs counter to their "Imago Worship".

Then he defends the Canonical Books of the O.T. as the Jews regard them, basing his views upon Josephus' *Contra Ap.* 1 and Levita's third preface to his *Masōreth Hammasōreth*.[3] Philo's *De Legatione ad Caium* and *De exitu Israelitarum ex Aegypto*, 1, prove "that the Jewes being more zealous of their lawes than other nations, are ready to suffer many deaths before they will derogate anything from their law, or do contrary unto it".[4] He stresses the care for every letter of Scripture bestowed upon the Hebrew Bible by the Jews,[5] and quotes St. Augustine's description of them as "capsarios et librarios Christianorum". Neither Christ nor the apostles mention any of the (apocryphal) books. The learned Christian Fathers provide further evidence for their rejection, and finally Nicolas of Lyra and Paul Burgensis.[6] The first Papist objection is thus refuted that "we have mangled god his word and cutt away many godly

---

[1] See n. 4, p. 107.
[2] Lightfoot's *Horae Hebraicae et Talmudicae*, and Pococke's *Porta Mosis*, e.g., are important first steps in the systematic opening up of Rabbinic texts for the serious and independent study of Christian scholars.
[3] Ed. Ginsburg, p. 120.
[4] Fol. 11b. A similar statement is made again on fol. 156 in glowing terms.
[5] He quotes from Levita's figures for the number of occurrences of every single letter of the Hebrew alphabet in the O.T.
[6] Much space is devoted to a justification of the Hebrew Canon. See also n. 1, p. 95.

parts of the canonicall and divine scripture".[1] Throughout the treatise evidence is adduced in this sequence—Jews, Jesus, early Fathers, mediæval Fathers, and contemporary Papists.

The second objection concerns the use of the Hebrew and Greek texts (O. and N.T.) instead of the Catholic vulgar Latin version. He sets out to prove that the Hebrew text is "the most true and authenticall scripture of god and the safest rule for interpretation thereof". After that he will prove that neither the LXX nor the Vulgate "doth so purely express the divine and infallible truth of god his holy word. But as well the one as the other in infinit places errounious and faulty. So shall it clearly appeare that we do well in following the Hebrew, and not amisse in refusing those interpretacons."[2] "Only this is that which we stand upon that the Hebrew in those places where no corruption and falshood can be proved ought to be of greatest authority and accompted the undoubted and certaine trueth of the spirit of god to be preferred before any translation whatsoever. . . . But this we shall never obtaine so long as they [our adversaries] thinke their vulgar laten bible according to the decree of the counsell of Trent to be true and authenticall scripture, for that saith one thing, where the Hebrew being pure and faultless saith another " . . . He is firmly convinced that it is "the very word of God and the originall patterne of every translation". "Seeing then the Hebrews had the true authenticall scripture among them and that in their owne tongue it cannot be doubted that the Hebrew text and writing therof was the pure word of god: Againe what writing of god his word can be more divine than that wherof the Inditer was god himself? in his owne words. what more authenticall, then that wherof the prophetts annoynted of god and endued with his spirit were the penners, and as it were his secretaryes and scribes in their owne tongue?"[3] Every interpretation must fully and justly agree with the original text, he avers, and illustrates this axiom with a mistranslation of the LXX in Ps. lxxiv, which was made worse by the Latin translator who used it, having a copy of the LXX in front of him which read καταπαύσωμεν for the already incorrect κατακαύσωμεν "let us burne". The same applies to Jer. xxxi. 12. The best and most accurate translation cannot equal the original word of God, let alone such faulty translations as have just been quoted. He goes on to touch briefly upon the translations of the "Jewish Church" itself, necessitated by long captivity and troubles. And yet, "with great care, studdy and industry they alwaies preserved and held the knowledge of the Hebrew tongue among them by the benefit and help of art and learning . . . and therfore the Hebrew text they placed faire in the midst like a Queene with the translations about it as it were handmaids attending on her." In this context he quotes from Levita the reading of the weekly portion in the synagogues.[4] "And thereupon if I be not deceived first came and sprung the custome of reading 2 lessons in Christian churches on holy dayes . . ."[5]

---

[1] Fol. 28b.
[2] Fol. 29a. b.
[3] Fol. 33a.
[4] Fol. 37b. The number 53 is taken from Levita's *Tishbī* which is incorrect for 54. Lively quotes Acts xiii. 15 in support of this ancient custom.
[5] Fol. 38a.

Jewish themes

Jesus himself quoted Ps. xxii in Hebrew and not in Greek, Matthew likewise adheres to the Hebrew, Origen sets the Hebrew text in the Hebrew character "in the first place as cheife and principall and rule to examine the rest by" in his Hexapla. Jerome and Augustine are important witnesses to the "Hebrew truth".

He now proceeds to inquire whether the same may be said for the LXX and the vulgar Latin. By carefully chosen examples he shows the inadequacy and inaccuracy of the Greek translation. In Gen. v Methuselah is credited by the LXX with having lived fourteen years after the Flood. How is this possible since he was not in the Ark with Noah, asks Lively? "But out of the Hebrew text it had bin easy to have convinced that notable errour." Other examples include Gen. xlvi. 20, 22, 27; Is. xxiv. 23; Ezek. v. 12. In view of these errors he feels constrained to examine the claim that the LXX translators were inspired, and agrees with Aristeas and Josephus that they were not prophets, nor does he credit them with more than the translation of the Pentateuch. In this view he follows Josephus and Philo.[1] He comes to the conclusion that the Protestants are justified in making an English translation from the Hebrew, seeing that Jerome did not slavishly follow the LXX's translation.

His next task is to examine the vulgar Latin version. He begins with Genesis and goes through the whole O.T., analysing and noting all discrepancies. "Thus in the first booke of scripture have bin noted many places more corrupt and faulty in the laten byble then either in the first tongue or many other translations therof...."[2] Only a competent Hebrew scholar could demolish all the inaccurate translations, and only an expert controversialist could choose his arguments so well, especially quoting Catholic authorities against the sole authority of the Vulgate. A notable example is Deut. xii. 15, where he dismisses the Latin as a gloss which would be more suitable in the margin than in the text.[3]

Since the Psalms have great religious value, he devotes much space to their examination, with the result that "in no other parte of the ould scripture faults and errours are so rife, so many so grosse as in this. The cause therof is this that the Latin psalmes were translated into that tongue not out of the Hebrew fountaine but the Greek translacon which is itself full of errours." He cites Catholic objections to the Psalms in Latin, and then gives a number of examples some of which have been already discussed.[4]

He likewise finds much fault with Solomon's writings in the Latin version, which leads him to this verdict—"If the latin version of Solomon's writings were authenticall he would not deserve to be called wise, he which had an understanding hart such as never was before nor after and so large as the sande on the sea shore and which excelled in wisdome all the children of the East,

---

[1] Fol. 62 f.
[2] Fol. 75a.
[3] Fol. 78 f. Among other telling examples we find Nu. xxxvi. 7, with Paul of Burgos as witness against the Vulgate; Jos. xi. 13, 19; Jud. i. 9; I Sam. iii. 3, with Nicolas of Lyra as witness against the Vulgate; Esth. i. 5, and Jb. ii. 21.
[4] Pp. 98, 109.

and all the Egyptians besides .. ."¹ The prophets fare no better under his scrutiny.²

Next, he shows numerous cases in which the Church Fathers themselves quote passages from the O.T. in a Latin translation which differs from the Vulgate. This is clear proof for him that the Vulgate cannot have enjoyed the absolute authority for over a thousand years which the Papists claim for it. His examples range over the whole period of the Latin Church, and include Epistles and Papal decrees. Gildas is quoted to show that in England the Vulgate was not authoritative, as is also evident from quotations used by English divines of the eleventh and twelfth centuries from older Latin versions made from the Greek. By contrast the Hebrew text deserves more authority, seeing that it is much older. But length of use is no argument, for, says he, "No custome ought to prevayle against the trueth of God".³ He stresses that he was driven to pointing out Jerome's errors "by the importunitie of absurd men who abuse his name to maintayne errour against the truth".⁴

Finally, he defends the Jews against Papist accusations of falsification of Scripture. Their whole history and tradition of preserving the text intact speak eloquently against it. In his usual painstaking way he cites Rabbinic sources, Church Fathers, and especially Arias Montanus, in their defence, and finally the Massoretes and their work.⁵ Towards the end of his treatise he returns to the charges Gregory Martin levelled against the Protestants, and refutes them with arguments taken from Catholics who prefer the Hebrew text to the Latin version, notably Pagninus and Pico della Mirandola. He ends up by exclaiming—"Let judgment be given whether we be iustly accused and rayled on by our adversaries or no. In that we leaveing the greeke and latin translacons of the ould Testament flee to the hebrew text for more sounde and perfect knowledge of gods heavenly wisdome... what madness were it to choose the worse and refuse the better?"⁶

If we compare Lively's defence with that of Fulke, a striking difference in scope and treatment emerges. Where Fulke deals with O.T. passages in his *Answers to the Preface* of Gregory Martin's accusation, he covers part of the ground on which Lively, not being concerned with the N.T., concentrates. His argument is sound and convincing. That it is partly identical with that used by Lively is inevitable. But Lively is fuller, and adduces any and every piece of evidence which he can find. Fulke uses both Bomberg Bibles, that edited by Felix Pratensis as well as that edited by Jacob ben Ḥayyim. But Lively gets more out of them, and finds additional proof in Arias Montanus and the Jewish commentators, so that he can sum up the case about $k\bar{a}^{\flat}ar\bar{\imath}$ or $k\bar{a}r\bar{u}$ (Ps. xxii. 17) thus:

---

¹ Fol. 101.
² Is. ii. 22; xxviii. 21; xxxiii. 3. In the last named passage he attacks the Latin translator for following Symmachus who sees in *hāmōn* an angel "which some of the Jewes suppose to be Gabriel the Angell. And so instead of a sounde translation we have a Judaicall fable. . . ." Ezek. viii. 14; xix. 14; Am. i, 1. etc.
³ Fol. 128.
⁴ Fol. 135b.
⁵ See pp. 99ff, 103ff.
⁶ Fol. 226.

"Thus we see that they were and are yet two diverse readings of this place the one, they have pierced, the other, as a lyon, And though I graunt that the later is more usuall and commonly received among the Jewes yet seeing the other which we Christians imbrace being a trueth as reason proveth remaineth still in some hebrew bibles there is no let by this place but that the hebrew text may be called pure and uncorrupt neither do we in translating the right word followe either the Greek word or the Latin but the hebrew text both written and printed in some bookes."[1] Lively defends the Hebrew Truth, not only against Gregory Martin, but against all Catholic adversaries, thus giving his defence a much wider scope and striking power.

Unlike Muenster,[2] he makes no excuses for adducing evidence from Hebrew sources, nor does he find it necessary to apologize for his extensive use of Jewish writers and their works. He is, with very few exceptions, remarkably free from bias against the Jews, whose yeoman service for the cause of God's word he gratefully and gracefully acknowledges. He combines solid and careful learning with sincere faith and a life-long devotion to the service of truth wherever it is to be found.

---

[1] Cp. Fulke, *loc. cit.*, pp. 43 f, 78 f; Lively, 187b.

[2] See Rosenthal, *Muenster*, p. 357 f, with n. 28. As for Lively, see n. 2, p. 111. There is one strong rejection of Jewish interpretation in his *A True Chronologie*, where he reproduces criticism by Pererius and Temporarius, and adds—"All this is true I confesse; the Church of God for other matters is much beholding to the Hebrew Rabbines being great helps unto us for understanding holy scripture in many places, as well of the new testament as the olde: but touching the knowledge of the Persian Empire, wherein they should haue bin most cunning, they were as blinde as beetle...." Josephus is exonerated because he read Latin and Greek histories and is therefore better informed. In conclusion a passage may be quoted from his *On the Translation* . . . , fol. 140b–141—"God has granted helps towards the true understanding of his word in the originall tongues. . . . To this end the knowledge of the Hebrew tongue hath bin to this day continually preserved among the Jewes of whom no smale number have bin converted unto Christianity in sundry ages so that the Church cannot be said to have wanted the knowledge of that tongue yea even such as were never converted have bin ready for gaine and commodity to teach Christians the understanding therof. . . ." One wonders whether he owes his competent knowledge of Hebrew, especially his ability to handle and quote so expertly Talmudical passages and Maimonides, to the services of Philip Ferdinand, a converted Jew who taught Hebrew for a time privately in Cambridge before he removed to Oxford where Dr. John Rainolds favoured him. See Rosenthal, *Rashi*, pp. 148, 164, with notes. Cp. also the careful study by S. Stein, *Phillipus Ferdinandus Polonus* in *Essays in honour of the Very Rev. Dr. J. H. Hertz*, 1943. Be that as it may, the application of his considerable and accurate Hebrew learning is all his own. It establishes his competent scholarship and is unique among Hebraists in sixteenth-century England.

8
ANTI-CHRISTIAN POLEMIC IN MEDIEVAL BIBLE COMMENTARIES

THE rebuttal of christological interpretations of chapters and verses of the Hebrew Bible is not, as might at a first glance appear, a mere by-product of the activity and intention of the medieval Jewish commentators. It is an integral part of their work. Understood as such it represents a positive, important facet of the aim of all Jewish exegesis: to promote the knowledge and understanding of the true meaning of the Bible and thereby to keep the Jewish people, frequently subjected to fierce attack and persecution, alive and strong. The commentators were responsible spiritual leaders who wrote their commentaries in order to strengthen the faith of their generation in the future redemption, and to foster their trust and confidence in the truth of Judaism and in the divine promise of the coming of the Messiah and the Kingdom of God. Rashi, Samuel b. Me'ir (Rashbam), Ibn Ezra, Qimḥi, Moses b. Naḥman (Ramban), Abravanel and many others in Spain, Northern and Southern France and Germany—most of them disciples of Rashi—were alive to the great issues of their time and strove valiantly to maintain a living Judaism. This struggle amidst a hostile, aggressive Christian environment—characterized by the Crusades and religious disputations—was thus a positive force even where defensively arrayed around the plain, literal meaning of the Bible as against christological typology and the allegorizing tendency proferred by contemporary Latin exegetes; it displays itself in a Jewish-Christian dialogue which flourished the more vigorously the more hostile the Church showed itself, and in disputations forced upon an unwilling Jewry. On the other side, the Church tried not only to convert the Jews; it was also combatting Judaizing tendencies discernible in various sects and heresies in its own midst.

Anti-Christian polemic as we find it throughout the medieval commentaries is, in fact, a part of the *wikkūaḥ*-literature of the Middle Ages, especially from the eleventh century onwards. It is bold, fearless and direct; it exhibits the same courage and determination as that exhibited by Jewish representatives at the disputations in Paris, Barcelona and Tortosa. R. Yeḥiel of Paris, Ramban[1], Albo and others asserted the Jewish position freely,

[1] Cf. e.g. I. F. BAER, *le-viqqoreth ha-Wiqquḥim shel rabbi yeḥi'ēl mi-Paris we-shel rabbi mosheh ben naḥman*, Tarbiz ii, 2, pp. 172 f. The disputations

when they refuted the Christian arguments for the divine nature of Jesus and his Messiahship in front of an illustrious assembly of the highest dignitaries of Church and State. They applied the method of *peshaṭ* to the messianic passages in the Hebrew Bible and appealed to past and contemporary history. The same applies to such specific anti-Christian tracts as Joseph Qimḥi's *sēfer ha-Bĕrīth*, Lippmann Mühlhausen's *Sēfer niṣṣāḥōn* and many others. Admittedly it was less dangerous to write about these matters in commentaries. But the Church was not slow in spotting this polemic and subjected the manuscripts of these commentaries to close scrutiny. The offensive passages were made illegible. Yet, sufficient manuscripts escaped the censor, and critical editions of Rashi, Rashbam, Abraham ibn Ezra, Ramban and others, based on such manuscripts, enable us today to correlate this polemic with its authors' positive exposition of the Bible and to appreciate the living issues reflected in medieval exegesis[2]. It is clear that it was

have been thoroughly investigated by BERNHARD BLUMENKRANZ in a number of comprehensive studies, as e.g.: *Die jüdischen Beweisgründe im Religionsgespräch mit den Christen in den christlich-lateinischen Sonderschriften des 5. bis 11. Jahrhunderts* (*Theologische Zeitschrift* iv, 2, 1948, pp. 119-147). The second part of this basic study deals with the Jewish arguments as found in these tracts. Also *Altercatio Aecclesiae contra Synagogam* (Strasbourg 1954). He stresses the importance of exegesis in this matter and relates the shifts in arguments to the changed situation created by the Crusades and inner-Christian struggles. See also his *Les auteurs chrétiens latins du moyen âge sur les Juifs et le Judaïsme* in *REJ*, NS., ix, xi, xiii, xiv where he gives valuable information about these authors and their anti-Jewish writings. Cf. also his new critical edition, with introduction, of *Gisleberti Crispini Disputatio Judei et Christiani*, Utrecht/Antwerp, 1954 and his *Juden und Jüdisches in christlichen Wundererzählungen. Ein unbekanntes Gebiet religiöser Polemik* (*Theol. Zeitschr.*, X 1954, pp. 417-46).

[2] The following critical editions were used in preparing this paper. *Rashi: Parshandatha* ed. J. MAARSEN, Part II (Isaiah), Jerusalem 1933; Part I (Minor Prophets), Jerusalem 1936. To my regret I could not obtain Part III (Psalms). A. J. LEVY, *Rashi on Ezekiel xl-xlviii*, Philadelphia, 1931. For the psalms I had to rely on S. Poznanski's *Eliezer of Beaugency* (Introduction), and on JUDAH ROSENTHAL's contribution to the Rashi vol. published by the World Jewish Congress, Hebrew portion, pp. 45 ff. under the title *Ha-Pulmus ha-'anti-noṣeri be-Rashi 'al ha-Tenakh*. *Rashbam* (R. Samuel b. Me'ir): Commentary on the Pentateuch, ed. D. ROSIN, Breslau, 1881. *Abraham b. Ezra*: M. Friedlaender, *Essays on the writings of Abraham ibn Ezra*, IV, London, 1877. *Radaq* (R. David Qimḥi): Isaiah i-xxxix, ed. L. FINKELSTEIN, New York, 1926; Hosea, ed. H. COHEN, New York, 1929; Nahum, ed. W. WINDFUHR, Giessen, 1927.

Psalms: S. SCHILLER-SZINESSY, *The First Book of Psalms with the Longer Commentary of R. David Qimchi*, Cambridge, 1883; S. I. ESTERSON's edition of psalms xlii-lxxii *HUCA*, X, 1935, pp. 309 ff. No critical edition of the third and fourth books exists, but the fifth book was critically edited by J.

Anti-Christian polemic in Bible commentaries

the correct understanding of the Bible, together with the fulfilment of the *miṣwoth* according to the *Halakhah*, that secured Jewish survival.

It is well known that the close attention to grammar and lexicography from Gaon Saʿadya onwards enabled medieval Jewish commentators to get at the *peshaṭ*, the natural, plain, simple meaning of Scripture, not as is sometimes stated, the rationalist meaning. Logical or rational this exposition is, but not rationalistic in the philosophical sense of the term[3]. It is less often realized, however, that the retreat of the *derash*—it could not be given up since Judaism cannot ever dispense with it—and the consequent stress on the *peshaṭ* was directly caused and made inevitable by the Christians' attack and their attempt at converting the Jews. In turn, the application of this method reacted on the Christian exegetes who had to answer the challenge. They recognized the plain sense as one of the four legitimate ways of Christian interpretation of Holy Writ; *historia* corresponds to *peshaṭ*. It is well to remember—as Isaak Heinemann has reminded us[4]—that Origen and his circle speak of the Jews as a *carnalis populus*, as *amici literae*, and call the literal meaning the *sensus Judaicus*. In the later Middle Ages, when the Jewish-Christian controversy (we leave the Jewish-Muslim one out of account) was once again a live issue, we find that the *sensus Judaicus* was the best, sharpest and most effective weapon that the Jews could wield in the positive defence of Judaism. The Christians found support for their own

---

BOSNIAK, The Commentary on the fifth Book of Psalms, New York, 1954. Radaq's anti-Christian remarks were collected and are appended *inter alia* to Th. Hackspan's edition of Lippmann Mühlhausen's *Sefer Niṣṣaḥon*, Nuremberg 1644 under the title *Tosefeth teshuvoth Radaq*. I also used the Isny edition 1541, and the Cremona edition, 1561, and the Latin translation by Genebrardus under the title: *Responsa simul et argumenta, quae Rabbi David Kimhi contra Christianos suis ad Psalmos commentariis inseruit*, being pp. 63-105 of his treatise *R. Joseph Albonis, R. Davidis Kimhi, et alius cuiusdam Hebraei anonymi argumenta, quibus nonnullos fidei Christianae articulos oppugnant*, Paris 1566. MS. Add. 1574 of the Cambridge University Library has been subjected to Christian censorship and the offensive passages have either been erased or blacked out; but they are legible under ultra-violet light. The variants are unimportant, e.g. we find אמונתם for ישו הנוצרי, or האיש אותו.

[3] So, e.g. B. SMALLEY, *The Study of the Bible in the Middle Ages*[2], Oxford 1952, p. 103, where she refers to the Jewish teachers of Hugh of St Victor as belonging to "the contemporary North French school of rationalist exegetes founded by Rashi".

[4] *Die Wissenschaftliche Allegoristik des jüdischen Mittelalters* (*HUCA* xxiii 1, 1950-51).

use of the *peshaṭ* in Augustine who allowed the literal meaning, so long as the Christians adhered to the *sensus mysticus*. The twelfth century Victorines, Hugh and Andrew of St. Victor[5], provide the most telling example. Sa'adya asserts that we must accept the literal meaning except when it contradicts sense perception and reason, another unequivocal passage in Scripture, or trustworthy tradition[6]. It is a well known fact that the medieval Jewish religious philosophers distinguished between the external and the inner, real meaning of Scripture, but they were careful to exclude the application of the latter to the laws.

If proof were needed that the concentration on the *peshaṭ* was the direct answer to the christological challenge we need only look at Abraham b. Ezra's introduction to his Commentary on the *Torah*, where he opposes his own method of interpretation to four others. The first method is there attributed to "the sages of the uncircumcised" who maintain that the whole *Torah* consists of riddles and allegories, not only the whole of Genesis but also all the laws and statutes and ordinances. Everything is a hint, an allusion (*remez*). Thus the twelve tribes typify the twelve apostles, the woman with seed the Church, etc. Ibn Ezra castigates this method as vanity and hot air and insists that every commandment, every word must be interpreted in conformity with what is written, while admitting that the *Torah* contains secrets like the tree of knowledge or paradise. He appeals to the reason implanted in us by

[5] See the important researches of BERYL SMALLEY: *Andrew of St. Victor, Abbot of Wigmore: A Twelfth century Hebraist* (*Recherches Théologiques Anciennes et Médiévales*, x, pp. 358 ff.); *The School of Andrew of St. Victor* (ibid. xi, pp. 145 ff.). The use of Jewish exegesis is clear from such remarks as *in Hebreo, tradunt Hebrei*, etc. See especially pp. 149 f., 153, on Herbert of Bosham (*ibid.*, xviii). Cf. also the detailed, informative study by R. J. LOEWE, *Herbert of Bosham's Commentary on Jerome's Hebrew Psalter* (*Biblica* xxxiv, pp. 44-77; 159-192; 275-298) which traces Herbert's sources. Dr. SMALLEY states in her *The Study of the Bible ...*, p. 110 that Richard criticises Andrew for 'judaizing', *i.e.* accepting the Jewish exposition as the literal sense of prophecy. It is interesting to note that Bernard of Clairvaux used the term *judaizare* for Christian moneylenders, thus equating it with usury. Despite H. HAILPERIN's justified criticisms (cf. *Historia Judaica*, iv, pp. 163 ff.) this book is remarkable both for its comprehensiveness and its wealth of relevant, hitherto largely unknown detail, especially on the Hebrew attainment of the Victorines (Hugh, Andrew, Richard), and its legacy in the works of Peter the Comestor, Peter the Chanter and Stephen Langton.

[6] Cf. *K. al-amānāt wa-l-i'tiqādāt*, ed. S. LANDAUER, Leiden 1880, p. 212, S. ROSENBLATT's English translation (*Yale Judaica Series*), p. 265, and A. ALTMANN's abridged English version (*Philosophia Judaica*, Oxford 1946) pp. 157 f.

Anti-Christian polemic in Bible commentaries

God, to testify to the *peshaṭ*[7]. The guiding principle, from Talmudical times onwards had to be *'eyn miqra' yoṣe' miydey peshuṭo*; it does not only mean that every verse in the *Torah* must be explained in accordance with its literal, plain sense, but also that it can never lose its plain meaning whatever hidden or inner meaning is attributed to it[8]. Heinemann is therefore right when he speaks of *Mehrdeutung*, but not *Umdeutung*, *i.e.* it is legitimate to give a verse more than one meaning, but it is not permitted to explain the literal sense away by an allegorizing interpretation. Allegory must be distinguished from metaphor, a metaphorical exposition of anthropomorphisms is necessary, since God is not a body. It is only the *Song of Songs* that is generally accepted to be an allegory. The philosophical exposition of the Bible in its non-preceptive part is, however, often *Umdeutung* rather than *Mehrdeutung*.

In our context it is significant that the medieval commentators link the *peshaṭ* with the "answer (or rejoinder) to the Christians" and thus establish a clear connection between the literal method and anti-Christian polemic. They were in fact less concerned with convincing Christians than with reassuring and fortifying Jews. But they could do so only by providing their generation with an answer to the Christian claims so formulated as to uphold the Jewish position in a manner at once satisfying and convincing for a Jew when hard pressed.

It is for this reason we find such expressions as Rashi's *lephi mashmaʿo we-litheshuvah la-Minim* or Rashbam's *peshaṭ zeh teshuvah la-Minim*. *Minim* here means Christians just as in the anti-Christian tracts, where *min* is contrasted with *ma'amin*, i.e. the Jew who has the right belief. Sometimes we find *noṣerim* (so often in Qimḥi's commentary on *Psalms*), or *toʿim*, the designation for the Crusaders in the Hebrew reports concerning the Crusades, or *ṭoʿanim*, i.e. objectors, in Abraham b. Ezra, or the abbreviation *ʿakum*. At times Rashi defines his *minim* by the addition of *ha-Mesithim 'eth yisra'el laʿavodhah zarah* in order to indicate the grave danger that threatened his generation[9].

---

[7] See M. FRIEDLAENDER, *op. cit.* (note 2, above), pp. 1 ff. of the Hebrew appendix.

[8] In a forthcoming article R. LOEWE will, so he informs me, show grounds for questioning whether it is legitimate to render *peshuṭo* as *literal, plain* sense in this context and will suggest an alternative explanation.†

[9] In his comment on *Prov.* ii: 12, quoted by JUDAH ROSENTHAL, *op. cit.*, p. 49. This article is throughout relevant for the question under discussion.

Jewish themes

Here we must restrict ourselves to the consideration of the actual commentaries on the Bible, and leave aside the records of the religious disputations, as well as the specific anti-Christian tracts and the anti-Christian polemic contained in such religious-philosophical works as Sa'adya's *'Emunoth we-dhe'oth* and Maimonides' *Moreh*[10].

How topical and relevant Qimḥi's anti-Christian utterances were, can be gathered from his regular use of the phrase "if somebody were to object you must answer" or "the Christians interpret this psalm [as referring] to Jesus" (or "to that man" or "to their faith"), but you must answer them...". That this is not simply a rhetorical figure of speech, but was dictated by necessity and constituted a very real practical help in the Jewish-Christian controversy is clear from the context of contemporary history[11]. It also seems to point to an actual dialogue between individual Jews and Christians, not necessarily of the learned only on both sides, and proves the whole controversy to be a real life issue, a common daily life feature. If it had been a purely literary discussion, Qimḥi might have been expected to specify the Christian opponents by name[12]. It is obvious that the terminology employed by the Jews often corresponds to that of their Christian opponents, e.g. *gufanith* equals *corporealiter*, *ruḥanith spiritualiter*. Once Qimḥi makes a pun when he declares the Christian interpretation—*ruḥanith*—to be *ruaḥ*, wind. Again, the occurrence of these terms need not presuppose the study of Latin commentaries, but rather reflects the personal contact of Jews with Christian exegetes, just as expressions like *Judaei dicunt, Hebraei tradunt* point to oral communication. Even where a literal quotation can be traced to Rashi or Rashbam it is not necessarily always derived from their commentaries, but can have been communicated to the Victorines or Herbert of Bosham by word of mouth—notwithstanding the Hebrew attainment of these medieval Christian Biblical scholars.

[10] Characteristic examples are given by W. BACHER in his *Die Bibelexegese der jüdischen Religionsphilosophen des Mittelalters vor Maimûni*, Strasbourg 1892 and *Die Bibelexegese Moses Mainmûni's*, Strasbourg 1897.

[11] In J. KATZ' forthcoming book *Exclusiveness and Tolerance* a chapter will be devoted to this whole aspect of the subject, so Mr. Loewe informs me.†

[12] This does not render a detailed investigation of the Latin commentaries of his contemporary Christian scholars superfluous. Later in this paper a passage will be quoted in which Qimḥi attacks Jerome: but it is difficult to say whether a Christian divine told him, or whether he was acquainted with the Vulgate directly or through quotation in a commentary or polemical treatise.

II.

What were the issues at stake in this battle for the truth of the Bible, its meaning and significance? Broadly speaking, there were two main Christian claims with a positive and a negative side to them. The first was, as is well known, that Jesus was the son of God, a divine-human being, and was the Messiah promised in the Hebrew Bible. The second issue was the Christian claim that by his coming Jesus had set aside the *Torah* in its material sense and had given it a purely spiritual existence and meaning. Christ's law was claimed to be much superior to Moses' law, as e.g. in a commentary coming from the school of Peter Abelard[13].

The first problem, that revolving round Jesus, is dealt with by practically all medieval Jewish commentators, but most extensively by Qimḥi, who was not a disciple and champion of Maimonides for nothing[14]. He correctly raises in objection the Jewish concept of

[13] Cf. A. LANDGRAF, *Commentarius Cantabrigiensis in Epistolas Pauli e Schola Petri Abaelardi* (Notre Dame, Indiana, 1937-45), ii (1939), pp. 278-280. The passage runs in full (ii, 278) *Moyses enim, qui homo spiritalis erat non solum legem ad historiam intelligebat, sed etiam mistice*, with reference to *Ex.* xxxiv: 33; *Is.* ix: 6 and *Zech.* ix: 9, and p. 279: *Lex autem Moysi ad tempus data fuit, que tandem evacuata est. Lex vero Christi tamquam perpetua est, cui alia lex non succedet.*

[14] His commentary on Psalms abounds in philosophical explanations. In the introduction he discusses the nature of prophecy and of prophets as distinct from men inspired by the *ruaḥ ha-Qodesh* in the manner of Maimonides (cf. *Guide*, ii, xxxvi). In the body of the commentary the influence of Abraham b. Ezra is also very marked. Examples of philosophical comment are: *Ps.* viii: 2, the tetragrammaton is distinct from the other divine names in that it is not an attribute (SCHILLER-SZINESSY, *op. cit.*, p. 25); v. 5, against those who maintain the eternity of the world (p. 26) צבאות equals גלגלים, a cosmological explanation. *Ps.* xv: 2 gives Qimḥi an opportunity to state that philosophical demonstration can prove the existence and unity of God. On xvi: 8 he quotes *Guide* iii, li. Concerning xvii: 15 he claims that he only who has studied psychology can understand these matters. Moses' intellect was *intellectus in actu*; the whole passage seems to come from the *Guide*, III, li. On xix: 2 he refers to *Guide* II. v; commenting on v. 8 he compares the soul to a stranger in the body like in a foreign land. On xxv: 9 he quotes Ibn Gabirol's *Sefer tiqqun middoth ha-Nefesh* (also on xxxv: 10 and xxxvii: 8, 23); on v. 10. Maimonides. *Ps.* xxviii, like xxvii, contains a request to God to free the Psalmist from the needs of the body so that he might concentrate on those of the soul, *i.e.* the service of God through which transgressions are atoned and the soul draws near to God. Here is his definition of עבודת האלהים (on v. 5): והיא להבין בחכמת הטבע ובפעלותיו ומעשה ידיו בשמים ובארץ; ומשם יתבונן כח מעשה אלהים שהכל מאתו, והוא הסבה הראשונה ... The importance of the study of physics in the service of religion may he noted. On xxxvi: 11 he defines the wise (philosophers) as those who occupy themselves with the *Torah*, its commandments and with metaphysics, in contrast to the ישרי לב who confine their study to the two first mentioned

Jewish themes

the absolute, simple unity and uniqueness of God. The divinity of Jesus interested the Jews, however, less than his alleged messianic character. The refutation of this Christian claim is accompanied by the positive assertion that none of the messianic prophecies and promises had been fulfilled during the second Jewish commonwealth—in the lifetime of Jesus—but that the final redemption is still to come and, what is more, is imminent. It is thus clear that Christian attack and persecution provided a strong incentive for the messianic expectancy of the time, and constituted an additional argument for the messianic interpretation of many a prophetic passage in the Bible. *Peshaṭ* is joined by the appeal to history, in order to prove the fallacy of the Christian claim and to strengthen the Jewish belief in the divine promise of final redemption[15].

and consequently attain to דעת הבורא by way of tradition only. Similarly, he states on cxi: 10 that first comes למוד התורה and then - חכמת הפילוס ופיא which confirms and establishes the former correctly. Here we have the philosophical justification of religious truth. In the long introduction to cxix Qimḥi discusses the several ways to תיקון המדות, the strongest of them all being the seventh: ראיית השכל וידיעתו; but there remains an eighth way, that of tradition, and we are obliged to believe in it in every respect. On cxxxvi: 4 he speaks of the forms as the separate intelligences which are neither bodies nor like bodies, and which the human eye cannot comprehend. A similar, more extended philosophical comment is offered on cxlviii, strongly reminiscent of Maimonides' *Guide*. These examples may suffice to show how philosophical comment is employed by Qimḥi as a legitimate means to bring out the meaning of the psalms, in conjunction with *peshaṭ*, contemporary events, messianic hope and the final redemption.

[15] Reference will be made to such interpretations below, when discussing Rashi, and some such comments may be mentioned here from Qimḥi's commentary on *Psalms*: x: 16, on the Exile and the return of the kingdom to Israel; xii, on the future redemption; xiii and xiv, on the Exile; xxi is dealt with later under Qimḥi; xxii, on the Exile and redemption; xxiii, on David, or Israel's return from Exile; xxiv: 9 on the redeemer; xxv, xxvi and xxvii are concerned with this world and the world to come; contrary to previous interpreters, Qimḥi refers *Ps.* xxix to the future, to the days of the Messiah, possibly to the wars of Gog and Magog. xxxvi: 8 (חסדך) refers to the world to come. cviii is interpreted messianically, although most of it is identical with lvii and lx which refer to David, this psalm refers to the seed of David to whom will fall the kingdom at the time of the final redemption of Israel; cxvii refers to the messianic redemption; cxviii either to David or to the time of the Messiah. cxx: 2 refers to the nations in whose midst Israel suffers in Exile, also v. 6; likewise cxxi: 3, 4, while v. 8 refers to the return from Exile to the land of Israel; cxxii is מאמר בני הגלות; v. 6 refers to ערלים וישמעאלים; on cxxiii Qimḥi expresses his trust in God "who alone will redeem us from Exile;" cxxiv refers to Israel in Exile, as does cxxvi which also points to the time of redemption; cxxvii contains an allusion to King Messiah; v. 2 is interpreted messianically with a reference to Muslims and Christians and the war that will be waged between them until the redeemer comes. cxxviii is understood of the Exile and redemption and ensuing peace for Israel. cxxix and cxxx express the hope of redemption as on

Undoubtedly prompted by the Christian attitude to the *Torah*, Abravanel[16] at length deals with the question whether the *Torah* will be abrogated in its entirety, or in part, or not al all when the Messiah comes. It shows —as we also find in Qimḥi— how the validity of the *Torah* is bound up with the person and coming of the Messiah.

To repeat, the Jewish commentators intended by their polemic to give courage and hope to their sorely tried generation: and in rejecting the claim that Jesus shared in the divine nature of God the father, they clarified and emphasised the Jewish concept of the one and only God. In refuting, in the light of past and contemporary history, the claim that Jesus was the promised Messiah, they heightened the eschatological expectancy of their generation and offered practical support for its successful resistance to Christian pressure even if this meant dying a martyr's death in defence of the ancestral faith. The troubled state of affairs was, to the Jews of the Middle Ages, a clear sign that the promised redemption of Israel and mankind was at hand, that persecution and suffering foreshadowed divine intervention to secure personal and national

previous occasions. cxxxiii refers to the Messiah, the rebuilt temple, and the world to come. cxxxv refers to Solomon or King Messiah; v. 14 means that Israel is now in Exile but God will lead him back to his inheritance. v. 20 and cxxxvi: 1—Israel and all mankind will worship and praise God. cxxxvi: 23 is referred to the Babylonian exile or more correctly to the present one. cxxxvii: 7-9 refers to the Babylonian exile; the psalmist also foresaw ברוח הקדש the exile of the Second Commonwealth, when Titus destroyed the Temple and the Roman empire, the children of Edom, led Israel into exile. cxlv, *end* refers to the ingathering of the exiles, as does cxlvi; v. 2 means that God only can send salvation to Israel and to every individual. Just as He sent Cyrus to redeem Israel from the Babylonian exile, so will He redeem Israel in the future through the kings of the nations, if Israel in Exile puts his trust in God alone. Qimḥi stresses throughout this psalm God's rule over all the nations after the redemption of Israel from his present Exile. It is worth noting that Qimḥi naturally reflects the tension between particularism and universalism so characteristic of Judaism. cxlvii is interpreted with reference to the Exile and redemption from Exile which for Qimḥi is an article of faith. cxlviii: 14 manifests God's omnipotence as exemplified in His redeeming and gathering Israel from the nations. cxlix refers to the war with Gog and Magog, with Israel praying for redemption. cl hints at the thirteen *middoth* by which God rules the world (an echo of the *Guide*). God will be magnified and sanctified by the nations for delivering Israel. Turning briefly to Isaiah, we note that Qimḥi sees in xxiv, contrary to traditional exegesis, a prophecy of the future, as is clear from the end of the chapter. xxv: 5, Israel will be saved; xxvi: 1 refers to the time of salvation; v. 20 refers to Gog and Magog; xxvii again points to the time of salvation.

[16] Cf. E. I. J. ROSENTHAL, *Don Isaac Abravanel...*, *Bulletin of the John Rylands Library*, xxi, 2, Oct. 1937, pp. 445 ff., especially 464-67, 470 f.

salvation. The contemporary scene explains the frequent references to the present Exile and the marked underlining of the messianic, redemptive import of many passages in the prophets, in *Daniel* and in the *Psalms*[17].

III

What has been said may now be illustrated by reference to Rashi, Rashbam, Abraham b. Ezra and in particular to David Qimḥi's commentary on the Psalms.

It is not surprising that Rashi, who for all his profound learning was also a man of affairs and an acute observer of the contemporary scene, should relate prophecies to his own age. For him *Micah* vii: 8 refers to "Babylon and guilty Rome". By Rome he understands Christian Rome, which as such is the target of his attack in the form of the fulfilment of an ancient prophecy. His commentary on *Isaiah* contains many references to Rome, e.g. xxiii: 1, the *Kittim*; *ibid.* v. 5 is Tyre to be understood as *edhom rumi* or literally Tyre (*ṣor mammash*)[18]? But on xxvi: 5 and xxvii: 10 he leaves no doubt[19]. While Rashi does not refer *Zech.* ix: 4 to the Second Commonwealth, as the Christians do, but to the days of the Messiah, he allows the last verses only of the book of Daniel to apply to the final redemption and sees in the bulk of the book allusions to political events at the time of the Maccabees[20]. Passages like *Is.* xi: 12, xxiii: 18, xxiv: 16, 18, chapters xxvi, xxvii, xxviii and xxxiv point to the Messiah and the future redemption of Israel[21], as does *Jer.* xxxi: 39[22]. He opposes the Christian interpretation of *Is.* vii: 14 (*ha'almah*)[23] and of ix: 5f. He is at one with

---

[17] See notes 15, 16, above, and what is said of Rashi and Abraham b. Ezra, *infra*.

[18] Cf. MAARSEN, *op. cit.*, pp. 60 f.

[19] Cf. *ibid.*, pp. 65, 69. Qimḥi cites this as one explanation without mentioning Rashi by name.

[20] Cf. I. F. BAER, *Rashi we-ha-Meṣi'uth ha-historith shel zemanno*, (*Tarbiz*, xx, 1950, pp. 320 ff., especially 326 ff.; also JUDAH ROSENTHAL, *op. cit.*, pp. 49 ff.

[21] Cf. MAARSEN, *op. cit.*, pp. 38, 62, 63, 65, 67 (סימני ישועה וגאולה), 68, 71, 86.

[22] Cf. S. POZNANSKI's introduction to his edition of Eliezer of Beaugency's Commentaries on Ezekiel and the Minor Prophets, Warsaw, 1910-13, p. xx.

[23] Cf. MAARSEN, p. 23. Rashi refers it to the wife of the prophet who will, ברוח הקדש, call him עמנואל. Qimḥi also refers it to the wife of the prophet, or to Ahaz, which seems to him to be the correct view since if she were the prophet's wife she would be named נביאה as in *Is.* viii: 3 and he is the son of the king in accordance with *Is.* v: 8. העלמה is young in years, she is not a virgin כדברי התועים, *i.e.* the Christians. Qimḥi also quotes his father's ס' הברית for

other exegetes in admitting *sar shalom* only as the name to be given to Hezekiah, whereas all the other names refer to God; *me'attah we'adh 'olam* cannot refer to Jesus, who was born 500 years later[24]. Of equal relevance are some of his comments on certain psalms. E.g. he understands *ben* in *Ps.* ii to mean the beloved (*haviv*) of God, which implies a rejection of the Christian claim that Jesus is meant. Or, he rejects the traditional interpretation of *Ps.* ix on linguistic grounds and applies it to the future redemption of Israel (v. 2); v. 14 *haneneni* means "now in the Golah", and *meromemi* "at the time of your redemption". Vv. 14-20 of *Ps.* x are applied by him to Israel after the dominion of Ishmael and Rome over the nation has been broken and they have been driven from his [Israel's] land; God will then be king for ever (v. 16). *Ps.* xxi is referred by the Rabbis to King Messiah, but Rashi thinks it right to refer it to king David after his marriage to Bathsheba. *Ps.* xxii: 2 is a prayer by David for the future; v. 27 points to "the time of our redemption, the days of our Messiah". *Ps.* lxviii is explained historically and as pointing to Israel's future redemption.[25] As in his interpretation of *Ps.* xxi, in that of the Servant Songs in *Isaiah* Rashi departs from the Rabbis, and it is quite likely that he did so in order to avoid any possibility of a Christological application. He applies chapters lii and liii of *Isaiah* to the people of Israel as a whole, not like the Rabbis to the Messiah, nor with the Christians to Jesus as Messiah. On the other hand, chapters xlix and l have the prophet himself in mind.[26] *Jer.* xi: 19 refers to the prophet, not to the Church as the Christians say, and *Zech.* vi: 12 has in mind, Zerubbabel, not Jesus.[27] Here again Rashi differs from the Rabbis, who apply this verse to the

---

an answer to the Christians. The sign was given to Ahaz, not to Jesus who lived more than 400 years later. Cf. also B. BLUMENKRANZ, *Die jüdischen Beweisgründe* ... (see no. 1, above) 11, pp. 134 ff.

[24] Cf. MAARSEN, pp. 31 f. with his notes on עולם ... מעתה: ולתשובת המינים שהוא שם לטעותם יש להשיבם מהו מעתה והלא לא בא אותו טעות עד לסוף שנה מאות שלש 300 years should be 500 years, according to the ס' נצחון. By טעות Jesus is meant. Rashi interprets xi: 12, xxiii: 18 messianically; xxiv on the future redemption of Israel; xxvi: 6 refers to King Messiah like *Zech.* ix: 9; v. 17 likewise, and this contains "signs of salvation and redemption". xxvii: 2, xxviii: 16, xxxiv are all interpreted messianically.

[25] Cf. on psalm xxi: 2 POZNANSKI, *op. cit.*, p. xx, who adds from an uncensored MS. לפי פשוטו ולתשובת המינים; v. 2 does not refer to Jesus, as the Vulgate translates. The messianic references are culled from מקראות גדולות.

[26] Cf. JUDAH ROSENTHAL, *op. cit.*, pp. 52 f.

[27] *Ibid.*

Messiah. The Church refers the whole matter to Jesus, but Rashi sees in it an allusion to the Second Commonwealth.[28]

Rashbam offers a unique interpretation of the controversial passage in *Gen.* xlix: 10 '*ad ki yavo shiloh*: "*until Judah come to Shiloh* means until the king of Judah, i.e. Rehoboam, the son of Solomon, comes to Shiloh which is the name of a place, near Shechem". He goes on to say: "this *peshaṭ* is an answer to the Christians, for it is only written as the name of a town ... it is not written *shello*, as the Jews say, nor *sheliaḥ*, as the Christians say".[29]

Abraham b. Ezra may once more be quoted with an interesting explanation of *Gen.* xxvii: 40.[30] He first gives examples of how Edom served Judah in the days of Hyrkanus II and Agrippa, identifies the *Kittim* with Rome and ends thus: "there were a few men who believed in a man they made into God ... Rome believed in the days of Constantine who had renewed [*i.e.* established] the whole religion and placed a representation of that man [*i.e.* Jesus] upon his standard. But there were not in the world any who observed the new law except a few Edomites, therefore Rome is called Edom".

IV

More evidence of anti-Christian polemic could be adduced from many medieval commentators, such as the successors of Rashi in Northern France, Joseph Bekhor Shor, Joseph Qara, Eliezer of Beaugency and others. In his valuable introduction to Eliezer's commentaries S. Poznanski has shown their important

---

[28] *Ibid.* For further examples see this study. For Rashi, Rome represents the Church; in his comment on *Micah* vii: 8 (MAARSEN, ad loc.) he refers to it by the term רומי החייבת; and the Christians are idolaters, who try to pervert the Jews to idolatry.

[29] Cf. RASHBAM's Commentary, ed. D. ROSIN, pp. 71 f. with n. 6, quoting (p. 72) the Vulgate's *mittendus est*; also A. POSNANSKI, *Schiloh*, Leipzig, 1904, p. xv and S. POZNANSKI, *op. cit.*, p. xxxix. Rashi read *shello* and referred it to the Messiah whose is the kingdom, or *shay lo* who deserves homage (cf. *Schiloh, loc. cit.*) Further examples from Rashbam's commentary are: on *Ex.* iii: 22 he remarks חהו עיקר פשוטו ותשובה למינים and *Ex.* xx: 13 (ed. ROSIN, p. 111, with notes 18, 19). The Vulgate is referred to by the term לשון לטין; also *Lev.* xi: 3, 34 and xix: 19. Rashbam uses the expressions ולפי פשוטו של מקרא... and ולמינים אמרתי and also לפי דרך ארץ ותשובת המינים, which seems to indicate personal contact. Passages like *Ex.* xi: 2 and *Deut.* xxii: 5, 9 show his emphasis on the *peshaṭ*. Cf. also D. ROSIN, *R. Samuel b. Meir als Schriftklärer*, Breslau, 1880, especially pp. 61, 77 ff.

[30] Cf. מקראות גדולות, *ad loc.* I owe this reference to Dr. E. WIESENBERG.

contribution to biblical exegesis and has collected a large number of such anti-Christian comments.[31]

All in common have a strict adherence to the *peshaṭ* and a refusal to admit an allegorical interpretation. They go far beyond Rashi, on whom they lean heavily. *Peshaṭ*, now based on a far better knowledge and appreciation of the language of the Bible than hitherto, implies, as stated before, rational as well as historical argument. Naturally, we have to realize that logic is not necessarily an adequate and successful weapon when used against an opponent where faith is concerned. The value of this anti-Christian polemic in Bible commentaries consists, to repeat, largely in the practical help it provided for Jewish life and thought which were equally in danger from Christian conversionist zeal at all times during the Middle Ages, and not infrequently from open persecution also.[32] This is clear from the often quoted formula "an answer to the Christians" or from Qimḥi's more personal phrase "you must answer".

Qimḥi's "answers" deserve detailed and careful study in the light of contemporary Christian exegesis, since Narbonne was the seat of an archbishop. It has already been stated that his familiarity with Christian exegesis is evident from his rejoinders, and that his knowledge may to a large extent at least be oral and not necessarily based on his personal study of Christian commentaries. I must content myself in what follows with presenting some of the more telling comments selected in the main from his commentary on the *Psalms*.

---

[31] Cf. S. POZNANSKI, *op. cit.*, pp. xxxvii on Joseph Qara's comment on *Deut.* xiv: 1; many passages in Joseph Bekhor Shor's Commentary, e.g. on *Lev.* xviii: 5; *Deut.* xxviii: 63; xxxi: 16; xxxii: 21 and, in particular, on *Num.* xii: 8 (p. lxix) against the Christian claim that Moses' words are אליגוריא ... כלמר חידה ומשל ואינו מה שהוא אומר ומהפכין הנבואה לדבר אחר ומוציאין הדבר ממשמעותו לגמרי ... שאע"פ שהעתיקו את התורה מלשון הקדש ללשונם (*i.e.* Vulgate) לשמוע ואזנים לראות ועינים לדעת לב הק' להם נתן לא According-ing to POZNANSKI, J. Bekhor Shor commented on almost all the passages which the Christians claim as foundations for their faith; in particular he polemized against their concept of the trinity, images, Jesus' birth without a father, etc. POZNANSKI cites many examples from the בעלי התוספות which are relevant to our question, especially pp. ci; cviii, introduced by תשובה למינים, and finally Eliezer of Beaugency's "answers", e.g. on *Is.* ix: 5 against the Christian claim that all the names refer to Jesus, the son of God (p. clxiii): אבל ודאי שקר בימינם וזייפו ספריהם לקרא ויקרא שמו להסב .... כל השמות יל הילד or on *Ezek.* v: 4: הם רשעי ישראל ובני פריצי עמנו כגון ישו וחבריו שהתעו את ישראל ונכשלו ונהרגו.

[32] Cf. note 11, *supra*.

Ps. ii.[33] "It is not right to say 'son of God' of flesh and blood, for the son is of a kind with the father. He to whom God says *you are my son* must be of His kind and God must be like him. Further, if anybody were to say: *I have today born you* and the born one is of the same kind as the begetter, then answer them: 'in divinity it is not possible [to assume] father and son, for the Deity cannot be divided. God is no body that can be divided. His unity is absolute without addition, distraction or divisibility'. You must tell them further that 'we can speak of father and son only if the father is first in time and the son goes forth from the strength of the father. Hence the son must be later than the father. But then no tri-unity is possible. If both were co-existent all the time you should call them twin brothers, not father and son, begetter and born'. Answer him who says it is not possible to call any one son of God who is not of the [same] kind of divinity that we can speak of God metaphorically only, as e.g. when we say *the mouth of God, the eyes, the ears of God*. We call him who fulfils His mission and His commandments 'son of God', just as a son fulfils the commandments of his father ... 'Again, you say of God that the father said to the son *ask of me and I will give you nations as your inheritance*. If the son is God why should he ask his father? Has he no power over nations and the ends of the earth like Him?' ... They might point out that this happened after He had become flesh. God has referred to his humanity, promised so-to-speak inheritance to the son as man. But this is not so, because he had no kingdom while in the flesh nor any dominion over any nation. If they say that the psalm speaks of their faith ... [then reply to them] that the majority, be they Jews or Muslims, have not accepted it. Now, I have taught you what answer to give them concerning this psalm. You must add from your own knowledge in accordance with these matters. If asked for an interpretation choose between the two, refer it either to David or to the Messiah, as I have explained". Two obvious points arise out of this anti-Christian comment. The first is that Qimḥi takes not only the text of the psalm, but also the Christian interpretation literally. On this basis, his rejoinder is logically sound. The second point is that style and expression leave no doubt that Christians tried to convince Jews of the truth of the Christian exposition and that Qimḥi was con-

---

[33] Cf. SCHILLER-SZINESSY, *op. cit.*, pp. 11 f. The same argument is used by Qimḥi in his comment on *Ps.* xlv.

cerned to provide his generation with a rationally convincing answer. In other words, this was by no means a merely academic exercise between the learned on both sides. Similarly, Qimḥi's comment on *Ps.* vii: 8[34] contains this "answer": "the Christians mistakenly interpret this verse (as applying) to Jesus and refer *waʿadhath leʾummim* to the nations who have turned to his faith..."

Ps. xv, Commenting on v. 5 Qimḥi continues: "I have enlarged on this point for you so that you can find an answer in it to the Christians, who say that David did not discriminate between an Israelite and a Gentile, but that all interest was forbidden.[35] This is not possible (or, not right) for David did not forbid what Moses our Teacher permitted by the command of God. In fact, the *Torah* says: *you shall not add to it* [*sc.* the commandments] *nor take away from it* (*Deut.* iv: 2)".

In his comment on *Ps.* xix: 10 Qimḥi objects to the Christians "who hold that the *Torah* which was given on Mount Sinai had a limited duration, namely until the time of Jesus' coming only. Until his time it was in the flesh, *corporealiter* (*gufanith*), but when he came he commanded to understand it in the spirit, *spiritualiter* (*ruḥanith*). But their words are words of wind and vanity. For those commandments which in their view are allegorical and cannot be understood in their literal meaning [have in point of fact] been clearly revealed by God and not in an allegory (*mashal*). Therefore, the other commandments also must be understood by man according to their literal meaning, not as an allegory. For if the commandments were allegorical men would be in doubt. One would say the hidden thing is such and such, and another such and such, but Scripture says explicitly..."[36] Qimḥi expresses here lucidly what was the generally accepted and defended Jewish position with regard to the permanent validity of the *Torah* of Moses.

Qimḥi applies *Ps.* xxi either to David or to King Messiah of the future; the Christians to Jesus.[37] "But (writes Qimḥi) you shall

---

[34] Cf. SCHILLER-SZINESSY, p. 23. This passage is not contained in the separate *Answers*.

[35] Cf. *ibid.*, p. 41 and the note on כל רבית אסור. This was a favourite Christian objection, as we know from many Jewish *answers*.

[36] Cf. *ibid.*, pp. 58 f. Qimḥi ends his rejoinder with *Deut.* xxx: 11-14. Cf. also the quotation in n. 13, above.

[37] Cf. *ibid.*, pp. 62 f.

answer them verse by verse. All his words are dependent on others.³⁸ Take for example the phrase *Oh Lord in thy strength the king rejoices*, indeed, for without the power of the father the son will have none. But if he is weak then he is not God . . . *He asked life from you*: this cannot refer to his humanity for he did not live long; if [it refers] to his divinity what has He given him which he has not already had? Or, *great is his glory through your salvation*: but without your salvation his glory is not great. Hence he is not God. *For the king trusts in the Lord*, if this refers to his divinity, there is no need for him to trust in another and he has no need of the grace of the Most High..." We have here a combination of *peshaṭ* with logic and an appeal to history. This kind of argument no doubt appealed more to Jews than it convinced Christians.

To *Ps.* xlv.³⁹ "The Christians apply this psalm to Jesus the Nazarene. *The daughters of kings* are interpreted allegorically as meaning the nations which have turned to the religion of the Christians." Qimḥi again proceeds verse by verse in order to demolish the Christian argument. He points to the impossibility of applying to God companions, or a tri-unity. He rejects the Christian interpretation of *shegal* (v. 10) as entirely inappropriate to God,⁴⁰ and polemizes against their exposition of v. 17 as being equally inapplicable to an incorporeal, transcendent deity.⁴¹ His method is again to employ the logic of common sense, and, by his use of the same weapons, to prove that even on the Christians' own premises their interpretation is inadmissible because it would be incompatible with the Jewish concept of God.

Again in his anti-Christian polemic in connection with their interpretation of *Ps.* lxxii he denies that it can be applied to Jesus. How urgent it was to refute the Christian claim emerges from his use of such terms as "you must shatter their words in front of

---

³⁸ Genebrardus translates "Haec enim verba omnia sunt hominis ab alio pendentis" which makes better sense, but is difficult to get out of the Hebrew text: כל דבריו הם תלוים באחרים

³⁹ Cf. ESTERSON, *op. cit.*, pp. 333 f.

⁴⁰ Cf. *ibid.*, p. 334: ולא יאמר לו נצבה שגל לימינך אפילו דרך משל כי שגל היא כמו שפירשנו לשון משכבי אשה ולא יתכן זה על אלוה׃

⁴¹ Cf. *ibid.*: ועוד איך יאמר תחת אבותיך יהיו בניך ואם יאמר לך יש לאלוה בנים והם המאמינים בו כמו בנים אתם לה׳ אלהיכם [דברים יד׳א], אמור לו אם יש לו בנים אין לו אבות׃ ואם יאמר האב כמו שהם אומרים אב ובן ורוח הקדש כבר השיבונו על זה, במזמור למה רגשו גוים [ב׳א]׃ ועוד תשובה אחרת אם יאמר אב אפילו לדבריהם לא יתכן לומר אבות בלשון רבים׃

them and reply: 'you say that in this verse is contained the trinity of God, the king, and the son of the king. But as you identify Jesus with Solomon there are actually four'." He then proceeds to examine the Christian claim under the aspect of the dual nature of Jesus as God and as man, and finds the claim absurd on both counts. What follows in the psalm can on no account refer to Jesus, for there was no peace in his time, and after him the wicked and sinners increased even more. Neither did Jesus rule from sea to sea, nor did all peoples worship him.[42]

To *Ps.* lxxxvii. "The Christians explain this psalm concerning Jesus (a variant reading is "their faith") and say: '*his foundation* that is Jesus. In Zion Jesus was formed and born; ... the man born there is the most high, and God is the Most High. *Glorious things are announced of you*: why? because you are the city of God in which he will be born'. You must answer them: 'first of all, how does it say *his* foundation, with the personal suffix *o*, when he has so far not been mentioned in the verse?' Next, if they construe *the most high* of the one born and refer *and he* to the man born who was mentioned, then you must object to them: 'indeed the verse speaks of 'man' and 'man' points to many men, yet he was only one. The psalm also says *and he will establish her*; what is it that he established? Jesus in Jerusalem? They will then answer you: 'it does not speak of wood and stone, but he came to establish Zion and Jerusalem in the spirit, that is, the faith through which they who believe in him are saved from that day onwards.' But you must object to them: 'how can this be understood now materially, now spiritually? ... Further, the cities mentioned are (to be understood) materially, not spiritually ... Finally, it says of these cities, *this man will be born there*. If this be so, do you say that in every one of these cities there was born one God?[43]

To *Ps.* cx.[44] "The Christians apply this psalm to Jesus. In the first verse they read *'adhonay la'dhonay*, pointing the *nun* with

---

[42] Cf. ibid., pp. 442 f. The use of the term כסילות reflects Christian objections to Jewish exegesis, only in reverse. Qimḥi again points out that neither Jews nor Muslims worship Jesus; they deny him. He shows a good knowledge of Christian claims and arguments, e.g. the Christians claim that Jesus continually prays for himself. The Jews say this would be absurd if he were God. The Christians then meet this objection by saying that Jesus prays for all who believe in him. He refutes this by asking why he should pray if, as the son of God, he is God.

[43] Cf. נצחון 'ס, ed. *Hackspan* (cf. note 2), p. 199

[44] Cf. BOSNIAK, *op. cit.* (note 2), pp. 66 ff. (Hackspan, p. 200).

qameṣ, and say it means two, *i.e.* father and son, and the spirit is the third. Another error is that they read (v. 3 *'immekha* for *'ammekha*, and refer *qodhesh* to Jesus, born from the womb. Answer them that Jerome, their translator, made a mistake, for *la'dhoni* is written with the *nun* pointed *ḥireq*, and is said of David. All the books from east to west have *nun ḥireq* and likewise *'ammekha* with *pathaḥ* to the *'ayin*. Do they not say that our *Torah* is a witness for them? Answer their error of belief in this way: 'if both father and son are divine, then the one does not need his companion, for he who is in need of somebody else is not called God' . . ." Qimḥi then deals in similar vein with the other identifications — erroneous, as he holds, — with Jesus, and ends up by denying the Christian claim that the *Torah* was of limited duration. This he refutes, and this time he quotes as proof *Malachi* "the seal of the prophets"[45]: *remember the law of Moses my servant* (iii: 22), *and I will send you Elijah the prophet* . . . (v. 23). He asserts that the *Torah* was commanded to Moses on Sinai, not to Jesus. "From this you can see that the *Torah* from Sinai will never be changed, but as it was given to our Teacher Moses so it will remain for ever. Elijah has not yet come and will not come until the time of the Messiah". Then he returns to the attack: v. 5, *he shall shatter kings in the day of his wrath*: where are the wars which Jesus has waged, and where the kings whom he has vanquished?" . . ." v. 7 says: *he shall lift up the head*, but unto this day he has not lifted up his head". The right interpretation requires reference of this psalm to David, *'al derekh ha-peshaṭ*. Here again, he combines the *peshaṭ*, buttressed by a grammatical analysis, with an appeal to history.

Further illustrations could be given from *Ps.* cxix: 129. Qimḥi rejects the Christian claim that the *Torah* is a *mashal* and has a fixed time of validity.[46] Further, on *Ps.* cxxvi: 5 he compares the *Torah* to a seed of blessing[47], and again on cxxix: 8.[48] In both cases

[45] Cf. BOSNIAK, חותם; other MSS read אחרון or סוף.

[46] Cf. *ibid.*, pp. 141 f. and on v. 152 p. 147. Cf. also his comment on *Ps.* xix, above, and n. 37. On v. 160 (cf. *ibid.*, p. 149) he again stresses the eternal validity of the *miṣwoth*: אין להם זמן [זמן קצוב v. 152] כמו שאומרים הנוצרים התועים ...

[47] Cf. *ibid.*, p. 165, הזורעים בדמעה refers to the keeping of the *Torah* in Exile, and the harvest will be הגמול הטוב for which the Jews hope. See also his comment on vv. 4 and 6.

[48] Cf. *ibid.*, p. 174. By implication the Christians are meant by הגוים: כן יהיו הגוים כי כל תורתם ואמונתם הבל וריק כחציר גגות וכן יבלו כחציר גגות אבל תורת ישראל המשיל לזרע ברכה.

he seemingly permits himself an allegorical explanation, clearly overstepping the boundary between allegory and metaphorical comparison which he is generally very careful to observe throughout his commentaries. His deep concern for the permanent validity of the *Torah* as the possession and obligation of Israel may account for his apparent departure in the two instances just quoted. They seem to be isolated cases; they are certainly different from the examples cited in connection with his interpretation of *Pss.* ii, lxxii and lxxxvii together with his censure of the Christian method adopted in cx, partly literal, partly spiritual. For he is at pains to show that the method of *peshaṭ* is the only correct one and that the Christian resort to a spiritual, allegorizing and typological interpretation is contrary to the text and meaning of Scripture. This opposition which he shares with the other Jewish exegetes, is, indeed, fundamental to the Jewish position; it cuts at the very root of Christian Biblical exegesis and shows clearly how incompatible the two methods are. To depart from the *peshaṭ* as one absolutely essential method of interpretation opened the door wide to sectarian and heretical tendencies with their inherent danger of antinomianism. The religious philosophers and the Qabbalists were therefore careful not only to conform in their own lives to the *Halakhah*, but (at least the majority of them) also to refrain from a philosophical or mystical interpretation of the preceptive part of the *Torah*, notwithstanding their attempt at unravelling the *mysteries of the commandments* metaphysically or mystically. If we apply this to Qimḥi's metaphorical interpretation of *ben* in *Ps.* ii and relate it to his inevitable adherence to antianthropormophism we realize that he was bound to uphold the immaterial, incorporeal nature of God. Significantly he has recourse to *mashal*, metaphorical interpretation in the strict sense of using a comparison, on the principle of *dibberah Torah ki-leshon beney 'adham*, but not to [*derekh*] *ruḥanith*, the spiritual *Umdeutung*. It is true that the frontier between metaphorical and spiritual, *i.e.* typological, allegorical, mystical, exposition is not always clearly marked, but it is a legitimate distinction and one which is borne out if we compare the Jewish and Christian interpretations of the Bible.

The anti-Christian polemic must not be considered in isolation; it is, as has been claimed, an integral part of the medieval Jewish explanation of the Bible as a whole. We must, therefore, not assume that the collection of Qimḥi's anti-Christian remarks on certain psalms into a separate treatise is in itself an indication of such isolation. The collection was made for practical purposes. We must equally take account of his systematically pursued messianic and eschatological interpretation as a necessary complement. There is his vindication of the future redemption of Israel, his reference, whenever feasible, to the end-time, the time of salvation for Israel and of what is left of the other nations, after the war of Gog and Magog.[49]

The whole body of medieval exegesis is an eloquent witness to the relentless struggle between a powerful Church and a Jewry at bay. Inasmuch as it is part of a comprehensive whole, the spirited defence of Judaism made possible by the skilful application of the method of *peshaṭ*, helped to strengthen the Jews in their faith and practice and enriched the understanding and appreciation of the biblical heritage. If we grasp this simple but fundamental fact everything falls into place: the fervent belief in the coming of the promised Messiah and in final redemption and salvation; the eternal validity of the *Torah*, which was neither abrogated by Jesus nor will it be set aside when the Messiah, heralded by Elijah, will come. Both beliefs receive sanction from the unflinching faith in the simple, absolute unity and uniqueness of God.

There is no need to defend, still less to apologise for the language in which this polemic was couched. There is no pulling of punches, but at least there is no abuse. These commentators were as much the children of their own age as were their Christian opponents, and we must understand them in the context of contemporary society. Their work reflects the spiritual climate of the Middle Ages, when theological preoccupations dominated the lives of Jews and Christians alike. They coloured social and economic thought no less than political action. Biblical exegesis, both Jewish and Christian, mirrors the life and thought of two faiths locked in battle, one on the offensive, aggressive, demanding, the other on the defensive, suffering from discrimination and sometimes outright persecution. Neither was willing to depart from their respective theological positions. The anti-Christian polemic contained in the *corpus* of Jewish biblical exegesis is a witness to the relevance, and the topical urgency of the problems discussed. Appeal to the literal, plain meaning of the Bible and to reason

[49] See the passages enumerated in n. 15, above.

and history resulted in the Jews standing firm, with few, but notable exceptions, and in their holding their own. And despite official hostility, there was much personal contact between Jewish and Christian scholars, in a sincere desire to discover the truth of the Hebrew Bible for both of them, as being the word of God, Holy Writ.[50]

---

[50] Paper read at the Institute of Jewish Studies, then at Manchester, in January 1959.

9

'JÜDISCHE ANTWORT'

I. Voraussetzungen für die jüdische Auseinandersetzung mit der christlichen Religion

1. *Die aufgezwungene Verteidigung*

Schon der Titel dieses Kapitels besagt, daß in der Beziehung des Judentums zum Christentum ein religiös-schöpferisches Element fehlt. Zwar bestanden selbst in Zeiten systematischer Judenverfolgung freundschaftliche Beziehungen zwischen einzelnen gelehrten Juden und führenden christlichen Geistlichen und Gelehrten, welche für beide Teile fruchtbar und geistig anregend waren und zweifellos zu besserem gegenseitigem Verständnis der heiligen Schriften der beiden Religionen führten. Aber das Judentum als solches verfügt über keine eigenständige, spontane Stellungnahme zum Christentum, das aus ihm hervorgegangen ist und mit dem es das gemeinsame Erbgut des Alten Testamentes verbindet. Jede Erörterung des Verhältnisses zwischen der Synagoge und der Kirche muß aber von der wichtigen Tatsache ausgehen, daß das Alte Testament die unentbehrliche Grundlage bildet für gegenseitige Freundschaft wie auch Feindschaft. So steht von Anfang an das jüdisch-christliche Mit- und Gegeneinander in einem Zwielicht, in einer Art feindlicher Brüderschaft, gekennzeichnet durch das Grundgebot der Nächstenliebe, das beiden Religionen eigen ist, aber auch durch Haß und Feindschaft der siegreichen, mächtigen Kirche gegen die unterlegene, der Bekehrung sich widersetzende Synagoge. Vom Standpunkt der Kirche aus war die Bekehrung der Juden natürlich verständlich, ja sogar nötig. Aber die Juden haben mit steigender Bitternis auf den Bekehrungseifer reagiert, der mit der Ausbreitung des Dominikaner- und Franziskaner-Ordens immer stärker – und gefährlicher – wurde. Die wesentliche Rolle, die bei den Bekehrungsversuchen – von der päpstlichen Kurie und der hohen Geistlichkeit gutgeheißen und gefördert – getaufte Juden in Wort und Schrift spielten, hat die jüdische Haltung stark beeinflußt und die jüdische Antwort polemischer und auch ausfälliger gemacht.

Die Juden wurden immer mehr in die Enge getrieben, Massentaufen – besonders anläßlich der blutigen Verfolgung der spanischen Juden im Jahre

1391, wie 1096 in Deutschland anläßlich des ersten Kreuzzuges — waren an der Tagesordnung. Das unberechenbare Nebeneinander von Toleranz und Verfolgung, begleitet von Ausnahmebestimmungen gegen die Juden zu allen Zeiten, vergrößerte die Unsicherheit der jüdischen Existenz in einer Atmosphäre des Kampfes um Leib und Seele. Besonders gefährlich für die Juden wirkte sich das Bündnis zwischen geistlicher Autorität und weltlicher Macht aus. Trotziges Beharren im angestammten Glauben, Taubheit und Blindheit gegenüber der christlichen Botschaft brachten es oft mit sich, daß die örtliche Geistlichkeit der weltlichen Gewalt hilfreiche Waffen lieferte, wenn es sich darum handelte, Vorwände zu Ausschreitungen gegen die Juden oder gar zu ihrer Vertreibung zu haben. Denn die rechtliche Lage der Juden, ob als kaiserliche Kammerknechte oder als Schutzberechtigte von weltlichen und geistlichen Fürsten im Mittelalter, war unsicher und meist von wirtschaftlichen Erwägungen abhängig. Die wirtschaftliche Rolle der Juden war, unbeschadet ihrer Nützlichkeit, ja Notwendigkeit, leicht dazu angetan, den Haß und Neid der christlichen Bevölkerung herauszufordern, besonders wenn es sich um jüdische Geldhändler und Steuerpächter handelte. Religiöser Fanatismus und wirtschaftlicher Druck der auf jüdischen Kredit angewiesenen christlichen Bevölkerung bildeten zusammen einen fruchtbaren Anlaß zu antijüdischen Maßnahmen.

Dieser Rückblick war nötig als Hintergrund für unsere ins einzelne gehende Betrachtung der jüdischen Antwort auf den Versuch der Kirche, der Synagoge durch die Bekehrung ihrer Mitglieder ein Ende zu bereiten und den Juden das Seelenheil durch den Glauben an den göttlich-menschlichen Jesus als den verheißenen und bereits erschienenen Messias zu ermöglichen. Dabei ist ferner noch zu bedenken, daß nicht nur Tatsachen und auf der rationalen Ebene liegende Gründe das gegenseitige Verhältnis zwischen Juden und Christen, besonders unter den Gebildeten, bedingten, sondern auch — und diese Erscheinung kann nicht hoch genug bewertet und in Rechenschaft gezogen werden — irrationale Elemente eine unheilvolle Rolle gespielt haben. Die im Mittelalter weitverbreitete Magie und der volkstümliche Glaube an ihre Wirksamkeit sind weitgehend verantwortlich für die wachsende antijüdische Haltung der breiten Volksmassen, welche die Verleumdung der Hostienschändung und die Lüge der Blutschuld ohne weiteres ernst nahmen und daher leicht gegen die jüdische Bevölkerung zu blutigen Ausschreitungen aufgestachelt werden konnten. Bekanntlich hat die Blutschuldlüge, der angebliche Ritualmord um die Osterzeit, bis in unsere Zeit ihr Unwesen getrieben.[1] Die Kurie und die hohe Geistlichkeit haben sich zu allen Zeiten eindeutig gegen solche grundlosen Beschuldigungen gewandt, aber diese haben trotzdem willige Ohren bei der breiten Masse gefunden, deren Glaube stark mit Aberglauben gemischt war; und die Ortsgeistlichen haben oft solche irrationalen Gefühle angefacht und geschürt, was viel zum Entstehen einer antijüdischen Atmosphäre beigetragen hat.

'Jüdische Antwort'

In einer solchen Atmosphäre hat sich vom 12. Jahrhundert ab der Kampf der Kirche gegen die Synagoge mit steigender Heftigkeit abgespielt, um dann vom 13. Jahrhundert an für das Judentum gefährliche Formen anzunehmen. Die literarische Auseinandersetzung beginnt natürlich schon mit den Kirchenvätern und hat ihr Echo im *Talmud* gefunden. Aber der Talmud ist von der Kirche erst vom Jahr 1239 an im Glaubenskampf benützt worden. Damit ist die christlich-jüdische Auseinandersetzung in ein neues Stadium getreten, wobei getaufte Juden weitgehend die Sprecher der Kirche waren und den Kampf unwilligen Rabbinern aufgezwungen haben. Obgleich ihr Angriff der *Haggada*, dem nicht religionsgesetzlich gültigen und als verpflichtend anerkannten Teil des Talmuds, galt, war damit Herz und Rückgrat der jüdischen Existenz schwer gefährdet worden. Denn diese Existenz war nur auf der Grundlage des Talmuds möglich und gesichert.

Die Lage der Juden wurde von jetzt an immer schwieriger. Die Unsicherheit der materiellen Existenz dehnte sich auf die geistige und religiöse aus und selbst der Bestand des Judentums geriet in immer größere Gefahr. Das ist wichtig bei der Beurteilung der literarischen Fehde, die Gegenstand unserer Darstellung ist. Denn es handelt sich keineswegs nur um Texte und Protokolle, um Kommentare zu biblischen Büchern, insbesondere zu messianischen Verheißungen, um Briefe und Streitschriften im eigentlichen Sinn und um offizielle Berichte über Disputationen. Sie alle haben ihren *Sitz im Leben* nicht nur der beiden Religionen, sondern vor allem ihrer Bekenner. Die Überredungskunst eines Vicente Ferrer (von 1412 ab) und eines Josua de Lorca, der bei seiner Taufe den christlichen Namen Hieronymus de Santa Fide annahm, war nicht weniger gefährlich wie eine schwache Antwort der zum *Streitgespräch in Tortosa* versammelten geistigen Führer des spanischen Judentums, besonders Aragoniens (1413–14). Die Verbrennung des Talmuds in Paris ein paar Jahre nach der »Disputation« von 1240 war im Grunde das Signal zur Verbrennung von Ketzern, Christen sowohl als auch jüdischen Neu- und Scheinchristen. Die Zensur nicht nur des Talmuds, sondern der ganzen hebräischen Literatur stellt das sichtbare Zeichen der Kontrolle der Kirche über die Synagoge dar. Innerhalb des Judentums gab es auch Dunkelmänner, welche glaubten, der Gefahr der christlichen Missionstätigkeit am besten dadurch begegnen zu können, daß sie die Anhänger des Moses Maimonides (1135–1204) ihrer philosophischen Ansichten wegen in den Bann schlugen und sogar die Hilfe der Inquisition zuerst in Montpellier und dann in Paris im Jahre 1233 in Anspruch nahmen und Maimonides' philosophische Schriften verbrennen ließen. Zwar fand diese Maßnahme die scharfe Verurteilung selbst der gemäßigten Antimaimonisten, aber sie ist doch symptomatisch für die Einstellung derjenigen jüdischen Kreise, die angesichts der von außen drohenden Gefahr glaubten, die Reihen schließen und jede freiere Regung des Geistes unterbinden zu müssen.

Jewish themes

Die Auseinandersetzung zwischen Christentum und Judentum im Hochmittelalter war den Juden von der Kirche aufgezwungen worden. Christliche Bekehrungsversuche gingen Hand in Hand mit der Bekämpfung judaisierender Tendenzen innerhalb des Christentums selbst und der Ausrottung aller Häretiker. Diese Tatsache macht es verständlich, warum die Kirche die jüdische Auslegung des Alten Testamentes bekämpfen mußte. Am Gegenpol finden wir die systematischen jüdischen Angriffe auf das Neue Testament vom 12. Jahrhundert an: sie sind mehr als zum Gegenangriff übergehende jüdische Abwehr und Rechtfertigung; sie müssen auch im Zusammenhang mit der Bekämpfung judaisierender Ketzer im Christentum betrachtet werden. Daraus ist also ersichtlich, wie wichtig im Kampf um den rechten Glauben und um das Seelenheil der Rechtgläubigen die richtige Auslegung der Bibel zu allen Zeiten war, besonders aber im Hochmittelalter, in der Epoche der Renaissance, der Reformation und der Gegenreformation.

Uns geht hier nur die jüdische Abwehr und Rechtfertigung an. Von einem richtigen Zwiegespräch, einem Dialog ebenbürtiger Teilnehmer kann keine Rede sein, ganz abgesehen von der eingangs erwähnten Tatsache, daß das Judentum offiziell keine Notiz vom Christentum genommen und kein selbständiges Verständnis von ihm gehabt hat. Gezwungen und zaghaft setzten sich die Rabbiner mit der christlichen Auslegung der beiden Religionen heiligen Schrift des Alten Testamentes auseinander.

2. Hauptprobleme des theologischen Streites

Worum ging es dabei? Diese einfache Frage kann nicht allgemein für alle Zeiten des christlich-jüdischen Religionsgesprächs beantwortet werden. Zwar haben sich die Grundlehren, um die es ging, nicht geändert, aber je stärker und drohender der christliche Angriff seit dem 13. Jahrhundert wurde, desto mehr sahen sich die jüdischen Verteidiger gezwungen, den Nachdruck auf die eine oder andere Frage zu legen und einen Unterschied zwischen Glaubensartikeln im christlichen Sinn und Grundlehren zu machen, vor allem in der Messiasfrage. Solche Hauptfragen wie die Natur Gottes, d. h. auf jüdischer Seite seine absolute einfache Einheit und Einzigkeit, oder die ewige Gültigkeit und Verbindlichkeit der *Tora* als Gesetz, welches das ganze Leben des Juden als einzelnem und in der jüdischen Glaubensgemeinschaft regelt, sind nie einem Wechsel unterworfen worden. Aber von Nachmanides an, dem jüdischen Streiter im *Streitgespräch von Barcelona* im Jahre 1263, hat sich ein Wandel in der Bewertung der Messiasfrage angebahnt, der seinen Ausdruck in Chasdai Crescas (1350–1410), Simon ben Zemach Duran (1361–1444) und vor allem in Josef Albo (einem Schüler Crescas', gestorben 1444), findet. Für

Albo ist der Glaube an den Messias ein abgeleitetes, nicht ein Grundprinzip des Glaubens. Auf diese Weise hoffte er, dem christlichen Messias-Anspruch sozusagen die Spitze abzubiegen dadurch, daß er dem Christentum den Offenbarungscharakter abspricht, weil es gegen die Einheit des göttlichen Wesens durch seinen mit der geoffenbarten jüdischen Religion im Widerspruch stehenden Gottesbegriff verstößt.[2] Dies ist mindestens teilweise durch die christliche Betonung des Messias bedingt. In der Tat ist die Frage, ob der von den Propheten verheißene Messias schon gekommen ist oder nicht, die Hauptstreitfrage bei den Religionsgesprächen. Die Kirche erhebt den Anspruch, daß Jesus von Nazareth der verheißene Messias ist, während die Juden das verneinen, indem sie auf die Bedingungen hinweisen, die auf Grund der prophetischen Verheißungen der Messias erfüllen muß und welche Jesus nicht erfüllt hat; also ist der Messias nicht während der Zeit des zweiten Tempels, d. h. zu Lebzeiten Jesu, erschienen. Nach judischer Auffassung war Jesus nicht der Messias, welcher erst in der Zukunft kommen wird. Der Wortstreit geht nicht nur bei den Disputationen gerade um diese messianische Frage, auch in den Streitschriften und Bibelkommentaren nimmt sie einen breiten Raum ein.

So wichtig diese Frage ist, sie ist gleichwohl nicht die einzige, die die beiden Religionen unversöhnlich trennt. Daher finden wir in den hebräischen Bibelkommentaren vor allem die beiden andern Hauptfragen (nach dem Wesen Gottes und der Dauer des mosaischen Gesetzes) ausführlich erörtert, während in den Streitgesprächen und den Streitschriften hauptsächlich die letztere zur Sprache kommt. Für die Juden ist der Talmud die autoritative Auslegung des mosaischen Gesetzes. Für die Christen ist sein haggadischer Teil durch allegorische Deutung beweiskräftig für die Messianität Jesu. Außerdem enthält nach der Meinung der Christen der Talmud ausfällige Bemerkungen über Jesus, Gotteslästerung und Absurditäten, weshalb er, wenn nicht verbrannt, zum mindesten von diesen Anstößigkeiten gereinigt werden müsse. Aus diesem Grund waren die Juden gegen ihren Willen gezwungen, zu diesen Aussagen Stellung zu nehmen. Soweit es sich um die Bibel handelt, bestehen sie auf dem Wortsinn und lehnen die christliche Auslegung, sei sie allegorisch oder typologisch, ab. Was den Talmud betrifft, so machen die Juden eine grundsätzliche Unterscheidung zwischen gesetzlichen, verbindlichen Stellen, welche den Hauptteil der Traktate des ausgedehnten Werkes ausmachen, und dem nicht-gesetzlichen, haggadischen Teil, welcher Geschichten und Legenden erbaulichen Charakters enthält, deren Mehrzahl eine Moral im Sinne der jüdischen Ethik lehren. Manche sind einfach erzählender Natur ohne spezifisch religiös jüdische Beziehung, wie man sie bei allen Völkern antrifft.

Die zur Antwort christlicher Ansprüche und Einwendungen verpflichteten geistigen Führer der Juden haben einen schweren Stand gehabt und waren dieser heiklen Aufgabe weniger gewachsen als der Bibelexegese, bei der sie auf dem festen Grund der Sprachwissenschaft und der eindeutigen jüdischen Tradition ihren Stand nehmen konnten. Es ist eine Ironie des Schicksals, daß die diesem Wortstreit zugrundeliegende Taktik der Kirche von getauften Juden zugetragen und mit Hilfe der christlichen scholastischen Methode dialektisch glänzend entwickelt wurde. Die jüdischen Argumente hatten größeres Gewicht, wenn sie von Nachmanides in Barcelona (1263) gehandhabt wurden, wobei ihm eine freundlicher gesinnte weltliche Autorität zur Seite stand. Dieselben Argumente verloren an Schlag- und Überzeugungskraft bei der Disputation von Tortosa 150 Jahre später, nicht so sehr, weil die dortigen jüdischen Vertreter weniger geübt und ihrem Gegner nicht gewachsen waren, sondern vielmehr weil die Lage der Juden sich katastrophal verschlechtert hatte, weil sowohl die weltliche Autorität ihnen feindlich gesonnen war, als auch die geistliche Gewalt des spanischen Gegenpapstes Benedikt XIII., seiner Kirchenfürsten und der von Dominikanern und Franziskanern glänzend geschulten Gelehrten ihnen entgegenstand. Die Kombination geistlicher Waffen und einer prekären wirtschaftlichen Stellung, die christlichen Neid und Haß hervorrief und bei den führenden jüdischen Familien persönlichen Vorteil über die Standhaftigkeit und Treue zum angestammten, unter Feuer stehenden Glauben stellte, mußte sich äußerst ungünstig auf den Bestand des Judentums auswirken. Von Tortosa führt eine gerade Linie zur Vertreibung der Juden aus Spanien im Jahr 1492, obgleich es in dieser Zeit nicht an wackeren Kämpfern für die jüdische Sache wie dem genannten Josef Albo und Don Isaak Abravanel gefehlt hat.

II. Polemische Kommentare zur Bibel

1. Grundsätze der Bibelauslegung

Wir beginnen mit einer Darstellung der christlich-jüdischen Auseinandersetzung, wie sie uns in den hebräischen Bibelkommentaren entgegentritt. Die jüdische Antwort auf den christlichen Anspruch, Jesus Christus sei der verheißene Messias gewesen, habe das mosaische Gesetz abgeschafft, durch seinen Opfertod die Erbsünde getilgt und den Alten, auf dem mosaischen Gesetz gegründeten, Bund durch den Neuen Bund ersetzt, welcher auf dem Glauben an ihn ruht und durch ihn der Menschheit Erlösung gewährt, diese jüdische Antwort war in erster Linie an die Adresse der Juden gerichtet und dazu bestimmt, sie in ihrem Glauben zu festigen und die messianische Hoffnung in ihnen wachzuhalten. Die Kommentarliteratur ist sehr ausgedehnt, und wir müssen uns auf den christlichen Kulturkreis in West- und Mitteleuropa beschränken. Die antichristliche Polemik ist natürlich der Kirche nicht entgangen, und sie hat sie einer gründlichen Zensur unterzogen, um zu verhindern, daß die des Hebräischen kundigen christlichen Leser in ihrem Glauben wankend würden. Kein mittelalterlicher hebräischer Bibelkommentar ist frei von antichristlicher Polemik mit dem Ziel, eine Anwendung der messianischen Verheißungen auf die Zeit Jesu zu bestreiten und ihre Erfüllung in der Endzeit zu begründen. Je gefährdeter die jüdische Existenz ist, desto dringender wird diese Auslegung und desto enger ist sie mit dem unmittelbaren oder wenigstens baldigen Kommen des verheißenen Messias verbunden. So wirft diese Literatur ein interessantes Licht auf die christlich-jüdische Auseinandersetzung und zeigt, wie lebensnah und für das Fortbestehen des jüdischen Lebens unerläßlich sie war. Die jüdische Bibelexegese hat sich, wie schon erwähnt, auf die Erklärung und Erhellung des einfachen Wortsinns des hebräischen Textes konzentriert und die metaphorische und allegorische Erklärung auf die Bekämpfung des Anthropomorphismus beschränkt. Dieser Aspekt der Bibeldeutung ist erst in der Auseinandersetzung mit dem Christentum zu voller Entfaltung gekommen, auch wenn er von allem Anfang an ein innerjüdisches Erfordernis war. Denn die christliche Lehre von der Menschwerdung Gottes in der Person Jesu Christi war unvereinbar mit der jüdischen Gottesauffassung. Deshalb mußte die körperliche Darstellung Gottes in der hebräischen Bibel umgedeutet werden mit Hilfe des rabbinischen Satzes »die *Tora* (hier die ganze Heilige Schrift) spricht in der Sprache der Menschen«. Die talmudischen Weisen haben ferner den Grundsatz aufgestellt, daß kein Schriftvers seinen Wortsinn verlieren darf, auch wenn ihm darüber hinaus noch ein verborgener, innerer Sinn gegeben wird. In der Auseinandersetzung mit dem Christentum hat dieses Erklärungsprinzip eine immer größere Rolle gespielt; seine Anwendung hat den Juden eine wirksame Waffe im Kampf um den Sinn der Bibel und um das Verstehen der in ihr offenbarten religiösen Wahrheit geliefert. So finden wir beim Kirchenvater Origenes die Bezeichnung der Juden als »ein körperliches Volk« und als »Freunde des Buchstabens«; der Wortsinn wird geradezu »der jüdische Sinn« genannt. Die Juden haben die christlichen Bibelerklärer gezwungen, zum Wortsinn Stellung zu nehmen, und der heilige Augustin hat den Wortsinn erlaubt, solange die Christen sich an den »mystischen Sinn« hielten.[3] In seinem Pentateuch-Kommentar spricht Abraham ibn Ezra (etwa 1092—1167), der bedeutendste Bibelerklärer der spanischen Schule vor und neben Nachmanides, von fünf Erklärungsweisen:

1. »Die erste ist die Methode der unbeschnittenen Weisen (d. h. der Christen), die sagen, die ganze *Tora* sei Rätsel und Gleichnisse, sowohl alles, was im Buche *Genesis* steht, als auch alle Gebote und gerechten Satzungen. Jeder fügt dieses hinzu oder nimmt jenes weg nach seinem eigenen Gutdünken, einmal um es zu verbessern, ein anderes Mal, um es zu verschlechtern. So sind ›die sieben Völker‹ eine Anspielung auf verborgene Dinge ... Auch die Zahl der Stämme ist eine Anspielung auf die Zahl der Apostel, die abtrünnigen (durch die Zensur entfernt und durch ›die

12 Sternbilder< ersetzt). Aber dies ist alles eitel und nichtig; es gibt nichts dergleichen. Die Wahrheit ist, jedes Gebot, Ding und Wort zu erklären, wie sie geschrieben sind. Wenn sie dem Verstand nahe liegen, ist es auch in Ordnung, daß Dinge Geheimnisse enthalten, und sie sind in ihrem Wesen wahr, auch Rätsel, wie die Sache des Paradieses und des Baums der Erkenntnis ... Der zuverlässige Zeuge in unserem ganzen Kommentar ist der Verstand des in unser heiliges Innere gepflanzten Herzens (d. i. Verstandes), und wer der Vernunft widerspricht, ist wie einer, der unser Empfinden verleugnet. Denn die *Tora* (oder das Gesetz) unserer Väter ist Menschen des Verstandes (wörtlich: des Herzens) gegeben worden. Finden wir etwas in der *Tora* geschrieben, das die Vernunft nicht ertragen kann, so fügen wir (erklärend) hinzu oder verbessern nach Vermögen auf Grund des Sprachgebrauchs, welchen der erste Mensch bestimmt hat. Das machen wir auch mit den Geboten so, wenn etwas seinem Wortsinn nach der Vernunft nicht (zu erfassen) möglich ist, wie (Deut. 10, 16) >so beschneidet denn die Vorhaut eures Herzens<; denn über die Gebote ist geschrieben (Lev. 18, 5), >die der Mensch üben soll, daß er durch sie lebe< ...«[4]

Die fünfte Erklärungsweise ist seine eigene, sich auf die Gesetze der hebräischen Sprache stützende philologische Methode, um den einfachen Wortsinn zu ermitteln. Nur in der Erklärung der Gebote stützt er sich auf die Früheren.[5]

Der einflußreichste mittelalterliche jüdische Exeget R. Salomo ben Isaak (Raschi), der Rabbi Salomo der christlichen Bibelerklärer (1040—1105), fügt vielen seiner Erklärungen den Ausdruck bei »nach dem Wortsinn und als Antwort für die Ketzer (d. i. Christen)«. So fügt er in seinem Kommentar zu Sprüche 2, 12 dem »Ketzer« als Erklärung hinzu »die Israel zum Götzendienst verführen«. Dem Ketzer wird der Gläubige, d. h. der gläubige Jude entgegengesetzt. Andere Bezeichnungen für die Christen sind »Nazarener«, oft von dem bedeutenden David Kimchi (um 1160—1235) in seinem Psalmenkommentar benutzt, oder »Irrende« (in den hebräischen Berichten über die Judenverfolgungen während der Kreuzzüge) oder »Einwände Erhebende« (so Abraham ibn Ezra). Die Bezeichnung »Götzendiener«, für Christen natürlicherweise beleidigend, ist oft durch einen andern Ausdruck *(akum)* verschleiert, um bei der Zensur keinen Anstoß zu geben; wörtlich bedeutet er »Anbeter von Sternen und Sternbildern (des Tierkreises)«. Wie aktuell die gegen die christliche Auslegung gerichtete jüdische war, geht auch aus einer Wendung hervor, die David Kimchi gerne benutzt: »sollte jemand einwenden, so mußt du antworten«, oder: »die Christen beziehen (diesen Psalm) auf Jesus«, wofür oft »jener Mann« oder auch »ihr Glaube« steht. »Einwand« und »Antwort« scheinen auf tatsächliches christlich-jüdisches Gespräch, zum mindesten zwischen einzelnen Vertretern beider Religionen, hinzudeuten. Ob die Ausdrücke »körperlich« und »geistig« im Gespräch verwandt oder nur in der Literatur vorkommen, ist weniger wichtig als ihre Verwendung durch die Juden; sie sind christliche Ausdrücke.

2. Auslegung des Jakobssegens

Diese grundsätzlich verschiedene Deutungsweise soll an einigen besonders wichtigen biblischen Stellen klargemacht werden. Zuerst besprechen wir die im Jakobssegen (Gen. 49, 10) enthaltene Weissagung betreffend Juda, weil sie nicht nur in der Kommentarliteratur, sondern auch in den Streitschriften und vor allem in den Disputationen von Barcelona und Tortosa eine große Rolle spielt. Die Stelle lautet: »nicht weicht das Szepter von Juda, der Herrscher nicht von seinem Schoß (oder: der Herrscherstab (Gesetzesstab) nicht von seinen Füßen), bis er nach Schilo kommt und Nationen ihm gehorchen.«

Die in den Disputationen gegebene Auslegung beiseite lassend, beginnen wir mit Raschi, der Schilo als Name des Messias versteht im Sinn der aramäischen Übersetzung des Onkelos »dessen das Reich ist« oder im Sinne von *schaj lo* »dem Huldigung gebührt«, einer midraschischen Auslegung folgend, die dem R. Mose ha-Darschan aus Narbonne (um 1060) zugeschrieben wird und auch von Raimund Martini in seinem *Pugio fidei* zitiert wird. Messianisch deuten Schilo noch andere jüdische Ausleger.[6] Sie haben alle gemeinsam, daß sie den Vers auf die messianische Zukunft am Ende der Tage beziehen und nicht auf Jesus, wie das die Christen tun. Denn, so argumentieren diese, die Herrschaft ist längst von Juda geschwunden und auf Jesus Christus übergegangen. Um dem vorzubeugen, haben einige jüdische Ausleger die hebräische Konjunktion *adh ki* auseinandergezogen und entweder »das Szepter ... und der Gesetzesstab von seinen Füßen *ewiglich, sobald* Schilo kommt« oder »*ewiglich; denn* ...« übersetzt. Messianisch, aber Schilo nicht als Namen des Messias, faßt die Stelle auch Rabbi Samuel (ben Salomo aus Falaise, um 1175–1250), der erklärte, *schiloh* bedeute: »Ruhe«, nach Klagelieder 1, 5: »Ihre Feinde leben ruhig *(schalu)*. Wenn der Messias erscheint, wird Frieden und Sicherheit herrschen.«[7]

Wahrscheinlich in antichristlicher Absicht haben wieder andere Ausleger Schilo nicht messianisch und als auf eine Person bezüglich, sondern als den Ortsnamen Schilo mit dem Heiligtum gleichen Namens verstanden. So finden wir bei Samuel ben Meïr (Raschbam, dem Enkel Raschis, um 1085–1158) folgende Erklärung, die auch von anderen Auslegern von ihm übernommen worden ist:

2. »Das Szepter wird nicht von Juda weichen‹, das Königtum, welches ihm verliehen wurde, so daß alle seine zwölf Brüder sich vor ihm bücken sollen. Nicht soll verschwinden diese ganze Größe und Herrschaft und der Gesetzesstab von seinem Samen, bis Juda nach Schilo komme, d. h. bis der König von Juda kommen wird – er ist Rehabeam Sohn Salomos, der kommt, um das Königtum in Schilo, welches nahe bei Sichem ist, zu erneuern. Aber dann fielen die zehn Stämme von ihm ab und wählten (sich) den Jerobeam (b. Nebat) zum König und dem Rehabeam ben Salomo blieben nur Juda und Benjamin (treu). ›Und ihm ist die Sammlung der

Völker‹, die Stämme, die seinem Vater Salomo untertänig waren, wie es in 1. Kön. 5, 4 geschrieben steht ... ›Neben der Terebinthe, die bei Sichem stand‹ (Gen. 35, 4) war nämlich ein geräumiges Grundstück, geeignet für die Versammlung von Menschen und zur Ehrung der darangrenzenden Stiftshütte von Schilo. Diese wörtliche Deutung ist eine Antwort an die Christen (wörtlich ›Ketzer‹), es steht nämlich nichts geschrieben außer Schilo als ein Stadtname ... und es ist hier nicht *schelo* geschrieben, wie die Juden (wörtlich ›Hebräer‹) sagen, noch *scheliach*, wie es die Christen (wörtlich ›Nazarener‹) sagen ...«[8]

Eine andere Auslegung erklärt den Vers dadurch, daß ihr Verfasser, nach Posnanski Jakob ben Abraham am Rhein (um 1165), die Zeitwörter *sur* und *bo'* anders übersetzt:

3. »Im (Talmud) Jeruschalmi wird der Vers Gen. 49, 10 folgendermaßen erklärt: *lo jasur* es wird nicht erblühen, nach Jer. 2, 21 *surej*, ›die blühenden wilden Reben‹, d. h.: Das Szepter aus Juda und der Aufseher und König über Israel, d. i. David, wird nicht erblühen, bis Schilo untergeht, wie: ›und ist die Sonne untergegangen ... (Lev. 22, 7)‹. Schilo ist die Stiftshütte, d. h. es wird kein König in Israel sein, bis die Stiftshütte von Schilo zerstört ist, dann wird ihm das Szepter und der Gesetzesstab gehören ... wie geschrieben steht: ›und er (Gott) verstieß die Stiftshütte in Schilo‹ (Ps. 78, 60) ... ›und wählte David, seinen Knecht‹ (Ps. 78, 70).«[9]

Schließlich soll eine dritte Deutung von *Schilo* Erwähnung finden. David Kimchi leitet das Wort in seinem Wörterbuch von einer Wurzel *schi-j-l (schil)* ab und sagt:

4. »Seine Bedeutung ist ›sein Sohn‹ und die Prophezeiung geht auf David vom Stamme Juda oder auf den Messias und es gehört zum Ausdruck ›und auf die Nachgeburt, die zwischen ihren Füßen hervorgeht (Deut. 28, 57)‹ ... und beide Wurzeln und ihre Bedeutung sind ein und dasselbe.«[10]

In seinem Kommentar zur Genesis erklärt er die Stelle so:

5. »›Nicht wird das Szepter weichen‹, der Herrscher wird Stab (Rute) genannt, weil er über das Volk herrscht und sie zurechtweist, wie der Mensch mit der Rute züchtigt. Das ist die Weise der Herrscher, die das Szepter in ihrer Hand haben ... ›Und der Gesetzesstab zwischen seinen Füßen‹, d. h. von seinen Kindern, wie es Deut. 28, 57 heißt ... und der Herrscher wird Gesetzesstab genannt, weil er die Gesetze gibt. Und er (der Vers) sagt: nicht wird die Fürstenwürde von Juda weichen, bis ihm mehr zukam, daß er König wurde; dies geht auf David. *Schilo* bedeutet ›sein Sohn‹ von ›und auf ihre Nachgeburt‹ *(schiljah)* (ebenda). ... bis der kommt, dem die Königsherrschaft gehört und der Sinn ist, wie einer zum andern sagt: nimm dies jetzt, bis ich dir mehr gebe. *jikhat* (Versammlung, Gehorsam) ist hier ein Hauptwort und gleicherweise Sprüche 30, 17 ›der Mutter zu gehorchen‹, was ›Gehorsam und Dienst‹, bedeutet, besagend, daß die Völker ihm gehorchen und dienstbar sein sollen, wie das bei David war und um so mehr beim König Messias (dereinst) sein wird.«[11]

David Kimchis Gleichsetzung von »sein Sohn« *(schilo)* mit »Nachgeburt« *(schilja)* haben nicht nur jüdische Ausleger nach ihm angenommen, sondern auch Raimund Martini, der sich ausdrücklich auf Kimchis Wörterbuch bezieht. Aber er hat darin einen Beweis für die christliche Lehre von der unbefleckten Empfängnis und Marias Jungfräulichkeit bei der Geburt Jesu gesehen:

6. »die Benennung Silo hängt somit mit Silya zusammen, das die lateinischen Ärzte als secunda oder secundina, Nachgeburt, bezeichneten und das sich lediglich aus dem Muttersamen allein bildet, so daß, wenn der Hl. Geist, durch Jakob und Mose sprechend, den Messias Silo nannte, er nichts so deutlich hat sagen wollen, als daß Christus dem Leibe nach nicht aus väterlichem Samen, sondern einzig und allein aus der Mutter Substanz mit Hilfe des Hl. Geistes geboren werden sollte.«[12]

Levi ben Abraham aus Villefranche de Conflent (1250—1315) beginnt seine Auslegung der Stelle mit dem Satz:

7. »Was die Christen (wörtlich: die Ketzer der Völker) an den Vers ›nicht wird das Szepter von Juda weichen‹ (als den Sinn) anhängen, ist offenbare Absurdität, denn nach seinem Wortsinn ist es unmöglich, daß in Juda einer (als Herrscher) aufgetreten ist bis David kam, und eine lange Zeit vor Jesus hat das Königtum des Hauses David bereits aufgehört...«[13]

3. Auslegung von Jesaja 53

Die Auslegungen des 53. Kapitels des Propheten Jesaja (genauer von Kap. 52, 13 an) sind vor vielen Jahren im hebräischen Original mit einer englischen Übersetzung herausgegeben worden.[14] Es genügt daher, weiter unten nur die Deutung des Nachmanides im Anschluß an seinen hebräischen Bericht über das Religionsgespräch zu Barcelona zu Wort kommen zu lassen. Im allgemeinen gilt für die Erklärung der Propheten, was für die eben referierte Auslegung des Jakobssegens gilt: die Juden haben jede Beziehung auf die Zeit des zweiten Tempels und damit auf Jesus abgelehnt und mit Hilfe ihrer philologischen und historischen Deutung versucht, den Wortsinn zu eruieren. Ihre Beweisführung mag uns Heutige, in der modernen Bibelkritik geschulte, nicht überzeugen. Aber in unserem Zusammenhang ist es wichtig, in diesen mittelalterlichen jüdischen Deutungen klar ihre alleinige Absicht zu erkennen: ihrer Generation Mut und Hoffnung zu machen und sie in ihrem Glauben gegen christliche Bekehrungsversuche zu bestärken und zu erhalten und dadurch den Weiterbestand des Judentums zu sichern. Nur so können wir verstehen, warum etwa Raschi nur die letzten Verse des Buches Daniel auf die Erlösung am Ende der Tage bezieht, alles andere aber als Anspielungen auf die Zeit der Makkabäer erklärt. Jesaja, Kapitel 26—28 und 34 wie auch die Stellen 9, 12; 23, 18 und 24, 16, 18 weisen auf den künftigen Messias und die Erlösung des Volkes Israel hin. Daß Jes. 7, 14 eine junge, verheiratete Frau und nicht eine Jungfrau unter *alma* zu verstehen ist — entgegen der christlichen Auffassung, die sich auf die griechische Übersetzung stützt — ist die allgemeine jüdische Ansicht. Nur über die Identität der jungen Frau, ob die Frau des Propheten (Raschi) oder des Königs Achas (Kimchi) gibt es verschiedene Meinungen. Nach Kimchi wurde dem König ein Zeichen gegeben und kann die Verheißung nicht auf Jesus gedeutet werden, der mehr als 400 Jahre später lebte.[15] Dasselbe gilt von Jes. 9, 5: nur »Friedensfürst« bezieht sich auf »Denn ein Kind ist uns geboren ...«, die andern Namen sind Bezeichnungen für Gott. »Von nun ab bis in Ewigkeit« im nächsten Vers kann sich auch nicht auf Jesus beziehen, der 500 Jahre später geboren wurde. In seiner Psalmenexegese bemüht sich Raschi ebenfalls, die christliche Deutung zu widerlegen und scheut sich nicht, aus sprachlichen Gründen gegen die Überlieferung eigene Wege zu gehen. Oft beginnt oder endet er seine Erklärung mit dem Ausdruck »gemäß seinem (des Verses) Wortsinn und als Antwort für die Christen (wörtlich: Ketzer)«. Ps. 9, 14: »Gib Gunst mir, Ewiger, sieh mein Elend von den Hassern« bezieht sich auf die Jetztzeit im Exil, während: »der du erhebst von Todes Pforten« die Zeit der Erlösung im Auge hat. Während die jüdische Tradition Psalm 21 auf den König Messias bezieht, glaubt Raschi, daß David nach seiner Heirat mit Bathseba gemeint ist. Sach. 6, 12 spreche von Serubbabel, nicht von Jesus, meint Raschi, wohl um der christlichen Auslegung zu begegnen, denn die Kirche bezieht die ganze Verheißung auf Jesus, während die jüdische traditionelle Auslegung den künftigen Messias darunter versteht. Die meisten Ausleger identifizieren Edom mit dem christlichen Rom; so finden wir, daß Raschi Micha 7, 8 auf »Babylon und das schuldige Rom« bezieht, ebenso auch viele Stellen bei Jesaja (23, 1, 5; 26, 5; 27, 10). Seine Nachfolger in Nordfrankreich haben die Methode der wörtlichen Deutung mit gegenchristlicher Absicht vervollkommnet.[16] Beispielsweise leugnet Josef Bekhor Schor in seinem Pentateuchkommentar (zu Num. 12, 8), daß Moses Worte

8. »eine Allegorie seien, d. h. Rätsel und Gleichnis und nicht was er (tatsächlich) sagt, und sie verdrehen die Prophezeiung in etwas anderes, und sie lassen das Wort völlig aus seinem Wortsinn heraustreten ... Obgleich sie die Tora aus der heiligen Sprache in ihre (d. h. die Vulgata) übersetzen, hat ihnen der Heilige, gepriesen sei er, nicht ein Herz zur Erkenntnis, Augen zum Sehen und Ohren zum Hören gegeben.«[17]

4. Der Psalmenkommentar des David Kimchi

Von besonderem Interesse in unserem Zusammenhang sind eine Reihe antichristlicher Äußerungen in David Kimchis *Psalmenkommentar*, die auch gesondert gesammelt der Hackspanschen Ausgabe des *Sefer Nizzachon* des Lipman von Mühlhausen beigefügt sind.[18] Wir haben eingangs die verschiedenen Probleme, die trennend zwischen Judentum und Christentum stehen, gesondert aufgeführt. In Wirklichkeit gehören sie natürlich eng zusammen, denn das Wesen des Messias, wie es das Christentum in der göttlich-menschlichen Person Jesu sieht, kann nicht getrennt von dem Wesen Gottes begriffen werden. Aber aus methodischen und praktischen Gründen ist es geboten, das Problem der Natur Gottes gesondert vom Problem des Wesens des Messias zu behandeln. Ebenso verhält es sich mit der Frage des Alten Bundes, in der Offenbarung des Gesetzes vom Sinai herab verkörpert, und der des Neuen Bundes, der vom Christentum als eine Offenbarung in der Menschwerdung Gottes in Jesu Christi verstanden wird und daher in der Annahme mündet, daß der Neue Bund das Gesetz des Alten Bundes abgeschafft habe. Die Juden haben bezeichnenderweise in jeder Form ihrer »Antwort« darauf bestanden, nach dem Wesen des Messias zu fragen, ehe sie die für sie eng damit zusammenhängende Frage des Kommens des Messias behandeln wollten. Das werden wir besonders bei der Darstellung der öffentlichen Religionsstreitgespräche sehen.

Diese Verflochtenheit der drei Hauptprobleme — die Frage der Erbsünde ist nur eine Teilfrage des Messiasproblems in unserem Zusammenhang — zeigt sich auch im *Psalmenkommentar* des David Kimchi. Im Psalm 2 finden wir den Ausdruck »Sohn« von Gott auf den Menschen angewandt; Vers 7 lautet: »Mein Sohn bist du, ich hab dich heut gezeugt«. Dazu bemerkt Kimchi:

9. »Es ist nicht richtig, von Fleisch und Blut ›Sohn Gottes‹ zu sagen, denn der Sohn ist von derselben Art wie der Vater. Zu wem Gott sagt ›du bist mein Sohn‹, muß von Seiner Art sein und Gott muß wie er sein. Weiter, sollte jemand sagen: ich habe dich heute geboren und der Geborene ist von gleicher Art mit dem Zeuger, dann antworte ihnen: ›in der Gottesnatur ist es nicht möglich, Vater und Sohn (anzunehmen), denn die Gottheit kann nicht geteilt werden. Gott ist kein Körper, der geteilt werden kann. Seine Einheit ist absolut, ohne Hinzufügung, Wegnahme oder Teilbarkeit.‹ Du mußt ihnen ferner sagen, daß wir nur dann von Vater und Sohn sprechen können, wenn der Vater zuerst ist in zeitlichem Sinn und der Sohn aus der Kraft des Vaters hervorgeht. Daher muß der Sohn später sein als der Vater; dann ist aber keine Dreieinigkeit möglich. Wären beide die ganze Zeit koexistierend, sollte man sie Zwillingsbrüder nennen, nicht aber Vater und Sohn, Zeuger und Geborenen. Antworte dem, der sagt, es sei nicht möglich, irgend einen ›Sohn Gottes‹ zu nennen, der nicht von der (gleichen) Art von Göttlichkeit ist, daß wir von Gott nur metaphorisch (gleichnishaft) sprechen können, so beispielsweise wenn wir sagen ›der Mund Gottes‹, ›die Augen oder die Ohren Gottes‹. Wir bezeichnen denjenigen, welcher Seine Aufgabe und Seine Gebote erfüllt, als ›Sohn Gottes‹, genau so wie ein Sohn die Gebote (Befehle) seines Vaters ausführt... Wiederum sagst du von Gott, der Vater habe zum Sohn gesagt, ›verlange von mir und Ich will dir Völker als dein Erbe geben‹. ›Wenn der Sohn Gott ist, warum sollte er seinen Vater bitten? Hat er keine Gewalt über Völker und die Enden der Erde wie Er?‹... Sie mögen darauf

hinweisen, dies sei geschehen, nachdem er Fleisch geworden ist. Gott nahm Bezug auf seine Menschlichkeit, und hat dem Sohn als Menschen sozusagen Erbschaft versprochen. Doch das ist nicht der Fall, denn er hatte kein Königreich, solange er Fleisch war, noch irgendwelche Herrschaft über irgend ein Volk. Sagen sie, der Psalm spreche von ihrem Glauben... (dann erwidere ihnen), daß die Mehrzahl (der Menschen), seien sie Juden oder Moslems, es nicht anerkannt haben. So, jetzt habe ich dich gelehrt, wie du ihnen in bezug auf diesen Psalm antworten sollst. Du mußt aus deinem eigenen Wissen gemäß diesen Dingen (etwas) hinzufügen. Wenn um eine Erklärung gefragt, wähle zwischen den beiden, beziehe es entweder auf David oder auf den Messias, wie ich es erklärt habe.«[19]

Wir haben hier ein gutes Beispiel für Kimchis Methode der wörtlichen Erklärung. Denn Kimchi nimmt nicht nur den hebräischen Psalmtext, sondern auch seine christliche Erklärung wörtlich und setzt sich mit beiden rein logisch auseinander. Mit andern Worten, er, der ein Schüler des Maimonides und also philosophisch geschult war, hat christliche Glaubensartikel wie die Dreieinigkeit und die göttlich-menschliche Natur Christi buchstäblich verstanden. Das gilt durchweg für die jüdisch-christliche Auseinandersetzung im Mittelalter.

Über den jüdischen Anspruch, daß die Tora ewig gültig und verpflichtend sei, äußert sich Kimchi in seiner Kommentierung des 19. Psalms, Vers 10:

10. »Er widerspricht den Christen, welche die Ansicht vertreten, daß die Tora, die auf dem Berg Sinai gegeben wurde, eine begrenzte Dauer habe, nämlich nur bis zum Zeitpunkt des Kommens Jesu. Bis zu seiner Zeit war sie ›im Fleisch‹, aber als er kam, befahl er, sie ›im Geist‹ zu verstehen. Ihre Worte sind jedoch Wind und Eitelkeit. Denn diejenigen Gebote, die ihrer Ansicht nach allegorisch sind und nicht in ihrem wörtlichen Sinn verstanden werden können, (sind tatsächlich) von Gott klar offenbart worden, aber nicht in einem Gleichnis. Deshalb müssen die anderen Gebote vom Menschen auch gemäß ihrem wörtlichen Sinn und nicht allegorisch verstanden werden. Denn wenn die Gebote allegorisch wären, würden die Menschen im Zweifel sein. Der eine würde sagen, das Verborgene ist so-und-so, und ein anderer so-und-so, die Hl. Schrift sagt aber ausdrücklich...«[20]

Kimchi schließt seine »Antwort« mit dem Abschnitt Deut. 30, 11–14. Kimchi hat hier klar und eindeutig die jüdische Einstellung zur ewigen Gültigkeit der Tora Mosis zum Ausdruck gebracht. Psalm 21 spreche von David oder dem König Messias, nicht aber von Jesus, wie es die Christen behaupten. Er sagt:

11. »Du mußt ihnen Vers für Vers antworten... Nimm zum Beispiel den Ausdruck ›O Ewiger, durch deine Kraft freut sich der König‹ – gewißlich, denn ohne die Kraft des Vaters wird der Sohn keine haben. Aber wenn er schwach ist, dann ist er nicht Gott... Oder, ›groß ist sein Ruhm durch deine Hilfe‹ – aber ohne deine Hilfe ist sein Ruhm nicht groß. Folglich ist er nicht Gott. ›Ja, vertraut der König auf den Ewigen‹ – bezieht sich dies auf seine Göttlichkeit, dann hat er nicht nötig, auf einen andern zu vertrauen und er bedarf keineswegs der Gnade des Allerhöchsten.«

'Jüdische Antwort'

Für die Christologie ist Psalm 45 besonders wichtig. Deshalb geht Kimchi in seiner Widerlegung der christlichen Auslegung sehr ins einzelne:

12. »Die Christen wenden diesen Psalm auf Jesus den Nazarener an. ›Die Königstöchter‹ (v. 10) sind allegorisch gedeutet als die Völker, die sich der christlichen Religion zugewandt haben. ›Die Liebste steht zu deiner Rechten...‹ sagt man nicht von ihm, selbst nicht im Gleichnis, denn *schegal* ist, wie wir es erklärt haben, ein Ausdruck des Beischlafs mit der Ehefrau und das ist unzulässig in Bezug auf Gott. Ferner, wie kann man sagen ›Statt deiner Väter sollen deine Söhne sein‹ (v. 17)? Sagt man zu dir, Gott habe Söhne, so sind es ›die an ihn glauben‹, wie: ›Kinder seid ihr dem Ewigen, eurem Gott‹ (Deut. 14, 1). Deshalb sage zu ihm: wenn er Söhne hat, so hat er keine Väter. Sollte er sagen ›der Vater‹, wie sie vom Vater, Sohn und Hl. Geist sprechen, so haben wir schon darauf in (unserer Erklärung von) Psalm 2, 1 entgegnet. Es gibt noch eine andere Erklärung: wenn er vom Vater spricht, so ist es sogar nach ihrer Erklärung unstatthaft, von Vätern in der Mehrzahl zu reden.«[21]

Besonders wichtig war die Widerlegung der christlichen Auslegung von Psalm 72. Kein hebräischer Psalmenkommentar des Mittelalters konnte dem aus dem Wege gehen. Wir bringen Kimchis Erklärung:

13. »Die Christen deuten diesen Psalm auf ihren Glauben (andere Lesart: auf Jesus den Nazarener) und sagen: es sei Salomo, unter welchem Friede war, und er ist des Königs Sohn. (Der Vers 4) sagt ›er bringt Heil den Armen‹, daß er denen, die in die Hölle hinabsteigen, Heil bringe. ›Er kommt herab wie Regen auf die Flur‹ (6). Das ist die Gottheit, die vom Himmel herabkommt. Doch wie kann man von einem Menschensohn sagen, er steige herab und woher steigt er herab? (Deshalb) mußt du ihre Worte vor ihnen zerschmettern und zu ihnen sagen: ›ihr sagt, daß in diesem Vers die Dreieinigkeit Gottes, des Königs und des Königsohns, ausgesprochen ist, doch sagt ihr auch, daß Salomo auf die Gottheit bezogen ist; wenn dem so ist, dann sind es vier (Gottheiten). Ferner, warum bittet er, daß der Vater dem Sohn Recht und Gerechtigkeit schenken soll? Wenn das auf das Fleisch (d. h. das Menschsein) geht, ist das Fleisch nicht des Sohn des Königs, denn der Sohn ist auf Grund ihres Glaubens die Gottheit. Geht es aber auf die Gottheit, dann hat er ja, worum er bittet, und das wäre Torheit. Ferner, ›mögen die Berge Frieden auf das Volk tragen‹ (v. 3); aber es war kein Friede in seiner (d. h. Jesu) Zeit... Ferner, ›es blüht in seinen Tagen der Gerechte und reicher Friede...‹ (v. 7), aber in den Tagen Jesu gab es weder Gerechte noch reichen Frieden. ›Von Meer zu Meer wird er herrschen‹ (v. 8). Geht dies auf sein Menschsein, (so war es nicht so), denn er herrschte nicht einmal über ein Dorf. Geht es aber auf seine Göttlichkeit, dann gäbe es keine Grenze für seine Herrschaft, denn seine (d. h. Gottes) Herrschaft reicht über die ganze Welt, über Himmel und Erde. ›Und seine Feinde lecken Staub‹ (v. 9) (geht) auf Israel, die seine Feinde waren. Wie werden sie seinen Staub lecken? In Wirklichkeit verfolgten sie ihn, bis sie ihn dem Tod auslieferten; sie herrschten über ihn, nicht er über sie, so daß sie seinen Staub leckten... ›Es beugen sich ihm alle Könige, und alle Völker dienen ihm‹ (v. 11). Das war nicht so, denn zwei Teile der Völker dienen ihm (oder verehren ihn) nicht, weder Israel noch die Ismaeliten (d. h. Moslems), sondern verleugnen ihn. Woraufhin ist ›er lebe‹ (v. 15) gesprochen? Wenn auf sein Menschsein, er lebt ja nicht, ist in der Tat nach kurzem Leben gestorben; wenn auf sein Gottsein, dann wäre es nicht nötig, darum zu beten,

daß er lebe... ›Daß er immerzu für ihn bete‹ — warum ist das nötig? Die Gottheit braucht nicht für sich zu beten. Sagst du aber, der Sohn bete vor dem Vater für alle, die an ihn glauben, warum soll er beten, ist der Sohn nicht Gott? ›Er gibt ihm Gold aus Scheba‹; wie sollte er das nötig haben?«[22]

Dasselbe gilt von Psalm 110. Kimchis Methode, den Wortsinn durch eine Verbindung von Philologie mit Geschichte und einfacher Logik zu ermitteln, zeigt sich hier besonders klar.

14. »Die Christen deuten diesen Psalm auf Jesus. Im ersten Vers lesen sie *adonaj ladonaj* (des Ewigen Spruch an meinen Herrn = Gott), sie meinen damit Vater und Sohn. Wie (ist das möglich)? Nur dadurch, daß sie (die Vokalisation) ändern, denn es ist geschrieben *adonaj la'doni;* und der Geist ist der dritte. (D. h., daß *adoni* im Singular auf den König David nach der traditionellen Auslegung des überlieferten Textes geht.) Ein anderer Irrtum besteht darin, daß sie *imecha* (d. h. mit dir = Jesus), für *ammecha* (d. h. dein Volk) lesen und unter *behadrej kodesch* den Heiligen (*kadosch* = Jesus), den vom Mutterschoß Geborenen verstehen. (Vers 3 lautet: Dein Volk zum Fürstentum am Tag, da du geboren, in heilger Hoheit...)[23] In Bezug auf den Irrtum ihrer Lesart mußt du ihnen sagen, daß ihr Übersetzer Hieronymus einen Fehler gemacht hat... Sagen sie nicht, unsere Tora sei ein Zeugnis für sie? Wenn dem so ist, dann sollten sie an den Zeugen glauben... Auf den Irrtum ihres Glaubens erwidere ihnen: wenn Vater und Sohn Gottheit sind, bedarf der eine keines Gefährten, denn nicht wird der Gott genannt, der eines andern bedarf. Und wie kann der Vater zum Sohn sagen ›sitz zu meiner Rechten‹ (v. 1)? Wenn er (Jesus) so seiner Rechten und Hilfe (Gottes) bedarf, dann ist ihm (Jesus) Schwäche eigen, aber Gott ist nicht schwach und mangelt nicht der Kraft...« Kimchi tut auf diese Weise den christlichen Anspruch, daß unter Melchisedek (v. 4) Jesus zu verstehen sei, ab: Gott bringt keine Opfer dar, sondern der Mensch bringt Gott Opfer dar. Dann beweist er aus Mal. 3, 22 f., daß »die Tora nie geändert werden wird, sondern wie sie auf dem Berg Sinai dem Mose gegeben wurde, so wird sie für ewig bleiben. Elia ist noch nicht gekommen und wird auch nicht kommen vor der Zeit des Messias. Ferner sagt v. 5 ›zerschmettert Könige an seines Zornes Tag‹ — wo sind die Kriege, die Jesus geführt, und wo die Könige, die er besiegt hat? Und wie kann ›er richtet unter Völkern‹ (auf Jesus gehen), wo er doch nicht kam, um zu richten, sondern um die Seelen zu retten...«[24]

Diese Beispiele mögen genügen, um die Dringlichkeit und Wichtigkeit der jüdischen »Antwort« auf die christliche Auslegung der hebräischen Bibel zu zeigen. Die Antwort war, wie die persönliche Anrede »so antworte ihnen« oder die Gleichsetzung von Wortsinn und »Antwort an die Christen (Ketzer)« deutlich macht, in erster Linie für die Juden gemeint,[25] um sie, wie schon gesagt, gegen Bekehrungsversuche gefeit zu machen und um ihnen Mut und Hoffnung auf das baldige Kommen des Messias zu geben. Ob die Christen davon überzeugt werden konnten, daß ihre Auslegung falsch und unzulässig war, ist eine andere Frage. Fest steht nur, daß mit dem intensiven Studium des Hebräischen seit der Gründung des Dominikaner- und des Franziskaner-Ordens die jüdische Auslegung Christen auf dem Weg des eigenen Studiums zugänglich wurde. Prompt ließen sie, oft mit Hilfe der Inquisition,

Anstößiges durch eine gründliche Zensur entfernen. In vielen Fällen kann man heute die zensurierten Stellen unter ultraviolettem oder infrarotem Licht lesen. Die kritischen Ausgaben der Kommentare Raschis und Kimchis enthalten die antichristlichen Auslegungen.

Es soll nicht unerwähnt bleiben, daß man ein tieferes Verständnis der christlichen Glaubensartikel kaum von den gelehrten Juden erwarten kann. Das geht aus den oben gegebenen Beispielen ihrer Reaktion auf die Dogmen der Dreieinigkeit und der göttlich-menschlichen Natur Jesu klar hervor. Die jüdische Ablehnung war aber eindeutig scharf und bestimmt und hat ihren — innerjüdischen — Zweck weitgehend erfüllt, ob es sich um Bibelausleger oder um die Religionsphilosophen handelt, denen wir uns nun kurz zuwenden wollen.

III. Stellungnahmen jüdischer Philosophen

Die Auseinandersetzung mit dem Christentum war natürlich nicht ausschlaggebend für die Abfassung religionsphilosophischer Werke und spielt im Gesamtrahmen dieser philosophischen Darstellung der Grundlehren des Judentums eine untergeordnete Rolle. Diese Schriften sind in erster Linie geschrieben worden, um die Offenbarungsreligion vernunftmäßig zu rechtfertigen und zwar für die sich mit der Philosophie Beschäftigenden, die leicht in Zweifel geraten konnten. Darum hat Maimonides (1135–1204) sein philosophisches Hauptwerk *Führer der Verwirrten* (nicht »Irrenden«, sondern eher »Unschlüssigen«) genannt. Daß vor allem die Trinitätslehre, aber auch christliche Ansprüche betreffend Jesus und die Tora, sowie christliche Bibelexegese behandelt werden, zeigt allerdings deutlich, wie sehr diese Fragen zum jüdischen Denken und Fühlen im Mittelalter gehörten und wie sehr die jüdische »Antwort« ein Teil der intellektuellen und religiösen Ausrüstung der jüdischen Gebildeten war. Selbst in Spezialwerken, die sich nur an einen kleinen Kreis philosophisch Gebildeter wendeten, fanden sie einen Platz, und auch wenn sie auf philosophischer Ebene und mit philosophischen Argumenten behandelt wurden, fehlte der polemische Ton nicht. Andererseits hat die christliche Gotteslehre ihren berechtigten Platz bei der Erörterung der jüdischen Gotteslehre, ebenso wie das neue »Gesetz« Jesu bei der Behandlung der Frage des offenbarten und des menschlichen Gesetzes.[26]

1. Gaon Saadia

Uns interessiert hier zuerst der Gaon Saadia (882–942), der erste systemative jüdische Denker im islamischen Kulturkreis. Trotzdem wir uns auf den christlichen Westen beschränken, müssen wir seiner gedenken, weil ihn der Verfasser der ersten systematischen Streitschrift gegen das Christentum, der seine Aufmerksamkeit dem Neuen Testament zugewandt hat, Jakob ben Reuben (um 1170), in seinem *Buch der Kriege Gottes* zitiert. Unser Hauptzeuge allerdings wird der bereits erwähnte Josef Albo sein, der bei dem Religionsgespräch in Tortosa eine bedeutende Rolle gespielt hat und dessen religionsphilosophisches Werk *Grundlehren* (was soviel bedeutet wie Glaubensartikel im Christentum jener Zeit) zweifellos dieser Disputation und der durch sie geschaffenen Lage viel verdankt.

Indem Saadia die Einzigkeit und Einheit Gottes zu beweisen sucht, weist er nicht nur den Dualismus, sondern auch die christliche Trinitätslehre zurück. Dies tun auch die islamischen Religionsphilosophen und Theologen, von deren Argumentation Saadia beeinflußt war. Aber er dehnt die theoretische Widerlegung des christlichen Dogmas auf die praktische Anwendung dieses Dogmas in der christlichen Bibelexegese aus. So besteht er auf der absoluten Einheit des Wesens Gottes, dessen Attribute des Lebens, der Macht und des Wissens dieser Einheit keinen Eintrag tun. Denn sie sind, wie Maimonides es später ausdrückte, nicht Attribute des Wesens, sondern nur des göttlichen Handelns. Deshalb, so meint Saadia, sind die Christen im Irrtum, wenn sie eine Unterscheidung im Wesen Gottes auf Grund dieser Attribute machen und ihm Dreieinigkeit zuschreiben. Denn sie unterscheiden zwischen dem Wesen Gottes und seinem Leben und Wissen als zwei vom Wesen verschiedene Dinge. Saadia lehnt dann Augustins Dreiheit des menschlichen Lebens — in Analogie zur Dreieinigkeit Gottes — ab, indem er auf der Unkörperlichkeit Gottes besteht. Eine Dreiteilung aber bedeute Körperlichkeit, die wir von Gott keinesfalls annehmen dürfen. Er macht dies klar durch die Betonung der Verschiedenheit des menschlichen Seins vom Leben und von der Erkenntnis. Die absolute Einheit Gottes macht eine solche Unterscheidung unmöglich. Er, der Schöpfer, hat allein alles auf einmal geschaffen. Selbst nicht geschaffen, kann man in seinem Handeln — durch seine Attribute der Macht und der Weisheit, die eins sind mit seinem ewigen Leben — keinen Unterschied von seinem Sein sehen. Aber der Mensch ist am Leben und stirbt, er ist wissend und ein anderes Mal unwissend, also kann man ihn nicht Gott vergleichen. Nun finden wir aber in der Hl. Schrift, daß Gott körperlich dargestellt wird; sie spricht von seinem Mund, von seiner Hand oder von seinen Augen. Alle diese sind aber nur Redensarten, um dem Menschen die Größe, Macht und das Wissen Gottes klarzumachen.[27] An diese Ausführungen knüpft Saadia logischerweise eine kurze Behandlung des Wesens Jesu an, indem er die Anschauungen von vier verschiedenen christlichen Sekten referiert.[28] Seine Widerlegung erfolgt später im Zusammenhang mit den Fragen der Außerkraftsetzung des Gesetzes und des Kommens des Messias.

'Jüdische Antwort'

Nach Auffassung der jüdischen Tradition sind die in der Tora Mosis enthaltenen Gesetze nicht aufhebbar. Saadia stimmt mit dieser Tradition überein und belegt ihre Richtigkeit mit Bibelstellen, wie Ex. 31, 16 »... für ihre Geschlechter als einen ewigen Bund« oder Deut. 33, 4: »Die Weisung (Tora), die uns Mose hat geboten, das Erbteil der Gemeinde Jakobs«. Er setzt sich dann mit sieben Argumenten auseinander, die zu beweisen suchen, daß kein Gesetz ewig sei, und geht zu einer Widerlegung der Ansicht über, daß Glaube an Propheten und Gesetzgeber an deren Wunder gebunden sei: die Wunder, sagt Saadia, sind nur die Rechtfertigung des Propheten und seines göttlichen Auftrags, sie folgen auf die Verkündung, gehen ihr nicht voraus. Nachdem er mehrere Schriftstellen angeführt hat, die nach seinem Ermessen falsch verstanden wurden, weil diejenigen, die sie zitierten, die Eigentümlichkeiten der hebräischen Sprache nicht verstanden haben und daher irregeführt wurden, schließt er mit der bekannten Stelle Jer. 31, 31, die von christlicher Seite als auf den Neuen Bund des Christentums hinweisend verstanden wird: »Sieh, Tage kommen, ist des Ewigen Spruch, da schließe ich mit dem Haus Israel und dem Haus Juda einen neuen Bund.«

15. »Ihnen antwortete ich: warum seht ihr euch nicht an, was auf diesen Vers folgt? Dort wird ausdrücklich gesagt, daß der neue Bund, der vorher erwähnt wurde, die Tora selbst ist. Sagt doch die Schrift: ›(v. 33) Sondern dies ist der Bund, den ich mit dem Haus Israel schließen will nach jenen Tagen, ist des Ewigen Spruch: ich lege meine Weisung in ihr Inneres und schreibe sie auf ihr Herz.‹ (Der neue Bund) wird nur darin vom ersten Bund verschieden sein, daß er nicht gebrochen werde, wie es beim ersten Mal geschah, wie die Schrift sagt: ›(v. 32) ... wo sie dann meinen Bund übertraten, wiewohl ich ihr Herr geworden, ist des Ewigen Spruch.‹«[29]

Als nächstes widerlegt er zehn Einwände, die die Annullierung des Gesetzes beweisen wollten. Dabei zeigt er sich als ein Ausleger der Bibel von ganz außergewöhnlichem Format. Ohne jede polemische Absicht und Ausdrucksweise, macht er objektiv klar, wir die Ausnahmen nur scheinbar das mosaische Gesetz verletzen und lediglich durch besondere und einmalige Umstände bedingt sind. Zum Beispiel:

16. »Die zweite (Einwendung) betrifft die Tatsache, daß Kains Strafe für den Mord an Abel war, ›ein Flüchtling und Wanderer (Gen. 4, 12)‹ zu werden. Nachher aber war die über jeden Mörder verhängte Strafe der Tod. Jedoch stellt dies keine Abschaffung (des Gesetzes) dar, denn wenn der Allweise befiehlt, daß der Mörder getötet werde, geschieht dies nur durch Richter und Zeugen. Diese gab es aber nicht zur Zeit, da Kain Abel erschlug, deshalb konnte die Todesstrafe nicht über ihn (Kain) verhängt werden, und Gott mußte ihn auf andere Weise bestrafen. Siehst du nicht, wie Gott zu Noa sagte: ›Wer Menschenblut vergießt, durch Menschen sei sein Blut vergossen (Gen. 9, 6)‹. ... Die vierte betrifft die Darbringung von Opfern am Sabbat, trotzdem zuvor jede Arbeit an diesem Tag verboten worden war. Auch das ist keine Annullierung; im Gegenteil, es half, die Abschaffung zu verhindern. Denn

das Gesetz betreffend Opfer ging dem über den Sabbat (zeitlich) voran, weshalb es unstatthaft gewesen wäre, hätte das Sabbatgesetz es gestört, zumal dies gleichbedeutend mit der Abschaffung gewesen wäre. Folglich waren die Darbringung von Opfern und die Beschneidung erlaubt, während alle anderen Arten von Arbeit verboten waren. (Opfer und Beschneidung) waren nämlich vor dem Sabbat(gebot) befohlen... Die siebente ist das Wort Gottes, er sei gepriesen, an Hiskia: ›Denn du sollst sterben und nicht leben (Jes. 38, 1)‹ und später: ›... siehe ich füge zu deinen Tagen noch fünfzehn Jahre hinzu (v. 5)‹. Doch ist auch dies keine Abschaffung, denn Gott kann einen Befehl erlassen, um einem Menschen zu drohen oder ihn zu tadeln. Achtet jener darauf und nimmt den (göttlichen) Tadel auf sich, dann wird die Drohung zurückgezogen. Das wissen wir von der Erzählung der Einwohner Ninives (Jona) und von jedem Reumütigen, der sich (Gott) unterwirft.«[30]

Zum Schluß sei kurz Saadias Anspruch angeführt, keine der Verheißungen hätten Bezug auf die Zeit des zweiten Tempels gehabt, noch seien sie in dieser Zeit in Erfüllung gegangen. Dies folgt auf seine mit Schriftstellen bewiesene Beschreibung der Erlösung in der Endzeit. Er behauptet, diese Verheißungen seien nicht an Bedingungen gebunden, sondern absolut. Dies ist gegen diejenigen gerichtet, die meinen, die Erlösung sei so lange unmöglich, als die Juden Sünden begehen. Das wäre aber eine unstatthafte Einschränkung, ja Verneinung der Macht Gottes. Saadia vergleicht nämlich die Erlösung mit Gottes Schöpfung; also muß sie stattfinden, wenn Gott es so bestimmt hat. Er bringt dann 15 Widerlegungen falscher Ansichten: fünf aus der Hl. Schrift, fünf aus der Geschichte und fünf aus rationaler Beobachtung. Aus der ersten Gruppe führen wir an:

17. »... das erste Argument ist, daß gemäß der Heilsbotschaften ganz Israel im Heiligen Land gesammelt werden soll, kein einziger soll in fremdem Land bleiben. So steht geschrieben: ›... und ich will sie sammeln aus den Ländern und sie auf ihren eigenen Boden (d. h. das Land Israel) bringen ... (Ez. 34, 13)‹. Zur Zeit des zweiten Tempels kehrten jedoch nur 42 360 von ihnen (nach Israel) zurück, wie die Hl. Schrift sagt: ›Die ganze Volksschar zusammen war 42 360 (Neh. 7, 66)‹. Das zweite (Argument) ist, daß Israel von den Meeresinseln gesammelt werden sollte, wie es in der Hl. Schrift heißt: ›... und von den Inseln des Meeres (Jes. 11, 11)‹. Als jedoch Israel zum ersten Mal in die Verbannung ging, fuhren sie zu keiner dieser Inseln, also konnte keine Rede davon sein, daß sie von ihnen zurückkehrten. Drittens, die Völker sollten Mauern um Jerusalem bauen, wie es in der Hl. Schrift heißt: ›Da baun der Fremde Söhne deine Mauern, und ihre Könige bedienen dich (Jes. 60, 10).‹ Aber nicht nur haben sie nichts für uns in der Zeit des zweiten Tempels gebaut, sie haben uns sogar behindert, so daß wir dauernd mit ihnen im Streit waren während der Bautätigkeit. (Folgt ein Zitat: Neh. 4, 11 f.) Viertens, die Tore der Stadt (Jerusalem) sollten Tag und Nacht offen stehen dank der Sicherheit, die ihre Einwohner genießen ... (folgt Jes. 60, 11). Doch finden wir, daß zur Zeit des zweiten Tempels die Tore vor Sonnenuntergang geschlossen wurden und erst spät am Vormittag wiedergeöffnet zu werden pflegten, wie Nehemia berichtet: ›Die Tore Jerusalems sollen nicht geöffnet werden, bis die Sonne heiß ist ... (7, 3). Fünftens, daß kein Volk übrigbleiben wird, das Israel nicht dienen werde, wie in der Hl. Schrift gesagt ist: ›Denn Volk und Königreich, das dir nicht dient, geht unter (Jes. 60, 12).‹

Jedoch bezweifeln wir nicht, daß sowohl Israel als auch ihre Felder während der Zeit des zweiten Tempels unter dem Joch von Königen standen, wie es in der Hl. Schrift heißt: ›Sieh, wir sind Knechte heute und das Land, das du unsern Vätern gegeben hast ... (Neh. 9, 36).‹ Dies ist die Erklärung gemäß des Textes der Hl. Schrift (in ihrem Wortsinn).«[31]

Bezeichnenderweise sind die fünf historischen Argumente auch auf dem Alten Testament gegründet, ebenso auch die fünf Argumente der Erfahrung. Auszugsweise lauten sie:

18. »Das erste (Argument) ist, daß gemäß den Propheten alle Geschöpfe letztlich an die Einheit Gottes glauben ... (Sach. 14, 9). Jedoch sind sie heute noch in Irrtum und Unglauben befangen. Zweites (Argument): Jes. 62, 8 sagt voraus, daß die Gläubigen von der Zahlung von Steuern und der Lieferung von Geld und Nahrung an andere befreit sein werden. Aber in Wirklichkeit sehen wir ein ganzes Volk (Israel) Steuern zahlen und gehorsam und dienstbar einem jeden Volk, in dessen Gewalt es fällt. Drittens der Krieg soll unter Menschen abgeschafft werden ... (Jes. 2, 4). Jedoch sehen wir die Völker untereinander kämpfen und Krieg führen so heftig als möglich. Sollte jemand diese Aussage dahin verstehen, daß sie (die Völker) nicht länger wegen der Religion Krieg gegen einander führen, so muß man ihn darauf hinweisen, daß sie in der Tat so erbittert als je über ihre Religionen streiten. Viertens würden die Tiere miteinander in Frieden leben, so daß sogar der Wolf mit dem Lamm zusammen weidet, ... der Löwe frißt dem Rind gleich Stroh ... sie sollen weder schädigen noch zerstören ... (Jes. 11, 6–9). Doch sehen wir noch jetzt ihr Benehmen gemäß ihrer Natur ... und noch keine Veränderung in ihnen. Sollte aber jemand auch dies als ein Gleichnis erklären, daß es nämlich ausschließlich bestätigen will, daß die Bösen mit den tugendhaften Menschen Friede schließen würden, so ist die Situation in Wirklichkeit das gerade Gegenteil. Denn heute begehen die Starken größere Ungerechtigkeit und Unrecht gegen die Schwachen als je zuvor.« Das fünfte Argument betrifft Sodom, das nach Ez. 16, 53, 55 wiederhergestellt werden soll, was auch noch nicht geschehen ist. Saadia schließt mit den Worten: »Alle diese Tatsachen ... beweisen schlüssig, daß die Heilsprophezeiungen noch nicht erfüllt worden sind.«[32]

Seine Widerlegung der Ansicht, daß sich die Verheißungen auf die Zeit des zweiten Tempels beziehen, ist nicht nur gegen Juden gerichtet, sondern auch gegen die christliche Auslegung der messianischen Bibelstellen. So sagt Saadia:

19. »Diese Christen ... bestimmen die Zeit (der Erfüllung) 135 Jahre vor der Zerstörung des zweiten Tempels. Deshalb (bedarf es) ihnen gegenüber ... noch einer andern Widerlegung, d. i. worauf der Prophet anspielt in dem Ausdruck ›siebzig Wochen‹ (Dan. 9, 24), der nach unserer Ansicht als 490 Jahre zu verstehen ist.« Das ist die übliche jüdische Chronologie auf Grund der Danielstelle. Die Zahl 135 Jahre stammt aus dem Talmud, wo Jesus als ein Schüler des Josua ben Perachja angesehen wird (*Sanhedrin* f. 107 b). Dann folgt die ebenfalls allgemeine jüdische Auslegung der anderthalb Wochen Dan. 9, 27: »Endlich wird die letzte Woche teils eine Zeit des Friedens zwischen dem jüdischen Volk und einigen der Könige sein, teils eine solche der Verletzung (von Verträgen) und von Krieg unter ihnen allen. So sagt die Hl. Schrift: ›Und er wird stark im Bund für viele auf eine Woche, und zur halben Woche schafft er ab Schlacht- und Mehlopfer (Dan. 9, 27).‹ Das Land

wird dann verwüstet werden und viele seiner Bewohner werden umkommen, wie es ebendort gesagt ist: ›Und (wendet sich) zu dem geflügelten Greuel der Verwüstung, bis die beschlossene Vernichtung sich ergießt über den Verwüster.‹ Daher umfaßt diese Zeit von 70 Wochen sowohl Perioden des Wohlstands und Gedeihens als auch der Abschaffung jüdischer Herrschaft und der Tätigkeit von Priestern und Propheten. Denn die Hl. Schrift sagt am Anfang der eben zitierten Stelle aus: ›daß der Frevel vollendet und die Sünde erfüllt ist, die Missetat gesühnt und ewig Heil herbeigeführt, daß Gesicht und Begeisteter besiegelt und Hochheiliges gesalbt ist (Dan. 9, 24)‹ ... Dann läßt uns die Hl. Schrift wissen, daß am Ende der Zeit jeder gesalbte Priester ausgerottet werden wird, so daß keiner mehr da sein wird. Sie sagt nämlich: ›und nach den 62 Wochen wird ein Gesalbter ausgerottet und hat keinen (Nachfolger) (v. 26)‹. Die Schrift beabsichtigt nicht eine bestimmte Person (Jesus nach den Christen), wenn sie dies aussagt, sondern meint jeden gesalbten Priester im Sinne des Ausdrucks in der Tora (folgt Lev. 4, 3; 16; 6, 15) ... Diese Menschen (die Christen) behaupten, daß in der Schriftstelle ›ein Gesalbter soll ausgerottet werden ...‹ eine bestimmte Person gemeint ist. Aber das ist aus mehreren Gründen unhaltbar. Ein Grund ist, daß der Ausdruck *maschiach* (Gesalbter) nicht allein auf eine bestimmte Person Bezug hat, sondern auf jeden Priester oder König angewandt werden kann. Weiter, jedes Mal wenn der Ausdruck ›soll ausgerottet werden‹ gebraucht wird im Sinne von ›zu töten‹, wird er nur von einem Menschen gebraucht, der den Tod verdient hat, wie in der Aussage der Hl. Schrift: ›wer immer es ißt, soll ausgerottet werden (Lev. 17, 14)‹. Außerdem hat dieses Ereignis angenommenermaßen gleichzeitig mit der Zerstörung des Heiligtums zu erfolgen, mit der es verbunden ist (folgt Dan. 9, 26).«

Mit anderen Worten, die Christen beziehen die Danielstelle mit Unrecht auf Jesus als den Messias, da er nach jüdischer Zeitrechnung, wie wir gesehen haben, nicht zur Zeit der Zerstörung des Tempels gelebt hat oder gestorben ist. Saadia beweist dies mit der Behauptung, daß seit der Verkündigung Daniels bis zum Tode Jesu nur 285 Jahre verflossen seien, aber in Wirklichkeit 490 Jahre vergehen müssen, nämlich 70 Jahre bis zum Wiederaufbau des (zweiten) Tempels und die 420 Jahre seines Bestehens. Ihre Berechnung geht fehl in der Annahme, daß die persische Herrschaft über Palästina ungefähr 300 Jahre gedauert habe, bis die griechische Herrschaft sie ablöste. Sie nehmen 17 persische Könige an, während auf Grund von Dan. 11, 1 f. nur vier regiert haben können.[33]

2. Moses Maimonides

Moses Maimonides (1135–1204) hat mehrfach zum Christentum und seinem Stifter Stellung genommen. In seinem *Führer der Verwirrten* erwähnt er die Trinitätslehre bei der Behandlung der Attribute Gottes:

20. »Du mußt wissen, daß Gott keineswegs ein Wesensattribut besitzt und daß, ebenso wie er unter keinen Umständen ein Körper sein kann, er auch kein Wesensattribut besitzen kann. Sollte aber einer glauben, daß er einzig ist, jedoch eine

'Jüdische Antwort'

Anzahl von Wesensattributen besitzt, so würde er zwar in seinen Worten ausdrücken, Er sei Einer, aber in seinem Denken würde er glauben, daß Er viele wäre. Dies gleicht dem, was die Christen sagen: daß er Einer ist, aber auch drei, und daß die drei einer sind.«[34]

In seinem *Sendschreiben an* (die Juden von) *Jemen* sagt er von Jesus, er mache durch seine Schriftauslegung die Tora mit all ihren Geboten und Verboten zunichte.[35]

Die wichtigste Stelle findet sich in seinem halachischen Werk *Mischne Tora* Buch xiv »Richter« im 5. Teil »Könige und Kriege«, Kapitel 11, 3, 4 über den Messias. Dieses Kapitel hat so sehr unter der christlichen Zensur gelitten, daß nur wenige Ausgaben des hebräischen Textes Maimonides' beachtliche Ansichten über den Stifter der christlichen Religion, die Abschaffung des jüdischen Gesetzes und über die Rolle des Christentums und des Islam in der Verbreitung des Monotheismus und der Vorbereitung der Menschheit auf die messianische Zeit enthalten.

Die Stelle über Jesus lautet:

21. »Aber wenn er (d. h. der Messias) nicht vollen Erfolg hat oder getötet wird, ist es klar, daß er nicht der in der Tora verheißene Messias ist. Er muß wie alle anderen ... Könige aus dem Hause Davids betrachtet werden, die starben und die der Heilige, Er sei gepriesen, hat erstehen lassen, um die Menge zu prüfen, wie geschrieben steht (folgt Dan. 11, 35). Selbst von Jesus von Nazareth, der wähnte, er sei der Messias, aber durch das Gericht getötet wurde, hatte Daniel prophezeit, wie geschrieben steht: ›... und die abtrünnigen Buben deines Volkes erheben sich, das Gericht zu bestätigen; aber sie werden straucheln (Dan. 11, 14)‹. Denn hat es je ein größeres Straucheln gegeben ...? Alle Propheten haben bekräftigt, daß der Messias Israel erlösen werde, sie retten, ihre Zerstreuten sammeln und die Gebote bestätigen werde. Er (d. h. Jesus) aber veranlaßte, daß Israel durch das Schwert vertilgt, ihr Rest zerstreut und erniedrigt wurde. Er war verantwortlich dafür, die Tora zu ändern, die Welt zum Irrtum zu veranlassen und einem anderen außer Gott zu dienen. Doch geht es über den menschlichen Geist hinaus, die Absichten des Schöpfers zu begreifen; denn unsere Wege sind nicht Seine Wege, noch unsere Gedanken Seine Gedanken. Alle diese Angelegenheiten, die sich auf Jesus von Nazareth und auf den Ismaeliten (d. i. Mohammed), der nach ihm kam, beziehen, dienten nur dazu, den Weg für den König Messias frei zu machen, und die ganze Welt auf die Verehrung Gottes mit vereinten Herzen vorzubereiten, wie es geschrieben steht (folgt Zeph. 3, 9). Auf diese Weise sind die messianische Hoffnung, die Tora und die Gebote allgemein verbreitete Gesprächsgegenstände geworden — Gesprächsgegenstände (unter den Einwohnern) der fernen Inseln und vieler Völker, unbeschnitten an Herz und Fleisch. Sie diskutieren diese Gegenstände und die Gebote der Tora. Einige sagen, ›Diese Gebote waren wahr, haben aber ihre Gültigkeit verloren und sind nicht länger verbindlich‹; andere erklären, sie hätten eine esoterische (verborgene) Bedeutung und es bestehe nicht die Absicht, sie wörtlich zu nehmen, daß der Messias schon gekommen sei und ihre verborgene Bedeutung offenbart habe. Wenn jedoch der wahre König Messias erscheinen und erfolgreich sein wird, ... werden sie sofort einen Widerruf leisten und erkennen, daß sie nichts als Lügen

von ihren Vätern ererbt und ihre Propheten und Vorfahren sie in die Irre geführt haben.«[36]

Zu Lebzeiten des Maimonides konnte jeder in der rührigen Auseinandersetzung zwischen Judentum, Christentum und Islam — mit Ausnahme einer kurzen Verfolgung Andersgläubiger durch die fanatischen Almohaden in Spanien und Nordafrika, vor welcher er selbst fliehen mußte, um der Zwangsbekehrung zum Islam zu entgehen — offen schreiben. Es war der christlichen Zensur vom 13. Jahrhundert an vorbehalten, anstößige Stellen im jüdischen Schrifttum auszumerzen.

3. Josef Albo

Schließlich müssen wir Josef Albos (gestorben 1444) antichristlichen Ausführungen in seinem *Buch der Glaubensgrundsätze* (Ikkarim) Raum geben.[37]

Obgleich das 25. Kapitel des 3. Buches einen integrierenden Bestandteil des ganzen Werkes bildet, ragt es hervor als eine in sich geschlossene, prinzipielle Auseinandersetzung mit dem Christentum. Zudem hat es die Form eines »Dialogs« mit einem christlichen Gelehrten, über dessen Identität wir nichts wissen. Er mag wie Albo an der Disputation von Tortosa teilgenommen und privat mit Albo über die Vorzüge und Nachteile der beiderseitigen Religionen diskutiert haben. Dieser Umstand ist aber unwichtig, von größerer Bedeutung ist die Tatsache, daß Albo weitgehend von seinen jüdischen Vorgängern abhängig ist, vor allem von seinem Lehrer Chasdai Crescas und von Simon ben Zemach Duran. Wir teilen aus dem langen Kapitel das Maßgebende mit: Der Christ geht von den vier aristotelischen Ursachen der Materie, der Form, der wirkenden und der Endursache aus und findet die Tora Mosis in allen vier Aspekten mangelhaft:

22. »Sie ist mangelhaft in Bezug auf die Materie, weil sie Erzählungen und andere Dinge enthält, die nicht Tora, d. h. Anleitung und Weisung sind. Dagegen enthält das Gesetz Jesu nichts, das nicht Tora ist. Im Hinblick auf die wirkende Ursache, weil sie (d. i. die Tora Mosis) die göttlichen Geheimnisse, die auf die Dreieinigkeit anspielen, sehr verhüllt annimmt, so daß es unmöglich ist, aus ihr die Vollkommenheit des Schöpfers und Seine Attribute zu verstehen. Er sagt, dies könne man aus der Tora Jesu des Nazareners verstehen, welche klar macht, daß Gott Vater, Sohn und Hl. Geist ist und daß sie alle eines sind. In Bezug auf die Endursache, weil sie das geistige (oder seelische) Glück, das das menschliche Ziel ist, nicht postuliert, sondern nur körperliche (oder sinnliche) Glückszustände. Andererseits postuliert die Lehre Jesu geistiges Glück und nicht materielle Segnungen. Im Hinblick auf die formale Ursache, weil sie (die Tora Mosis) gebührender Weise drei Dinge umfassen soll: die Beziehungen zwischen Mensch und Gott, d. i. Zeremonialgesetze ...; die zwischenmenschlichen Beziehungen, d. i. Zivilgesetze ..., die für die bürgerliche Gemeinschaft nötig sind; und Gebote, die den Einzelnen selbst betreffen ...«

'Jüdische Antwort'

Albo folgt hier Thomas von Aquins Dreiteilung der Gesetze des Alten Testamentes in seiner *Summa*, was schon aus der Benützung der lateinischen Termini hervorgeht. In allen drei Teilen ist, so sagt der Christ, das alte Gesetz mangelhaft. Der jüdische Opferdienst ist unrein, während das Gesetz Jesu rein ist: Brot und Wein anstelle von geschlachteten Tieren mit Fleisch, Fett und Blut. Das jüdische Gesetz erlaubt Zinsen vom Fremden zu nehmen, was der bürgerlichen Gesellschaft von Schaden ist. Unbedachter Totschlag wird ungleichmäßig bestraft, während im Neuen Bund die Strafe dem Richter überlassen bleibe. Endlich verlangt das persönliche Moralgesetz im Judentum nur rechtes Handeln, wogegen Jesus Reinheit des Herzens verlangt und den Menschen vor der Höllenverurteilung rettet. Albo entgegnet:

23. »Dies war meine Antwort: alle diese Aussagen sind das Gegenteil der Wahrheit, ohne Einsicht, Verständnis und Wissen um die Wege der Tora. Bevor ich auf seine Worte erwidere, will ich eine Vorbemerkung machen, worüber kein Vernunftwesen im Zweifel sein kann, nämlich, daß alles, wobei der Glaube eine Rolle spielt, dem Verstand vorstellbar sein muß, selbst wenn es von seiten der Natur unmöglich ist ... Natürliche Unmöglichkeiten wie die Spaltung des Roten Meers oder die Verwandlung des Stabes in eine Schlange und die übrigen Zeichen und Wunder, die in der Tora vorkommen oder in den Propheten erwähnt werden, kommen in den Bereich des Glaubens, nachdem ihre Vorstellung dem Verstand möglich ist, dahingehend, daß es in der Macht Gottes steht, sie in die Existenz zu bringen. Hingegen etwas, das dem Verstand unmöglich ist, sich vorzustellen, wie daß etwas gleichzeitig ist und nicht ist, oder ein Körper zu ein und derselben Zeit an zwei verschiedenen Orten ist ..., kann nicht geglaubt werden und kann nicht als im Vermögen Gottes angesehen werden. So ist es unvorstellbar von Gott, daß er einen andern sich in jeder Beziehung Gleichen schaffen kann, oder ein Quadrat zu bilden, dessen Diagonale seiner Seite gleich ist ..., denn an unmögliche Dinge zu glauben, gibt der Seele keine Vollkommenheit. Der Verstand wäre dem Menschen vergebens gegeben worden, und der Mensch hätte keinen Vorsprung vor den Tieren, da der Verstand nicht glauben könnte, was in den Bereich des Glaubens gehört. Nach dieser Vorbemerkung sage ich, daß seine Behauptung, die Tora Mosis sei mangelhaft in Bezug auf die Materie, auf sein ungenügendes Wissen um die Tora Mosis hinweist. Denn in der Tora Mosis ist kein Wort und keine Erzählung, die nicht notwendig sind, um einen Gedanken oder eine ethische Regel zu lehren oder eines der Gebote der Tora zu erläutern ... Wenn er sagt, dem sei nicht so im Gesetz Jesu, so finden wir nicht, daß Jesus ein Gesetz gegeben hat, sondern daß er ja selbst geboten hat, die Tora Mosis zu beobachten. Die Evangelien sind kein Gesetz, sondern eine Erzählung des Lebens Jesu. Die Zeichen, die er, wie sie sagen, in seinem Leben vollbracht hat, sie und ähnliches, finden wir, wurden (auch) von den Propheten ausgeführt, die kein Gesetz gaben. Was in den Evangelien an ethischen Regeln und an Belehrung des Volkes, seine Handlungen zu bessern, vorkommt, all dies ist in Gleichnissen und Rätseln vorgebracht. Das geschieht aber nicht nach Art eines Gesetzes, denn es ist schwer, die Absicht einer Sache zu ermitteln, die in Form von Rätsel oder Gleichnis gesagt ist.« Albo vergleicht dann die klare Prophetie Mosis mit den dunklen Gleichnissen und Rätseln der Prophezeiungen eines Sacharja, die der Vollkommenheit ermangeln und der Erklärung bedürfen. Er fährt fort: «Es ist klar, daß das Gesetz der Tora nur auf der höchsten Stufe der Prophetie (gegeben) sein darf, denn daraufhin

preist die Hl. Schrift die Prophetie Mosis, indem sie sagt: ›von Mund zu Mund rede ich mit ihm und sichtbar, nicht in Rätseln (Num. 12, 8)‹. Daraus sehen wir, daß eine gesetzliche Rede in Rätselform einen Mangel im Hinblick auf ihre Materie aufweist (er meint das Gesetz Jesu). Das ist aber das (genaue) Gegenteil dessen, was der Christ dachte.«

Dem Einwand in Hinblick auf die wirkende Ursache begegnet Albo auf folgende Weise: »Die Tora stellt ausdrücklich das Grundprinzip der Einheit und Unkörperlichkeit Gottes fest und macht klar, daß Gott nicht mit dem Verstand erfaßt werden kann, indem sie sagt: ›denn der Mensch schaut mich nicht und lebt (Ex. 33, 20)‹. Sie schreibt, daß, was von Gott erfaßt werden kann, mit Hilfe der Eigenschaften geschieht, mit denen er seine Geschöpfe regiert, wie Er dies Mose erklärt hat, der sagte: ›... tue mir doch Deine Wege kund, auf daß ich Dich erkenne, damit ich Gunst in Deinen Augen finde (Ex. 33, 13)‹. Gott tat ihm kund, daß die dreizehn Eigenschaften (d. h. Attribute), mit denen er seine Geschöpfe regiert, die Wege sind, die zu erkennen dem Menschen mehr oder weniger möglich sei, gemäß der Verschiedenheit der Stufe, welche er erreicht hat. Doch Seine Wesensattribute können unmöglich erfaßt werden. Die Tora Mosis schreibt nichts über die Dreieinigkeit, weil das eine Ansicht ist, die der Vernunftwahrheit nicht entspricht. Denn die Tora gibt (dem Menschen) keine Idee zu eigen, die nicht wahr ist, wie daß eines drei und drei eines seien, indem sie wesensmäßig gesondert existieren, wie sie meinen (d. h. die Christen). Was nämlich die Philosophen von Gott aussagen, daß er Verstand (Intellekt), verständig (intelligent) und zu verstehen (intelligibel) und dabei (absolut) eins ist, ist keineswegs von dieser Art. Denn sie meinen nicht, daß in ihm drei Dinge sind, die wesensmäßig eine gesonderte Existenz haben, Gott behüte! Aber sie meinen, daß das eine Ding (d. h. Gott) bei drei Namen in drei verschiedenen Aspekten genannt wird. Gott ist einfacher Intellekt ohne jede Zusammensetzung, aber da er Intellekt ist, muß er notwendig verstehen, daher ist er intelligent. Doch erfaßt er nichts außer Sich selbst, denn es wäre widersinnig, (anzunehmen) daß seine Vollkommenheit von einem andern abhängen sollte, der ihn aus der Potentialität (Möglichkeit) in die Aktualität (Wirklichkeit) übergehen ließe. In dieser Hinsicht ist er immer intelligibel durch seine Wirksamkeit. Trotz all dem wird jedoch seine Einheit keineswegs zu einer Vielheit. Es ist also unmöglich, daß in Ihm drei gesonderte Dinge existieren, jedes als ein eigenes Wesen existierend – wie sie (die Christen) sagen ›distintos en personas‹ (in verschiedenen Personen)‹ – aber daß sie (doch) eines sind, es sei denn zwei sich widersprechende (Dinge) sind zugleich wahr. Das verstößt aber gegen die ersten Grundsätze, und der Verstand kann sich eine solche Existenz nicht vorstellen. Daher leugnet die Tora die Körperlichkeit (Gottes) und warnt davor, an sie zu glauben (folgt Deut. 4, 15).« Dem Einwand in Bezug auf die Endursache begegnet Albo folgendermaßen: »Daß sie (die Tora) das geistige Glück nicht erwähnt, ist nicht der Fall, denn sie erwähnte es in einer Anspielung für die Weisen ... Daß sie es nicht klar gemacht hat, geschah, weil die Tora nicht nur den Weisen und Intelligenten gegeben wurde, sondern dem ganzen Volk, groß und klein, weise und töricht. Darum gehört es sich, daß in ihr solche Dinge vorkommen, die für alle verständlich und glaubwürdig sind.« Er spricht dann von den Wundern, die ständig Israel widerfahren sind, belegt dies mit Stellen aus der Hl. Schrift und dem Talmud und hält dem gegenüber: »die Christen haben kein dauerndes Zeichen, das auf die Wahrheit ihres Glaubens hinweist. Der Beweis, den sie vom Glück ihrer Gläubigen erbringen, ist gar kein Beweis, da wir finden, daß mehr als 2000 Jahre bevor die Tora Mosis gegeben wurde, alle Völker mit Ausnahme einzelner Erwählter, wie die Erzväter und dergleichen, dem Götzendienst ergeben waren, aber trotzdem alle glücklich waren, jedes einzelne in dem ihm eigenen Königreich in Ruhe und Sorglosigkeit lebend. Selbst nach der Gesetzesoffenbarung waren alle Völker, außer Israel, Götzendiener, und jedes gedieh in seinem Reich. Der Erfolg Sennacheribs (= Sancherib) und Alexanders (des Großen) und ihre Herrschaft über Israel ist doch kein Beweis dafür, daß ihre Religion besser als der Glaube Israels war. In der Tat behaupten heute noch die Christen, daß das Gesetz der Ismaeliten ein konventionelles, kein göttliches Gesetz sei. Doch sind sie (die Moslems) erfolgreich und herrschen über einen großen Teil der Welt. Dann ist es aber offensichtlich, daß der Erfolg eines Volkes kein Beweis für die Qualität (= Wahrheit) seines Glaubens ist. Vielmehr ist der Beweis für die Wahrheit eines Glaubens das andauernde Geschehen von Wundern, wie diese dauernd in Israel vorkamen, solange es in seinem eigenen Lande lebte. Jedoch finden wir dies nicht so im Fall der an die christliche oder an die ismaelitische Religion Glaubenden. Was sie (die Christen) über das Glück der Seele im Jenseits sagen, darüber streiten wir, ob es so ist oder nicht, und was für einen Beweis dafür gibt es? Und was ihren (der Tora Mosis) Mangel in Bezug auf die Form betrifft, so ist seine Behauptung völlig unsinnig und das Gegenteil der Wahrheit. Denn die Tora ist in allen drei Teilen, die er erwähnt, von äußerster Vollkommenheit. In den Zeremonialgeboten, d. h. dem Gottesdienst, ist sie sehr vollkommen, denn sie befiehlt das Gebet: ›Ihr sollt dienen dem Ewigen, eurem Gott, dann wird Er dein Brot und dein Wasser segnen (Ex. 23, 25)‹ ... Sie ermahnt uns auch, Gott zu lieben und zu fürchten (folgt Deut. 6, 5 (Liebe); Lev. 19, 14 (Furcht); Deut. 6, 13 (Furcht und Dienst)).« Die Verteidigung der Opfer, teilweise mit Maimonides' Begründung, müssen wir beiseite lassen. In ihrem Verlauf wendet sich Albo gegen die Bezeichnung des Sakraments von Brot und Wein als Opfer, da es ja »den Körper ihres Gottes« darstelle. Mit Gründen der Logik und der Sinneswahrnehmung verwirft er das Dogma der Transsubstantiation als etwas dem menschlichen Denken Unverständliches und schließt mit folgenden Worten: »Wie ist es möglich, so etwas zu glauben, das der Verstand ablehnt und die Sinne widerlegen? Daher ist es für einen Juden schwierig, seinen Verstand zu zwingen, an solche Dinge zu glauben, die dem Verstand unbegreiflich sind, denn wie kann der Mensch glauben, was er nicht verstehen, ja sich gar nicht vorstellen kann? Denn der Jude ist an wahre Meinungen gewöhnt, die die Sinne nicht verwerfen und die nicht gegen erste Grundsätze streiten, wie sie in der Tora Mosis stehen, von der alle gestehen, daß sie göttlich sei und in aller Öffentlichkeit im Beisein von 600 000 Menschen offenbart wurde (d. i. die Gesetzesoffenbarung am Sinai).«[38]

Sich auf widersprechende Aussagen über Jesu Geburt und Herkunft in den Evangelien stützend, weist Albo dann nach, daß die Apostel die Bibel des Alten Testamentes nicht richtig gekannt haben, und zieht daraus den Schluß — auf Grund ihrer falschen Zitate und Auslegungen —, daß das Gesetz Jesu ein konventionelles, kein göttlich offenbartes sei. Wir wollen einige Sätze aus dem langen Argument anführen:

24. »Es ist ihm (dem Juden) besonders schwierig, an (gewisse) Dinge im Gesetz Jesu zu glauben, wenn er sieht, daß das, was sie als ein Grundprinzip und einen Glaubensartikel festlegen, nämlich daß Jesus der Messias Sohn Davids war, unsicher ist (wörtlich: daß es bei ihnen unbekannt ist, ob er der Sohn Davids war oder nicht). Denn Kapitel 1 des Evangeliums Matthäi leitet die Abstammung Josefs, des Gemahls der Miriam, oder ihres Verlobten nach ihren Worten, von Salomo und

David ab und sagt von ihm, daß er königlicher Abkunft sei. Aber im 3. Kapitel des Evangeliums Lukas heißt es von ihm, daß er nicht königlicher Abkunft war und von Nathan, dem Sohn Davids, abstamme... Außerdem, wie kann ein Jude, beschlagen in den heiligen Büchern, der sieht, wie die Schriftstellen, die sie nennen – im Evangelium und ihren übrigen Büchern –, nicht den Beweis liefern, den sie beanspruchen, sich dazu bringen, ihren Worten Glauben zu schenken, wie die Erwähnung im 1. Kapitel Matthäi (1, 22), daß Jesus von einer Jungfrau geboren wurde, um aufrecht zu erhalten, was geschrieben steht: ›Siehe die junge Frau soll schwanger werden ... (Jes. 7, 14)‹. Das ist doch wohl bekannt, sogar Schulkinder wissen es, daß diese Schriftstelle auf (König) Ahas gesagt wurde ungefähr 600 Jahre vor Jesus als ein Zeichen, daß die Königreiche Aram (Syrien) und Israel zugrunde gehen werden, aber das Königreich Juda werde bestehen unter Königen aus dem Haus Davids. Wie aber konnte die Geburt Jesu von einer Jungfrau ein Zeichen für Ahas sein? ... So gibt es noch andere Schriftverse, die sie im Evangelium anders als sie sind bringen und im Gegensatz zu deren (wahren) Absicht. All dieses entfremdet den Menschen vom Glauben, daß die Tora Jesu göttlich sei, vielmehr ist sie von Menschen erlassen, die nicht in den heiligen Schriften bewandert sind und die Absicht der Schriftstellen nicht erfaßten ..., auch (weiß er), daß der vollkommene Gottesdienst zu jeder Zeit und an jedem Ort die Aufrechterhaltung und Erfüllung der Gebote ist.« Dann stellt Albo die positiven Gesetze der Tora als die vollkommensten hin: »Sie ermahnt uns zur Menschenliebe in den Worten: ›liebe deinen Nächsten wie dich selbst (Lev. 19, 18)‹. Sie verwirft den Haß: ›du sollst deinen Bruder nicht hassen in deinem Herzen (Lev. 19, 17). Den Fremdling betreffend sagt sie ›ihr sollt den Fremden lieben (Deut. 10, 19)‹.« Albo zitiert dann weitere falsche Aussagen oder Deutungen, die sich die Apostel haben zuschulden kommen lassen, und sagt: »Aber selbst wenn wir annehmen, daß die Apostel, wie sie beanspruchen, Autorität hatten, die (Zivil-)Gesetze zu ändern, wer hat dem Papst Autorität gegeben, die Sabbatgebote zu ändern, die nicht zu diesen Gesetzen gehören ... Niemand kann das Sabbatgebot, das göttlich ist, abschaffen, umso mehr, als es eines der Zehn Gebote ist. Ist es doch ein Gebot, das Jesus und all seine Schüler beobachtet haben.« [39]

Schließlich setzt sich Albo mit der Anklage gegen die ethischen Gebote der Tora auseinander:

25. »Er (der Christ) sagt, die Tora Mosis ermahne nur zu geziemendem Benehmen, aber nicht zur Reinheit des Herzens. Das ist das Gegenteil der Wahrheit, denn sie (die Tora) sagt ja: ›beschneidet die Vorhaut eures Herzens (Deut. 10, 16)‹ und ›du sollst den Ewigen, deinen Gott, mit ganzem Herzen lieben (Deut. 6, 5)‹, und ›du sollst deinen Nächsten lieben wie dich selbst (Lev. 19, 18)‹ ... Der Grund, warum sie richtiges Handeln gebietet, ist, daß die Reinheit des Herzens für nichts gilt, außer das Handeln stimmt mit ihr überein. So ist das Grundprinzip die Absicht des Herzens; sagt (doch) David: ›ein reines Herz schaffe mir (Ps. 51, 12)‹, und dergleichen gibt es mehr Stellen, als angeführt werden können. Daher finden wir, daß die Tora Mosis in allen Arten von Vollkommenheit vollkommen ist im Gegensatz zu der Meinung des Christen ... Hieronymus, der christliche Übersetzer, irrte sich in der Übersetzung von *temima* (vollkommen) durch ›ohne Fehl‹. Er tat dies, damit man der Tora Mosis nicht Vollkommenheit zuerteilen könnte, so daß er sagte, sie sei mangelhaft und die Tora Jesu habe sie (erst) vervollkommnet. Dem ist aber nicht so, denn die Bedeutung von *temima* ist notwendigerweise *schelema*

(vollkommen). So kommt in dem Abschnitt von der roten Kuh (Num. 19, 2) der Ausdruck *temima* vor, aber trotzdem muß (dazu noch) gesagt werden ›an der kein Fehl ist‹, was zeigt, daß *temima* eines ist und ›ohne Fehl‹ ein anderes. Unsere Lehrer haben schon erklärt, daß *temima* (an der angeführten Stelle) ›vollkommen an Röte bedeutet‹ (*Sifre, Numeri*, 123) und das zeigt, daß die Bedeutung von *temima* an jeder Stelle (der Hl. Schrift) äußerste Vollkommenheit in einer bestimmten Art ist.« [40]

Albo schließt mit der Bemerkung, daß daher die Tora Mosis in allen vier Aspekten vollkommen und frei an Mangel sei.

Es ist für Albo charakteristisch, daß in dieser Auseinandersetzung mit einem christlichen Gelehrten mit keinem Wort vom jüdischen Messias gesprochen wird und die messianischen Verheißungen der Propheten unerwähnt bleiben. Das mag darauf zurückzuführen sein, daß Albos christlicher Gesprächspartner sich tatsächlich auf die vierfache Unvollkommenheit des mosaischen Gesetzes beschränkt und Albo ihm nur auf seine diesbezüglichen Einwände geantwortet hat und daß wir tatsächlich eine Art Dialog mitten in einem den Glaubensprinzipien des Judentums gewidmeten Buch vor uns haben. Der wahre Grund dürfte aber vielleicht anderswo zu suchen sein. Die Messiasfrage war der Hauptgegenstand der öffentlichen Streitgespräche. Unter dem verheerenden Eindruck von Tortosa mag Albo wohl absichtlich der Messiasfrage in seinen *Ikkarim* gewissermaßen eine untergeordnete Rolle eingeräumt haben. Denn er weist der jüdischen Messiaslehre nicht den ersten Rang einer Grundglaubenslehre zu, sondern der Glaube an den Messias und sein Kommen ist ein notwendiges Erfordernis.

26. »Ebenso ist der Glaube an das Kommen des Messias von dieser Art und Weise (d. h. wie der Glaube an die Wiederauferstehung). Es ist eine Unterabteilung der dritten Grundlehre, nämlich Lohn und Strafe, und ist eine Glaubenslehre, die in der (jüdischen) Nation akzeptiert ist und an die jeder Bekenner zur Tora Mosis glauben muß ... Aber er ist kein Grund- noch ein abgeleitetes Prinzip (d. h. Glaubensartikel) des mosaischen Gesetzes.« [41]

Denselben Gedanken spricht Albo im Zusammenhang mit dem Christentum aus. Er geht davon aus, daß es nur drei »Glaubensartikel« oder Grundprinzipien im Judentum gibt – nach seiner Meinung –: die Existenz Gottes; Lohn und Strafe; und Offenbarung oder prophetische Sendung Mosis. Alles andere, was wir Grundlehren nennen würden, sind für Albo nur Unterabteilungen. Dagegen sind »(der Glaube an) das Kommen des Messias und die Wiederauferstehung der Toten Glaubensartikel (*ikkarim* = Grundprinzipien), die ausschließlich dem Christentum eigen sind, dessen Existenz ohne sie nicht vorstellbar ist«.[42] Wir sind also wohl zu dem Schluß berechtigt, daß Albo im Hinblick auf das Christentum den Messiasglauben nicht unter die jüdischen primären Glaubens»artikel« aufgenommen hat und der »Tora Jesu« den Charakter eines göttlich offenbarten Gesetzes abgesprochen hat.

IV. Der ungleiche Kampf der Disputationen

Was wir bisher betrachtet haben, ist trotz seiner Lebensnähe und höchst praktischen Bedeutung aber doch mehr oder weniger privat oder halb-offiziell gewesen: Auseinandersetzung zwischen individuellen Juden und Christen und jüdische Verteidigung zur Festigung Israels in der Zerstreuung oder »Verbannung«. Weil selbst diese Art von Auseinandersetzung die Gefahr widerspiegelte, die dem Judentum vom Christentum drohte, und die jüdische Verteidigung und Selbstbehauptung für die Juden, die sich daran beteiligten, nicht ohne Gefahr — persönlich wie auch kollektiv — war, stellen die öffentlichen Streitgespräche, zu denen die Juden von Kirche und Staat gezwungen wurden, eine wirkliche Lebensgefahr für Judentum und Judenheit im strengen Sinn des Worts dar. Kann man von dem literarischen Streit bis zum Zeitpunkt der Religionsdisputationen im allgemeinen sagen, daß er sich in einer wenn nicht immer freundlichen, so doch zum mindesten neutralen Atmosphäre abspielte, in der sich die Juden frei und ebenbürtig fühlten, so setzt mit den Disputationen und ihrem Zwang eine Periode öffentlichen Angriffs ein, der von feindseligen Maßnahmen gegen Juden und Judentum begleitet oder gefolgt war. Es beginnt jetzt ein ungleicher Kampf, dessen Ausgang im voraus dahingehend entschieden war, daß das Christentum den Sieg über das angegriffene Judentum unbedingt erringen mußte. Einschüchterung und Strafandrohung im Falle der Weigerung, die gestellten Fragen zu beantworten, versetzten die Juden von vornherein in eine peinliche, gefährliche Situation der Schwäche und Hoffnungslosigkeit. Daß sich die jüdischen Teilnehmer dem ungleichen Kampf offen und kritisch stellten, zeugt mindestens für ihren persönlichen Mut und ihre Glaubensstärke.[43]

1. Rabbi Jechiel contra Nikolaus Donin. Paris 1240

Die Disputation von Paris im Jahre 1240 unter dem Vorsitz des judenfeindlichen Königs Ludwig des Heiligen, bei der die Königinmutter Blanche gebieterisch zugegen war, war mehr ein Inquisitionsverhör als eine Diskussion selbst zwischen ungleichen Vertretern der beiden Religionen. Von den vier vorgeladenen Rabbinern war R. Jechiel, ein bedeutender Kenner und Ausleger des talmudischen Rechts und ein angesehener Lehrer und geistiger Führer der französischen Judenheit, der Hauptsprecher, der die von dem getauften Nikolaus Donin in 35 Artikeln vorgebrachten Fragen beantwortete.[44] Neben den weltlichen Herrschern waren bedeutende Kirchenfürsten wie die Erzbischöfe von Paris, Sens und Senlis und andere hohe Geistliche anwesend. Die Verlesung der Anklage und die darauf gegebene Antwort dauerten drei Tage, vom 25. bis zum 27. Juni 1240. Die 35 Artikel sind identisch mit der Anklageschrift, die Donin im Jahre 1236 dem Papst Gregor IX. vorgelegt hatte; sie ist ausschließlich gegen den Talmud gerichtet. Die Hauptpunkte betreffen die Autorität des Talmuds bei den Juden; blasphemische Äußerungen über Gott und gegen Christus, Maria und die Christen; die Entbindung von Gelübden durch die liturgische Formel am Vorabend des Versöhnungstages und anti-christliche Gebete in der jüdischen Liturgie. Donin setzte die im Talmud kritisierten *Gojim*, hauptsächlich Heiden, einfach mit den Christen gleich. Tatsächlich finden sich im Talmud abfällige Äußerungen über Jesus und Maria.[45]

R. Jechiel verteidigte die Autentizität und Autorität des Talmuds, der die Juden 1500 Jahre lang geleitet habe und ohne den sie weder die Bibel verstehen noch dem Judentum treu bleiben könnten. Der Hl. Hieronymus, ein guter Kenner des Talmuds, habe nichts gegen ihn vorgebracht. Er leugnete auch, daß die beanstandeten Äußerungen gegen die Gojim sich gegen die Christen wendeten. Darunter seien die Heiden des Altertums gemeint. Der im Talmud genannte Jesus sei ebensowenig der Jesus der Evangelien – beide haben eine verschiedene Abstammung – wie die in ihm vorkommende Maria die Mutter Jesu. Nach *Sanhedrin* 67 a ist Jesus, der Sohn Satedas, Sohn Panderas, in Lud am Vorabend des Passahfestes gehängt worden. Er ist nach der jüdischen Tradition nicht mit dem Jesus der Evangelien identisch, der ein Schüler R. Josua ben Perachias war, der ihn verwarf. Er lebte also 200 Jahre vor der christlichen Zeitrechnung. Ähnlich lebte Maria 400 Jahre nach Jesus. Wie nicht alle, die den Namen Ludwig in Frankreich tragen, Könige sind, so brauchen diejenigen, die den Namen Jesus tragen, auch nicht identisch zu sein. (Die angebliche Identität der beiden Jesus ist erst im Mittelalter vorgenommen worden.)

Die Vorwürfe gegen die jüdische Liturgie als antichristlich weist er dadurch ab, daß er »das frevelhafte Reich« auf die heidnischen Reiche Ägypten, Assyrien und Babylonien bezieht, nicht aber auf den christlichen Staat, wie Donin behauptete. Auch sind unter den *minim* des Talmuds nicht die Christen zu verstehen, sondern abtrünnige Juden. Damit versetzte er Donin einen Hieb. Gegen den Vorwurf der Gotteslästerung und ungereimter Erzählungen konnte Jechiel lediglich sagen, daß dies haggadische Auslegungen und Geschichten seien, die nicht wörtlich zu nehmen seien, sondern richtig gedeutet, positiv gewertet werden könnten.

Aber es gelang Jechiel nicht, die dem Talmud drohende Gefahr abzuwenden: Der Talmud wurde im Jahre 1242 auf Grund einer päpstlichen Verordnung verbrannt, möglicherweise Tausende von Exemplaren.[46] Der Kampf gegen den Talmud nahm immer schärfere Formen an, entweder wurde er in Bausch und Bogen verdammt, oder die Päpste verlangten wenigstens, daß die angeblich anstößigen Stellen ausgemerzt wurden.[47]

2. Nachmanides contra Paul Christiani. Barcelona 1263

Auch in Barcelona [48] im Jahre 1263 war die Rolle des Vertreters der Juden lediglich, die vom Vertreter des Christentums an ihn gestellten Fragen zu beantworten. Unter dem Vorsitz des Königs Jakob I. von Aragonien hatte R. Moses ben Nachman (bekannt als Nachmanides) aus Gerona, bedeutender Bibelerklärer, Mystiker und Talmudist, die Kernfragen der christlich-jüdischen Kontroverse zu beantworten, die Fray Paul Christiani im Beisein des Ordensgenerals der Dominikaner, Fray Raimond de Peñaforte, durch dessen Einfluß er Christ geworden war, an ihn stellte. Die Diskussion nahm vier Sitzungen in Anspruch und wurde am 4. August in die Hauptsynagoge von Barcelona verlegt, wohin sich der König mit seinen Höflingen und den hohen christlichen Würdenträgern und Mitgliedern des Franziskaner- und Dominikaner-Ordens begab, um eine die Juden zum Übertritt zum Christentum ermahnende Missionsansprache zu halten. Nachmanides hielt vor einer großen Gemeinde eine Predigt – als Antwort auf die christlichen Reden – unter dem Titel *Die Tora des Ewigen ist vollkommen*.[49]

Beide Seiten beanspruchten begreiflicherweise den Sieg. Wir haben einen hebräischen Bericht von Nachmanides selbst, auf Wunsch des Bischofs von Gerona verfaßt, und ein lateinisches Protokoll. Doch stimmen beide Seiten in den Hauptpunkten überein. Es ist natürlich, daß Nachmanides' »Zugeständnisse« im christlichen Bericht »Bekenntnisse« geworden sind. Der König empfing Nachmanides am Ende in Audienz und gab ihm eine Geldsumme, die er sich von einem jüdischen Geldhändler in Barcelona leihen ließ, und sagte zu Nachmanides, er habe noch nie jemand, auf dessen Seite das Recht nicht war, so glänzende Einwände vorbringen gehört.

Es ist klar, daß die Kirche bei jeder von ihr oder auf ihr Verlangen inszenierten Disputation von Anfang an darauf bestand, daß die Religion Christi über jeden Zweifel erhaben wahr sei und deshalb nicht zur Debatte stand. Sie erwartete, oder zum mindesten erhoffte, daß die vor das Tribunal zitierten jüdischen Gelehrten diese Wahrheit anerkannten und die logische Folgerung aus der christlichen Auslegung, die sie nicht widerlegen könnten, zögen und sich zum Christentum bekehrten, von ihren Gemeinden darin gefolgt. Nachmanides bat zu Beginn der Disputation den König und Peñaforte um volle Redefreiheit, was ihm gewährt wurde, solange er nicht geringschätzig über das Christentum spräche. Er erwiderte, er wisse gebührend zu reden, aber müsse darauf bestehen, nach seinem Willen die Diskussion zu führen. Er sagte:

27. »Die Auseinandersetzung zwischen Christen und Juden geht um viele Dinge aus dem Gebiet der gesetzlichen Bräuche, von denen kein Glaubensprinzip abhängt. Ich will aber ... nur über Dinge disputieren, von denen der ganze Glaube ab-

'Jüdische Antwort'

hängt ... So kamen wir überein, zuerst über den Gegenstand des Messias zu sprechen, ob er – nach dem Glauben der Christen – schon gekommen sei, oder ob er – nach dem Glauben der Juden – erst in der Zukunft kommen werde. Nachher wollen wir darüber sprechen, ob der Messias wirklich Gott oder völlig Mensch, von Mann und Weib geboren, sei; danach, ob die Juden an der wahren Tora festhalten oder die Christen.« Auf Fray Pauls Anspruch, er werde aus dem Talmud beweisen, daß der Messias bereits gekommen sei, erwiderte Nachmanides u. .a: »Ist es denn nicht eine bekannte Tatsache, daß Jesus ... vor der Zerstörung des Tempels geboren wurde und gestorben war? Aber die Weisen des Talmuds lebten nach der Zerstörung ... und vor allem R. Aschi, der Verfasser des Talmuds, ungefähr 400 Jahre später. Hätten jene Weisen an die Messianität Jesu geglaubt, daß er wahr und sein Glaube wahr seien, und hätten sie die Worte geschrieben, aus denen Fray Paul das beweisen wollte, wie hätten sie da an der jüdischen Religion festhalten können ...? Denn sie waren Juden und hielten das jüdische Gesetz ihr ganzes Leben lang, sie, ihre Kinder und Schüler ... Warum sind sie nicht abtrünnig geworden und zur Religion Jesu übergegangen, wie das Fray Paul getan und aus ihren Worten verstanden hat, daß der Glaube der Christen – Gott behüte – der wahre sei, und gegangen und auf Grund ihrer Worte abtrünnig geworden ist? Aber sie und ihre Schüler, die die Tora aus ihrem Mund empfangen haben, lebten und starben als Juden wie wir heute. Sie lehrten uns das mosaische Gesetz und jüdische Sitte, denn all unsere Handlungen beruhen heute (noch) auf dem Talmud ... denn der ganze Talmud ist nur dazu da, uns die Bräuche der Tora und des Gebotes zu lehren ... Hätten sie jedoch an Jesus und seine Religion geglaubt, wie konnten sie nicht tun, wie Fray Paul tat, der ihre Worte besser versteht als sie selbst?« Dann folgt ein Argument über die oben besprochene Stelle Gen. 49, 10, die Nachmanides dahingehend auslegt, daß das Königtum zwar unterbrochen war, aber nie von Juda für immer weichen werde. »Fray Paul wandte ein, sie sagten im Talmud, der Messias sei bereits gekommen, und brachte jene Haggada aus dem *Midrasch Echa* (Klagelieder) ..., daß der Messias geboren wurde, als der Tempel zerstört wurde. Ich erwiderte: Diese Haggada ist entweder nicht wahr oder es gibt eine andere Erklärung für sie aus den Geheimnissen der Weisen. Doch will ich sie (um des Argumentes willen) annehmen in ihrem Wortsinn, wie du gesagt hast, da sie zum Beweis für mich dient. Nun, sie sagt, daß am Tage der Zerstörung des Tempels der Messias geboren wurde. Wenn dem so ist, war Jesus nicht der Messias, da ihr sagt, er sei vor der Zerstörung geboren und umgebracht worden. Doch fand seine Geburt in Wahrheit fast 200 Jahre vor der Zerstörung statt, aber nach eurer Rechnung 73 Jahre. Dann verstummte der Mann ... Die Weisen sagten nicht, er sei gekommen, sondern (nur) er sei geboren worden. Denn am Tag, da Mose, unser Meister, geboren wurde, ist er nicht als Erlöser gekommen, sondern (erst) als er zu Pharao mit dem Gebot des Ewigen kam und zu ihm sagte: ›So sagt der Ewige; sende mein Volk ... (Ex. 8, 1)‹; dann ist er gekommen. Ebenso, wenn der Messias zum Papst kommen und zu ihm auf Geheiß Gottes sagen wird: ›sende mein Volk‹, dann wird er gekommen sein. Aber bis zum heutigen Tag ist er noch nicht gekommen, noch gibt es (bis jetzt) überhaupt einen Messias. Denn David, der König, war am Tag, da er geboren, kein Gesalbter, sondern (erst) als Samuel ihn salbte. So wird der Messias am Tage, da Elia ihn salbt – auf Befehl Gottes – Messias genannt werden; am Tag, da er darauf hin zum Papst kommt, uns zu erlösen, dann wird er (Erlöser) genannt und dann ist er gekommen. Wandte jener Mann (Fray Paul) ein, der Abschnitt ›Siehe, mein Knecht soll Glück haben (Jes. 52, 13)‹ erzählt die Angelegenheit des Todes des Messias, wie er in die Macht seiner Feinde kommt und sie ihn unter die Frevler geben, wie es mit Jesus geschah. Glaubst Du, daß dieser Abschnitt vom Messias handelt? Ich sagte zu ihm: nach dem wahren Wortsinn spricht er (der Abschnitt) von nichts anderem als dem Volk Israel in seiner Gesamtheit; denn so nennen sie die Propheten: ›Israel, mein Knecht (Jes. 41, 8)‹ und ›Jakob, mein Knecht (Jes. 44, 1)‹. Erwiderte Fray Paul: ich aber sehe in den Worten eurer Weisen, daß er vom Messias spricht. Ich antwortete ihm: es ist wahr, daß unsere Weisen in den haggadischen Schriften ihn auf den Messias deuten. Aber sie haben niemals gesagt, er werde durch die Hand seiner Feinde getötet werden, denn du wirst nie in irgend einer der Schriften Israels finden – nicht im Talmud und nicht in Haggadot –, daß der Messias Sohn Davids getötet wird, noch wird er in die Macht seiner Feinde übergeben oder unter Frevlern begraben. Selbst der Messias, den ihr euch gemacht habt, ist nicht begraben worden. Ich will euch den Abschnitt in guter, klarer Deutung erklären, wenn ihr wollt. Dort steht überhaupt nicht, daß er getötet werde, wie es mit eurem Messias war. Sie aber wollten nicht (s) hören.« Nachmanides hat den Abschnitt ausführlich gesondert erklärt, mit zahlreichen Belegstellen aus der Hl. Schrift (Jesaia, Jeremia, Psalmen). Wir geben den wichtigen Schlußabsatz der Erklärung wieder: »... denn zur Zeit der Erlösung wird der Messias erkennen und das Ende verstehen, daß die Wendung gekommen ist, sowie die Endzeit, die der Gemeinde derer enthüllt werden wird, die auf ihn harren ... Siehe, im Abschnitt wird nicht erwähnt, daß er in die Hand seiner Feinde gegeben werde, noch daß er getötet und an ein Holz gehängt werde, sondern daß er ›Samen sehen werde, noch lange lebe (Jes. 53, 10)‹ und ›hoch wird er ... und ragen soll empor sein Königtum (Num. 24, 7)‹ unter den Völkern, ›mächtige Könige (Ps. 135, 10)‹ werden ihm zur Beute.« Dann intervenierte der König, nachdem Fray Paul darauf bestanden hatte, auf Grund der Haggada des Talmuds sei der Messias geboren (*Sanhedrin* 98 a), und Nachmanides dies zwar zugegeben hatte, aber erklärte, er glaube nicht daran. Die Szene war inzwischen in ein Kloster verlegt worden, und Nachmanides wollte gerne Fragen stellen, was ihm aber der König verwehrte, da Fray Paul der Fragesteller sei und er (Nachmanides) ihm zu antworten habe. So wandte er sich an die ganze Versammlung und setzte ihnen auseinander, warum er nicht an die von Fray Paul zitierte Haggada glaube: »Wisset, daß wir drei Arten von Büchern haben. Das erste ist die Bibel, und wir glauben alle an sie mit vollkommenem Glauben. Das zweite ist Talmud genannt, und er ist ein Kommentar zu den Geboten der Tora, denn in ihr gibt es 613 Gebote, wovon nicht ein einziges nicht im Talmud erklärt worden ist. Wir glauben an ihn (den Talmud) in bezug auf die Erklärung der Gebote. Ferner haben wir noch ein drittes Buch, Midrasch genannt, d. h. *sermones* (Predigten), genau so wie der Bischof aufsteht und eine Predigt hält und einer aus der Hörerschaft findet sie gut und schreibt sie auf. Wer an dieses Buch glaubt, gut; wer aber nicht daran glaubt, schadet es auch nichts ... Auch heißen wir dieses ›Buch der Haggada‹, d. h. *razionamiento* (Erzählung), d. i. sie (die Haggadot) sind nichts als Sachen, die einer seinem Freund erzählt. Aber ich akzeptiere diese Haggada (die Fray Paul angeführt hat) in ihrem Wortsinn, wie ihr es wünscht, weil sie ein klarer Beweis dafür ist, daß euer Jesus nicht der Messias war, wie ich euch gesagt habe, daß er nicht an jenem Tag (der Tempelzerstörung) geboren wurde. Denn seine ganze Sache war schon geraume Zeit vorüber.«

Seiner eingangs geäußerten Absicht entsprechend, versuchte Nachmanides dann die Diskussion auf die grundsätzlichen Unterschiede zwischen den beiden Religionen zu lenken: »Der Kernpunkt des Streites und der Meinungsverschiedenheiten zwischen Juden und Christen besteht in dem, was ihr über das Dogma der Gottheit sagt, eine sehr bittere Sache. Du, unser Herr, der König, bist ein Christ, Sohn eines Christen, und hörst alle deine Tage Kleriker (und Franziskaner und Dominikaner von der Geburt Jesu sprechen) und dein Gehirn mit dieser Sache füllen..., doch die Sache, die ihr glaubt — und sie ist ein Grundprinzip eures Glaubens — kann der Verstand nicht akzeptieren und die Natur nicht zulassen; auch haben die Propheten nie so gesprochen.« Über das Wunder der Geburt sagt er: »(es ist schwer zu verstehen), daß der Schöpfer des Himmels und der Erde in den Leib einer gewissen Jüdin eingehen, dort sieben Monate wachsen und klein geboren werden sollte und nachher heranwachsen und später seinen Feinden ausgeliefert werden sollte und sie ihn zum Tode verurteilen und töten lassen und ihr danach sagt, er sei am Leben und zu seinem ersten Ort zurückgekehrt; das kann der Verstand eines Juden oder überhaupt eines Menschen nicht ertragen. Ihr sprecht eure Worte vergebens und umsonst, denn das ist der Kern unserer Meinungsverschiedenheit. Aber laßt uns wieder vom Messias sprechen, wenn das euer Wille ist. — Sagte Fray Paul: Glaubst du, daß er gekommen ist? da sagte ich: nein, aber ich glaube und weiß, daß er nicht gekommen ist und nie hat es einen Menschen gegeben, der selber oder von dem (andere) gesagt hätten, er sei der Messias, außer Jesus. Es ist mir unmöglich, an seine Messianität (zu glauben), denn der Prophet sagt vom Messias: ›und seine Herrschaft (im Bibeltext steht ›und er wird herrschen‹) von Meer zu Meer, vom Strom bis zu der Erde Enden (Ps. 72, 8)‹. Aber er (Jesus) hatte keine Herrschaft, sondern war zu Lebzeiten von seinen Feinden verfolgt und hat sich vor ihnen verborgen, aber am Ende fiel er in ihre Hände und konnte sich nicht retten; wie soll er ganz Israel retten? Selbst nach seinem Tode war die Herrschaft nicht sein, denn die Herrschaft Roms war nicht seinetwegen, sondern bevor man an ihn glaubte, herrschte die Stadt Rom über den größeren Teil der Welt. Nachdem sie den Glauben an ihn angenommen hatten, gingen viele Herrschaften zugrunde, und jetzt besitzen die Verehrer Mohammeds ein Reich, das größer ist als das ihrige (d. h. des christlichen Roms) war. (folgen Schriftbelege über das messianische Friedensreich aus Jeremia (31, 33) und Jesaja (11, 9; 2, 4)). Von den Tagen Jesu bis heute ist die ganze Welt voll Gewalt und Raub, und die Christen vergießen mehr Blut als die andern Völker ...«[50]

Die angeführten Stellen aus dem Religionsgespräch müssen genügen, um einen Eindruck seines Charakters zu vermitteln und die Gestalt des jüdischen Sprechers zu kennzeichnen. Trotz der vielen Wiederholungen, unvermeidlich solange sich die Diskussion um die Messianität Jesu drehte, oder vielleicht gerade deshalb wird die Intensität des Kampfes deutlich. Keine Seite gibt Terrain auf, die Vertreter beider Religionen gebrauchen immer wieder die gleichen Argumente und stützen sich immer auf die gleichen Belegstellen. Bei Nachmanides kommt klar zum Ausdruck, wie sich die Positionen versteift, allerdings auch zu beachtlicher Höhe entwickelt haben. Soweit die Bibel zur Debatte steht, hält die jüdische Seite am Wortsinn und der geschichtlichen Situation der Prophezeiungen fest. Soweit die Haggada herangezogen wird, sei es aus dem Talmud oder aus dem Midrasch, sind die Rollen vertauscht worden. Die Christen beziehen diese Erzählungen auf Jesus, ihnen einen Rang nahe zur Bibel, wenn nicht ihr ebenbürtig einräumend. Der Grund dafür liegt nahe: sie müssen Beweisgründe für ihren Anspruch der Messianität Jesu heranziehen, welche die Juden nicht so leicht parieren können. Deshalb haben wir die bedeutsamen Ausführungen des Nachmanides über die drei verschiedenen Gruppen von Schriften und ihre relative Verbindlichkeit und Beweiskraft zitiert. Seine Geschicklichkeit steht außer Frage: zuerst erklärt er diese Erzählungen als unverbindlich und dann dreht er den Spieß sozusagen um und »beweist« aus ihrer wörtlichen Auslegung das Gegenteil dessen, was sein christlicher Gegner aus ihnen herausliest. Gegen seinen Willen muß er immer wieder zur Messiasfrage Stellung nehmen; es nützt ihm nichts, daß er die Frage der Gottnatur für wichtiger hält und an ihr klarmachen will, welch ein Abgrund das Judentum vom Christentum trennt. Die Dreieinigkeit und die Göttlichkeit Jesu — an sich und gleichzeitig mit seiner Menschhaftigkeit — lehnt er wie seine Vorgänger und Nachfolger schroff ab. Das Mysterium Christi ist dem Juden unbegreiflich, nicht nur, weil ihm — mit Ausnahme Efodis — die Subtilität der Dogmen nicht zugänglich ist, sondern in erster Linie, weil diese Dogmen der jüdischen Auffassung diametral entgegenlaufen. Wäre dem nicht so, würden die Juden nicht immer zum gesunden Menschenverstand und zur einfachen Logik ihre Zuflucht genommen haben. Aus praktischen Gründen mußte die Kirche sich aber auf den Messiasglauben in der Diskussion beschränken trotz der Angriffe auf den Talmud, seine angebliche Gotteslästerung und geringschätzende Behandlung von Jesus und Maria und seine Absurditäten. Denn nur auf dem Weg über die Anerkennung der Messianität Jesu war der Übertritt der Juden zur katholischen Kirche möglich. Hat der Jude einmal Jesus Christus als den von den Propheten der Bibel verheißenen Messias anerkannt, muß er an ihn glauben, selbst in der christlichen Form als an ein göttlich-menschliches Wesen.

Die Verurteilung des Talmuds hat schlimme Folgen für die Juden gezeitigt. Nachmanides selbst mußte einen hohen Preis für seine offene Bekämpfung christlicher Dogmen zahlen: die Dominikaner haben ihn der Lästerung des christlichen Glaubens bezichtigt und seine exemplarische Bestrafung gefordert. Der König, der, wie wir gesehen haben, seinen Mut und seine Geschicklichkeit bewundert hatte, begnügte sich, trotz kirchlichen Druckes, mit einer verhältnismäßig milden Bestrafung, einer zweijährigen Verbannung aus Spanien. Nachmanides zog es aber vor, wie vor ihm Jechiel von Paris, seine Heimat für immer zu verlassen und sich im Heiligen Lande anzusiedeln, wo er, schon ein Siebziger, seinen großen Pentateuch-Kommentar schrieb.

Man hat die Ansicht geäußert, es gäbe in der ganzen Literatur keine nutzlosere Lektüre als die Streitgespräche zwischen Juden und Christen, und wenn man eine Disputation gelesen habe, habe man davon für alle Zeiten genug gelesen.[51] Das mag vom Standpunkt der schöpferischen Literatur, besonders der religiösen Literatur, richtig sein. Aber diese Religionsgespräche spiegeln das Neben- und Gegeneinander der beiden Religionen, besonders im Hochmittelalter, schlagend wieder. Und so nutzlos ist ihr Studium gerade im

Zeitalter des Ökumenismus doch nicht, zeigen sie doch anschaulich, wie das Trennende stärker denn das Verbindende ist, aber auch, wie die beiden Religionen miteinander verhaftet und im letzten Grund in der Gegenwartssituation aufeinander angewiesen sind.

3. Josef Albo und Astruc Halevi contra Hieronymus de Santa Fide. Tortosa 1413–14

Die Ausführlichkeit der Behandlung von Barcelona erlaubt es, die an Dauer und Umfang viel größere Disputation von Tortosa mehr summarisch zu skizzieren, zumal wir von jüdischer Seite nur einen unvollkommenen Bericht haben, der lediglich die ersten fünf der 69 Sitzungen umfaßt.[52] Daneben haben wir noch im *Schewet Jehuda* des Ibn Verga[53] eine kurze Inhaltsangabe des Berichtes, den einer der jüdischen Teilnehmer, Bonastruc Desmaestre, seiner Gemeinde Gerona gegeben hat. Von christlicher Seite haben wir einen offiziellen Bericht, ausgearbeitet von den Sekretären des Gegenpastes Benedikt XIII. unter der Aufsicht des christlichen Disputanden, Maestre Geronimo de Santa Fide, früher Josua de Lorca, und angeblich in Gegenwart von acht Juden. Sie enthalten auch Memoranden, die beide Seiten auf Befehl des Papstes als Grundlage für die Diskussion zu unterbreiten hatten, um sicher zu sein, was sie gesagt hatten. Das wichtigste jüdische Gutachten wurde von R. Astruc Halevi (R. Astruc Levy von Alcañiz) vorgelegt, in Erwiderung der Argumente, die Hieronymus in seinem Beweis aus dem Talmud, daß der Messias in der Person Jesu bereits erschienen sei, vorgebracht hat. Y. F. Baer vertritt die Ansicht, daß im Gegensatz zu den Berichten über Barcelona »in Tortosa eine objektiv einwandfreie Berichterstattung vorliegt.«[54] Doch hat sich zwischen den beiden Ereignissen nicht nur die Zuverlässigkeit der Verhandlungsberichte verbessert, die Lage der Juden hat sich auch in noch größerem Maß verschlechtert. Der gewandte Ankläger hatte nämlich den Papst öffentlich aufgefordert, die jüdischen Gelehrten, die die Verbindlichkeit des Talmuds auf dessen gesetzliche Bestimmungen – wie Nachmanides und vor ihm Jechiel – beschränken wollten, der Häresie zu überführen und dementsprechend zu bestrafen. Die Drohung mit der Inquisition, die auch über jüdische Rechtgläubigkeit – von der Kirche definiert! – zu wachen hatte, muß auf die jüdischen Vertreter und Zuhörer einschüchternd gewirkt haben.

Ein wichtiges Moment in dem ungleichen Wortstreit ist die einwandfrei bewiesene Tatsache, daß Raymund Martin in seinem *Pugio Fidei* sich der Fälschung von *Midraschim* schuldig gemacht hat.[55] So berichtet er Aussprüche eines gewissen R. Rachamon aus einem Midrasch *Bereschit rabba* des R. Mose ha-Darschan, die sich in keinem in jüdischem Besitz befindlichen Text finden lassen. Hieronymus (Josua de Lorca) benützte Martins antijüdische Schrift und war daher außerstande, die von den Juden beanstandeten Beweisstellen zu beschaffen, wenn sie dies verlangten, weil sie in ihren Exemplaren nicht vorhanden waren. (Am Ende des 15. Jahrhunderts bekämpft Don Isaak Abravanel (1437–1508) Josua de Lorcas Mißbrauch der Haggada in seinem *Jeschuot meschicho*, in dem er alle messianischen Beweisstellen aus Talmud und Midrasch gesammelt hatte, wie er es für die biblischen messianischen Verheißungen in seinem Daniel-Kommentar *Quellen der Erlösung (Majenej ha-jeschua)* und einem alle andern Bibelstellen umfassenden Werk *Verkünder der Erlösung (Maschmia jeschua)* gemacht hatte, um seiner niedergeschlagenen Generation Mut zuzusprechen.)

Das Thema der Disputation, die sich in Tortosa unter großem Pomp in den Jahren 1413 und 1414 über eineinhalb Jahre hinzog, war natürlich dasselbe wie in Barcelona. Nur war Hieronymus gescheiter und gewandter als Fray Paul. Auch trat er viel rücksichtsloser und schärfer auf, was aus seiner Drohung ebenso hervorgeht wie aus dem Beginn seiner »Fragen« mit der Stelle Jes. 1, 18 und 20: »Wohlan denn, laßt uns rechten, spricht der Ewige, wenn ihr euch aber weigert und widerspenstig seid, sollt ihr vom Schwert verzehrt werden.« Diese Worte zitierte er, nachdem der Papst sich folgendermaßen an die Juden gewandt hatte:

28. »Ihr, gelehrte Juden, sollt wissen, daß ich nicht (hierher) gekommen bin, noch nach euch geschickt habe, um zu beweisen, welche der beiden Religionen wahr ist, denn es ist mir klar, daß meine Religion und mein Glaube wahr sind, aber eure Lehre war (zwar) wahr, ist aber zunichte geworden. Ihr seid nur gekommen, weil Geronimo (de Santa Fide) erklärt hat, er wolle aus dem Talmud eurer Rabbinen, die mehr wissen als ihr, beweisen, daß der Messias bereits erschienen ist. Deshalb sollt ihr vor mir nur über diesen Gegenstand allein sprechen.« Die eigentliche Disputation begann am dritten Tag mit dieser Rede des Hieronymus: »In eurem Talmud ist geschrieben: ›6000 Jahre wird die Welt bestehen, 2000 Jahre der Nichtigkeit, 2000 Jahre der Tora, und 2000 Jahre der messianischen Zeit (*Sanhedrin*, f. 97 a, b, Goldschmidt, IX, S. 66)‹. Aus diesem Ausspruch ist es also klar, daß in den letzten beiden 2000 Jahren der Messias gekommen ist. Wer ist er – wenn nicht unser Erlöser (wörtl. Retter)? ... Sagte Don Vidal Benveniste: ›Unser Herr, Papst, wir wollen die Bedingungen des Messias kennen (lernen), dann wird es klar werden, ob er bereits gekommen ist. Finden sich bei dem, der gekommen ist, die messianischen Bedingungen, dann wollen auch wir uns zu ihm bekennen.‹«

Aber da die Frage des Kommens des Messias zur Debatte stand, mußten die Juden zu der Haggada Stellung nehmen und sie entgegneten deshalb mit dem Schluß der Haggada: »wegen unserer Sünden aber, die zahlreich sind, sind schon viele davon vergangen« – das weist deutlich darauf hin, daß er noch nicht gekommen ist ... Wenn nun der Messias bereits gekommen wäre, hätte es heißen müssen: »und am Ende des vierten Jahrtausends wird der Messias kommen« oder »und zu Anfang des fünften Jahrtausends oder zu der und der Zeit wird der Messias kommen«; nunmehr ist es möglich, daß er erst am Ende kommt ... Sagte R. Josef Albo: »... und sie (die Weisen des Talmuds) sagten, es gebe zwei Termine für das Kommen des Messias, entweder die Zeit, die Gott verheißen hat, oder die Zeit, wenn Israel durch Reue und Buße dafür vorbereitet ist. Deshalb setzt der Ausdruck keine bestimmte Zeit für das Kommen des Messias und sagt ›und 2000 Jahre der messianischen Zeit‹. Sind die Juden dessen würdig, kommt er am Anfang, wenn nicht am Anfang sondern in der Mitte, kommt der Messias in der Mitte der Zeit, und wenn sie erst am Ende würdig sind, dann kommt er am Ende. Aber nicht werden die 2000 Jahre vergehen, ohne daß er kommt«. Erwiderte der Papst: »Und warum sagt ihr nicht, wenn die Christen dessen würdig sind, wird er sofort erscheinen, aber wenn nicht, werde er bis zum Ende der 2000 Jahre säumen?« Da sagten die Abgesandten: »Wir sagen nur, daß der Erlöser für den kommt, der im Exil verweilt. Denn wer in Ruhe lebt, wozu braucht er einen Erlöser? Der Messias ist eine Notwendigkeit für ein Volk, das in der Verbannung und Knechtschaft lebt.«[56]

Auf die zwölf Fragen über den Messias, die Hieronymus an die Juden gestellt hat, antworten sie — im Einklang mit der jüdischen Tradition, wie es auch Maimonides in dem wegen seiner Äußerungen über Jesus und das Christentum oben zitierten proskribierten *Mischne Tora* getan hat —, daß der verheißene Messias nur ein guter Mensch und Prophet sei, ohne irgend etwas Göttliches zu besitzen; er werde Israel aus dem Exil befreien, so daß das Volk Gottes leichter und vollkommen das Gesetz Gottes befolgen und so zum ewigen Leben gelangen könne. Sie leugnen, daß der Messias den Tod erleiden muß, um die vom Judentum nicht als Erbsünde anerkannte Sünde Adams zu sühnen. Sie geben zu, daß sie noch nicht verziehen ist, da es immer noch viel Elend und Bestrafung unter den Menschen gibt, aber beschränken die Tätigkeit des Messias auf die Erlösung des jüdischen Volkes. Er wird kein neues Gesetz bringen, weil Lehre und Gesetz Mosis, unabänderlich und ewig, völlig genüge. Auch versichern sie, daß Israel in sein Land zurückkehren werde, um es wieder in Besitz zu nehmen. Sich die Worte Raimund Martins zueigen machend, schreibt Hieronymus das noch fortdauernde Exil lediglich der »grundlosen Feindschaft« (*Joma* 9 b, Ausdruck aus dem Zusammenhang gerissen) gegen den Stifter der christlichen Religion und gegen die Kirche zu.[57] Nach der Wiederaufnahme der Diskussion nach längerer Pause waren nur noch drei der 22 jüdischen Gelehrten bereit, weiterzudisputieren. Die andern sollten nur Belehrung erhalten. Es ging nun um fünf Punkte in der Diskussion über den Talmud: 1. über die Falschheiten, Häresien und Scheußlichkeiten, die in ihm enthalten sind; 2. über das Verbrechen des Wuchers, den sie in fluchwürdiger Weise ausübten; 3. über die Synagogen, die sie ohne päpstliche Erlaubnis gebaut oder vergrößert und verschönert haben; 4. über ihre (sozialen) Beziehungen zu den Christen und 5. über die öffentlichen Ämter, die eben diese Juden nur im Mindestmaß unter den Christen bekleiden sollen. Darüber wolle der Papst Verordnungen erlassen »zum Lob, zum Ruhm und zur Ehre Gottes und zur Zierde des ganzen christlichen Glaubens«.[58]

Abgesehen vom ersten Punkt, ging es bei den andern um wichtige Gegenwartsfragen, die zeigen, wie brennend die Judenfrage war und wie sehr sich die Lage der Juden Spaniens seit Barcelona verschlechtert hatte. Bei der Erörterung des ersten Punktes hat vor allem R. Ferrer — nicht zu verwechseln mit dem erfolgreichen Missionsprediger Vicente Ferrer, der während der Verhandlung in Tortosa Spanien durchzog, um Juden massenweise zu bekehren — die jüdische Position deutlich auseinandergesetzt. Er war der letzte jüdische Sprecher, nachdem zuvor das Gutachten Astrucs, das grundlegend war und die gleiche Linie einschlug, verlesen und diskutiert worden war. Er führte aus, daß Christen und Juden darin einig gehen, daß sie ihre Dogmen oder Grundlehren *(Ikkarim)* auf Grund von Glaube und Tradition besitzen. Daher ist der Talmud im Sinne dieser Grundlehren zu interpretieren. Dabei ergibt sich, daß der Jude auf Grund seiner Glaubenslehren den Messias in der Zukunft erwartet, genauso wie es für den Christen ein Glaubensartikel ist, daß der Messias schon gekommen ist. Die jüdische Erwartung dauert fort, solange das Exil währt.[59] R. Astruc hatte diese Stellung schon vorher präzisiert durch die Betonung des Glaubenselements und der für den Juden verbindlichen traditionellen Auslegung gegenüber dem Wissen. Dies muß im Lichte der vom christlichen Dogma beherrschten Disputation und im Zusammenhang mit dem Verhalten der Juden während der langen Verhandlungen verstanden werden. Denn sie haben — diesem Grundsatz treu — oft die Fragen des Hieronymus übergangen oder ihr Nichtwissen bekannt. So verteidigt sich R. Astruc nach seiner Rückkehr — er hatte Tortosa verlassen, um in seiner Gemeinde nach dem Rechten zu sehen — gegen die Beschuldigung, daß die Juden ihre Unwissenheit nur vorschützten damit, daß er darauf hinwies, daß sie seit zehn Monaten aus ihren Wohnsitzen abwesend sind; ihre Fähigkeiten »verringert und gleichermaßen völlig zerstört sind«; großer Schaden in den Gemeinden (ohne Hirten) entstanden sei; sie ihre Frauen und Kinder verloren haben; sie an Lebensmitteln knapp sind, weil sie ohne Geld sind, dabei aber große Ausgaben haben: »Das ist die Lage derer, die mit Magister Hieronymus und seinesgleichen disputieren müssen, die alle im Gegensatz dazu in ungeheurem Wohlstand und großen Annehmlichkeiten leben.«[60] R. Astruc hätte hinzufügen können, daß die in die Hunderte von Seelen gehenden Taufen, die am Ende mancher Sitzungen verkündet worden sind, einen demoralisierenden Eindruck auf die anwesenden Juden, Vertreter wie auch Zuhörer, machen mußten, zumal sich unter den Neubekehrten bedeutende jüdische Adlige befanden, die mit ihren ganzen Familien zum Christentum übertraten. Die Disputation hat das ihr von der Kirche gesteckte Ziel teilweise erreicht trotz der Versuche der gelehrten Juden, ihren Glauben zu verteidigen.

'Jüdische Antwort'

V. Hebräische Streitschriften

Wir wenden uns zum Abschluß der sehr ausgedehnten hebräischen Streitschriftenliteratur zu. Sie ist ebenso wie die eingangs behandelten Kommentare — abgesehen von Briefen an Abtrünnige oder an solche Juden, die den Übertritt zum Christentum erwogen — hauptsächlich mit der Auslegung von messianischen Verheißungen in Bibel, Talmud und Midrasch gegen ihre christliche Deutung beschäftigt. Hinzu kommen Angriffe auf Widersprüche im Neuen Testament und seine Interpretation. Diese sollen uns hier allein beschäftigen.

1. Efodi an den Konvertiten David Bonet Bongiorno

Zuerst zu nennen ist der Brief *Sei nicht wie deine Väter (al-tehi kaabotecha)* 1396, den Profiat (Perfet) Duran, oder Efodi genannt, an seinen Freund David Bonet Bongiorno schrieb als Erwiderung auf dessen Aufforderung, sich wie er zum Christentum zu bekennen.

Der jüngere Freund hatte sich von Paul von Burgos, dem früheren Salomo Halevi, von der Wahrheit des Christentums überzeugen lassen. Efodis Brief ist mit solcher Ironie und Geschicklichkeit abgefaßt, daß er zuerst von den Christen für eine Verteidigung der Taufe und der Überlegenheit des Christentums gehalten wurde. Sobald der Irrtum erkannt war, wurden die vorhandenen Exemplare vernichtet. Efodi schreibt:

29. »... Gesegnet sei der Messias, der dir gegeben ein einsichtiges Herz und ein hörendes Ohr ... Töricht, der da sagte, der Verstand und das Gesetz seien zwei Leuchten; der Verstand hat vielmehr gar nicht darein zu reden mit seinen Schlüsseln und Beweisen, der Glaube allein geht aufwärts, und wer ihn bezweifelt, geht als Sünder in die Hölle. Da ich nun gesehen, mein Bruder, daß deine Absicht wohlgemeint ist und deine Handlungen um Gottes willen geschehen, ... so will ich dich denn auch aufmerksam machen auf die Grundsätze des Glaubens, welchen du im Lichte und in der Herrlichkeit des Messias, der dich umstrahlt, erwählt. So sei nicht wie deine Väter, welche an den *einen* Gott glaubten, von welchem sie eine jede Vielheit entfernten, die sich in dem Satze »Höre Israel« geirrt und unter *echad* (eins, einzig) die reine Einheit verstanden haben, nicht aber etwa eines durch Zusammensetzung, in Art, Gattung, Verhältnis, oder dem etwas hinzugefügt werden könnte. Du aber nicht also; glaube vielmehr, daß Eines drei und drei Eines sind, innerlich und wesentlich vereint, was der Mund nicht auszusprechen und das Ohr nicht zu fassen vermag ... Sei nicht wie deine Väter, welche bei Gott keine Veränderung möglich hielten, darauf irrig den Ausspruch bezogen (folgt Mal. 3, 6), jede Verkörperlichung mit aller Kraft ihres Denkens von ihm fernhielten, in ihm vielmehr nach philosophischer Spekulation einen reinen Geist sahen, die Schriftstellen, welche nach ihrem buchstäblichen Sinne zur Verhüllung für die Schwachsichtigen dienen sollen, tiefer erklärten. Du aber nicht also! Bewahre, daß du eine Verkörperlichung von ihm fernhalten solltest; glaube vielmehr, daß er, nämlich eine seiner drei Personen, Fleisch geworden, als sein Blut zur Sühne für sein Volk

vergossen werden mußte. Danke ihm dafür, daß er den Tod erduldet, um dich zu retten; seine Weisheit hat eben keine andere Art deiner Rettung gefunden. Sei nicht wie deine Väter (betreffend die Schöpfungsgeschichte). Nimm vielmehr alles nach seinem Wortsinne, nur daß du noch eine Seelenstrafe, die Erbsünde, auf den Menschen ladest, so daß er von seinem Sturze sich nicht aufhelfen kann und den Händen des Satans völlig übergeben ist, bis sein Erlöser kommt und ihn befreit ... Sei nicht wie deine Väter, welche sich viel mit der Spekulation beschäftigten ... und so sich die Wahrheit zu begründen suchten. Du aber nicht also! Fern sei es von dir, ... du müßtest nämlich den Schluß gelten lassen: der Vater ist Gott, Gott ist der Sohn, folglich ist der Vater der Sohn.« Ähnlich behandelt Efodi das Dogma von der Transsubstantiation und sagt, es gäbe so viele Leiber des Messias als Hostien auf den Altären und gleichzeitig Ruhe (Jesus im Himmel) und Bewegung (sein Leib in die Hostie verwandelt auf den Altären) am selben Gegenstand, was unmöglich sei. »... Halte fest an diesem Glauben, der dich zum ewigen Leben führt, und Gott wird mit dir sein, denn du issest das Brot, deinen Gott. – Ach, deine Väter haben Brot der Mühseligkeit gegessen, waren oft auch durstig und hungrig; du aber hast deine Seele gerettet, issest und wirst satt deines Heilands in dir. – Sei nicht wie deine Väter, denen Moses Lehre zum Erbteile war, die die geistige Welt zu erlangen bestrebt waren durch Gesinnung und Tat, die die Lehre hoch hielten, ihren Geboten und Verboten dauernde Verbindlichkeit beilegten. Du aber nicht also, du müßtest dich ja schämen; beachte keines der Ge- und Verbote! Freilich haben die Apostel, als Nachkommen Abrahams, die Lehre genau beobachtet, selbst nach dem Tode des Messias und nachdem sie in seinem Namen getauft waren. Aber diese und andere Widersprüche wirst du schon lösen; weiß ich ja, daß der heilige Geist auch aus euch spricht und nichts euch verborgen bleibt. Dankt dem Messias, der euch erwählt. Sei nicht wie deine Väter, die selbst die Gebeine eines Hohenpriesters für unrein hielten! Gehe vielmehr und hole die Gebeine, sie werden dir Wunder und Zeichen tun. Du hast ja viele bei dir, alle Heiligen, auch Propheten, so forsche bei den Toten! ... Darauf wollte ich dich aufmerksam machen, da ich weiß, daß du die Wahrheit liebst und dich nicht von den Lüsten dieser Welt verführen lässest, vielmehr ganz hingegeben bist deinem Glauben, dem Glauben an den Messias; in seinem Lichte schaust du Licht. Du achtest nicht auf die Demütigung, die dir auferlegt wird, nicht auf die Schmach, mit der du als getaufter Jude belegt wirst. Dir genügt, daß deine Seele der unbeschreiblichen Wonne teilhaft wird, daß du das Antlitz des Königs (Gottes) sehen wirst und bei ihm weilend seine Hausgenossen ... Ich bin hingegeben meinem Gotte mit ganzem Herzen und ganzer Seele auf immer, auf seinen wahren Messias hoffend und vertrauend, er ist meine Stärke, meine Freude und mein Heil. An diesem Glauben halte ich fest und habe ich mich darin nie geändert; was ich jetzt glaube, war mein Glaube schon seit zwanzig Jahren und wird es bleiben!«[61]

Was immer man über diesen Brief denken mag, er ist ein wichtiges Zeitdokument. Zeigt er doch nicht nur die merkwürdige Mischung von Herz und Verstand, von Verachtung und Bewunderung, von Trauer und Stolz, sondern auch den zeitgeschichtlichen Hintergrund, gegen den alle Bemühung um die Rettung der Seelen – das Ziel der missionseifrigen Kirche –, zusammen mit weniger edlen Motiven auf beiden Seiten, und andererseits die zwiespältige Stellung der Marranen oder Scheinchristen und der überzeugten Neuchristen gesehen werden muß, wollen wir die christlich-jüdische Auseinandersetzung jener Zeit, ja aller Zeiten verstehen. Niemand kann oder will Übertritt aus Überzeugung bestreiten, noch Zweifel am Bekehrungseifer der Getauften haben oder das traurige Geschick der Zwangsgetauften und derer, die ihre Taufe bereuten, außer Auge lassen. Ein ungeheurer Gewissenskonflikt und ein ständiges Schwanken zwischen dem neuen und dem alten Glauben, ein inneres Ringen um ehrliche Loyalität stehen dem Streben nach Karriere im christlichen Staat — man denke nur an die adlige Familie De la Cavalleria [62] — gegenüber.

2. Efodis Auseinandersetzung mit der christlichen Lehre

Doch wenden wir uns vom Persönlichen zweier Freunde, durch den Glaubenswechsel des einen plötzlich getrennt, zu den Streitschriften im eigentlichen Sinn, die mit Bedacht zur Stärkung der eigenen Seite von Juden verfaßt worden sind, und betrachten wir Efodis *Buch der Schande der Völker* (oder Christen).[63] Während die meisten polemischen anti-christlichen Schriften des Mittelalters ihr Material weitgehend der — wie wir gesehen haben — gleichfalls polemisch gerichteten Kommentarliteratur entnehmen und in Dialogform verfaßt sind — gleichviel ob es sich um tatsächliche Gespräche oder nur um ein literarisches Mittel handelt —, ist Efodis Streitschrift in zwölf Kapiteln eine systematische und sachlich gehaltene jüdische Auseinandersetzung mit dem Neuen Testament und der ganzen christlichen Lehre. Efodi zeigt eine seltene Vertrautheit mit den Evangelien — viel intensiver als Jakob ben Reuben, der erste Polemiker, der systematisch das Neue Testament angreift. Außerdem kennt er die christliche theologische Literatur, was aus Zitaten und Hinweisen auf Nikolaus von Lyra oder Petrus Lombardus, und auf anti-jüdische Schriften von zum Christentum bekehrten Juden wie Petrus Alfonsi und Fray Paul hervorgeht. Er zitiert die Namen der neutestamentlichen Schriften aus dem Spanischen; aber ohne genaue Untersuchung kann nicht festgestellt werden, ob er die Schriften in einer vorhandenen hebräischen Übersetzung aus dem Spanischen oder aus der Vulgata benützt oder selbst übersetzt hat. Er weist auf jeden Fall der Vulgata, der lateinischen Bibelübersetzung des Kirchenvaters Hieronymus (340/350—419/420), viele Übersetzungsfehler nach, einige absichtlich aus christologischen Gründen, die meisten aus ungenügender Kenntnis des Aramäischen und Hebräischen herrührend. Obwohl Efodi auf seinen oben zitierten Brief hinweist, ist sein Stil in der »Schande der Christen« durchaus ruhig und würdig. Von Interesse ist auch, daß er durchweg zwischen Jesus, seinen Jüngern und den Kirchenlehrern unterscheidet. Jesus war für ihn ein »törichter Frommer« (Ausdruck gebraucht in anderem Zusammenhang in *Mischne Sota*, III, 4), seine Jünger nennt er »Irrende« und die Kirchenväter »Irrende, die andere in die Irre führten«. Das bedeutet, daß seine Einstellung zu dem Menschen Jesus, soweit die jüdische Lehre dies möglich machte, durchaus positiv war. Seine Jünger folgten Jesu Lehre, aber begingen Irrtümer in ihrem Verständnis; während die Lehrer der Kirche von Hieronymus an bis in die Tage Efodis mit Hilfe der Dogmen, die sie aus der Lehre Jesu durch Mißverständnis entwickelt haben, andere in die Irre führten. — Efodi beginnt mit dem Anspruch auf die Göttlichkeit Jesu und sagt:

30. »Erstes Kapitel, um den Beweis zu erbringen, daß es nicht die Absicht des imaginären (oder: angeblichen) Messias noch seiner Schüler war, daß er Gott war, wie es die nach ihnen Kommenden denken ... In allem, was in den Evangelien und Briefen geschrieben steht, finden wir nicht, daß sie ihn Gott nennen, sondern immer ›der Herr Jesus‹ oder ›unser Herr Jesus‹ ... und nie ›unser Gott Jesus‹. Vielmehr mehr dachten sie, er sei der Auserlesene der menschlichen Gattung, höher als unser Meister Mose, und deshalb nannte er sich selbst und nannten seine Jünger ihn ›Sohn Gottes‹ (Poznanzki bemerkt, daß in einer Handschrift diese Version ausgestrichen und darüber geschrieben sei »und *nicht* nannten seine Jünger ihn ›Sohn Gottes‹«), um auf die Überlegenheit seiner Stufe hinzuweisen, während unser Meister Moses nach ihrer imaginären Ansicht auf der Stufe des ›Knechtes‹ stand (folgen Num. 12,7 und Jos. 1,1), doch Jesus war auf der Stufe des ›geliebten Sohnes‹.« (Zum Beweis führt Efodi Matth. 16, 13—17 — Prophet, Elia und (durch Petrus) ›Messias des lebendigen Gottes‹ — und Hebr. 3, 5 f. an) (105).

Er zitiert dann aus dem Johannesevangelium 10, 30 und 14, 9 und sagt, diese Stellen bedeuten nur Jesu Gottnähe, nicht aber seine Göttlichkeit. Auch aus seinem Hilfeschrei (Matth. 17, 34) und Mark. 10, 18 gehe dasselbe hervor. Er zitiert auch die Briefe an die Korinther und Kolosser, die Apokalypse, die Briefe Johannis und Judas, um zu beweisen, daß die Späteren mit Unrecht aus Jesus Gott gemacht haben. Er polemisiert gegen Nikolaus von Lyras *Postille zu Jesaja* (7, 16), der meinte, daß alles Gleichnis und Metapher sei, was in der Tora und den Propheten stehe, und auf Jesus den Erlöser hinweise, mit der Bemerkung, daß Gottes Zeichen vor und nicht Jahrhunderte nach dem Ereignis stattfinden. Er hält Hieronymus entgegen, daß er Jes. 7, 14 die Verben, die in der Gegenwart gebraucht sind, falsch in die Zukunft gesetzt hat —, um sie auf Jesus beziehen zu können (109).

Das zweite Kapitel behandelt das Dogma der Dreieinigkeit. In der Darstellung des Dogmas folgt Efodi Nikolaus von Lyra und vor allem Petrus Lombardus und kritisiert nicht so sehr das Dogma selbst, wie er es so sarkastisch im Brief *Sei nicht wie deine Väter* getan hat, sondern die Tatsache, daß es verschiedene Dreieinigkeiten bei den christlichen Gelehrten gebe, wie: »Vater, Sohn und Hl. Geist«; »Seele (Geist), Wasser und Blut«; »Weisheit, Macht und Wille« (148). Die letztgenannte Definition mag Efodi aus der Diskussion zwischen Maimonides im *Führer der Verwirrten* und Fray Paul beziehungsweise Raimond Peñaforte bekannt gewesen sein. Bei Nachmanides sind Wille, Weisheit und Macht natürlich nicht Wesensattribute, sondern solche des göttlichen Wirkens.

'Jüdische Antwort'

Im dritten Kapitel geht es um die Fleischwerdung Gottes in Jesus und um die Erbsünde. Die christliche Lehre wird mit Hilfe von Nikolaus von Lyra (Postille zum Römerbrief) und Petrus Alfonsi objektiv dargestellt, wenn auch Efodi vor allem Nikolaus' Darstellung ungenügend findet. Die christlichen Ansichten gehen auf den Römerbrief des Paulus (5, 5–21) zurück, den Efodi zitiert. Er lehnt die Beschränkung der Erlösung auf die an Jesus Glaubenden ab und zitiert Matthäus (9, 12 ff.; 15, 24; 18, 2 ff.) als Gegenargument, verstärkt durch Matth. 19, 16 ff.; 23, 13–39 und Luk. 18, 25. Nur die schlechten Taten der Pharisäer verschlössen ihnen die Tore des Himmels. Himmel und Hölle habe es vor Jesus Tod gegeben und die Christen hätten Unrecht, wenn sie sagen, Abraham habe auf der ersten Höllenstufe gestanden, denn da kann niemand ruhen, und Abraham bezeugte ausdrücklich, daß er in Ruhe und Frieden war. Daraus schließt Efodi, daß die Erbsünde nicht im Wege stehe, sondern jeder Mensch für seine guten Taten belohnt und für seine schlechten bestraft werde. Deshalb habe Jesus – nach Matth. 19, 17 – zur Erfüllung der Gebote ermahnt, wie auch aus Matth. 23, 2 f. klar sei (149–153). Er wirft Jesus vor, daß er unter geistiger Unsterblichkeit nicht dasselbe verstanden habe wie die wahren Toragläubigen, nämlich die Unsterblichkeit der reinen Seele als separater Intelligenz, und er zitiert Luk. 16, 23 zum Beweis.

Im vierten Kapitel (157–164) beweist Efodi, daß »Jesus nie daran dachte, gegen die Tora zu streiten, sondern sehr ihre Aufrechterhaltung und Ewigkeit wollte, und daß seine Jünger sie ebenfalls für ewig (gültig) für das Volk hielten, dem sie geboten war« (157). Er bringt Beweisstellen aus den vier Evangelien (besonders Matth. 5, 30–44; 23, 2 f.; Luk. 16, 17). Jesus sei nicht wegen der Zerstörung der Tora zum Tode verurteilt worden, sondern weil er – nach Matth. 26, 63–6 – zugegeben habe, daß er der Messias und Sohn Gottes sei, also der Gotteslästerung schuldig war. Aber die Kirchenlehrer (wörtlich »die in die Irre Führenden«) behaupten, auf Grund von Matth. 15, 1–3, 11, er habe gegen die Tora verstoßen, »aber das ist eine Lüge, denn seine Jünger beobachteten die Gebote der Tora und hüteten sich vor verbotenen Speisen ... seine Absicht mit seinem Ausspruch war vielmehr nur: ›die verbotenen Speisen machen lediglich auf Grund einer göttlichen Warnung unrein‹« (159). Daß Jesus seinen Aposteln – nach Luk. 10, 3–7 – das Essen verbotener Speisen erlaubte, sei nur geschehen, weil er sie in die Welt sandte. (Mit andern Worten: im Lande Israel waren seine Jünger und Apostel an die Speisegesetze der Tora gebunden.) Efodi akzeptiert diese Auslegung jedoch nicht, da sie mit Matth. 10, 5–15 in Konflikt steht. Jesu Feindseligkeit gegen die Pharisäer sei in seiner Sorge um die Erfüllung der Tora verankert gewesen, er griff sie an, weil sie ihre Gebote nicht beobachteten (160). Außerdem sei seine Ermahnung an die Jünger ganz eindeutig auf die positive Erfüllung der Gebote gerichtet (Luk. 16, 17; Mark. 7, 6–15; Matth. 23, 3–5). Die Apostelgeschichte beweise, daß seine Jünger nach dem Tode Jesu ebenfalls bestrebt waren, die Tora zu erfüllen (Matth. 10, 11—16; 28; 21, 26; 28, 16—8). Nach weiteren Belegstellen faßte Efodi so zusammen:

31. »All das zeigt, daß Jesus und seine Jünger an die Ewigkeit der Tora glaubten, sie irrten nur in der Sache dieses Messias und wähnten, er sei Sühne und Erlösung von der Ursünde ... diejenigen irrten auch, die glaubten, er werde das Königtum Israel wieder zurückgeben ...« (161).

In bezug auf Gen. 15, 6 beschuldigt er dann Paulus einer falschen Auslegung, die die Völker irregeführt habe; denn Glaube allein sei nach der Tora nicht genug. Für ihn war Paulus — nach seiner eigenen Aussage — der Apostel an die Heidenvölker. Er zitiert Deut. 29, 28 zum Beweis dafür, daß die Juden ewig an die Tora gebunden sind, und sagt, die Jünger stellten die Verbindlichkeit und Ewigkeit der Tora für die Juden nicht in Frage.

32. »Deshalb trugen seine Jünger von den Kindern Israels gute Sorge, die Gebote zu erfüllen ... Nur weil sie die Völker zum Glauben an Jesus führen wollten und sahen, daß sie ihre Mission nicht erfüllen konnten, wenn sie ihnen das Joch der Tora aufbürdeten, kamen sie überein, daß der Glaube allein genüge, sie zu erlösen, und daß sie ihnen nicht das Joch der Werke auferlegen sollen. Weil es aber zum Brauch Israels gehörte, Proselyten, die unter den Schutz der Schwingen der Schechina (Bezeichnung für Gott) kommen, zu taufen ... und sie sahen, daß das Joch der Beschneidung für sie (die Heiden) sehr schwer war, kamen sie überein, daß für sie die Taufe allein genügend sei. So vollzogen sie eine solche Taufe im Namen des Vaters, des Sohnes — das ist Jesus — und des Hl. Geistes, denn so sagte Jesus zu ihnen in Matth. 28, 9 und Mark. 16, 15—6, gemäß des (jüdischen) Gesetzes, Proselyten zu taufen« (162).

Im *Talmud Jewamot* f. 46 a ist beides, Taufe und Beschneidung, für Proselyten vorgeschrieben (Goldschmidt IV, 469). Deshalb zitiert Efodi den Galaterbrief (5, 2—3), wonach, wer beschnitten ist, die ganze Tora halten muß. Röm. 2, 17—26 überzeugte ihn, daß Paulus nur die — im Fleisch — Unbeschnittenen von der Erfüllung des Gesetzes entband (164).

Im fünften Kapitel setzt sich Efodi mit dem christlichen Versuch auseinander, Proselyten durch die Außerkraftsetzung der Tora zu gewinnen, und beschreibt, wie diese Erleichterung der Ausbreitung des Glaubens an Jesus geholfen hat. Er wendet sich gegen falsche Auslegung und Übersetzung von Bibelstellen wie Ps. 27, 11 und vor allem Jes. 42, 4, das Matth. 12, 21 übersetzt: »und die Heiden werden auf *seinen Namen* hoffen«, während die wörtliche und richtige Übersetzung heiße »auf *sein Gesetz*«. Zur christlichen Auslegung von Jer. 31, 30—2 nimmt Efodi genau wie vor ihm Saadia Stellung (siehe oben), gegen Paulus in Hebr. 8, 10, der wie Hieronymus »verwirrt« ist und die Stelle als zukünftiges, neues Gesetz versteht. Efodi dagegen meint, es handelt sich beim neuen Bund um das alte Gesetz: »Dieser neue Bund ist die Tora selbst; das einzig Neue ist, daß die Tora jetzt nicht mehr umgangen werden wird wie der mit den Vätern geschlossene Bund, sondern ihre Gesetze werden beobachtet werden« (166 f.). Dann setzt er sich mit der Dreiteilung der Gesetze auseinander, genau so wie Albo im 25. Kapitel des 3. Buches seiner *Ikkarim*, das wir oben ausführlich besprochen haben. Albo ist wohl von ihm abhängig, vorausgesetzt Efodi schrieb seine Polemik, ehe Albo sein Buch verfaßte. Das ist wohl mit Sicherheit anzunehmen, denn Simon ben Zemach Durans *Bogen und Schild* gegen Christentum und Islam, ein Teil seines Kommentars zu den Sprüchen der Väter unter dem Titel *Der Schild der Väter*, ist in seinem antichristlichen Teil ganz von Efodi abhängig, mindestens zwei Drittel stimmen mit der *Schande* überein.

Im sechsten Kapitel (171—178) beschreibt Efodi dann die Transsubstantiationslehre, sich weitgehend auf Petrus Lombardus' *Sententiae* berufend. Zum Wein führt er Jes. 51, 17 an und zum Brot Hos. 11, 4 und 9, 7, wahrscheinlich, um zu zeigen, daß sie die Quelle für Jesu Gebot waren. Im Anschluß an 1. Kor. 10, 16 f.; 20 f. und 11, 23—29 sagt Efodi, daß diese Stellen keineswegs aussagen, es fände eine tatsächliche Umwandlung von Brot und Wein in den Leib und das Blut Christi statt, vielmehr diene das Sakrament lediglich dazu, die Gläubigen an Jesus zu erinnern und ihren Glauben zu festigen, wodurch sie das ewige Leben gewinnen werden (175 f.). Seine Beschreibung ist, soweit mir bekannt, wohl dank seiner Quelle Petrus Lombardus, ein ganz seltenes Zeugnis jüdischen Verständnisses der christlichen Lehre und ihrer Symbolik im Mittelalter.

Das siebte Kapitel (178—180; 37—41) handelt von der Taufe, ausgehend von Matth. 3, das nach Efodi den Brauch der Reuigen Büßer im Judentum schildert. Er macht dann klar, daß Johannes und nach ihm Jesus die Taufe anders verstehen und gebrauchen als die Juden, trotzdem sie diese ebenso vollziehen wie es bei den Juden im Fall von Proselyten üblich war: jetzt bedeutet sie den Glauben an Jesus, der nie an Juden, sondern nur an Heiden gedacht hat, gemäß Matth. 28, 19; 1. Kor. 10, 1 f. Efodi stützt sich wieder auf Petrus Lombardus und bringt die wichtige Stelle Gen. 14, 18 f. über Melchisedek, der Abraham über Brot und Wein segnete. Merkwürdigerweise zitiert Efodi nicht den Hebräerbrief (7, 1—17). Er wendet sich gegen die »In die Irre Führenden«, weil sie die Melchisedek-Geschichte als ein Gleichnis ansehen, was schon daran scheitere, daß Abraham ihm als dem Priester des Allerhöchsten Gottes den Zehnten all seiner Erzeugnisse ablieferte (39). Genauso wollen sie das Tauchbad, wo immer es im Alten Testament vorkommt, auf Unreinheiten, besonders auf die von der Berührung mit einem Toten verursachte Unreinheit, metaphorisch und symbolisch beziehen, um diese Deutung auf die Taufe Jesu, der eine Hebegabe für die Toten war, anzuwenden, wie Paulus 1. Kor. 15, 20 sagt. Er lehnt diese willkürliche Deutung ab mit den Worten Jer. 23, 36: »...so hattet ihr die Worte des lebendigen Gottes verdreht«.

»Die Worte des lebendigen Gottes« ist bei Efodi ein wichtiges Auslegungsprinzip: Verstoß dagegen durch die christliche geistige und mystische Auslegung als Gleichnis ist unzulässig. So wendet er sich im zehnten Kapitel (47 f., 81–96) gegen »die Irrtümer, Verwirrungen und unberechtigten Dinge, die Jesus, seine Jünger, Apostel und die Kirchenväter nach ihnen in bezug auf die Bibel und ihre halachische Erklärung« begangen haben (im Gegensatz zu den »Worten des lebendigen Gottes«) und worin sie ihr geringes Verständnis zeigen. Sie seien ungebildete Menschen gewesen, die die Hl. Schrift mißverstanden. Er wendet sich vor allem gegen falsches Zitieren alttestamentlicher Verse und Worte im Neuen Testament (82–89). Es versteht sich von selbst, daß dabei auch die Genealogie Jesu und seiner Mutter eine wichtige Rolle spielt. Er wird hier manchmal scharf in seiner Ablehnung, da auch er keine Deutung messianischer Verheißungen auf die Zeit Jesu dulden kann. Wäre die christliche Interpretation des Alten im Neuen Testament richtig gewesen, dann hätten die Juden Jesus anerkennen müssen und es auch zweifellos getan (87). Er geht systematisch durch alle vier Evangelien und vergleicht sie mit Jes. 59, 10: »Wir tappen wie die Blinden die Wand entlang und tasten wie der Augenlose«. Er meint, was sie die vollkommene Tora Jesu heißen, gleiche mehr einer törichten Frömmigkeit, wie etwa das Gebot, seine Feinde zu lieben. »Es ist nicht recht, dergleichen Tora zu nennen, denn durch ihre Beobachtung würde die politische Gemeinschaft zugrunde gehen« (90). Im zwölften Kapitel behandelt Efodi schließlich systematisch die Übersetzungsfehler des Hieronymus – eine ungeheure Zahl. Er schreibt ihnen den Grund für den Vorwurf der Bibelfälschungen zu, den die Christen gegen die Juden erheben, denn sie weigern sich in ihren Streitschriften, den hebräischen Text zu zitieren. Er zeigt dies an vielen Beispielen (120–122).

In den nicht gestreiften Kapiteln beschreibt Efodi u. a. die sieben christlichen Sakramente, den Papst, die Geburt Jesu und seine Zeit. An Kenntnis und Verständnis der christlichen Lehren auf Grund des Neuen Testaments und der Kirchenväter kommt ihm keiner der andern Verfasser von Streitschriften gleich, weder vor noch nach ihm. Es ist erstaunlich, daß seine ernste, tiefschürfende, auf wirklicher Kenntnis beruhende Kritik am Christentum so gut wie unbekannt ist. Aus diesem Grunde haben wir geglaubt, ihm den Vorzug geben zu müssen, und so viel Raum eingeräumt, daß es nicht möglich ist, die andern mittelalterlichen Streitschriften auch nur kurz zu würdigen.[64]

3. Trokis Auseinandersetzung mit Christologie und Trinitätslehre

Zum Schluß muß Isaak Troki (gest. 1594) kurz zu Worte kommen, dessen *Befestigung im Glauben* sein Erscheinen Religionsgesprächen mit Christen seiner Zeit verdankt.[65] Zwar ist das Buch kaum über Profiat Duran (Efodi) hinausgegangen, aber es hat weite Verbreitung gefunden und ist dadurch viel mehr bekannt geworden. Seine Eigenart besteht in der klaren Anordnung und der systematischen Antwort auf die christologische Auslegung des Alten Testamentes in seiner Ganzheit. Das Buch zerfällt in zwei Teile: der erste, weit größere Teil behandelt in den ersten 43 Kapiteln die christlichen Einwände gegen die jüdische Bibelauffassung in einer erschöpfenden, jede Beweisstelle anführenden Entkräftung. Gleichzeitig weist Isaak Troki aus der Bibel nach, warum die Juden Jesus nicht als Messias anerkennen konnten, und zeigt, warum das schon 1500 Jahre dauernde Exil nicht Gottes Strafe für die Verwerfung Jesu als Messias sei. Die Kapitel 44—50 des ersten Teiles bringen Trokis Einwürfe gegen das Christentum und dessen Beweisführung im Neuen Testament. Der zweite, kürzere Teil ist einer eingehenden Kritik des Neuen Testaments in der Reihenfolge seiner Schriften gewidmet, wobei der Verfasser manches wiederholt, was er im ersten Teil schon im Zusammenhang mit seiner Widerlegung der christlichen Auffassung angeführt hat.

Es ist nicht verwunderlich, daß Troki keine neuen Beweisgründe anführt. Trotzdem er Karäer war — d. h. die rabbinische mündliche Lehre, vor allem in ihrem gesetzlichen Teil ablehnte — ist seine Bibelexegese keineswegs von der karäischen, sondern ganz von der des rabbinischen Judentums abhängig: er steht ganz in der langen Tradition der anti-christlichen Polemik und Apologetik, die im Westen ihren Höhepunkt im Hochmittelalter in Süd- und Nordfrankreich und Spanien erreicht hat. Diese polemische Literatur ist ihrerseits von der im Osten unter der Herrschaft des Islams entstandenen und ausgebildeten hebräischen Sprachwissenschaft abhängig, wie auch von Saadias Polemik, die das Judentum gegen Islam und Christentum verteidigen mußte. Einwurf und Antwort waren ein für alle Mal, und vom Anfang des christlichen Kampfes gegen das Judentum und um die Seele der Judenheit an, in ziemlich starren Grenzen festgelegt. Was bei Troki neu ist, ist höchstens die Tatsache, daß er, der nach der Reformation gelebt hat, sich sowohl gegen die Katholiken wie auch gegen die Protestanten wenden mußte. Soweit ich sehe, bestehen keine grundsätzlichen Unterschiede zwischen der römisch-katholischen und der protestantischen Einstellung zum Judentum und auch nicht im Eifer beider Konfessionen, die Juden zum Christentum zu bekehren.

Es ist geltend gemacht worden,[66] daß Troki mit Antitrinitariern in Verbindung stand. In der Tat zitiert Troki im ersten Teil der *Befestigung im Glauben* Martin Czechowicz und seine Schrift *Abhandlung dreier Tage (S. 91)* und benützt die jüngste Bibelübersetzung Alten und Neuen Testaments von Simon Budny (ebd.). Er sagt (S. 283):

33. »Ich will nun beginnen, den zweiten Teil des Buches zu schreiben, welcher den Nachweis der Unrichtigkeit der Aussprüche der Verfasser des Evangeliums enthält ... Wisse, ... daß ich den größten Teil dieser Aussprüche nach der Über-

setzung des jüngsten Übersetzers, Simon Budny, angeführt habe, ... weil diese Übersetzung richtiger ist, als die der Übersetzer, die vor ihm gewesen.«

Czechowicz und Budny waren Sozinianer; Budnys Übersetzung wurde von römisch-katholischer Seite angegriffen. Doch daß Troki diese beiden gegen das Neue Testament und seine traditionell-orthodoxen Ausleger heranzieht,[67] besagt nichts über ihre Stellung zu den messianischen Verheißungen und ihrer christlichen Auslegung, sondern höchstens zu den angeblich die Dreieinigkeit beweisenden Stellen. Doch auch dies ist keineswegs eindeutig, was die folgenden Zitate aus Kapitel 9 und 10 des ersten Teils zeigen mögen:

34. »›Im Anfange erschuf Gott die Himmel ...‹ (Gen. 1). Die Christen, sowohl die Anhänger des Papstes zu Rom, auch Katholiken genannt, als auch die Anhänger Martin Luthers, auch Evangelische genannt, führen diesen Vers als Beweis für ihren Glaubensgrundsatz der Dreieinigkeit an, indem sie behaupten, das Wort *Elokim* (= *Elohim*, Gott), das in der Pluralform steht, deute auf die Dreieinigkeit, nämlich den Vater, den Sohn und den Heiligen Geist hin, die, obwohl drei, doch nur eins sind. Antwort: Es ist allen Kennern der hebräischen Sprache bekannt, daß das Wort *Elokim* sowohl die Bedeutung Gott, Engel als auch menschlich(e) Richter und Vorgesetzte in sich schließt. (Folgen Belegstellen für jede Bedeutung — Gen. 1, 1; Richter 13, 21; Ex. 22, 8 —.) Würde man das Wort *Elokim*, das von Gott ausgesagt wird, auf die Dreieinigkeit hindeuten, wie die Christen vorgeben, so müßte ... auch bei den Engeln und den Richtern, die ... mit dem Wort *Elokim* bezeichnet werden, die Dreieinigkeit anzutreffen sein, ja selbst unser Lehrer Mosheh, von welchem Ex. 7, 1 gesagt wird, ›sieh ich habe dich gesetzt zum *Elokim* dem Pharao‹, müßte zusammengesetzt sein aus Vater, Sohn und Heiligem Geiste, was jedoch eine gewaltige Lüge wäre, die jeder Vernünftige zurückweisen muß. Hierzu kommt, daß das Wort *Elok* (= *Eloah*) in der Einzahl steht, und wird nur von Gott und nicht wie *Elokim* von noch sonst jemand gebraucht; (folgen Deut. 32, 15 und Ps. 50, 2). Nun ist bekannt, daß beide Wörter ... eines und dasselbe bedeuten, indem wir Jes. 44, 6 finden ›außer mir ist kein *Elokim*‹ und kurz darauf V. 8 ›gibt es einen *Elok* außer mir (?)‹, während aber nach ihrer unrichtigen Meinung in dieser Benennung, d. h. in der Benennung *Elok* ein Widerspruch gegen den Glauben der Dreieinigkeit enthalten ist. Allein, daß die Hl. Schrift den Ausdruck *Elokim* in der Mehrheit vom Schöpfer braucht, obschon dieser die Einheit im wahrsten Sinne des Wortes ist, geschieht im Hebräischen als Kundgebung der göttlichen Majestät, Größe und Herrlichkeit. Die göttliche Lehre spricht hier von Gott in menschlicher Weise ... Darum heißt es auch ›erschuf *Elokim* ...‹ nämlich (das Zeitwort) in der Einzahl und nicht ›erschufen‹ (in der Mehrzahl) (folgen Jes. 19, 4; Gen. 39, 10; Ex. 21, 4 und 22, 13). Auch in andern Sprachen finden wir, daß der geringere den Vornehmeren, ehrenhalber, in der Mehrzahl anredet ... ›Und Gott sprach: Wir wollen machen einen Menschen, in unserem Ebenbilde, nach unserer Ähnlichkeit, und sie sollen herrschen ...‹ (Gen. 1, 26). Auf den ferneren Beweis, den sie von diesem Verse heranbringen, indem sie behaupten, daß das Wort *naaseh* (wir wollen machen), welches in der Mehrzahl steht, auf die Dreieinigkeit hindeute, weil es, wäre dies nicht der Fall, hätte *eeseh* (ich werde machen) in der Einzahl heißen müssen, diene zur Antwort: Würde das Wort *naaseh*, wie sie behaupten, auf die Dreieinigkeit hindeuten, warum heißt es später, ›und Gott erschuf den Menschen, in seinem Ebenbilde‹ (V. 27) in der Einzahl, und so mögen sie uns denn auch kund tun, welcher von den Dreien

den Menschen nach seinem Ebenbilde geschaffen; denn hätten alle Drei den Menschen insgesamt geschaffen, so hätte es ja nach ihrer Meinung heißen müssen, ›sie erschufen‹ in der Mehrzahl? Allein das Wort *naaseh* in der Mehrzahl ist gleichfalls ein *pluralis excellentiae* ...« (78–80).[68]

Schluß: Trennendes und Einendes

Ob diese Art von Polemik stichhaltig ist oder nicht, steht nicht zur Debatte. Vieles in der polemischen Literatur und auch bei den öffentlichen Streitgesprächen Gesagte ist oft nichts anderes als ein Versuch, dem Gegner einen Sprung im Wortgefecht voraus zu sein. Es ist dabei wichtig zu betonen und zu beherzigen, daß es ja gar nicht so sehr um Frage und Antwort oder Anklage und Gegenklage ging als vielmehr um das Bemühen, die Juden zum Christentum zu bekehren, ob es sich um die mittelalterliche Kirche oder um beide Kirchen seit Luther handelt. Es ist auch gleichgültig, daß in der Zeit Trokis die Lage der Juden im allgemeinen besser war als vorher. Denn der Glaubenskampf ging, wenn auch die Inquisition eine Sache der Vergangenheit war, im übrigen unverändert weiter. Christliche Wahrheit stand gegen jüdische Wahrheit, denn beide Seiten mußten (und müssen) auf der Wahrheit ihres Glaubens bestehen. Verstandesmäßig läßt sich die Frage des Wahrheits*grades* (wenn man so sagen könnte) wohl nie lösen lassen, jedenfalls solange nicht, als Christen und Juden überzeugte Gläubige sind. Deshalb scheint doch etwas Wesentliches, ja Ausschlaggebendes in der Hartnäckigkeit zu stecken, mit der die jüdischen Polemiker weniger über die Frage, ob Jesus der verheißene Messias war, diskutieren wollten als über grundlegende Fragen wie die Natur Gottes und die Natur Jesu, auch wenn praktisch diese Grundfragen in der Messianitätslehre eingeschlossen waren.

Die jüdische Antwort, die wir in diesem Kapitel dargestellt haben, ist nur ein Ausschnitt aus einem viel größeren Komplex von Kommentaren, Streitschriften, Briefen und Disputationen. Selbst wenn mehr Raum gewesen wäre,[69] würde das Bild kaum anders erschienen sein. Es ging um brennende Fragen, die, auch wenn sie heute nicht mehr (oder noch nicht wieder?) so brennend sind, im Grunde und wesentlich die gleichen geblieben sind. Die wachsende Verweltlichung und Veräußerlichung unseres Lebens kann den früheren Glaubensstreit nicht vergessen machen, mindestens nicht über Nacht. Doch darf vielleicht der Gedanke geäußert werden, daß gerade angesichts der drohenden Gefahr beide Religionen ja schließlich um ihre Existenz kämpfen müssen und auf Grund ihres gemeinsamen Erbes vielleicht doch einen Weg suchen sollten, gemeinsam der Gefahr zu begegnen.

So möge der letzte Satz aus Trokis *Befestigung im Glauben* auch dieses Kapitel beschließen, so predigthaft er klingen mag: Absichtlich alle theologische Subtilität und alles die beiden Religionen wohl immer Trennende beiseite lassend, kann er doch ausdrücken, was hinter diesem Handbuch als etwas Juden und Christen Einendes steht:

»Ebenso wolle Er mich glücklich erleben lassen die Verheißungen seiner Propheten: ›Alsdann werde ich verwandeln die Sprache der Völker in eine geläuterte, daß sie Alle anrufen den Namen Gottes und ihm dienen einmütig‹ (Zeph. 3, 9). ›Und sein wird der Herr König über die ganze Erde, an selbigem Tage wird der Herr sein Einer und sein Name Einer‹« (Sach. 14, 9).

Anmerkungen

[1] Vgl. J. Trachtenberg, The Devil and the Jews, New York 1961; W. P. Eckert u. E. L. Ehrlich, Judenhaß – Schuld der Christen ? ! Essen 1964.

[2] Book of Principles *(Sefer Ha-ikkarim)*, hebr. Text und englische Übersetzung von I. Husik, Philadelphia 1946, I, Kap. 26; besonders III, Kap. 25 (S. 224 ff.) Vgl. J. Guttmann, Die Philosophie des Judentums, München 1933 (englische Übersetzung der vermehrten hebr. Ausgabe von D. M. Silvermann, London 1964).

[3] Vgl. I. Heinemann, Die wissenschaftliche Allegoristik des jüdischen Mittelalters, Hebrew Union College Annual XXIII (1950–51).

[4] Meine Übersetzung aus dem hebräischen Text, herausgegeben von M. Friedlaender, Essays on the Writings of Abraham b. Ezra, IV, London k. D. (1877?), Appendix, S. 1 f.

[5] A. a. O., S. 5.

[6] A. Posnanski, Schiloh, Leipzig 1904, S. 126–136.

[7] A. a. O., S. 133; aus dem *Alten Nizzachon* (um 1300), hrsg. v. J. C. Wagenseil, *Tela ignea Satanae*, Altdorf 1681, III, S. 32.

[8] Pentateuchkommentar, hrsg. v. D. Rosin, Breslau 1881, S. 71 f.

[9] A. Posnanski, a. a. O., hebr. Teil 41 (S. XVI), aus *Sefer ha-asufot*.

[10] Radicum liber sive Hebraeum Bibliorum lexicon, hrsg. v. J. H. R. Biesenthal u. F. Lebrecht, Berlin 1847.

[11] A. Posnanski, a. a. O., Hebr. Teil, S. XXVII.

[12] A. a. O., S. 361 aus Raimund Martins *Pugio Fidei*, verfaßt 1278, hrsg. v. Carpzow, Leipzig 1687, Pars II, Kap. IV, S. 312 ff.

[13] A. a. O. (Posnanski), S. XXVII.

[14] S. R. Driver u. Ad. Neubauer, The fifty-third chapter of Isaiah according to the Jewish interpreters, I. Text, hrsg. v. A. Neubauer; II. Übers. v. Driver u. Neubauer, Oxford 1876.

[15] Vgl. für die Kommentarliteratur E. I. J. Rosenthal, Anti-Christian polemic in medieval Bible commentaries, The Journal of Jewish Studies, 11 (1960), S. 115 bis 135, wo die einschlägige Literatur angeführt ist, besonders die Arbeiten von B. Blumenkranz und J. Rosenthal. Vgl. auch Anm. 25.

[16] Vgl. S. Poznanskis hebr. Einleitung zu seiner Ausgabe von Eliezer von Beaugency's Kommentaren zu Ezechiel und den 12 Propheten, Warschau 1910–13, und meinen Aufsatz.

[17] A. a. O., S. LXIX.
[18] Th. Hackspan, Nürnberg 1644 unter dem Titel *Tosefeth teschuwoth Radak*. Vgl. auch die lateinische Übersetzung des Genebrardus, *Responsa simul et argumenta, quae Rabbi David Kimhi contra Christianos suis ad Psalmos commentariis inseruit*, Paris 1566. Vgl. auch Anm. 2, S. 116 f. meines Aufsatzes.
[19] The First Book of Psalms with the Longer Commentary of R. David Qimchi, hrsg. v. S. Schiller-Szinessy, Cambridge 1883, S. 11 f. Vgl. auch Kimchis Erklärung von Ps. 45, in meinem Aufsatz, S. 130.
[20] A. a. O., S. 58 f.
[21] Kimchis Kommentar zu Ps. 42—72 wurde herausgegeben von S. I. Esterson (Hebrew Union College Annual, 10 (1935), S. 309 ff.)
[22] Ebd., S. 442 f.
[23] Nach d. Übers. von H. Torczyner, Die Heilige Schrift, Frankfurt 1937, IV, der ich im allgemeinen in den Zitaten aus der Bibel folge.
[24] J. Bosniak, The Commentary on the fifth Book of Psalms, New York 1954, S. 66 ff. (Hackspan, S. 200).
[25] Vgl. Anm. 15 und Judah Rosenthal, Die antichristliche Streitschriftenliteratur bis zum Ende des 18. Jahrhunderts (hebr.). Eine Bibliographie, in: Aresheth, II (Jerusalem 1960), S. 130—179; III (1961), S. 433—439.
[26] Über göttliches und menschliches Gesetz vgl. E. I. J. Rosenthal, Griechisches Erbe in der jüdischen Religionsphilosophie des Mittelalters, Stuttgart 1960, 2. u. 3. Kap.
[27] Saadia, *Kitab al-amanat wa-l-itikadat*, hrsg. v. S. Landauer, S. 85 ff., engl. Übers. des arab. u. hebr. Textes von S. Rosenblatt, New Haven 1948, S. 102 ff. Vgl. Jakob Guttmann, Die Religionsphilosophie des Saadia, Göttingen 1882, wo die Polemik systematisch dargestellt ist (S. 101—107).
[28] J. Guttmann, a. a. O., S. 108—113.
[29] Saadia, hrsg. v. Landauer S. 135 / Rosenblatt 167.
[30] Ebd., L. 136 ff. / R. 167 ff.
[31] Ebd., L. 249 f. / R. 315 f.
[32] Ebd., L. 251 / R. 318 f.
[33] Ebd., L. 252 ff. / R. 320 ff. Vgl. auch W. Bacher, Die Bibelexegese d. jüd. Religionsphilosophen des Mittelalters vor Maimûni, Budapest 1892, S. 42 ff.
[34] M. Maimonides, The Guide of the Perplexed, übers. v. S. Pines, Chicago 1963, I, Kap. 50, S. 111.
[35] Aus W. Bacher, Die Bibelexegese Moses Maimûnis, Straßburg 1897, S. 174.
[36] The Code of Maimonides: Book Fourteen, übers. a. d. Hebr. v. A. M. Herschman, New Haven 1949, S. XXIII f. d. Einleitung. Es war nicht möglich, einen unzensurierten hebr. Text einzusehen und zu übersetzen.
[37] A. a. O., III, Kap. 25. Husik benutzte unzensurierte, vollständige Handschriften und Drucke des hebr. Textes. Auch in Genebrardus (s. Anm. 18 oben), der Titel lautet: *R. Joseph Albonis, R. Davidis Kimhi, et alius cuiusdam Hebraei anonymi argumenta, quibus nonnullos fidei Christianae articulos oppugnant.*
[38] Die ganze Stelle findet sich in: Husik, S. 229—234.
[39] Ebd., S. 234 ff.
[40] Ebd., S. 242 ff.
[41] Ebd., I, S. 186.
[42] Ebd., I, S. 135 f.
[43] S. oben, S. 309 ff.
[44] Der hebräische Bericht ist von Wagenseil, a. a. O., fehlerhaft herausgegeben und

kritisch von S. Grünbaum, Thorn 1873, u. d. Titel *Wikkuach de rabbi Jechiel* (Streitgespräch), engl. Übers. d. Wagenseilschen Textes v. O. S. Rankin, Jewish religious polemic, Edinburgh 1956, worin er wichtige Texte in englischer Übersetzung bringt. Vgl. Enc. Jud., Berlin 1930, Bd. V, s. v. Disputationen. A. Lewin, Die Religionsdisputation d. R. Jechiel v. Paris 1240 am Hofe Ludwigs d. Heiligen, ihre Veranlassung und ihre Folgen. Monatsschr. f. Gesch. u. Wissensch. d. Judentums, 18 (1869), S. 99–110, 145–156, 193–210; A. Kisch, Die Anklageartikel gegen den Talmud und ihre Verteidigung durch R. Jechiel ben Joseph vor Ludwig d. Heiligen in Paris, Monatsschr. f. Gesch. u. Wissensch. d. Judentums, 23 (1874), S. 10–18, 62–75, 123–130, 155–163, 204–212. Die 35 Artikel basieren auf der von Donin dem Papst Gregor IX. vorgelegten Anklageschrift gegen den Talmud, *Extractiones de Talmut*. Der lateinische Bericht enthält auch die Confessio magistri Vivo (d. i. Jechiel) und die des mag. Juda, seines Kollegen. Vgl. Isidore Loeb, La Controverse de 1240 sur le Talmud. Revue des Etudes Juives, I (1880), S. 247–261; II (1881), S. 248–270; III (1881), S. 39–51; auch Y. F. Baer, Zur Kritik der Streitgespräche des R. Jechiel von Paris und des R. Moses b. Nachman (Hebr., Tarbiz II, 2, S. 172 f.); B. Blumenkranz, Die jüdischen Beweisgründe im Religionsgespräch mit den Christen in den christlich-lateinischen Sonderschriften des 5. bis 11. Jahrhunderts (Theol. Ztschr. IV, 2 (1948), S. 119–147) für die frühere Zeit. Ferner: Judah Rosenthal, The Talmud on Trial: the disputation at Paris in the year 1240, The Jewish Quarterly Review, XLVII, S. 57 bis 76, 145–169; S. W. Baron, A Social and Religious History of the Jews, New York u. London 1965–67, IX, S. 79–83, mit wichtigen Anmerkungen.

45 Vgl. auch Enc. Jud., Bd. IX, s. u. Jesus von Nazareth.
46 Vgl. S. W. Baron, a. a. O., IX, S. 66.
47 *Wikkuach de rabbi Jechiel*, hrsg. v. S. Grünbaum, S. 4 f.
48 Nachmanides' hebr. Bericht in *Kitwej Rmbn*, hrsg. v. H. D. Shevel, I, Jerusalem 1963. Vgl. S. W. Baron, a. a. O., IX, S. 83–87 mit Anmerkungen; Y. F. Baer, Amm. 44 oben; C. Roth, The Disputation of Barcelona (1263), The Harvard Theological Review, 43 (1950), S. 117 ff.; P. Denifle, Quellen zur Disputation Pablos Christiani mit Moses Nachmani zu Barcelona, 1263 (Hist. Jahrb. d. Görres-Ges., VIII (1887), S. 225–244). Eine engl. Übers. des hebr. Berichtes findet sich in O. S. Rankin, a. a. O., S. 157 ff., auf der Edition M. Steinschneiders basierend.
49 *Kitwej* ..., hrsg. v. Shevel, S. 139 f.
50 Ebd., S. 303–313.
51 S. Schechter, Studies in Judaism, I, London 1896, S. 126.
52 Abgedruckt in: Jeschurun, hrsg. v. Jos. Kobak, VI (Bamberg 1868) unter d. Titel *Wikkuach Tortosa*, S. 45–55.
Über die Disputation besteht eine große Literatur, u. a.; F. Baer, Studien zur Geschichte der Juden im Königreich Aragonien während des 13. und 14. Jahrhunderts, Berlin 1913, besonders S. 12 f. u. 29 ff. Vgl. auch: ders., A History of the Jews in Christian Spain, Philadelphia 1966, Bd. 2, Kap. XI, S. 170–243; sehr wichtig. (Ursprünglich hebr. erschienen Tel-Aviv, 2. A. 1959). Ders., Die Disputation von Tortosa (Spanische Forschungen d. Görres-Ges., Erste Reihe, 3. Bd., Münster 1931, S. 307–336). Ders., Die Juden im christlichen Spanien, Berlin 1929, I, 1, S. 786, 799, 810 ff.; S. W. Baron, a. a. O., IX, S. 87–94 mit wichtigen Anmerkungen. F. Ehrle, Martin de Alpartils Chronica Actitatorum temporibus Domini Benedicti XIII, Bd. I, Paderborn 1906, S. 580 ff., 16. Die große Judendisputation von Tortosa und San Matteo (7. Febr. 1413 bis 13. Nov. 1414), auf der Vatikan-

Handschrift des lateinischen Protokolls beruhend – sehr wichtig. Auf einer schlechteren Handschrift fußend A. Posnanski, Le colloque de Tortosa et de San Mateo, Revue des Etudes Juives, LXXIV u. LXXV, 1922.

[53] S. ibn Verga's *Shewet Jehudah*, hebr. Text und deutsche Übers. v. M. Wiener, Hannover 1855, neue Textausgabe v. Azriel Schochet, mit Einltg. v. Y. F. Baer, Jerusalem 1947.

[54] Die Disputation von Tortosa (s. Anm. 52), S. 326, Anm. 33.

[55] Y. F. Baer, Die gefälschten Midraschim des Raimund Martin (hebr. Gedenkschrift für Gulak und Klein; Jerusalem 1942, S. 28–49).

[56] A. Schochet, S. 97 ff.; Wiener, S. 70 ff., 139 ff., auch J. Höxter, Quellenbuch zur jüdischen Geschichte und Literatur, Frankfurt 1928, II. Teil, S. 105 ff.

[57] Vgl. A. Posnanski, a. a. O.; F. Baer, Die Disputation ...; F. Ehrle, a. a. O.

[58] F. Ehrle entnommen, auf Grund der Vatikan. Handschrift. Über den Wucher vgl. S. Stein, A Disputation on Moneylending between Jews and Gentiles in Meir b. Simeon's Milchemeth Mizwah, Narbonne, 13th Cent., The Journal of Jewish Studies X (1959), S. 45–61, bes. das Zitat in engl. Übers. S. 51–57.

[59] Aus F. Baer, Die Disputation ..., Beilage IV.

[60] F. Ehrle, a. a. O., S. 591 aus der Vatikan-Handschrift.

[61] Der Brief ist aus A. Geiger, Das Judentum und seine Geschichte, Breslau 1910, auszugsweise zitiert, S. 482 ff. Der ganze Brief ist abgedruckt in: F. Kobler, A Treasury of Jewish Letters, Philadelphia 1954, I, S. 276 ff. F. Baer, Die Juden im christl. Spanien, I, 1, S. 799, bestreitet mit Recht, daß Efodi die Zwangstaufe angenommen hat, da er sich unmöglich nach seiner Rückkehr zum Judentum hätte in Spanien zeigen können; er war in Tortosa anwesend.

[62] S. W. Baron, a. a. O., IX, S. 92.

[63] Textausgabe von A. Posnanski in: Ha-zofeh, III (1913–14), 99–113; 143–180; IV, 37–48; 81–96; 115–124. S. 125–132 enthalten bibliographische Angaben des Herausgebers. Das *Gojim* des Titels, gewöhnlich Heiden oder Andersgläubige bedeutend, wird hier wohl Christen im Sinne haben, da die ganze Abhandlung sich gegen das Neue Testament richtet. *Gojim* = Christen ist der volkstümliche Gebrauch.

[64] Wenigstens seien die wichtigsten Streitschriften und die Literatur darüber hier angeführt: das bereits erwähnte »Bogen und Schild« des Simon b. Zemach Duran ist nur in einigen Ausgaben seines »Schild der Väter« aus Zensurgründen zu finden. Ich benützte die Ausgabe Livorno 1763. Jakob b. Reuben's »Kriege Gottes« wurde von Judah Rosenthal herausgegeben, Jerusalem 1963. Derselbe Gelehrte hat noch andre solche Traktate im hebr. Original veröffentlicht: *Herew Piphioth* (A Two-edged Sword), ein Streitgespräch zwischen einem *nokhri* (Christen) und einem *iwri* (Juden) des Jair b. Shabetaj da Correggio (2. H. d. 16. Jhs.), Jerusalem 1958; *Wikkuach Jehudi-Nozri misof hameah hat 'w* (Jüdisch-christliches Streitgespräch vom Ende des 15. Jahrhunderts), erschienen in: Sura, I, Jerusalem 1954; nach 1472 zwischen Elias Hajjim b. Benjamin von Genzano di Roma und Fra Francesco di Acquapendente, einem Franziskaner, in Orvieto. Vgl. oben Anm. 25. Wichtig ist Josef b. Nathan Official's *S. Josef ha-mekanne* (Buch Josefs d. Eiferers), das Judah Rosenthal herausgibt. Über ihn vgl. Zadok Kahn, Le Livre de Joseph le Zélateur, Revue des Etudes Juives, I (1881), S. 222 ff.; III, 1881, S. 1 ff., und E. Urbach in seinem umfassenden Aufsatz, ebd. C (1935), S. 61 ff. Etudes sur la Littérature Polémique au Moyen-Age. Das Buch enthält vieles aus hebr. Kommentaren und früheren Steitschriften; es ist vom Verfasser des hebr. Berichts des Streitgesprächs in Paris geschrieben und

polemisert u. a. gegen 43 Verse aus dem Neuen Testament (Kahn). Urbach weist gegen Kahn nach, daß dessen Datum für das Buch — 1274 — nicht stimmt, da es in einem aus dem Jahr 1269 stammenden Werk genannt ist. Vgl. auch Isidore Loeb, Polémistes chrétiens et juifs en France et en Espagne, Revue des Etudes Juives, 18. Glänzende Darstellung in: S. W. Baron, a. a. O., IX, Kap. XXXIX, und besonders Anm. 7, S. 293–297 (jüd. Polemiker), u. Anm. 4, S. 288–292 (christl. Polemiker). Vgl. auch oben Anm. 6, 15; 15, 44 (O. S. Rankin). S. Krauss, Das Leben Jesu nach jüdischen Quellen, Berlin 1902, eine weitverbreitete, volkstümliche anti-christliche Schrift, die auch J. C. Wagenseil in seinem *Tela ignea Satanae*, Altdorf 1581, hebräisch mit lateinischer Übersetzung bringt *(Libellus Toldos Jeschu)*. Krauss'sche Versionen und Übersetzung sind zuverlässiger.

[65] *S. Chizzuk Emunah*, hrsg. u. übers. von D. Deutsch, Sohrau/Breslau, 2. A. 1837, aus dem die Zitate stammen.

[66] Vgl. A. Geiger, Nachgel. Schriften, 3. Bd., Berlin 1876, S. 178–223, und Judah Rosenthal, Marcin Czechowic and Jacob of Belzyce. Arian-Jewish Encounters in 16th century Poland, Proceedings of the American Academy for Jewish Research, New York 1966, S. 77–97, bes. S. 92 ff. Isaak Troki betreffend.

[67] Ebd., S. 195 f.

[68] Der Abschnitt aus Kap. 10 ist ausführlicher in Höxter, a. a. O., IV, S. 69 f. zitiert. Vgl. auch das Kapitel von G. Müller in diesem Handbuch für ein anderes Zitat aus Troki.

[69] Nur ein Bruchteil der reichen und vielfältigen Literatur zur Auseinandersetzung zwischen Judentum und Christentum kann in diesem Kapitel benützt werden. Die folgenden Literaturhinweise sollen es dem Leser ermöglichen, den Hintergrund und die Ereignisse selbst kennenzulernen:
S. W. Baron, A. Social and Religious History of the Jews, Vols. III–VIII, bes. IX–XII, New York u. London, 1965–67. Sehr wertvolle Anmerkungen mit erschöpfenden Literaturangaben; S. Dubnow, Weltgeschichte des Jüdischen Volkes, Berlin 1927, Bd. V.; H. Graetz, Geschichte der Juden, München 1853–75, Bd. 6–8; J. R. Marcus, The Jew in the medieval world. A Source Book, New York 1960; J. Parkes, The Conflict of the Church and the Synagogue (Meridian Books), New York 1961; ders., The Jew in the medieval Community, London 1934; I. Abrahams, Jewish Life in the Middle Ages, New York 1958; J. Trachtenberg, The Devil and the Jews, New York 1961; M. Güdemann, Geschichte des Erziehungswesens und der Cultur der abendländischen Juden während des Mittelalters und der neueren Zeit, Wien 1880–88, 3 Bde.; S. Grayzel, The Church and the Jews in the XIIIth Century, Philadelphia 1933; C. Roth, A History of the Marranos, New York 1959; R. T. Herford, Christianity in Talmud and Midrasch, London.

10

THE STUDY OF THE BIBLE
IN MEDIEVAL JUDAISM

The study of the Torah or Pentateuch is a biblical commandment. In Deut. vi the father is enjoined to teach his children all the commandments, statutes and ordinances; and teaching comprises both what the text says and what it means. Interpretation is known by the term *derash*. Its justification is derived from the verse in Deut. xiii: 'thou shalt inquire, and make search and ask diligently...' Rules of interpretation were developed to enable the rabbis to establish laws and regulations to meet the needs of the day. Minute investigation of the biblical text was called for, and far-fetched interpretation was sometimes needed to derive such laws from the Bible. But this method succeeded in preserving the Bible as the Word of the living God and as the perpetual foundation of Judaism. In this way, there arose gradually a 'fence round the Torah', considered necessary in response to the commandment to Israel to be 'a holy nation unto the Lord'. Holiness is understood in its basic meaning of separateness; unless Israel is

The study of the Bible in medieval Judaism

separate it cannot attain holiness. The fence developed into the oral Torah, eventually codified in the Talmud. The written Torah comprises not only the Pentateuch but all the Canon of Old Testament Scripture. Adherence to the whole Torah as *Halakhah*, the way to God, secured Jewish survival. Yet there was modification, adaptation, change and even abrogation in a continuous attempt to preserve the biblical heritage. Flexibility was essential, and it could only be maintained by ever fresh study and reinterpretation. The bulk of post-biblical Hebrew and Jewish literature is in fact interpretation of the Bible. Leo Baeck expressed this truism thus: 'It is a principle in Judaism that truth has to be discovered in, and through, the Bible. The book of "revelation" must again and again be revealed by the teacher. For every sentence and story in this book not only tells something, it also means something. It does not merely describe what has been and now ceased to be. It manifests something permanent that attains actuality again and again.'

The rabbis of the first centuries of the Common Era coined a terminology of interpretation which reflects the dynamic character of their diligent search for the truth of the Bible. This was not a theoretical ideal, or an intellectual exercise of the contemplative life; it was a wrestling with a text which was alive with meaning, a practical guide to individual and social conduct, a 'tree of life' for the Jewish people. 'Turn it and turn it, for all is in it' aptly describes the fundamental importance of the Torah and the constant, ceaseless activity of those qualified to interpret it. The fruit of this endeavour is to be found in the Midrash literature, apart from the Aramaic and Greek versions of the Old Testament. As the Torah contains preceptive matter, formulated in laws and statutes, and moral, edifying instruction and stories, these *Midrashim* are *halakhic* or *aggadic*, legal exposition and homily. Thus, we have two different approaches and methods side by side, the literal and the homiletical, figurative interpretation of the Bible. To guard against creative imagination running wild and undermining the obligatory character and significance of the preceptive side, the rabbis asserted a basic hermeneutic principle: 'No verse in Scripture can lose its literal (plain, simple) meaning.' This *peshat* or literal meaning must not be explained away by an allegorical or mystical interpretation; it always remains basic. But alongside it, *derash* or homiletical, figurative, meaning can be deduced from the text as a legitimate additional meaning.

Jewish themes

In the period under discussion, this principle of biblical exegesis assumed great importance, and *peshat* became the dominant method of interpretation in the West from the eleventh century onwards.

This survey of medieval Jewish exegesis in the Christian West is necessarily brief. But even its general character cannot become clear unless we realize—against the background of this sketch of the purpose of exegesis—that it is but a part of a continual activity of long standing. Together with the observance of Jewish law, the fulfilment of the commandments as developed and interpreted in the *Halakhah*, continuous exposition of the basic teachings of the Hebrew bible in literary form guaranteed the meaningful survival of Judaism as a distinct religious way of life, an enclave in Christian and Muslim Europe. Living within the 'fence round the Torah' the Jews were sometimes tolerated but often persecuted as a separate group. This group, which did not profess either of the regnant religions, was determined to live a life of its own in accordance with its own religious and cultural heritage, intent to preserve and, if necessary, to defend it against attack and especially against any attempt at conversion. The 'fence' was not an impenetrable wall; it was more like a rampart. The Jews, while maintaining their separateness, were open to the spiritual currents and movements of the times. They drew into their own civilization what appealed to them among the ideas and institutions of the world around them, striving for a synthesis between the indigenous and the extraneous in religious thought—both in theology and in philosophy—and to some extent in social organization. This was effected by interpretation. For this reason it is important to see this activity clearly. Its task was twofold. Its principal object was to explain the tenets of biblical religious culture to each generation in order to give the life of the community and the individual member guidance and direction, and to strengthen their faith in the existence and absolute, simple unity of God, his revelation in history through the Torah, his promise of the kingdom of God on earth and the final redemption at the end of days through the Messiah, son of David. The second objective was the defence of these concepts against Muslims and Christians in so far as these two daughter-religions claimed to have superseded Judaism.

Our concern in this section is only with the Christian claim, or more specifically with the arguments the Jewish commentators on the Hebrew

The study of the Bible in medieval Judaism

bible used against it. In particular, two issues were of vital importance from the days of the Church Fathers to the end of the medieval period: the divine–human nature of Jesus and his Messiahship and, connected with it, the validity of the Torah. In fact, the double purpose of Jewish exposition is basically one and the same, but it is so to speak a struggle on two fronts, an internal and an external one.

Internally, traditional normative Judaism had to be maintained: against the sectarian tendencies of the Karaites, who denied the oral Torah of rabbinic Judaism; against extreme rationalism; and against mysticism in so far as it developed into antinomianism. Externally, the Christian claim that Jesus was the Messiah promised in the Old Testament, and that he had replaced the Torah, had to be refuted. Since it was less relevant to convince the Christians than to confirm the Jewish belief that the Messiah was still to come and with him final redemption, and thus to fortify the Jews to withstand Christian attack and attempts at conversion, medieval Jewish exegesis was primarily concerned with the exposition of Judaism for the Jews. But Christian endeavours to convert the Jews, persecution, and general insecurity imposed on the Jewish leaders the task of emphasizing the simple unity of God, Messianism and imminent redemption. Hence we meet with a strong element of anti-Christian polemic, coupled with the stress on the literal as against the spiritual meaning of Scripture, in particular of its messianic passages in the Torah, in the prophets, especially in Isaiah, and in the Psalms. The twofold aspect of this exegesis is seen in its methods and also in its terminology. Both testify to the relevance and topicality of such exegesis.

Leaving aside the Jewish–Muslim controversy and Jewish commentaries written in Arabic, we confine ourselves to the Jewish–Christian issue and to the commentators writing in Hebrew. They give us a clear idea of the mental climate of the time; of close personal relations between Jews and Christians—closer, it appears, the more hostile the attitudes and measures of the Church against the Jews became. They also show us how great the messianic expectancy was among the Jews and what a vital part the eschatological teaching of the Hebrew prophets played in the daily lives of the hard-pressed Jews. All this goes to show how relevant the Bible was in those days and what a practical and active part its exposition played in the preservation of Judaism and in the survival of the Jews. But before we can tell the story of this exegesis we must briefly mention what made it possible for the Jews of Spain, southern and especially northern France and Germany to develop the literal interpretation of the Hebrew bible into a fine art and a powerful instrument, and to lay the foundations for the modern scientific study of the Bible.

As has been stated at the beginning, the literal interpretation is not the invention of the medieval commentators. Already the Church Fathers opposed to the *sensus Judaicus* (by which they mean the literal sense) the *sensus mysticus*. For the disciples of Origen the Jews were a *carnalis populus, amici litterae*. Jerome shared this view, although he made a valiant attempt, with the help of Jewish teachers, to get back to the *Hebraica veritas* in his Vulgate. Augustine also showed a more positive attitude to the literal meaning, as long as the spiritual or mystical sense was the one accepted by Christians. Dr Smalley has shown in her researches in the school of St Victor how the *peshat* found an entry into the exegetical work of Hugh and Andrew of St Victor, and how Jewish explanations are quoted by them, by the Chanter, by Langton and the Comestor; and Raphael Loewe has traced Herbert of Bosham's indebtedness to medieval Jewish exegesis, to mention only two of the more recent investigations. We shall come back to this question later in this section. Suffice it to say that even in the later middle ages, Jewish exegesis was always connected with the literal sense, and while it promoted a more accurate understanding of the Hebrew text it hampered Christian missionary activity and militated against the Christological interpretation, especially of the messianic prophecies. But it was on this ground of *peshat* that Jews and Christians met as Bible scholars in a common search for the truth of the Bible, irrespective of their theological presuppositions.

In the middle ages, the pioneering efforts in grammatical and lexicographical studies of Saadya Gaon (880–942) laid the foundation for the exegetical work of the Spanish Jews, who in turn enabled the French school in north and south to give an entirely new meaning and content to the method of *peshat*. Saadya established Hebrew philology as the prerequisite for the study of the literal sense of the Bible, a method he employed in his Arabic translation and in his Arabic commentaries on the Pentateuch, Isaiah, Proverbs and Job, which are extant in critical editions with French translation. He naturally brought the traditional

The study of the Bible in medieval Judaism

rabbinic interpretation to bear on the text, to which he also applied the findings of reason. For he was steeped in Islamic culture and made full use of the secular knowledge of his time, the result of the renaissance of Greek science and Hellenistic philosophy. On the one hand, he stressed the paramount importance of the literal meaning. On the other, he allowed the inner, hidden meaning only if the literal sense ran counter to reason or established tradition, or was in opposition to another scriptural passage. In his case, the close attention to, and concentration on, the plain meaning of Scripture was forced upon him by the Karaites, who, as their name implies, went back to the Bible for guidance while rejecting the rabbinic interpretation of it as it crystallized in the *Halakhah*. These sectarians were a grave danger to rabbinite traditional Judaism, and Saadya, rising to its defence, employed the weapons of his opponents. Another danger threatened from the rationalist thinkers of Islam; hence Saadya clearly defined when and where a departure from the literal meaning was justified, or required. He contrasts the secular knowledge of the philosopher, consisting of three 'roots' (sense-perception, reason and logical deduction), with the knowledge of the religious thinker, who adds a fourth 'root', true trustworthy tradition deriving from the Torah and the Books of prophecy. He insists on the complementary unity of reason, of Torah as divine instruction, and of tradition based on prophecy, i.e. instruction through revelation. He thus laid the foundations of Jewish medieval religious philosophy, which, like every manifestation of the Jewish mind, is in a very special sense interpretation of the Bible. Rational inquiry and speculation are limited by the overriding demands of divinely revealed truth. We shall touch upon the philosophical interpretation of the Bible later in this section.

Saadya's aim in his exegesis, as we learn from his commentaries, is to show the theological and ethical significance of the Bible as a guide to God and to moral or social conduct. For him the Bible is a unity and so is every one of its books. Thus, his comments supply missing links as his translation does also by supplying suitable adverbs or conjunctions. Indeed, his translation shows the well-known characteristic of all translation: that it is interpretation, the translator's understanding of the original text. He says at the end of the introduction to his version of the Pentateuch that his translation is 'a simple, explanatory translation of the text of the Torah, written with the knowledge of reason and tradition'.

Jewish themes

In his commentary on Proverbs he defines wisdom and analyses its various aspects. He is always lucid and to the point and deals with special topics like wisdom, justice, or knowledge in a little excursus, keeping the literal interpretation separate. It is to him that medieval Jewish religious philosophy owes the division of the commandments of the Bible into those of revelation and those of reason. Space does not permit much detail, but it must at least be mentioned that Saadya prefaces his comments with an introduction which sets out the contents of the book and points to its difficulties in order to facilitate its understanding. His approach is throughout rational, and he has recourse to metaphor, but not to allegory, typology or symbolism. In this he may have been reacting against Christian biblical exegesis.

With the decline of Babylonian Jewry the centre of cultural activity shifted to Muslim and Christian Spain, and biblical studies flourished there under the influence of Saadya and of Arab linguistic and philosophical studies. Hebrew grammar and lexicography were developed to a high degree, and a lasting and scientifically sound foundation was laid for the systematic study of the Hebrew language. The interpretation of the Hebrew Bible greatly benefited from this linguistic approach. The demarcation line between *peshat* and *derash* became more pronounced, and the literal meaning was worked out by close attention to Hebrew grammar and syntax. Besides, the text was examined in the light of past history, to which greater attention was now paid. Naturally, it was largely directed at the historical books of the Bible, until towards the end of the period Don Isaac Abravanel widened the scope of historical studies by including extra-biblical and non-Hebrew sources, as we shall see below.

The intensive study of the Hebrew language in the West begins with Menahem ben Saruk (c. 960) and his able critic Dunash ibn Labrat, and it culminates in Abraham ibn Ezra and the Kimhi family. Menahem wrote his *Dictionary* (*mahbereth*) of biblical Hebrew in Hebrew, which was also the language Dunash used in his objections. A century later Rashi, the most influential of the medieval Jewish exegetes, mainly relied on Menahem in his own linguistic observations and comments. It was important for the application of his findings to the interpretation of the Bible that Menahem, sometimes in opposition to Saadya, attempted a systematic presentation of the Hebrew roots, their formation and meaning, on the basis of reason and study, as he puts it in the introduction to his dictionary. He also tried to find the meaning of a root from the context. It seems that he recognized the well-known characteristic of Hebrew poetry, parallelism, at least as far as synonymous parallelism between the two verse halves is concerned. For him, as for Saadya, the unity of the Hebrew language is a fact, and he often explains a biblical word by a Mishnaic one. Needless to say both authors have recourse to the Targum, the Aramaic version of the Pentateuch.

Dunash, a disciple of Saadya, severely criticized Menahem in the light of a comprehensive and systematic investigation of Hebrew morphology, grammar, and syntax and a comparative study of Hebrew, Arabic and Aramaic, the Massorah and the traditional rabbinic rules of interpretation. Undoubtedly his critique of Menahem marks an advance, even though his empiricism sometimes led him astray. He was on the way to discovering the principle of triliteralism in Hebrew roots; he flatly rejected single-letter roots and tried to replace biliteral by triliteral roots. His terminology was more exact and he distinguished, more successfully than Menahem, the form and significance of Hebrew words.

Of their successors, divided into adherents and opponents, Hayyuj, a disciple of Menahem, outshone his master and Dunash; he was the first scientific Hebrew grammarian in the strictest as well as the widest senses of this term. He established the triliteral theory of Hebrew roots scientifically, applying them to the so-called weak verbs, and succeeded in establishing definite laws and rules for the vowel changes and the different grammatical forms. What followed his work is only a development and modification of his results. He tells us in the introduction to his important treatise on the weak verbs that he based his investigations exclusively on the text of the Hebrew Bible, drawing, as a rule, conclusions from what he found there to what he did not find in the Bible. In this way he illuminated many problems of morphology and verbal structure. His contribution to a better understanding of the Hebrew noun, based on extensive Massoretic studies, also deserves mention. Throughout he employed, in his works written in Arabic, the terminology of Arabic grammar. The man who completed Hayyuj's work was Ibn Janah, known by his Hebrew name, Rabbi Jonah. He, too, engaged in linguistic studies in order the better to understand the Hebrew bible. He looked upon himself as one who added to and completed the work of his master Hayyūj. Beyond this work he gathered his own advanced researches and original observations into his *magnum opus* in two parts: a grammar and dictionary. His *Book of roots* was for centuries largely forgotten because of David Kimhi's dictionary of the same title. But even Kimhi's father largely depended on R. Jonah. In our context, R. Jonah's contribution to biblical exegesis is significant. For he also paid systematic attention to matters of biblical style and diction, thus furthering a correct understanding, and critically evaluated the traditional rabbinic exegesis from the point of view of his linguistic attainment.

Moses ibn Gikatilla was the first to translate Hayyuj's principal studies into Hebrew, and Abraham ibn Ezra recorded many of Gikatilla's philological interpretations of biblical passages in his own grammatical and exegetical writings. Moses wrote in Arabic, as did Judah ibn Balaam. These two were the most important Bible commentators of Spain before Abraham ibn Ezra. Both applied to their exegesis the linguistic findings and aids of Hayyuj and R. Jonah. Moses ibn Gikatilla's writings are no longer extant and we have only extracts from his commentary on Isaiah and the Psalms quoted by Abraham ibn Ezra. These comments represent an attempt to give a historical explanation, coupled with an exposition based on grammatical analysis. He refers some psalms to the Exile and the prophecies in Deutero-Isaiah to the Second Commonwealth, to quote two examples. Similar comments on passages in the Minor Prophets are quoted by Abraham ibn Ezra. We possess a modern edition of Judah ibn Balaam's commentary on Isaiah; in this he seems to be dependent on Saadya. He also wrote a commentary on the Psalms. With regard to the miracles reported in the Bible Judah holds fast to the traditional, literal view, opposing Moses ibn Gikatilla's rationalistic interpretation.

Before dealing with the greatest Spanish exegete, Abraham ibn Ezra, we turn for chronological reasons to the school of biblical exegetes in northern France. It is significant that many representatives of this school were at the same time engaged in expounding the Talmud. Their knowledge of the traditional rabbinic exegesis was, therefore, unsurpassed and it was brought to bear on the literal interpretation. At times, the traditional homiletical interpretation (*derash*), as it is enshrined in the Midrash-collections, was by some accepted as *peshat*, and

The study of the Bible in medieval Judaism

the borderline between the two methods became at times rather fluid. The linguistic foundation of their method of *peshat* was not as pronounced and systematically applied as among their Spanish co-religionists, and often the historical interpretation was in the foreground. This naturally varied with the individual exegetes. Yet with all of them, the attention to the plain, simple, literal meaning of Scripture was paramount. It resulted in highly competent commentaries of permanent value and significance. Their output was extensive and covers practically the whole of the Hebrew Canon. Its importance is by no means confined to the Jewish tradition. For they were in personal contact with the Christian exegetes of France and England and, together with the work of Abraham ibn Ezra and David Kimhi, their commentaries were of considerable help to the reformers and the biblical exegesis of the Reformation, in particular to its choicest fruit, the Authorized (King James) Version of the English Bible.

Another important aspect of their literal interpretation is that it was closely linked with the refutation of Christian exegesis, in particular the Christological exposition of the messianic prophecies in Isaiah and of the Psalms. On the Jewish side this centred round the concept of the absolute, simple unity and uniqueness of God, round the Christian claim of the divine–human nature of Jesus, who fulfilled for the Christian the messianic prophecies of the Old Testament, and round the eternally binding character of the Torah as the revelation of God, who made a covenant with the people of Israel.

By far the greatest and most enduring impact was made by Rashi (Rabbi Solomon ben Isaac of Troyes, 1040–96), who commented on almost the entire Hebrew Bible. Though he was more famous for his great commentary on the Talmud, his biblical commentaries, especially that on the Pentateuch, have always had a special appeal and fascination for countless generations of Jews. Christian exegetes from his day onwards, from the Victorines to the humanists and translators of the Authorized Version, carefully noted his direct, simple, often homely explanations, more often with approval than rejection, and he was aptly called by Reuchlin *ordinarius Scripturae interpres*. Nicholas of Lyra quoted him so often that Reuchlin remarked that not many pages would remain over if one took away references to 'Rabi Salomon' from Nicholas's *Postillae*. His exegesis figures largely in the Latin translation of Sebastian Münster, who so decisively influenced the Puritan scholars and translators. Rashi's comments can be detected in Tyndale, Coverdale and the Genevan and Bishops' Bibles, important forerunners of the King James Version, whose chief architect, John Reynolds, refers to him—as Reuchlin had—as 'the author of their ordinary gloss' in his commentaries on Haggai and Obadiah.

What is it that appealed so much to Rashi's contemporaries and subsequent generations? It was his combination of the method of *peshat* with the best in the rabbinic *derash*. Rashi was not uncritical of traditional exegesis and often opposed the literal meaning to it. But he was not rigid in the application of the *peshat*, aware as he was of its significance for a correct understanding of the Bible. He wrote for the people, learned and ordinary folk alike, and the occasional homily from tradition helped to establish the strictly literal, direct, plain meaning. He was not out to instruct merely to increase knowledge, but by instruction to strengthen the faith of his generation and to foster their hope of redemption and their belief in messianic fulfilment. We must remember that he was active in an atmosphere which produced the crusades, and he saw with his own eyes what that meant for the Jews. Many a comment on a passage in the Pentateuch, in Isaiah, Jeremiah, Ezekiel or the Psalms is concluded with the statement that his interpretation is according to the plain sense and serves as 'an answer to the Christians'. References to contemporary events and institutions are not wanting, for example, to the crusades, and to conversions and persecution in his comments on Isa. liii. 9 or Ps. 38: 18. They show that Rashi was not a recluse, an academic, but a man who lived with his people and mixed with Christians in his native Troyes and on his travels. Besides, they are a vivid testimony to the relevance of the Hebrew Bible for his time.

For what was more important than refuting Christian exegesis was providing the Jews with a Jewish interpretation. Thus the second psalm refers to David, not to Jesus, and Ps. 45 refers to Israel and not to the Church. Rashi shares with other Jewish exegetes of the period the interpretation of Edom as Rome; he identifies the *Kittim* with Christian Rome. Against the Christian interpretation of Zech. ix. 4 as referring to the second commonwealth, Rashi refers it to the days of the Messiah. In general, he tried to combat Christian interpretation even if he had to depart from traditional exposition. This is clear from his interpretation of Psalms 9 and 10 or 21 and of the 'servant songs' in

Isa. lii–liii, or of Zech. vi. 12. There can be little doubt that, except where he was forced to reject the rabbinic exposition on linguistic grounds, as in Psalm 9, it was the contemporary Jewish–Christian controversy which led Rashi to an interpretation in opposition to the rabbis. Yet the anti-Christian slant is only the negative side of his exegesis. The Christian interpretation—referring a prophecy or a psalm to Jesus or the Church—is countered by the positive assertion that it refers to a biblical historical person or event and, if plausible linguistically and historically, that it contains a promise of the future redemption of Israel. Thus, he says that Ps. 22: 27 points to 'the time of our redemption, the days of our Messiah'. Psalm 68 foretells Israel's final redemption. Verses 10–14 of Ps. 10 refer to Israel when the rule of Ishmael (Islam) and Edom (Rome) has come to an end and they have been driven from the land of Israel; then God will be king for ever. These examples must suffice to show the twofold character of anti-Christian polemic as we find it in Rashi and his successors, notably David Kimhi. They also indicate the strength of messianic expectation among the Jews and their eschatological preparedness. In this context it must not be forgotten that eschatology is also partly at the back of the crusading movement. Thus, the exegetical literature of the middle ages is, as has been claimed at the beginning of this section, among other things a source of knowledge of the state of mind of the period.

An unexpected by-product of Rashi's commentaries and of those of his school is the large number of French glosses which have preserved many a medieval French word for which there is no evidence in French contemporary literature. They have been collected and analysed by Blondheim, Darmesteter and Brandin, and number over 3,000 in Rashi alone. Rashi used these words to explain to his readers—another indication that he had not only scholars like himself in mind—difficult Hebrew phrases or words.

Primarily an exegete, Rashi did not leave separate grammatical treatises. Nor was he a systematic linguist, and we have seen that he relied on Menahem ben Saruk's *Mahbereth* in many cases. But he had a well-developed sense of the peculiarities of the Hebrew tongue, and his commentaries are full of grammatical observations, prompted by his close study of the context and similar passages elsewhere in the Bible and by his frequent use of the Targum of Onqelos on the Pentateuch. Rashi often coined his own terminology; Hayyuj and R. Jonah were unknown to him. Steeped in traditional lore as Rashi was, he studied and made use of the Massorah as well. His success can be measured by the unusually large number of manuscripts of his commentaries on the several books of the Bible, especially on the Pentateuch, and of the many super-commentaries, begun by his pupils and continued for many generations. Fortunately, enough of these manuscripts have escaped the vigilance of Christian censorship and we can recover Rashi's original text. Critical editions of his commentaries on Isaiah, the Minor Prophets and the Psalms, based on such uncensored manuscripts, were only published some twenty years ago. Incidentally, his commentary on the Pentateuch was the first Hebrew book to be printed, in 1475. This no doubt facilitated the acquaintance of the humanists and reformers with his exegesis, apart from the Latin tradition, briefly touched upon earlier on in this chapter.

Rashi inaugurated in northern France the movement towards the literal interpretation and the refutation of Christological exposition of many messianic passages within biblical commentaries. There were also public disputations, based on scriptural passages, and special pamphlets. These too were devoted to the Christian claims that the Messiah promised in the Old Testament had already come in the divine–human person of Jesus and that the Law had been superseded; they too provoked Jewish denials. This is not the place to go into detail about the disputations and pamphlets. They are mentioned to indicate at least the background to the Jewish–Christian controversy carried on in commentaries on the books of the Old Testament. To this literary struggle must be added, alongside the public disputations forced upon the Jews (in 1240 in Paris, 1263 in Barcelona, 1413 in Tortosa), the burning of the Talmud as a manifestation of the relentless campaign of the Church to convert the Jews. It is, therefore, the more remarkable that the growing hostility of the Church did not prevent friendly intercourse between Christian and Jewish scholars who met to discover the truth of the Bible, which was for both sides the Word of God. These meetings were a true dialogue between students of the Bible. For while the Jews gave their Christian partners the Jewish interpretation which they could not obtain unaided from the original texts, the Christians in turn acquainted the Jews with the Vulgate, the interpretation of the Church Fathers, and their own interpretation according to the fourfold method of biblical interpretation dating back to the Venerable Bede and

The study of the Bible in medieval Judaism

Rabanus Maurus, to which we shall refer when discussing the mystical exegesis of the Kabbalists.

In this context it is not possible to discuss, even very briefly, the Jewish–Christian controversy outside the strictly exegetical literature, such as the tenth-century anonymous *Altercatio Aecclesie contra Synagogam* or *Gisleberti Crispini Disputatio Iudei et Christiani* of the last decade of the eleventh century. The first tract is directed as much if not more against judaizing heretics as against Jews, and is one of many such writings. Crispin's *Disputatio* had a considerable circle of readers until the middle of the twelfth century when the censor altered the text and transformed the Jew from an attacker into a passive, pale figure on the defensive. This reflects the changed situation caused by the crusades, which forced the Jews on to the defensive. Nor can we consider Moses Nachmanides' report of his role in the disputation at Barcelona with Paul, a Jewish convert to Christianity, as his opponent. The questions discussed were those which we meet again and again in the Jewish commentaries under discussion. This shows that these theological questions formed a live issue at a time when the western world, though divided between three religions, was at one in its fervent faith in God. It was thus by no means a purely academic question who was the *verus Israel*, the Church or the Synagogue; or whether the Messiah had already come in the person of Jesus, as the Christians claimed, or was still to come, as the Jews maintained. Both parties appealed to Scripture as sole authority, or to Scripture and Reason. In our context, the most sustained Jewish 'answer to the Christians' is to be found in David Kimhi's commentary on the Psalms and in Don Isaac Abravanel's three messianic treatises, two of which will occupy us a little later.

First, we must consider one or two of Rashi's successors in the field of exegesis. All without exception adhere to the *peshat* method of interpretation, and most of them combine it with a refutation of the Christological interpretation. In this respect they show a growing familiarity with the Vulgate, but it is difficult to decide whether they read the Vulgate themselves or obtained their knowledge from their Christian partners in conversation.

Joseph Bekhor Shor stands out among them; he combats Jerome, pointing out his mistakes and stressing the correct meaning arrived at by the application of the method of *peshat*, especially in Jerome's translation of the Psalms. His references to the history of Israel and to contemporary events show historical sense, an open mind and acute observation. He criticized the Christians' interpretation of almost all the passages which they claimed for their faith, more so than any other Jewish exegete before him. He was concerned about the anthropomorphisms in the Bible, just as was Saadya, who went far beyond the Targum in this matter. His attempt at whitewashing the patriarchs is ingenious, but very far-fetched, and his explanation of the miracles in the Old Testament is rationalistic. Many of his comments are based on the customs of his age and country. Like Rashi, he sometimes admits the *derash*, but more often prefers the sense required by Hebrew usage.

Brief mention must be made of Samuel ben Meir's commentary on the Pentateuch. He was a grandson of Rashi and on the basis of Rashi's commentary developed the literal interpretation to a fine art. His linguistic ability was exceptional without being systematically trained and scientifically developed; he relied on Menahem ben Sarūk, but not uncritically, thanks to a natural gift for languages and a profound knowledge of the whole Bible. Like his grandfather, who taught him and whom in all deference he often criticized, he wrote his commentary for a practical purpose: the instruction of the people to strengthen their loyalty to their inherited faith. With reverence for tradition he combined independent judgement, which he often followed against traditional exegesis. Thus, he disagreed with both Jewish and Christian exegesis of Gen. xlix. 10, since neither is consonant with the strictly literal meaning. *Shiloh* does not refer to Jesus as the promised Messiah; the Vulgate is wrong in translating *qui mittendus est*. So is the Jewish interpretation. The right explanation is that Shiloh is the name of a town, near Shechem, to which the king of Judah, namely Rehoboam, the son of Solomon, is to come. In two other places he opposes the translation of the Vulgate: in Exod. xx. 13 and Deut. xxxii. 39. These and a number of anti-Christian passages are not to be found in the printed editions of the Hebrew Pentateuch with rabbinic commentaries; they only occur in a critical edition of Samuel ben Meir's commentary on the Pentateuch, based on an uncensored manuscript.

Next, we pass to Abraham ibn Ezra (*d.* 1167), who in a long, unsettled life of travel mediated the achievements of the Spanish school of exegesis to the Jews of Italy and northern France. During his stay in England he composed two largely exegetical works, one on the Sabbath, the other on the reasons underlying the biblical commandments and their division. His weightiest commentary is on the Pentateuch as a whole; a second recension of the important introduction exists. A separate long commentary on Exodus, particularly rich in grammatical observations, and commentaries on Isaiah, the Minor Prophets, Psalms, Job, Esther, Ruth, Song of Songs, Ecclesiastes and Daniel illustrate his originality, wide range of knowledge, independent judgement and remarkable insight into the theological and ethical content of the Bible. On the foundations of the Spanish school, of Saadya's work in linguistics and exegesis, and of the sum total of secular knowledge of Muslim Spain, Abraham ibn Ezra composed commentaries which betray an exceptional mind and a colourful personality. He often shrouds his innermost thoughts in riddles and speaks of secrets hidden in commandments, stories and expressions. He is fond of allusions and hints, but is at pains to demonstrate with great learning and skill the literal meaning, especially of the preceptive part. His commentary on the Pentateuch ranks next to Rashi's in popularity; it has also produced many super-commentaries. But his commentary was in fact much more in need of explanation, through its terseness and its allusions. Daring in his independent approach, in his insistence on the *peshat* and rejection of the *derash*, and much in advance of his time in his literary criticism of the text of the Pentateuch and of Isaiah, he still stood four-square on the ground of traditional acceptance of the Pentateuch as Mosaic. But he held that some additions were made after Moses to the Pentateuch and that we have to distinguish a Second Isaiah from the first, although the latter opinion is more hinted at than openly expressed. But there applies to him what holds good for the religious philosophers as well: they accepted the revelation of the Torah on Sinai in the sight and hearing of the assembled children of Israel as an axiom of faith, because it was for the Jew a historical fact, not a myth. It would be wrong to make of Abraham ibn Ezra a Bible critic centuries before Higher Criticism. He was not only essentially a medieval man, but also a responsible spiritual leader of a community fighting for survival. Only in respect of one biblical book, the Song of Songs, did Abraham ibn Ezra adopt the allegorical method of interpretation, following Jewish tradition unquestioningly. He says in the introduction to his commentary that a secret meaning is contained and sealed up in this most excellent of all the songs of Solomon. But even in this commentary the allegorical method is only one other method next to the literal exposition, true to the general principle stated at the beginning of this chapter. For he says that he provides a threefold commentary: in the first place he explains every obscure word, next he sets out the contents according to its simple meaning, and in the third instance according to the method of *derash*.

His own method of interpretation is explicitly stated in the introduction to his commentary on the Pentateuch, and is set against four methods. The method practised by the *Geonim*, the spiritual leaders of Babylonian Jewry, contains unnecessary extraneous matter; yet he shows in his own commentaries a high regard for the greatest among them, Saadya Gaon. The method of the Karaites falls short of the true understanding of Scripture because it leaves out of consideration the accumulated tradition which, he holds, is of great help to the contemporary commentator. The method of Rashi and his school pays too much attention to the *derash* contained in Midrashic literature; it does not sufficiently follow the results of the scientific study of the Hebrew language and the dictates of reason. He allows the 'method of Midrash' only as a means of finding the inner connection of passages and chapters. Only by the strictest application of the laws of language and logic can we hope to penetrate to the plain, literal meaning of the text. For that reason, he completely rejects the allegorizing interpretation of the Christian sages, as he puts it, who say that the whole Torah consists of riddles and allegories, not only the whole of Genesis, but also all the laws and statutes and ordinances. To them, everything is a hint, an allusion. Thus, the twelve tribes typify the twelve apostles, and other words and passages are typologically interpreted to point to the Church as the heir of the Jews. We find the same attitude in David Kimhi, who, in his commentary on the Psalms, employs Christian terminology to refute Christian claims. Ibn Ezra denounces this method as vanity and hot air and insists that every commandment and every word is to be interpreted according to the scriptural wording. He admits that the Torah contains secrets, such as the tree of knowledge or paradise, and he appeals to the intellect implanted in us by God, to be a witness to the *peshat*. Once again, we see how closely linked are the literal meaning and the refutation of the Christian, spiritual, interpretation.

The study of the Bible in medieval Judaism

This is particularly striking in the case of David Kimhi (1160–1235), the son of Josef, a noted grammarian and exegete, and a brother of Moses who taught him. David began with grammatical studies and wrote his commentaries only afterwards. They were incorporated in the first printed Hebrew bibles, next to Rashi's. David Kimhi composed commentaries on all the prophets, on Chronicles and on Psalms. Of his commentary on the Pentateuch only that on Genesis has so far survived. The Kimhis completely share Ibn Ezra's attitude and method. David Kimhi is equally distinguished as a grammarian and lexicographer and as a Bible commentator. Of special interest is his commentary on the Psalms, which contains an introduction dealing with the phenomenon of prophecy (distinguishing it from inspiration by the Holy Spirit), and 'answers to the Christians'. He appended these to his comments on certain psalms claimed by the Christian interpreters to refer to Jesus. These 'answers' were collected into a separate treatise and frequently copied. Critical editions have been prepared of parts of Kimhi's commentaries over the last seventy years, based on manuscripts which had escaped censorship and which contain the refutation of Christological interpretation applied to parts of Psalms 2, 15, 19, 21, 45, 72, 87, and 110. A Latin translation by the Christian Hebraist Genebrardus was printed in 1566 at Paris.

It need not be stressed that these statements were by no means academic exercises; their topical relevance is also clear from Kimhi's introductory formulas, such as 'if somebody were to object, you must answer', or 'the Christians interpret this psalm as referring to Jesus' (or 'the Nazarene', 'that man'), or 'to their faith', 'but you must answer them [i.e. object]'. Kimhi insists, against the Christian claim that 'son' of Psalm 2 means Jesus, on the absolute, simple, undivided unity of God which makes it impossible for God, who is not body, to be divided as would be necessary on the Christian interpretation, since the Son is of the same kind as the Father. Moreover, the Son must be later than the Father, hence tri-unity is not possible. For if both were co-existent from all time one ought to call them twin brothers, not father and son. We can, he asserts, speak only metaphorically of God. He then deals with the Christian claim that the phrase *ask of me and I will give you nations as your inheritance* refers to Jesus. The logic of his rejoinder can hardly be denied, but in matters of faith this is not necessarily conclusive.

But since he, like all the Jewish exegetes who 'answered' Christian interpretation of this sort, was not aiming primarily to convince the Christians of the fallacy of their claim, but rather wished to provide an answer which would enable the Jews to withstand Christian proselytising activity and would fortify them in their inherited faith, his answers are not without interest. Says he:

if the son is God why should he ask his father? Has he no power over nations and the ends of the earth like him? They might point out that this happened after he had become flesh; God had referred to his humanity and promised, so to speak, inheritance to the son as man. But this is not so since he [Jesus] had no kingdom while in the flesh, nor any dominion over any nation. If they [the Christians] say that the psalm speaks of their faith...[object to them] that the majority, be they Jews or Muslims, have not accepted it.

This argument of the minority is also used by Ibn Ezra in his comment on Gen. xxvii. 40.

Another example is Kimhi's objection to the Christian interpretation of Psalm 19. The Christians maintain 'that the Torah has a limited time of validity, namely only until the time of Jesus' coming. Prior to his coming it was *corporealiter*, but when he came he commanded that it be understood *spiritualiter*. But their words are wind and vanity. For the commandments, which in their view are metaphorical and cannot be understood in their literal meaning, have been revealed by God with a clear exposition, not in a metaphor. Therefore, the other commandments must also be understood by man according to their literal meaning, not as an allegory.' He quotes Deut. xxx. 11–14 to prove that the commandments are actual and clear; if they were allegorical, men would be in doubt about them, and one would explain the hidden meaning one way and another another way.

Kimhi's arguments in the other psalms mentioned are similar in nature. He insists on the *peshat*, and on the basis of the unity and uniqueness of God denies the divine nature of Jesus; he asserts the continuing validity of the Torah and denies the messianic character of Jesus, since he has not fulfilled the prophecies concerning the Messiah at the end of days. The means which he employs are an appeal to grammar, e.g. in Psalm 87, and to history, and his demand for consistency when he denies that one can explain one passage of a psalm *corporealiter* and another *spiritualiter*. The few examples quoted show how he uses Christian terminology. Lack of space does not permit further examples

The study of the Bible in medieval Judaism

in full, but I must at least refer to his denial that Psalm 110 refers to Jesus. He again resorts to grammatical objections which are incontrovertible and to prophetic passages (Malachi) which to his mind prove that the Torah will never be abrogated or changed, but will remain for ever as it was given to Moses on Sinai—adding that it was not given to Jesus. Elijah has not yet come again and will not come until the time of the Messiah (the Jews believe that Elijah will herald the coming of the Messiah and the final redemption). Kimhi insists that the *peshat* demands that this psalm be referred to David.

Assuredly, this polemic is only a small part of medieval Jewish exegesis. But it is an integral part of it, since its complement is the messianic interpretation which, as already stressed, occupies such a large space in the commentaries of Rashi and Kimhi and the others. They countered the Christian claim to the messiahship of Jesus with the positive assertion that the promises of the Messiah contained in the prophets, especially in Isa. ix and xi, and of the final redemption of Israel suffering in exile have still to be fulfilled. They see, therefore, references to their own time and to the redemption in many psalms as well, not only in the prophets. This is strikingly demonstrated by Kimhi in his commentary on the Psalter, for example on Psalms 10, 12, 29 and especially those contained in the fifth book, such as 108 and parts of 119–150. In addition, we meet with many a philosophical interpretation, often dependent on Maimonides' *Guide to the Perplexed*, for example in his definition of prophecy, in his teaching on the soul and the hereafter or in his exposition of the meaning of wisdom. In his ethics Kimḥi leans on Ibn Gabirol and especially on Bahya ibn Pakuda, and a Neoplatonic strain is unmistakable. While such comments will have been appreciated by those of his readers who were acquainted with the religious philosophy of their day, Kimhi was not forgetful of the ordinary reader and tried to serve his needs as well. While strengthening his faith in redemption he gave him hope of messianic deliverance from exile if the Jews showed true repentance of their sins, were devout in loving service of God—he gives a moving definition of the 'servant of God'—by loyally fulfilling the commandments, which are not meant metaphorically and are still and will always remain obligatory. We see here again how the defence of Judaism against Christian claims and attempts at conversion was uppermost in his mind, as it was in that of many other exegetes whom we have met in this section.

Jewish themes

The same features characterize the last great representative exegete at the end of our period, Don Isaac Abravanel (1437–1509). If anything, the Jewish position was by now much worse; the danger threatening from Dominican zeal was at its height, defection rife, and despair and despondency among those loyal to their religion and tradition growing deeper from day to day until 1492 brought the expulsion of the Jews from the Iberian peninsula. We must confine our attention to Abravanel's work as commentator; to this he brought many accomplishments which put him in a class apart from his predecessors, on whom he naturally leant. Philosophy and philosophical Bible exegesis are subordinated to a conservative reiteration of tradition and strict adherence to its sufficiency. He had learnt much from his Jewish predecessors, but also from Christian exegetes such as Jerome, Bede, Isidore of Seville, Albertus Magnus, Nicholas of Lyra and Paul of Burgos, a convert from Judaism. His method is scholastic in that he carefully reviews previous exegesis before giving his own explanation. He shows sound sense in his criticism, born of an unrivalled knowledge of affairs in the service of that king of Spain who decreed the expulsion of the Jews, and of other princes. His knowledge of past history, which he gained from Latin chronicles, is considerable and used judiciously, together with Jewish historical writings (*Josippon* or Pseudo-Josephus, Abraham ibn Da'ud's *Chronicle*). There is something of the humanist of the next age in him, something approaching the scientific spirit of the Renaissance. He anticipated what we call today the science of introduction to the Old Testament by his close attention to questions of date and authorship of the historical books of the Bible and of the hagiographa. His method of interpretation is naturally that of the *peshat*, and his strictures on his predecessors such as Rashi, Nachmanides and Abraham ibn Ezra were hardly justified, except in a purely formal sense and in so far as he sifted traditional material more critically, thanks to his greater resources. As a son of his age, he was more conservative in his attitude to rabbinic material, searching as his historical and literary criticism of it is. But Judaism had been forced back on itself, with terror, intimidation, discrimination and persecution growing in volume. Hence his insistence on the *peshat* within the confines of the text itself, and his reluctant recourse to a figurative interpretation where, and only where, a literal interpretation is contrary or inaccessible to human reason. For him the divinely revealed Torah is clear in its own terms; our understanding of it is aided by traditional exegesis used with discernment. His presentation—prefaced by a number of questions and an exposition of difficulties which are to be dealt with on the basis of previous Jewish and Christian exegesis—is orderly and systematic. His principal aim is the same as that of his Jewish predecessors, only its urgency is greatly heightened by the contemporary situation. Thus, he wanted 'to rouse his people Israel from the sleep of exile' by expounding to them the good tidings of the prophet Daniel. He demonstrated again and again with all the knowledge at his disposal that not one of the messianic prophecies had been fulfilled in Jesus during the second commonwealth. For him, that period was but an interlude and the first exile was still in being; soon, he was confident, to be terminated by the grace of God, who would send his promised Messiah to gather the exiles from the four corners of the earth and to redeem the land of Israel. In this vein he collected in a special treatise all the messianic passages in Scripture which might inspire hope in his generation, just as he held up Daniel as an example and preached repentance. As with his predecessors, the second purpose was the refutation of the Christian claim to the messiahship of Jesus, which the Dominicans maintained energetically in sermons which the Jews were forced to attend, and in treatises such as those of Geronimo de Santa Fé. Abravanel could claim to have provided a better answer than Nachmanides at Barcelona.

To illustrate his method of exegesis, his inquiry into the general character and meaning of Scripture under the four categories of Aristotelian philosophy may be sketched very briefly. Applying the three categories of purpose, matter and form to the Jewish and Christian division of the Canon, he tries to show the superiority of the Jewish division into Law, Prophets and Writings over the four parts of the Christian division into legal, historical, prophetic and Wisdom literature. David must not, in his view, be counted among the prophets, for his Book of Psalms is only written under the influence of the Holy Spirit, as are the Writings. Therefore the Christian designation of *sapientes* is inadequate as it places these books on the same level as the writings of Aristotle and other philosophers.

That he should refer to contemporary events is only natural. Of poignant interest is a reference to the Marranos, or neo-Christians, many of whom secretly still practised their Judaism. Thus we read in his messianic treatises *The Salvation of His Anointed* and *The Wells of Salvation* (Commentary on Daniel):

...that in the midst of all the anguish and persecutions many of our nation leave the religious community and this is heresy, for through the wickedness of the nations hundreds of thousands of Jews have forcibly left the Lord... *until all kingdoms are changed to heresy* shows that this refers to all nations in general or to the wicked in particular, be it to Rome where our own eyes see in the kingdom of Spain that heretics increase and where they burn them because of their heresy *in thousands and myriads*...Also all the priests and bishops of Rome in this time run after profit, accept bribes and do not care for their religion...

These were clear signs that the Messiah would soon come and with him the end of the exile and the promised redemption. The prophecy of Daniel was about to be fulfilled. Rome, the fourth empire, was full of sin and corruption; it staggered to its destruction. Then the fifth empire, that of the king Messiah, would dawn upon mankind and bring redemption to the righteous of the Jews and of all nations.

Although the method of *peshat* had gained and maintained ascendancy over the figurative method, there were groups in medieval Jewry who raised their powerful voice in defence of a strictly rational interpretation of Scripture in order to bring out the inner, hidden (and to them real and true) meaning. For they would not admit that Reason could be in conflict with Revelation. Truth is one and indivisible, and revealed truth, contained in Scripture, contains nothing which runs counter to philosophical truth established by demonstrative proof. We have seen how Saadya dealt with this problem, balancing Reason with trustworthy tradition based on Revelation. Among his successors this balance was not always maintained, and often tilted towards a philosophical interpretation which set aside the plain meaning. This is not the place to argue about the possibility of complete agreement between the revealed truth, set forth in a comprehensive, prophetic law, and the Greek-Hellenistic philosophy and its man-made law. In our context, it is significant that the starting-point for the religious philosophers and exegetes alike was the Bible as revealed truth which had to be accepted as the basis of their speculation. Maimonides' *Guide* is largely philosophical interpretation of the Bible in an attempt to reconcile its doctrines with Aristotelian philosophy. For him the Bible contained what philosophy taught. This necessitated at times a figurative interpretation and meant setting aside the literal meaning. But Maimonides (1135–1206) was careful not to touch the basic tenets of his faith nor to undermine the foundations of the Torah. This is evident from his acceptance in its literal sense of the creation out of nothing, against Aristotle's assumption of the eternity of matter. Since Aristotle did not convince the metaphysician Maimonides, the traditionalist believer had no difficulty in accepting the Word of God as it stood. But God being incorporeal, anthropomorphisms had to be metaphorically explained away. Angels were Aristotle's separate intelligences. On the other hand, providence or reward and punishment were religious doctrines absolutely necessary for the life and faith of the people of Israel, the ordinary believer as well as the elect few.

It is understandable that a storm broke over this allegorical interpretation of biblical doctrines and that contemporary Jewry was divided into followers and opponents of Maimonides. The fact that the Church relied on allegorical interpretation of the Old Testament complicated the situation. In any case, the continued existence of Judaism demanded the wholehearted fulfilment of the commandments, and any tampering with the literal sense carried with it the danger of antinomianism. But the addition of a philosophical interpretation to the literal one received a tremendous stimulus through Maimonides' masterly exposition, and we find in David Kimhi's commentaries frequent philosophical comments, including even Maimonides' interpretation of prophecy as a natural phenomenon, the most controversial of all his teachings and that which aroused most hostility among the traditionalists. Abravanel did not defend Maimonides as Kimḥi had done, but occupied a middle position. He respected the author of the *Guide* as his master so long as he could square the philosophical explanation with the traditionally accepted one based on the *peshat*. He accepted Reason as the handmaid of Revelation, but he could not subscribe to the philosophers' opinion that agreement between the two was possible and that it was rational man's duty to achieve it. For him 'the way of the sages of Israel in their wisdom received by tradition is as far removed from the ways of the philosophers in their speculations and thoughts as East is from West'. This is most marked in his concept of prophecy as the free gift of God to any man he chooses, irrespective of his natural disposition and moral and intellectual preparation and perfection. Maimonides differed from

Alfarabi, who furnished him with his psychological theory, only in his insistence that God could, if he so wished, withhold the gift of prophecy even from a man whose imagination and intellect were perfect. Yet in many a detail Abravanel followed Maimonides. The inescapable fact remains, as the poet-philosopher Judah Ha Levi (Hallewi, 1085–1141?) said, that the God of Abraham is not the God of Aristotle. A personal God of love, mercy and forgiveness, who in his goodness created the world for the good of man, and did so not of necessity but of his own free will, is the indispensable basis of Judaism, Christianity and Islam. Even the strictest of the Aristotelians among the Jews, Gersonides (Levi ben Gerson, 1288–1344), maintained this, though he accepted the eternity of matter. But he upheld voluntarism in God and creation in time and was a most acute exegete, combining *peshat* with a strictly Aristotelian philosophical interpretation.

The rational explanation of those biblical commandments which human reason could understand, as provided by Maimonides, did much to retain the loyalty of those whose contact with the regnant philosophy of the day had caused doubt and confusion in their minds. Before Maimonides, Saadya's division of the commandments—taken over from Muslim theology—into commandments of reason and commandments of revelation was widely accepted. The divinely revealed law contained both to perfection and both were equally obligatory for the faithful. Maimonides replaced this division by that into ceremonial laws, the reasons for which man cannot know, and judicial laws. In this as in others of his doctrines he influenced the scholastics, notably Alexander of Hales, Albert the Great and Thomas Aquinas, who often refers to 'R. Moyses'. Contact is not limited to such fundamental problems as the knowledge and perception of God, the creation out of nothing, divine attributes, angels and prophecy, but in the case of Thomas Aquinas extends even to Maimonides' detailed discussion of the biblical commandments in the third book of his *Guide*. A few illustrations may show this.

Thomas adds to Maimonides' two sources of the knowledge and perception of God, Revelation and Reason, a third, intuitive vision. It is the perception of God which for both leads man to his ultimate happiness in the hereafter. Both religious thinkers agree that the necessary foundation even for that knowledge which we can gain in this world already is faith. Thomas states the five reasons of 'R. Moyses' why this is so. Both accept Avicenna's doctrine that in God existence and essence are identical. Thomas goes some way with Maimonides in the latter's description of the divine attributes, but differs from him in his assumption that God's qualities are identical with his essence and then develops his own theory in conscious opposition to that of Maimonides, which he explicitly states.

A similar agreement in large measure can be seen in the question of the creation of the world. Thomas accepts Maimonides' arguments against its eternity, but seems to think that the creation out of nothing can be proved by demonstration, whereas Maimonides cannot find conclusive proof, and relies solely on faith which raises the philosophical possibility to religious certainty. Thomas uses Maimonides' exposition of the biblical creation story, but disagrees with the latter's view that the celestial bodies possess a soul. He also opposes his views on the angels and on prophecy, but agrees with his evaluation of the prophetic character of Moses as unique, that is, outside the natural disposition.

In dealing with the reasons for the biblical commandments Thomas Aquinas, like Alexander of Hales, sees in the ceremonial laws—going beyond Maimonides—a mystical significance in that they serve as a pointer to Christ. Thomas entirely agrees with Maimonides' explanation of the sacrifices and other specifically Jewish laws like circumcision or Sabbath observance. In the matter of judicial laws Thomas often accepts Maimonides' exposition, but he excludes the moral laws from them.

The philosophical exegesis was not only combated by those who adhered to the *peshat* and upheld the sufficiency of tradition, but also by the adherents of the *Kabbalah*, the Jewish mystics, from the twelfth century onwards. Like the rationalist thinkers, the mystics insist on the inner, hidden meaning of Scripture which they place above the literal sense and which they reach by a combination and manipulation of the letters making up a word in the text of the Bible and by computations based on the numerical value of the letters of the Hebrew alphabet. They recognized the literal meaning because they were, with few exceptions, anxious to remain loyal to Jewish tradition and to maintain normative Judaism intact and flexible. The century between 1150 and 1250 saw the mystical movement in Germany transplanted there from the East by the Kalonymos family. Eleazar of Worms made a notable contribution to biblical exegesis by his mystical explanations of the secrets hidden in the Torah, incorporating the teachings of Judah the Devout. The eschatological element was strong under the impact of the crusades, and the ideal of piety or devotion was expressed in the exegesis of the Bible as the 'tree of life' of Judaism. The German *Hasidim* ('pious', 'devout') had a tendency to asceticism and, according to I. F. Baer, were influenced in their social teaching and organization by a similar Christian movement, the Franciscan 'spirituals'. The mystical movement gathered momentum in Spain in the thirteenth century and the resultant literature centres in the Bible. The main influence was Nachmanides (Moses ben Nachman, 1195–1270), whose commentary on the Pentateuch contains mystical allusions and hints in addition to the primary exposition according to the *peshat*. His disciple Bahya ben Asher also wrote a commentary on the Pentateuch from 1291 onwards, which contains explanations employing four different methods of exegesis, *peshat, midrash, sekhel* and *kabbalah*. The first two are the well-established methods, the third is the philosophical exegesis which Bahya accepts as long as it does not run counter to the text and tradition. The fourth is the new method, which he stresses and which he develops on the basis of earlier mystical works. The four methods roughly correspond to those adopted by the basic mystical work of the middle ages, the *Zohar*, which exercised such a tremendous influence over the Jews for centuries and is at the centre of the kabbalistic vogue in the sixteenth century among Christians. They are, adapted to Jewish concepts and needs, the Christian methods of *historia* (*peshat*), *tropologia* (*derash*), *allegoria* (*remez*, 'allusion', 'hint') and *anagogia* (*sod*, 'mystery', 'hidden secret'). Bahya combines in his term *kabbalah* both *remez* and *sod*. The *Zohar* is now ascribed to Moses de Leon, who, according to G. Scholem, came from philosophic enlightenment to mysticism. The *Zohar* is the answer of the late thirteenth century to rationalism; it interprets the Torah mystically and, according to G. Scholem, attempts to preserve the substance of naïve popular faith. The Torah is a vast *corpus mysticum* wherein the Kabbalists 'discover layer upon layer of hidden meaning'. An investigation of its literary sources has underlined the basic unity of Jewish exegesis, which allows of several meanings alongside each other while stressing now the one and now the other. All the commentators discussed in this section occur in quotations in the *Zohar*: Rashi, Kimḥi, Ibn Ezra, Nachmanides, and there is evidence of a sound knowledge of the grammatical and lexicographical literature. The mystics pursued the same aim as the philosophers and the traditionalists, though their ways were different from each other, namely to draw near to God in knowledge and love. All four methods of biblical exegesis are pressed into the service of this task.

Medieval Jewish exegesis succeeded in keeping alive the spirit of the Bible; together with the fulfilment of the commandments, it preserved Judaism for the Jews; it also made an important contribution to Christianity by helping to establish that *Hebraica veritas* at which the Reformation aimed in its struggle for the authority of the Word of God.

Select Bibliography

Bacher, W., 'Die Bibelexegese vom Anfang des 10. bis zum Ende des 15. Jahrhunderts', in Winter u. Wünsche, *Die Jüdische Litteratur...*, Band 2 (Trier, 1894).
Driver, S. R. and Neubauer, Ad., *The fifty-third chapter of Isaiah according to the Jewish interpreters*. Texts and translations (Oxford, 1876).
Heinemann, I., 'Die wissenschaftliche Allegoristik des jüdischen Mittelalters', *Hebrew Union College Annual*, XXIII (1950–1).
Loewe, H. and Trend, J. B. (eds.), *Isaac Abravanel* (Cambridge, 1937).
Loewe, R. J., 'Herbert of Bosham's Commentary on Jerome's Hebrew Psalter', *Biblica*, XXXIV (1953).
Poznanski, A., *Schiloh* (Leipzig, 1904).
Poznanski, S., *Eliezer of Beaugency's commentaries on Ezekiel and the minor prophets* (Warsaw, 1910-13) (Hebrew introduction espec.).
Rosenthal, Erwin I. J., 'Rashi and the English Bible', *Bulletin of the John Rylands Library*, XXIX, i (1940).
'Don Isaac Abravanel: financier, statesman and scholar', *ibid.* XXI, ii (1937).
'Sebastian Münster's knowledge and use of Jewish exegesis', *Essays presented to Dr J. H. Hertz*, ed. I. Epstein, E. Levine and C. Roth (London, 1943).
'Edward Lively: Cambridge Hebraist', *Essays and studies presented to Stanley A. Cook*, ed. D. Winton Thomas (London, 1950).
'Anti-Christian polemics in medieval Bible commentaries', *Journal of Jewish Studies*, XI (1960).
'Medieval Jewish exegesis: its character and significance', *Journal of Semitic Studies*, IX, 2 (1964).
Scholem, G., *Major trends in Jewish mysticism*[3] (London, 1955).
Smalley, B., 'Andrew of St Victor, abbot of Wigmore: a twelfth-century Hebraist', *Recherches Théologiques Anciennes et Médiévales*, X.
'The School of Andrew of St Victor', *ibid.* XI.
The study of the Bible in the middle ages[2] (Oxford, 1952).

PART II
MEDIEVAL JEWISH RELIGIOUS PHILOSOPHY

II

MAIMONIDES' CONCEPTION OF STATE AND SOCIETY[1]

When we think of the great influence Maimonides has exercised on philosophy it is only fitting to lay stress on his own sources. This is necessary so that we may be able to see him in his true proportions. It is generally held that M. is an Aristotelian[2]; only H. Cohen comes to the conclusion that his Ethics is Platonic.[3] I cannot decide here which of the two views is the right one as regards Maimonides' philosophy as a whole nor present a third alternative by claiming that his philosophy is essentially Jewish. I intend rather to demonstrate the Maimonidean point of view compared and confronted with that of his Islamic environment in matters politico-philosophical, and I make an earnest attempt to see him in his true perspective in his political conception.[4]

There are, broadly speaking, two main sources for Maimonides' conception of State and Society, i.e. Jewish tradition and Greek philosophy as transmitted through the Islamic philosophers, the Falasifa.[5] Muslim philosophy, which it is well to remember, is as

---

[1] Abstract of lecture delivered without the notes on occasion of the Maimonides' octocentenary celebrations of the University of Cambridge.
I must acknowledge my debt to Dr. Leo Strauss with regard to the influence of Plato on Islamic " political " philosophy, by his first drawing my attention eight years ago to Averroes' paraphrase on Plato's " Republic ". Without that I could not have seen the connection between Alfarabi and Averroes and between Averroes and Maimonides, and could not have arrived at my conclusions. I regret I could not make use of his book, just published, *Philosophie und Gesetz*, Berlin, 1935, which gives the research in Maimonides a decisive turn throwing light on the influence of Plato on Jewish and Muslim philosophy, based on an exhaustive study of the sources.

[2] So J. Guttmann, in *Die Philosophie des Judentums*, München, 1933. H. A. Wolfson in *JQR.*, N.S., ii, who calls M. a " Hellenist " in contrast to the " Hebraist " Judah Halevi.

[3] In *Charakteristik der Ethik Maimunis* (Moses b. Maimon, i, Berlin, 1908). Platonic influence has been acknowledged in details, but not in principle, despite Steinschneider and Dieterici and lately in full by Leo Strauss.

[4] " Political " is here used in the Aristotelian sense, i.e. comprising Ethics as dealing with the relations between men and " Politics " proper.

[5] In the short time at my disposal I could not make use of all available sources. I had to leave aside Ibn Sina completely and used only Averroes' paraphrase on Plato. His commentary to the Ethica ad Nicomachum of Aristotle, considered by himself as the first theoretical part to Plato's *Politeia*, has especially to be consulted for a full analysis. See also my article in *JRAS.*, Oct. 1934, pp. 737–744. I hope to deal with this problem at length in my publication of the " Paraphrase ".

much under the influence of the *Shari'a*, the Canon law of Islam, as Jewish philosophy is under that of the *Torah*.[1] It is, therefore, necessary to speak first of what we might call the Common Ground on which Maimonides and his Muslim sources both stand. Though the *Shari'a* cannot be likened throughout to the Jewish Divine Law, *Torah*, they both have in common the absolute supreme authority, theoretically, and this alone is decisive for our problem. The precepts of the Law are absolutely binding, the letter of the Law is unalterable, doubt is only admissible as to the interpretation of the Law, and this can only be decided by *Ijma*. In this respect both Jews and Muslims agree. This Law is perfect. To turn to Judaism, Jewish tradition holds that, long before there was a Jewish State, the Law was revealed by God to Moses in the presence of the whole community. It implied the subordination of individual and tribal wishes to one supreme Divine will, laid down in the Law and binding divergent interests to serve one purpose—the obedience to the will of God. Society had thus been in existence before the State. What we call Judaism dates from the time of Ezra, who endowed with political power by the King of Persia, forced the observance of the Law upon the purely Jewish nation. This historic event actually made the Torah supreme authority in the State and decided the whole course of Jewish history up to the present day. The Law has always been and must always remain the essence of Judaism, the central authority and creative factor. This is as true of Maimonides as of any great teacher the Jews have produced for themselves and for mankind. This Law and its history is the one constituent force in Maimonides. It is noteworthy that he was from the outset in a different position from the Muslim philosophers. He did not write for the sake of philosophic speculation or for the enlightenment of an intellectual artistocracy alone, but in his capacity as Nagid of the Jews of Egypt and as the unquestioned halachic authority of the day he deeply influenced and determined the course of Judaism in the future whether he met with approval or opposition. The leading contemporary intellect among the Muslims, Averroes, remained in the sphere of theoretical philosophy and so did his precursors. Maimonides was a teacher who felt the responsibility not only to serve the Jewish religion with a philosophic justification,

---

[1] Torah means teaching rather than law, but the conventional term is used here throughout. It is, however, not applied to the Pentateuch alone, but comprises everything which constitutes Jewish traditional law.

to harmonize revelation with reason, but he was called upon to be the spiritual leader of the Jewish communities throughout the Islamic world in troubled times. In speaking of his personality and his work, we must therefore remember his activity, the root of which is to be found in the Ethical teachings of Judaism alone.

The question of Common Ground is bound up with what I have said about Maimonides being an Aristotelian or a Platonist. It cannot be answered categorically, due, in the first place, to the uncertainty of discerning in every instant whether the Muslims had handed to them and transmitted to the Jews the genuine philosophy of Aristotle and Plato or rather seen both in the light of Neoplatonism.[1] For al-Kindi took what was an extract of the *Enneads* IV–VI of Plotinus as the so-called *Theology* of Aristotle. Alfarabi lent his authority to its Aristotelian genuineness and, moreover, wrote a treatise, under Neoplatonic influence, entitled *The Book of the agreement between the ideas of the two philosophers, the Divine Plato and Aristotle*.[2] In it he tries to prove that there is no contradiction between Plato and Aristotle. It is for our question of the greatest importance that Alfarabi mentions in this essay two different " political " treatises of Plato, *Bulitiya* and *Siyasa*.[3] Moreover, Alfarabi has written two treatises, *madina fadila*,[4] the "Ideal State", and *siyasa madaniyya*,[5] "Politics". The latter is known to the Jews as *Sefer ha-Hathhaloth* in accordance with the other title of Alfarabi's *siyasa*.[6] Maimonides not only quotes frequently Alfarabi and mostly this treatise, but recommends it also to his translator Samuel ibn Tibbon next to the study of Aristotle himself.[7] It is clearly from this quarter that Maimonides became acquainted with Plato and his ideas. Therefore, any exposition of his political ideas has to start from Alfarabi, who has influenced all subsequent Muslim philosophers.[8]

---

[1] All philosophers concerned are influenced by the Theory of Emanation. Quotations later on in this paper show, however, clearly that the original works of Plato have been used at least by Alfarabi and Averroes.

[2] Dieterici, *Alfarabi's philosophische Abhandlungen*, Introduction and Arabic text.

[3] Dieterici, loc. cit., p. 7 *et passim*.   [4] Ed. Dieterici.

[5] German translation by Dieterici, MS. Brit. Mus. (Arabic and Hebrew, quotations from Hebrew). In reading it I remembered L. Strauss' statement on the importance of Plato's *Laws*. I could now identify many a passage in Averroes' *Paraphrase* I could not find in the *Politeia*.

[6] *Kitabu-l-mabadi*.

[7] Steinschneider, *Alfarabi*, p. 63; Hebr. Uebers, §13, n. 291b.

[8] I am unable to treat this subject in full as it deserves in this short paper. I can only mention a few salient points in my treatment of Maim. A detailed and well documented account must be reserved for another occasion.†⍌

Although I cannot claim at the present moment to have arrived at final and definite conclusions, I hazard an opinion on the question of the respective influence of Plato and Aristotle on Islamic and Jewish philosophy as follows: if one were to say that Aristotle was the unquestioned authority in the field of Logic, Physics, and Metaphysics whereas Plato is to be looked upon as the master in the field of Ethics and Politics, it would perhaps simplify matters too much, but it comes near the truth.

II

The first question is—why must there be a State? Maimonides gives the same answer as all Muslim philosophers: because Man cannot live by himself, cannot provide his subsistence alone, he must form with others a community in mutual help and assistance and is therefore a social being. This argument is but the well-known statement of Aristotle, modelled upon Plato.[1] Society is thus the natural result and indispensable for Man's existence. The sum of the individuals constitute Society, but adding one to the other mechanically does not yet guarantee the maintenance of individual and social life. For human faculties and tendencies are not only manifold but even divergent, and, moreover, the process of providing the necessary means of subsistence is so complex that there is naturally need for organization and leadership. This is the real meaning of Aristotle's "zoon politikon", the equivalent of which is in Arabic *madani* (citizen).[2] The leader must be a person " who keeps the right balance and establishes a common rule binding all alike. If their actions and customs continually comply with this rule (*sanan*), the natural differences are covered up by the great harmony, and society is in perfect order ".[3] The State as organized society has not only to guarantee Man his bodily

---

[1] *Guide*, ii, ch. 40; iii, ch. 27 (ed. S. Munk). Following the Arabic text it becomes clear that Maimonides borrowed his terms for political institutions from the Islamic philosophers, like *ijtima*, *mudabbir*, etc. This argument is used in all Arabic " political " treatises, but Ibn Khaldun states this reason only for the material existence (see my *Ibn Khaldun's Gedanken über den Staat*, München,1932, p. 4). It will have to be shown what and how much Ibn Khaldun owes for the shaping of his thought to Islamic " political " philosophy. Cf. Plato, *Rep.*, 369B.

[2] Alfarabi, *mad. fad.*, p. 54, *siyasa*, 206 a.r. Averroes 2a (quoted from Munich MS. (M); see also the Latin translation of Jacob Mantinus, cf. my article in *JRAS.*).

[3] *Guide*, ii, ch. 40; i, ch. 72; *mad. fad.*, ch. 26, pp. 53-4. Probably written under the influence of Plato's repeated statement that Man should concentrate on one profession; note Plato's distinction of the various " Stände " as the result.

welfare, but also that Man can satisfy his intellectual needs. Thus it appears that the State is not an end in itself but exists for the sake of Man.

III

The next question is—what aim has Man to reach? The answer is: perfection.[1] Individual human perfection, however, is possible only in a perfect society, i.e. in a well-organized State in which Law and Order are guaranteed, where there is social justice and freedom for the socially-minded individual who contributes his proper share to the common weal. Man is composed of body and soul, the relation of which is like that of matter and form.[2] The essence of soul is reason. Man is Man by possessing the rational faculty.[3] The aim of Man is to reach Happiness, i.e. highest intellectual perfection.[4] So far Alfarabi, Averroes, and Maimonides agree. Maimonides discerns four kinds of human perfection which represent four degrees progressing from the lowest to the highest.[5] The first is that of property and wealth, i.e. worldly goods. The second is that of the body appertaining to Man as animal. The third concerns the true nature of Man—the ethical perfection which is a social virtue and bound to be of value only in society. The last and highest perfection is the true human perfection, Man possessing the intellectual virtues which enable him to conceive of the *Intelligibilia*, which give us sound ideas on Metaphysics. This alone is the ultimate aim and makes Man actually perfect, secures his immortality, and through it Man is Man. He does not share it with anybody else.[6] Apart from this division into four kinds of per-

---

[1] Alfarabi sees in this the reason for the formation of society, *mad. fad.*, p. 54. Pp. 73 ff. contain the manifold reasons which lead to a society other than perfect. Averroes says Man needs the help of others so that he is able to acquire what is necessary for his material existence, but at the same time the virtues which alone make out his perfection. This is not the place to enter on a detailed definition of this term nor on a discussion of the philisophical questions involved. This applies also to Alfarabi's four different forms of *intellectus* and the different faculties of the soul (*mad. fad.*, pp. 34–45) and to Averroes' detailed exposition of the arts and sciences appertaining to *practical* and *theoretical* Reason. I cannot take account of the difficult problem of prophecy either, important as it is, especially because a treatment of Ibn Sina is indispensable, but must refer to the thorough presentation of this question by Z. Diesendruck (*Jewish Studies in Memory of I. Abrahams*, N.Y., 1927).
[2] Averroes, M. 23b.   [3] Loc. cit.   [4] Alfarabi, *siyasa*, 206a r.
[5] Cl. Plato, *Laws*, 743e; Aristotle, *Eth. Nic.*, i, 8 f.
[6] *Guide*, iii, ch. 54, cf. *siyasa*, 207b r.

fection, Maimonides discerns the perfection of the body and of the soul. Averroes also discerns four kinds of human perfection, speculative, dianoetic, and ethical virtues and practical arts.[1] The highest is speculative virtue, for the sake of which the others exist and prepare. The practical arts have been instituted out of necessity to satisfy Man's needs, whereas the theoretical sciences as the object of the theoretical reason in Man are higher. It is, thus, Man's aim to rise from a sensual to a rational being.[2] "He who is engaged in speculation surpasses him who exercises one of the practical arts and is, therefore, worthy to be master. The different perfections existing in different people make it necessary that they unite."[3] For Man reaches his aim only by being part of the State.[4]

IV

If Man attains his purpose completely only in a perfect society it is evident that such a society has to be ruled over by a perfect leader. Yet this condition is not sufficient without a Law which is in itself perfect. By means of such a Law and no other the ruler is able to guide the community. We have here the transformation of the philosopher of Plato into the prophet. Maimonides distinguishes three kinds of emanation of the "Active Intellect" caused by God according to the constitution of Man. If the Active or Divine Intellect emanates on to the Passive Intellect, i.e. the *rational* faculty alone, there comes into being a scholar. If the Active Intellect emanates on to the *imaginative* faculty it produces leaders and lawgivers.[5] That Man is a prophet whose rational and imaginative faculties are influenced alike provided his imagination is of its utmost perfection.[6] Alfarabi says that the first condition of leadership is highest human perfection. God reveals himself to a philosopher-prophet, i.e. the Active Intellect emanates first on to the passive human intellect making Man wise (a philosopher) and then on to the imaginative faculty, thus making him a prophet.[7]

[1] Averroes, M. 2a, esp. 27a, based on *Laws*, vii. Maim. fully agrees with that; see also n. 4, p. 195.
[2] Averroes, M. 24b, 25b.   [3] Loc. cit., 25b.   [4] Loc. cit., 23b.
[5] This is in accordance with Maimonides' views, shared by Averroes, that politics as a practical art is outside the sphere of theoretical reason. Averroes, M. 25b (politics as leading practical art); M. 21a (concerning lawgiver); cf. Weiss, *Führer*, ii, p. 248, n. 8.
[6] *Guide*, ii, ch. 37.
[7] *Mad. fad.*, pp. 58–9. Maim. states that some of the Falasifa share his opinion on prophecy. Cf. also Averroes, M. 23b, on the subject.

Maimonides' conception of State and Society

Averroes replaces the equation between philosopher and prophet by that between philosopher, king, lawgiver, and *qohen*, by which he means *Imam*. He accepts Plato's condition that the rulers should be philosophers, because if the State is to be wise alike in the practical arts and the theoretical sciences it is important that only those who possess both, i.e. philosophers, shall rule it. Such a philosopher has to possess in addition to his excellent training in both the arts and sciences the ethical and dianoetic virtues so that he may attain to his ultimate perfection. The king must, if his art of government is to be perfect, possess the same qualities.[1] For the lawgiver these conditions are equally essential. Whether prophecy is also required in a ruler is for Averroes a matter of serious deliberation.[2] Among the qualities necessary for the king there are, according to Averroes, ten appertaining to the soul; his bodily conditions are the same as for Plato's guardians. He agrees entirely with Alfarabi on this point, who mentions thirteen qualities.[3] In Plato's *Laws*[4] we find seven which partly correspond to them, whereas Maimonides also mentions thirteen qualities necessary for the ruler if he is a prophet, corresponding to the thirteen attributes of God which he shall imitate.[5] A comparison between Maimonides and the Muslims shows that his conditions are purely and exclusively *ethical*. Averroes stresses that *speculative* perfection cannot be achieved without *ethical* perfection as preparation for attaining the aim. On the same level stands another statement to the effect that the philosopher cannot reach highest perfection except in a perfect society. If such a society does not exist he loses his perfection if he retires into solitude.[6] Alfarabi makes it a condition for the inhabitants of the *Ideal State* that they all must attain a knowledge of the principles of *Existing Things* and of the praiseworthy actions the doing of which procures Happiness. Happiness is the absolute Good and everything which helps to reach it is good; everything which hinders is bad.[7] Averroes in reviewing the various opinions existing on the aim of Man gives us the religious teaching

---

[1] Averroes, in commenting on the different constitutions described in the *Politeia*, assigns to the ruler of the Ideal State five qualities (wisdom, perfect intelligence and imagination, adequacy, power of perseverance, and full bodily vigour to perform exacting duties). He who possesses all of them is absolute king and his rule is truly a royal government. Cf. M. 31*b*.
[2] Averroes, M. 21*a*.   [3] Loc. cit.; *mad. fad.*, pp. 59–61.
[4] *Laws*, 709–710.   [5] *Guide*, i, ch. 54.
[6] Averroes, M. 22*a*. This agrees with Maimonides' view that the third, i.e. ethical perfection is possible in society only.
[7] *Siyasa*, 206*a* r., 207*b*, l.

of his day that this aim is what God willeth. This Divine will can only be perceived by a prophet. Prophecy is twofold, abstract knowledge alone, such as the Law commands with regard to the perception of God, and action such as recommended by Ethics. "Its intention is thus like that of philosophy . . . Therefore men think that these laws only follow Metaphysics. It is, therefore, evident that Good and Evil, Profitable and Detrimental, Beautiful and Hideous, in the opinion of all these are existing by Nature not by supposition and that everything which leads to the aim is good and beautiful whereas everything which stands in its way is evil and hideous."[1] What a contrast is served by the following quotation from the Guide: "The thirteen 'middoth' (attributes of God) are necessary for ruling the states as the ultimate virtue of Man is to imitate God as much as is in his power, i.e. that we liken our actions to His actions."[2] Or a passage out of the "Eight Chapters": "And he (Man) shall set himself always one aim and that is the perception of the Lord inasmuch as is in his power to recognize it, and all his actions, movements and his rest he shall cause to lead to this aim so that there are no vain actions, i.e. an action which does not lead to this aim."[3]

V

To achieve this is only possible under the guidance of the Divine Law. According to Maimonides the Law is part of the Divine Wisdom to preserve mankind whose existence He desires. Thus, some individuals are born leaders. Amongst them are those who have been inspired with this leadership—the prophet and the lawgiver; others have the political power of putting into practice the precepts of prophet and lawgiver—the sovereign and the pretender to prophecy. A law is instituted by Man if it aims exclusively at the best order in the state and removes injustice and violence. It secures Man a certain material happiness, but no attention is paid to the perfection of the rational faculty and there is no room for speculation. Yet, a Law is Divine and guidance comes from God if it is directed towards the best order of the body and the faith alike. Besides, its foremost concern is to spread sound views con-

---

[1] Averroes, M. 23*b*, cf. *siyasa*, 205*b*, r. Averroes took almost verbally this passage over from Alfarabi, with the difference of substituting בטבע לא בהנחה for בטבע או ברצון in *siyasa*.
[2] *Guide*, I, ch. 54. [3] Ch. 8.

cerning God and the angels, to promote Man's wisdom and understanding, and to draw his attention to perceiving all *Existing Things* in their true form.[1] Thus the whole law intends two things, the best order of body and soul. The best order of the soul consists in sound ideas for the masses according to their capacity. The best order of the body is effected by the improvement of the ways of living with one another. This end is reached in two ways. First, by eliminating mutual violence in that no individual is allowed to follow his own wishes and the tendency of his faculty. Man is obliged to do that which is beneficial to the community. Every human being must acquire these social qualities. The best order of the soul is superior to and nobler than that of the body, but the body takes precedence in Nature and in time. The right guidance of society and the best order of the affairs of all its citizens are indispensable for the achievement of the first and foremost well-being, that of the soul. " The first perfection consists in the good health of his corporeal conditions and in his free disposal over everything he needs for his material well-being. The final perfection is that he becomes *rational in act*, i.e. in possession of the active intelligence, and thus comprehends what is Man's faculty to know of all *Existing Things in toto*. This ultimate perfection has nothing in common with actions or qualities; it is only ideas to which speculation leads and which reflection demands."[2] " The true Law is unique, there is no other and it is the Law of our master Moses which came to us to bring us the double perfection."[3] " The Law has given us the most important of the true ideas through which we reach ultimate perfection and called upon us to believe in them in general, i.e. in the existence of God, His unity, His knowledge, power, free will, and eternity which we can only understand after a careful study of other ideas. There are still other notions the belief in which is necessary for the best order of the affairs of the State."[4] These principles of belief do not belong to the sphere of the individual alone but are essential for the political order. They are, however, very remote from the naïve belief of the majority and are accessible only to the metaphysicists. But Maimonides would not be a Jew if he were satisfied with the perception of *Existing Things*, the domain of the scholar, so that, whereas he first defined

[1] *Guide*, ii, ch. 40.
[2] *Guide*, iii, ch. 27; cf. also Judah Halevi, *Kitab al-Khazari*, ed. Hirschfeld, p. 166.
[3] *Guide*, iii, ch. 27; ii, ch. 39.   [4] *Guide*, iii, ch. 28.

the prophet as being perfect in imaginative and rational faculty alike, he now attributes to him a higher degree of rational faculty. He states that for him who concentrates on a perception of God after having accomplished the perception of the " Intelligibilia " as such, the next higher and final step in the true perception is to realize, with the help of the fully developed rational faculty, the Divine Rule over the " Intelligibilia ", and through that to ascertain in transcendental speculation the existence of God. This degree is prophetical. Thus, highest human perfection consists in true worship of God. This true worship is effected in a rational act, i.e. the true perception of the Divine.[1]

VI

To understand Maimonides' conception of State and Society it is necessary to consider briefly the place of " Social Ethics " in his system. " It is known that through good morals human society and its formation gain perfection which is necessary for the good order of human relations."[2] Other commandments aim at eliminating violence and injustice. Criminal law and punishment are necessary because clemency in such a case would only endanger or even ruin the state.[3] Capital punishment is inflicted very rarely, but e.g. on the son who beats or curses father or mother, because of the ruinous effect on the family-life, the principal basis of the State.[4] Referring to Aristotle, he affirms that Man needs friends throughout his life. The closest ties, however, are only to be found among relatives, especially parents and children. " A common ancestor inspires them with love, mutual assistance and attachment which is one of the greatest intentions of the law."[4] It is, therefore, that prostitution has been legally forbidden because of its ruinous effect on family.[5] Next follow property-rights and rules relating to trade and commerce between men. These commandments are of evident importance for

---

[1] *Guide*, iii, ch. 51.   [2] *Guide*, iii, ch. 35.   [3] *Guide*, iii, ch. 41.
[4] *Guide*, iii, ch. 49; cf. Plato, *Republic* and *Laws* with regard to marriage and marriage laws, especially laws for the right relations between parents, children, and relatives. One might think even of Ibn Khaldun's *asabiyya* (loc. cit., pp. 1–3 and *passim*). Maim. uses the same stem here '*sb*.
[5] Cf. Judah Halevi, loc. cit., pp. 166ff., on social relations and the duties of the individual in society. Although the starting-point is here purely religious, the effect is primarily a social and political one. Quite similarly Maim. thinks of the social value of the three feasts which teach Man to feel compassion with others and cause men to unite more with their fellows. (*Guide*, iii, ch. 46.)

the maintenance of individual and social life, as well as for peace and order in the State.

Finally, we have to consider briefly Maimonides' treatment of the Messiah and the Messianic kingdom as expounded in the final chapter of his *Mishneh Torah*, which he sums up as follows: " His rule will be firmly established and then the wise will be free for the study of the Law and its wisdom, and in those days there will be no hunger nor war nor hatred nor rivalry, for Goodness will be spread all over, all dainties will be scattered like dust and there will be no toil on earth but for the knowledge of the Lord alone." His views in detail fully agree with the traditional belief. But the Messianic idea was of actual practical import. Messianic movements spread over the Islamic empire, caused by persecutions, and Maimonides' reasoned and calm admonitions were bitterly wanted as we can see from his letters. It is evident that Maimonides did not accept the Messianic doctrine because it was just one of the precepts in which a Jew had to believe, no, it is for him an integral factor. For the Messianic kingdom which has to take shape in our world is but the materialization of the aim for which Man is striving. This aim is the perception of God and consequently the imitation of His ways. Imitation necessarily means a lagging behind the model. Setting imitation as aim gives Man a task he will have never discharged at a given moment. It is, therefore, not right to see in Maimonides the true disciple of Aristotle who saw Man's aim in complete self-sufficiency. For self-sufficiency is something static, it is synonymous with pure contemplation. But self-perfection is dynamic, Man has constantly to strive for it and might yet never attain to its full possession. And it is here that Maimonides' Messianism is an essential factor in his system. Naturally, stress is laid on the intellectual perfection which is, to repeat it, dependent on the best order of Society as it is only guaranteed in a reign of peace and justice, i.e. the Messianic kingdom. It is as much man's activity as it is the will of God in his mercy which in their co-operation secure the coming of the Messiah.

VII

Let me try to draw some conclusions from the preceding exposition. I shall not repeat the minor points of contact between Maimonides and Alfarabi and Averroes. It should be clear that the philosophic starting-point is almost identical in the three thinkers and that there is unanimity in some important thoughts and their exposition in detail, as e.g. in the conceptions of prophecy, the valuation of learning and its progressive degrees up to Metaphysics, and in their idea of the Highest Good. It is also clear that the ethical teachings of Judaism and the most firm rooting of Maimonides in that tradition, together with his emphasis on the Divine Law, have caused him to give the philosophic ideas he inherited and acquired a marked turn towards Judaism. I venture to say that he adapted philosophy more to Judaism than vice versa.[1] It will have to be shown how far Alfarabi and Averroes have accepted Plato's conception of the Law as compared with the Islamic conception of the *Shari'a*. That Platonic ideas have deeply influenced them is beyond any doubt, but it is not so certain whether they have been conscious of the resemblance existing between Plato's conception of origin and meaning of the Law and their own. So much, however, is certain that they both mention that the ruler has to depend on Laws and they both differentiate between a comprehensive general Law and individual ordinances instituted when need arises by the ruler who happens to be in office.[2] Averroes, drawing largely on Alfarabi's *siyasa*, emphasizes the preponderance of this principal Law over individual ordinances which are meant only to meet a particular situation and which should rather result naturally from the application of the principal Law as being, so to speak, incorporated "in potentia" in it.[3] Plato draws the same distinction. Yet the question remains whether they have just commented on Plato or made his ideas their own, incorporated them in their own philosophy and applied them to their Divine Law.[4] One thing is, however, evident that Alfarabi drew from the "Laws" of Plato at least as much as from his "Republic".[5]

---

[1] As I have hitherto limited my research to certain parts of the extant works of Alfarabi and Averroes, I am unable at the moment to assess definitely their influence on Maimonides in detail.†

[2] *Siyasa*, 207a, r.   [3] Averroes, M. 14b.

[4] Whether we have to assume direct influence or just "common ground" can only be decided after a careful study of the whole material. It is the merit of Leo Strauss to have discovered the influence of Plato's *Laws* on Islamic thought.†

[5] We have to interpret the meaning of the term "hanhagath ha-Medinith" in the title of Averroes' *Paraphrase* as applying to the *Laws* as well as to the *Republic*. This is due to the large extent to which Averroes drew from Alfarabi's *siyasa*. I have to revise my opinion on the influence of Plato and Aristotle on Alfarabi and Averroes respectively as stated in my article in *JRAS.*, loc. cit., p. 744. For I see now that Averroes follows Plato in his "political" conception at least as closely as Alfarabi does. He is much more influenced by Alfarabi's comments on Plato than I thought in 1933 when I wrote my article.

Both these philosophers have in common with Maimonides that their starting-point is the Divine Law already in being. Plato's task in founding a State as perfect as possible is to establish such a Law first. But for him, too, this Law has not only its origin in God but is in its statutes divine as its aim is to make the citizens ready for the Highest Good, for a following of God. Therefore, he thinks that only he who serves the established Law, by rigorously obeying it, should be the first man in the State, and he likens his office to a ministry to the gods.[1] Plato's Law is only then a true one if it promotes the common interest of the whole community.[1]

That there is a remarkable resemblance in principle between the Law of Plato and the Jewish and Muslim Law is for us obvious. Whether we are justified in speaking of a direct influence of Plato on the conceptions under review here has to be shown by a detailed investigation. We have certainly not to attach too much importance to a passage in the already quoted letter of Maimonides to Samuel ibn Tibbon to the effect that the study of Plato was unnecessary as his philosophy was outweighed by that of Aristotle. For much in Aristotle is derived from his teacher Plato, and there still remains the question of Neoplatonism with its harmonizing of the two systems. Apart from that it would suffice that Maimonides recommended Alfarabi's *siyasa* which is at least in its political part a commentary on Plato's political philosophy. That Maimonides also recommends the study of the works of Averroes has been questioned,[2] but we have also the contention of one of his commentators that he was under the influence of Averroes.[2] Without committing myself to a definite answer, I venture to say that some of the passages I have quoted alone show such an agreement as to make it difficult not to suppose an influence. At any rate, if one speaks of influence on Maimonides, in matters politico-philosophical, one has to think of Plato, not of Aristotle. Plato's conception of the aim of the State and of the Law is so much nearer to him who had such a clear idea of the central position of the Law and its moral effect on a perfect State. As much as he himself and the Falasifa revered Aristotle in due acknowledgment of their debt to him, it was Plato whom they called *illahi*, Divine. Not deciding at present whether they all, and in particular Maimonides, arrived at the philosophic justification of the supreme " political " authority

---

[1] *Laws*, iv, 715, in particular, but the whole book iv has to be considered for this question.
[2] Cf. Steinschneider, *Hebr. Ueberss.*, § 16, n. 42.

of the Law with or without the help of Plato, it is in this that Maimonides has made a definite contribution and has set a seal to the research of the Falasifa. His is the clearest and profoundest formulation of the meaning of the Divine Law for the life of Man as a citizen and for the community. Many voices have paid tribute to his eminence at a certain juncture in the life of the Jews and of Mankind. The approach to philosophy, its central problems and the attempt to solve them, are certainly different to-day from what they were in his day. But to that which will last of his work will undoubtedly belong his truly historic insight and momentous perception that the Divine Law is the sole guarantor of a life in a perfect society whose members have to reach the ultimate perfection which is implied in the words of Isaiah: " For the Earth shall be full of the knowledge of the Lord as the waters cover the sea."

12

AVICENNA'S INFLUENCE ON JEWISH THOUGHT[1]

"It happens occasionally in our time that he who studies the sciences a little has no power to hold two candles in both his hands, the light of his Faith (i.e. religious law) in his right hand and the light of his wisdom (i.e. philosophy) in his left. For when the light of philosophy is kindled the light of religion goes out."

This quotation from the *Exalted Faith* of Abraham ibn Daud of Toledo, who died a martyr's death about 1180, aptly illustrates the danger to which the educated Jews and Muslims were exposed in the Middle Ages. To meet this danger, outstanding intellects from the ninth to the fifteenth centuries applied themselves to the task of guiding the perplexed—if I may borrow the title of Maimonides' great work—of their generation, perplexed by the seeming contrast and even contradiction between the teachings of the Bible and the theories of Plato, Aristotle and the Neo-platonists.

Medieval philosophy was not a "Creation out of nothing": it was, from the start, faced with and exclusively conditioned by the existence of Revelation, a revelation which had taken place in history. Arabic translations of the original works of Plato and Aristotle and their Neo-Platonic commentators, complete or in the form of Alexandrian summaries, were read by men whose thought and life were filled with the "Emanation" of this historic revelation, the Law, be it the Torah of Judaism or the *Shari'a* of Islam. The result of the meeting of these two worlds was a distinctly religious philosophy.

But was there no religion in Greek and Hellenistic philosophy? Do Plato and Aristotle not only speak of gods and the necessity of their worship, but even of One God, the God of Plato's "Laws", Aristotle's Prime Mover? Yet, while the relation to God is not absent, it is rational man who occupies the central position in their speculation. Sovereignty belongs to Reason, as does authority, and not to God and His Law as in Judaism and Islam. Is not Plato's postulate of the Imitation of God, then, the same as that of the Islamic and Jewish philosophers ? The answer is : No, because—to limit myself to the subject of this lecture—Plato's God, though sharing the attribute of Justice with the God of Judaism and Islam, is not the Personal God of Love, Goodness and Benevolence and Mercy who has revealed His will to be obeyed absolutely and voluntarily by observance of His Law.

It is for this reason that Medieval Philosophy is religious philosophy. This is, naturally, not to deny that it has made a notable contribution to all the usual branches of philosophy as well, and not only by handing on to the West Aristotelian Logic, Physics, Psychology and Metaphysics, partly in its pure and partly in its revised form, revised by Alexander Aphrodisiensis, Plotinus, Themistius and Proclus. With this aspect I cannot deal here in any detail, since it does not belong to a consideration of the impact Avicenna had on Jewish thought. Yet, owing to the character of Jewish and of Islamic civilisation, the reception and adaptation of Greek and Hellenistic philosophy promoted the growth and development of a theology hardly distinguishable from philosophy, and of ethics which has its basis in Revelation rather than in Reason.

The particular value and the specific significance of Islamic and Jewish religious philosophy, therefore, consist in the vindication of Revelation as Divine Law and the recognition of the inadequacy of Reason fully to understand God. At the same time, it was at pains to demonstrate that Revelation teaches nothing that is contrary to Reason : it had therefore to have recourse to the device of a two-fold meaning of Scripture, an obvious, literal meaning and a hidden, inner meaning. The Jewish thinkers taking over this distinction from the Mu'tazila through the medium of the first systematic interpreter of Judaism, Saadya, found justification for this procedure in the Talmudic saying: " the Torah speaks in the language of man ".[2] At the same time, man has a duty to perceive God. It follows from this that man gifted with reason is obliged to search for the hidden, the real meaning. Whilst this is accessible only to the philosopher who is fully trained in the sciences, ordinary mortals have to be content with the plain meaning of Scripture and joyfully to obey its commandments.[3]

But we must not forget that Revelation was more than a premiss in logic for the Falasifa and the Jewish philosophers; it was a reality of deep significance in their daily lives as Jews or Muslims. Their superior intellect did not place them above the Law. Not only the ethical laws, but also the ceremonial, or judicial laws, as Maimonides calls them,[4] are binding upon the few elect no less than on the masses. The Law is more than a pedagogue, a guide to moral perfection. To apply one's reason to its study will lead to understanding of its inner meaning and through that an ever deepening understanding of the ways of God with the goal of intellectual perfection. We will return to this point later on. For the moment, we repeat that it is Divine Revelation which conditions speculation, prescribes its topics and limits its scope. The statement—earlier on—that Revelation teaches nothing that is contrary to Reason means that there is only One Truth. But Revelation is not only superior to philosophy in that it teaches with absolute and eternal validity right and true opinions about God, the angels, nature and man by means of prophets. It also lays down laws about man's duties to God and his fellow-men at which reason would arrive only after a long search. More than that, it embodies commandments which though inaccessible to reason, yet enable man to obey the will of God and draw near to him by their fulfilment. In other words, to its infallibility is added its all-comprehensiveness and effectiveness.

It will thus be clear that much of speculative thought takes the form of Scriptural exegesis.

It is against this background that we have to examine the influence of Avicenna upon Jewish thought. Whilst it is always difficult to assess influence where thought-processes are concerned, it is particularly so in our case.

For, in the first place, Jewish religious philosophy flourished in an environment both congenial and akin, with the Jews taking their full share in Islamic civilization, speaking and writing in Arabic. Judaism was faced with the same problems as Islam due to essential similarity. Sectarian and heretical attack on the meaning of Scripture had to be warded off with the same arguments often. Apart from at least partially similar internal problems, there was a good deal of religious controversy. The Muslim charge of falsification of Scripture had to be met. The Muslim claim to possess the true revelation in absolute perfection through Muhammad, the seal of the prophets, raised the awkward question of the immutability of the will of God, for the Jews could not admit that Revelation was limited in time and imperfect in character, that Muhammad had superseded Moses. Here already it is clear how closely related theological and philosophical questions are. Christianity must remain outside our inquiry.

Further, Biblical exegesis was a traditional science of long standing before Judaism came into contact with Islam. The development of Oral out of the Written Law and the insistence on their unity and equally divine, binding character was possible through definite rules of interpretation, which, incidentally, can in Islam sometimes be traced to Jewish influence, at any rate are often parallel. It is therefore only natural that rationalist attack upon the Koranic representation of Allah with human " attributes " should take the same form if applied to the Bible. But here it is well to remember that the struggle against anthropomorphism was waged in Judaism many centuries earlier already.[5]

This leads us to a further point: Jewish-Hellenistic philosophy was the first to encounter the challenge of Plato and Aristotle and their schools. It is difficult to prove direct survival and transmission of the ideas of Philo of Alexandria. But even if we make full allowance for the human mind reacting alike or similarly to a like or similar challenge, there does seem to be a possibility that certain of these ideas travelled via the Stoics and Syrian-Christian philosophers to the Falasifa and from them to the Jewish thinkers.[6]

Further, I have already mentioned Saadya, and his indebtedness to his Islamic environment for arguments in his defence of Judaism. The influence he exerted on subsequent Jewish thinkers is generally acknowledged, both in acceptance and rejection of his ideas.[7] Finally, there is the further complication of wholesale borrowing from earlier writers without acknowledgment. Ideas, once put to paper, became the common property of those they reached. Fatherhood is usually disclosed, however, when they are opposed. Applied to our case, this means that only the most minute comparison of texts leading to the clear establishment of literary dependence can determine whether a Jewish thinker has taken over an Avicennian idea or opinion direct or through al-Ghazali who in his attack on the Falasifa extensively quotes Avicenna's views.

Of more importance is the fact that Avicenna is not the first great Muslim thinker. He is preceded by the dominant mind of al-Farabi, on whom he leans heavily, as we heard from his *Autobiography* quoted by Prof. Arberry (in the first lecture of this Course). Be that as it may, Avicennian views can be traced in the writings of Jewish thinkers in Spain, Italy and Southern France from the first half of the twelfth century onwards. They are also to be found in Spinoza, who most likely adopted them from Maimonides. Maimonides does not quote Avicenna in his *Guide* by name, but in a letter to his translator, S. b. Tibbon, he recommends to study the books of al-Farabi in the first place and, naturally, Aristotle, but not without his commentators. The writings of Avicenna, however, do not approach al-Farabi's, although they are useful and deserve to be studied, and he chides an opponent for thinking that Avicenna's treatise on Eschatology was philosophical.

In view of the religious character of Jewish philosophy as just sketched, all too briefly, we shall now examine in some detail whether and how Avicenna influenced Jewish thinkers in their concepts of God, His nature and attributes, of the soul and at some length Avicenna's theory of prophecy and view of Revealed Law compared with Maimonides. Ideas about Reward and Punishment, Resurrection, Redemption and Providence must remain outside our discussion.

Avicenna wrote a separate treatise devoted to Psychology. The statements of al-Farabi about the soul and its parts and faculties, the different kinds of intellect and related questions, are contained in his treatise on the *Ideal State*, and on *Political Government*. Further passages occur also in smaller tracts, the attribution of parts of which to him is sometimes questioned. It is therefore rather tempting to see in Avicenna the source for an identical or similar statement in Abraham ibn Daud or Maimonides. Yet, due to the fact that the former means by the term true philosophers both al-Farabi and Avicenna, and in view of the verdict of the latter on the respective importance of the two, I am content to defer judgment until a comparative study of reliably edited texts can settle this question. Suffice it to say that Avicenna either accepted or developed further al-Farabi's notions based on Plato, Aristotle and Galen, and that their views were adopted by the Jewish thinkers. To my knowledge, Crescas is the only one who disagrees with Avicenna as to which part of the soul—which as Form is substance—is immortal. According to Avicenna, it is the acquired intellect. The soul is created with the body but does not perish with it. Whilst Ibn Daud and Maimonides agree with him, Crescas holds that the immortal part is the substance of the rational soul itself: not through intellectual attainment but through loving attachment to God who loves His creatures and wills their perfections.[8]

Turning now to God, we note that Avicenna's view of God as a necessary Being in whom existence and essence are identical, is accepted by the Jewish thinkers.[9] In all created beings, however, existence is an accident superadded to the essence. This is the view of Maimonides and also of Spinoza as was demonstrated by Wolfson.[10] From this concept of God as necessary existence formulated by Avicenna follows God's absolute, pure and simple Unity. Avicenna here follows al-Farabi. But he expands the argument and his diction is more concise. With the question of Divine attributes[11] I cannot deal further, nor can I go into detail in respect of the cosmological and ontological proofs for the Existence of God beyond this brief reference.

Maimonides deals with this problem in 25 propositions in the form of an Introduction to the second part of his *Guide*. They represent a succinct summary of the main doctrines of Aristotle based on the latter's writings and to some extent on Avicenna's exposition, as was already stated by Munk for Propositions 19–21. These 25 propositions are a perfect illustration of the use of Aristotelian philosophy to prove the existence of the God of the Bible, His unity and incorporeality. It is significant in this context that Maimonides insisted against Aristotle on the Creation out of nothing as an act of God's Free Will. This, however, is a complicated question outside the scope of this lecture. Suffice it to say that the philosopher has to accept the teachings of the Prophet. The Commentators of Maimonides' *Guide* were not slow to discover where he followed Avicenna, nor have they hesitated to explain Maimonides with the help of Avicenna, unless they followed Averroes and his criticism of Avicenna. Their attitude to Maimonides' views is consequently conditioned by their attitude to Averroes as against Avicenna.[12]

Before we go on to a discussion of the theory of Prophecy as the central problem in the relationship of Revelation and Philosophy, it may be useful to assess in a preliminary fashion the importance of Avicenna for Jewish thought on God, leaving on one side the evident indebtedness of a number of thinkers in the realm of psychology to his treatise on the soul, some having incorporated whole chapters in their own writings. There can be no doubt that Avicenna's principal contribution to the Divine Science, the Arabic term for Metaphysics, is the notion of the necessary Being whose essence and existence are identical, who is not subject to change, is immaterial, is not the Prime Mover, but the Prime Cause and the Creator of the whole creation. It would lead us too far to show in detail how Maimonides' Concept of God, whilst agreeing partly with Avicenna, goes beyond it.

Prophecy is dealt with by Avicenna in the last part of his Metaphysics, which has as its subject Practical Philosophy comprising Ethics, Economics and Politics.

Abr. b. Daud concludes his *Exalted Faith* likewise with a short summary of Practical Philosophy with its threefold division. Avicenna seems to be the first philosopher to have adopted this Aristotelian division and from him the Jewish thinkers have taken it over. It found its way into a little Hebrew treatise by Palqera, sandwiched between parts of al-Farabi's " Encyclopedia ", lifted out of Avicenna's " Divisions of the Sciences ", a similar work. (This Hebrew book is a good illustration of that appropriation of literary production not covered by copyright of which I spoke earlier on. It is only a few years since the origin of the various parts, particularly that coming from Avicenna, was ascertained, though Steinschneider already suspected al-Farabi as the author of a part of it).[13] Avicenna's " Divisions " is of particular interest to us, together with the last part of his Metaphysics, and the ninth part of his *Isharat*, the last metaphysical treatise he wrote according to his biographer. For it shows us why prophecy is included in Practical Philosophy.

One reason is to be sought in its definition : it is a natural, psychological phenomenon ; the other is that prophecy and *Shari'a* are necessary for the life and survival of mankind. Both of these will now be considered in their bearing on Jewish thought, especially Maimonides. Be it said at once that some of his commentators remarked adversely that in his treatment of prophecy he was dependent upon al-Farabi and Avempace. The latter can hardly be correct, as far as we can make out from his extant writings. On the other hand, Abu Bakr ibn al-Sa'igh can not easily be misprinted for Ibn Sina. Maybe they mean Abu Bakr ibn Tufail, who is often confused with Avempace. But this I hope to investigate soon.

Only the barest minimum can be given here of the theory of prophecy as evolved by the Falasifa and accepted by some Jewish thinkers, particularly Ibn Daud and Maimonides. This theory is closely linked with their views about the soul and their Theory of Knowledge. It is fully developed by al-Farabi, especially in his two afore-mentioned Political treatises and can be summed up as follows :

He distinguishes practical and theoretical reason in man, who is consequently endowed with imaginative and rational faculties. These are in him only potentially and must be brought into actuality by the emanation of the Active Intellect, also called Holy Spirit. (The Neo-Platonic theory of Emanation is contained in Plotinus' *Enneads*, taken by the Falasifa to be the *Theology of Aristotle*,[14] mentioned in the previous lecture). Only if this Active Intellect emanates on to the Passive human intellect and makes man into a philosopher, and then on to his imaginative faculty making him perfect in both intellect and imagination, does man reach the highest possible stage, becoming a prophet.[15] As such, he is capable of leadership, which is necessary to guarantee the law and order of society into which man—helpless by himself—must organize himself. He calls man, therefore, a citizen, *madani* being the Arabic for *zoon politikon*.[16] But why is a philosopher-prophet needed ? The answer lies in the destiny of man : to reach the Highest Good which consists in the knowledge and perception of God in a rational act. This, possible for the philosopher only, can be realized in none but the Ideal State based on the Divinely revealed Law, the Islamic counterpart to Plato's Ideal State ruled over by the philosopher-king. For al-Farabi there is identity between prophet, philosopher, King and Imam.[17]

Turning to Avicenna,[18] we find the prophet defined as the highest human being, possessed of ethical and intellectual perfection, thanks to the emanation of the Holy Spirit—just as in al-Farabi. He is capable of working miracles and—here Avicenna seems to go beyond al-Farabi—of spontaneous perception, which distinguishes him from the philosopher who requires training and the use of syllogism, demonstration, etc. Thus endowed, he can receive revelations, i.e. he hears the word of God and sees His angels. This explains why imagination in perfection is a necessary condition in prophets.

It is very difficult to decide whether Maimonides has taken over this psychological explanation of prophecy which is, to repeat, a natural disposition in man, from al-Farabi or from Avicenna. One scholar, L. Strauss,[19] is of the opinion that since he agrees with Avicenna in the point of superiority over the philosopher, it is Avicenna whom he follows. In 1935,[20] without knowledge of that book, I compared Maimonides with al-Farabi only and came to the conclusion that he was the source. My reasons are the following:

Maimonides says of this divine emanation, that it produces philosophers if it reaches man's rational faculty only, i.e. his theoretical reason. If, on the other hand, it affects his imaginative faculty only, i.e. his practical reason, it produces political leaders and lawgivers. The prophet, finally, is he whose imaginative and rational faculties are both acted upon,[21] first the rational faculty and then the imaginative one which must be perfect from birth. He thus not only combines the qualities of philosopher, political leader or ruler and lawgiver in his person, but he is by far superior to the two other classes of men and is perfect in the ethical and intellectual virtues. In Avicenna, no mention is made of the rational and imaginative faculties being successively acted upon. He distinguishes between degrees of prophecy, but not between types of public men. It appears that the distinction of three classes is Maimonides' own, with the significant pre-eminence of the lawgiver over the mere ruler.[22] Al-Farabi speaks only of two, philosopher and prophet.

In like manner, Maimonides reproduces the arguments for the necessity of political organisation under the leadership of a prophet, the transmitter and expounder of the Divine Law which alone enables man to reach ultimate perfection and happiness in the perception of God and the imitation of His ways.[23]

If one compares the statements in al-Farabi, Avicenna and Maimonides, one is led to the conclusion that Maimonides knew and used the views of both, but interpreted and adapted them to his own. He was, one must not forget, a foremost teacher and systematizer of Jewish Law as well. The tradition of Halakhah, its preceptive part, no less than of Haggadah, containing the theological and ethical teachings of Post-biblical Judaism—this tradition is the starting-point and centre of his thought. He combined with this native tradition a profound respect for and understanding of Aristotelian philosophy with not a little of Plato in it. Both traditions he strove to harmonize, and it would be fatal to divorce the philosopher from the Halakhist. He is one, not a split personality. This holds good for thinkers like Averroes as well to a large extent, less perhaps for al-Farabi and Avicenna.

What is of greater importance, however, is where Maimonides modifies this theory of the Falasifa. For, although the natural disposition to receive the two-fold emanation may be there, God can if He so wishes withhold the gift of prophecy. Incidentally, Abraham ibn Daud already adduces scriptural proof for this very opinion.[24] Another modification concerns the performing of miracles, with which I cannot deal now. Both of these modifications, however, are less relevant than Maimonides' express exclusion of Moses from the category of prophets just described in agreement with the Falasifa. Where the other prophets hear the voice of God, see His angels and have dreams and visions, Moses experiences the presence of God awake and composed, in direct communion. What is more, he received the Divine Law and was bidden to speak to and teach, to judge and lead the Israelites. Neither before nor after him has anything similar taken place with any of the other prophets. God has created man and wants to preserve human kind and for this reason he sent his prophet with the Law Divine, as Avicenna also teaches.[25] God therefore put into man's nature the ability to govern: first, in order of time and excellence, is the inspired prophet and lawgiver, and after him comes the ruler with power to put into effect the precepts of the former. This law is directed towards the best order of body and faith alike, in contrast to the man-made law which is concerned with man's phyical well-being and good order of the State alone. The Divine Law, concerned with the improvement of the mind and the perfection of man's rational faculty to lead him to his true destination, teaches sound views about God and the angels, thus deepening man's understanding and leading him to the perception of all Existing Things. In his own words: " the true law is unique, there is no other. It is the law of our master Moses which came to us to bring us the double perfection (i.e. of body and soul) ". " The Law has given us the most important of the true ideas through which we reach ultimate perfection and called upon us to believe in them in general, i.e. in the existence of God, His Unity, His Knowledge, Power, Free Will and Eternity which we can only understand after a careful study of other ideas." This and more is needed, not only to lead the individual to happiness and bliss, but also for the well-being of society. Needless to say, these ideas are only accessible to the speculative philosopher, who alone of the faithful can achieve intellectual perfection. This means that he must advance beyond the perception of Existing Things until he recognizes the Divine rule over the Intelligibles and finally perceives God. Yet he does not stop at the static contemplation of the Divine Power. Though this rational act constitutes the highest human perfection, it must be linked with the active striving to become like God " by likening our actions to His actions ". For by imitating His ways we effect the good rule of the State.[26]

It will be clear from this brief account, that Maimonides shares with the Falasifa many an important idea about prophecy and its essential part in political affairs and social life. The Codifier of Jewish Law is here at one with the philosopher.

What remains to be discussed is Avicenna's opinion of the character of Politics as part of Practical Philosophy in connection with Prophecy. In his " Divisions of the Sciences " he contrasts, under the heading " Politics ", kingship with that part dealing with prophecy and *Shari'a*. The former is dealt with in Plato's "Republic" and Aristotle's "Politics" and the latter in "The Laws"[27] This is significant in that it throws light on how the Falasifa from al-Farabi to Averroes linked in their minds the Islamic Ideal State based on the *Shari'a* with the Ideal State of Plato's. Avicenna treats in the last part of his Metaphysics of the Ideal State *and* the Caliphate. In his treatise on *Prophecy*, he speaks of the two-fold task of the prophet to ensure through politics the good order of the physical world and through science (or philosophy) that of the rational world. There is no mention here of the *Shari'a*; instead, he refers to Plato's Laws where he is reported as saying that he who does not pay attention to the meaning of allegories of the prophets will not obtain the Divine kingdom. He speaks of the Greek prophets like Pythagoras, Socrates and Plato who hide in their books their secrets in allegories.[28] The relationship between Theory and Practice, Knowledge and Action, has exercised the Falasifa no less than their Greek and Hellenistic masters.

Far from drawing a lesson from Plato's Laws, Maimonides expressly contrasts the divine law with "the laws of political governments like the laws of the Greeks which are made by political leaders and not by prophets".[29] Thanks to al-Farabi's political treatises, one of which he quotes several times, Maimonides shares with the Falasifa the reception of the Platonic idea of the philosopher-king which they so characteristically adapted to their own ideas conditioned by the dominant position of the Divine Law revealed by a Prophet.[30] No doubt, Greek political concepts have sharpened their mind to the political significance of their Revealed Law. This is particularly striking in the case of Averroes, as I have shown in another place, and cannot repeat here since it falls outside the scope of this Lecture.[31] They deduced from their Revelation the right not only, but even the duty, to concentrate on the perception of God through the study of physics and metaphysics and saw no contradiction between what their Law taught and what philosophy sought. But at the same time they were deeply conscious of the gulf that separated their God from the Greek god. Nor could they overlook that Torah and *Shari'a* were perfect by virtue of being Divine Revelation, whereas the Ideal State of the Greeks to be based on Law was still to be founded. In this context a view of Avicenna's may be quoted which, though hardly compatible with his view about Plato's *Laws*—rather suspect, as it stands in that treatise on Prophecy—throws light not only on his own attitude but also on the similarity between him and Maimonides, between Muslim and Jewish religious philosophy. It comes from the last but one chapter of his *Isharat*, assigned to a group of writings designed to reveal " the secrets of Eastern Philosophy ".[32] Describing the various stages on the way to bliss of the seeking after Truth and God—they are identical—he states, in similar terms to his treatment in *Metaphysics*, the necessity of political and social organization supported by Law. This Law is the Divine law sent through the prophet who teaches the masses about God and His unity, reward and punishment in the Hereafter, worship and obedience. The reward of the seeker after God is perfection achieved in the contemplation of God in various stages leading to mystical union. So much is certain, that only the *Shari'a* in the Ideal State can provide the setting for the few elect speculative philosophers to attempt union with God. But l mention this type of Avicennian writings—to which the treatise on Prophecy belongs—for another reason as well. They seem to have been read widely by Jews. One of them—his allegory *Haiy b. Yaqzan*—was translated into Hebrew both in rhyme and prose. The rhymed version comes from the poet, philosopher and exegete, Abr. b. Ezra. Another was quoted earlier on (with Maimonides' rebuke of his correspondent). But they are important within the field of Islamic philosophy as well. For it is possible that two Muslim philosophers in the West—Avempace and Ibn Tufail—were influenced by them, and possibly al-Ghazali as well. But if I may be allowed to use a favourite phrase of Averroes : here is a topic for investigation. This will have to cover Averroes himself, for he, together with the two first-named, has devoted a special treatise to the problem of the possibility of the union of the human with the Active Intellect. Whether the term " Eastern " should be translated " Illuminative " matters rather less than to find out the real character of this undoubtedly mystical movement which Hajji Khalfa represents as playing the same part in philosophy as Sufism plays in religion.[33] Goldziher thinks it is equivalent to the "esoteric" philosophy of the "Theology of Aristotle" and to be identified with the "inner" philosophy which deals with the mysteries of religious law and has its representatives among the Ikhwan al-safa.[34] The secrets hinted at in the books of Pythagoras, Socrates and Plato, referred to above, are no doubt related to the secrets of Eastern philosophy—by this term it is quoted in Hebrew sources. Neoplatonic and Neopythagorean writings, perhaps even Gnostic ones, must be compared. Plato is considered as the chief of the Ishraqiyyun.

Finally, I should like to refer once more to the link-up of prophecy with politics. The origin of this idea is as yet unknown though one suspects that its history does not start with al-Farabi only. Where has he taken it from? One possible source seems to be Philo of Alexandria. For him Moses is the ideal ruler. He combines in his person the offices of the prophetic Lawgiver with Judge and Leader.[35]

The person of Moses is sufficient to suggest the possibility that Philo connected prophecy with lawgiving and rulership. Whether and how this concept was transmitted to the Falasifa is, to repeat, shrouded in darkness. That Stoic ideas made their way into Syrian-Christian philosophy is established. That the Church Fathers made full use of Philo's allegorical interpretations is well known. Eusebius might be the intermediary, or at least one of them. Qaraite familiarity with Philo is significant.[36] Yet, there need not be any connection at all, just a parallelism. After all, Philo looked upon the Mosaic Law with the eyes of one who knew Plato's and Aristotle's political writings. What is more, his unbounded enthusiasm for the Mosaic Law as a divinely-revealed Ideal constitution of the Ideal Polity is evoked in contrast to the man-made constitutions discussed by Aristotle, as is stressed in a recent work on Philo by Wolfson. It is certainly striking to compare Philo's remarks about this perfect law with those quoted from Maimonides. It is unlikely that the latter knew directly of the former. Why, then, drag all this into a lecture on Avicenna's influence on Jewish Thought? For one very good reason: to illustrate how difficult it is to establish beyond doubt the indebtedness of one writer to another within a cultural environment inviting parallel development. The example of Philo and Maimonides shows an almost identical reaction to the same challenge. But he would be bold who claimed direct Philonic influence on Maimonides.

Yet, allowing for a parallelism in attitude and therefore in reaction, there can be little doubt that in some important concepts Jewish thought owes a good deal to Avicenna's Islamic interpretation of Greek and Hellenistic ideas. Even in the matter of the Divine Law, Avicenna may have helped Maimonides to see the fundamental difference between the Torah of Moses and the Laws of Plato more easily, and at the same time to appreciate the character of the Torah as the Ideal Constitution.

SHORT BIBLIOGRAPHY

In addition to the literature listed in the preceding notes, the reader may wish to consult the following works:—

A.—*Sources:*

Saadya: *k. al-amanat wa-al-i'tiqadat*, ed. S. Landauer, Leiden, 1880.
Saadia Gaon: *The Book of Beliefs and Opinions*, trans. by S. Rosenblatt, Yale Univ. Press, New Haven 1948;
Saadya Gaon: *The Book of Doctrines and Beliefs*, abridged translation by A. Altmann, Oxford 1946.
Yehuda Hallewi: *k. al-khazari*, ed. and trans. by H. Hirschfeld, London 1931.
Maimonides: *k. dalalat al-ha'irin*, ed. S. Munk, Paris 1856-66 (Hebrew: *Moreh nebukhim*);
———: *The Guide of the Perplexed*, trans. by M. Friedlander, London 1885.

B.—*Selected Literature:*

Guttmann, Julius: *Religion und Wssenschaft im mittelalterlichen und im modernen Denken*, Berlin 1922;
———: *Die Philosophie des Judentums*, Munchen 1933.
Husik, I.: *A history of mediaeval Jewish philosophy*, Philadelphia 1946.
Munk, S.: *Mélanges de philosophie juive et arabe*, Paris 1859.
Neumark, D.: *Geschichte der jüdischen Philosophie des Mittelalters*, I; II, 1; II, 2, Berlin 1907-28.
Vajda, G.: *Introduction à la Pensée Juive du Moyen Age*, Paris 1947.

NOTES

[1] The purpose of this lecture is to give a reasoned summary of the principal points of contact between Avicennian and Jewish medieval thought. In the absence of an authoritative monograph, the present writer had—apart from the study of the relevant sources—to content himself with a critical perusal of books and articles dealing with various aspects of Jewish philosophy written since 1845. He gladly acknowledges his indebtedness to these treatises and their authors, both dead and living, as will be apparent from the notes and the short bibliography.

In general, only such instances are treated which appear to point to Avicennian influence, not counting ideas taken over by Avicenna from al-Farabi. Some of the earlier authorities could not be aware of the dominant position of al-Farabi in Islamic philosophy, which fully to appreciate we have only learnt in recent years. Since it would be outside the purpose and scope of this series of lectures, I have not taken issue with their statements, but simply left out of account what appeared to me to go back to al-Farabi rather than to have originated in Avicenna.

It is hoped that this summary may stimulate others to write a comprehensive monograph on the relationship between Avicenna and his Jewish followers and critics. Special reference will have to be made to Moses Narboni's as yet unpublished commentary on al-Ghazali's *maqasid al-falasifa* and to Palqera's writings, in particular to his commentary on Maimonides' *Guide*, entitled *Moreh haMoreh*, with its frequent quotations from Avicenna.

[2] According to W. Bacher (*Die Bibelexegese Moses Maimuni's*, p. 19, *n.* 4), Judah b. Quraish applied this saying in this sense first.

[3] *Cf.* Erwin I. J. Rosenthal: *Saadya Gaon: An Appreciation of his Biblical Exegesis* in: *Bulletin of the John Rylands Library*, XXVII, 1; 1942.

[4] *Cf.* Erwin I. J. Rosenthal, *Mediaeval Judaism and the Law* in: *Law and Religion*, edited by E.I.J.R., Sheldon Press, London, 1938, p. 200, n. 2; and, for the problem under discussion generally, p. 190 ff. and 196 ff.

[5] E.g. in the *Targumim*, the Aramaic translations of the Bible. *Cf.* also Erwin I. J. Rosenthal, *Saadya's Exegesis of the Book of Job* in: *Saadya Studies* edited by E.I.J.R., Manchester 1943, esp. pp. 183–191; and S. Rawidowicz, *Saadya's Purification of the Idea of God*: *ibid.*, pp. 139–165.

[6] It is also possible that Qaraite authors, *e.g.* al-Qirqisani, acted as transmitters of Philonic ideas. A possible intermediary source is David b. Marwan al-Muqammas, who is quoted by Judah b. Barsillai in his commentary on *The Book of Creation* as having taught Saadya. Only a fresh, thorough investigation can perhaps throw light on this difficult, yet very important question. I hope to attempt such an enquiry, based upon the writings of Poznanski and Hirschfeld, at a later date. See also *n.* 35 and 36, below.

[7] *Cf.* the Saadya Anniversary publications (*Jewish Quarterly Review*, 1943), esp. contributions by Wolfson, Efros and Heschel; *Saadya Anniversary Volume*, published by the American Academy for Jewish Research, New York, 1943; *Rab Saadia Gaon*, edited by L. Finkelstein, Jewish Theological Seminary of America, 1944, and *Rab Saadya Gaon*, edited by J. L. Fishman, Jerusalem, 1943 (Hebrew), and, in addition to the articles quoted above in *Saadya Studies* edited by E.I.J.R., that by A. Altmann on *Saadya's Theory of Revelation*. *Cf.* also Georges Vajda in: *Revue des Etudes Juives* IX (CIX), July 1948/June 1949, pp. 68–102, who examines critically the views of Efros, Heschel and Wolfson on the basis of Islamic sources: a very important contribution.

[8] Crescas, *Or Adonay* II. vi, 1, quoted in H. A. Wolfson's basic, masterly *Crescas' Critique of Aristotle*, Cambridge (Mass.), 1929, p. 486. My treatment follows closely this authoritative exposition of the problem of Divine attributes in general and in particular. It will have to be borne in mind that al-Farabi is the first to conceive of the soul as a substance, in which view he is followed by Saadya (see *k. al-amanat wa-al-i'tiqadat*, ed. S. Landauer, p. 116). Or do both follow a Mu'tazilite source? *Cf.* also *Or Adonay* III, ii. 2 and Wolfson's interpretation, *loc. cit*, p. 295, with *notes* 8–11 on p. 667. The treatment of the soul, its nature and parts, by S. Horovitz is still basic and the reader may be referred for details to his *Die Psychologie des Aristotelikers Abraham b. Daud*, where he traces A. b. Daud's Psychology partly to al-Farabi, partly to Avicenna, esp. pp. 224, 231, 253, 255 ff., 265, 274 ff., 283 f. *Cf.* also S. Landauer, *Die Psychologie d. Ibn Sina* in: *Zeitschrift der Deutschen Morgenlaendischen Gesellschaft* XXIX, 1875. Steinschneider discusses this treatise as Book VI of Avicenna's *Physics* in §4 of his *Heb. Uebers.*, p. 18 f. See also p. 27 for Hillel b. Samuel of Verona, Lewi b. Gerson and Simon b. Semah Duran in their relationship to Avicenna's Psychology.

[9] This is already in substance the view of Saadya, though in their formulation the later Jewish thinkers closely follow Avicenna. *Cf.* H. A. Wolfson, *Notes on Proofs of the Existence of God in Jewish Philosophy* in: *Hebrew Union College Annual*, vol. I, 1924, pp. 575–596, esp. 584, 586, 588–592. See also his important study, *Crescas on the Problem of Divine Attributes* in: *Jewish Quarterly Review*, N.S., VII.†

Jewish themes

¹⁰ In his *Spinoza* (Cambridge (Mass.) 1934) I, 121 ff., esp. 124 f., on Existence and Essence with reference to Avicenna, Maimonides, Crescas and Spinoza with relevant quotations. On p. 188 Wolfson discusses the fourfold classification of Being (which we called Existence) in connection with Shem Tob's Commentary on Maimonides *Moreh* II, Introduction. On p. 194 Wolfson traces the Avicennian version of the proof for the existence of God from Maimonides through Thomas Aquinas to Kant.

¹¹ The best treatment of this important problem of medieval philosophy is still to be found in D. Kaufmann's *Geschichte der Attributenlehre, etc.*, Gotha 1877. Although al-Farabi and Avicenna are not always kept separate and their respective influence remains an open question, the book is indispensable for a historical understanding. See esp. for Judah Hallewi, p. 133 and 147, *n.* 77; for Abr. b. Daud, pp. 333, 341 and 347 with notes; for Maimonides, pp. 370 ff., 379, 415, 428 and 434 with relevant notes. The passages in Avicenna are taken from his *k. al-najat* or from al-Shahrastani. Wolfson discusses in his Spinoza, II, the question of God's Knowledge on p. 18 and cites Maimonides, *Moreh* III, c. 20, to the effect that God's knowledge extends to the species directly and only indirectly to the individuals of the species. Narboni declares this to be the view of Avicenna.

¹² Crescas uses al-Tabrizi's arguments contained in the latter's Commentary on the 25 Propositions of Maimonides. A comparison between Maimonides on the one hand and Avicenna (*k. al-najat, k. al-shifa* and al-Shahrastani) and al-Ghazali (*k. maqasid al-falasifa*) on the other is instructive, especially in view of Maimonides' commentators and critics. It cannot be undertaken here for lack of space, but I should like to refer to a few examples discussed by Wolfson in his already quoted *Crescas' Critique of Aristotle*. Pp. 482 ff. deal with " the impossibility of an infinite series of causes and effects " (important for the proof for the existence of God as the uncaused First Cause and Necessary Existent). Crescas, so Wolfson tells us, took this proof from al-Tabrizi, who follows closely Avicenna's version (*k. al-najat*, p. 62). With regard to the motion of the celestial sphere, Avicenna is of the opinion that it is a motion in position, not in place (al-Shahrastani, p. 398). This view is shared by Abr. b. Daud (*Exalted Faith*, I. 3) and quoted in Wolfson, *loc. cit.*, p. 505. On p. 506 he cites Judah Messer Leon's Commentary on Aristotle's *Categories* III, 2, for a reference to Avicenna's view. Further, the view propounded in Maimonides' Proposition 10, that in every body there are the two essential principles of Matter and Form, is the same as that of Avicenna, *k. al-najat*, p. 55. *Cf.* also Wolfson's interesting quotation from Abravanel, who traces Avicenna's view to Plato's *Timaios*, that the celestial sphere is likewise composed of matter and form and only eternal because God made it thus (p. 597, n. 24). The same Avicennian view is to be found in Abraham b. Daud and Bahya b. Paquda. Further examples are given by Wolfson on pp. 582-585.

¹³ In his noteworthy monograph on *al-Farabi*, pp. 176-178 (St. Petersburg 1869). L. Strauss traced part of Palqera's *Reshit hokmah* to Avicenna's *aqsam al-'ulum* in his *Eine vermisste Schrift Farabis* (*Monatsschrift f. Gesch. u. Wissenschaft d. Judentums*, 1936, pp. 96-106.)

¹⁴ *Cf.* Erwin I. J. Rosenthal, *Maimonides' Conception of State and Society* in: *Moses Maimonides*, edited by I. Epstein, London 1935, p. 193.

¹⁵ al-Farabi, *madina fadila*, pp. 58 f. See *op. cit.* previous note, p. 197 and also E. I. J. R., *Some Aspects of Islamic Political Thought* in: *Islamic Culture*, XXII, 1, January 1948, p. 6 f.

¹⁶ al-Farabi, *madina fadila*, p. 54.

¹⁷ *k. tahsil al-sa'ada*, p. 43 (Hyderabad 1345 A.H.) and *op. cit., n.* 15, p. 8.

¹⁸ See Landauer, *loc. cit.*, p. 410 f.; al-Shahrastani, pp. 418 f, Avicenna, *risala fi ithbat al-nubuwwat* in: *tis' rasa'il* and al-Ghazali's treatment of Avicenna's theory of prophecy in his *tahafut*, p. 27 ff. (edited by P. Bouyges, 1927).

¹⁹ *Philosophie und Gesetz*, Berlin 1935, pp. 103 ff. The whole treatment of Maimonides' theory of prophecy deserves careful notice. *Cf.* also Z. Diesendruck, *Maimonides' Lehre von der Prophetie* in: *Jewish Studies in Memory of Israel Abrahams*, New York, 1927.

[20] See n. 14, above, pp. 191-206.
[21] ibid., p. 197 f. See Maimonides, Moreh II, c. 36.
[22] Moreh II, c. 37 and esp. 40.
[23] Moreh I, c. 54 and thamaniya fusul, c. 8.
[24] Exalted Faith, p. 74. His theory of prophecy is modelled upon al-Farabi and Avicenna as was shown by Jakob Guttmann already in his monograph entitled Die Religionsphilosophie des Abraham b. Daud aus Toledo, Goettingen, 1879. It deals fully with all aspects of Abr. b. Daud's philosophy and Avicenna's influence on it.
[25] Cf.: k. al-isharat wa-al-tanbihat, p. 200 (edited by Forget) and risala fi ithbat al-nubuwwat, p. 85. Both passages are also referred to by Strauss, op. cit., p. 112 f.
[26] Cf. op. cit. (n. 14), pp. 200-203. The relevant passages are taken from Moreh, II, cs. 39, 40; III, cs. 27, 28 and 51.
[27] Cf.: aqsam al-'ulum in: tis' rasa'il, p. 73 f. See also Strauss, op cit., p. 111 ff.
[28] p. 85 f.
[29] Moreh II, c. 39. See also op. cit. n. 4, pp. 199-205.
[30] He avoids the term "king", though he uses the term sultan for "ruler", which his Hebrew translatoi Samuel b. Tibbon actually renders by melekh. It is possible that Maimonides prefers the term mudabbir, political leader. He may have Moses in mind and also reserve the term "king" to the king Messiah of the house of David. For Philo Moses, the Ideal Ruler, was king, just as some Jewish exegetes refer melekh in Deuteronomy XXXIII, 5, to Moses. This point requires further study.
[31] Cf. op. cit., (n. 15) p. 10 ff.
[32] See A. F. M. Mehren, Traités mystiques d'Avicenne, Leyden, 1889, p. 11 of Arabic text and his rather paraphrastic rendering on pp. 55 ff.; also his articles on Avicenna's philosophy in Le Muséon, 1882, 1883, 1885.
[33] Quoted by L. Gauthier in his Ibn Thofail, etc., p. 59 ff., the passage occurs in kashf al-dhunun, ed. Flügel, III, 87, l. 4 ff.
[34] In the notes to his edition of the k. ma'ani al-nafs, p. 29 ff. See also his remarks on Avicenna and Jewish thinkers on pp. 18+, 52+, 54+ f., 57+ f., 61+.
[35] In spite of the vast literature on Philo, no agreement exists as yet among the experts as to what in Philo constitutes his own ideas and what is Hellenistic, particularly Stoic, and what is Jewish past and contemporary thought. Yet, with the help of Goodenough's The Politics of Philo Judaeus (Yale 1938), especially c. V, and Wolfson's monumental two volumes Philo (Cambridge Mass., 1947), as well as H. Leisegang's Der Heilige Geist, etc., I, 1919, it may be possible to determine at least whether there is any evident connection between Philo's 'Holy Spirit' and the Holy Spirit identified with the Active Intellect of the Falasifa and their Jewish followers, chief among them Maimonides. In this connection, a remark of Abr. b. Daud's in his Exalted Faith, p. 58 (ed. Weil), is of particular significance. In speaking about the Active Intellect that mediates prophecy, he mentions that what the philosophers call Active Intellect the adherents of Islam call the Holy Spirit, *but before them all the prophets* (of Israel) *called it Holy Spirit.* The well-known passage in Numbers XI. 14-29, esp. vv. 17 and 25, with its close connection between prophecy and judge-and-rulership must be looked into in this context. I hope to go into this question at a later date. See also next note.
[36] See S. Poznanski, Philon dans l'ancienne littérature judéo-arabe in Revue des Etudes Juives, L, 1905, pp. 10-31. H. Hirschfeld published Arabic fragments of Philo's writings, found in the Cairo Genizah, in: JQR XVI and XVII. It will have to be ascertained where the Qaraites obtained their knowledge of Philo. It is possible that David b. Marwan al-Muqammas acted as transmitter. Yet, even if Qaraite transmission might be established this would not necessarily account for their having transmitted it to al-Farabi. Plotinus seems the more likely source for al-Farabi, and al-Farabi with Avicenna for Abr. b. Daud and Maimonides.

13

TORAH AND 'NÓMOS' IN MEDIEVAL JEWISH PHILOSOPHY*

The blending of the Hebraic and the Hellenic mind was more than a subject for inquiry *more academico* for Leon Roth. The Jew who wrote on Maimonides and Spinoza and the Professor at the Hebrew University of Jerusalem who translated classical Greek philosophical works into Hebrew considered the twofold scholarly tradition in which he was reared as equally meaningful for our time. The universality of the Torah and the rationality of the *nómos* in their mutual penetration in affinity and contrast do not only form the central theme of medieval religious philosophy in Judaism, but do so in a special way, particularly in the thought of Abraham ibn Da'ud and Moses Maimonides. It may, therefore, not be inappropriate to discuss briefly the meeting-point of the two realms of faith and reason, as a tribute to a philosopher and friend whose untimely death has left not merely a gap in our lives, but also a challenging legacy to try to resolve the perpetual tension between the universal and the particular in the lives of those of us who are committed to Judaism.

Whereas Abraham ibn Da'ud speaks, in the introduction to his *'Emūnāh rāmāh*, of the difficulty of the co-existence of faith and philosophy, Maimonides in his *Moreh nebhūkhīm* (II, 40) expresses and in part resolves their conflict through his distinction between a divine and a human law, the law of revelation and the law of human reason. His identification of the latter with 'the laws of the Greeks' (*ibid.*, II, 39) not only gives us the source – Greek philosophy – but also the ultimate reason why the challenge of philosophy to religious tradition took the specific form of revealed *versus* human law. For this challenge would neither have been felt nor accepted if there had not existed some important common ground between revealed faith and human reason. Both have the same aim in regard to man as a *zóon politikón*: to help him attain his highest good – *eudaimonía*, happiness or blessedness.[1] As far as philosophy is concerned, this task mainly falls to the share of practical philosophy (ethics, politics and economics), and to this end the philosopher has devised a *nómos*, a law guiding the citizen of the *pólis*. Religion uses the same means to enable the believer, as a member of a religious community, to reach his goal – in the case of the Jew the Torah. But here the affinity ends, and the contrast becomes apparent once the aim and the way to it are defined. The Jew starts from the fact of revelation, from God; but the Greek starts from man and his sovereign reason. The Torah shows the way to God; it is in the perception and love of God that the Jew attains happiness and bliss. Without obedience to the will of God expressed in the Torah there can be no happiness; for man is not only a rational being, he is also (and in the first place) a religious entity and a creature made in the image of God, whom to serve in love is his sole purpose. Why, then, does the medieval Jew stand in any need of a philosophy invented by the sovereign intellect of self-sufficient man? In point of fact, it is only a certain type of Jew who does need it – the Jew who looks out from the fortress of the Torah, and has come into contact with philosophy; not the fervent yet naive believer whose happiness and perfection is guaranteed by the spontaneous fulfilment of the *miṣwōth*. Every Jew is enjoined to study the Torah which is identical with *ḥokhmāh*, wisdom. He accepts this wisdom unquestioningly because it comes from God. For the intellectual *élite* wisdom has, however, also another connotation, which stems from the Greeks. Faith is no longer the only guide to the God whom to know and to love we are all, as Jews, commanded in the Torah. If practical philosophy constituted the totality of philosophy the Torah would, indeed, be entirely sufficient to lead rational man to his end. For according to Maimonides' definition, the divinely revealed law guarantees the religious human being twofold happiness, *viz.* wellbeing in this world as well as salvation, the bliss of the immortal soul, in the life everlasting. Practical philosophy guarantees the former only, through law and order in the *pólis*. But Plato demands more: for him, that man alone attains to perfection and happiness whose right doing springs from right beliefs and sound convictions. It is here that the conflict between faith and reason arises, but it is precisely here that this conflict – so the medieval religious thinkers hold – can be resolved. And yet, although divine and human law travel part of the way together in respect of what they have in common – the concern for man in this life on earth – it is theoretical philosophy (physics and metaphysics) alone that can help the believer to justify his right beliefs and convictions (i.e. the religious doctrines of the Torah), through demonstration. But demonstration is, ultimately, insufficient to solve the secrets of the Torah, commonly described in the twin concepts of *ma'asēh berē'shīth* and *ma'asēh merkābhāh*. For while the literal meaning of Scripture must be abandoned if incompatible with demonstrative proof, in the case where the metaphysician is unable to demonstrate his opinion – Maimonides means, of course, Aristotle's view of the eternity of matter – the believer is obliged to accept and to uphold the biblical account of the creation of the world *ex nihilo* as revealed truth. On the other hand, God's incorporality is established by philosophical proof, hence anthropomorphic language must be explained allegorically.[2] It is obvious that Jewish medieval thinkers started from the Torah; and while Bahya ibn Paqūda[3] sought to show – in his *Duties of the Heart* – that the Torah fully satisfies both the Jew's faith and his intellectual striving as well, Abraham ibn Da'ud[4] was equally convinced, as was Maimonides after him, that although the Torah was the best guide to man's *haṣlāḥāh* (*eudaimonía*) – a better one than the practical philosophy of the Greeks – it is faith and its doctrines which must occupy first place in the intellectual study of the Torah in order to reach the highest perfection. Doctrines are only accessible to the inquirer trained in metaphysics, in so far as their deeper understanding is concerned. In this attitude Abraham ibn Da'ud is in agreement with both Plato and Aristotle. As we have seen, Plato demands right beliefs and sound convictions, and Aristotle sees in the intellectual virtues the highest that man can achieve. And yet, Abraham ibn Da'ud goes further, in his insistence that to know God is a religious duty as being a direct divine command.

It seems more correct, then, to speak of the *intellectualism* of Jewish medieval thinkers, and not of their rationalism; for intellectualism grants primacy to faith with its religious commandments, whereas rationalism insists on the primacy of sovereign reason. Intellectualism recognises frontiers in the endeavour of reason to unravel the secrets of God and His universe, and where reason fails the believer humbly accepts by faith even what he cannot fully grasp intellectually. Acceptance means, in this context, acceptance of the literal meaning. Only where the literal meaning runs counter to clear proof must it be abandoned for a rational explanation which aims at bringing out its inner, sometimes hidden meaning. For the out-and-out rationalist reason can, and must, plumb the deepest depths.

Abraham ibn Da'ud uses the Ten Commandments as a telling illustration of the difference between revelation in the form of the Torah and philosophy (in form of the *nómos*). Philosophy, he says, is silent about the first five commandments, which are concerned with our knowledge and worship of God. Nevertheless, as already stated, he considers philosophy necessary for the proper understanding of religious doctrines. It is only on this theoretical basis that ethics and politics are firmly established, and can fulfil their purpose: the good order of the world and the preservation of human civilisation. Hebraic and Greek ideas are so closely intertwined in his thought that he does not always present them in their right order or context. Thus, he declares the biblical commandment *'Thou shalt love thy neighbour . . .'* to be the first of the political laws and not one of the moral laws. This is, no doubt, due to the influence of Greek political philosophy which, together with its ethics, provided that link which was necessary to open the world of the Torah to the otherwise alien world of Hellas. There can be no doubt that Plato and Aristotle taught the medieval Muslim world and, in its wake, the Jewish thinkers the political character and significance of the divinely revealed law. For this reason, Abraham ibn Da'ud admits that the second half of the Ten Commandments is comprised also by practical philosophy – but, he adds, in a less comprehensive manner. Both the Decalogue and practical philosophy deal with inter-human relations in society and state; but human reason is bound to frame laws relative to time, place and economic and social circumstance, without the absolute, timeless perfection of the divine Lawgiver who made His law known through Moses, the greatest of the prophets. Naturally, practical philosophy is more concerned with personal and social interests and concerns in this world than with such religious demands as love of neighbour, abstemiousness and personal, inward piety. Piety is devotion to God in worship and good deeds towards our neighbour. Worship is more than prayer and fasting; it must permeate our entire daily life. We might at once point out that worship, i.e. the cult, is a Platonic demand equally, as being a civic duty. Nevertheless, Abraham ibn Da'ud's inward piety – like Baḥya's 'duties of the heart' – is something much more than the civic duty of public worship, and goes beyond the prescribed measure of the law. It is precisely this *plus* of religious commandments which bestows upon the divine law its superiority over man-made laws. Through its addition of *'Love thy neighbour'* the Torah guarantees the best order for the world in a way which even the best *nómos* can never provide. In this context Abraham ibn Da'ud's religious interpretation of *sōphrosýne* is rather illuminating: to be content with what God has granted us without coveting what is our neighbour's. To repeat, man as the servant of God is a more perfect human being than is the *zōon politikón* of the *pólis* and its *nómos*. And yet, the very concept of perfection and happiness (or blessedness) is a

Greek concept, though it has been adapted to indigenous Islamic and Jewish concepts and has been transformed in the process. Even more important is another addition: the biblical command to *love* God.†We have seen that for the Jewish disciple of Plato and Aristotle this is not possible without first *perceiving* the Creator and Ruler of the universe with man in it as a rational being. Man shows his love for God by serving his Master in obedience to His will as expressed in the Torah. Thus, man must at the same time love his neighbour by fulfilling his social and moral obligations under the Torah. The laws of revelation are a constant reminder to man to fear and to love God. With Plato, Abraham ibn Da'ud demands that the cogitative part of the soul must dominate and rule the other parts in order to guarantee justice, for the Greeks the foremost political virtue. Nevertheless, despite his recognition of the indispensability of the rational perception of God with the help of philosophy, Abraham ibn Da'ud classes the pious observer of the traditional commandments yet higher, even though such a pietist is not, or may not be intellectually capable of understanding their reasons. For the Jew's obedience is founded on, and grounded in a historical event which is prior to philosophy in both time and rank – the revelation of the Torah from Sinai in the presence of the whole people of Israel. This divine event is supported by the exemplary nature of Moses, the announcer of the law, and by the truth of his miracles performed in public sight. Abraham ibn Da'ud combines this traditional outlook with an intellectualism which maintains that there is nothing in the Torah which contradicts reason. Reason is therefore permitted full play in the interpretation of revelation. Such rational inquiry is, indeed, a religious duty. The fact that the Torah embodies teaching about God and contains religious doctrines and principles, clearly shows that it is concerned with the spiritual, inner well-being of the believer as the creature of God. This is something that philosophy does not do. Although the primacy of faith cannot be questioned and the significance of the ethical teaching of the Torah is continually stressed, the priorities of faith and philosophy are not always or consistently observed. This is due to the fact that the two realms are fundamentally different from each other even though they overlap and are complementary. This is a real dilemma: and it is one by no means confined to the Middle Ages. It was already present in Philo, who attempted a similar solution; but it meets us in its acutest form in Maimonides, and with him more concisely and sharply than in Abraham ibn Da'ud. Without Maimonides, there would be no modern Jewish philosophy in Spinoza, Moses Mendelssohn, Hermann Cohen and Franz Rosenzweig.

Needless to say, Sinai as the historical proof of God's existence no less than of the divine origin of the Torah of Moses, is as valid for Maimonides as for any other Jewish thinker. But the disciple of Aristotle felt bound to add to the incontrovertible proof of tradition the demonstrative argument of the metaphysician. He was convinced that the Torah did not teach anything which contradicted Aristotle's teaching, and he would not depart from the literal sense of Scripture unless Aristotle forced him to. Things were not always so clear cut – or, should we perhaps add, so obliging – as in the case of the creation. Since Aristotle's argument in favour of the eternity of matter did not convince Maimonides, he did not accept Aristotle in place of the plain sense of the creation story in *Genesis*. But how dangerous and precarious his position was between tradition and Aristotelian metaphysics is shown by his admission that, if Aristotle had been able to offer incontrovertible proof for his opinion, the Torah would have had to be abandoned. This would have disastrous consequences for the truth of the biblical prophets and the justification of miracles. Since I have discussed this problem elsewhere[5] and since it is moreover not directly relevant to the present theme, it must suffice here to emphasise that in order to uphold such fundamental biblical teachings as messianism and reward and punishment, Maimonides gave precedence to inherited religious principles over those of metaphysics (*Mōrēh* II, 40 and III, 54). Especially in the latter passage, Maimonides takes a decisive step further when he postulates that it is man's supreme duty to imitate the thirteen attributes of God, even though he emphasises – with Aristotle – intellectual perfection as man's greatest achievement. I would therefore hold that since the imitation of

God alone leads to the perception and love of God – the religious person's true fulfilment and attainment of the highest blessedness – Maimonides recognises the primacy of revelation.[6] God's attributes are, in his view, all attributes of action and not of the divine essence; and it is the Torah which conveys the perfect teaching of how to achieve that imitation.

Before recapitulating Maimonides' distinction between divine and human law, it is necessary briefly to digress. For the obvious objection must be met that the concept of the *Imitatio Dei* is also a philosophical postulate, defined in Plato's *Theaetetus* (176b) as 'becoming just, holy and wise'. When we remember that justice is the primary political virtue, we shall not be surprised to see Maimonides introduce his demand – justified by the *Siphrē* – by the following significant formula: 'His actions [i.e. the thirteen *middōth*] are necessary for the government of states' (I, 54).[7]

The importance of justice for state and society, which applies equally to Plato's ideal *Republic* and to the state of God with the Torah as its constitution and law, must not lead us to assume that medieval Jewish (and Muslim) thinkers identified their own ideal state with the Greek *pólis* as visualised by Plato. This is not only clear from what we found in Abraham ibn Da'ud – love of neighbour and inward piety – but even more apparent in Maimonides' distinction between the laws in force in the two states, in regard to their respective scope and ultimate purpose. Human law aims at the good order of the state and its affairs, and tries to keep injustice and strife away from it; to regulate inter-human relations, and to enable the citizens to attain what they consider to be their happiness. In contrast to the law in the philosopher's state, the divine law goes beyond it in extent as well as in content, for it aims at man's spiritual as well as his physical well-being and salvation. Its regulations are not only concerned with man's material interests and needs, but also (and in the first place) with right convictions and views about God, the angels, the divine order of the world, God's providence and reward and punishment. Its intention is to make man wise and give him insight so as to enable him to gain true knowledge of reality (II, 40). We note that Maimonides overlooks the fact that Plato, no less than he himself, demands right beliefs and convictions. But there is definitely more to the Torah than to the *nómos*, in virtue of the former's inclusion of purely religious matters. In another passage (III, 27) Maimonides emphasises that it is only the law of Moses, as being the divinely revealed law, that provides for our twofold blessedness in body and soul, in this world in the political community and in the life everlasting. The law announced by the prophet stems from God's unfathomable will; it reflects God's love, mercy, compassion and justice. But this does not mean that medieval thinkers denied the *relative* excellence of the philosopher's law, as is clear from their awareness of the political and social relevance of any and every law. Even Judah Hallevi who, like Ghazālī, recognised practical philosophy only, admitted this; and at the end of the period Albo found much of human law implied and included within divine law, as we shall see later on. It is not only Plato's *Republic*, but also Aristotle's *Nicomachean Ethics* with its ideas of equity, which impressed medieval religious thinkers. Nevertheless they were all convinced that equity, and not absolute justice, must be the norm wherever it is fallible man who makes laws; the divine law is by contrast immutable and absolutely just, not subject to changing times and varying circumstances, nor in need of improvement – only of clarification and interpretation.

The Torah was there at the beginning of all philosophical speculation and always remained in the centre, superior in its fundamental difference over the *nómos*. It served as a barrier between revelation and philosophy which no attempt at harmonisation, no esoteric interpretation could ultimately remove. And yet our picture would be incomplete and distorted if we simply confronted the ideas of Jewish medieval thinkers starting from the Torah, both written and oral, with the original Platonic and Aristotelian writings. For it was precisely the development and modification of Platonic and Aristotelian ideas among Neoplatonists and Stoics and the other Hellenistic schools which had made their reception by Jews and Muslims possible. The religious penetration and expansion of classical Greek ideas, especially among the commentators of Plato and Aristotle, played a decisive role: with the result that we cannot be dogmatic about the relative strength of 'religious' or 'philosophical' concepts, and the priority in every instance of their medieval reception and transformation.[8] The precise meaning of 'happiness' is not merely a question of semantic development of the term *eudaimonía*. Nowhere is this clearer than in the controversial question of the meaning and interpretation of prophecy, to be met with in Muslim and Jewish thinkers. Though very relevant to our question of Torah *versus nómos*, it cannot be even outlined here. I must content myself with the statement – substantiated in earlier studies[9] – that Maimonides explicitly exempts the prophecy of Moses, and thus the character of the Torah, from the psychological explanation of Fārābī (be its origin middle-platonic or Stoic). There is a profound difference between the prophet sent by God and the natural prophet.[10] Even in the case of the other prophets Maimonides would not allow that the gift of prophecy has to be automatic simply because its natural conditions – perfect imagination and perfect intellect – are extant in any given person; God has the power to withhold the actualisation of the prophetic nature, if He so wills.

To sum up what we have outlined so far it must, therefore, suffice to state that the law promulgated by the prophet, on divine instruction, is superior to the law devised by the philosopher. The same applies to the nature and degree of human happiness. Maimonides follows Fārābī in distinguishing between absolute – true – happiness, and relative – alleged, imaginary – happiness. True happiness is only attainable in the perfect state under the Torah; the other, inferior kinds of happiness are relegated to the states under the *nómos*, corresponding to Plato's imperfect constitutions.[11] This points to the primacy of revelation, the practical and political implications of which Maimonides stresses – clearly under Greek influence, in particular on the basis of Plato's *Republic* and Aristotle's *Nicomachean Ethics*. The Torah aims at the attainment of every person's happiness and perfection – though its degree is in proportion to the individual's intellectual level – and he says of it: 'only this law do we call divine, the other political constitutions as e.g. the *nómoi* of the

Greeks ... are the work of statesmen (or, governors), but not of prophets' (II, 39). He also stresses another distinctive quality of the divinely revealed law: that it observes the right proportion, and is free from all exaggeration and excess. This not only reminds us of Aristotle's definition of virtue, but also seems to have a polemical significance, being possibly directed against both Christian monasticism and Muḥammad's sensuality (II, 36, 40).

In the wake of the battle that raged round the *Guide to the Perplexed* and the growing precariousness of the Jewish position, a decided swing back to the traditional outlook characterises the post-Maimonidean era, towards the end of the Middle Ages. Crescas[12] rejected the need for the philosophical justification of the biblical concept of God and of the relationship between God and man. The love of God is, for him also, man's highest good; but it can be achieved by the spontaneous fulfilment of the divine commandments of the Torah, and need not be preceded by the intellectual perception of God. He thus restored the undivided sovereignty and authority of revealed religion in a manner reminiscent of Judah Hallevi and Baḥya. His disciple Albo illustrates in his '*Iqqārīm* the self-sufficiency of religion with the help of philosophy, especially its practical part. Despite his dependence on Maimonides and Crescas, and consequently a marked absence of intellectual independence, his treatment of the Torah and its aim – the attainment of human happiness – is illuminating. Its main points may fittingly conclude our brief survey.

Albo's reduction of Maimonides' thirteen principles of faith to three 'root principles' is chiefly important in our context for its relegation of prophecy to the position of a secondary principle, derived from the revelation of the Torah. This not only avoids the dilemma posed by the psychological interpretation of prophecy; but it also reduces philosophy from its challenging position to one of illustration, in order the better to demonstrate (for throughout his theological treatise Albo uses the systematic methodology of philosophy) the superiority of revelation. His defence of Torah-religion is that of an unquestioning traditionalist who no longer feels the challenge of metaphysics to be dangerous. Thus, he can say: 'faith in God and His Torah leads man to eternal bliss and to the union with the spiritual'.[13] Such union in perfection is possible for the prophet only, not for the philosopher; experience attests this for Israel through tradition. Naturally, he agrees with the earlier Muslim and Jewish thinkers that prophecy is indispensable for man's attainment of his highest good. But, as stated, he derives prophecy from the Torah, for it is only the divine law that announces to man how he can attain his highest good, namely through his knowledge of the things that please God and through doing them. Man needs divine guidance – through the Torah – in order to learn what is true and good and what leads him to blessedness. Because of this need of divine guidance the Torah is a 'root principle'. In other words, Albo starts from God and His will and not from man and his desires and striving, just as do his predecessors; but for him tradition is sufficient, and it no longer requires philosophical justification and confirmation.

But philosophy, as already stated, is useful to spotlight this self-sufficiency of the Torah. Like Maimonides, Albo distinguishes between divine and human law, except that he subdivides the latter into natural and positive-conventional law, which together serve the same purpose as does that part of the divine law which, for Abraham ibn Da'ud, was contained in the latter five of the Ten Commandments. Albo is the first Jewish thinker who directly refers to Aristotle's *Politics*, either from direct knowledge or through Thomas Aquinas.[14] Natural law is common to all men, since it is necessary to maintain human life. We know that for the Stoa the law of nature (*lex naturae*) was identical with the divine law (*lex aeterna* or *lex divina*), but at the same time we remember that 'divine' in their case had nothing to do with the personal God of love, mercy and justice of the Bible. Jewish medieval thinkers derive the law of reason – which, for the Stoa, was identical with the law of nature – likewise from revelation, since all laws stem from the will of the one good God. They even assign the seven Noachide laws to revelation although they are common to all nations out of absolute necessity.

Torah and 'nómos' in Jewish philosophy

It is well known that they admit that reason would, after a long time had elapsed, have arrived at the laws of reason by its own effort, but only in their general outline, thus leaving man in the dark as to their particular application. This application we learn from the divine law which is, therefore, superior to human law. Moreover, the divine law not only commands what reason also postulates – justice, equity, truth and ethical conduct – and forbids what reason rules out – murder, theft, adultery and fornication. It also demands divine worship, religious feasts, purity and dietary laws. Whereas Sa'adya assigned the last group to laws of revelation (for he divided laws into those of revelation and those of reason) Maimonides recognises solely laws of revelation; and he distinguishes – with Aristotle – between general and specific laws, the reason for which man cannot always understand.

If we compare Jewish with Stoic law we realise that the revealed law comprises both natural and positive law, but denies man all power to promulgate any laws. Judaism would hence never acknowledge the ultimate validity of a *ius civile* issuing from some human legislator. But the very term 'rational laws' used by Sa'adya suggests that Islamic dialectical theology (*Kalām*) has mediated a Stoic concept to him. Nevertheless, he denies their independent existence, deriving them no less than what he calls laws of revelation – the ceremonial laws – from God.

This digression has been necessary in order to understand Albo's classification of laws. He avers that the principles of the divine law, like that law itself, are validated by experience – the historical experience of Sinai – and he rejects Aristotle's principles of positive or conventional law: choice and purpose ('*Iqqārīm* I, 93 ff.). He says,[15] in principle, the same as does Maimonides about the peculiar properties of the divinely revealed law which alone leads mankind (not only the Jew) to ultimate happiness and bliss. But his language is, naturally, that of his own age; it is conditioned as much by Thomas Aquinas, with his use and adaptation of Aristotelian legal philosophy, as by Maimonides and Crescas, with the additional flavour of rabbinic thought and expression in place of the philosophical superstructure as a justification of revelation.

The student of political thought in the Middle Ages will notice that, contrary to the main tradition of Greek-Hellenistic and Muslim-Jewish political philosophy, Albo – like Ibn Bājja – envisages the attainment of the highest good even in imperfect states based on bad constitutions. From the context – the Torah as the perfect guide to happiness – it would, however, appear that he was possibly thinking of the Jew in the Diaspora living according to the prescriptions of the Torah, and achieving the happiness of his soul and immortality by joyfully fulfilling the commandments. This is what he says:

> The purpose of the divine law is to lead men straight to the true blessedness which is spiritual happiness (*literally*, the happiness of the soul) and immortality. It shows them the ways they must follow to obtain it, teaches them the true good so that they strive to attain it, and teaches them true evil, too, so that they guard against it. It accustoms them to give up the kinds of imaginary happiness, so that they no longer crave for them nor are grieved at losing them. It also lays down ways of justice (*or*, equity) so that the political community may be ordered in a proper and perfect manner. As a result, the evil order of their community will not prevent them from attaining true blessedness, nor from striving to attain it and the ultimate aim of mankind which is the purpose of the divine law. Herein it goes beyond the conventional law.[16]

True and false, good and evil, what is done and not done – all these are contained in the divine law. Like Maimonides, Albo makes the divine law provide for true opinions and ethical action; but such provision is the function of the divine law alone. Just as we cannot rely on the human lawgiver in matters of what is seemly and unseemly, so we cannot trust him in matters of our deepest convictions, for example in the matter of the creation or the eternity of the world. For human reason is without certainty in this matter, nor can the observance of a human law that lacks all certainty fill the citizen with joy.[17] The rabbinic *simḥāh shel miṣwāh*, joy experienced through fulfilment of a commandment, is reserved for the Torah. This is the legacy of the Rabbis; and it was Crescas who brought it to the fore again.

NOTES

* This essay is a summary in English of parts of the first three chapters of my *Griechisches Erbe in der jüdischen Religionsphilosophie des Mittelalters* (*GE*), Stuttgart, 1960, and I am indebted to the publisher (W. Kohlhammer) for permission to use the book and quote from it. Lack of space forbids a full exposition with the necessary evidence *in extenso*; the reader may, therefore, be referred to the German publication for a justification of the views here expressed, especially the chapters entitled: '*Torah und Nomos I: Die Glückseligkeit als menschliches Ziel*' and '*Torah und Nomos II: Glaubenslehren, Herzensfrömmigkeit und praktische Philosophie*'. There will also be found the necessary references to the literature utilised, and to my earlier studies in problems of political philosophy in Islam and Judaism, from 1935 onwards.
1 Cf. Averroes' Commentary on Plato's *Republic*, ed. E. I. J. Rosenthal, p. 185.
2 Cf. *GE*, pp. 21 f., 56 with relevant notes. It is important to note that Maimonides links the question of creation with that of revelation and prophecy.
3 Cf. *K. al-hidāya*, ed. Yahuda, p. 5. The passage is reproduced and commented on in *GE*, p. 97, n. 5. Cf. also, for Baḥya's attitude generally, *ibid.*, pp. 41–4.
4 Cf. *GE*, pp. 44–9 and *passim* for a full account with reference to AbD's text (*S. ha-'emūnāh ha-rāmāh*, ed. S. Weil, pp. 98–104) and his indebtedness to Plato, Aristotle and Avicenna.
5 Cf. *GE*, pp. 22 f. with n. 18; *Mōrēh* II, 25. Julius Guttmann's selection of the *Mōrēh* – translated from the Arabic by C. Rabin – in *Philosophia Judaica* (East and West Library, London), especially his Introduction, is important. A rationalistic interpretation is given by Leo Strauss in his *Philosophie und Gesetz* and in *The Literary Character of the Guide for the Perplexed* (in *Essays on Maimonides*, ed. S. W. Baron). Cf. now also the new English translation of the *Guide* by S. Pines with an Introductory Essay by L. Strauss (Univ. of Chicago Press, 1963).
6 Cf. *GE*, chapter *Sendungsprophetie und Natürliche Prophetie*, especially pp. 55 f.
7 *Siphrē, Deut.*, 49 on 11: 22 (cf. 10: 12), ed. Finkelstein, p. 114. Cf. *GE*, pp. 28 f. with notes 4 and 5, and my *Political Thought in Medieval Islam* (*PT*), chapters 1, 5–7 and 9. The question of *eudai-*

monía is discussed in *GE, Exkurs I: Begriff und Bedeutungswandel der Eudämonie*, pp. 69–78 with notes, pp. 103 ff.

8 I have dealt with this problem briefly in *GE*, pp. 25 f. and at greater length in my *PT*.

9 Cf. my *Maimonides' Conception of State and Society* (in *Moses Maimonides*, ed. I. Epstein, 1935); *PT* for a similar view of Averroes as regards Muḥammad, and my studies mentioned there, dealing with Fārābī, Ibn Bājja (Avempace), Avicenna and Averroes, as also *GE, Exkurs I* and *II* (*Bemerkungen zur Theorie der Prophetie bei den mittelalterlichen islamischen und jüdischen Philosophen*), pp. 79–86, with notes pp. 105–7; also *GE*, pp. 32 f., especially note 22, p. 94.

10 Cf. *GE* as in note 6, above, the whole chapter.

11 Cf. *GE*, pp. 31 ff. with notes.

12 Cf. Julius Guttmann, *Die Philosophie des Judentums*, 1933, pp. 237 ff., whose interpretation I am following in *GE*, pp. 51 f. Hebrew version (*Ha-pīlōsōfīāh shel ha-Yahadūth* ², 5713), pp. 205 f. English translation of the latter, by David M. Silverman, 1964, p. 224 f.

13 Cf. *Sēfer hā-'iqqārīm*, ed. I. Husik, 4 f., where the passage is translated (I, 173): 'and causes his soul to cleave to the spiritual substance (*dābhār ha-rūḥānī*)'.

14 Cf. *GE*, p. 53 with notes 18–22, which deal with Albo's attitude to Aristotle, citing the relevant passages in the *Nicomachean Ethics*. For want of space, I can here merely refer the reader to my treatment of Sa'adya in *GE*, pp. 34–40 and *passim*, with notes on pp. 95 f.

15 Cf. *GE*, p. 54, with notes 24–27, for a fuller treatment than is here possible.

16 Cf. *Sēfer hā-'iqqārīm*, I, 79 f. My translation differs slightly from Husik's. Cf. also *ibid.*, I, 146, 148, 152, 158; III, 59, 109, 230, 265 f. and my *GE*, n. 24, p. 99.

17 *Sēfer hā-'iqqārīm*, I, 80 f.; III, 46 f. and *GE*, n. 25, pp. 99 f.

PART III
'WISSENSCHAFT DES JUDENTUMS'

14

ISMAR ELBOGEN AND THE NEW JEWISH LEARNING*

In 1872 the *Hochschule für die Wissenschaft des Judentums* first opened its doors to students in Berlin. In 1874 Ismar Elbogen was born in Schildberg in the Prussian province of Posen. For most of his mature life he served the *Hochschule*, the embodiment of WdJ, as professor, organiser, administrator, warm-hearted and wise counsellor of generations of students, and as a dynamic scholar of outstanding qualities of character and intellect. With indomitable courage and determination he strove to further the knowledge and understanding of Judaism, its basic teachings, history and fate. An exile in the United States, his new home from 1938, he died in 1943 in the fulness of a life crowded with ceaseless work, and of selfless devotion to the scientific study, explanation and presentation of Judaism. His legacy is of permanent value: it is a monument to German Jewry in its most creative last period, a solid contribution to WdJ through important publications spanning 46 years of original research, and a popular presentation of the ebb and flow of Jewish life and thought which reflects the integrity of mature, well-informed scholarship and the warm heart of a devout, practising Jew.

Elbogen is not the only scholar from Posen (Poznan) who has risen to eminence, but he was perhaps the most approachable, worldly-wise, influential and lovable personality of them all. Those of us who were privileged to study and work with him see and hear him in every page of his writings. His work reflects the warm humanity, the wit, even the sarcasm, the clarity and rare insight of his philosophically trained mind. A man of strong feeling, telling in argument and repartee, he was never unkind or abusive, never out to destroy a scholarly reputation. He welcomed criticism as long as it was not uncharitable (*lieblos* is the word he used).

---

*"The New Jewish Learning" is an inadequate rendering of the German *Wissenschaft des Judentums* (WdJ), founded by Leopold Zunz. Throughout this article it will be referred to as WdJ or *Wissenschaft* and only rarely as "science". For "science" usually means natural sciences whereas WdJ belongs to the humanities (*Geisteswissenschaften*). The term "New Jewish Learning" stands for the new, critical study and evaluation of Judaism in contrast to the old *Lernen* or *Talmud Torah*. Ismar Elbogen deserves a full-length biography; within the confines of this Year Book it could not be given. But I have gladly accepted the Editor's invitation to write a contribution on the occasion of the twentieth *Jahrzeit* to focus attention on Elbogen's dominant position within WdJ. A glance at the bibliography, published by the professor's widow (Ismar Elbogen 1874-1943. A Bibliography by Regi Elbogen in *Historia Judaica*, VIII, 1 April 1946), reveals a very large number and amazing variety of publications of which a representative selection, including all the larger studies and books, has been used for this tribute. We regret that a description of Elbogen's important extra-scholarly activities, for example in and for the Grossloge UOBB and the Centralverein deutscher Staatsbürger jüdischen Glaubens, would have gone beyond the limits set by this essay.

Jewish themes

To do full justice to Ismar Elbogen's personality and life's work is not possible within the confines of an essay. But it is hoped to convey at least an impression of both by concentrating on Elbogen as a representative, dominating figure of WdJ. He was not only one of its most successful and creative practitioners, he was also a most penetrating interpreter of its aims and objects, its zealous advocate and fearless defender. For him WdJ was the only effective means to preserve and continue Judaism, as he wrote in his study on the *Hochschule*[1] on the occasion of the consecration of its own home in 1907. He was representative of the spirit that animated its founders who intended the teaching of WdJ to be free from religious and political bias. Ruefully he remarked that the *Hochschule*, which neither belonged to nor served any party[2], had all parties as its enemies.

We might legitimately ask why Elbogen identified himself so completely with the *Hochschule* in a lifelong fight for its continued existence and development as a strictly academic institution. The answer provides us not only with the key to the real motive force of his life and work but also explains the philosophy underlying WdJ and guiding its practitioners in Elbogen's time. Elbogen passionately believed in Reason and its healing power. He believed not only in Reason, but also in reasonableness, the reasonableness of Man, and the triumph of humanity, of the community of rational, humane human beings over unreason, irrational prejudice and inhumanity. His optimism remained undaunted to his last breath, as two of his most important contributions movingly testify: for the significance of Elbogen's faith becomes apparent if we remember that the first of these two books, his *Geschichte der Juden in Deutschland*, was published under the Nazis in 1935 by the "Jüdische Buchvereinigung" in Berlin, and the second, *A Century of Jewish Life*, in 1944 in the U.S.A. He had revised the Epilogue to this book at which he had worked the last five years of his life a month before his death in 1943 — as the late Alexander Marx tells us in a fine introductory *Appreciation*.

But to say that Elbogen believed in the power of Reason does not, of course, mean that Reason was his God. No, Elbogen believed in Reason, in rational inquiry in the same way as our great medieval thinkers, foremost among them Maimonides, had believed, namely, on the firm foundation of their faith in God, the God of Revelation, the God of History. Elbogen believed in the permanence of Judaism because he had unbounded faith in the God of Judaism. The triumph of Reason was the triumph of God. Here lies the unity of Elbogen's life and work; his guiding idea was his confident faith and hope in the ultimate vindication of

---

[1] Cf. Die Hochschule, ihre Entstehung und Entwicklung (Festschrift zur Einweihung des eigenen Heims), I. Elbogen und J. Höniger, 1907.
[2] *Ibid.* p. 13 a.o.: ... 'eine einheitliche feste Anschauung wurde ihnen nicht mitgegeben ... Die Lehrvorträge boten Gelegenheit ... und zugleich die Ausrüstung, die Begründung der Lehrmeinungen zu prüfen, zwischen ihnen zu wählen.'

Judaism as a witness to God. Hence his single-minded devotion to the service of WdJ as the way to the renewal of Judaism, to its conscious realisation in the lives of the Jews. Hence his repeated appeals to his generation to support *die Wissenschaft,* for "on the cultivation of its *Wissenschaft* rested the continued existence of Judaism".[3] WdJ had to be practised as a strictly academic discipline — subject to the then prevailing canons of literary and historical criticism — based on a thorough knowledge of the sources in their original languages. But this did by no means confine it to a mere theoretical exercise, the pastime of intellectuals. Elbogen insisted on the close connection of *Wissenschaft und Leben.* We can justifiably apply to WdJ the principle of the *Sitz im Leben* that has guided the scientific study of the Hebrew Bible from the days of Gunkel and his investigation of the Psalms. This means that literature can only be understood from its origin in the soul and mind of a people and from a given historical situation of that people. It is the task of WdJ to examine the teachings of Judaism and their place in the life of the Jewish people throughout their chequered history, with the tools of philological and historical criticism.

Elbogen was naturally aware of the origins of WdJ in the 19th century with its struggle for emancipation. He never lost sight of its practical implications and purpose. Its method, too, was that of the 19th century: philological-historical criticism. He sees its connection with the general trend of German scholarship and courageously criticises its early endeavours in the spirit of Wilhelm v. Humboldt.[4]

Characteristically, two 19th-century German thinkers, W. v. Humboldt and Schleiermacher, have deeply impressed themselves on the mind of the Jew Elbogen. There can be little doubt that it was Elbogen's practical mind and his insight into the dynamism of Jewish history and the continuity of Judaism through the ages which tempered his 19th-century idealism. Yet, it is significant that it was these two commanding minds of a past age in German philosophy and *Wissenschaft* which have fashioned Elbogen's essentially historical outlook and metaphysical presuppositions,

---

[3]*Ibid.,* p. 3: 'Dafür war in unserer Glaubensgemeinschaft damals die rechte Einsicht noch nicht erschlossen. Erst neuerdings, seitdem der Kampf gegen die Existenz des Judentums mehr mit den Waffen der Wissenschaft geführt wird, beginnt die Erkenntnis sich Bahn zu brechen, dass der geistige Gehalt des Judentums, dass sein Schrifttum erhöhter Pflege und nachdrücklicher Förderung bedürfen, dass die Glaubensgemeinschaft leidet, wenn die Glaubenslehre verkümmert'.

[4]Cf. zum Jubiläum der "Gesellschaft zur Förderung der Wissenschaft des Judentums" in MGWJ 72, 1928, pp. 1-5. Some of his critical remarks are worth noting: ‚Sie [die wissenschaftliche Erforschung des Judentums] hatte ihre grosse Zeit, blieb aber nicht auf der Höhe, sie hatte Neuland zu bearbeiten, und, beglückt durch die Entdeckerfreude, häuften die Gelehrten Fund auf Fund, ohne den Ertrag recht zu verarbeiten. Baustein kam zum Baustein, aber nie sah man ein Gebäude, selten ein harmonisch abgetöntes Mosaik. Einzelheit stand neben Einzelheit, selten gab es eine Zusammenfassung... der Überblick über das Ganze fehlte, der Geist, der hinter den Tatsachen liegt, ward nicht erkannt...' (p. 3).

whereas his friend and colleague Leo Baeck owed so much of his own outlook as a creative thinker to Dilthey of the 20th century.

It is, therefore, worthwhile to examine Elbogen's attitude to the past and contemporary WdJ a little more closely. Again and again he returns to the important role WdJ must play in the life of contemporary Jewry, especially German Jewry. His words read like variations on a theme, pronounced in lectures or written in papers on special occasions, mostly anniversaries of Jewish scholars like Zunz, Geiger, Graetz and others, or of Jewish institutions like the *Hochschule,* the *Gesellschaft zur Förderung der Wissenschaft des Judentums* and the *Akademie für die Wissenschaft des Judentums.* These were anything but occasional statements in form of generalities and platitudes, of uncritical eulogies, of oratorical fireworks so popular with audiences on festive occasions. Elbogen treated his audiences as responsible adults whom he wanted to instruct and win over for active support for WdJ which was cultivated by these three institutions devoted to teaching and research. In this connection I should like to borrow an apt characterisation that Kurt Wilhelm made in a letter to me: Elbogen was the "*Shtadlan* of German Judaism". To avoid possible misunderstanding I must define this term *Shtadlan* in relation to Ismar Elbogen.

He was not the spokesman and representative, self-appointed or chosen by general consent, of the Jews of a region or land before the rulers of the day, like Joselmann of Rosheim. *Shtadlan* applies to the scholarly and communal activities of a man who was deeply conscious of the responsibility of a Jewish scholar at the time of grave danger to Judaism from within and without and who was always ready to advise on any problem of private or public Jewish concern. He took a leading part in the defence of Judaism and the Jews as the foremost representative of WdJ.

In *Ein Jahrhundert Wissenschaft des Judentums*[5], he discusses earlier unsatisfactory attempts at defining WdJ. To him, its justification is solely in its striving to further our understanding of a *living* Judaism and its development on a historical basis. Commenting on an encounter between the founder of WdJ, Leopold Zunz, and the greatest Jewish historian, Heinrich Graetz[6], Elbogen characterises Graetz as "a feeling Jew for whom Judaism at all times and in all lands formed a unity, as a member of this living organism", who was not merely an "erudite investigator digging up dead bones". Elbogen thinks that herein lies the essence of WdJ as "the science of a living Judaism in the stream of development as a sociological and historical unity". It is "therefore a

---

[5]In: Festschrift zum 50jährigen Bestehen der Hochschule für die Wissenschaft des Judentums in Berlin, 1922, pp. 138 ff.

[6]*Ibid.*, p. 141: when Graetz was introduced to Zunz as the author of a Jewish History, Zunz remarked: „Wieder eine jüdische Geschichte?" whereupon Graetz replied: „Allerdings, aber dieses Mal eine jüdische".

science with a purpose, it has to solve a practical task... Its aim is and remains a living Judaism, this must form the focus towards which all rays are aiming..."[7] In all his endeavours Elbogen was guided by this concept of a living Judaism which could only be understood through the cultivation of WdJ; it gives unity of design and outlook to his writings with whatever aspect they deal. This disciple of Graetz went beyond the master whom he admired and revered. Salo Baron rightly pointed out that Graetz was a romantic like his model Ranke; he took no notice of economic history, he is subjective in his treatment of the sources.[8] Elbogen stresses the sociological approach and in his own historical writings evaluates the totality of available sources in all its facets, economic, social, cultural, religious and national.

Concerned as he was with the aim and practical implications of WdJ, he nevertheless attempted a definition in yet another of his studies, *Neuorientierung unserer Wissenschaft*.[9] This was a lecture addressed to a wider audience on the occasion of the centenary of Zunz's first public appearance on behalf of WdJ, "its hour of birth". Zunz describes in his *Zeitschrift für die Wissenschaft des Judentums* the essence of this new science to which he had then given its name. Significantly, Elbogen states that he would prefer to call it "Jewish theology" in the sense of Schleiermacher's definition as a "positive science in respect of a definite conceptual formation of the consciousness of God [in man]".[10] Elbogen continues: "in our sense theology is a science on a philological-historical foundation with a strictly scientific method"... "The frontiers of theology are nowhere drawn very narrowly, and in face of the intimate connection between the religious and the national in Judaism they will always remain open even more widely." He thought WdJ would possess a better method as a theological discipline, "it would gain a centre towards which the entire research activity gravitated and from which it would be systematically applied over its entire realm".[11]

If we were to classify Elbogen we should call him rather a theologian than a historian. His abiding interest belonged to Judaism and its literature which he interpreted on a philological-historical basis. Yet, his interests were so wide and so catholic that the man defies neat classification. His love and his labours belonged to this *Wissenschaft* which was as

---

[7]*Ibid.*, 'sie ist demnach eine Zweckwissenschaft'. [Es handelt sich um die] 'Lösung einer praktischen Aufgabe'. 'Ihr Ziel ist und bleibt das lebendige Judentum, dieses muss den Brennpunkt bilden, nach dem alle Strahlen hinzielen...'
[8]S. W. Baron, Graetzens Geschichtsschreibung in: MGWJ 62, 1918, pp. 5-15.
[9]In: MGWJ 62, 1918.
[10]In the original German: "eine positive Wissenschaft in Bezug auf eine bestimmte Gestaltung des Gottesbewusstseins" (*ibid.*, p. 90).
[11]*Ibid.*: 'die Wissenschaft würde einen Mittelpunkt erhalten, um den sich die gesamte Forschertätigkeit gruppierte, von dem aus sie systematisch in dem ganzen Gebiete betrieben würde'. Further, in *Die Hochschule*, p. 20: 'dieses Wissen [vom Judentum] muss ein Kennen und ein Erkennen sein, aus historischer Kenntnis und spekulativer Erkenntnis sich zusammensetzen'.

all-embracing as Judaism itself. Elbogen's concept was not only one of width and breadth, but also of depth. He was not satisfied with the philological and historical basis, necessary as that was, but demanded also a "philosophical part". This speculative part "has as its task the systematic presentation of the contents of Judaism".[12] He pleaded for "conceptual penetration of the investigated material", the absence of which he deplored. He never tires of admonishing his hearers and readers, both academic and lay, especially the leaders and the intellectual *élite* of the Berlin Jewish Community, to take WdJ seriously. "It is the task of *Wissenschaft* to work through the material, to formulate from it abstract concepts and formulae, and universally valid laws." Again, he refers to W. v. Humboldt for support when he complains that there is too much attention to detail, too much collecting of material and too little systematic thinking which alone "would bring back to us the great points of view".[13] In his direct, homely, often pithy style Elbogen managed to drive home his point, to invest his informed, positive criticism of what was wrong or lacking in the WdJ of his day with that relevance and urgency which was needed to rouse a largely smug and indifferent generation. In this activity he had allies in his colleagues and friends, such powerful minds as Leo Baeck, Eugen Mittwoch, Julius Guttmann, Eugen Täubler and Tur-Sinai (Torczyner). The twin institutions of the *Gesellschaft zur Förderung der WdJ* and of the *Akademie für die WdJ* owed practically everything to these outstanding scholars. The *Gesellschaft* published not only the *MGWJ*[14] but also a series of basic works under the title of *Grundriss der Gesamtwissenschaft des Judentums*. The *Akademie* was primarily a research institute under the direction of Eugen Täubler. Elbogen published in 1928 an important essay on the occasion of the jubilee of the *Gesellschaft*[15], in which he described the hopes for WdJ and a living contemporary Judaism as the result of this new departure. For the *Gesellschaft,* as later the *Akademie,* was founded to give a new direction to Jewish learning commensurate with the position of German Judaism and Jewry, in the context of the humanities and their study in German universities, a point of capital importance which is stressed by all.

To understand the aims of Elbogen and his colleagues it is necessary to consider the general situation of Judaism in Germany during the first three decades of the present century. The legacy of Bismarck's German

---

[12]*Die Hochschule*, p. 21.
[13]*Neuorientierung*..., p. 92: 'Wissenschaft kann nicht gesammelt, sondern nur geistig erarbeitet werden'.
[14]Monatsschrift für die Geschichte und Wissenschaft des Judentums.
[15]Cf. n. 4, above. 'Ein neues Programm der *Gesellschaft:* das Schöpferische in der WdJ wieder anzuregen, den Stoff zusammenzufassen und mit Geist zu durchdringen... Sie rief zu neuer Arbeit auf, nach neuen Methoden, nach neuen Gesichtspunkten, nach Wiederherstellung des Zusammenhangs mit dem Leben, des Zusammenhangs mit den Geisteswissenschaften...'

Empire confronted German Judaism and Jewry with a new phenomenon. The opposition to Jews in political and in economic life which — oversimplified — can be summed up in the one word *Radau-Antisemitismus* now took on a new, much more dangerous, because subtler, form and appearance. Antisemitism became the preoccupation of some of Germany's foremost intellectuals who were no longer satisfied with attacking Jews for this or that alleged misdemeanour, but carried their attack right into the essence of Judaism and its basic teachings. It was the Jews' continued adherence to Judaism which blocked their complete identification with Germany and their unqualified acceptance as equal citizens, so they averred. This "scientific" antisemitism, represented by Heinrich von Treitschke and a number of lesser lights, had to be met with scholarly weapons. Elbogen and others, like Benno Jacob[16], sprang willingly to the defence of the honour of Judaism through the *Centralverein*, and WdJ received a certain apologetic colouring. That this was inevitable does not make it any less regrettable. Elbogen's innate dignity and nobility of mind never deserted him when he took up the cudgels on behalf of Judaism and his fellow-Jews. But it sometimes deflected him from more strictly academic tasks for which he was so superbly fitted. No minority can keep apologetics out. One of the fruits of this defence was a work in several volumes, *Die Lehren des Judentums,* published by the *Verband der deutschen Juden* in the hope "to remove prejudice and to bring about a just appreciation of Judaism in a wider circle".[17] The work consists of extracts from the basic sources with short introductions, several of which Professor Elbogen contributed. He stressed the important contributions that practitioners of WdJ had made, first in the struggle for emancipation and later in the defence of Jewish right, honour and liberty.[18] This was an integral part of that *Sitz im Leben* of true learning, on which he insisted. It counteracted the danger to which every researcher is exposed: that of losing himself in his studies and forgetting that the sources stem from living authors grappling with real problems of mind and body. Nevertheless, the higher purpose of every *Wissenschaft* must never be forgotten. Love of Judaism, the honest conviction of its eternal cultural values and of its relevance here and now, must inspire the scholars. Graetz, Elbogen said, was so successful "because he has always been truthful [and genuine], animated by the

---

[16]Cf. Kurt Wilhelm's fine study in Year Book VII, 1962: *Benno Jacob, a Militant Rabbi*, pp. 75-94.
[17]From the preface of Dr. S. Bernfeld, the editor, p. 9. (Die Lehren des Judentums. Erster Teil: Die Grundlagen der jüdischen Ethik, Berlin 1920).
[18]Why was sufficient support for the *Hochschule* not forthcoming? Elbogen answers: 'Der Kampf gegen die wüsten Ausschreitungen des Judenhasses, die Sorge um die Selbsterhaltung nahm alle Kräfte in Anspruch und drängte das Interesse für das geistige Erbe der Väter in den Hintergrund. Eine solche Anschauung wäre freilich eine arge Verblendung gewesen! Die Pflege der Wissenschaft hat sich mehr als einmal als Kampfmittel für das Recht und die Ehre der Juden bewährt, mehr als einer unter

confidence of a genius and the loyalty of a man of sterling character, and because he has never cast furtive glances to left or right".[19]

Yet WdJ is there to serve every Jewish generation in its particular situation. Hence the paramount importance — for Elbogen — of popular presentation. He says: "the power must not be underrated which was needed in order to change the gold of scholarly labour into small coin".[20] His contribution to the *Festschrift* on the occasion of the fiftieth anniversary of the *Hochschule* in 1922 (from which this quotation is taken) is of great importance on several other counts as well. Thus, whenever Elbogen speaks or writes about WdJ, he quotes Zunz as chief witness to the relevance of *Wissenschaft* for the respected position of the Jew as a full and equal citizen.[21] Elbogen characterized WdJ with real insight, identifying himself with its lofty aim, but freely admitting how far it had failed to attain its design. Zunz's dream was not fulfilled, WdJ remained a *Fachwissenschaft* of the few. Yet, "its foundation was a providential deed for modern Judaism; it has proved itself as a cultural factor of the first rank. We owe to its labours the thorough improvement of Jewish education, the transformation of the Jewish view of life *(Lebensanschauung)*, religious renewal and last but not least the enlightenment of public opinion concerning Jewish ways and Jewish fate".[22] He deplores the absence of an independent Jewish point of view *vis-à-vis* the criticism of text and canon of the Hebrew Bible, which is growing in severity.[23] He is dissatisfied with the present state of affairs: we do not yet possess a real history of Hebrew and Jewish literature, in which field he laboured so successfully. We lack a systematic evaluation of any branch of Jewish learning, an often recurring theme with him. This he attributes to the inability of achieving the integration of Talmudic learning (which he possessed in no small measure) with modern *Wissenschaft*; they have remained two separate disciplines. He castigates as "a false romantic doctrine" *(romantische Irrlehre)* the view "that exclusively that kind of erudition [*Talmud Torah*] can claim a genuinely Jewish

---

den Männern, die am Tempel der jüdischen Wissenschaft bauten, hat für Recht und Freiheit seiner Glaubensbrüder eine Lanze gebrochen, hat Verunglimpfungen des Judentums mit den Waffen der Wissenschaft nachdrücklich und wirkungsvoll zurückgewiesen.' Nevertheless, it was a fact 'dass bei aller Liebe zum Judentum seine Wissenschaft ziemlich leer ausging, dass von all den reichen Gaben für jüdische Zwecke nur seltene und kärgliche Brosamen auf ihren Tisch fielen'. (From *Die Hochschule* ..., pp. 68 f.).

[19]*Ein Jahrhundert Wissenschaft des Judentums*, p. 113.
[20]*Ibid.*, p. 114.
[21]*Ibid.*, p. 107. Zunz said: "Die Gleichstellung der Juden in Sitte und Leben wird aus der Gleichstellung der Wissenschaft des Judentums hervorgehen". Elbogen pleads for a revival of Hebrew in the interests of the development of WdJ and of the resonance needed to maintain contact with living Judaism. No less necessary is the cultivation of European languages: to retain the link with the *allgemeine Wissenschaft*.
[22]*Ibid.*
[23]*Ibid.*, p. 117.

character, but that WdJ [allegedly] represents a false way. A compromise under the slogan *Torah und Wissenschaft* would damage both sides". For he sees no solution in setting up an extraneous *Wissenschaft* in addition to the traditional study of the *Torah*. Rather the traditional *Lernen* "must be imbued with the spirit of critical *Wissenschaft*".[24] Underlying this sharp separation of the new from the old Jewish learning is Elbogen's respect for Reason and his realisation that Judaism cannot survive and flourish without our intellectual affirmation. Here lies the rub, and here is, to my mind, the origin of the problematical position in which many of us find ourselves today: we are hard put to buttress our emotional attachment to Jewish traditional belief and practice with an unequivocal intellectual affirmation of faith and observance. Very few Jews today would deny the cultural values of Judaism which for well over a century WdJ has been actively engaged in presenting to generation after generation of "modern" Jews whose unquestioning faith has steadily decreased and often ceased to exist. Everybody who has known Ismar Elbogen is convinced that he passionately believed in the regenerative power of the critical approach to the sources of Judaism; and that nothing was further from his mind and his intention than to undermine that faith in which he himself was so securely rooted. Elbogen's religiosity, his deep faith and devotion to historical Judaism are mirrored on every page of his writings. But the problem is there for us, though it was not there for him. Religionless Judaism would have been unthinkable for the representative modern Jewish scholar who had received a thorough traditional education from a learned father; it is an undeniable fact with us and not to be ignored.

One of Elbogen's insistent demands was that WdJ must be part of "general science" *(allgemeine Wissenschaft)*. Actually this had already been voiced by Zunz and first attempted by him. Zunz, says Elbogen, "has the merit of having made the critical investigation of Judaism a branch of general research within the totality of the *Wissenschaften*. He has freed it from its onesidedness and dogmatism". With all this Elbogen could appreciate the value of traditional *Talmud Torah* and respect the erudition of its devotees. But it lacked two indispensable elements: system and criticism. This counts for more than mere erudition. Elbogen puts it in one of the happy, incisive turns of phrase so typical

---

[24]*Ibid.*, p. 104. Elbogen continues: 'Die Verbindung zwischen jüdischer Gelehrsamkeit und Wissenschaft kann nur dann gedeihlich wirken, wenn sie legitim, nicht wenn sie morganatisch ist. Die Wissenschaft hat es lediglich mit Erkenntnis zu tun und nicht nach den Folgen der Erkenntnis fürs Leben zu fragen. Orthodoxie und Wissenschaft schliessen einander aus, wenn auch von orthodoxer Seite bisweilen wertvolle Einzelbeiträge zur Wissenschaft geleistet worden sind'. He actually stresses the fact that the Hildesheimersche Rabbiner-Seminar had, at an early stage, defined its position with respect to the impetuous criticism of the Pentateuch (131f.). He apparently refers to David Hoffmann. To my mind a legitimate marriage between orthodoxy and Wissenschaft took place – and was possible only – in the Middle Ages. We need only think of Maimonides.

of him: "true *Wissenschaft*... sharpens the judgement that one can be tremendously erudite and yet no scholar". For, "the aim of all *Wissenschaft* — the perception and presentation of reality — can only be attained through critical research... we must not accept any result out of mere loyal faith without testing its origin, without examining the reliability of its tradition..."[25]

On this principle of free inquiry and rigorous, critical testing of tradition, teaching and research had to be based in order to press the claim of WdJ and to achieve its dream: to be recognized as an equal among the academic disciplines as taught at the German universities. To this end *Hochschule, Gesellschaft* and *Akademie* were founded, maintained and developed. It is Elbogen who has repeatedly and persistently given the clearest and most forceful expression to this vital objective. He was no less outspoken in his condemnation of the lack of interest and, consequently, of material support on the part of the Jewish community.[26] The growth of the *Hochschule* was stunted; its hand-to-mouth existence hampered the expansion of its teaching staff. Thanks to the selfless efforts of the small band of professors it achieved much more than could reasonably be expected; it broadened its curriculum, thereby increasing the burden for its staff both in teaching and administration. Though administration was a duty all had to perform, Elbogen carried the heaviest burden. In fact, he *was* the *Hochschule,* its embodiment. Naturally, he could not have shouldered this burden without the loyal support and active participation of his colleagues.

He had joined the *Hochschule* in 1902, charged with teaching the "History and Literature of the Jews and of Judaism". In 1906 he was appointed to two chairs simultaneously, adding to his subject "Ethics and Religious Philosophy of Judaism", no mean task, especially for a man like Elbogen who in teaching, research and writing insisted on a thorough knowledge and understanding of the original sources. It is a sign of the important position he held within the *Hochschule* that he was asked to write the story of its first quarter of a century. This became the *Festschrift* of 1907, mentioned above. A few programmatic statements from it throw light on the man no less than the scholar: "The existence of Judaism is linked with its *Wissenschaft;* it alone guarantees the untarnished preservation of its basic ideas, the continuous purification of its forms, the living progression of its spirit... The care for *Wissen-*

---

[25]Neuorientierung unserer Wissenschaft in *MGWJ* 62, 1918, p. 83: '...wahre Wissenschaft versagt keinem Verdienst die Anerkennung, aber sie schärft... das Urteil dafür, dass einer unheimlich gelehrt und doch kein Gelehrter sein kann. Daher vermag sie jener Gelehrsamkeit bei allem Reichtum des Inhalts nicht den Charakter der Wissenschaft zuzusprechen, es fehlen ihr die Elemente, welche das Wissen zur Wissenschaft erheben, Systematik und Kritik'.

[26]With the notable exception of the Berlin Community, from 1892 onwards, cf. *Die Hochschule...*, p. 69.

schaft belongs to the noblest and most significant tasks of our religious community. The future of Judaism is the future of its *Wissenschaft*, the continued existence of Judaism is bound up with the investigation of its literature and the cultivation of its spiritual life. The *Wissenschaft* is a source of renewal of ethics, of the revival of the religious spirit, it is a means to unite opposing religious views[27]... WdJ needs incessant, untiring, loving care if it is to give to the religious community that for which it is called [into being and asked to do], if it is to furnish the weapons for the fight for our right and our honour also in future. [It needs support] if it is, in the face of indifference and desertion, to highlight the cultural values which we possess and defend as Jews."[28]

In this struggle Elbogen and his colleagues encountered strong opposition from the traditionalists of the old school of *Talmud Torah*, as was to be expected. It is needless to emphasize that the other side was as keen on "right and freedom", on civic equality, on the defence of Jewish honour and on being considered as loyal "German citizens of the Jewish faith". But they were apprehensive lest the new Jewish learning should lead to a weakening of Jewish loyalty in the sense of strict observance of the traditional way of life; and this not without justification. True, Ismar Elbogen as the representative figure of the critical approach was personally no less attached to tradition, and in his own life practised traditional Judaism just as much as did the conservative element in German Jewry. But the religious crisis was and is a universal world phenomenon, though it affected and affects Torah-Judaism differently from, say, Christianity.

The problem is ever present; the burning issue of the validity of tradition in theory no less than in practice is at the back of WdJ as the legitimate expression of the "modern" age in Judaism. It was given to Elbogen to state the problem and the case for a living Judaism in our time with his customary clarity: "The singularity of our *Wissenschaft* only lies in its material, not in the method or way of thinking of the scholars. He only can practise WdJ with success who is permeated with (i.e. convinced of) the basic direction and method of general *Wissenschaft*. This will certainly not be without consequences for the religious viewpoint... How the individual religious community faces this is not a problem of *Wissenschaft* but a question of its vitality. The religious community rests on too firm a basis to be uprooted through a new scientific discovery or hypothesis. We may have confidence in Judaism

---

[27]*Ibid.*, p. 96, where Elbogen quotes Geiger: "Es gibt kein anderes Mittel, die Alten und die Neuen im Judentume innerlich zu verbinden, als welches in den *geistigen Gütern* des Judentums selbst gelegen ist".
[28]*Ibid.*, p. 97, and *Neuorientierung*..., p. 89: 'Das lebendige Judentum will erforscht, in seinem Bestande und seiner Struktur, seinen Lehren und Bestrebungen, seinen Entwicklungstendenzen und -möglichkeiten ergründet und bestimmt werden. Die WdJ bedarf daher neben dem historischen auch eines philosophischen Teils'.

that it will also in future find the right way to safeguard its continued existence as it had had the strength to maintain itself for three thousand years of history in the face of all changing spiritual movements."[29]

From the days of Zunz his demand that WdJ should be represented by a Chair at one or more German universities was raised again and again until it crystallized in the demand for the establishment of a Jewish theological Faculty. What was really at stake was official recognition of WdJ as a partner in Higher Education, be it in the shape of a whole Faculty or a single Chair. Success seemed near, non-Jewish support for the establishment of a Chair for *Jüdische Wissenschaft* was at last freely given, and only the outbreak of the First World War prevented the Ministry of Education *(Kultusministerium)* from acceding to such a request — signed by sixty leading German theologians and philologists, among them Theodor Nöldecke and Julius Wellhausen — and thus "to remove an old injustice".[30]

It was not until some years after the establishment of the Weimar Republic that Jewish-Christian co-operation — initiated by Hugo Gressmann of the *Institutum Judaicum* of Berlin University — was established in the academic field. This co-operation took the form of a series of lectures by Jewish scholars during the academical year 1925—1926, which were published in 1927.[31]

In his Introduction Gressmann stressed the strictly and exclusively scholarly character of the Institute and claimed that it filled a long-felt gap in the University. He went out of his way to concede the same right to Judaism which the Church claims in demanding Protestant and Catholic theological Faculties: It is wrong to exclude Judaism from the *universitas literarum*. To remedy this untenable position he issued an invitation to the professors of the *Hochschule* to help him to present objectively the true image of Judaism just at a time when antisemitism was strong. He rightly avers that "true objectivity always presupposes love, and for this reason the Jewish scholar is always at an advantage vis-à-vis the Jewish religion". Moreover, these guest lectures are intended "as a recognition of *jüdische Wissenschaft*".[32] The lecturers were Elbogen, Juda Bergmann, Michael and Julius Guttmann, and Leo Baeck. Elbogen gave the first lecture on "Ezra and Post-exilic Judaism" and after expressing thanks to Hugo Gressmann, he commented on the difficulties facing the lecturers because the subject "concerns the most intimate and private [side] of man, the religious". He defines the object of these lectures as giving a cross-section *(Querschnitt)* of

---

[29]*Neuorientierung...*, p. 84.
[30]*A Century of Jewish Life*, p. 417.
[31]Under the title: *Entwicklungsstufen der jüdischen Religion*, Giessen 1927.
[32]Hugo Gressmann, *Einführung*: "...die einzige Mission, die es [das *Institutum Judaicum*] treibt, ist die der Wissenschaft" (p. 1); cf. also pp. 2 ff.

religious life, a glimpse into Jewish *piety (Frömmigkeit)* of different times.³³

This excursion into the *universitas literarum* on an equal footing was, alas, transitory, since only a few years separated this breakthrough from the confinement of WdJ within the segregated Jewish community, followed by its extinction, in Hitler's Germany. But it was a symbol, however fleeting, of a long cherished dream come true: the recognition of Judaism as a relevant factor in general culture. To Elbogen it may have seemed like a milestone on the road first trodden by Moses Mendelssohn who, as Elbogen said in a speech at a celebration in Dessau in honour of the bicentenary of Mendelssohn's birth, "re-established the connection of Judaism with general culture".³⁴

A year earlier, Elbogen had sketched the character and task of the *Gesellschaft zur Förderung der Wissenschaft des Judentums* as "the exponent of a new time".³⁵ The *Gesellschaft* was founded in 1903 to pave the way for a systematic presentation of the results of individual research in comprehensive works. "It appealed for a fresh approach, it called for new methods, new points of view, to reforge the link with life, with the humanities *(Geisteswissenschaften)*... It sought contact with the public at large in order to force the scholars to express themselves in the language of general culture *(Bildung)*." What was needed was a link-up with the general ideas of the time, a confrontation of Judaism — critically understood — with current concepts and ideas. Jewish and general education were not opposites, but complementary. "It is no accident that the first book published by the *Gesellschaft* was Leo Baeck's *Essence of Judaism*, that the first article of the *Monatsschrift* was Hermann Cohen's lecture on "The establishment of Chairs for Ethics and Religious Philosophy at the Jewish-Theological Seminaries". Those were programmatic manifestations, signals on the new way... Likewise, the *Grundriss der Gesamtwissenschaft des Judentums* was to achieve that great systematization. For it was the general demand of the times to summarize the results of research in systematic monographs so that research could become the common possession of all educated people *(aller Gebildeten)*..."³⁶ The *Gesellschaft* hoped to arouse interest among the educated

---

³³*Ibid.*, p. 13.
³⁴In *Zeitschrift für die Geschichte der Juden in Deutschland*, 1, 1929, p. 187: 'Er wollte nur in seinen Büchern forschen und wurde ein Umgestalter und Schöpfer, er wollte nur ein Wahrheitssucher sein und wurde Lehrer und Wegbereiter... Diesen Weg zur Philosophie hatte ein Jahrhundert vorher Spinoza beschritten, aber ausserhalb des Judentums vollendet, während Moses Mendelssohn im Judentum verblieb, das Judentum treu liebte, die Verbindung des Judentums mit der allgemeinen Kultur wiederherstellte, es für neue Gedanken, für neue Anregungen empfänglich machte und den Weg für die gesamte neuere geistige Entwicklung des Judentums bahnte'. Cf. also Elbogen's *Geschichte der Juden in Deutschland*, s.v. Mendelssohn.
³⁵Cf. n. 15, above.
³⁶*Ibid.*, p. 4.

German Jews, especially through the "Grundriss" and to promote understanding for WdJ and for Judaism.

But it could not produce the scholars needed for this gigantic undertaking, particularly not those who possessed not only the necessary specialized knowledge of the various branches of Jewish literature and history but also perception and insight in order to write definitive, comprehensive studies of mature scholarship in readable form. With this object in mind, the *Akademie* was founded in close co-operation with the *Gesellschaft*. This co-operation was secured not least through the personal union between the *Präsidium* of the *Gesellschaft* and the directors of the various sections of the research institute of the *Akademie*. One of the common ventures of both institutions was the monumental edition of the works of Moses Mendelssohn with Elbogen, Guttmann and Mittwoch as editors, each responsible for a group of the writings. Reading Guttmann's annual reports on the work of the *Akademie*, published in the *Korrespondenzblatt*, one is struck by the unfortunate hand-to-mouth existence of what should have been the pride of German Jewry. One would have thought that it was but commonsense and sheer self-preservation to enable our foremost Jewish scholars to train sufficient collaborators for the task in hand. But financial stringency made this impossible. This is the more surprising since Julius Guttmann made it clear[37] that it was German Jewry which demanded the *Akademie*. No professional sponsorship brought the *Akademie* into being, specialists in WdJ were only invited after the foundation, which was the result of the efforts by Franz Rosenzweig and Hermann Cohen. In his characteristic manner Elbogen, commenting favourably on Rosenzweig's *Zeit ist's*, exclaimed that we needed academicians before we could set up an academy! Eugen Täubler, the first scientific *(wissenschaftliche)* director of the *Akademie,* created the research institute which was to become the real performer of its work.[38] This institute means something entirely new for WdJ. "The scholarly *(wissenschaftlichen)* institutions which it possessed so far, served teaching *(Lehre)*, not research *(Forschung)*... The *Forschungsinstitut's* principal job is to win new forces and to develop new forms of research, it wants new men to serve a central *wissenschaftliche* idea in an intimate working fellowship, complete in itself."

These words of Julius Guttmann show the essential unity of outlook and aim that bound him to Elbogen as well as to their colleagues. They

---

[37]In his contribution *Die Akademie für die WdJ zu ihrem zehnjährigen Bestehen* to the "Festgabe zum zehnjährigen Bestehen", Berlin 1929. See Fritz Bamberger, Julius Guttmann, in LBI Year Book V (1960), pp. 14/15. Cf. also Ernst Simon, *Franz Rosenzweig und das jüdische Bildungsproblem* in: "Korrespondenzblatt der Akademie...", 1930, pp. 1-13, and Gershom Scholem, *Wissenschaft vom Judentum Einst und Jetzt* in: Bulletin of the LBI, No. 9, 1960, pp. 10-20, especially pp. 18 ff.

[38]Cf. Eugen Täubler, *Das Forschungsinstitut für die WdJ. Organisation und Arbeitsplan* in "Korrespondenzblatt...", 1, 1920. See Selma Stern-Täubler, Eugen Täubler and the WdJ, in LBI Year Book III (1958), pp. 50 ff.

collaborated wholeheartedly in the three principal institutions of WdJ and with single-minded devotion, against considerable odds of financial stringency, Jewish indifference and defection, and antisemitic attack. That they have achieved so much in spite of all obstacles is in no small measure due to their vision and determination, and to Elbogen's indefatigable drive and enthusiasm in particular. Impeccable scholarship was to help their generation to regain their Jewish self-respect, and to win the respect of the outside world, undermined by antisemitism.

From its inception in 1919 Elbogen was closely associated with the *Akademie*, its organisation, direction and research. He was in charge of the *Literarhistorische Sektion* (section for literary history) whose principal objective was the preparation and publication of a *Corpus scriptorum grammaticorum et exegetarum*. It is a sad reflection on the situation prevailing in Jewish scholarship that such a collection – in critical editions – of our Jewish grammarians and Biblical exegetes has not yet materialized, although it is one of the basic requirements of modern research.

Elbogen contributed to the *Festgabe* on the occasion of the tenth anniversary of the foundation of the *Akademie* the important article on the history of Jewish literature.[39] He remarks that Zunz was the first to see and speak of the entire Jewish literature in any and every language as an organic whole. But for Zunz this literature was completed, it was something of the past. "Zunz approached Jewish literature with the intention of issuing its death certificate, but under the touch of his reviving hand it woke up to a new life, recuperated and set out on a sturdy growth." In the wake of Zunz and Karpeles, data were collected, but "it [the history of Jewish literature] only rarely advanced to the comprehension of the creative power [of that literature]. Strictly literary-historical points of view, the investigation of literary forms and genres as well as of the influence of personality in literature have come off badly. It has laid the foundations and erected the outer walls but has hardly touched the work in the interior".[40] Jewish literary history "must proceed from the material to the hand which has written it down, but then to the head which has thought it out, or to the heart which has felt it!"[41]

The history of Jewish literature was Elbogen's special field to which he made his principal original contribution. But the preceding pages have shown, I hope, that to decide what the main contribution of Ismar Elbogen to WdJ was, would be a difficult choice. Was he a historian *à la* Graetz, or a literary historian in the wake of Zunz, with special emphasis on the liturgy, or the consummate popularizer, the changer of the gold of original

[39]*Zum Problem der jüdischen Literaturgeschichte.*
[40]*Ibid.*, p. 72.
[41]*Ibid.*, p. 75.

research, to which he himself contributed so much, into small coin for the educated Jewish and non-Jewish lay public? Indeed he was all these together. His warm personality had many facets, all bound together by a catholic interest in Judaism as a whole, on the basis of integrity of character belonging to a Jew whose love of God and of his fellow-men was the very essence of his being. It is for this reason that I said earlier that to think of Elbogen as a theologian would perhaps be more in keeping with his rare personality and his massive achievement. He defies definition and neat labels. The driving force of his many activities was his deep religious faith, and in all his scholarly work he applied the historical method on the basis of linguistic analysis of the original sources, complemented by a metaphysical-theoretical superstructure (which he acquired when he prepared and wrote his doctoral dissertation at the University of Breslau on the *Tractatus de intellectus emendatione of Spinoza*, 1898). In short, he practised precisely what he demanded of WdJ as the servant of a renewed, vigorous, modern Judaism.

This will be borne out by a brief survey of his scholarly achievement. He began his Jewish research in Breslau with a history of the *Amidah (Achtzehngebet)* which won him the prize offered by the Breslau Rabbiner-Seminar.[42] This work has already all the marks of Elbogen's mature scholarship: his attention to grammar and literary usage, his historical method which based sound conclusions lucidly on the established facts of a text critically examined, without wild conjectures and unsubstantiated brilliant guesses[42a]. He prefaces the thorough investigation of the *Amidah* with a programmatic statement about the right approach to the study of the liturgy, stresses the importance of the Talmud as 'the most important source for the history of the *Amidah*' and tells us that he leaned on the "learned studies" of Rapoport, Zunz, Landshut and S. Baer. (Elbogen always lectured on the Talmud, in addition to his official subjects). This first study led to his *Studien zur Geschichte des jüdischen Gottes-*

---

[42]*Geschichte des Achtzehngebetes* in: MGWJ, 1902 and, as a separate treatise, Breslau, 1903. In that modesty which he retained all his life, Elbogen ended the Introduction to his first major publication on the Liturgy thus: 'Sollte dennoch in dieser Abhandlung manche gute und neue Bemerkung gefunden werden, sollte mancher wichtige neue Gesichtspunkt hervortreten, so verdanke ich den Hinweis darauf in allererster Reihe meinem verehrungswürdigen Lehrer, Herrn Seminarrabbiner Dr. Lewy in Breslau, der nicht nur durch seine Vorlesungen und seine private Anregung, sondern besonders auch im Anschluss an die Lectüre dieser Arbeit mich ausserordentlich gefördert hat'. This was Israel Lewy who held the Chair for Talmud at the *Hochschule*, as the colleague of Steinthal, Cassel und Abraham Geiger, but moved later to Breslau. In 1934, Elbogen refused a *Festschrift* in his honour on the occasion of his sixtieth birthday. But his colleagues in the *Gesellschaft* insisted on dedicating the 4. Heft of the MGWJ to him.

[42a]It displays that modesty and caution which betray the true scholar. At the end he confesses that the terms of the award forced him to publish a study 'the results of which appeared to me, in the course of time, partly doubtful, just as its problems became ever more complicated, even almost insoluble the more I pondered over them and worked at them'.

dienstes[43], followed by a large number of individual articles on various aspects of the liturgy[44], and culminated in his authoritative *Der Jüdische Gottesdienst*, first published in 1913, with additional notes again in 1924 and a third time, with further additional notes, in 1931. Death, unfortunately, prevented the author from bringing out a new, revised edition. A detailed evaluation of Elbogen's extended work on the liturgy cannot be given here. Suffice it to describe his method in the conception and execution of which he has no peer. He always goes back to the oldest texts and, on that basis, he subjects tradition to a critical examination in which he pays special attention to the terminology.

To my knowledge, Elbogen was the first scholar to recognize the importance of individual prayer *(Gebet des Einzelnen)*: "Every true prayer is... individual, personal... On the other hand, no genuine religion can give up a communal service which is the expression of its essence and teachings as well as a criterion of its value". A grave conflict ensues. "The community cannot take into consideration the special, subjective petitions of the individual, and the individual cannot be satisfied with the general contents of the communal prayer. It is the task of all religions to find a way out of this dilemma, if they do not want to give up living piety *(lebendige Frömmigkeit)*."[45]

An example might illustrate how much research was bound up with polemics. Modern Christian theologians claim that the Jewish religion in New Testament times was "strongly externalized", that "prayer was strangled and narrowed down by rules so much that individual piety could not at all arise." In his answer, Elbogen accuses them of a tendentious attitude, for it is precisely Judaism which has for the first time introduced the "worship of the heart", "a regular service of prayer without sacrifices and images".[46] Elbogen then shows that Judaism solved the dilemma by offering an opportunity to the individual for his personal petitions at the end of the communal service.

Elbogen's *magnum opus, Der Jüdische Gottesdienst* — to characterize it, though all too briefly — is a mine of information, systematically arranged, closely, yet lucidly argued, written in a fluent, attractive style and comprehensive within the limits of the liturgical texts available to the author. Of his many smaller liturgical studies one at least must be mentioned, *Die messianische Idee in den alten jüdischen Gebeten*.[47] In a few pages

---

[43] Band 1, Heft 1.2 der "Schriften der Lehranstalt f. d. WdJ", 1907.
[44] Cf. the Bibliography quoted in n. * at the beginning of this article.
[45] *Studien* ..., p. 40.
[46] *Ibid.*, p. 41. The crucial quotation runs in the original German: 'Würden die Kritiker der "religionsgeschichtlichen Schule" mehr bestrebt sein, sich eine kompetente *Beurteilung* der jüdischen Religion zu eigen zu machen, als eine tendenziöse *Verurteilung*, dann würden sie sich wohl in acht nehmen, eine solche Ungereimtheit gerade von derjenigen Religion zu behaupten, die zuerst "den Gottesdienst des Herzens", den opferlosen und bilderlosen regelmässigen Gebetskultus eingeführt hat'.
[47] In: *Judaica. Festschrift zu Hermann Cohens 70. Geburtstag*, 1912, pp. 669-679.

Jewish themes

Elbogen masterly describes the old basic prayers which incorporate both the prophetic idea of the future of mankind and the narrower idea of Israel's redemption and share in the kingdom of God.

In this connection mention should be made of his lecture — already referred to — at the *Institutum Judaicum* on Ezra's significance for the nature and history of post-exilic Judaism. Speaking of Ezra's introduction of assemblies in which first the Torah and later also the Prophets were read and expounded, he claims: "This is the first example that the Holy Scriptures of a people were taken away from the privileged and became the possession of the whole community. Nor is it accidental that it remained the only example and, through numerous translations, passed into world literature, and that it became, quite apart from its religious significance, one of the most successful teachers of the human race... This was the victory over the priesthood by the lay element just at a time when such a great external position had been granted to the priesthood... The other tremendous achievement of that time is the [emergence of] religious individualism with its noblest flower, the life of prayer..." He ends his lecture with the words: "Sanctification of the divine Name, to love God even with the surrender of life — this is the last word of the religion of *Torah*."[48]

It was in the strictly historical field that his rare gifts bore fruit richly, even exuberantly. This applies to his original contributions, breaking new ground in his evaluation of the Hebrew reports on the Jewish fate during the Crusades and in his interpretation of Hebrew sources concerning the early history of the Jews in Germany.[49] Philological exactitude, sound historical sense, caution and judgement, combined with a sure feeling for what is important and permanent as against the trivial and transient, we expect of every good historian. Elbogen added two qualifications which are indispensable to the historian of Judaism: technical mastery and insight into the spirit of Rabbinic sources, and a competent, first-hand knowledge of general history, its driving forces and guiding ideas, based on a sound philosophy of history. Salo Baron said of Graetz that he wanted to understand the history of the people he described as an isolated entity.[50] Not so Elbogen; he not only declared that the history of the Jews could only be studied and understood as part of general history, but himself wrote history from this point of view. He had revived the *Zeitschrift für die Geschichte der Juden in Deutschland* in 1929 and remained one of its editors till 1938. He sent it on its way with the programmatic declaration that "a close connection existed between the entire history of the Jewish population of Germany and the

---

[48]*Esra und das nachexilische Judentum* (cf. n. 31), pp. 25 f.
[49]ZGJD (cf. n. 34): *Hebräische Quellen zur Frühgeschichte der Juden in Deutschland*, pp. 34-43, and *Zu den hebräischen Berichten über die Judenverfolgungen im Jahr 1096* in: Festschrift zum 70. Geburtstag Martin Philippsons, 1916, pp. 1-19.
[50]Cf. n. 8, above.

general history of the German lands, the German rulers and the German citizenry *(Bürgertum)*".⁵¹ For him, the German Jews were an integral part of Germany. But while Jewish history belongs, always and everywhere, to general history, Elbogen objected to the title of Simon Dubnow's History of the Jewish people as *"World* History...", "for no single people has a world history".

In his extensive critical review of Dubnow's work, which at that time (1926) had appeared in a German translation in Berlin,⁵² Elbogen i.a. acknowledges that Dubnow has a historian's sense of reality but deplores his commitment to the attitude of the Enlightenment *(Aufklärung) à la* Voltaire, his failure to recognize metaphysical forces in world happenings and his inability to understand the impact of religion in Judaism. This leads him to "the most disastrous basic error of the book. The author has the perfectly and solely legitimate intention of building Jewish history on sociological considerations but combines this correct approach with a grossly exaggerated valuation of the national." Elbogen further criticizes Dubnow's undiscriminating use of the term "autonomous" which — for Elbogen — means something quite different in different periods of Jewish history. The same doubt applies to Dubnow's term 'nationality'; and the term *'Judaismus'* is "a consequence of the grossly exaggerated application of the term 'nation'. The expression 'Jewish religion' is avoided whenever possible, to the detriment of clarity and precision; it is replaced by the expandable concepts of *'Judaismus'* and 'Jewish-national culture'."

By contrast, we note Elbogen's lucidity and exactitude, his predominantly religious approach and insight. These legitimate manifestations of Dubnow's secularism are quite alien to Elbogen and in his view entirely inapplicable to Judaism. Elbogen rejects Dubnow's distinction between "political" and "spiritual" nation: "... these things belong so intimately together that they cannot be separated, and even Dubnow has not been able to separate them despite his strong emphasis on the contrast".

Apart from these objections to principles and method, Elbogen registers his disagreement with a number of details: he takes Dubnow to task for his misunderstanding of the conflict between Sadducees and Pharisees, and of the character of the Pharisees in particular. He sums up this part of his review thus: "A splendid formulation [by Dubnow], except that it is most improbable that the old Pharisees would have understood it".⁵³ Elbogen himself is always careful not to read the views and interpretations of a later age into the past; he interprets the

---

⁵¹*Zum Geleit*, p. 2.
⁵²*Zu S. Dubnows Geschichtswerk* in: MGWJ 70, 1926, pp. 145-155.
⁵³*Ibid.*, p. 151: 'Eine prachtvolle Formulierung, nur ist es sehr unwahrscheinlich, dass die alten Pharisäer sie verstanden hätten'. See also Elbogen's contribution to the *Festschrift* for Israel Abrahams (Jewish Studies in Memory of I.A., 1927), pp. 298-312, under the title *Einige neuere Theorien über den Ursprung der Pharisäer und Sadduzäer*. His

sources of a given period in their own political, economic, social, cultural and religious setting. This is not only evident in his studies on some definite historical problem, but also determines his historical writings which cover, as in his *A Century of Jewish Life,* a whole epoch, or, as in his *Geschichte der Juden in Deutschland,* the history of Jewish life in Germany from Roman times to the advent of Hitler, or, as in his *Geschichte der Juden seit dem Untergang des jüdischen Staates,* the entire history of the Jews in antiquity, in the Middle Ages and in modern times till 1917.

To read these books is, without exaggeration, a great experience, quite apart from the accurate knowledge the reader gains of tendencies and movements, of "men who made history" and of significant facts and figures. The exposition is aglow with life in all its variety and perplexity, because our author is not only immensely learned, but fair-minded, wise and understanding. He captures the open-minded reader by his sanity and by his humanity. Take for example Elbogen's last work which spans a most controversial period of Jewish life, thought and experience, from the emancipation to Hitler's *Total War Against The Jews,* up to the year 1943 in the middle of World War II. It would be too easy to condemn the book because it is not — in the view of some — what it set out to be, namely, a continuation of Graetz. That it cannot be, for many reasons. The setting is different, so is the atmosphere, the mental climate. Elbogen, though basically holding the same concept of Judaism as Graetz, approaches Jewish history as part of world history. From this presupposition he distributes light and shade differently, puts the emphasis on different parts of the whole. To his wider vista he adds a remarkable freedom from bias, he has no axe to grind, he does not ignore the opinions of others: he records objectively, dispassionately the foibles and the passions as part of life which he sees as a whole from the vantage-point of this faith in God, in Reason, and in Justice. Hence his objectivity is not colourless or indifferent, it does not make him into a sceptic. He has a great sense of humour, a witty phrase illumines men and events, movements and periods. The specialist may find mistakes, or may disagree with an interpretation here and there; but as far as I can see, there are few, if any, errors of judgement.

We should also duly appreciate his so-called popular writings. He has a special gift of proceeding from analysis to synthesis, of writing a fascinating story which grips and holds the reader. There is nothing second-

---

criticism of Dubnow's whole concept of Jewish history is summed up in the conclusion: 'Einem so einzigartigen Phänomen wie das jüdische Volk nun einmal ist, in seiner ganzen langen Geschichte mit einer einzigen Formel gerecht werden zu wollen, heisst die Quadratur des Zirkels lösen. Sie hat den Vorzug der Konsequenz, scheitert aber an den Tatsachen. So wird man Dubnows grandiosem Bau seine Anerkennung zollen, wenn man auch an der Auffassung mancherlei auszusetzen hat.'

hand about the man or his writing. It is amazing how much Elbogen has contributed to our knowledge of Judaism and Jews, scattered over periodicals, *Festschriften,* newspapers, encyclopedias, quite apart from his major works. Among the latter I count all those publications which he addressed to a wider public and not only to specialists. He has written much, but never said.too much, never used one word too many. He was a master of style, often a terse phrase is engraved on the reader's mind. Many of his statements and memorable formulations are untranslatable.

When discussing sexual ethics in the second volume of *Die Lehren des Judentums* (The Teachings of Judaism) he says: "The ideas and precepts of Judaism on the relationship of the sexes are focussed from the start on the contrast with the world around. There is no female godhead — an advantage, not a defect of the Jewish religion". Apologetic-polemical undertones are not absent. Thus he stresses that the Jewish religion condemns and punishes any kind of unchastity and unnatural sexual relations "such as were widespread not only in the ancient Orient, but also among Greeks and Romans". Marital fidelity and adultery were much more strictly understood among the Jews than among any other people of antiquity "because immorality is a denial of God". "God is for Judaism a God of ethics, and not of sensuality". This is more telling in the original German: "Gott ist für das Judentum ein Gott der Sittlichkeit und nicht der Sinnlichkeit".[54]

In conclusion, it remains to substantiate by a few quotations what has just been claimed for Elbogen the historian. He wrote the introductory article *Deutschland* in the *Germania Judaica*[55] from which I quote his criticism of Hahn[56]: "Instead of formulating a rule, we ought — with Täubler — to take into consideration the small number of known details and the variety of life. One can understand the Jewish situation only if one comprehends it in a natural manner and in the context of contemporary reality. Such designations as hawking (old clothes or second-hand trade), retail trade, and wholesale trade between localities should probably not be applied at all to the early Middle Ages. It is, moreover, totally wrong to designate — as Hahn does — the activity which one calls trade journeys in the case of Christian merchants, as hawking and peddling in the case of Jews". Unless the Jews had participated in the regular retail trade in the towns they could simply not have survived, they could not have maintained their shops nor their landed property. Otherwise we could not explain the existence of such large communities as Worms, Mainz and Cologne already before 1096, since only few Jews

---

[54]Die Lehren des Judentums. Zweiter Teil: Die sittlichen Pflichten des Einzelnen, pp. 68 f.
[55]Breslau, 1934. Von den ältesten Zeiten bis 1238. This work is being continued by the LBI under the editorship of Zvi Avneri.†
[56]Hahn's study bears the title: *Zur Handelsbedeutung der Juden in Deutschland vor Beginn des Städtewesens.* Cf. *Germania Judaica,* p. xliv. n. 113.

could have made a living from money and foreign trade. Besides, the solidarity that existed between burghers and Jews can only be explained on the assumption of daily trade relations on a large scale. Elbogen states that "the following exposition is at pains to draw a picture from the sparsely extant sources". He made the same stringent demands on himself, and after extracting the gold from the original sources — to vary his own phrase — he changed it into small coin in such a way that the value in gold was preserved in what appears to be an effortless, popularizing construction.

Elbogen's books are no light weights which the critical wind of expert scrutiny sweeps away. His *Geschichte der Juden in Deutschland* is a solid house built of stones carefully chiselled by an expert craftsman who was also an artist. He says in the short preface: "The history of the Jews in Germany is only a small segment of the history of the Jews altogether, and only an insignificant factor in the history of the German people. He who wants to tell it in a short space must presuppose a good deal of the history of the two peoples and refer the reader to the great descriptions of German and Jewish history. This history shall be told here according to the sources, not in its [every] detail, but [showing] its dynamism, its active forces, and the passions which are at work in it — in nobody's favour, to nobody's harm, for the good of all".[57] Then he tells the story without fear or favour in a sober, dignified way, good-humouredly, in a homely, pleasing style until he reaches the triumph of Nazism which "made a political dogma out of the anthropological theory of the myth of race". And yet, his unshakable faith and optimism make him end this tale of success and failure, of achievement and dashed hopes, of confidence and despondency, of courage and cowardice, thus: "Once again the German Jews are facing the problem of having to prove themselves, again the prophet's call rings out to them 'You are my witnesses, says the Lord'. It is up to them to answer with the old word of readiness 'Here am I!'."[58]

He tells the story in such a way that the interaction of German and Jewish history becomes manifest. He shows how the Westphalian Peace affected the legal and religious position of the Jews, how the absolutism of the princes *vis-à-vis* the estates, coupled with the development of industry and commerce, benefited the Jews because they were useful. He demonstrates the position of the Court Jews in connection with the transition to trade in goods *(Warenhandel)*. In recounting, with his customary restraint, the experiences during the Crusades he remarks: "... it was easier to finish off a bunch of Jews than to free oneself inwardly from one's sins, and so the fanatical crowd raved and raged

[57]In the original German: '– niemand zu Liebe, niemand zu Leide, jedermann zu Nutz und Frommen'.
[58]Wieder einmal stehen die deutschen Juden vor der Frage der Bewährung, wieder ergeht an sie der Prophetenruf "Ihr seid meine Zeugen, spricht der Ewige". Es ist an ihnen, mit dem alten Wort der Bereitschaft zu antworten: "Hier bin ich!".'

against the Jews".[59] It required courage to describe, under the nose of the Nazis, the suffering of medieval German Jewry, yet it must have been balm for the wounds of his fellow-Jews who were persecuted and humiliated by Hitler's hordes. Or, he stresses the otherworldliness of medieval Jews while outwardly clinging to material gain and earthly joys.[60] Of the polemical *Book of Disputation* of R. Lipmann of Mulhouse Elbogen says: "He wants to remove errors, not men; the motto "[our Christian] faith or [your] life" is not Jewish. Despite everything which separates Jew from Christian he has never forgotten that they were both human beings. When the others raved against him like brute fiends *(Unmenschen)*, the Jew has submitted to death and expulsion as [being] God's will, and he has resigned himself to his hard fate".[61] Dealing with the Jewish position under the territorial princes, Elbogen writes: "These centuries were milder, they no longer engineered the mass murder of Jews, but subjected them to humiliation *(beugten ihnen das Rückgrat)* and accustomed them to put up with mockery, scorn and insult, with being pelted with stones, and beaten, and with it all to fawn and to cringe. The pliable, whining pariah took the place of the heroically suffering Jew".[62]

Finally, we turn to Elbogen's last book, *A Century of Jewish Life*. The profound changes in material civilisation and spiritual culture, in the individual's attitude to religion have affected a divided Jewry more intimately and fatefully than any other human group. Self-containment and self-reliance have given way to an allegiance to many gods and idols, once the faith and trust in the One God of our fathers was allowed to wither or has been wilfully abandoned. The problems resulting from this situation have been filtered in this book through the perceptive mind of a whole Jew. Though deeply rooted in traditional Judaism and in the idealism of nineteenth-century liberalism, Elbogen never stood still. He was able to write with sympathy and understanding of Jewish nationalism although his own outlook was essentially that of Moses Mendelssohn, the closing lines of whose *Jerusalem* conclude his *Geschichte der Juden seit dem Untergang des jüdischen Staates*.[63]

[59]*Ibid.*, p. 59. Elbogen goes on: 'Auf die *Glaubenseinheit* war es abgesehen; die Juden aber standen unerschütterlich fest in ihrem *Einheitsglauben*'.
[60]*Ibid.*, p. 97, continuing Elbogen writes: 'Aber all das irdische Getriebe galt nur der Erhaltung der körperlichen Existenz, das wahre Leben sahen sie in der Befolgung des göttlichen Gebots. Und wahrlich, dieses Geschlecht hat ein bewundernswertes Erziehungswerk vollbracht, eine totale Opferbereitschaft geschaffen, die ohnegleichen dasteht . . .' (98).
[61]*Ibid.*, p. 101.
[62]*Ibid.*, p. 120.
[63]"Und noch jetzt kann dem Hause Jakobs kein weiserer Rat erteilt werden als eben dieser. Schickt Euch in die Sitten und in die Verfassung des Landes, in welches Ihr versetzt seid, aber haltet auch standhaft bei der Religion Eurer Väter. Tragt beider Lasten, so gut Ihr könnt." − Elbogen's book was published in 1919 and has this *Vorwort:* 'Der Schützengraben, aus dem die Anregung zur Abfassung dieser Schrift

Elbogen gives a sober account of Jewish activities in an expanding European economy, in banking, industry, trade and commerce and of the entry of Jews into science and scholarship, into European culture, between 1850 and 1880. The problem of that time leads him to the pertinent question: can Judaism turn into a religious community in the midst of a general religious crisis while Judaism "changed into a synagogal and congregational form", when "not group affiliation, but the individual's sense of responsibility now determined the intensity of his reaction and the direction of his energy"? The leadership passed from rabbis to laymen who "though of proven integrity... possessed no strong Jewish consciousness... In the Synagogues the peace of the churchyard prevailed, there was no public opinion, there was no leaven of criticism".[64]

The chapter on "Theodor Herzl and political Zionism" vividly conveys Herzl's impact on his generation and contains such flashes of insight as this: "It was perhaps providential that Herzl had no Jewish affiliations, for now no party could regard him as a renegade and all could give him their trust, which he did receive in the fullest measure".[65] Or, "Herzl dead was used by those who had embittered his life as a weapon against Wolffsohn and Nordau".[66]

His independence and sense of fairness are evident in his refutation of the charge against the *Hilfsverein* in the language controversy, proffered by official Zionist historiography.[67] But at the same time he objectively summed up the controversy thus: "... the episode demonstrated two things: first, the Palestinian Yishuv had, for the first time, shown independence and had demonstrated that it would not allow itself to be governed by its 'benefactors', and secondly, the Zionist Organisation suddenly realized the necessity of building up its own school system".[68]

Of the objections raised against Jewish immigration into England after the Russian pogroms he writes: "The charge was made that they kept themselves separate and did not enter upon mixed marriages, as if, with

---

kam, liegt hinter uns, die Judenfrage aber hat von ihrer Schärfe nichts verloren; sie wird erneut mit heftiger Leidenschaft in der Öffentlichkeit behandelt, und jeder Beitrag zu ihrer Klärung darf auf Beachtung rechnen. Die vorliegende Darstellung versucht die Schicksale der Juden im Zusammenhang mit der allgemeinen Geschichte verständlich zu machen, die treibenden Kräfte der geschichtlichen Entwicklung deutlich herauszuarbeiten, ein möglichst klares, anschauliches und wissenschaftlich-sachliches Gesamtbild zu zeichnen. Ein verspätetes Kriegsbuch, das dem Frieden und der Verständigung dienen will'. This is an apt illustration of the *Sitz im Leben* of WdJ, Elbogen's outstanding contribution to it and, together with his endorsement of Mendelssohn's *Credo*, indicative of his primarily religious attitude which allows Diaspora Jewry to practise a dual, not a divided loyalty.

[64]*A Century of Jewish Life*, pp. 93 ff.
[65]*Ibid.*, p. 279.
[66]*Ibid.*, p. 306.
[67]*Ibid.*, p. 724, n. 47.
[68]*Ibid.*, p. 308.

the exception of the few aristocrats who were interested in rich Jewish heiresses, the English were so eager to intermarry with Jews. It was not long before these same guardians of the temple expressed concern over the fact that the immigrants did not remain Jewish enough, that they gave up too many traditions which they had brought with them..."[69] He gives a vivid, factual account of the inhuman sufferings of Russian Jewry, only surpassed by the Nazis' calculated, scientifically prepared and executed bestiality.

He who wants a thumbnail sketch of the Jewish position just before World War I would do well to read the few pages on "Defense Organizations and Philosophical Literature", including a fine appreciation of Hermann Cohen. Under the heading "The Deep-Rooted Prejudice" Elbogen discusses the ample Jewish contribution, active or financial, to cultural pursuits, but concludes: "Their contributions were accepted; their fellowship was rejected". Quoting W. Sombart's views: "The European states grant to their Jewish citizens full equality of rights; but tact and intelligence will prevent the Jews from making full use of this equality", Elbogen rather bitterly comments: "Should Jewish research workers or judges neglect their abilities in order not to become worthy of promotion? Or should Jews acquiesce when they realize that baptism opens all the roads which are barred to loyal Jews?"[70]

Lastly, Elbogen after mentioning the guarantees written into the Peace Treaties after World War I comments: "It was only the laws and not the people that were changed, and so this hope was not fulfilled".[71]

What better salute could we offer to Ismar Elbogen, *zikhrono lib'rakhah,* on the occasion of the twentieth anniversary of his death than to quote the concluding paragraph, a witness to his optimistic and deeply religious nature at a time of great mental anguish, and to his unquenchable faith in the God of Israel at a time of generally failing faith: "The dominion of wickedness will be broken, but we shall still be far from the Millenium. Strenuous and unstinted efforts will be needed to heal the wounds the world bleeds from. Though trained in martyrdom, the Jewish people never before has experienced such a cataclysm as has our generation. But we go on! We trust in the unswerving help of our God and the God of our fathers! Through all the moral and spiritual crises of the last hundred years we have not given up our identity. We have saved our faith, saved our morale, saved our mental faculties. Battered from all sides, we were capable of giving to the world some of the greatest luminaries of the period. We don't despair! As long as Israel believes, Israel will not perish! We trust in God, and we go on!"

---

[69]*Ibid.*, p. 312.
[70]*Ibid.*, pp. 424 f.
[71]*Ibid.*, p. 509.

A generation separates us from Ismar Elbogen. A whole world, his world, has gone to ruin. Where is the Jewish faith, the trust and the confidence of the present generation? His lifelong labours have borne fruit and are still with us, even if WdJ has not led to that renewal of Judaism for which he raised his voice and wielded his pen with so much energy, ability and single-mindedness of purpose. Yet, even if Elbogen's concept of Judaism is today no longer shared by many nevertheless conscious Jews, WdJ carries on, notably in Israel, and may well achieve for a religionless Judaism what Elbogen hoped it would do for a historical Judaism centred in faith in the God of the Universe in whom he and our forefathers had implicit trust in loving service.†

APPENDIX OF ADDITIONAL NOTES

p. 3: cf. now K. H. Bernhardt, *Das Problem der altorientalischen Königsideologie im Alten Testament...*, Supplement to *Vetus Testamentum*, VIII (1961), for a reasoned, well-argued refutation of the presence in ancient Israel of the Near Eastern kingship ideology.

21: cf. also L. Strauss, 'On Abravanel's Philosophical Tendency and Political Teaching' in *Isaac Abravanel; Six Lectures*, ed. H. Loewe and J. B. Trend (Cambridge, 1937); I. F. Baer, 'Don Isaac Abravanel...' (Hebrew) in *Tarbiz*, VIII (1937); and the full-length study by B. Netanyahu, *Don Isaac Abravanel, Statesman and Philosopher* (2nd ed., Philadelphia, 1968). In view of these studies I did not write the intended monograph.

62: cf. vol. I, chapter 7.

64: should be Menahem di Recanati, as suggested in vol. I, chapter 6, p. 129, n. 6.

65: cf. vol. I, chapter 6.

66: cf. now S. Stein, 'Phillipus Ferdinandus Polonus' in *Essays in Honour of Dr J. H. Hertz* (London, 1943), pp. 397 ff.

68: as corrected in vol. I, chapter 6, p. 129, n. 4, it should read 'Muenster must obviously have seen Pagnino's translation'.

84: and her *The Study of the Bible in the Middle Ages* (2nd ed., Oxford, 1952). Cf. also vol. I, chapter 10.

86: reprinted as chapter 5 in vol. I.

121: cf. now S. L. Skoss, *Saadia Gaon, the Earliest Hebrew Grammarian* (Philadelphia, 1955).

134: cf. now G. E. Weil, *Élie Lévita. Humaniste et Massorète* (Leiden, 1963).

169: published as 'The "Plain" Meaning of Scripture in Early Jewish Exegesis' in *Papers of the Institute of Jewish Studies*, ed. J. G. Weiss, volume I (Jerusalem, 1964), pp. 140–85. It does not deal with the Middle Ages.

170: published Oxford, 1961; chapter IX.

277: cf. now chapters 12 and 13 in vol. I, and chapters 2–6 in vol. II ('Islamic Themes'); also, my *Griechisches Erbe in der jüdischen Religionsphilosophie des Mittelalters* (*GE*) (Stuttgart, 1960).

278, n.1: cf. vol. II, chapter 1.

n.2: cf. *Averroes' Commentary on Plato's 'Republic'* (*ACR*) (3rd ed., Cambridge, 1969), I.ii.1, p. 22.

286, n.1: cf. vol. I, chapter 13, and *GE*, pp. 55–68.

For a different interpretation of Maimonides and his political thought, consult now the 'Introductory Essay' by Leo Strauss and the 'Translator's Introduction' in the new English translation from the Arabic by Shlomo Pines, *The Guide of the Perplexed. Moses Maimonides* (Chicago and London, 1963).

n.4: cf. chapters 4 and 5 in vol. II.

305: cf. also A. Altmann, 'Essence and Existence in Maimonides' in *Studies in religious philosophy and mysticism* (Ithaca, N.Y., 1969).

Appendix of additional notes

314: cf. G. Vajda, *L'Amour de Dieu dans la Théologie Juive du Moyen Age* (Paris, 1957), especially pp. 118–40.

347: now *Germanica Judaica*, II, 1; II, 2 (Tübingen, 1968).

352: the reader is referred to the recent anthology *Wissenschaft des Judentums im deutschen Sprachgebrauch*, ed. Kurt Wilhelm (2 vols., Tübingen, 1967); in particular, to the editor's 'Zur Einführung in die Wissenschaft des Judentums', and Sinai (Siegfried) Ucko's 'Geistesgeschichtliche Grundlagen der Wissenschaft des Judentums' (originally published in *ZGJD*, V, 1934).

INDEX

Abbasid caliphs 95
Abelard, Peter 171
Abimelek (Abimelech) 122
Abraham 122, 138, 231, 233
Abraham, 'sapiens' R. 131
Abraham de Balmes—*see* Balmes
Abraham bar Chiyya (Ḥiyya) 45, 49 n.1, 137 n.33, 158 n.1
Abraham ibn Dā'ūd—*see* Ibn Dā'ūd
Abraham ibn Ezra—*see* Ibn Ezra
Abraham Halevi (ha-Lewi)—*see* Ibn Dā'ūd
Abraham Saba' 131, 132 n.18, 139 n.37, 140, 141 n.42
Abraham Sepharadi—*see* Abraham Saba'
Abrahams, Israel 242 n.69
Abravanel, Don Isaac 21–54, 56, 154, 154 n.4, 165, 173, 192, 224, 250, 257, 306 n.12, 353
  his attitude to Maimonides 50–3 *passim*, 267–9
  biography 25–7
  his commentaries 29ff.
  his exegetical method 31–42 *passim*, 49, 53, 54, 96, 119, 264–6
  his faith in approaching salvation 46–9
  influenced by or opposing earlier Christian exegetes 30, 35
  influenced by or opposing earlier Jewish exegetes 29, 31, 32, 33 n.1, 52
  his messianic treatises 39 n.1, 41–3, 43 n.3
  polemics against Christian exegesis 36, 42, 45
  his political thought 40, 40 n.2
  and prophecy 37, 37 n.3
  quotes classical authors 31
  his use of history 43, 44, 45, 49, 49 n.1, 54
Abravanel, Josef 27
Adam, Michael 68
Adonijah 8, 11
Adret, Solomon ben Abraham 42 n.2
Aggada—*see* Haggadah
Ahab 9, 12 n.20
Ahaz 174 n.23, 214
Airay, Henry (Oxford) 82
Akitu festival (Mesopotamia) 16
Albert the Great (Albertus Magnus) 30, 264, 268
Albo, Joseph xii, 24, 45 n.3, 50, 165, 190, 191, 192, 204, 233, 317, 324 n.14
  and Aquinas 210f.
  defends Torah 210–15
  and subdivision of human law 320f.
  three fundamental doctrines and Messianism 215, 319f.

true happiness 322
—*see also* Messiah; Nómos
Alexander Aphrodisiensis 291
Alexander the Great 31, 45, 213
Alfārābī—*see* Fārābī, al-
Alfarghānī (Alfraganus) 158
Alfonso, King of Naples 27
Alfonso, King of Spain 25
Al-Ghazālī—*see* Ghazālī, al-
Al-Kindī 277
Al-Muqammas, David ben Marwan 305 n.6, 307 n.36
Al-Qirqisani 305 n.6
Alley, Bishop 62
'*Almah* 174, 174 n.23, 198
Alt, A. 5, 5 n.4, 11, 11 n.19
Al-Tabrizi 306 n.12
Altmann, Alexander 168 n.6, 305 n.7, 353
Amidah 342
Amos 51
Anatoli, Jacob 158
Anderson, C. 61
Andrew of St. Victor 168, 168 n.5, 248
Andrews (Andrewes), Lancelot (Dean of Westminster) 149 n.3
Anointing 8, 9, 10, 11, 14
Anthropomorphism xiii, 99, 105, 105 n.2, 107, 111 n.5, 169, 183, 193, 258, 267, 293, 311
Antichrist 30, 44
Anti-Christian polemic, medieval x–xiii, 36, **165–85**, 192–203—*see also* Abravanel; Controversy, religious, writings on; D. Kimḥi (Qimḥi); Rashi
Antinomianism 267
Antiochus Epiphanes 45
Antipope—*see* Benedict XIII
Antisemitism
  German 333, 338, 341
  medieval (economic, social, theological) 187–242
Apikorsim 46
Aquinas, Thomas 211, 306 n.10
  and Albo 320–1
  and Maimonides 268–9
Arabic—*see* Bible, Hebrew: Arabic
Arberry, A. J. 294
Arias Montanus 163
Aristeas 162
Aristotle viii, ix, xiii, 29, 36, 46 n.1, 53, 265, 267, 268, 275, 277, 278, 279 n.5, 284, 285, 286 n.5, 287, 290, 293, 294, 295, 299, 301, 303, 311–15 *passim*, 317–21 *passim*, 323 n.4, 324 n.14

Index

Astronomy 45
Astruc Halevi (of Alcañiz), at Tortosa disputation 223-6
Athaliah 8, 16
Augustine 151, 160, 162, 168, 193, 248
Avempace—*see* Ibn Bājja
Averroes—*see* Ibn Rushd
Avicenna—*see* Ibn Sīnā
Awwalun 121 n.2

Ba'al ha-Turim—*see* Jacob ben Asher
Baasha 10
Babel 33 n.1, 48
Bacher, Wilhelm 21 n.1, 86 n.1, 90 n.1, 97 n.1, 108 n.1, 109 nn.1,2, 113 n.2, 120, 121, n.1, 124, 131 n.15, 170 n.10, 239 n.35, 271, 305 n.2
Bedarsi, ha-—*see* Yedayah
Baeck, Leo 245, 330, 332, 338, 339
Baer, I. (Y.) F. 21 n.1, 165 n.1, 174 n.20, 223, 240 nn.44,48,52, 241 nn.53,55,57,61, 270, 353
Baer, Seligmann 342
Baḥya ben Asher 270
Baḥya ibn Pakuda (Paqūda) 33 n.1, 90 n.1, 263, 306 n.12, 311, 313, 319, 323 n.3
Balmes (Palmis), Abraham de 131, 156, 157
Bamberger, Fritz 340 n.37
Barnett, Jacob 66, 66 n.5
Baron, Salo W. 240 nn.44,46,48,52, 241 n.62, 242 nn.64,69, 331, 331 n.8, 344
Bathsheba 198
Bede, the Venerable 30, 256, 264
Begrich, J. 15 n.27
Bekhor Shor (Schor), Joseph 176, 177 n.31, 198, 257
Benedict XIII (Antipope) 24, 192, 223
Benveniste, Vidal 224
Bergmann, Juda 21 n.1, 338
Berlin University, *Institutum Judaicum* 338
Bernard of Clairvaux 168 n.5
Bernfeld, Simon 333 n.17
Bernhardt, K. H. 353
Beroald, Mathew 152
Beza, Theodore 59
Bible, Aramaic—*see* Targum
 English: Authorized Version x, 57, 58, 61, 62, 66, 68-77 *passim*, 82, 83, 134, 137, 140, 140 n.40, 142, 144, 253, 254; Bishops' Bible 59-62 *passim*, 68-80 *passim*, 127, 254; Genevan Bible 58-62 *passim*, 67, 69-78 *passim*, 80, 127, 254; Great Bible 59, 60, 64, 67, 69-77 *passim*, 127, 144; Matthew's Bible 58, 60, 60 n.3, 67, 70-9 *passim*, 127; Sebastian Münster's influence 127-45; Rashi's influence 56-85; Revised Version 69-76 *passim*
 Greek 107, 161, 162
 Hebrew 3ff., 128, 155, 161, 162: Arabic, importance to exegesis of vii; authorship of 36, 37; Christological interpretations, rebuttal of 165ff., 187-242; commentary, polemical 192-203; division of 36, 38; exegesis, Northern France, school of 252-8, of Rashi 56-81, 253-7, study of, in medieval Judaism 252-71, of Abraham b. Ezra—*see* Ibn Ezra, of Isaac Abravanel—*see* Abravanel, Don Isaac, of David Qimḥi—*see* Kimḥi, D.—*see also* Anti-Christian polemic; 'higher criticism' of 334; literal interpretation of 193, 200, 202, 248-71;—*see also* Bible, Massoretic
 Latin 150, 162, 163—*see also* Münster (Muenster), Sebastian; Vulgate
 Massoretic 108-16 *passim*, 128, 163, 251, 256—*see also* Bible, Hebrew
 Peshitta 107
 Vulgate 58, 65, 68, 73, 74, 76, 107, 136, 140 n.40, 141, 144, 161, 162 n.3, 163, 176 n.29, 198, 229, 248, 256, 257, 258
Biblia Hebraica 112-15 *passim*
Bibliander, Theodor 59, 59 n.5
Bignon, Peter 63 n.3, 148
Bildad 118 n.2, 123 n.3
Bilson, Bishop 62
Bismarck 332
Blanche of Castile (Queen Mother, France) 216
Blondheim, David Simon 255
Blood libel 188
Blumenkranz, Bernhard 165 n.1, 174 n.23, 238 n.15, 240 n.44
Bodley, John 61
Bomberg, Daniel 128, 130, 131 n.14, 163
Bonastruc Desmaestre 223
Bongiorno, David Bonet 227
Bosniak, J. (ed.) 166 n.2, 181 n.44, 182 nn.45-8, 239 n.24
Braganza, Duke of 26
Brandin, L. 255
Broughton, Hugh 148 n.3, 150, 150 n.4, 153, 154, 154 nn.1,4,5, 157, 158, 159
Buber, Martin 3 n.1, 6, 6 n.7, 15 n.27, 17 n.32, 129 n.7
Buddeus 35
Budney, Simon 235, 236
Bullinger, Heinrich 59, 59 n.5
Burleigh, Lord (Cambridge Chancellor) 148
Buxtorf, Johannes B., the younger 35, 149 n.4

Index

Calonymos—*see* Kalonymos
Calvin, John   59, 155, 156
Cambridge, Biblical studies—*see* Lively, Edward
Canaan, Canaanites   4 n.3, 5
Caro, Joseph   159 n.3
Carpzow, Johann G.   35
Cassuto, Moses David (Umberto)   6 n.7
Cavallerius (Cevallerius), Rodolphus—*see* Chevalier, Anthony
Cavallero family   229
Cecil, Sir William   61
Censorship, Christian   xiii, 167, 189, 193, 194, 202, 209, 210, 256, 257, 261
Chanter, The—*see* Peter the Chanter
Chevalier, Anthony (Rodolphus Cavallerius)   63, 63 n.2, 68, 151, 156
Christ—*see* Jesus
Christiani, Pablo (Paul) (convert)   23, 42, 218–23, 224, 229, 230
Christianity   x, xi, xiv, 21–5 *passim*, 30, 35, 42, 44, 45, 47, 128, 137, 172 n.15, 187–242, 247, 253, 260, 262, 268, 270, 303, 319—*see also* Anti-Christian polemic; Constantine the Great; Controversy, religious, writings on; Conversion to Christianity; Disputations; Jesus; Messiah, Messianism; New Testament
Christmann, Jacob   158
Chronicles   38 n.1, 40, 44 n.1
Chronicles of the Latins   30, 31 n.1, 43, 54
Coddaeus, Guilelmus   149 n.4
Cohen, Hermann   166 n.2, 275, 315, 339, 340, 351
Comestor, The—*see* Peter the Comestor
Commandments, classification of   91, 91 n.2—*see also* Ten Commandments
Constantine the Great   43, 44 n.3, 47, 176
Controversy, religious, writings on   227–38—*see also* Anti-Christian polemic; Disputations
Conversion to Christianity   xi, xii, xiii, 165, 167, 177, 226, 232, 233, 248, 254, 256, 257, 262, 263, 266
Coverdale, Miles   58, 59, 60, 60 n.3, 67, 69–77 *passim*, 127, 254
Cradock, Richard   147 n.1
Creation   93
Crescas, Chasdai   50, 190, 210, 295, 305 n.8, 306 nn.10,12, 319, 321, 323
Crispin, Gilbert   257
Crusades   50, 165, 169, 188, 254, 255, 257, 270, 348
Cyrus   172 n.15
Czechowicz, Martin   235, 236, 242 n.66

Dagesh   143

Dan   36, 37
Daniel   30, 35, 40, 41, 43–8 *passim*, 51, 152, 153, 153 n.3, 158 n.1, 197, 208, 209, 265, 266
Darmesteter, Arsène D.   255
David, King   4, 5, 8–12 *passim*, 14, 19, 36, 37 n.1, 38, 38 n.1, 172 n.15, 175, 178, 179, 182, 196, 197, 198, 200, 202, 254, 265
his throne's continuity   7, 11, 14 n.24, 18, 19, 38 n.1, 196, 263
Deborah   142 n.47
Decalogue—*see* Ten Commandments
De la Mare, William   84 n.1
Denifle, P.   240 n.48
Derash   167, 244, 245, 250, 252, 254, 258, 259, 260
Derenbourg, Hartwig D. (ed.)   89 n.1, 97 n.1
Deutsch, D. (ed. trans.)   103 n.1, 242 n.65
Diesendruck, Zvi   279 n.1, 306 n.19
Dieterici, Fr. (ed.)   275 n.3
Dilthey, Wilhelm   277 nn.2–5, 330
Diodorus Siculus   158
Dioscorides   157 n.1
Disputations   xi, xii, xiii, 165, 165 n.1, 189, 191, 192, 195, 204, 210, 215, 216–26, 256, 257
Donin, Nicolas (Nikolaus)   216–17
Driver, S. R.   12 n.20, 238 n.14, 271
Drusius, Junius   156, 157 n.1
Dubnow, Simon   242 n.69, 345
Dunash ibn Labraṭ   250, 251
Duran, Profiat (Efodi)   xiii, 227–34
criticism of New Testament   229–34
Duran, Simon ben Zemach   190, 210, 233, 305 n.8

Eck, Johannes   128
Eckert, W. P.   238 n.1
Edom   5, 39 n.1, 43, 47, 176, 198, 254, 255
Efodi—*see* Duran, Profiat
Efros, Israel   305 n.7
Ehrle, F.   240 n.52, 241 nn.57,58,60
Ehrlich, E. L.   238 n.1
Einleitungswissenschaft   35
Elbogen, Ismar   xiv, 158 n.1, 327-52
Elbogen, Regi   327 n.
Eleazar of Worms   130, 130 n.11, 269
Eliezer of Beaugency   174 n.22, 176, 177 n.31
Eliezer ben Yehudah   132 n.19
Elihu   94, 98, 116–19 *passim*, 125
Elijah   9, 182, 184, 263
Eliphaz   118 n.2
Elisha   9
Elizabeth I, Queen   60 n.1
Elokim   236
Erasmus   156

Index

Eschatology 255
Esterson, S. I. (ed.) 166 n.2, 180 n.39, 239 n.21
Eudaimonia 310, 318
Eusebius 158, 303
Exegesis, Biblical x—*see also* Bible, Hebrew
Exile 33 n.1, 35, 36, 36 n.3, 38 n.1, 40, 44, 45, 48, 51, 172 n.15, 174, 182 n.47
Exodus 32 n.1
 importance of recurrent mention 6
Eyre 149, 149 n.4
Ezekiel 51, 158
Ezra 17, 36 n.3, 38 n.1, 39 n.2, 276, 344

Fagius, Paul 65, 83, 134 n.26, 151
Falaquera—*see* Palqera
Falasifa (Islamic philosophers) viii, ix, 275, 280 n.7, 287, 288, 292, 293, 294, 297, 299, 300, 301, 303, 307 n.35
Fārābī, al-, Abū Naṣr viii, ix, 51, 268, 275 n.1, 277–82 *passim*, 301, 303, 304 n.1, 305 n.8, 306 nn.11,15,16, 307 nn.24,36, 318, 324 n.9
Felix Pratensis 163
Ferdinand and Isabella (Spain) 24, 26
Ferdinand, Philip (Phillipus Ferdinandus Polonus) 66, 82, 83, 164 n.2, 353
Fernando, King of Naples 27
Ferrer, Rabbi 226
Ferrer, Vicente 24, 189, 226
Finkelstein, Louis (ed.) 166 n.2, 305 n.7
Fishman, J. L. (ed.) 305 n.7
France—*see* Bible, Hebrew: exegesis, Northern France
Frankfort, H. 3 n.1, 7 n.11
Friedländer, Michael (ed.) 166 n.2, 169 n.7, 238 n.4
Fuerst (Fürst), J. 27 n.2, 35 n.3
Fulke, William, of Pembroke 148, 148 n.2, 163, 164 n.1
Future life ix

Gad 37
Galen 295
Galling, K. 12 n.20
Gauthier, L. 307 n.33
Geiger, Abraham 241 n.61, 242 n.66
Geiger, Ludwig 63 n.4, 64, 68 n.3, 128 n.3, 330, 337 n.27
Gemara 33 n.1
Genebrard (Genebrardus) 150, 166 n.2, 180 n.38, 239 n.37, 261
Geonim 260
Germany—*see* History, German Jewish
Geronimo de Santa Fe—*see* Hieronymus de Santa Fide

Gersonides (Levi ben Gerson) 29, 31–4 *passim*, 44 nn.3,4, 45, 53, 58, 65, 96, 119, 130, 268, 305 n.8
Gesellschaft zur Förderung der Wissenschaft des Judentums 329 n.4, 330, 332, 336, 339, 340
Ghazālī, al- 294, 302, 305 n.1, 306 nn.12,18, 317
Gikatilla, Moses ibn 252
Gilby, Anthony 59
Gildas 163
Ginsburg, Christian D. 154 n.3, 160 n.3
Gnosticism 303
God *passim*
 Avicenna's view of 295
 Jewish concept of 173, 347
 his kingship ix, 6, 6 nn.8,9, 7, 255
 love of x
 nature of xi, xiii, 184, 190, 191, 212, 227, 238, 261, 267, 268, 269, 290–2, 294, 295, 296, 300—*see also* Anthropomorphism; Saadya Gaon, on God's nature
 his promise to the Patriarchs 5, 8
 his relationship with Israel 4, 6-10 *passim*, 13–17 *passim*, 19, 20, 48, 49, 54, 173, 253
 his relationship with Solomon 7
 son of God xii, 6, 6 n.8, 178, 261, 262
 unity of—*see* nature of
 —*see also Elokim*
Gog and Magog 172 n.15, 184
Goldschmidt, Lazarus (trans.) 232
Goldziher, Ignaz 302
Goodenough, E. 3 n.1, 307 n.35
Graetz, Hermann 242 n.69, 330, 330 n.6, 331, 333, 344, 346
Grayzel, Solomon 242 n.69
Gressmann, Hugo 12, 338, 338 n.32
Grindal, Edmund, Bishop 59 n.5, 61, 63, 84
Grünbaum, S. (ed.) 240 nn.44,47
Grünberg, S. (ed.) 21 n.1
Güdemann, Moritz 242 n.69
Gunkel, Hermann 329
Guppy, Henry 60, 60 n.2
Guttmann, Jakob 21 n.1, 90 n.1, 238 n.2, 239 nn.27,28, 275 n.2, 307 n.24
Guttmann, Julius 304, 323 n.5, 324 n.12, 332, 338, 340, 340 n.37
Guttmann, Michael 338

Hackspan, Th. (ed.) 181 nn.43,44, 239 nn. 18,24
Hagar 141
Haggadah (*Aggada*) 42, 42 nn.1,2, 138, 138 n.36, 221, 224, 245, 299
 Christian attack on 189
 Jewish refutation of Christian claim 219–21

Index

Hagiographa 32, 36, 37, 38 n.1, 47
Hahn 347
Hailperin, H. 168 n.5
Halakhah 42, 167, 183, 245, 246, 249, 299
Harding (Oxford) 149 n.3
Hasidim 270
Ḥayyūj, Judah ben David 251, 252, 255
Hebraica veritas x, 128, 129, 134, 145, 148, 151, 154, 157, 164, 248, 271
Hebrew monarchy—see Monarchy, Hebrew
Heinemann, Isaak 167, 169, 238 n.3, 271
Hellenism—see Torah and nómos
Heller, B. 86 n.1
Henry of Costessy 84 n.1
Herbert of Bosham 168 n.5, 170, 248
Herford, R. Travers 159 n.1, 242 n.69
Herodotus 157 n.1, 158
Herschman, A. M. 239 n.36
Herzl, Theodor 350
Heschel, Abraham J. 305 n.7
Hezekiah 8, 13, 40, 175, 206
Hieronymus—see Jerome
Hieronymus de Santa Fide (Fe) (formerly R. Joshua of Lorca) 24, 41, 189, 217 223-6, 265
Hillel ben Samuel of Verona 305 n.8
Hilles, R. 59 n.5
Hirsch, S. A. 63 n.4, 84 n.1
Hirschfeld, Hartwig 86 n.1, 87 n.1, 88 n.2, 91 n.2, 283 n.2, 307 n.36
History, German Jewish 348
Hitler, Adolf xiv, 339, 346—see also Nazism
Hochschule (Lehranstalt) für die Wissenschaft des Judentums 327, 328, 330, 334, 336, 338, 342 n.42
Hoffmann, David 335 n.24
Ḥokmah (wisdom), kinds of 89, 89 n.3, 90, 91, 92, 93, 310
Höniger, J. 328 n.1
Hooke, S. H. 15, 15 n.28, 16
Horovitz, S. 305 n.8
Hosea 12 n.20
Höxter, J. 241 n.56
Hugh of St. Victor 167 n.3, 168, 248
Huldah 16
Humboldt, Wilhelm von 329, 332
Husik, Isaac 239, nn.37,38, 304

Ibn Bājja viii, 297, 302, 322, 324 n.9
Ibn Balaam, Judah 252
Ibn Da'ud (Dā'ūd), Abraham ha-Lewi, of Toledo 129, 133, 139, 158, 158 n.1, 159 n.5, 264
   on divine attributes 306 nn.11,12
   on divine v. human law 312
   on highest perfection (happiness) 311-16 passim
   influenced by Avicenna 294f., 307 nn. 35ff.
   on practical philosophy 296f., 299, 307 n.24
   religion and reason in 290, 309, 312-14, 323 n.4
   on the soul 305 n.8
Ibn Ezra, Abraham 29, 32, 33 n.1, 35, 52, 53, 58, 64, 65, 68, 69, 70, 74, 76, 77, 129 n.6, 130, 131, 133, 137, 140-3 passim, 152, 155, 156, 157, 159, 159 n.1, 165, 166, 168, 169, 171 n.14, 174, 174 n.17, 176, 193, 194, 250, 252, 253, 262, 264, 270, 302 (trans.)
   —see also Edward Lively; Sebastian Münster
   in England 259
   his method of interpretation 258-60
Ibn Gabirol, Solomon 171 n.15, 263
Ibn Gikatilla—see Gikatilla
Ibn Janāḥ (Gannah, R. Jonah) 68, 143, 251, 252, 255
Ibn Khaldun (Khaldūn) 278 n.1, 284 n.4
Ibn Kuraish (Quraish), Judah 305 n.2
Ibn Labraṭ, Dunash—see Dunash
Ibn Rushd viii, ix, x, 275-82 passim, 285, 286 nn.1,3,5, 287, 296, 299, 301, 301 n.31, 302, 323 n.1, 324 n.9, 353
Ibn al-Sa'igh 297
Ibn Sīnā 269, 323 n.4, 324 n.9
   his influence on Jewish thought 290-307
Ibn Tibbon, Samuel 277, 287, 294, 307 n.30
Ibn Ṭufail 297, 302
Ibn Verga, Solomon 223
Ijmā' (Ijma) 276
(Ihkwān al-ṣafā') (the) Ikhwan al-safa 303
Immigration, Jewish, into England 350
Inquisition 24, 25, 189, 202, 223, 237
Isabella of Spain—see Ferdinand and Isabella
Isaiah 8, 10, 30, 33 n.2, 39, 40, 47, 136, 197, 198, 259, 288—see Anti-Christian polemic, medieval
Isaiah, Second 259
Ishraqiyyun (Ishrāqiyyūn) 303
Isidore of Seville 30, 30 n.1, 264
Ishmael—see Islam
Islam vii, viii, ix, x, xiv, 21, 22, 107, 204, 209, 210, 213, 233, 235, 249, 255, 259, 262, 268, 275, 313, 316, 321—see also Averroes; Avicenna; al-Fārābī; Maimonides, his political conceptions; Muslims
Israel (Patriarch) 122
Israel (Children of):
   as Chosen People 48, 49, 50
   consolation for 47
   kingship—see Kingship in Israel

Index

Israel (*cont.*)
 redemption of—*see* Redemption
 her survival 49, 206, 207, 254
 —*see also* God, his relationship with Israel

Jacob 195, 205
Jacob ben Abraham, on the Rhine 196
Jacob ben Asher (*Ba'al ha-Turim*) 133, 142
Jacob of Belzyce 242 n.66
Jacob, Benno 333
Jacob ben Ḥayyim of Tunis 130, 130 n.13, 131, 163
Jacob ben Reuben (*c.* 1170) 204, 229
Jacobsen, Thorkild 9
Jaime I, of Aragon 218
Jechiel (Yeḥi'el), R. of Paris 165, 216–17, 222, 223
Jehoahaz 8
Jehoiada 8, 15, 16, 17
Jehoshaphat 18
Jehu 8, 9
Jellinek, Adolf J. (ed.) 133 nn.21,22
Jeremiah 37, 39, 39 n.2, 40, 119 n.1, 122, 158
Jeroboam 10
Jeroboam II 12 n.20
Jerome (Hieronymus) 30, 30 n.1, 37 n.1, 58, 70–8 *passim*, 129 n.5, 130, 135, 151, 157 n.1, 162, 163, 170 n.11, 182, 202, 214, 229, 230, 232, 234, 248, 257, 264
Jerusalem 48
 destruction of 39
 —*see also* Temple
Jesus xi, xiii, 23, 30, 35, 42, 47, 158–60, 172, 175f., 177 n.31, 179–82, 194, 197ff., 203, 211, 213, 220f., 228f., 233, 254f., 261, 269
 abolished the Law xii, 23, 42, 184, 192, 200, 231, 247, 256, 262, 265
 divine nature of xi, xiii, 42, 166, 171, 193, 201, 225, 230, 253, 256, 262f.
 promised Messiah in Christian exegesis opposed by Jewish exegetes xi, 23, 30, 35, 47, 128, 134, 136, 138 n.36, 153, 153 n.3, 166, 171, 188, 191f., 198, 209, 219–22, 225, 235, 247, 253
 son of God xii, 178, 188, 199, 201
Jezebel 12 n.20
Joash 8, 15, 16
Job—*see* Saadya Gaon, *Job*
John (New Testament) 233
Johnson, A. R. 3 n.1, 18 n.36
Jonah 206
Jonah, Rabbi—*see* Ibn Janāḥ
Joseph 132 n.18, 139
Joseph ben Gorion (Pseudo-Josephus) 30, 31, 31 n.1, 43, 44, 44 n.1, 48 n.1, 139, 139 n.37, 158 n.1, 264

Joseph ben Kalonymos 131 n.15
Josephus, Flavius 43, 44 n.1, 81 n.1, 158, 158 n.1, 159, 160, 162, 164 n.2
Joshua 4, 5, 6, 13–17 *passim*, 20, 36
Joshua of Lorca—*see* Hieronymus de Santa Fide
Joshua ben Peraḥya 207, 217
Josiah 8, 13, 15, 17 n.32
Judah ibn Balaam—*see* Ibn Balaam
Judah Halevi (J. Ha-Lewi, Yehuda Hallewi) 49, 49 n.1, 123 n.4, 268, 283 n.2, 284 n.5, 306 n.11, 317, 319
Judah he-Ḥāsīd (the Devout; the Pious) 270
Judaism—*see* Torah; *see also* Disputations
 answer to Christianity xii, xiii, xiv, 187–242
 medieval vii, 244–71
Judaizing 165
Judges 4, 5, 37, 37 n.1, 38

Kabbalah (*Qabbalah*), Kabbalists 51 n.2, 183, 257, 269, 270
Kahn, Zadok 241 n.64
Kalām vii
Kalonymos (Calonymos) 131, 269
Kant, Immanuel 306 n.10
Kara, Joseph—*see* Qara
Karaites 87, 87 n.1, 88 n.2, 235, 247, 249, 260, 303, 305 n.6, 307 n.36
Karpeles, G. 341
Katz, J. 170 n.11
Kaufmann, D. 306 n.11
Kaufmann, Y. 3 n.1, 5, 6 n.7
Kethībh and *Qerē* 81 n.1, 130, 154, 155
Keturah 141
Khalfa, Hajji 302
Khalīfa 10
Khilāfa ix
Kilbye, Richard 62, 66, 83, 84
Kimḥi (Qimḥi), David 32 n.2, 58, 63, 64, 65, 68, 68 n.3, 74, 77, 129 n.6, 130, 131 n.14, 132 nn.17,19, 133, 136–41 *passim*, 143, 143 n.48, 144, 154, 156, 157, 157 n.1, 159, 159 n.1, 165, 169–74 *passim*, 177–84 *passim*, 194, 196, 197, 198–203, 252, 253, 255, 257, 260–3 *passim*, 267, 270
Kimḥi (Qimḥi), Joseph 166, 261
Kimḥi (Qimḥi), Moses 261
Kimḥi family 250
King, kingship in Israel **3–20**
 anointing and succession 8, 9
 central problem of 3
 chosen by God 7, 9, 20
 and the Covenant 3, 14–16, 19–20
 duties of 8, 10, 11, 12, 17–20 *passim*
 election method 8, 9, 12

360

Index

King (cont.)
 functions of 8, 12
 God's promise to Patriarchs 5, 8
 historical continuity 4, 6–9 passim, 11, 14, 15
 mediator between God and people 8, 16, 20
 messianic connections 8, 10, 19, 20, 195, 195 n.2, 196, 197, 214
 opposition to 5, 6, 11, 12 n.20
 origins of 4, 5
 parallels among neighbours 4, 5, 9, 13, 20
 relationship with God 6–11 passim
 in Sukkoth celebration 4, 4 n.2
 and the Torah 8, 12, 13, 14, 16–20 passim
Kisch, A. 240 n.44
Kittim 176, 254
Kobak, Jos. (ed.) 240 n.52
Kobler, F. (ed.) 241 n.61
Koran—see Qur'an
Krauss, Samuel 121 n.1, 242 n.64

Lambert, M. 91 n.2
Landauer, S. 168 n.6, 239 nn.27,29, 305 n.8, 306 n.18
Landgraf, A. (ed.) 171 n.13
Landshut, L. 342
Langton, Stephen 168 n.5, 248
Lateran Council (1215) 22
Law of Moses—see Torah
Leisegang, H. 307 n.35
Leo Africanus 30
Leo Judae 61, 67, 68, 69
Leon, Judah Messer 306 n.12
Leon, Moses de 270
Leveen, Jacob 86 n.1
Levi ben Abraham, of Villefranche de Conflent 197
Levi (Lewi) ben Gerson—see Gersonides
Levita, Elias (Elijah) 65, 128, 129 n.8, 134 n.26, 137, 143, 151, 154–8 passim, 160, 160 n.5, 161, 161 n.4, 353
Levita, James 66
Levy, A. J. (ed.) 166 n.2
Levy, J. 155 n.3
Lewin, A. 240 n.44
Lewy, Israel 342 n.42
Lightfoot, John 150, 153 n.3, 160, 160 n.2
Lipmann (Lipmann of Mulhouse), Yomtob 131, 131 n.16, 166, 166 n.2, 199, 349
Lively, Edward (Cambridge Hebraist) 62, 63 n.3, 83, 147–64
 application of Tiqqūn Sōpherim and 'Iṭṭūr Sōpherim 155
 defence of O.T. 148–54 passim
 and Hebraica veritas 148 passim
 and Hebrew grammar and lexicography 152, 156f., 159
 and Hugh Broughton 150, 153–5
 indebted to Elias Levita 155
 and Jewish calendar 159
 his writings 147
Loans, Jacob ben Yeḥiel 64
Loeb, Isidore 240 n.44
Loewe, Raphael J. 168 n.5, 169 n.8 170 n.11, 248, 271
Lombardus, Petrus 229, 230, 233
Louis IX (St. Louis), King of France 216
Luke 214
Luther, Martin 58, 67, 127, 129. 144, 236, 237
Lyra, Nicholas de 30, 33 n.1, 35, 35 n.1, 45, 57, 58, 67, 70, 71, 74, 144, 160, 162 n.3, 229, 230, 231, 253, 264

Maarsen, J. (ed.) 166 n.2, 174 nn.18,21,23, 175 n.24
Maccabees 45, 174
Macedonia 45
Maimonides, Moses (Rambam) ix, xii, xiii, 28, 29, 33 n.1, 64, 91, 133, 159, 159 nn.1,3, 164 n.2, 170, 171, 171 n.14, 189, 200, 203, 204, 213, 225, 230, 292, 335 n.24, 353
 Abravanel's attitude to 33 n.1, 34, 37 n.3, 40 n.2, 43 nn.1,2, 46 nn.1,2, 49 n.2, 50–3
 and Christianity 208–10
 common ground between philosophy and revealed law 275–7
 comparison with Ibn Rushd 281–2
 dependence on al-Fārābī 278f.
 human happiness and perfection 282–4
 and Ibn Sīnā 294–7 passim, 301
 imitatio Dei 282
 Messiah and Messianic kingdom 285
 his political conceptions 275-88
 on prophecy, law and state 297–300
 D. Qimḥi under influence of 171, 171 n.14, 263, 267
 social ethics 284
 theory of prophecy 280
 Torah v. Nómos 276, 287
 —see also Nómos; Torah
Maimunists and Antimaimunists 52, 189, 267
Malachi 182
Malter, H. 86 n.1
Mantinus (Mantino), Jacob 278 n.2
Marcus, J. R. 242 n.69
Marranos 24, 25, 41, 41 n.2, 228, 265
Martin, Gregory 148, 148 n.2, 155, 163, 164
Martin, Raymund (Raimund di Martini) 45, 195, 197, 223, 224, 225
Martinius, Peter 62, 147 n.1, 149, 149 n.4, 156, 156 n.3
Marx, Alexander 328

361

Index

Mary (New Testament) 197, 217, 222, 234
Maschkowsky, Felix 57 n.2
Matthew (New Testament) 213, 214
Matthew—*see* Bible
Mehren, A. F. M. 307 n.32
Melchizedek 233
Melekh, meaning of 6
'Men of the Great Assembly' 39 n.2
Menahem ben Sarūk (Sarūq) 64, 129 n.6, 250, 251, 255, 258
Mendelsohn, I. 4, 4 n.3
Mendelssohn, Moses 315, 339, 339 n.34, 340, 349
Mercier 156
Merx, A. 31 n.3
Messiah, Messianism ix, xi, xii, 23, 24, 30, 31, 39 n.1, 40–4 *passim*, 46–9 *passim*, 131 n.16, 132 n.18, 134, 136, 136 n.32, 138, 138 n.36, 144, 152, 153, 165, 166, 171–6 *passim*, 178, 179, 182, 184, 188–93 *passim*, 195–206 *passim*, 207, 208, 209, 213, 214, 215, 219, 222, 224–8 *passim*, 230, 231, 234–7 *passim*, 247, 248, 253–8 *passim*, 262, 263, 265, 266, 207 n.30—*see also* Abravanel; Albo; Kimḥi; Kingship, messianic connections; Maimonides; Rashi; Saadya
Methuselah 162
Michael (angel) 138
Michalski, A. J. 35 n.1, 57 n.2
Midrash, in Christian exegesis xi, 42, 133, 133 n.22, 136, 136 n.30, 138, 219, 220, 221, 223, 224, 227, 245, 252, 260, 270
Mirandola, Pico della 163
Mishnah 117, 120 n.1
Mittwoch, Eugen 332, 340
Monarchy, Hebrew—*see* Kingship in Israel
Mohammed—*see* Muḥammad
Monotheism, Hebraic 3
struggle against paganism 3
Moses ix, xi, 4, 6, 6 n.7, 8, 13, 14, 16, 17, 17 n.32, 20, 39, 119 n.1, 121, 135, 171, 171 n.14, 177 n.31, 182, 198, 205, 230, 236, 299, 300, 303, 307 n.30, 313, 314—*see also Torah*
Moses of Coucy 130, 130 n.12, 131, 132 n.19, 133 n.20, 137, 137 n.33, 141 n.44, 143 n.48
Moses ben Naḥman (Ramban)—*see* Nachmanides
Moses HaDarshan 142 n.47, 195, 223, 305 n.1
Moses Narboni 305 n.1
Mowinckel, S. 6 n.7, 17 n.32
Muḥammad (Mohammed) ix, 52 n.2, 209, 221, 293, 319, 324 n.9
Müller, G. 242 n.68

Mullinger, J. P. 65 n.2
Munk, S. 278 n.1, 295, 304
Münster (Muenster), Sebastian 60, 60 n.3, 61, 64–70 *passim*, 83, 127–45, 151, 154 n.1, 156, 157, 164, 164 n.2, 253, 353
his influence on English Bible versions 127ff.
his Jewish sources 128, 130, 131, 131 nn.13–15, 132 nn.17–19, 133, 136f.: Hebrew grammars and dictionaries 130, 131, 132 n.17, 137 n.33, 141 n.43, 143 n.48; historical Jewish writings 139; uses *Minor Midrashim* and Talmud 138
on the defensive 133
praise for Moses 134f.
Muslims 47, 87, 172 n.15, 200, 201, 317—*see also* Islam
Mutakallimūn 91
Muʿtazila 291
Muʿtazilite 305 n.8
Mysticism 302—*see also* Ḥasidim; Kabbalah; Zohar

Nachmanides (Moses ben Naḥman; Ramban) 23, 29, 33, 33 n.1, 41, 42, 43 n.1, 52, 58, 64, 65, 96, 130, 133, 137–41 *passim*, 159 n.1, 166, 190, 192, 193, 218–23, 230, 257, 264, 270
Nāgīd 9, 9 n.17, 10, 11, 11 n.19, 19, 20, 276
Nathan the prophet 8, 8 n.14, 37, 214
Nationalism, Jewish—*see* Zionism
Nazism 348, 349, 251—*see also* Hitler, Adolf
Nebuchadnezzar 31
Nehemiah 38 n.1
Neoplatonism 277, 287, 290, 297, 303, 317
Neopythagorean writings 303
Netanyahu, B. 353
Neubauer, Adolf 66 nn.4,5, 139 n.38, 158 n.1, 238 n.14, 271
Neumark, D. 304
New Christians—*see* Marranos
New Testament xi, xiii, 128, 134, 134 n.27, 148 n.2, 152, 190, 204, 227, 229, 230, 231, 233–6 *passim*
New Testament, Syriac 159 n.1
New Year, identification of Passover with 15, 15 n.28, 16
Nimrod 138
Noachide Laws 135, 320
Nöldecke, Theodor 338
Nómos viii, ix, x, 309–24
Nordau, Max 350
North, C. R. 3 n.1
Noth, M. 5, 5 n.6, 7, 19, 19 n.37
Nyberg, H. 115

Index

Occupations, medieval Jewish xii, 347
Octateuch 14
Oesterley, W. O. E. 95 n.3
Old Testament xi, xii, 54, 56, 128, 134–7 *passim*, 144, 147 n.1, 148, 149, 151, 152, 154, 155, 160, 162, 163, 187–90 *passim*, 207, 211, 227, 233, 234, 235, 256, 267—*see also* Bible
Onqelos (Onkelos) 78, 129 n.8, 140, 140 n.40, 195
Origen 167, 193, 248
Overall, John 62
Ovid 31

Pagnino (Pagnine), Santes 60, 61, 68–78 *passim*, 129, 129 n.4, 163, 353
Palqera (Falaquera), Shemtob ben Joseph 296, 305 n.1, 306 n.13
Parker, Matthew (Archbishop of Canterbury) 60, 60 n.1, 61, 63, 65, 67, 68, 72, 84, 127, 145, 148, 148 n.3
Parker Correspondence 59, 60, 63 nn.2,3, 148 n.5
Parkes, James 242 n.69
Parkhurst, Bishop 59, 59 n.5
Parallelism 251
Passover 15, 16, 32 n.1
 identification with New Year 15, 15 n.28, 16
Paul (New Testament) 232
Paul of Burgos (formerly Rabbi Solomon Halevi (Hallewi)) 24, 30, 45, 160, 162 n.3, 227, 257, 264
Pedersen, Joh. 3 n.1, 6 n.7, 12 n.20, 15 n.27
Pellicanus, Conrad 64, 65
Pennaforte, Raimund (Peñaforte, Raimond de) 23, 218, 230
Pererius 164 n.2
Persecution xii—*see also* Russia, pogroms; Spain, persecutions
Persia 45, 164 n.2
Peshat 32, 167, 168, 169, 171 n.14, 172, 176, 177, 180, 182, 183, 184, 245, 246, 248, 250, 252, 253, 254, 257, 259, 260, 262, 263, 264, 266, 268, 269, 270
Peter the Chanter 168 n.5, 248
Peter the Comestor 168 n.5, 248
Petrus Alfonsi 229, 231
Pharisees 231
Philistines 5
Philo of Alexandria viii, 158, 160, 162, 293, 303, 304, 307 nn.30,35,36, 315
Philosophers, Jewish 203–15—*see also* Torah and *nómos*
Philosophy, religious vii, viii, ix, x, 249, 250, 296, 302—*see also* Avicenna; Falāsifa; Ibn Dā'ūd; Maimonides, his political conceptions; *Torah* and *nómos*
Pines, Shlomo 323 n.5, 353
Plato viii, ix, x, 40, 95, 275 n.1, 277–81 *passim*, 284 n.4, 286, 286 nn.4,5, 287, 288, 290, 293, 295, 298, 299, 301, 302, 303, 306 n.12, 311–14 *passim*, 316, 317, 318, 323 n.4, 353
Playfere 149 n.2
Pliny 157 n.1
Plotinus 277, 291, 297, 307 n.36
Pocoke, Edward (the elder) 83, 149, 149 n.4, 157, 157 n.1, 160, 160 n.2
Pogroms, Russian 350, 351
Pope, the 44, 44 nn.2,4, 219, 234, 236—*see also* Benedict XIII (Antipope); Rome; Silvester
Porphyry 30, 30 n.1, 45
Porteous, N. W. 3 n.1
Posnanski, A. 176 n.29, 196, 238 nn.6,9,11,13, 240 nn. 52,57,63, 271
Potiphar's wife 141
Poznanski, S. 166 n.2, 174 n.22, 175 n.25, 176, 176 n.29, 177, n.31, 230, 238 n.16, 271, 307 n.36
Prayer 343
Proclus 291
Prophecy, Prophet ix, 51, 53, 267, 268, 280–4 *passim*, 294, 296–9 *passim*, 301, 302, 303, 307 n.35, 318, 319, 320, 344
Proverbs—*see* Saadya Gaon, on Proverbs
Psalms 38, 39, 198ff., 262, 263
Pseudo-Jonathan 78
Pseudo-Josephus—*see* Joseph ben Gorion
Ptolemy 158
Pythagoras 301, 303

Qabbala—see Kabbalah
Qara (Kara), Joseph 176, 177 n.31
Qimḥi—*see* Kimhi
Qur'an (Koran), David in 10

Rabah 122
Rabanus Maurus 257
Rabbanites 87, 87 n.1, 88 n.2
Rachamon, Rabbi 223
Rainolds (Reynolds), John 61, 62, 66, 80–4 *passim*, 150, 164 n.2, 254
Rambam—*see* Maimonides
Ramban—*see* Nachmanides
Rankin, O. S. 240 n.44, 242 n.64
Rapaport, S. J. 342
Rashbam (Samuel ben Meir) 165, 166, 169, 170, 174, 176, 176 n.29, 195, 258
Rashi (Rabbi Salomon; Shelomoh ben Yiṣḥaq; R. Solomon ben Isaac of Troyes) 29, 32,

Index

Rashi (*cont.*)
　33 n.1, 35 n.1, **56–85**, 127, 129 nn.4 5,6, 130, 132 nn.17,19, 133, 137, 139, 140–5 *passim*, 152, 157, 159, 159 n.1, 165, 166, 169, 170, 172 n.15, 174–7 *passim*, 194, 195, 197, 198, 203, 219, 250, 258, 259, 261, 263, 264, 270
　his commentaries 56ff.
　his exegetical method 253–7, 260
Rationalism—*see* Reason
Rawidowicz, Simon 90 n.1, 305 n.5
Reason vii, viii, ix, 28, 33, 52, 89, 90, 91, 91 n.2, 103, 105, 111, 125, 266, 267, 280, 290–3 *passim*, 310, 311, 312, 314, 320, 321, 322, 335
Recanati, Menachem di 129 n.6, 130, 130 nn.10,11, 131, 143, 143 n.49, 353
Rechabites 6, 12 n.20
Redemption 20, 32 n.1, 33 n.1, 35, 41, 44, 44 n.4, 46, 47, 48, 50, 171–5 *passim*, 184, 207, 255, 263, 266, 344
Reformation 253, 271
Rehoboam 176, 258
Religious philosophy—*see* Philosophy, religious
Renaissance 30
Resh Laqish (Lakish)—*see* Simeon ben Laqish
Resurrection 46, 46 n.2
Reuchlin, Johannes 57, 63, 63 n.4, 64, 65, 68, 68 n.3, 81, 83, 84, 133, 156, 253, 254
Revelation viii, ix, xi, 28, 33 n.1, 91, 91 n.2, 93, 259, 266, 267, 290–4 *passim*, 301, 310–14 *passim*, 316–21 *passim*, 328
Richard of St. Victor 168 n.5
Robertson, E. 8 n.13
Rome 41, 42, 44, 44 nn.2,3,4, 174, 176, 176 n.28, 198, 254, 255, 266
Rosenblatt, S. (trans.) 168 n.6, 239 n.27
Rosenthal, Erwin I. J. 148 nn. 1,5; 150 n.2, 151 n.2, 154 nn.1,4, 164 n.1, 173 n.16, 238 n.15, 239 n.26, 271, 305 nn.3–5,7, 306 nn.14, 15, 323 nn.1,7
Rosenthal, Judah 166 n.2, 169 n.9, 174 n.20, 175 n.26, 238 n.15, 239 n.25, 240 n.44, 241 n.64, 242 n.66
Rosenzweig, Franz 129 n.7, 315, 340
Rosin, D. 166 n.2, 176 n.29
Roth, Cecil 41 n.2, 240 n.48, 242 n.69
Roth, Leon 309
Ruaḥ Haq-qodesh 36, 37 n.3
Ruth 37, 38

Sa'adya (Saadya, Saadia) Gaon vii, viii, xii, 142, 144, 152, 167, 168, 170, 232, 235, 258, 259, 260, 291, 293, 305 nn.8,9, 321, 324 n.14, 353

　against doctrine of trinity 204
　on commandments 91, 91 n.2, 95, 268
　the *Dahriyya* 118 n.1
　his exegetical method 86–96, 248–51 *passim*, 266
　his faith 125
　founder of Jewish philosophy 86
　on God's nature 98, 105, 106, 107, 116, 116 n.4, 117, 118, 120, 122, 123, 124, 206f.
　on *ḥokmah* 89, 92
　indebtedness to Targum 106–11
　on instruction 92, 93
　on *Job* 88, 88 nn.1,3, 93 n.3, 94, 94 n.1, 95 n.2, **97–125**
　on knowledge 90
　his linguistic comments 119–22 *passim*
　on Messianic promises and redemption 206–8
　as philosopher 203–8
　on *Proverbs* 94, 95, 95 n.3, 117 n.2, 118 n.1
　on reason 90, 91, 92, 94, 99, 100, 103, 105, 107, 111 n.8
　on reward and punishment 124, 125
　on a ruler's duties 94, 95
　on *Torah* 90, 91, 92, 94, 95, 205f.
　on tradition 90, 91, 99, 105
　his translation method 98–107 *passim*, 115–18 *passim*
St. Louis (France)—*see* Louis IX
Salomon, Rabbi—*see* Rashi
Samuel 4 n.3, 5, 8–12 *passim*, 37, 37 n.1
Samuel ben Me'ir—*see* Rashbam
Samuel ha-Nagid 142
Samuel ben Solomon of Falaise 195
Sandys, Edwin, Bishop 59, 60, 63 n.2, 65
Sarachek, J. 43
Satan 93, 106, 121, 121 n.4, 122
Saul 5, 8, 9, 10, 12, 14, 37 n.1
Scaliger, Joseph 82, 150, 150 n.4, 157, 158
Scaliger, Julius 156
Schechter, Solomon 240 n.51
Schiller-Szinessy, Solomon (ed.) 166 n.2, 171 n.14, 178 n.33, 179 n.34, 239 n.19
Schleiermacher, F. E. D. 329, 331
Schmiedl, A. 106 n.1
Schochet, Azriel (ed.) 241 nn.53,56
Scholem, Gershom 270, 271, 340 n.37
Schwartz, I. 121 n.2, 122 nn.2–5
Sekhel 270
Selden, John 82
Sennacherib 213
Sexual ethics 347
Sforno, Obadiah 64
Shari'a (Islamic law) viii, ix, x, 276, 286, 290, 297, 301, 302
Shelomoh ben Yiṣḥaq—*see* Rashi

364

Index

Shevel, H. D. (ed.)   240, n.48
Shiloh   195, 196, 197, 258
Shtadlan   330
Siegfried, A.   57 n.2
Silvester, Pope   43
Simeon ben Laqish (Lakish) (Resh Laqish)   121, 157 n.1
Simon, Ernst   340 n.37
Simon, Père Richard   149 n.4
Skoss, S. L.   353
Smalley, Dr Beryl   84 n.1, 167 n.3, 168 n.5, 248, 271
Smith, Miles   62
Socrates   301, 303
Solomon   4, 7-12 *passim*, 14 n.24, 18, 40, 46 n.1, 162, 172 n.15, 181, 200
Solomon Halevi (Hallewi)—*see* Paul of Burgos
Sombart, W.   351
Soul, immortality of the   294, 295, 305 n.8
Spain   21ff., 189
  Biblical studies in   250
  Christian servants forbidden   24
  Christianity, conversion to   23, 24, 41—*see also* Marranos
  expulsion of Jews   25, 26, 27, 35
  Inquisition   24, 25
  Jewish community organization   23
  Jews' function in   22
  massacre of Jews   23
  persecutions of Jews   23, 24, 25, 28, 41, 187
  religious disputations   23, 24, 41, 42, 216-26, 256, 257
  return to Judaism   23
Spinoza   294, 295, 306 n.10, 315, 339 n.34
State and society, conceptions of   300, 301, 316—*see also* Maimonides, his political conceptions
Stein, Siegfried   164 n.2, 353
Steinschneider, Moritz   29 n.1, 275 n.3, 277 n.7, 287 n.2, 296, 305 n.8
Stern-Täubler, Selma   340 n.38
Steuchus   129, 129 n.5, 141
Steuernagel, Karl   12
Stoa, the   320
Stoics   293, 303, 307 n.35, 317, 321
Strauss, Leo   275 nn.1,3, 277 n.5, 298, 306 n.13, 307 nn.25,27, 323 n.5, 353
Strype, John   63 nn.1,3, 149 nn.1,3
Sufism   302
Sukkoth   4, 13, 15
Symmachus   163 n.2

Tabernacles—*see Sukkoth*
Talmon, S.   5 n.5
Talmud   xi, 42, 56, 81, 117, 120 n.1, 133, 136, 138, 157 nn.1,2, 159, 189, 191, 193, 196, 212, 217, 219, 220-7 *passim*, 232, 252, 256
Targum   58, 64, 65, 69, 70, 72, 74-7 *passim*, 95, 99, 101-12 *passim*, 115, 117, 119 n.4, 120, 122, 129, 137, 140, 140 n.40, 251, 255, 258
Täubler, Eugen   332, 340, 340 n.38, 347
Temple (Jerusalem)   18, 33 n.1, 38 n.1, 47, 47 n.2, 159, 172 n.15, 191, 197, 206, 207, 208
  ritual   17 n.32, 18, 19
Temporarius   164 n.2
Ten Commandments   52, 312, 313, 320
Terach   138
Themistius   291
Theodicy   97
Tindale—*see* Tyndale
Titus   172 n.15
Torah (*Ṭora*)   ix, x, xi, xii, 14, 19, 33 n.1, 34, 49, 52, 53, 168, 169, 171, 171 n.14, 173, 179, 182, 182 n.47, 183, 184, 190, 193, 194, 200, 202, 203, 205, 208-15 *passim*, 219, 231, 232, 234, 249, 253, 259, 260, 262, 263, 264, 267, 270, 276, 290, 291, 300, 301, 304, 335, 344
  authority of   28, 50
  command to read   12-15 *passim*, 18, 19
  Joshua in relation to   13, 14
  and *nómos*   309-24
  observance by kings and people of   8, 12-19 *passim*
  priests as the teachers of   17, 18
  reason and revelation   28, 29
  study of, in medieval Judaism   244-71—*see also nómos*
Torczyner (Tur-Sinai), H.   239 n.23, 332
Torquemada   25, 26
Trachtenberg, J.   238 n.1, 242 n.69
Transubstantiation   xiii, 213, 228, 233
Treitschke, Heinrich von   333
Tremellius, Immanuel   63, 63 n.2, 65-80 *passim*, 83, 151, 155, 156, 156 n.3, 157
Triliteral theory of Hebrew roots   251
Trinity   xi, xiii, 178, 181, 182, 199, 200, 201, 203, 204, 208, 210, 212, 222, 227, 230, 235, 236, 261
Troki, Isaac   xiii, 234-7
Tyndale, William   57, 58, 67, 69-77 *passim*, 254
Tyre   174

Ucko, Sinai (Siegfried)   354
Ugarit   4, 4 n.3, 5
Urbach, S. E.   21 n.1, 241, n.64
Ussher, Jacob, Archbishop   147 n.1, 149, 149 n.4, 158
Uza   138

365

Index

Vajda, Georges 305 n.7, 354
Van der Ploeg, J. 11 n.19, 18 n.34
Venn, J., 148 n.3
Ventura, M. 90 n.1
Victorines 170—*see* Andrew of St. Victor; Hugh of St. Victor; Richard of St. Victor
Virgil (Vergil) 31
Vowel points, battle of the 154, 155
Vulgate—*see* Bible, Vulgate

Wagenseil, J. C. 242 n.64
Wakefield, Thomas 148, 148 n.3, 151
Walsingham, Sir Francis 160
Weil, G. E. 353
Weiser, A. 17 n.32
Weiss 280 n.5
Wellhausen, Julius 338
Whitgift, John, Archbishop 148 n.4, 152 n. 4, 154 n.2
Whittingham, William 59, 59 n.4
Widengren, Geo 3, 4 n.2, 11–20 *passim*
Wiener, M. 241 nn.53,56
Wiesenberg, E. 176 n.30
Wilhelm, Kurt 330, 333 n.16, 354
Windfuhr, W. (ed.) 166 n.2
Wikkūaḥ-literature 165
Wisdom—*see* Ḥokmah
Wissenschaft des Judentums xiv, **327–52**, 354
Wolf, Lucien 66 nn.1,5, 67 n.1
Wolffsohn, David 350

Wolfgang, James 66
Wolfius, John 59
Wolfson, H. A. 275 n.2, 295, 303, 305 nn.7–9, 306 nn.10–12, 307 n.35
Wood, Anthony à 61, 62, 66
Würthwein, Ernst 8

Xenophon 158

Yahuda, A. 323
Yahwism 7
Yedayah ha-Bedarsi 42 n.2
Yeḥiel of Paris—*see* Jechiel
Yehudah Hallewi—*see* Judah Halevi
Yeivin, Shemuel 8 n.13
Yishuv, Palestinian 350

Zadok the priest 8
Zakkut (Zacut(o)), Abraham b. Samuel 158
Zapho ben Eliphas ben Esau 139
Zechariah 47
Zemirin, S. 8 n.13, 15 n.29
Zerubbabel 38 n.1, 48, 175
Zionism 349, 350
Zohar 270
  Christian interest in 270
Zunz, Leopold 327 n., 330, 330 n.6, 331, 334 n.21, 335, 338, 341, 342
Zürich Letters 59, 59 nn.3–5, 63 n.2
Zwingli, Rodolph 63 n.2

CONTENTS

For the reader's information, this is the list of contents for vol. II of *Studia Semitica*—'Islamic Themes'.

INTRODUCTION *page* vii

PART I · POLITICAL PHILOSOPHY IN MEDIEVAL ISLAM

1 Ibn Khaldūn: a North African Muslim thinker of the fourteenth century   3
   (*Bulletin of the John Rylands Library*, vol.24, no.2, October 1940, pp.307–20)

2 Some aspects of Islamic political thought   17
   (*Islamic Culture*, vol.XXII, no.1, January 1948, pp.1–17)

3 The place of politics in the philosophy of Ibn Bajja   35
   (*Islamic Culture*, vol.XXV, jubilee number, part I, 1951, pp.187–211)

4 The place of politics in the philosophy of Ibn Rushd   60
   (*Bulletin, School of Oriental and African Studies*, vol.XV, no.2, 1953, pp.246–78)

5 The place of politics in the philosophy of Al-Farabi   93
   (*Islamic Culture*, vol.XXIX, no.3, July 1955, pp.157–78)

6 Ibn Jaldūn's attitude to the *falāsifa*   115
   (*Al-Andalus*, vol.XX, 1, 1955, pp.75–85)

7 The concept of *eudaimonia* in medieval Islamic and Jewish philosophy   127
   (*Storia della Filosofia Antica e Medievale*, Firenze, 1960 (Atti del XII Congresso Internazionale di Filosofia, 1958), pp.145–52)

8 Some observations on the philosophical theory of prophecy in Islam   135
   (*Mélanges .... Henri Massé*, ed. Ali-Akar Siassi. Teheran University, 1963, pp.343–52)

PART II · RELIGION AND POLITICS IN MODERN ISLAM

9 The role of Islam in the modern national State   146
   (*The Year Book of World Affairs*, Stevens & Sons Ltd., London, 1962, pp.98–121)

Contents

10 Some reflections on the separation of religion and politics in modern Islam 171
(Islamic Studies (Karachi), vol.III, no.3, September 1964, pp.249–84)

11 Politics in Islam 207
(The Muslim World, vol. LVII, no. 1, 1967, pp.3–10)

APPENDIX OF ADDITIONAL NOTES 215

INDEX 217